Contents

KU-691-366

OPPOSITE BERLIN GRAFFITI **PREVIOUS PAGE** BEBELPLATZ

Introduction to
Berlin

Seemingly in a perpetual state of transformation, Berlin is an extraordinary city. For over a century, events here either mirrored or determined what happened in the rest of Europe, and – even 25 years after the world-changing fall of the Berlin Wall – change in the city is brisk. Only now is the process of healing the wounds of half a century of totalitarian blight beginning to come to an end, as Berlin reasserts itself as the capital of Europe's most powerful country and becomes a world destination where you hear foreign languages as often as you do German.

Light-hearted **sightseeing** is difficult in Berlin: this is a profoundly scarred place, with looming symbols of the war years, the remains of the Wall, and several museums that openly and intelligently probe twentieth-century German history. Even in its flashiest sections the city can still seem half-built, many of its modern buildings – on both sides of the former divide – somehow making it look less finished and more ugly. Unlike Paris, Amsterdam or Munich, Berlin isn't a city where you can simply stroll and absorb the atmosphere: you need to plan and target points of interest, using the excellent transport system for what can be longish distances.

Given the range and severity of the events Berlin has endured, it's no wonder it has grown to be very different from anywhere else in Germany. West Berlin's **unorthodox** character always made it a magnet for people seeking alternative lifestyles – gays and lesbians, artists and musicians, hippies and punks have all flocked here. Non-Germans have made a significant mark, too: Turks, Greeks and Italians, who originally came as "guest workers" in the 1960s, soon made Berlin Germany's most **cosmopolitan** city by far – as reflected in the wide variety of cuisine offered in the city's restaurants, cafés and bars. And a recent wave of fairly penniless young artsy types from all around Europe have greatly added to Berlin's international and creative character.

Part of Berlin's special energy comes from its **nightlife**. Nowhere in the city is more than a stone's throw from a bar, be it a corner *Kneipe* or a slick upscale café – indeed,

ABOVE BERLIN MITTE AT DUSK

CENTRAL BERLIN

N

0 500 metres

Berlin-Spandauer-Schiffahrtskanal
Westhafenkanal
SEESTRASSE
Spree
SEESTRASSE
SIEMENSSTRASSE
QUITZOWSTRASSE
FRIEDRICHSTRASSE
PERLEBERGER STRASSE
TURMSTRASSE
ALT-MOABIT
ALT-MOABIT
HUTTIGPFAD
KAISERIN-AUGUSTA-ALLEE
KAISERIN-AUGUSTA-ALLEE
BISMARCKSTR.
OTTO-SUHR-ALLEE
KANTSTRASSE
SAVIGNY-PLATZ
ERNST-REUTER-PLATZ
HARDENBERGSTRASSE
Berlin Zoo
KURFÜRSTENDAMM
Kaiser-Wilhelm-Gedächtnis-Kirche
CITY WEST
OLIVER-PLATZ
LIETZENBURGER STRASSE
WITTENBERG-PLATZ
KONSTANZER STRASSE
NIKOLSBURGER PLATZ
FEHRBELLINER PLATZ
HOHENZOLLERNDAMM
BARBAROSSA STRASSE
HOHENSTAUFENSTRASSE
VIKTORIA-LUISE-PLATZ
WILMERSDORFER STRASSE
NOLLENDORF-PLATZ
ANSBACHER
SCHÖNEBERG
KURFÜRSTENSTRASSE
POTSDAMER STRASSE
Tiergarten
STRASSE DES 17 JUNI
HOFJÄGERALLEE
GROSSER STERN
ALTONAER STRASSE
PAULSTRASSE
STRASSE DES 17 JUNI
TIERGARTENSTRASSE
Kulturforum
Sony Center
POTSDAMER PLATZ
Brandenburg Gate
Reichstag
WILHELMSTRASSE
WILHELMSTRASSE
STRESEMANNSTRASSE
MEHRING-PLATZ
FRIEDRICHSTRASSE
Checkpoint Charlie
LINDENSTRASSE
Jewish Museum Berlin
ORANIENSTRASSE
GNEISENAUSTRASSE
RITTERSTRASSE
ORANIEN-PLATZ
ANNENSTRASSE
KREUZBERG
SKALITZER STRASSE
KÖTTBUSSER PLATZ
REICHENBERGER STRASSE
URBANSTRASSE
Landwehrkanal
Landwehrkanal
YORCKSTRASSE
LEIPZIGER STRASSE
SPITTEL-MARKT
CHARLOTTENSTRASSE
UNTER DEN LINDEN
KARL-LIEBKNECHT-STRASSE
MITTE
MUSEUM ISLAND
Fernsehturm
ALEXANDER-PLATZ
Hackesche Höfe
SPANDAUER VORSTADT
FRIEDRICHSTRASSE
Hauptbahnhof
Museum für Naturkunde
CHAUSSEESTRASSE
GARTENSTRASSE
INVALIDENSTRASSE
INVALIDENSTRASSE
Gedenkstätte Berliner Mauer
BRUNNENSTRASSE
BERNAUER STRASSE
DANZIGER STRASSE
TORSTRASSE
ROSA-LUXEMBURG-PLATZ
PRENZLAUER ALLEE
KOLLWITZ-PLATZ
GREIFSWALDERSTRASSE
PRENZLAUER BERG
DANZIGER STRASSE
DANZIGER STRASSE
PETERSBURGER STRASSE
LANDSBERGER ALLEE
Volkspark Friedrichshain
MOLLSTRASSE
OTTO-BRAUN-STRASSE
KARL-MARX-ALLEE
KARL-MARX-ALLEE
FRIEDRICHSHAIN
WARSCHAUER STRASSE
Ostbahnhof
East Side Gallery
Spree
MÜHLENSTRASSE
HOLZMARKTSTRASSE
KÖPENICKER STRASSE
STRALAUER ALLEE
STRALAUER STRASSE
MÜHLENDAMM
STRALAUER PLATZ
BERSARIN-PLATZ
FRANKFURTER ALLEE
LAUSITZER-PLATZ
SCHLESISCHE STRASSE

OFFBEAT BERLIN

Beach bars Sip a cocktail by the River Spree in a *Strandkorb* (beach basket), with sand between your toes. **See p.204**

Graffiti art Learn to graffiti with Alternative Berlin, then find your own bit of wall to practice on. **See p.125**

Badeschiff barges Swim or sweat in the pools and saunas of the converted barges of the Badeschiff, bobbing on the inky River Spree. **See p.234**

Go-karting Career around the streets in a go-kart. **See p.24**

Flea markets Rummage through Berlin's flea markets for GDR memorabilia and vintage clothes. **See p.232**

their variety is one of the city's great strengths. And between them they are open pretty much nonstop: Berlin really is a 24-hour city, and you'll never be short of something to do. Yet despite this and the immense cultural offerings – back to back concerts and festivals throughout the year, some 180 museums and dozens of extraordinary historical monuments – Germany's capital still remains satisfyingly **inexpensive** by Western European standards generally, and certainly if compared to London, Paris or New York.

What to see

Though cut off by the Wall for thirty years, the eastern part of the city – the Mitte district – has always been Berlin's real centre and is its main **sightseeing**, and **shopping** hub. Most visitors begin their exploration on the city's premier boulevard **Unter den Linden**, starting at the most famous landmark, the **Brandenburg Gate**, then moving over to the adjacent seat of Germany's parliament, the **Reichstag**. Unter den Linden's most important intersection is with **Friedrichstrasse**, which cuts north–south. At its eastern end Unter den Linden is lined by stately Neoclassical buildings and terminates on the shores of **Museum Island**, home to eastern Berlin's leading museums, but its natural extension on the other side of the island is **Karl-Liebknecht-Strasse**, which leads to a distinctively GDR-era part of the city around **Alexanderplatz**, the eastern city's main commercial and transport hub. Northwest from here, the **Spandauer Vorstadt** was once the heart of the city's Jewish community, and has some fascinating reminders of those days, though today it's best known for the restaurants, bars, boutiques and nightlife around the Hackescher Markt.

Back at the Brandenburg Gate, a walk south along the edge of the gigantic **Tiergarten** park takes you to the swish modern **Potsdamer Platz**, a bustling entertainment quarter that stands on what was for decades a barren field straddling the death-strip of the Berlin Wall. Huddled beside Potsdamer Platz is the **Kulturforum**, an agglomeration of cultural institutions that includes several high-profile art museums. Also fringing the park are Berlin's diplomatic and government quarters, where you'll find some of the city's most innovative architecture, including the formidable **Hauptbahnhof**. The western end of the Tiergarten park is given over to a zoo, which is also the name of the main transport hub at this end of town. This is the gateway to **City West**, West Berlin's old centre and is best known for its shopping boulevards, particularly the upmarket **Kurfürstendamm**.

Schöneberg and **Kreuzberg**, the two residential districts immediately south of the centre, are home to much of Berlin's most vibrant nightlife. The former is smart and is popular as a gay area, while Kreuzberg is generally grungy and edgy. Beyond Kreuzberg's

TOP 5 ARCHITECTURAL HIGHLIGHTS

Hackesche Höfe Imagine these pretty, restored courtyards teeming with turn-of-the-century life. **See p.71**

Jüdisches Museum Designed by Daniel Libeskind, this is a dramatically awkward building for a difficult subject. See p.117

Olympic Stadium On a scale to rival Rome's Colosseum. **See p.158**

Reichstag Meaningful and deeply impressive, irrespective of its historical associations. **See p.37**

Sony Center The Roman atrium reinvented for the twenty-first century. See p.92

eastern fringes, and back in what used to be East Berlin is **Friedrichshain** which offers some unusual architectural leftovers from the Eastern Bloc of the 1950s, while to the north **Prenzlauer Berg** is one of the few places in which the atmosphere of prewar Berlin has been preserved – complete with cobbled streets and ornate facades. It flows fairly seamlessly into the attractive if sleepy district of **Pankow** to the north.

Berlin's **eastern suburbs** are typified by a sprawl of prewar tenements punctuated by high-rise developments and heavy industry, though the lakes, woodland and small towns and villages dotted around **Köpenick** offer a genuine break from the city. The leafy **western suburbs** are even more renowned for their woodland (the **Grunewald**) and lakes (the **Havel**), with more besides: attractions include the baroque **Schloss Charlottenburg**, with its adjacent art museums; the impressive 1930s **Olympic Stadium**; the **Dahlem museum complex**, which displays everything from German folk art to Polynesian huts; and the medieval town of **Spandau**. Further out, foremost among possible **day-trips** are **Potsdam**, location of Frederick the Great's **Sanssouci** palace, and the former concentration camp of **Sachsenhausen**, north of Berlin in Oranienburg.

When to go

Lying in the heart of Europe, Berlin's **climate** (see p.28) is continental: winters are bitingly cold, summers hot. April is the earliest in the year you should go for decent weather: any earlier and you'll need winter clothing, earmuffs and a decent pair of waterproof shoes; that said, the city (especially the eastern part) has a particular poignancy when it snows. The best time to visit is in May; June and July can be wearingly hot, though the famed Berlin air (*Berliner Luft* – there's a song about its vitality) keeps things bearable.

BERLIN'S MARVELLOUS MUSEUMS

Berlin boasts that it's Europe's only city with more museums than rainy days (some 180 and 106 respectively), which is great news weather-wise, but also means that all but the most committed museum nuts are spoiled for choice.

Most collections are expertly presented in striking buildings and nowhere is this more true than on **Museum Island** (see p.55), location of the city's headline acts. Here Middle Eastern antiquities and, to a lesser extent, German art and sculpture, are the main draws, while the latter also form the kernel of collections at Berlin's other main central museum agglomeration: the **Kulturforum** (see p.94). This is known for its Medieval and Early-Modern paintings and decorative art; the greatest concentration of twentieth-century art lies in the museums around **Schloss Charlottenburg** (see p.153) outside the city centre. In addition, the vast collection in the airy old warehouses of the **Hamburger Bahnhof** is an essential first stop for lovers of contemporary art – before embarking on an exploration of some of Berlin's six hundred or so private galleries (see p.106).

Perhaps unsurprisingly, many of Berlin's most compelling museums are concerned with its astonishing history (see box, p.264). If weighty topics don't appeal, then Berlin's generic museums are a good bet, especially for **kids**: the Natural History Museum (see p.86) is famous for dinosaur skeletons; while the technology (see p.122) and communication (see p.120) museums are both engaging push-button places. Unsuitable for kids, but entertaining for the rest of us, are the **photography** museum (see p.109) devoted to Helmut Newton's nude photos and the **gay** museum (see p.237) which evokes the city's debauched 1920s. But for something truly offbeat, the dusty old exhibits of the freakish **medical museum** (see p.106) are hard to beat.

OPPOSITE TIERGARTEN; **ABOVE** EGYPTIAN GALLERY IN THE NEUES MUSEUM

17
things not to miss

It's not possible to see everything that Berlin has to offer on a short trip – and we don't suggest you try. What follows is a subjective selection of the city's highlights, ranging from vibrant nightlife to local cuisine and outstanding architecture. Each highlight has a page reference to take you straight into the Guide, where you can find out more. The colour of each highlight's number matches its relevant chapter in the Guide section.

1 FERNSEHTURM
Page 62

Love or loathe its concrete curves, this incongruous Eastern-bloc relic has the best views over the city.

2 EAST SIDE GALLERY
Page 130

The Berlin Wall was always famous for its graffiti, and now, on the longest remaining stretch, vivid murals record its demise.

3 BERLINER WEISSE
Page 205

Few would argue this brew is one of the world's best, but since you order it in either green or red it must be one of the most unusual.

4 THE REICHSTAG
Page 37

Perhaps Germany's most famous landmark, this muscular Neoclassical building now has a magnificent glass cupola you can walk round for free.

8

9

10

5 MARKETS
Page 232

Berlin loves its markets, with numerous food markets in each district and several weekly flea markets.

6 HACKESCHE HÖFE
Page 71

A series of elegant early-twentieth-century courtyards filled with stylish cafés and boutiques.

7 BERLIN WALL MEMORIAL
Page 86

The only remaining completely preserved section of the Wall forms part of a memorial to all the suffering caused by Berlin's division.

8 BRANDENBURG GATE
Page 35

Portal to Berlin's most impressive street and witness to several historical episodes: Napoleon stole the Quadriga, the Soviets built the Berlin Wall around it, then the world watched as the Wall tumbled down beside it.

9 SANSSOUCI
Page 169

The prettiest of a series of fine Potsdam palaces that lie an easy day-trip from Berlin.

10 CURRYWURST
Page 195

Berlin snack bars serve every type of German sausage, but be sure to try *Currywurst*, their speciality.

11

12

13

14

15

16

17

Itineraries

Berlin is a sprawling city, with several main drags and no defined centre. These itineraries – three day-long options and one overnighter – will help you make the most out of the place, and are easily followed with the help of a public transit day pass (plus some single tickets for the night-owl tour).

IMPERIAL BERLIN

Brandenburg Gate Berlin's foremost landmark and one of its biggest tourist attractions. A must for first-time visitors. **See p.35**

Reichstag and Holocaust Memorials Climb the dome of this historic building to find great city views – make sure you book a tour ahead. Then pay your respects at three thought-provoking memorials. **See p.37 & p.38**

Lunch Reserve in advance and enjoy a gourmet lunch with a view at *Käfer Dachgarten* in the Reichstag (see p.188); opt for classic Austrian dishes at old-fashioned *Café Einstein* (see p.187); or for budget options try sushi at *Ishin* (see p.188) or head for one of the many places in the basement of the DaimlerChrysler quarter at Potsdamer Platz (see p.94).

Gendarmenmarkt and Unter den Linden Walk off your lunch by wandering the length of Unter den Linden, with side trips to the elegant plazas of Gendarmenmarkt (see p.47) and Bebelplatz (see p.42). Stop en route at the Berlin Story shop (see p.225) to browse its selection of books and DVDs about the city.

Boat trip For a change of pace and a different angle, take a boat trip along the River Spree from the quays beside Museum Island. **See p.25**

Hackescher Markt Finish the day with a wander around these pleasant urban courtyards and choose from a multitude of cafés, bars and restaurants. **See p.71**

GDR BERLIN

Gedenkstätte Berliner Mauer The Wall memorial on Bernauer Strasse has fascinating, and free, indoor and outdoor exhibitions. **See p.86**

Tränenpalast Discover what division really meant to the city at this former pedestrian border crossing. **See p.84**

DDR Museum Get hands on with GDR culture at this fun interactive museum. Nearby is the imposing Marx-Engels-Forum, whose Marx and Engel monuments offer a fascinating glimpse into East German communist ideology. **See p.64**

Fernsehturm Gape at the bleak GDR architecture of Alexanderplatz before taking a trip up the Fernsehturm for tremendous views over the city. **See p.62**

Karl-Marx-Allee Take in the vast dimensions of this communist boulevard where monumentalist, wedding-cake style architecture produced "palaces for workers, not American egg-boxes!" and pick a cardboard kit to make your own model version at the Karl Marx Buchhandlung. Admire the original Kino International, as featured in the film *Goodbye Lenin!* **See p.130**

Coffee Grab coffee and cake (or ice cream) at *Café Sybille*, which also hosts a small but informative museum about Karl-Marx-Allee. **See p.200**

ABOVE THE REICHSTAG AT NIGHT; **OPPOSITE** CRUISE ON THE RIVER SPREE

East Side Gallery Finish up at the largest remaining section of the Berlin Wall, one of the world's largest open-air galleries. **See p.130**

Sleep For a complete *Ostalgie* experience (see p.66), book a night at the GDR-themed *Ostel* in Friedrichshain, which is also well placed for the neighbourhood's nightlife. **See p.181**

BUDGET BERLIN

Breakfast Start the day at *Morgenrot*, a bohemian café in Prenzlauer Berg where you pay according to your income. **See p.202**

Bus it Hop on the underground for a couple of stops to Alexanderplatz then take bus #100 then #200 in a loop for a free sightseeing tour of some of the city's main sights. **See p.25**

Kaiser-Wilhelm-Gedächtniskirche On the #100 bus route and close to Zoo Station, this dramatically shattered memorial church has a small exhibition on Berlin at the end of World War II. **See p.110**

Daimler Contemporary Stop off at Potsdamer Platz to see the free contemporary art shows. **See p.94**

Lunch *Joseph Roth Diele*, a charming restaurant nearby, offers excellent lunch deals. **See p.196**

Topography of Terror Built on the grounds of the former SS Headquarters, this memorial of Gestapo horrors will leave you reeling. **See p.121**

Holocaust Memorials If you have time and energy, explore the moving Holocaust Memorials, a short walk away. **See p.38**

Evening drinks End your day at one of the *Weinerei* bars, low-key hangouts where you pay what you feel is fair for the wine. **See p.209**

NIGHT-OWL BERLIN

Dine in Spandauer Vorstadt Get your night started with dinner around Oranienburger Strasse, for example at *Amrit* (see p.190) or the *Schwarzwaldstuben* (see p.191).

The Reichstag Either walk along the river or hop on the S-Bahn for one stop to Brandenburger Tor for a late tour of Germany's parliament building. Take time to check out the incredible sunset and night views over central Berlin. Book ahead. **See p.37**

Potsdamer Platz The roof of the Sony Center includes an impressive light show best enjoyed from the cafés and bars in its atrium. **See p.92**

East Side Gallery Take bus #200, M48 or the underground to Alexanderplatz, admire the Fernsehturm (see p.62), then take the S-Bahn to Ostbahnhof to walk southeast along the length of the East Side Gallery. **See p.130**

Eastern Kreuzberg Take the underground one stop, or cross the Spree on the Oberbaumbrücke. Grab a burger at *Burgermeister* before exploring the neighbourhood's countless bars and clubs. **See p.125**

Kumpelnest 3000 When the clocks hit 5am, join sundry night-owls at this cool, late-night haunt; five stops on the elevated subway line through Kreuzberg (night buses run along the line when the underground stops). **See p.210**

S-BAHN POTSDAMER PLATZ

Basics

Getting there

The quickest and generally cheapest way of reaching Berlin from the UK and Ireland is by air, a journey of around ninety minutes. It is, however, possible to travel by train or by car via a ferry. Direct flights link Berlin to New York and Chicago, which can also prove useful routes for visitors from Australia and New Zealand, though changing flights at a major European hub such as London, Amsterdam or Frankfurt – the only option for South African travellers – will probably be less expensive.

Airfares vary considerably according to the **season**, with the highest being around June to August; fares drop during the "shoulder" seasons – September to October and April and May – and you'll get the best prices during the low season, November to March (excluding Christmas and New Year when prices are hiked up and seats are at a premium). Flying at **weekends** will also usually raise the price of a return fare.

Flights from the UK and Ireland

Direct **scheduled flights** to Berlin are available **from London** airports with British Airways, easyJet, Lufthansa and Ryanair. Other UK airports with direct flights to Berlin include **Birmingham** (Lufthansa); **Bristol**, **Edinburgh**, **Glasgow**, **Liverpool** and **Manchester** (easyJet); **Leeds** (Jet2); and **Nottingham** (Ryanair). In Ireland both Ryanair and Aer Lingus offer direct flights from **Dublin**

The published return fare of the national airlines can cost as much as £300, but in reality booking at least a couple of weeks in advance can easily halve this amount. Prices with the budget airlines – Air Berlin, easyJet and Ryanair – can start as low as £40 for a return, but you'll often need to book at least a month ahead to secure this and many extra fees will apply, from checking in bags to failing to print out your own boarding pass.

Flights from the US and Canada

There are several daily scheduled flights from **North America** to Berlin, with a choice of carriers and destinations. Both United Airlines and Air Berlin fly direct from **New York**; Air Berlin also offers direct flights from Chicago and Miami. If you are starting your journey from elsewhere in the US, you may well find a cheaper and better connection from Washington DC, Boston, Chicago, Miami, Los Angeles or Seattle via a major European hub. **Canadians** will also end up flying via a major European hub and are unlikely to make any real savings by flying to the US first.

The lowest discounted **scheduled fares** you're likely to get in low/high season flying midweek are US$500/$1100 from New York, Boston or Washington DC; US$550/$1500 from Chicago; US$850/$1750 from Los Angeles or Seattle, and US$950/$1750 from San Francisco. Canadians have fewer direct-flight options than Americans. The widest selections are out of Toronto and Montreal, with low/high season fares to Berlin from around Can$950/$1550; from Vancouver expect to pay from Can$1350/$1850.

Flights from Australasia and South Africa

There are **no direct flights** to Berlin from Australia, New Zealand or South Africa; most airlines use Amsterdam, Frankfurt, London or Paris as their European gateway. All involve either a transfer or overnight stop en route in the airline's hub city: flying times from the Antipodes are around 24 hours via Asia and thirty hours via the US; from South Africa the shortest flight times, including transfer, are around 17 hours.

Flights to Europe are generally cheaper via Asia than the US, and typical low season/high season economy fares from Australia start at around Aus$2300/$2900. Low season/high season scheduled fares from Auckland start at around NZ$2600/$3150. From South Africa you'll pay between ZAR8000 and ZAR12,000, depending on the season.

A BETTER KIND OF TRAVEL

At Rough Guides we are passionately committed to travel. We believe it helps us understand the world we live in and the people we share it with – and of course tourism is vital to many developing economies. But the scale of modern tourism has also damaged some places irreparably, and climate change is accelerated by most forms of transport, especially flying. All Rough Guides' flights are carbon-offset, and every year we donate money to a variety of environmental charities.

Trains

Travelling to Berlin **by train** costs little more but takes far longer than flying. By far the **fastest** and most popular train route to Berlin begins with **Eurostar** (UK ☎08432 186 186; outside the UK ☎+44 (0) 1233 617 575 ⓦeurostar.com) from London St Pancras to Paris Gare du Nord (3hr), with a change of stations to Paris Gare de l'Est for the onward overnight train to Berlin (10hr). Return tickets for the complete journey begin at around £90, depending on your seating and sleeping arrangements. You can get through-ticketing – including the London Underground journey to St Pancras – from mainline stations in Britain; typical add-on prices are £30 from Edinburgh or Glasgow, £20 from Manchester and £15 from Birmingham.

Rail passes

You can buy a **rail pass** for the entire German rail network from Deutsche Bahn (ⓦbahn.com). InterRail (ⓦraileurope.co.uk) and Eurail passes (ⓦeurail.com) – the latter for non-European residents only – include other European countries.

Buses

Travelling to Berlin by **bus** won't bring any major savings over the cheapest airfares, and the journey will be long and uncomfortable, interrupted every three to four hours by stops at motorway service stations. The one advantage is that you can buy an open return at no extra cost.

Services are run by **Eurolines** (ⓦeurolines.com) from Victoria Coach Station in London. There are two buses daily to Berlin; the journey takes around twenty hours and costs £101 return. Starting your journey outside London can add considerably to the time, but little to the cost – the complete journey time from Edinburgh is 37 hours, but tickets start from £116. There's about a twenty percent discount on these rates for anyone under 26, and if you are travelling elsewhere in Europe you might consider buying a **Europass**. **Busabout**, meanwhile, runs guided bus tours of Europe for young people and offer a hop-on, hop-off bus pass (ⓦbusabout.com).

Airlines, agents and operators

AIRLINES

Aer Lingus ⓦ aerlingus.com
Air Berlin ⓦ airberlin.com
Air Canada ⓦ aircanada.com
Air France ⓦ airfrance.com
Air New Zealand ⓦ airnewzealand.com
British Airways ⓦ ba.com
Cathay Pacific ⓦ cathaypacific.com
Continental Airlines ⓦ continental.com
Delta ⓦ delta.com
easyJet ⓦ easyjet.com
Germanwings ⓦ germanwings.com
Jet2 ⓦ jet2.com
KLM ⓦ klm.com
LOT (Polish Airlines) ⓦ lot.com
Lufthansa ⓦ lufthansa.com
Qantas Airways ⓦ qantas.com.au
Ryanair ⓦ ryanair.com
SAS (Scandinavian Airlines) ⓦ flysas.com
South African Airways ⓦ flysaa.com
Swiss ⓦ swiss.com
United Airlines ⓦ united.com

AGENTS AND OPERATORS

Harvey World Travel New Zealand ☎ 0800 758 787, ⓦ harveyworld.co.nz. Great deals on flights, hotels and holidays.
Martin Randall Travel UK ☎ 020 8742 3355, ⓦ martinrandall.com. Small-group cultural tours, usually accompanied by lecturers: an eight-day Berlin, Potsdam, Dresden package costs around £2500.
North South Travel UK ☎ 01245 608 291, ⓦ northsouthtravel.co.uk. Friendly, competitive travel agency, offering discounted fares worldwide. Profits are used to support projects in the developing world, especially the promotion of sustainable tourism.
STA Travel UK ☎ 0333 321 0099, US ☎ 1800 781 4040, Australia ☎ 134 782, New Zealand ☎ 0800 474 400, South Africa ☎ 0861 781 781; ⓦ statravel.co.uk. Worldwide specialists in independent travel; also student IDs, travel insurance, car rental, rail passes, and more. Good discounts for students and under-26s.
Trailfinders UK ☎ 020 7368 1200, Ireland ☎ 021 464 8800; ⓦ trailfinders.com. One of the best-informed and most efficient agents for independent travellers.
Travel CUTS Canada ☎ 1800 667 2887, US ☎ 1800 592 2887; ⓦ travelcuts.com. Canadian youth and student travel firm.
USIT Ireland ☎ 01 602 1906, Northern Ireland ☎ 028 9032 4073, Australia ☎ 1800 092 499; ⓦ usit.ie. Ireland's main student and youth travel specialists.

Arrival

All points of arrival lie within easy reach of the city centre via inexpensive and efficient public transport; the farthest of the city's two airports is just 25 minutes by train from Berlin's city-centre Hauptbahnhof, where trains from all over Europe converge. Some trains also stop at other major stations such as Bahnhof Zoo, Alexanderplatz

and the Ostbahnhof, which may be more convenient for your destination.

Public transport **tickets** are valid for the entire system of trams, buses and suburban and underground trains. If you plan to use public transport throughout your stay, then get a ticket that covers several days (see p.22) – all these can be validated to cover your journey from the airport and are available from ticket machines at all points of arrival. In addition, a handful of upmarket hotels offer courtesy **shuttles**.

By plane

Until the much delayed and anticipated completion of Berlin Brandenburg Airport (BER) airport in 2014, Berlin's air traffic (Ⓦ berlin-airport.de) will be shared between the **Schönefeld** airport, which lies on an adjacent site, and **Tegel** airport, 7km northwest of the city centre.

Tegel

Many scheduled and charter flights still arrive at the small and manageable **Tegel (TXL)** airport, where you'll find shops, currency exchange, left luggage facilities and several car rental companies on the land-side. (When flying out, note that once past security it's another story, with only the most rudimentary services.)

Several **buses** head from Tegel into the city. The TXL JetExpressBus (daily 5am–11.30pm, every 15–20min) heads to Hauptbahnhof (28min) and Alexanderplatz (40min). **Bus X9** (Mon–Fri 4.50am–11pm, every 5–10min; Sat & Sun 5.20am–12.30am, every 10min) goes to Bahnhof Zoo (20min), while **Bus #109** heads to S-Bahn station Charlottenburg and **#128** to U-Bahn station Osloer Strasse.

If you intend to buy a Welcome Card, City Tour Card or simply a weekly **ticket** (see p.22), do this from the ticket machine just outside the terminal – the bus driver can only sell single (€2.60) and day tickets (€6.70 for zones A and B). **Taxis** cover the distance in half the time (depending on the traffic) and cost about €20.

Schönefeld and Berlin Brandenburg

Schönefeld, 20km southeast of the city centre, mostly serves budget airlines and holiday charters. Beside it is its soon-to-be replacement, **Berlin Brandenburg Airport**, which will eventually consume it. The train station is a five-minute walk from the terminal; from here you can get the Airport Express **train** (daily 5am–midnight), which takes 30 minutes to reach the Hauptbahnhof, or the

S-Bahn (4.30am–11pm), which takes about 40 minutes but may be more convenient as it has more stops; the same BVG zone A, B and C (single €3.20; day pass €7.20) ticket is valid on either service (see p.22). Long queues at the ticket machines in the underground passageway can usually be avoided by buying tickets from identical machines on the platform. A **taxi** into the town centre from Schönefeld/BBI costs around €37.

By train

Trains from European destinations generally head straight to the swanky **Hauptbahnhof**, which has late-opening shops and all the facilities you would expect from a major train station. The station is also a stop on the major S-Bahn line, and on the U-Bahn network. Your train ticket may well include use of zones A and B of the city's public transport system (see p.22) at the end of your journey: if you're not sure, check with the conductor or at the ticket office.

By bus

Most international **buses** and those from other German cities stop at the **Zentraler Omnibusbahnhof** or **ZOB** (central bus station; Ⓦ iob-berlin .de), Masurenallee, Charlottenburg, west of the centre, near the Funkturm. Several city buses, including the #M49 service to the centre, and the U-Bahn from U-Kaiserdamm, link it to the Ku'damm area, a journey of about fifteen minutes. The bus station has an information booth, a taxi stand and a couple of snack places.

By car

Getting into Berlin **by car** is relatively easy as Germany's famed autobahns (*Autobahnen*) pass reasonably close to the city centre. It may, however, be a long trip – the autobahns are very congested and delays are the norm. From the west you're most likely to approach on autobahn A2, which will turn into A10 (the ring-road around Berlin), from which you turn off onto A115, a highway that eases you onto Kaiserdamm on the western side of the city, from where it is just fifteen minutes to Zoo station. From the south you'll approach on autobahn A9, but the route once you hit the A10 is the same. Drivers coming from the Hamburg area will approach from the north on M24, which also turns into A10, but this time you take the A111 into the Charlottenburg district of Berlin.

City transport

Berlin's public transport network is well integrated, efficient and inexpensive. The cornerstone of the system is the web of fast suburban (S-Bahn) and underground (U-Bahn) trains, which are supplemented on the streets by buses and trams. All are run by the BVG, whose network looks complicated at first glance but quickly becomes easy to navigate.

On board, illuminated signs and announcements ensure it's easy to find the right stop. **Tickets** are available from machines at stations and on trams, or from bus drivers – but in all cases be sure to validate them by punching them in a red or yellow machine when you travel. Apart from their colour the machines are identical, serve exactly the same function and are strategically placed by the entrance of every bus, tram or platform. Failure to punch your ticket will result in spot fines.

Public transport

The **U-Bahn** subway is clean, punctual and rarely crowded. Running both under- and over-ground, it covers much of the centre and stretches into the suburbs: trains run from 4am to around 12.30am, and all night on Friday and Saturday. Once they have closed down for the night their routes are usually covered by night buses – denoted by a number with the prefix "N".

The **S-Bahn** system is a separate network of suburban trains, which runs largely overground, and is better for covering long distances fast and effectively and complements the U-Bahn in the city centre. It runs until 1.30am on weeknights and all night on Friday and Saturday.

You never have to wait long for a **bus** in the city and the network covers most gaps in the U-Bahn system, with buses converging on Zoo Station and Alexanderplatz. Buses #100 and #200, between the two, are particularly good for sightseeing. **Night buses** mostly run every half-hour and routes often differ from daytime ones; maps of the night bus routes can be picked up at most U-Bahn ticket booths.

Berlin's quiet and comfortable **trams** are found for the most part in the eastern section of the city, where the network has survived from prewar days.

MetroBuses and **MetroTrams**, their numbers preceded by the letter M, are the core services, running particularly frequently and all night.

Information and maps

For more **information** about Berlin's public transport system, call or check their website (☎ 194 49, ⓦ bvg.de) which has complete listings and timetables for the U- and S-Bahn systems, plus bus, tram and ferry routes. There are also transport information offices at Zoo Station, the Hauptbahnhof, Friedrichstrasse and Alexanderplatz, where you can also buy a complete and highly detailed guide to services, and various souvenirs of the network.

Kiosks on the platforms at most U-Bahn stations also provide simple free **maps** of the U- and S-Bahn, trams and some bus services.

Tickets

The same **tickets are valid** for all BVG services, allowing transfers between different modes of transport as well as all other public transport services within the VBB (Verkehrsverbund Berlin-Brandenburg) system, which includes buses and trams in Potsdam, Oranienburg and even Regional Express trains (marked "RE" when operating within the city limits). Tickets can be bought from the machines on U- and S-Bahn station platforms. These take €5, €10 and €20 notes and all but the smallest coins, give change and have a basic explanation of the ticketing system in English. Plain-clothes inspectors frequently cruise the lines, meting out on-the-spot **fines** of €60 for anyone without a correct ticket or pass that has been validated by a red or yellow machine (see above). You can also buy tickets, including day tickets, directly from the driver on a bus (change given); if you have a ticket already, show it to the driver as you board.

The transport network is divided into three **zones** – A, B and C. Basic **single tickets (Einzeltickets)** cost €2.60 and allow travel in Zone A and B. Zone C covers the outskirts of town and includes Potsdam, Oranienburg and Schönefeld/BBI airport; a ticket for zones A, B and C costs €3.20. All tickets are valid for two hours, enabling you to split a single journey as often as you like, but can't be used for a return journey. A **Kurzstrecke**, or **short-trip ticket**, costs €1.50 and allows you to travel up to three train or six bus stops (no return journeys or transfers).

Buying a **day ticket (Tageskarte)**, valid from the moment you buy it until 3am the next morning, costs €6.70 for the entire network within zones A and B, and may work out cheaper, as might the excellent-value **seven-day ticket (Sieben-Tage-Karte)**, which costs €28.80 for zones A and B and €35.60 for zones A, B and C.

A small **group ticket (Kleingruppenkarte)** is available for a whole day's travel for up to five

---

MUSEUM PASSES AND DISCOUNTS

While the Welcome Card (see below) and City Tour Card (see below), provide useful discounts for museum visits on top of access to the public system, a couple of passes are even more effective at cutting admission prices at museums, particularly if you're keen to visit several. Best is the **Museum Pass Berlin** – a good-value €24 three-day ticket covering some fifty Berlin museums, including all the state collection. It's sold at all participating museums, as well as at the Visit Berlin information centres (see p.33).

Also worth bearing in mind is the **Bereichskarte**, a day-pass valid for all of Berlin's state museums in one of the four zones they are divided into – Museum Island (see p.55), the Kulturforum (see p.94), Charlottenburg (see p.155), and Dahlem (see p.160). These cost €12–18, depending on the zone, and can be picked up at any of the museums within the zone for which you wish to purchase a ticket.

---

people; it costs €16.20 for zones A and B and €16.70 for three zones.

Another ticket of relevance is the **Fahrrad** ticket, which enables you to wheel a bike onto U- and S-Bahn services. It costs €2.30 for a single journey in zones A, B and C and €5.30 for a day pass – but note that it only covers the bike and you'll need to buy the appropriate pass for yourself, too.

Other possibilities are the **Welcome Card** and the slightly cheaper **City Tour Card** (Ⓦcitytourcard .com). Both are available for 48 hours, 72 hours or five days and range from €16.90 for 48 hours in zones A and B to €36.50 for 5 days in zones A, B and C. Both cards also give concessionary rates at a host of attractions and discounts at participating tour companies, restaurants and theatres; the main difference between the two are their partners, so check to see which are more appealing. A **Museum Island** (*Museumsinsel*) version of the Welcome Card also covers all the Museum Island museums (see p.55): 72 hours in zones A and B for €34

If you're in Berlin for longer than a couple of weeks, consider buying a **monthly ticket** (**Monatskarte**); various types are available and explained in full in English via the information buttons on dispensing machines.

By car

Though there's practically no need for a **car** within the city, you might want one to tour outside Berlin. The most important **rules** to bear in mind when driving are simple: drive on the right; main roads have a yellow diamond indicating priority; and unless otherwise indicated, traffic coming from the right normally has right of way. Trams also always have the right of way, which frequently catches out unwary visiting drivers who are prone to cutting in front of trams at junctions – a frightening and potentially lethal error. Also, when trams halt at designated stops,

it's forbidden to overtake until the tram starts moving, to allow passengers time to cross the road and board.

Thanks to widespread car ownership and extensive road construction projects, Berlin suffers **traffic snarl-ups** that can compete with the worst any European city has to offer. Rush-hour jams start at around 5pm and are particularly bad on Friday afternoons when you shouldn't be surprised if a journey takes three or four times as long as you expect.

Finding **parking spaces** in central Berlin can be tricky and you'll almost certainly have to pay. Meters, identifiable by their tall grey rectangular solar-power umbrellas, generally charge €1–3/30min. You're supposed to move after an hour, and stiff fines are handed out to cars parked for longer than that or without tickets – even cars with foreign plates. Parking garages generally charge around €2/hr and allow you to stay for several hours.

Central Berlin has been designated an **Umweltzone** – a green zone, announced by a sign with the word printed on it – in which all cars must display an emission badge (*Umwelt Plakette*; Ⓦumwelt-plakette .de). These can be purchased online in advance (€30) or bought for around €15 from any of the many garages in Germany that offer TÜV auto-testing (the German equivalent of an MOT) – look for the TÜV logo. The badges work by using a traffic-light system – currently all vehicles with amber and red badges are banned in central Berlin. In practice this means if you are driving a pre-'93 petrol car, a pre-'97 diesel vehicle or a diesel van, you will probably have to have an expensive catalytic converter fitted or leave your vehicle on the fringes of the central city. Fines for having the wrong badge or none at all are currently €50. All rental cars will have badges fitted.

Car, scooter and go-kart rental

All the major **car rental** agencies are represented in Berlin. Some have booths at the airports and most have pick-up points in the centre, too. You should be able to get something for under €30 a day, though watch out for hidden costs such as limited mileage. Most rental places do good-value Friday afternoon to Monday morning deals. If you are willing to call to book, you may find better deals with **local operators** – Robben & Wientjes (❻robben-wientjes .de), say, which offers cars from €15/day and has branches at Prinzenstr. 90–91, Kreuzberg (❻030 61 67 70; U-Moritzplatz) and Prenzlauer Allee 96 (❻030 42 10 36; U-Prenzlauer Allee).

You could also zip around on a **scooter** with a company such as Rent A Scooter, Friedrichstr. 210 (U-Kochstrasse; from €6/hr; ❻030 24 03 78 65, ⓦrentascooter-berlin.de), or for a more expensive but far more unusual experience, go for a street-legal **go-kart** with Kart 4 You (❻0800 750 75 10, ⓦkart4you.de); three hours will cost €49–59.

Taxis and velotaxis

Berlin's cream-coloured **taxis** are plentiful, cruising the city day and night and congregating at useful locations. They're always metered: for the first 7km it's €3.20 plus €1.65/km, after which it's €1.28/km. Fares rise slightly between 11pm and 6am and all day Sunday. Short trips, known as *Kurzstrecke*, can be paid on a flat rate of €4 for up to 2km or five minutes, though this only works when you hail a moving cab, and you must request it on getting into the taxi. Taxi **firms** include: City Funk (❻030 21 02 02) and Funk Taxi Berlin (❻030 26 10 26).

Finally, if you're not in a hurry and want to go just a short distance, you might consider hailing a **velotaxi**, a modern version of a cycle rickshaw. Between April and October they are easy to find at the Brandenburg Gate and other key points. They cost €6 for the first kilometre, then €2.50 for each subsequent kilometre. The drivers double as guides and are usually well informed and chatty; they also offer tours (see box, p.25).

Cycling

An extensive network of bike paths makes **cycling** around Berlin quick and convenient. You can also take your bike on the U- and S-Bahn; useful if you wish to explore the countryside and lakes of the Grunewald. To take your bike on a train you'll need to buy a **Fahrrad ticket** (see p.23) for the underground system, available for short journeys, single journeys, day tickets or monthly tickets. There are also a number of cycling **tours** of the city (see p.25).

One good investment if you're going to explore the city by bike is the **cycle route map** published by the **German bicycle club** ADFC, available from their shop at Brunnenstr. 28 (Mon–Fri noon–8pm, Sat 10am–4pm; ❻030 448 47 24, ⓦadfc-berlin.de; U-Rosenthaler Platz) as well as most city bookshops. The ADFC also offers free listings of bike rental and bike shops, with current rates and contact details.

Bike rental

Bike **rentals** are available at dozens of outlets, including many convenience stores, around Berlin, with rates around €15/day and €50/week. The nearest to your accommodation will probably be the most useful; otherwise one good company with six branches in central Berlin is **Fahrradstation** (ⓦfahrradstation.com); with branches at Auguststr. 29a (Mon–Fri 10am–7pm, Sat 10am–3pm; ❻030 22 50 80 70; U-Weinmeisterstrasse), and at Bergmannstr. 9, Kreuzberg (Mon–Fri 10am–7pm, Sat 10am–4pm; ❻030 215 15 66; U-Gneisenaustrasse).

For a more unusual experience, try renting a **vintage bike** with Kreuzberg's Finding Berlin Tours, Schlesische Str. 29/30 (❻0176 99 33 39 13, ⓦfind ingberlin-tours.com; U-Schlesisches Tor) or Hello World Berlin, Pappelallee 10 (❻01512 125 68 62, ⓦhelloworldberlin.com) in Prenzlauer Berg. Both have a selection of town, road and single-speed bikes and allow you to select your bike online at prices ranging from €9–35/day. Finally, if you turn up early enough, you can snag a free day's fixie bike rental at the Freitag shop (see p.228) in the Spandauer Vorstadt.

In addition, the railway company Deutsche Bahn (DB) has a **Call-a-bike** scheme that involves its own fleet of rental bikes scattered within underground zone A of the city, and parked on street corners and at major points like the Brandenburg Gate and Potsdamer Platz. These silver-and-red, full-suspension bicycles can be rented at any time of day for €0.08/ minute (up to €15 for 24hr and €48 for a week), with no deposit or minimum charge. To use one you first need to register a credit card (❻0700 05 22 55 22, ⓦcallabike-interaktiv.de). Registering your mobile will mean it will automatically debit your account when you call. Once you've registered, it's just a matter of calling the individual number on the side of a bike and receiving an electronic code to open

---

TOP 5 BIKE RIDES
The Grunewald See p.161
The Müggelsee See p.150
Potsdam See p.167
Sanssouci See p.169
Tiergarten See p.101

SIGHTSEEING TOURS

Fierce competition between several English-language companies means that the standard of **walking tours** is very high in Berlin. Most operators offer 4hr city tours for around €12, usually with the option of more specialized jaunts – Third Reich sites, Cold War Berlin, Jewish life, Potsdam and Sachsenhausen and the like – and there are several companies offering tours with an alternative edge. **Bike tours** are a great way of exploring the sprawling city centre itself; if that sounds too much like hard work, consider hiring a **velotaxi rickshaw** and driver.

    Bus tours abound, though you may find that buying a day ticket and hopping on and off the #100 and #200 services with a guidebook is more flexible and cheaper. Most depart from the Kurfürstendamm between Breitscheidplatz and Knesebeckstrasse, making the rounds several times every day, though schedules are curtailed in the winter.

    Boats cruise Berlin's numerous city-centre canals and suburban lakes regularly throughout the summer, and companies offer a variety of short jaunts, including trips through the town centre and day-trips to the Wannsee or Potsdam. In most cases you can just turn up at quayside stops and buy a ticket on the spot; all city centre companies have central stops around the Spree Island. Several smaller companies run tours around the Havel lake by the Grunewald, which include trips to Potsdam, and tours of the waterways around Köpenick – find details at the Reederverband der Berliner Personenschiffahrt (W reederverband-berlin.de), the organization for operators of passenger boats in Berlin.

WALKING TOURS

Alternative Berlin T 0162 819 82 64, W alternativeberlin.com. Tours of the graffiti art and squats of Berlin's underbelly.
Finding Berlin Tours T 0176 99 33 39 13, W findingberlin-tours.com. See below.
Insider Tours T 030 692 31 49, W insiderberlintours.com. Reputable outfit for city tours.
New Berlin Tours T 030 510 50 03 01, W newberlintours.com. The city centre tour offered here is free, but generous tips are expected.
Original Berlin Walks T 030 301 91 94, W berlinwalks.com. Walking tours of the main areas.
Slow Travel Berlin T 0171 122 59 73, W slowtravelberlin.com. Tours of residential districts like Wedding and Prenzlauer Berg.

CYCLING TOURS

Fat Tire Bike Tours T 030 24 04 79 91, W fattirebiketours.com/berlin. This reputable specialist charges €24 for a guided 4hr pedal around central Berlin astride a beach-cruiser bike.
Finding Berlin Tours T 0176 99 33 39 13, W findingberlin-tours.com. Vintage bike tours of Berlin's hidden corners and culinary cycling tours, along with offbeat walking tours of Turkish Berlin.
Velotaxi Tours T 0178 800 00 41, W velotaxi.de. Tours, with a driver and guide, start at €22 for two people for 30min.

BUS TOURS

Bex Sightseeing T 030 880 41 90, W bex.de. A basic 2hr city bus tour costs about €22.
Tempelhofer Reisen T 030 752 30 61, W tempelhofer.de. Hop-on hop-off service looping around central Berlin. Day passes €22.
Zille bus tour W bvg.de. Nostalgic tours, using buses decorated in the style of the "Golden Twenties" originals that operated in the city between 1916 to 1928 – they even come with a driver in period

uniform. Adults €8/50min; children up to 10 free. Tickets can be bought on the bus and at underground ticket machines. Departs from the Brandenburg Gate. April–Oct.

BOAT TOURS

Berlin Wassertaxi T 030 65 88 02 03, W berliner-wassertaxi.de. The cheap and cheerful option.
Reederei Riedel T 030 67 96 14 70, W reederei-riedel.de. Several day-trips on the river Spree, taking in the Reichstag and the Landwehrkanal. Its Stadtkernfahrt (€11.50) lasts around an hour, or you can join the 3hr Brückenfahrt (€20), which runs a large loop around all of central Berlin, at a number of points around the city. The same company also runs the Tagestour Wannsee (€18), a day-trip out to the Pfaueninsel and the Wannsee in the west of the city, to the Müggelsee in the east, and on other lakes surrounding Berlin. March to mid-Dec.
Reederei Winker T 030 349 95 95, W reederei-winkler.de. Reliable boat tours.
Stern und Kreis Schiffahrt T 030 536 36 00, W sternundkreis.de. Tours around the Havel lake, with trips to Potsdam, and of the waterways around Köpenick starting from Treptower Park.

QUIRKY TOURS

Air Service Berlin W air-service-berlin.de. Splash the cash on a 30min helicopter flight over Berlin for €124.
Hi-Flyer Wilhelmstr./Zimmerstr T 030 226 67 88 11, W air-service-berlin.de. Take to the skies (150m high) in a tethered hot-air balloon. €19 for 15min. Daily: April–Oct 10am–10pm; Nov–March 11am–6pm.
Trabi Safari T 030 30 20 10 30, W trabi-safari.de. Unique tours that explore the city in a Trabant, the cute 26-horsepower hbreglass car of the GDR. You are shown how to operate the machine before setting off on a self-driven 90min tour in their fleet of jolly open-top cars. Daily day and night, starting at €79/person if you're in a group of four, or €89/person for two. Great recorded commentary.

the lock. To drop it off you can leave it on any street corner then ring up for a code to lock the bike and leave its location as a recorded message. This can all also be done using the Call-a-bike smartphone app.

The media

English is the second language in Berlin, so you won't have a problem finding a good range of English-language newspapers and magazines and – with a little searching – programmes on the TV and radio. You will also find a number of good listings magazines (see p.33) for what's-on information.

Newspapers

The best place to look for **British and US newspapers** is at the newsagents in the main train stations: Bahnhof Zoo, Hauptbahnhof, Alexanderplatz, Friedrichstrasse and the Ostbahnhof.

Berlin has four **local newspapers**. The *Berliner Morgenpost* is a staid, conservative publication, and *B.Z.* is a trashy tabloid. *Berliner Kurier* is another tabloid – less trashy but otherwise similar. The other main local paper is the *Berliner Zeitung*, originally an East Berlin publication, which covers national and international news as well as local stories. Of the **national** dailies, the two best sellers are the centrist *Die Welt* (Ⓦ welt.de), and the sensationalist *Bild* tabloid. At the other end of the political spectrum are the liberal Berlin-based *Tagesspiegel* and the left-of-centre *Tageszeitung*, known as *taz* (Ⓦ taz.de) – not so hot on solid news, but with good in-depth articles on politics and ecology, and an extensive Berlin listings section on Friday. It has the added advantage of being a relatively easy read for non-native German speakers. The fairly dry and conservative business paper, the *Frankfurter Allgemeine*, is also widely available in the city, while the reasonably left-wing Hamburg-based *Die Zeit* appears every Thursday.

Television

Germany has **two national public TV channels** – ARD and ZDF – which somewhat approximate BBC channels or a downmarket PBS; Berlin also has regional public channel RBB. Otherwise major commercial channels dominate, foremost among them Sat, RTL and VOX. All channels seem to exist on a forced diet of US reruns clumsily dubbed into German. With cable TV, available in larger hotels,

you'll be able to pick up the locally available **cable channels** (more than twenty of them, including MTV and BBC World).

Radio

Berlin's radio output is reasonable, and you can find good things on the dial. The only **English-speaking radio** stations are the BBC World Service (90.2FM) and NPR Berlin (104.1FM) with non-commercial news, talk and entertainment programmes. For **talk** radio try sophisticated Radio Eins (95.8FM). The best **local music** stations, depending on your taste, are Fritz Radio (102.6FM), with some decent dance and hip hop, and Star FM (87.9FM), with its diet of American rock. For indie music try Flux FM (100.6FM). Best of the classical music stations is Klassik Radio (101.3FM); Jazz Radio (106.8FM) offers jazz and blues.

Festivals

Berlin's festivals are, in the main, cultural affairs, with music, art and the theatre particularly well represented. Among the other events Volksfeste – small, local street festivals – are held in most districts between July and September and worth looking out if you're on a quest for open-air music, beer and Wurst.

We've included a selection of the best festivals below; for others, check the Visit Berlin website (Ⓦ visitberlin.de) and listings magazines (see p.33).

A festival calendar

JANUARY

Bread & Butter Ⓦ breadandbutter.com. **Mid-Jan.** The city's most prestigious winter fashion event. See p.218.

Grüne Woche Ⓦ gruenewoche.de. **Late Jan.** Berlin's annual agricultural show, held in the Messegelände, with food goodies to sample from all over the world.

Sechstagerennen Ⓦ sechstagerennen-berlin.de. **Late Jan.** A Berlin tradition since the 1920s, this six-day non-stop cycle race takes place in the Velodrome, Paul-Heyse-Str.

FEBRUARY & MARCH

Berlinale Ⓦ berlinale.de. **Early Feb.** The third largest film festival in the world. See p.223.

Lange Nacht der Museen Ⓦ lange-nacht-der-museen.de. **Mid-March.** Many of Berlin's museums extend their hours – most until midnight – with surprisingly sociable results.

Impro Ⓦ improfestival.de. **Late March.** Running since 2001, this ten-day event is the biggest improvisational theatre festival in Europe.

APRIL & MAY

Amaze Indie Connect W amaze-indieconnect.de. Late April.
Gaming festival that brings together fans and creators of indie games for three days of workshops, lectures, exhibitions and awards.

My Fest W myfest36.de. May 1. Open-air festival in Kreuzberg, with music and cultural events and a lot of food stalls (especially around Kottbusser Tor). Note that May Day demonstrations in the evening in the same area have a tendency to turn ugly, though the daytime is safe and fun.

Gallery Weekend W www.gallery-weekend-berlin.de. Early May.
Forty galleries and small venues dedicated to art and design open for one weekend to present exclusive exhibitions and contemporary international art.

Theatertreffen Berlin W theatertreffen-berlin.de. Early May.
Large, mainly German-speaking theatre event held in various theatres, which tends towards the experimental.

Carnival of Cultures W karneval-berlin.de. Mid-May. Colourful weekend street festival held since 1996, with four music stages featuring acts from around the world, plus food and handmade arts and crafts. The high point is a street parade with around 4700 participants from eighty nations.

JUNE

Fete de la Musique W lafetedelamusique.com. Late June. Bands from all over Europe and beyond come to play in bars, clubs and other venues around the city as part of an ambitious event across 520 cities the world over.

Christopher Street Day W csd-berlin.de. Late June. Parade with lots of floats, music and costumed dancers celebrating gay pride at the end of the week-long Berlin Pride Festival. Draws around half a million people.

German-French Festival W volksfest-berlin.de. Mid-June to mid-July. Mini-fair with food and music and a reconstruction of a different French town each year.

Köpenicker Sommer Second half of June. Featuring a re-enactment of the robbery of the Rathaus safe in 1906 (see p.146).

JULY

Classic Open Air W classicopenair.de. Early July. The Gendarmenmarkt makes the perfect setting for this five-day series of popular outdoor classical concerts. Previous events have included the Royal Philharmonic Orchestra London performing the complete James Bond title themes and The Scorpions performing with the German Film Orchestra Potsdam.

Mercedes Benz Fashion Week Berlin W berlin.mbfashionweek .com. Early July. Big fashion show (see p.218) that coincides with the summer outing of the more offbeat Bread & Butter Berlin (see p.218).

Gauklerfest W gauklerfest.de. Late July to early Aug. Juggling and street performers' festival on Unter den Linden.

German-American Festival W deutsch-amerikanisches-volksfest .de. Late July to mid-Aug. One of the most popular events of the year. Three weeks of eating junk food and gambling your euros on lotteries and other carnival games.

AUGUST

Tanz im August W tanzimaugust.de. Mid-Aug. Around two weeks of dance performances featuring companies and artists from all over the world.

Jewish Culture Days W juedische-kulturtage.org. Mid-Aug.
Concerts, lectures, readings and films that focus each year on Jewish culture in a particular country or place.

Lange Nacht der Museen W lange-nacht-der-museen.de. Late Aug.
More than one hundred of Berlin's museums stay open until at least midnight and put on various special events in a repeat of the January event (see p.26).

SEPTEMBER

International Literature Festival W literaturfestival.com. Early Sept. Berlin's biggest literary event celebrates "diversity in the age of globalization" and features an eclectic and international selection of poets, short story writers and novelists over nine days.

Berlin Music Week W berlin-music-week.de. Early Sept. Acclaimed five-day pop music awards and festival event. With shows in clubs all around town and big names playing the Berlin Festival (W berlinfestival.de) at Tempelhof; past headliners have included Moby, Björk and the Pet Shop Boys.

Feste an der Panke Mid-Sept. Pankow Volksfest that's often among the city's best.

Berlin Marathon W bmw-berlin-marathon.com. Late Sept. With around 40,000 participants from around 107 countries and the most marathon world records (for men and women) set here, this is one of the largest and most popular road races in the world. The route starts in the Tiergarten, looping around to Friedrichshain and Dahlem before finishing near the Brandenburg Gate. Closing date for entries is one month before the marathon.

Berlin Art Week W berlinartweek.de. Late Sept. Big contemporary art event. See p.218.

Berliner Liste W berliner-liste.org. Late Sept. Locally focused art event held at around the same time as Berlin Art Week. See p.218.

OCTOBER & NOVEMBER

Tag der Deutschen Einheit Oct 3. The "day of German unity" is celebrated with gusto, beer, sausages and music at the Brandenburg Gate.

Festival of Lights W festival-of-lights.de. Mid-Oct. Every autumn, Berlin's famous sights are transformed into a sea of colour and light, including the Brandenburg Gate, the Berlin TV Tower, Berliner Dom and more. The nightly light show comes with art and cultural events around the topic of light.

JazzFest Berlin W jazzfest-berlin.de. Late Oct/early Nov.
Longstanding jazz festival staged throughout the city. See p.215.

International Short film Festival W interfilm.de. Mid-Nov.
Five-day festival, founded in 1982, that showcases numerous competitions across all genres, as well as workshops, discussions and parties.

DECEMBER

Christmas Street Markets Dec. Folksy Christmas markets – with roasted almonds, mulled wine and local handicrafts – dot the city. The most significant are on Breitscheidplatz and Alexanderplatz, but the prettiest are around the Staatsoper at Unter den Linden, on the Gendarmenmarkt where evening performances add to the atmosphere, at Schloss Charlottenburg, or outside the city in Spandau's old town.

New Year's Eve Run W scc-events.com. Dec 31. Annual 6.3km run organized by the Berlin Marathon authorities, with free entry and prizes for fancy dress.

Silvester Germany's largest open-air New Year's Eve party takes place along the Str. des 17 Juni, between the Brandenburg Gate and the Siegessäule, to the sound of fireworks and pop music. Street stalls sell sparkling wine.

Culture and etiquette

Berliners are traditionally quite a gruff lot who don't suffer fools gladly, though much of this attitude is laced with a sardonic wit known as Berliner Schnauze – literally "Berlin snout". Learn to take all this in your stride: it's nothing personal, just an everyday way of dealing with urban living.

Another defining attribute for Berliners is their Prussian sense of orderliness and respect for rules and authority. Jaywalkers will more frequently be reprimanded by bystanders – "what if a child saw you?" – than by the police.

Thankfully, despite all this, Berlin is a famously tolerant place. This tolerance comes in part from the city's appeal to unconventional Germans who relocate from elsewhere in the country and partly from its large immigrant population. Staggering around in the small hours, drinking in the street, or being openly gay will neither raise an eyebrow nor turn a head. This open-mindedness also extends to a tolerance for **smoking** that is far higher than elsewhere in Western Europe – with many bars frequently ignoring bans.

Travel essentials

Addresses

In Berlin the **street name** is always written before the number and all addresses are suffixed by a five-figure postcode. Street **numbers** don't always run odd–even on opposite sides of the street – often they go up one side and down the other. Strasse (street) is commonly abbreviated to Str., and often joined on to

the end of the previous word. Other **terms** include Weg (path), Ufer (river bank), Platz (square) and Allee (avenue). Berlin apartment blocks are often built around courtyards with several entrances and staircases: the Vorderhaus, abbreviated as VH in addresses, is as the name suggests, the front building; the Gartenhaus (GH; garden house) and the Hinterhof (HH; back house) are at the rear of the building. EG means the ground floor, 1 OG means the first floor, and so on. Dachwohnung means the "flat under the roof" – in other words, the attic.

Climate

Temperatures in Berlin can vary between July highs of around 30ºC and January lows of about -18ºC. Though temperatures tend to average about 5ºC between November and March, they rise quickly to a 20ºC average between May and August, but these summer months are also the wettest – when around half the city's annual **precipitation** of 570mm falls.

Costs

By the standards of most European capitals, **prices** in Berlin are reasonable and well short of the excesses of Paris and London, even though the quality of what's on offer can easily compete. Nevertheless, for anyone heading out to Berlin's famous nightspots or shopping at its designer stores, visiting the city can become expensive.

Assuming you intend to eat and drink in moderately priced places and use public transport sparingly, the **minimum** you could comfortably get by on – after accommodation costs, which start at about €60 for a basic double room in the centre in high season – is around €25 (around £22/US$33) a day. For this you would get a basic breakfast (€4), a sandwich (€3), an evening meal (€10), two beers (€5) and one underground ticket (€3), though this budget would limit you to visiting free museums and making your own entertainment. A more realistic figure, if you want to see as much of the city as possible (and party at night), would be about twice that amount.

AVERAGE MONTHLY TEMPERATURES AND RAINFALL

BERLIN	Jan	Feb	Mar	Apr	May	Jun	Jul	Aug	Sep	Oct	Nov	Dec
Max/min (°C)	9/-12	11/-12	17/-7	22/-2	28/2	30/6	32/9	31/8	28/4	21/-1	13/-4	10/-9
Max/min (°F)	48/10	52/10	63/19	72/28	82/36	86/43	90/48	88/46	82/39	70/30	55/25	50/16
Rainfall (mm)	43	38	38	43	56	71	53	66	46	36	51	56

TOP 10 FREE (OR ALMOST FREE) BERLIN EXPERIENCES

Berlin Wall Memorial See p.12
Cycling the Tiergarten See p.101
East Side Gallery See p.130
Flea market browsing See p.232
Holocaust Memorial See p.38
Picnicking in Sanssouci See p.169
The Reichstag See p.37
Sachsenhausen See p.174
Sightseeing for free on buses #100 and #200 See p.25
Tränenpalast See p.84

Crime and personal safety

Crime in Berlin is very modest in comparison with other European cities of equal size, and if tourists encounter it at all it will most likely be **petty crime** such as pickpocketing or bag-snatching in one of the main shopping precincts.

As far as **personal safety** is concerned, most parts of the city centre are safe enough. Use common sense, but bear in mind that even the "rougher" neighbourhoods (say, eastern Kreuzberg or Friedrichshain) feel more dangerous than they actually are: the run-down U-Bahn stations at Kottbusser Tor and Görlitzer Bahnhof (both in largely immigrant districts), or S Bahn stations Warschauer Strasse and Ostkreuz, look alarming when compared to the rest of the system, but wouldn't stand out in many other European cities. The situation in suburbs is a little trickier, with immigrant gangs flexing their muscles in the western half of the city and neo-Nazi thugs an issue in the east. With caution it's fine, but all the same it's wise to be wary in **suburbs** like **Lichtenberg, Marzahn, Wedding or Neukölln**, where muggings and casual violence do occur, particularly to those who stand out.

If you do have something stolen (or simply lose something), or suffer an attack you'll need to register the details and obtain an official statement (*Anzeige*) at the local police station: a straightforward, but inevitably bureaucratic and time-consuming process. Note the crime report number – or, better still, get a copy of the statement itself – for your insurance company.

The two offences you might unwittingly commit concern **identity papers** and **jaywalking**. By law you need to carry proof of your identity at all times. A driver's licence or ID card is fine, but a passport is best. It's essential that you carry all your documentation when driving – failure to do so may result in an on-the-spot fine. Jaywalking is also illegal and you can be fined if caught.

Electricity

Supply runs at 220–240V, 50Hz AC; sockets generally require a two-pin plug with rounded prongs. Visitors from the UK will need an **adaptor**, and those from North America may need a transformer, though most portable electrical equipment – like cameras, laptops and mobile phones – are designed to accommodate a range of voltages.

Entry requirements

British and other EU nationals can enter Germany on a valid passport or national identity card for an indefinite period. US, Canadian, Australian and New Zealand citizens do not need a **visa** to enter Germany, and are allowed a stay of ninety days within any six-month period. South Africans need to apply for a visa, from the German Embassy in Pretoria (see below), which will cost around ZAR260 depending on the exchange rate. Visa requirements vary for nationals of other countries; contact your local German embassy or consulate for information.

In order to extend a stay once in the country you must contact the nearest **Bürgeramt** (Citizens' Office) to register your address, and then make an email appointment with the Ausländerbehörde (Alien Authority), Friedrich-Krause-Ufer 24; U-Amrumer Strasse (✉ abh@labo.berlin.de). Full guidance is provided at ⓦ berlin.de, though all the relevant info is in German only.

GERMAN EMBASSIES ABROAD

Australia 119 Empire Circuit, Yarralumla, Canberra 2600 ☎ 02 6270 1911, ⓦ canberra.diplo.de.
Canada 1 Waverley St, Ottawa, ON K2P 0T8 ☎ 613 232 1101, ⓦ ottawa.diplo.de.
Ireland 31 Trimelston Ave, Booterstown, Blackrock, Co Dublin ☎ 01 269 3011, ⓦ dublin.diplo.de.
New Zealand 90–92 Hobson St, 6011 Wellington ☎ 04 473 6063, ⓦ wellington.diplo.de.
South Africa 180 Blackwood St, Arcadia, Pretoria 0083 ☎ 012 427 8900, ⓦ pretoria.diplo.de.
UK 23 Belgrave Square, London SW1X 8PZ ☎ 020 7824 1300, ⓦ london.diplo.de.

EMERGENCY NUMBERS

Fire and ambulance ☎ 112
Police ☎ 110

USA 2300 M St NW, Washington DC 20037 ☎ 202 298 4000, Ⓦ germany.info.

EMBASSIES AND CONSULATES IN BERLIN

Australia Wallstr. 76–79 ☎ 030 880 08 80, Ⓦ germany.embassy .gov.au.

Canada Leipziger Platz 17 ☎ 030 20 31 20, Ⓦ canadainternational .gc.ca.

Ireland Jägerstr. 51 ☎ 030 22 07 20, Ⓦ embassyofireland.de.

New Zealand Friedrichstr. 60 ☎ 030 20 62 10, Ⓦ nzembassy.com.

UK Wilhelmstr. 70–71 ☎ 030 20 45 70, Ⓦ britischebotschaft.de.

USA Pariser Platz 2 & Clayallee 170 ☎ 030 830 50, Ⓦ germany .usembassy.gov.

Health

As a European Union member, Germany has free reciprocal health agreements with other member states, whose citizens can apply – well in advance of their trip – for a free **European Health Insurance Card** (EHIC; Ⓦ ehic.org.uk). The card will allow you to receive free or cut-rate treatment, but does not extend to repatriation. Without it, EU citizens will have to pay in full for all medical treatment, which starts at about €30 for a visit to the doctor. Non-EU residents should check the level of cover that they might have from existing insurance policies, but in almost all cases are advised to take out travel insurance (see below). If you need to make an insurance policy claim for health costs, be sure to keep all receipts relating to treatment.

If you need immediate medical attention, head for the 24-hour emergency room of a major **hospital**, such as the Charité Universitätsklinikum, Charitéplatz 1, Mitte (☎ 030 450 53 10 00; S-Bahn Hauptbahnhof). For **dental emergencies** one good clinic is the English-speaking Zahnärztlicher Notdienst (☎ 030 89 00 43 33, Ⓦ kzv.de). In an **emergency**, phone ☎ 112 for an ambulance (*Krankenwagen*).

If you need a **doctor**, phone Calladoc (☎ 01805 32 13 03, Ⓦ calladoc.com; calls cost €0.14/min), an

English-language service featuring practitioners who will discuss your symptoms and can refer you or send an English-speaking doctor. Doctor surgery hours are 9am to noon and 3pm to 6pm on weekdays except Wednesday afternoon.

To get a **prescription** filled, go to a **pharmacy** (*Apotheke*), signalled by an illuminated green cross. Pharmacists are well trained and generally speak English. There's a 24-hour pharmacy in the Hauptbahnhof, otherwise, outside normal hours (usually 8.30am–6.30pm), there will be a notice on the door of any pharmacy indicating the nearest one that's open. After hours you'll be served through a small hatch in the door, so don't be put off if it looks as though a place is closed.

Insurance

Though Berlin is a relatively safe city (see p.29) and EU healthcare privileges (see above) or your private medical plan may apply in Germany, an **insurance policy** is a wise precaution to cover against theft, loss and various other travel mishaps.

Internet

Berlin is very internet-savvy and online access is excellent. Virtually all hostels and hotels, a growing number of cafés, and all the main train stations have **wi-fi** hot spots (locally referred to as WLAN) – and there's a free one in the Sony Center (see p.15). Access to terminals in internet cafés averages at about €2/30min.

Laundry

All large hotels generally provide a laundry service – but at a cost. **Launderettes** scattered throughout the city are generally cheaper, with an average load costing around €5 to wash and dry. Hours tend to be daily 7am–10pm and addresses can be found by searching "*Waschsalon*"

ROUGH GUIDES TRAVEL INSURANCE

Rough Guides has teamed up with WorldNomads.com to offer great **travel insurance** deals. Policies are available to residents of more than 150 countries, with cover for a wide range of adventure sports, 24hr emergency assistance, high levels of medical and evacuation cover and a stream of travel safety information. Roughguides.com users can take advantage of their policies online 24/7, from anywhere in the world – even if you're already travelling. And since plans often change when you're on the road, you can extend your policy and even claim online. Roughguides.com users who buy travel insurance with WorldNomads.com can also leave a positive footprint and donate to a community development project. For more information, go to Ⓦ roughguides.com/travel-insurance.

at ⓦberlin.de. One popular chain is Schnell & Sauber (ⓦschnell-u-sauber.de).

Left luggage

There are **24-hour lockers** at both Tegel and Schönefeld airports as well as at the Hauptbahnhof, Alexanderplatz, Ostbahnhof, Friedrichstrasse, Potsdamer Platz, Gesundbrunnen, Zoologischer Garten, Südkreuz and Spandau train stations and the ZOB bus station. The Hauptbahnhof also has a left-luggage office. Charges for lockers range around €2–6/day, but note too that most **hotels and hostels** will hold guest baggage for the day free of charge.

Living in Berlin

Berlin, a politicized, happening city with a dynamic arts scene and tolerant attitudes, is a magnet for young people from Germany and all over Europe, and has a large English-speaking community.

Numerous **job agencies** offer both temporary and permanent work – usually secretarial – but you'll obviously be expected to have a good command of German. Useful internet sources include ⓦstepstone.de, ⓦmamas.de, ⓦjobs.de, ⓦjobnet.de and ⓦmonster.de.

Work permits (*Arbeitserlaubnis*) aren't required for EU nationals working in Germany, though everyone else will need one – and, theoretically, should not even look for a job without one. Applying for a long-term permit is to enter a world of complicated and tedious bureaucracy, and it's essential to seek advice from someone with experience in the whole process, especially when completing official forms. The best official place for advice is the **Auswärtiges Amt** (German Federal Foreign Office; ⓦauswaertiges-amt.de), whose website has the latest information – in English.

For non-EU nationals – North Americans, Australasians and everybody else – finding work legally is extremely difficult, unless you've secured the job before arriving in Germany. The best advice is to approach the German embassy or consulate in your own country (see p.29). Citizens of Australia, New Zealand and Canada aged between 18 and 30 can apply for a working holiday visa, enabling legal work in Germany for 90 days in a twelve-month period: contact German embassies for details.

For long-term **accommodation**, while newspapers advertise apartments and rooms, it's much quicker and less traumatic to sign on at one of the several **Mitwohnzentralen**, accommodation agencies that specialize in long-term sublets in apartments. Anyone who wants to stay in Germany for longer than three months – including EU citizens – must first **register** their residence (*Anmeldung*) at a **Bürgeramt** (Citizens' Office). The form for this requires a signature from your landlord.

Lost property

The **Police lost and found** department (*Fundbüro*) is at Platz der Luftbrücke 6, Tempelhof (Mon, Tues & Fri 9am–2pm, Thurs 1–6pm; ☎030 75 60 31 01; U-Platz der Luftbrücke). For items lost on **public transport**, contact the BVG Fundbüro, Potsdamer Str. 182, Schöneberg (Mon–Thurs 9am–6pm, Fri 9am–2pm; ☎030 194 49; U-Kleistpark). **Tegel** airport's lost property department can be contacted on ☎030 41 01 23 15; Schönefeld airport's is on ☎030 34 39 75 33.

Mail

Post offices of **Deutsche Post** (ⓦdeutschepost.de) and their unmissable bright yellow postboxes pep up the streetscape. One of Central Berlin's most conveniently situated **post offices** (*Postämt*), with the longest hours, is at Bahnhof Friedrichstrasse (under the arches at Georgenstr. 12; Mon–Fri 6am–10pm, Sat & Sun 8am–10pm). Other offices (generally Mon–Fri 9am–6pm, Sat 9am–1pm), often have separate parcel offices (marked *Pakete*), a block or so away; and you can also buy stamps from the small yellow machines next to some postboxes and at some newsagents.

When posting a letter, make sure you distinguish between the slots marked for various postal codes. Boxes marked with a red circle indicate collections late in the day and on Sunday. Mail to the UK usually takes three days; to North America one week; and to Australasia two weeks. A postcard or letter under 50g costs €0.75 to send worldwide.

Maps

Having a **map** is essential for getting around Berlin; the city is full of little side streets and its long-running boulevards tend to change names every couple of blocks. One comprehensive map is the convenient and ingeniously folded *Falk Plan*, which includes a map of the U- and S-Bahn system and an index of every street in Berlin and Potsdam. It's available at most bookstores and newsagents. For a complete account of the public transport system you should pick the *BVG & S-Bahn Berlin Atlas*, which has complete listings and timetables for the U- and S-Bahn systems and bus, tram and ferry routes. It's available at the larger U-Bahn and S-Bahn stations. If you just need to check the routes – particularly the bus and tram routes – you can consult the huge city map reproduced in all stations and bus shelters.

Money and banks

Germany uses the **euro** as its currency, which is split into 100 cents. At the time of writing, the exchange rate was approximately €1.16 to the pound, €0.75 to the US dollar and €0.69 to the Australian dollar. For the latest rates, go to ⓦxe.com.

Banks are plentiful, and their hours usually Monday to Friday from 8.30am to 5pm with later opening two days a week until 6pm. For currency exchange, the **Wechselstuben** (bureaux de change) at the main train stations and airports offer better rates than the banks and are open outside normal banking hours – usually daily 8am–8pm. If you do use a bank to change money it may be worth shopping around (including the savings banks or Sparkasse), as the rates of exchange and commission vary. The latter tends to be a flat rate, meaning that small-scale transactions should be avoided whenever possible.

Debit and **credit cards** are becoming a part of everyday life, though their use is not as widespread as in the UK or North America. Cash is still the currency of choice, particularly in bars and restaurants. However, major credit and debit cards are good in department stores, mid- to up-market restaurants, and an increasing number of shops and petrol stations.

Should you want to get **cash** on your plastic, the best way is from the many **ATMs**. You can withdraw as little as €20; however they do charge a minimum fee, often around €2.50, and charge two to four percent of the withdrawal as commission. In addition to credit cards, most bank debit cards, part of either the Cirrus or Plus systems, can be used for withdrawing cash, and carry lower fees than credit cards; note, however, that your home bank will almost certainly levy a commission for use of the card abroad. Various banks will also give an advance against your credit card, subject to a minimum of the equivalent of £60/US$100 – stickers in bank windows indicate which cards they're associated with. Make sure your personal identification number (PIN) will work overseas.

Public holidays

Opening hours on public holidays generally follow Sunday hours: most shops will be closed and museums and other attractions will follow their Sunday schedules. **Public holidays** fall on January 1, Good Friday, Easter Monday, May 1, Ascension Day (forty days after Easter), Whitsun, October 3, November 3 and December 25 & 26.

Phones

You can make local and **international calls** from most **phone boxes** in the city – marked international – which are generally equipped with basic instructions in English. Virtually every pay phone you'll find takes coins and **cards**. The latter come in €5, €10 and €20 denominations and are available from all post offices and some shops. Phone boxes with a ringing bell symbol indicate that you can be called back on that phone. In addition, many **phone shops**, found throughout the city, offer cheap international calls, calling cards and often internet services.. The cheapest time to call abroad is between 9pm and 8am.

Most British **mobile phones** should work in Germany, but if you haven't used your phone abroad before, check with your provider whether it will work in Germany, and what call charges are. Unless you have a tri-band phone, it is unlikely that a mobile bought for use in the US will work outside North America; most smart phones are tri-band though.

If you are in Germany for a while, consider buying a local **SIM card** for your mobile phone. These tend to cost around €15 and are best bought through a phone shop. To use a different SIM card in your phone, it will need to be unlocked, if it isn't already, to accept the cards of different providers. The phone shops will be able to advise where it is possible to do this locally. Expect to pay around €10 for instant service. Top-up cards can be bought in supermarkets, kiosks and phone shops and even in BVG ticket vending machines.

To **call Berlin from abroad** use the **international code** for Germany (❶49), followed by the city code (❶30) and then the number.

For **directory enquiries** in English call ❶118 37; the service costs an initial €0.20, then €1/ minute.

Time

Germany is one hour ahead of GMT, six hours ahead of US Eastern Standard Time and nine ahead of US Pacific Standard Time.

Tipping

Service is, as a rule, included in the bill. Rounding up a café, restaurant or taxi bill to the next euro or

CALLING HOME FROM ABROAD

Note that the initial zero is omitted from the area code when dialling the UK, Ireland, Australia, New Zealand and South Africa from abroad.

Australia 00 + 61 + area code + number.
Ireland 00 + 353 + area code + number.
New Zealand 00 + 64 + area code + number.
South Africa 00 + 27 + area code + number.
UK 00 + 44 + area code + number.
USA and Canada 00 + 1 + area code + number.

Neuen Kranzler Eck Kurfürstendamm 22; U-Kurfürstendamm. Mon–Sat 9.30am–8pm, Sun 10am–6pm.
Tegel Aiport Terminal A /Gate 2; buses #X9; 109; 128; TXL. Daily 8am–9pm.

USEFUL WEBSITES

ⓦ **berlin.de** The city's official site, with loads of general information, plus the latest events.
ⓦ **berlin-online.de** An excellent, all-purpose source for news, business, politics, entertainment, restaurants, listings and the like.
ⓦ **findingberlin.com** Online magazine run by a group of twenty-something creative types that provides a great feel for the aspects of the city they love.
ⓦ **slowtravelberlin.com** Articles suggesting ways to meander around offbeat Berlin.
ⓦ **uberlin.co.uk** British expat blog with lots on the music scene.

so is acceptable in most cases, though when you run up a particularly large tab you will probably want to add some more.

Tourist information

Before you set off for Berlin, explore the **German National Tourist Board** website (ⓦ germany .travel), and that of the **city tourist office** (ⓦ visit berlin.de), which is more detailed, has a helpful accommodation service and maintains an excellent events section detailing most mainstream cultural happenings in the city. They run five tourist information centres (see below) and a call centre (Mon–Fri 9am 7pm, Sat 10am–6pm, Sun 10am–2pm; ☏ 030 25 00 23 33), that provides information as well as accommodation bookings. They also produce a handy free map.

Berlin has two essential **listings magazines** – *Tip* (ⓦ tip-berlin.de) and *Zitty* (ⓦ zitty.de) – which come out on alternate weeks. *Zitty* is marginally the better of the two, with day-by-day details of gigs, concerts, events, TV and radio, theatre and film, alongside intelligent articles on politics, style and the Berlin in-crowd, and useful classified ads. Reading copies of these can be found in any bar. A third magazine, also with a good deal of listings information and possibly more useful if you don't speak any German, is the monthly English-language *ExBerliner* (ⓦ exber liner.com), which caters to Berlin's expats.

TOURIST OFFICES IN BERLIN

Brandenburg Gate Pariser Platz (south wing); U- & S-Brandenburger Tor. Daily: April–Oct 9.30am–7pm; Nov–March 9.30am 6pm.
Fernsehturm (TV Tower) Panoramastr. 1a; U-Alexanderplatz. Late May–Oct daily 10am–6pm.
Hauptbahnhof Europaplatz; U- & S-Bahn Hauptbahnhof. Daily 8am–10pm.

Travellers with disabilities

Access and **facilities** for the disabled (*Behinderte*) are good in Berlin: most of the major museums, public buildings and the majority of the public transport system are wheelchair friendly, and an active disabled community is on hand for helpful advice.

A particularly good meeting place with lots of useful **information** is the *Hotel MIT-Mensch*, Ehrlichstr. 48 (☏ 030 509 69 30, ⓦ mit-mensch.com; S-Bahn Karlshorst; €84 for a standard double room in peak season), which provides friendly lodging run by and for wheelchair users. For more formal and in-depth information check out **Mobidat** (ⓦ mobidat.net), a Berlin activist group that campaigns for better access for people with disabilities. They have a wealth of information on wheelchair-accessible hotels and restaurants, city tours for disabled travellers and local transport services. Their online database lists more than 40,000 buildings in Berlin, including hotels, restaurants and theatres, indicating their degree of accessibility. Less useful is the tourist office (see above), though they do have listings of suitable accommodation.

The public transport system is disabled-aware: four out of five buses and around half its trams have ramps to allow access – look for a blue wheelchair symbol on the side of vehicles. Trains are generally easy to board, but getting onto the platforms less so – most but not all U- and S-Bahn stations are equipped with lifts. The official U- and S-Bahn map indicates which stations are wheelchair-accessible; for more information check with the BVG first (see p.22).

Mitte: Unter den Linden and around

The natural place to start exploring Berlin is at its most famous landmark, the Brandenburg Gate. It lies at the head of its premier boulevard, Unter den Linden, and beside the iconic Reichstag, the German parliament. During the Berlin Wall years all three became rather forlorn symbols of malaise: the gate sat in the no man's land of the Wall, the road led nowhere and the building lay largely empty. But now, following reunification, regeneration and Berlin's reinvention as Germany's capital, they again provide a nucleus for a city that lacked a coherent centre for so long. Gratifyingly, you can do a walking tour of the entire district that's manageable in a day. It's worth starting early with a booking to view the Reichstag dome – or consider ending your day's exploration here: the building's open until midnight and Berlin's nocturnal cityscape is an attraction itself.

This important historical district was key in Berlin's eighteenth-century transformation from a relative backwater to the capital of Prussia, when it became one of Europe's biggest players. With Prussia's rise its architects were commissioned to create the trappings of a capital city – churches, theatres, libraries, palaces and an opera house – all on and around Unter den Linden. Safe **Baroque** and **Neoclassical** styles predominate, and there are no great flights of architectural fancy. These buildings were meant to project an image of solidity, permanence and power, perhaps to allay the latent insecurity of Prussia's relatively late arrival on the European stage.

However, almost every one of these symbols of Prussian might was left gutted by the bombing and shelling of World War II. Paradoxically, it was the postwar communist regime that resurrected them from the wartime rubble to adorn the capital of the German Democratic Republic. The result was a pleasing re-creation of the old city, though one motive behind this restoration was to give the East German state a sense of historical continuity by tacitly linking it with Prussia.

This **restoration** was so successful that looking at these magnificent eighteenth- and nineteenth-century buildings it's difficult to believe that as recently as the 1960s large patches of the centre lay in ruins. Like archeologists trying to picture a whole vase from a single fragment, the builders took a facade, or just a small fraction of one, and set about re-creating the whole. And even though much of what can be seen today is an imitation, it's often easy to suspend disbelief and imagine unbroken continuity.

The rejuvenation is at its most amazing on the **Gendarmenmarkt**, a square just south of Unter den Linden where, even in the 1980s, its twin Neoclassical churches – the **Französischer Dom** and **Deutscher Dom** – remained bombed-out shells. Also impressive is the reconstruction of the grand buildings in and around **Bebelplatz**, which under the noble rulers of Prussia – the Hohenzollern – became an impressive prelude to the awesome buildings of the Spreeinsel, which included their palace and Museum Island (see p.53).

Just south of the **Reichstag** and the **Brandenburg Gate** is the **Holocaust Memorial**, which perversely paves the way to the site of **Hitler's Bunker** – sitting within Berlin's prewar **Regierungsviertel** or "government quarter" along **Wilhelmstrasse** – where the Führer committed suicide. Almost nothing of Regierungsviertel survives today, but along the road there's a small but interesting exhibition on the **Stasi**, the East German secret police.

The Brandenburg Gate

U- & S-Brandenburger Tor

Heavily laden with meaning and historical association, the **Brandenburg Gate** (Brandenburger Tor) has come to mark the very centre of Berlin. Built as a city gate-cum-triumphal arch in 1791, it was designed by Carl Gotthard Langhans and modelled after the Propylaea, the entrance to the Acropolis in Athens. The Gate became, like the Reichstag later, a symbol of German solidarity, looking out to the monolithic Siegessäule, a column celebrating Prussian military victories and guarding the city's grandest thoroughfare. In 1806 Napoleon marched under the arch and took home with him the **Quadriga**, the horse-drawn chariot that tops the Gate. It was returned a few years later, and the revolutionaries of 1848 and 1918 met under its form; later the Gate was a favoured rallying point for the Nazis' torchlit marches.

After the building of the Wall placed the Gate in the Eastern sector, nearby observation posts became the place for visiting politicians – John F. Kennedy included (see p.79) – to look over the Iron Curtain from the West in what became a handy photo opportunity; the view was apparently emotive enough to reduce Margaret Thatcher to tears. With the opening of a border crossing here just before Christmas 1989, the east–west axis of the city was symbolically re-created. The GDR authorities, who rebuilt the Quadriga following wartime damage, had removed the Prussian Iron Cross from the Goddess of Victory's laurel wreath, which topped her staff, on the

1

grounds that it was "symbolic of Prussian-German militarism". When the border was reopened, the Iron Cross was replaced, which some, mindful of historical precedent, still viewed with a frisson of unease – but now it certainly seems harmless enough and is used as a popular backdrop for photos of posing tourists.

Pariser Platz

The Brandenburg Gate looms over **Pariser Platz**, whose ornamental gardens have been restored to reproduce the prewar feel, if not exact look, since the square is now surrounded by modern buildings. However, the millions of euros that have gone into this redevelopment have had some interesting results, despite the stringent building guidelines: windows have to be vertical in format and facades only a maximum of 49 percent glass – the rest should be stone – though the **Akadamie der Künste** deliberately flaunted the rule.

DZ Bank

Described as the "best thing I've ever done" by Canadian-born architect Frank O. Gehry, the **DZ Bank** is worth a second look, even if you can't do much more than crane your neck at its curvaceous interiors from the lobby. While the building's plain

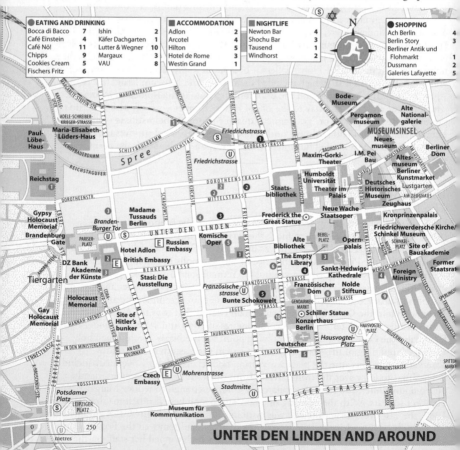

● EATING AND DRINKING			
Bocca di Bacco	7	Ishin	2
Café Einstein	4	Käfer Dachgarten	1
Café Nö!	11	Lutter & Wegner	10
Chipps	9	Margaux	3
Cookies Cream	5	VAU	8
Fischers Fritz	6		

■ ACCOMMODATION	
Adlon	2
Arcotel	4
Hilton	5
Hotel de Rome	3
Westin Grand	1

■ NIGHTLIFE	
Newton Bar	4
Shochu Bar	3
Tausend	1
Windhorst	2

● SHOPPING	
Ach Berlin	4
Berlin Story	3
Berliner Antik und	
Flohmarkt	1
Dussmann	2
Galeries Lafayette	5

UNTER DEN LINDEN AND AROUND

exterior almost mockingly follows the exacting building codes – it's only just fifty percent stone, its windows only slightly taller than wide – inside, beyond the huge blocks of Portuguese marble in the entrance, thousands of individually formed metal panels give the conference rooms at its heart an aquatic, undulating curvaceousness. The structure is also unusual in that it moves from a height of five storeys at the front to ten at the rear. Though owned by a bank, the building is mostly used as offices and event space; one of the thirty luxurious private apartments at the back is owned by Gerhard Schröder, the former German Chancellor (1998–2005).

Akadamie der Künste

Pariser Platz 4 • Daily 10am–10pm • Prices depend on exhibition; usually around €5 • ⓦ adk.de • U- & S-Brandenburger Tor

Shoulder-to-shoulder with the DZ Bank and every bit as eye-catching is the glassy **Akadamie der Künste** (Academy of Art). The building somehow slithered around local building codes by ostensibly copying the design of the prewar building that was here – though reconstructing it in glass and steel. Naturally a storm raged over how the building had been approved, but sensibly the courts upheld permission for it to stay. Inside you can see the last original structure from prewar Pariser Platz, tucked away at the back of building, and wander across sweeping concrete expanses for first-floor views of the platz. The building holds six temporary contemporary art exhibitions per year; the rest of the building includes offices, a café and a private club.

Hotel Adlon

On the southeast corner of the platz, the legendary **Hotel Adlon** (see p.177), once one of Europe's grandest hotels, has been rebuilt. The original was host to luminaries from Charlie Chaplin to Lawrence of Arabia and Kaiser Wilhelm II, and was regarded throughout the continent as the acme of luxury and style. The building was destroyed in the closing days of the war, and this new version, modelled loosely on its predecessor – the lobby fountain, for example, was salvaged from the original – attempts to scale the same heights of opulence. Even if you can't afford a drink here, let alone a room, have a look at the lobby and imagine the late eighteenth century when Berlin was the cultural capital of Europe. Culture of a very different sort graced the building in 2002, when Michael Jackson, who was staying in the bulletproof presidential suite, dangled his youngest child over the balcony in front of the world's press.

The Reichstag

Daily 8am–midnight; last admission 10pm • Free; entry requires advance booking (at least a day in advance in summer) for a particular time slot, which can be done online or at a booth on the opposite side of Scheidemannstrasse – the road that separates the Reichstag from the Tiergarten • ☎ 030 22 73 21 52, ⓦ bundestag.de • U-Bundestag

Directly behind the Brandenburg Gate a line of cobbles marks the course of the Berlin Wall where for 28 years it separated the Gate from the other great emblem of national unity, the **Reichstag** – now once again the seat of Germany's parliament. The imposing nineteenth-century Neoclassical Reichstag immediately impresses, its stolid, bombastic form wholly in keeping with its pivotal role in history.

However, designed by British architect Sir Norman Foster in 1999, the Reichstag's giant glass **dome**, supported by a soaring mirrored column, has become the building's main visitor attraction. A circular ramp spirals up the inside to a **viewing deck** with stunning 360-degree views of the city. In the foreground the Regierungsviertel buildings (see p.104) and the massive Tiergarten park dominate, but the Sony Center (see p.92), the Fernsehturm (see p.62) and the shimmering golden roof of the Synagogue on Orianienburgerstrasse (see p.77) arc other obvious landmarks. If you haven't booked in advance, reserve a table at the *Käfer Dachgarten* restaurant (see p.188), which has fairly good views itself, but, crucially, also gives you access to the dome.

1

THE REICHSTAG IN HISTORY

The Reichstag was built in 1894 to house a sham parliament answerable only to the Kaiser, but in November 1918, Philipp Scheidemann declared the founding of the German Republic from a window here, paving the way for the Weimar Republic, which lasted just fourteen years before the Nazis claimed power. Their coup came partly as a result of a fire in the Reichstag in 1933, seen across the world in flickering newsreels, which gave the Nazis an excuse to introduce an emergency decree suspending civil rights and effectively instigating a dictatorship. Debate as to who actually started the fire began immediately and continues to this day. In a show trial, an itinerant ex-communist Dutch bricklayer, **Marius van der Lubbe**, was successfully charged with arson and executed the following year, but it's more likely that the Nazis began the fire themselves. Equally famously, the Reichstag became a symbol of the Allied victory at the end of World War II, when soldiers raised the Soviet flag on its roof – even though heavy fighting still raged below. The building was left in tatters by the conflict, and only in 1971 was its reconstruction completed to house a museum of its own and Germany's history, but in 1990 the government of a reunified Germany decided to move its parliament back, though that didn't happen until April 19, 1999 – once all its interiors had been refashioned and a new **cupola** set atop the building. This ended up being more than just a stunning new refurbishment – it became part of a huge drive to improve energy efficiency. The Reichstag is the most energy-efficient parliament building in the world – all energy comes from renewables – meaning that the building has made history once again.

Having explored the inside of the Reichstag, wander around the outside of the building and try to spot the scores of patched bullet holes around some of its windows, dating from the last days of the Battle of Berlin. At the back of the building, beside the River Spree and the nearest corner of the Tiergarten, there is also a poignant series of **plaques** and **crosses** with the names (where known) of those who died attempting to swim or climb the East German border here.

The Holocaust Memorial

Memorial 24hr; tours in English Sat 3pm • Free; tours €3 **Information centre** Tues–Sun: April–Sept 10am–8pm, last admission 7.15pm; Oct–March 10am–7pm, last admission 6.15pm • Free; audio tours €4 • ☏ 030 26 39 43 36, ☒ holocaustmahnmal.de • U-Brandenburger Tor

The block of land immediately south of the Brandenburg Gate and Pariser Platz is officially dedicated to the National Memorial to the Murdered Jews of Europe. Generally known as the **Holocaust Memorial**, it was unveiled in 2006 after almost seventeen years of planning and controversy (see box, p.39), and six years of designing and building. The monument is the work of New York architect Peter Eisenman, who took inspiration from the densely clustered gravestones of Prague's Jewish graveyard. It involves 2711 dark grey oblong pillars of varying heights evenly and tightly spaced over the entire site – which is about the size of three football pitches. As there is no single entrance, visitors make their own way through the maze to the centre where the blocks are well above head height, tending to convey a sense of gloom, isolation and solitude, even though Eisenman insists he has created a "place of hope". At night, 180 lights illuminate the space, creating a sombre yet stunning spectacle.

The underground **information centre**, in the southeast corner of the monument, relates the life stories and plight of some Jewish victims of the Holocaust. Carefully researched and expertly presented, the small exhibition outlines the overall history of the Nazi hounding and extermination of Jews before moving on to the personal stories that lurk behind the monstrous statistics. Among them are notes left by those on their way to their death – including some thrown from the cattle wagons as they were transported to death camps. The **audio tour** is largely unnecessary, but does help flesh things out a little and acts as a donation to the foundation that built and runs the memorial, whose spiralling costs – the final tab was €27.6m – have landed it in some financial trouble.

1

MEMORIAL CONTROVERSY

Even by the standards of Berlin, which is well used to hotly debating most bricks-and-mortar city centre projects, the **Holocaust Memorial** was **controversial**. It was particularly criticized for its unnecessarily large scale and location, its use of prime real estate with little historical significance and its incredible costs for a city with tight finances. Another criticism was that the rectangular stones were too reminiscent of SS militarism; more compelling were arguments that memorials at former camps, like Sachsenhausen (see p.174), are more relevant, and that the brass cobbles (*Stolpersteine*) commemorating victims outside their former homes are more poignant and all-pervading.

One particularly contentious twist in the tale of the memorial's construction concerns **Degussa**, the company that provided anti-graffiti paint for the blocks. As this was a daughter company of IG-Farben – who produced Cyclon-B, the gas used in the Nazi gas chambers – some thought it wasn't appropriate to involve them in the project. After much debate, their tender was confirmed: it was argued that the whole nation was building the monument and that no organization or company should be hindered from contributing.

The Gay Holocaust Memorial

Across the road from the Holocaust Memorial, the fringes of the Tiergarten park hold another concrete oblong, dedicated as a **Gay Holocaust Memorial**. Officially called "The Memorial to Homosexuals Persecuted by Nazis", it remembers the 54,000 people who were convicted of homosexual acts under the regime; an estimated eight thousand of these died in concentration camps. Inaugurated by Berlin's gay mayor Klaus Wowereit (see p.239) in 2008, the 4m-high monument mimics those commemorating Jewish victims, but also contains a window behind which plays a film of two men kissing.

The Gypsy Holocaust Memorial

The most recently completed of the trio of Holocaust local memorials, the **Gypsy Holocaust Memorial**, lies in the northeastern corner of the Tiergarten park beside the Reichstag. Unveiled in 2012, a decade after its inception, it commemorates the half-million Roma and Sinti that died at the hands of the Nazis. Haunting violin music plays around a circular pond, surrounded by rough stone flags; at the centre is a rock upon which a single fresh flower is placed every day. According to Dani Karavan, the aptly named Israeli sculptor behind the project, this flower has supreme significance as the murdered Sinti and Roma lie in unmarked plots in huge cemeteries with only plants growing above them. The flower lies on a triangle, which represents the triangle the Nazis forced all gypsies to wear. Meanwhile the dark pond reflects the trees, the Reichstag and anyone who gazes into it – in that way the viewer becomes part of the memorial and part of the process of remembrance.

Hitler's bunker and around

A minute's walk south of the Holocaust Memorial, along Gertrude-Kolmar-Strasse, is its oddest possible bedfellow: the site of **Hitler's bunker**, where the Führer spent his last days, issuing meaningless orders as the Battle of Berlin raged above. Here Hitler married Eva Braun and wrote his final testament: he personally was responsible for nothing; he had been betrayed by the German people, who had proved unequal to his leadership and deserved their fate. On April 30, 1945, he shot himself, and his body was hurriedly burned by loyal officers. A roadside sign at the end of the **Ministergärten** (see p.39) provides a plan of the bunker detailing its rooms and their functions. Though it's often assumed that the bunker was glamorously furnished, the diagram accurately reveals how spartan the facility was.

1

The sign also maps the astonishing number of other bunkers that were once in the vicinity, the largest one being under the **Neues Reichskanzlei** (New Reich Chancellery), the vast building designed by Albert Speer in 1938 as part of the Nazi remodelling of the government area around Wilhelmstrasse. This gigantic complex ran to the north of and almost the length of Vossstrasse. Today nothing remains, for even though the Chancellery building survived the war, it was torn down in a fit of revenge by the conquering Soviet army, who used its marble to fashion the memorial on Strasse des 17 Juni (see p.103) and the huge war memorial at the Soviet military cemetery in Treptower Park (see p.128).

In den Ministergärten

The lands immediately west of Hitler's bunker were, during the Wall years, part of the death strip separating East and West Berlin. On reunification it was decided to resuscitate this part of the Regierungsviertel by inviting the government ministries from Germany's sixteen states to build on a street named **In den Ministergärten** in their honour. However, only seven took up the offer – the rest chose to avoid the historically charged site – with all opting for similarly dynamic modern designs replete with imposing entrances, atria and exhibition spaces. For the most part, however, they simply house offices and ministerial accommodation.

Wilhelmstrasse

South of In den Ministergärten, An der Kolonnade leads east to **Wilhelmstrasse** which, from 1871 to the end of the Third Reich, was Imperial Berlin's Whitehall and Downing Street rolled into one. Its many ministries and government buildings included the Chancellery and, after the Republic was established in 1918, the Presidential Palace. Today little remains, but trying to figure out what was where can be compelling, and information boards with photos and descriptions of the former buildings have helpfully been placed along the street. Most structures are fairly dull apartment buildings that once housed high-ranking East Germans; the only one that stands out is an apparent airport control tower that turns out to be the **Czech Embassy**. North of here is an exhibition on the **Stasi** and beyond it a road closure that announces the presence of the **British Embassy**. This counter-terrorism measure allows you to properly appreciate the eye-pleasing, quirky building by Michael Wilford; its austere stone facade is broken up at the centre by a riot of shapes in cool grey and violent purple – playful elements thought to reflect the British sense of humour and style.

Stasi: Die Ausstellung

Mon–Sat 10am–6pm • Free • ⓦ bstu.bund.de • U- & S-Brandenburger Tor

Accessed via a pathway opposite the junction of Wilhelmstrasse with Hannah-Arendt-Strasse, **Stasi: Die Ausstellung** (Stasi: The Exhibition) provides a sobering display on the feared East German Secret Police. The material is presented by the government commission responsible for sifting through and reconstructing Stasi files, and whose work includes the painstaking reassembly of documents hastily shredded as the GDR's regime came to an end. We are talking about sixteen thousand sacks of shredded documents: for almost two decades some thirty workers puzzled together around ten documents a day, but at that rate the work wouldn't have been completed until 2395. The project's saviour came with the invention of a remarkable E-Puzzler machine. The world's most sophisticated pattern recognizer, it compares the pattern, texture, thickness of paper and the shape of the fragments and can process ten thousand sheets an hour – bringing the estimated date forward to 2014. The exhibition is briefer than the one at the former Stasi headquarters on Normannenstrasse (see p.143), but it does contain several intriguing intelligence devices, including hidden cameras, tiny tape recorders, a big toolbox for producing counterfeit documents and even the proverbial toothpaste tube with a secret compartment. Aside from these cunning tools, however, the exhibit relates (in German only – ask to borrow a transcript in English) just what a powerful and frightening organization the Stasi was, and the amazing degree of observation, infiltration and control they practised in the GDR.

Unter den Linden

Berlin's grandest boulevard, **Unter den Linden**, runs east from the Brandenburg Gate towards the Spreeinsel and once formed the main east–west axis of Imperial Berlin. The street – "beneath the lime trees" – was named after the trees on its central island; the first saplings were planted by Friedrich Wilhelm, the Great Elector, during the seventeenth century to line the route from his palace to his hunting grounds in the Tiergarten (see p.101). The original trees were replaced by crude Nazi totem poles during the 1930s, so the present generation dates from a period of postwar planting.

Until 1989 the western end of Unter den Linden also marked the end of the road for East Berliners: a low barrier ran a hundred metres or so short of the Brandenburg Gate. From here it was possible to view the gate, beyond which the discreet presence of armed border guards and the sterile white concrete of the Wall signalled the frontier with West Berlin. This reduced Unter den Linden to little more than a grand blind alley, which – lined by infrequently visited embassies – gave it a strangely empty and decorative feel. Revitalization since 1989 has helped the boulevard reassume something of its old role and today it's busy and bustling, fringed by shops and cafés, though their presence is relatively muted.

Madame Tussauds Berlin

Unter den Linden 74 • Daily: Aug 10am–9pm; Sept–July 10am–7pm • €21, combination tickets with Berlin Dungeon (see p.64), Sea-Life Centre (see p.63) and Legoland (see p.93) offered • ☎ 0180 654 58 00, ⓦ madametussauds.com • U-Brandenburger Tor

The shiny faces and glassy eyes at **Madame Tussauds Berlin** belong mainly to German celebrities, though a clutch of Hollywood stars also get a look-in. Beyond the reliably long entrance queues, things kick off with Otto von Bismarck and Karl Marx, followed by Adolf Hitler sitting wild-eyed in a bunker, with Anne Frank and anti-Nazi campaigner Sophie Scholl close by to provide a kinder face for the era. Local political heroes and villains also make their appearances: John F. Kennedy; West German statesman Willy Brandt; East German leader Erich Honecker; Mikhail Gorbachev. All these waxworks feel pretty true to life; not so the laughably awkward renditions of Barack Obama and Angela Merkel. From the entertainment sections there's more local interest in the form of Marlene Dietrich and Bertolt Brecht, though it's the aggressive stance of former Germany goalkeeper Oliver Kahn that makes the greatest impression.

Russian Embassy

One of the first buildings you'll see as you head east from Pariser Platz is the massive **Russian Embassy**, rearing up on the right. Built in 1950 on the site of the prewar (originally Tsarist) embassy, it was the first postwar building to be erected on Unter den Linden and an example of the much maligned *Zuckerbäckerstil* or "wedding-cake style": a kind of blunted, monumental Classicism characteristic of Stalin-era Soviet architecture. Berlin has a number of such buildings, the most spectacular being those along Karl-Marx-Allee (see p.130).

Friedrichstrasse

Halfway along Unter den Linden, you come to its most important intersection as it crosses the busy shopping street of **Friedrichstrasse**. Before the war this was one of the busiest crossroads in the city, with Friedrichstrasse a well-known prostitutes' haunt lined by cafés, bars and restaurants. Nazi puritanism dealt the first blow to this thriving *Vergnügungsviertel* (Pleasure Quarter), and the work was finished by Allied bombers,

1

who effectively razed the street. Rebuilt considerably wider, what had once been a narrow, slightly claustrophobic street became a broad, desolate road. Since reunification, Friedrichstrasse has been extensively revamped. Bland modern edifices now house offices, malls and a series of fairly high-end boutiques that rub shoulders with more everyday shops, including several good bookshops.

Staatsbibliothek zu Berlin

Dorotheenstr. 27 • Mon–Fri 9am–9pm, Sat 10am–7pm; 90min tours Tues & Fri 5pm & first Sat in month 10.30am • Free, including tours • ⓦ staatsbibliothek-berlin.de • U-Französische Strasse

A block east of the intersection with Friedrichstrasse, Unter den Linden passes south of the **Staatsbibliothek zu Berlin** (State Library). First the Prussian, then GDR state library, it is a typically grandiose edifice dating from the turn of the twentieth century, with a facade that was extensively patched up after wartime shrapnel damage. Now twinned with the Staatsbibliothek in the Kulturforum (see p.94), it is mainly the haunt of Humboldt University students. Visitors who don't feel like delving into the volumes within can sit in the ivy-clad courtyard by the fountain. As you do so, admire a GDR-era sculpture showing a member of the proletariat apparently reading a didactic Brecht poem on a relief at the other side of the fountain.

Bebelplatz and around

Two blocks northeast of the Gendarmenmarkt, the lime trees no longer define Unter den Linden as it opens out into the imposing Neoclassical **Bebelplatz** that marks the start of Berlin's eighteenth-century showpiece quarter. Bebelplatz itself was conceived by Frederick the Great as both a tribute to ancient Rome and a monument to himself. He and the architect **Georg Wenzeslaus von Knobelsdorff** drew up plans for a space that would recall the great open squares of the Classical city and be known as Forum Fridericianum. It never quite fulfilled such lofty ambitions, although the architecture of many of the buildings did receive acclaim at the time. The centrepiece square is rather bleak and unimpressive; it has only just recovered from a spate of building work that put in an underground car park and gutted the **Dresdner Bank** on its south side. The bank has been converted to house the luxurious *Hotel de Rome*, the interiors of which were used in the film *Run Lola Run* (see p.277).

The Empty Library

At the windswept and otherwise featureless centre of Bebelplatz lies the **Empty Library**, a monument to the most infamous event to happen on the square. It was here that on May 10, 1933, the infamous **Büchverbrennung** took place, in front of the university, on what was then called Opernplatz. On the orders of Joseph Goebbels, Hitler's propaganda minister, twenty thousand books that conflicted with Nazi ideology went up in flames. Among them were the works of "un-German" authors like Erich Maria Remarque, Thomas and Heinrich Mann, Stefan Zweig and Erich Kästner, along with volumes by countless foreign writers, H.G. Wells and Ernest Hemingway among them. The most fitting comment on this episode was made with unwitting foresight by the Jewish poet Heinrich Heine in the previous century: "Where they start by burning books, they'll end by burning people." The ingenious monument itself, by Micha Ullmann, is simply a room with empty shelves set in the ground under a pane of glass; it is at its most spectacular at night when a beam of light streams out.

Alte Bibliothek

The **Alte Bibliothek**, a former royal library, crowds the western side of Bebelplatz with a curved Baroque facade that has given it the nickname *Die Kommode* ("the chest of drawers"). Built between 1775 and 1780, its design was based on that of the Michaelertrakt in Vienna's Hofburg. Lenin spent some time here poring over dusty

OPPOSITE REICHSTAG DOME INTERIOR >

1

tomes while waiting for the Russian Revolution, and, even though only the building's facade survived the war, it has all been immaculately restored.

Frederick the Great statue

Just north of the Alte Bibliothek and in the middle of Unter den Linden is a nineteenth-century statue of **Frederick the Great** by Christian Rauch, showing Frederick astride a horse. Around the plinth, about a quarter of the size of the monarch, are representations of his generals, mostly on foot and conferring animatedly. After World War II, the statue of *Der alte Fritz*, as Frederick the Great is popularly known, was removed from Unter den Linden and only restored to its city-centre site in 1981 after a long exile in Potsdam. Its reinstalling reflected an odd revaluation by Erich Honecker's GDR of the pre-socialist past: no longer were figures like Frederick the Great, Blücher, Scharnhorst et al to be reviled as imperialistic militarists, but were to be accorded the status of historic figures worthy of commemoration. Even Bismarck, the Iron Chancellor of Wilhelmine Germany, was recognized as having "in his *Junker* way played a progressive historical role".

Humboldt Universität

Over Unter Den Linden from the Frederick statue, the restrained Neoclassical **Humboldt Universität** was designed in tandem with the buildings around Bebelplatz and built in 1748 as a palace for Frederick the Great's brother. In 1809 the philologist, writer and diplomat Wilhelm Humboldt founded a school here that was to become the University of Berlin, and later be renamed in his honour. Flanking the entrance gate are statues of Wilhelm and his brother Alexander, famous for their exploration of Central and South America. Wilhelm is contemplating the passing traffic, book in hand, and Alexander is sitting on a globe above a dedication to the "second discoverer of Cuba" from the University of Havana. Humboldt Universität alumni include Karl Marx, Friedrich Engels and Karl Liebknecht, the socialist leader and proclaimer of the first German Republic who was murdered in 1919 (see p.251). The philologists Jacob and Wilhelm Grimm (better known as the Brothers Grimm) and Albert Einstein are some of the best-known former members of staff.

Staatsoper

Knobelsdorff's Neoclassical **Staatsoper**, on the east side of Bebelplatz, is among its plainer buildings, though it represented the pinnacle of the architect's career and was Berlin's first theatre. The building is best viewed from Unter den Linden, where an imposing portico marks the main entrance. Just under two centuries after its construction it became the first major building to fall victim to World War II bombing, on the night of April 9–10, 1941. The Nazis restored it for its bicentenary in 1943, but on February 3, 1945, it was gutted once again. Now, like virtually everything else in the area, totally reconstructed, it is one of Berlin's leading opera houses (see p.219).

Sankt-Hedwigs-Kathedrale

Mon–Sat 10am–5pm, Sun 1–5pm • Free • ⓦ hedwigs-kathedrale.de

Just behind the Staatsoper is another Knobelsdorff creation, the stylistically incongruous **Sankt-Hedwigs-Kathedrale**, which was built as a place of worship for the city's Catholic minority in 1747 and is still in use. According to popular legend it owes its circular shape and domed profile to Frederick the Great's demand that it be built in the form of an upturned teacup. This probably stems from the fact that the monarch "advised" Knobelsdorff; in truth, the building's shape was inspired by the Pantheon in Rome. Reduced to a shell on March 2, 1943, the cathedral was not reconstructed until 1963, a restoration that left it with a slightly altered dome and a modernized interior.

The **interior**, once you get past the hazy biblical reliefs of the entrance portico, is perhaps the most unusual aspect of the whole building. The greatest feature of the vast main hall is the split-level double altar – the upper one is used on Sundays and special occasions, while the sunken altar in the crypt, reached by a flight of broad stairs, is used for weekday masses. All this is complemented by the stainless-steel pipes of the ethereal-sounding organ above the entrance, and 1970s-style globe-lamps hanging from the ceiling. If you've survived the combined effects of all this, the crypt with its eight grotto-like side chapels and near-abstract charcoal drawings is a further attraction.

Opernpalais

East of Sankt-Hedwigs-Kathedrale lies a lawn dotted with dignified **statues of Prussian generals**. Among them are Scharnhorst, Yorck and Gneisenau, though it's Blücher, whose timely intervention turned the day at Waterloo, who looks most warlike – sabre in hand and with his foot resting on a cannon. The Baroque building behind is the eighteenth-century **Opernpalais**. It was known as the Prinzessinpalais (Princesses' Palace) before the war, for its role as the swanky town house of Friedrich Wilhelm III's three daughters.

Schinkel Museum

Friedrichwerdersche Kirche · Daily 9am–4pm · Free · ⓦ smb.museum · S-Hausvogteiplatz

By ducking under two sets of arches beside the Opernpalais, in the southeast corner of Bebelplatz, you'll come to the **Friedrichwerdersche Kirche** in which the **Schinkel Museum** fittingly celebrates the work of the man, who, more than anyone, gave nineteenth-century Berlin its distinctive Neoclassical stamp (see box below). The church itself is a rather plain neo-Gothic affair, a stylistic departure for Schinkel, who was largely infatuated with the Classical styles he had encountered on trips to Italy. Here, however, the inspiration came from churches he had seen on a visit to England in 1826. The museum gives a detailed history of the church, along with a full rundown of Schinkel's achievements, setting his work in the context of the times. A jumble of nineteenth-century German Neoclassical statuary crowds the ground floor.

Kronprinzenpalais

The Baroque **Kronprinzenpalais** on Unter den Linden dates from 1663, but is really defined by a 1732 facelift that gave it a more grandiose appearance to reflect its role as a residence for Prussian princes. With the demise of the monarchy in 1918 it became a national art gallery and a leading venue for modern art. In 1933 the Nazis closed it, declaring hundreds of Expressionist and contemporary works housed here to be

KARL FRIEDRICH SCHINKEL (1781–1841)

The incredibly prolific architect **Karl Friedrich Schinkel** was without doubt one of the most influential German architects of the nineteenth century. Nearly every town in Brandenburg has a building that Schinkel had, at the very least, some involvement in. His first-ever design, the **Pomonatempel** in Potsdam, was completed while he was still a nineteen-year-old student in Berlin. Despite this auspicious beginning, his architectural career did not take off immediately and for a while he worked as a landscape artist and theatre-set designer. Towards the end of the first decade of the nineteenth century he began submitting architectural designs for great public works, and, in 1810, he secured a job with the administration of Prussian buildings.

In 1815 he was given a position in the new Public Works Department, and during the years between 1815 and 1830 he designed some of his most renowned buildings such as the Grecian-style **Neue Wache** (see p.47), the elegant **Schauspielhaus** (see p.48) and the **Altes Museum** (see p.56) with its striking Doric columns: all vital to enhancing the ever-expanding capital of Brandenburg-Prussia. Later in his career Schinkel experimented with other architectural forms, a phase marked by the Romanesque **Charlottenhof** in Potsdam (see p.172).

1

examples of *entartete Kunst* or "degenerate art". Most of these were either sold off abroad or destroyed, and a number were bought at knock-down prices by leading Nazis, Göring among them. The Kronprinzenpalais has since played host to a variety of organizations and temporary exhibitions.

Deutsches Historisches Museum

Unter den Linden 2 • Daily 10am–6pm • €8 • ☎ 030 20 30 44 44, ⓦ dhm.de • S-Hackescher Markt

The **Deutsches Historisches Museum** (German Historical Museum) is spread across two buildings: the Baroque **Zeughaus** and a modern exhibition hall designed by Chinese-American architect **I. M. Pei**. Between them they chart German history from the Dark Ages to the present via eight thousand or so objects. You should allow at least two hours, and with only a relatively small proportion of the exhibition in English, the **audio guide** is recommended. There's also a very tasteful and little-known cinema and good restaurant, both entered from the Spree side of the museum.

The museum itself focuses overwhelmingly – perhaps inevitably – on military history, though it does try to show how big events or "epochs of change" affected the masses. It's all attractively set out and deals cleverly with difficult or contentious areas – such as the rise of nationalism and concepts of German nationhood – by simply providing a balanced summary of the main facts and avoiding interpretation.

Highlights from the early collection include an extraordinary assemblage of **armour** from the old Zeughaus days – including a 15kg jousting helmet – and an impressive collection of early sixteenth-century **bibles**, some of the first books to be printed anywhere. But the most engrossing exhibits are of later periods, following the French Revolution, where the museum offers a balanced view of Prussia, attempting to explain how it slid from being one of the most progressive parts of Europe to one of its most militarized powers. On display are several **helmets** – gruesomely memorable for their bullet holes – of soldiers killed in action in World War I.

The exhibition goes on to examine Weimar Germany and the rise of philosophical extremes, particularly communism and fascism, with insightful displays of propagandist art and leaflets. The **Nazi Third Reich** is explored in every deplorable detail – including the depiction of the war in Russian and American and Nazi **propaganda films**, the latter showing the *Blitzkrieg* arrive in Poland and mocking Jewish captives in chain gangs. It also covers the GDR years, where the exhibition splits to tell the parallel stories of the two Germanys.

THE ZEUGHAUS

Built by the Brandenburg Elector Frederick III between 1695 and 1730, the sturdy old Prussian Arsenal, or **Zeughaus**, is Unter den Linden's oldest building. Many of the building's decorative elements are the work of Andreas Schlüter, notably the walls of the **Schlüterhof**, the history museum's inner courtyard, where reliefs depict the contorted faces of dying warriors. There was much excitement at the Zeughaus on June 14, 1848, when, during revolutionary upheavals, the people of Berlin stormed the building looking for arms. A number of citizens were killed, and no weapons were found, but the incident gave the authorities an excuse to bring troops into the city and ban various newspapers and democratic organizations.

Just over thirty years later the Zeughaus was turned into a Prussian army museum. During the Nazi period it exhibited World War I propaganda – portraying the war as an undeserved defeat and making much of the dishonest conduct of enemies during the peace treaties – and hosted Remembrance Day speeches. At the March 1943 speech there was a failed attempt on Hitler's life; the Führer changed his plans, giving the suicide bomber, Rudolf von Gersdorff, just enough time to rush to the lavatory and defuse the bomb. From 1953, the heavily damaged building became a museum of German history, at first offering the GDR's version of events followed by, after reunification, a progressively more balanced, Western view in the Deutsches Historisches Museum (see above).

1

I.M. Pei Bau
The eye-catching swirling glass building behind the Zeughaus is the work of American-Chinese architect **I.M. Pei** – most famous for his glass pyramid at the entrance to the Louvre in Paris. Pei's hallmark geometric glass is here too, with the resulting play of light perhaps the most important factor in making the building work. Temporary exhibitions here usually delve into German social history in the last couple of centuries, and vary widely, though all seem to share first-class displays and even-handedness in the treatment of what are often subject matters.

Neue Wache
Karl Friedrich Schinkel's most celebrated surviving creation, the Neoclassical **Neue Wache**, is on Unter den Linden beside the Deutsches Historisches Museum. Built between 1816 and 1818 as a guardhouse for the royal watch, it resembles a stylized Roman temple and served as a sort of police station until 1918. In 1930–31 it was converted into a memorial to the military dead of World War I, and in 1957 the GDR extended the concept to include those killed by Nazis: as a "Memorial to the Victims of Fascism and Militarism". Until 1990 one of East Berlin's most ironic ceremonies was played out in front of the Neue Wache – the regular changing of the Nationale Volksarmee (National People's Army – the GDR army) honour guard, a much-photographed goose-stepping ritual that ended with the demise of the East German state. These days it serves as the "National Memorial to the Victims of War and Tyranny", and inside a granite slab covers the tombs of an unknown soldier and an unknown concentration camp victim. At the head of this memorial stone is a statue, depicting a mother clutching her dying son, an enlargement of a small sculpture by Käthe Kollwitz (see p.112).

Palais am Festungsgrab
The grand-looking building behind the Neue Wache, the **Palais am Festungsgrab** has had a chequered career. Built during the eighteenth century as a palace for a royal gentleman of the bedchamber, it later served as a residence for Prussian finance ministers, and during GDR days it was the Zentrale Haus der Deutsch-Sowjetischen Freundschaft or "Central House of German-Soviet Friendship". Today it houses the **Theater im Palais** (see p.220). West beside the **Palais**, the **Maxim-Gorki-Theater** (see p.220) is a one-time singing academy converted into a theatre after World War II.

Gendarmenmarkt
A five-minute walk south of Unter Den Linden brings you to the immaculately restored **Gendarmenmarkt** square, one of the Berlin's architectural highlights – it's hard to imagine that all its buildings were almost obliterated during the war and that rebuilding lasted until well into the 1980s. The Gendarmenmarkt's **origins** are prosaic. It was originally home to Berlin's main market until the Gendarme regiment set up their stables on the site in 1736 and gave the square its name. With the departure of the military, the Gendarmenmarkt was transformed at the behest of Frederick the Great, who ordered an architectural revamp of its two churches – the **Französischer Dom** and **Deutscher Dom** – in an attempt to mimic the Piazza del Popolo in Rome. The surrounding grid-like streets are testament to the area's seventeenth-century origins, when this pattern of building was the norm, and when a number of city extensions took Berlin beyond its original walled core. This area, once known as Friedrichstadt, became a Huguenot stronghold thanks to Prussian guarantees of religious freedom and rights that attracted them in numbers.

1

Französischer Dom
Gendarmenmarkt 5 • **Tower** Daily 10am–7pm • €3 • ⓦ franzoesischer-dom.de

Frederick the Great's Gendarmenmarkt revamp is at its most impressive and eye-catching in the **Französischer Dom** at the northern end of the square. Built as a simple place of worship for Berlin's influential Huguenot community at the beginning of the eighteenth century, the building was transformed by the addition, eighty years later, of a Baroque tower, turning it into one of Berlin's most appealing churches. The **Dom tower** has some fine bells, which ring out daily at noon, 3pm and 7pm. Bell-ringing concerts are sometimes performed at other times – ask at the desk for details. You can climb up the tower via a longish spiral of steps to an outside balcony with good views over the square – note that standing here when the bells ring will be a near-deafening experience.

Hugenottenmuseum
Tues–Sun noon–5pm • €2

In the church at the base of the Dom tower is the entrance to the **Hugenottenmuseum**, detailing the history of the Huguenots in France and Brandenburg. Exhibits deal with the theological background of the Reformation in France, the Revocation of the Edict of Nantes leading to the flight of the Huguenots from their native country, their settling in Berlin and the influence of the new arrivals on trade, science and literature. There is also a short section on the destruction and rebuilding of the Dom.

Französischen Friedrichstadtkirche
Tues–Sun noon–5pm • ⓦ franzoesische-friedrichstadtkirche.de

The Dom tower is so striking that a lot of visitors don't actually notice the church proper, the **Französischen Friedrichstadtkirche** (French Church in Friedrichstadt), which is modest enough in appearance that it looks more like an ancillary building for the tower. The main entrance to the church is at the western end of the Dom, facing Charlottenstrasse. The church, reconsecrated in 1983 after years of restoration work, has a simple hall-like interior with few decorative features and only a plain table as an altar.

Deutscher Dom
Tues–Sun: May–Sept 10am–7pm; Oct–April 10am–6pm • Free; free English-language audio guides available at the front desk (ID required as deposit)

At the southern end of the Gendarmenmarkt, the **Deutscher Dom**, built in 1708 for the city's Lutheran community, is the stylistic twin of the Französischer Dom. The Dom now hosts the fairly dull **"Wege-Irrwege-Umwege"** exhibition, which looks in detail at Germany's democratic history. A wander up through the Dom with its labyrinth of galleries is the highlight, and the reward for reaching the top is the chance to see a few scale-models of some early Norman Foster designs for the reconstruction of the Reichstag (see p.37).

Konzerthaus Berlin
Between the Gendarmenmarkt's two churches stands Schinkel's Neoclassical **Konzerthaus Berlin** (formerly called the Schauspielhaus). Dating from 1817, it was built around the ruins of Langhans' burned-out National Theatre, retaining the latter's exterior walls and portico columns. A broad sweep of steps leads up to the main entrance and into an interior of incredible opulence, where chandeliers, marble, gilded plasterwork and pastel-hued wall paintings compete for attention. Gutted during a raid in 1943, the building suffered further damage during heavy fighting as the Russians attempted to root out SS troops who had dug in here. It reopened in October 1984 and during Christmas 1989, Leonard Bernstein conducted a performance of Beethoven's Ninth Symphony in the theatre to celebrate the *Wende*, with the word *Freiheit* ("Freedom") substituted for *Freude* ("Joy") in Schiller's choral finale.

1

Schiller statue

The **statue of Schiller** outside the Konzerthaus was repositioned here in 1988, having been removed by the Nazis more than fifty years earlier, returned to what was then East Berlin from the West in exchange for reliefs originally from the Pfaueninsel (see p.163) and a statue from a Tiergarten villa. Outside Germany, Friedrich Schiller (1759–1805) is best known for the *Ode to Joy* that provides the words to the final movements of Beethoven's Ninth Symphony, but in his homeland he is venerated as one of the greatest German poets and dramatists of the Enlightenment. His works, from early *Sturm und Drang* dramas like *Die Räuber* ("The Thieves") to later historical plays like *Maria Stuart*, were primarily concerned with freedom – political, moral and personal – which was probably the reason why the Nazis were so quick to bundle him off the Gendarmenmarkt.

Bunte Schokowelt

Französische Str. 24 • Mon–Wed 10am–7pm, Thurs–Sat 10am–8pm, Sun 10am–6pm • Free • ☎ 030 20 09 50 80, ⓦ ritter-sport.de • U-Französische Strasse

Despite being fairly barefaced corporate propaganda for German chocolatiers Ritter Sport, **Bunte Schokowelt** (Colourful Chocolate World) can be excused – the company remains a family operation with some commendable ethical principles, and above all its dozens of varieties of chocolate are delicious. The key attraction here is that you can design your own chocolate bar and have it made on the spot; it takes about thirty minutes, during which time there's a little museum to browse – which includes a range of amusing Ritter Sport German TV ads from the 1950s onwards. There's also a pleasant café and many chocolatey bargains amid the extraordinary selection in the shop.

Jägerstrasse and around

Leading west from the Gendarmenmarkt, **Jägerstrasse** was the site of particularly heavy fighting during the 1848 revolution, but is best known as the centre of Berlin's nineteenth-century **banking quarter**. It was from here that the Mendelssohn Bank, a huge Jewish concern founded by the sons of philosopher Moses Mendelssohn, bankrolled much of Berlin's industrial revolution: a plaque on the north side of the street, outside no. 51, tells the story.

Nolde Stiftung

Jägerstr. 55 • Daily 10am–7pm • €8 • ☎ 030 40 00 46 90, ⓦ nolde-stiftung.de • U-Hausvogteiplatz

The Berlin branch of the **Nolde Stiftung** (Nolde Foundation) showcases the work of leading German Expressionist painter Emil Nolde. His vivid work and awkward lithographs were predictably banned by the Nazis, but he defiantly continued to work in secret in his home on Germany's Baltic coast, producing the wonderful work that's revealed in the changing temporary exhibitions here.

The Bauakademie and around

Before World War II the block to the east of the Friedrichwerdersche Kirche, on the banks of the Spree, was the site of the **Bauakademie** – Karl Friedrich Schinkel's architectural school. This 1836 building is widely considered to be one of modern architecture's true ancestors, rejecting the Classicism around it in favour of brick exterior and terracotta ornamentation. The building spoke of industrialization and a changing view towards design and construction, and even at the time it was thought to be one of Schinkel's finest creations; he seemed to agree, moving in and occupying a top-floor apartment until his death in 1841. The Kaiser however, hated it, referring to it as "the horrible red box that blots the view from the palace" (see p.53). The GDR regime also had no time for it, demolishing it in 1962 – despite its relatively light war damage – in favour of a prefab for its foreign ministry, which became one of the first

1

buildings to be demolished after the *Wende*. It was replaced by a grassy field with a rather lost-looking statue of Schinkel in the middle, but there are proposals to rebuild. As an advertisement and incentive, a corner section of the building has been reconstructed on its original site. The rest of the building has been recreated using scaffolding, wrapped in a canvas facade – in an attempt to stimulate enthusiasm and raise funds for reconstruction.

Foreign Ministry

Behind the Bauakademie and beside the River Spree lies the heavily guarded **Foreign Ministry**. The structure, though massive, projects an unassuming aspect by means of its plain glass facade, through which you can see a serene covered courtyard complete with trees and fountain. It illustrates one answer to a common problem facing architects for the new German capital: how to create large and significant civic buildings while avoiding any hints of Nazi monumentalism? A good example of the latter, and now also occupied by the Foreign Office, lies directly behind: the immense and imposing **Central Bank** built between 1934 and 1938. Having survived the war, it became the SED (Socialist Unity Party of Germany) headquarters and thus the nerve centre of the East German Communist party.

THE ISHTAR GATE

Mitte: Museum Island and around

At its eastern end, Unter den Linden leads to the Spreeinsel, the island in the River Spree that formed the core of the medieval twin town Berlin-Cölln. From the fifteenth century onwards, due to its defensive position, the Spreeinsel became the site of the *Residenz* – the fortress-cum-palace and church of the Hohenzollern family who controlled Berlin and Brandenburg. The church – the Berliner Dom – still stands, as do most of the structures on the island's northern tip, where in the 1800s the Hohenzollerns added a museum quarter. Known as Museum Island, this is home to some of the world's greatest museums: the Pergamonmuseum, with its jaw-dropping antiquities; the Altes Museum, and its superlative Greek vases; the Neues Museum, specializing in Ancient Egypt; the Altes Nationalgalerie, full of nineteenth-century European paintings; and the Bode-Museum, one of Europe's most important sculpture collections.

2

THE BRIDGES OF MUSEUM ISLAND

Unless you're hopping off bus #100 from Bahnhof Zoo or Alexanderplatz (alight at Schlossplatz) the most attractive way to get to Museum Island is from S-Bahn Hackescher Markt. From there walk west through the square, then through Monbijoupark to **Monbijoubrücke** beside the Bode-Museum or, by ducking under the railway arches, cross the Spree to the Alte Nationalgalerie on **Friedrichsbrücke**, another pedestrian bridge. Both bridges are replacements for ones destroyed by the German army during the Battle of Berlin – more interesting are a couple of the bridges that survived the war intact. Schinkel's **Schlossbrücke** at the eastern end of Unter den Linden is particularly impressive. It first opened on November 28, 1823 when not fully completed, lacking among other things a fixed balustrade, and 22 people drowned when temporary wooden barriers collapsed. Eventually cast-iron balustrades were installed, featuring graceful dolphin, merman and sea-horse motifs designed by Schinkel. The **Jungfernbrücke**, meanwhile, a drawbridge tucked away behind the former Staatsrat, is Berlin's oldest surviving bridge, built in 1798.

Just south of Museum Island likes the huge expanse and giant building site of **Schlossplatz**, where the *Residenz* once stood. This began as a martial, fortified affair – as much for protection from the perennially rebellious Berliners as from outside enemies – but over the years domestic stability meant it could be reshaped on a slightly more decorative basis. In a demonstrative break with Prussia's Imperial past the GDR tore down the war-damaged palace to make way for a huge parade plaza and some of its most important civic buildings: the **Palast der Republik** and the **Staatsrat**. Then, in another demonstrative break, this time with its communist past, Berlin's current administration decided to tear down the former and rebuild the **Schloss** – an ongoing project.

Schlossplatz and around

East of Unter den Linden, beyond the Schlossbrücke, is **Schlossplatz**, the former site of the Berliner **Schloss**, the old Imperial Palace, the remains of which were demolished by the communists after the war, and which, along with the Berliner Dom (see p.53), formed the Imperial *Residenz*.

The Humboldt Box

Schlossplatz 5 • Daily: April–Oct 10am–8pm; Nov–March 10am–6pm • €4 • ⓦ humboldt-box.com • S-Hackescher Markt

Despite its angular and futuristic look, the **Humboldt Box** museum is actually all about the past. It's here to promote the controversial rebuilding of Schloss (see p.54) and is chock-full of propaganda designed to encourage public donations. Nevertheless, the place is worth a look for some detailed history of the site and in particular a delightful scale model of Unter den Linden, Museum Island and the Schloss, all circa 1930: a tremendous amount of work has gone into getting the historical details correct: even tiny statues have been reconstructed using aluminium foil. The museum also has some original palace stonework, detailed plans of the proposed reconstruction and great views over current building works. The shop sells wonderful postcards of old Berlin.

Staatsrat

With the Palast der Republik gone, the only reminder of the GDR on Schlossplatz is the one-time **Staatsrat**, or State Council, an early 1960s building on the southern side of the platz, with some stylistic affinities to Stalin-era *Zuckerbäcker* architecture. Its facade incorporates a large chunk of the Schloss, notably the balcony from which Karl Liebknecht proclaimed the German revolution in 1918 (see p.251). The building is now the campus for the European School of Management and Technology.

THE SCHLOSS

Work began on the **Schloss** in 1443 and the Hohenzollern family were to live there for nearly half a millennium. It was constantly being extended and reshaped over the years; the first major overhaul came in the sixteenth century, which saw it transformed from a fortress into a Renaissance palace. Later the Schloss received a Baroque restyling, and subsequently virtually every German architect of note, including Schlüter, Schinkel and Schadow, was given the opportunity to add to it. For centuries it dominated the heart of Berlin, and until the 1930s no city centre building was allowed to stand any higher.

On November 9, 1918, the end of the Hohenzollern era came when Karl Liebknecht proclaimed a "Free Socialist Republic" from one of the palace balconies, now preserved in the facade of the Staatsrat building (see p.251), following the abdication of the Kaiser. Almost simultaneously, the Social Democrat Philipp Scheidemann announced a democratic German republic from the Reichstag, and it was in fact the latter that prevailed, ushering in the pathologically unstable Weimar Republic of the 1920s.

After the war the Schloss, a symbol of the still recent Imperial past, was an embarrassment to the GDR authorities who dynamited its ruins in 1950, even though it was no more badly damaged than a number of other structures that were subsequently rebuilt. In its place came the **Palast der Republik** (see p.54), which outlasted the regime that created it for almost a decade before being dismantled to make way for transitional projects and ultimately a re-creation of the Schloss, as detailed in the Humboldt Box museum (see p.54).

Neue Marstall

Immediately east of the Staatsrat lies the **Neue Marstall**, an unimaginative turn-of-the-twentieth-century construction built to house the hundreds of royal coaches and horses used to ferry the royal household around the city. During the 1918 November Revolution, it headquartered the revolutionary committee and sailors and Spartacists beat off government forces from it. A couple of plaques commemorate this deed of rebellious derring-do and Liebknecht's proclamation of the socialist republic. One shows Liebknecht apparently suspended above a cheering crowd of sailors and civilians, while the other, to the left of the entrance, has the head of Marx hovering over excited, purposeful-looking members of the proletariat.

Breite Strasse

Breite Strasse sweeps south beside the Neue Marstall, but before it arrives at the intersection with Mühlendamm – just over the Spree from the Nikolaiviertel (see p.66) – it passes the delicately gabled **Ribbeckhaus**. This late-Renaissance palace from the seventeenth century is one of the city's oldest surviving buildings and now houses a branch of Berlin's public library.

Berliner Dom

Am Lustgarten • Daily: April–Sept Mon–Sat 9am–8pm, Sun noon–8pm; Oct–March Mon–Sat 9am–7pm, Sun noon–7pm • €7, audio guide €3 • ⓦ berlinerdom.de • S-Hackescher Markt

Opposite the Palast der Republik and next to the Lustgarten, the **Berliner Dom** is a hulking symbol of Imperial Germany that managed to survive the GDR era. It was built at the start of the twentieth century, on the site of a more modest cathedral, as a grand royal church for the Hohenzollern family. Fussily ornate with a huge dome flanked by four smaller ones, it was meant to resemble St Peter's in Rome, but comes across as a dowdy neo-Baroque imitation.

The Berliner Dom served the House of Hohenzollern as a family church until 1918, and its vault houses ninety sarcophagi containing the remains of various members of the line. The building was badly damaged in the war, but laborious reconstruction has created a simpler version of its prewar self, with various ornamental cupolas missing from the newly rounded-off domes.

The main entrance leads into the extravagantly overstated **Predigtkirche**, the octagonal main body of the church. From the marbled pillars of the hall to the delicate plasterwork and gilt of the cupola, there's a sense that it's all meant to reflect Hohenzollern power rather than serve as a place of worship. As if to confirm this impression, six opulent Hohenzollern sarcophagi, including those of Great Elector Wilhelm I, and his second wife, Dorothea, are housed in galleries at the northern and southern ends of the Predigtkirche. The spiritual underpinnings of the society they ruled are less ostentatiously represented by statues of Luther, Melanchthon, Calvin and Zwingli, along with four German princes, in the cornices above the pillars in the main hall.

For an overhead view, head for the **Kaiserliches Treppenhaus** (Imperial Staircase), a grandiose marble staircase at the southwest corner of the building, which leads past pleasantly washed-out paintings of biblical scenes to a balcony looking out onto the Predigtkirche. Here you'll also find a small exhibition on the history of the building.

Back downstairs and to the south of the Predigtkirche is the restored **Tauf- und Traukirche**. At first sight this appears to be a marbled souvenir shop, but it is in fact a side chapel used for baptism and confirmation ceremonies.

THE PALAST DER REPUBLIK AND THE HUMBOLDT FORUM

It was no coincidence that the GDR authorities chose the site of the Imperial Schloss for their **Palast der Republik**, a piece of brutal 1970s modernism in glass and concrete, to house the Volkskammer, the GDR's parliament. This huge angular building with its bronzed, reflective windows was completed in less than a thousand days, and became a source of great pride to Erich Honecker's regime. As well as the parliament, it also housed an entertainment complex: restaurants, cafés, a theatre and a bowling alley. It would host craft fairs, discos, folk nights and Christmas festivities, and going there on a day out – something that all East German children were entitled to do once they'd turned 14 – was considered a highlight of growing up.

The interior was at once a showcase of East German design and a masterpiece of tastelessness, the hundreds of lamps hanging from the ceiling of the main foyer giving rise to the nickname, *Erich's Lampenladen* – "Erich's lamp shop". Shortly before unification asbestos was discovered, and on October 3, 1990, the building closed for almost thirteen years while it was stripped out. With only the glass and a skeleton of steel beams left inside, the Palast then became the chic venue for a guerrilla combination of **exhibitions, concerts** and **installations**, as well as a **nightclub** on the night of the fifteenth anniversary of the fall of the Wall.

In 2006, by order of the German Parliament, work started to dismantle the Palast. In its place a version of the original Prussian palace, dubbed the **Humboldt Forum** (🌐 sbs-humboldtforum .de), will be built, to house a mix of cultural and scientific institutions, probably including all the state museums in Dahlem (see p.160). The new palace will copy the original's dimensions and facade, but due to budget constraints, sadly not its central dome – which, in truth, made the building. Construction has started, but will take until at least 2019 and cost between €670 million and €1.2 billion.

Lustgarten

The **Lustgarten**, the lively green expanse leading up to the Altes Museum on the northern side of the Schlossplatz, is a great spot for picnics or resting your feet between museum visits and so relaxed that it's hard to believe its history. Built as a military parade ground (and used by Wilhelm I and Napoleon), it later saw mass protests (a huge anti-Nazi demo here in 1933 prompted the banning of demonstrations) and rallies (Hitler addressed up to a million people here). Bombed in the war and renamed Marx-Engels-Platz by the GDR, its current incarnation harks back to Peter Joseph Lenné's early nineteenth-century design with a central 13m-high fountain, as re-envisioned by German landscape architect Hans Loidl.

At the northern end of the Lustgarten, at the foot of the steps leading up to the Altes Museum (see p.56), is a saucer-shaped rock, carved from a huge glacier-deposited **granite boulder** found near Fürstenwalde, just outside Berlin, and brought here in 1828 to form part of the Altes Museum's rotunda. A mistake in Schinkel's plans meant that its 7m diameter made it too large, so, for want of a better plan, it was left here to become an unusual decorative feature.

Museum Island

The northern tip of the Spreeinsel, known as **Museum Island** (Museumsinsel), is the location of Berlin's most important museums. Their origins go back to 1810, when King Friedrich Wilhelm III decided Berlin needed a museum to house his rather scant collection of royal treasures. He ordered the reclamation of a patch of Spree-side marsh and commissioned Schinkel to come up with a suitable building; thus was created the **Altes Museum**, at the head of the Lustgarten. Things really took off when German explorers and archeologists began plundering archeological sites in Egypt and Asia Minor. The booty brought back by the Egyptologist Carl Richard Lepsius in the 1840s formed the core of what was to become a huge collection, and the **Neues Museum** was built to house it at the behest of King Friedrich Wilhelm IV. Later that century the imperial haul was augmented by treasures brought from Turkey by Heinrich Schliemann, for which the vast **Pergamonmuseum** was constructed.

During World War II the contents of the museums were stashed away in bunkers and mine shafts, and in the confusion of 1945 and the immediate postwar years it proved difficult to recover the scattered works. Some had been destroyed, others ended up in museums in the Western sector and others disappeared to the East with the Red Army. Gradually, though, the various surviving pieces were tracked down and returned to Berlin – with the notable exception of the **Priam's Treasure**, Schliemann's most famous find, which allegedly came from the ruins of the fabled city of Troy. This collection of nine thousand gold chains, elaborate silver pictures, gold coins and other amazing artefacts hit the front pages in 1993 when it finally resurfaced in Moscow, where it remains today.

Reunification brought together the impressive and long-divided collections of Museum Island, which is being completely restored and partially remodelled in an ambitious plan (wmuseumsinsel-berlin.de), begun in 1999 and due for completion in 2015, which will undoubtedly produce one of the world's greatest museum complexes.

INFORMATION AND TOURS

Admission Individually Museum Island museums cost €10 or €14; but a one-day Bereichskarte for all of them, available to buy at any of the museums, costs €18. The better-value Drei-Tage-Karte (three-day ticket; €24) covers the permanent exhibitions in all the city's state museums (see p.23) and a selection of the city's private museums too. Entry to Museum Island museums is also included on the Berlin Welcome Card and City Tour Card (see p.23). In all cases special exhibitions cost extra

Audio tours Most exhibits are in German only, but some collections do provide explanations and information sheets in English and most have excellent, multilingual audio tours included in the entrance price.

2

Altes Museum

Am Lustgarten • Tues, Wed & Fri–Sun 10am–6pm, Thurs 10am–8pm • €10, €18 with all other Museum Island museums on a Bereichskarte (see p.23) • ⓦ smb.museum • S-Hackescher Markt

At the head of the Lustgarten, the **Altes Museum** is – along with the Konzerthaus Berlin (see p.48) – one of Berlin's most striking Neoclassical buildings and perhaps Schinkel's most impressive surviving work, with an 87m-high facade fronted by an eighteen-column Ionic colonnade. Opened as a home for the royal collection of paintings in 1830, it is now host to the **Collection of Classical Antiquities**: small sculpture and pottery from the city's famed Greek and Roman collections. Greek Gods dominate the ground floor, but the upper floor contains a colossal range of Greek, Roman and Etruscan Art – urns, shields, sarcophagi, friezes – all chronologically and thematically arranged. Many are small works that lack the power and drama of the huge pieces on view at the Pergamon, but can captivate nonetheless: *The Praying Boy*, a lithe and delicate bronze sculpture from Rhodes, dating back to 300 BC, is the collection's pride and joy. Look, too, for the vase of Euphronios, decorated with an intimate painting of athletes in preparation – the series of Greek vases here is considered to be among the finest in the world.

Neues Museum

Bodestr. 1-3 • Mon–Wed & Fri–Sun 10am–6pm, Thurs 10am–8pm • €14, €18 with all other Museum Island museums on a Bereichskarte (see p.23) • ⓦ smb.museum • S-Hackescher Markt

The **Neues Museum** opened in 1855 to house the imperial Egyptian collection. Bombed out in the war, the building was slowly rebuilt and renovated under British architect David Chipperfield, who took great pains to preserve as many original features as possible, including fluted stone columns and battered faux-Egyptian ceiling frescoes. Entire wings had been destroyed in the war, including the central staircase, but rather than imitating every detail, plain concrete, bare brick and huge wooden rafters have been used for repairs, creating both a sense of history and an effective contrast to the original sections. Finally reopened in 2009, the building now houses Berlin's Egyptian Collection and its Museum for Pre- and Early History.

The most prized exhibit of the **Egyptian Collection** is the 3300-year-old *Bust of Queen Nefertiti*, a treasure that has become a symbol for the city as a cultural capital. There's no questioning its beauty – the queen has perfect bone structure and gracefully sculpted lips – and the history of the piece is equally interesting. Created around 1350 BC, the bust probably never left the studio in Akhetatenin in which it was created, acting as a model for other portraits of the queen (its use as a model explains why the left eye was never drawn in). When the studio was deserted, the bust was left there, to be discovered some three thousand years later in 1912 and then officially unveiled in Berlin in 1924; this also marked the beginning of an ongoing diplomatic struggle by the Egyptian authorities to have it returned to Egypt.

Elsewhere in the collection, atmospheric lighting is used to particularly good effect on the Expressionistic, almost Futuristic, *Berlin Green Head* of the Ptolemaic period. Don't miss the interesting pieces from the Schliemann excavations of Troy, though the best pieces (some represented here as replicas) remain in Russia, carted away as spoils of war; delicate negotiations for their return continue.

A bit of a comedown after all the Egyptian excitement below is the **Museum for Pre- and Early History** in the attic, with a rather underwhelming collection of archeological discoveries from the Berlin area.

Alte Nationalgalerie

Bodestr. 1–3 • Tues, Wed & Fri–Sun 10am–6pm, Thurs 10am–8pm • €10, €18 with all other Museum Island museums on a Bereichskarte (see p.23) • ⓦ smb.museum • S-Hackescher Markt

Tucked just behind the Neues Museum is the **Alte Nationalgalerie**, a slightly exaggerated example of post-Schinkel Neoclassicism that contains the **nineteenth-century** section of Berlin's state art collection. The main body of the museum, built in

1876, resembles a Corinthian temple and is fronted by an imposing equestrian statue of its royal patron, Friedrich Wilhelm IV.

Particularly noteworthy among the Alte Nationalgalerie's collection are several works of the "**German Romans**": mid-nineteenth-century artists like Anselm Feuerbach and Arnold Böcklin, who spent much of their working lives in Italy. Böcklin's eerie, dreamlike *Isle of the Dead* retains its power even today. A highlight of this school is the Casa Bartholdy **frescoes**, softly illuminated paintings by Peter Cornelius, Wilhelm Veit and others that illustrate the story of Joseph. The broad canvases of Adolph von Menzel strike a rather different note: though chiefly known during his lifetime for his detailed depictions of court life under Frederick the Great, it's his interpretations of Berlin on the verge of the industrial age, such as *The Iron Foundry*, that make more interesting viewing today.

Other rooms contain important **Impressionist** works by van Gogh, Degas, Monet and native son Max Liebermann, plus statues by Rodin. But it's on the top floor, in the **Galerie der Romantik**, with its collection of nineteenth-century paintings from the German Romantic, Classical and Biedermeier movements, that the collection is at its most powerful. The two central rooms here contain work by **Karl Friedrich Schinkel** and **Caspar David Friedrich**. Schinkel was the architect responsible for the Neoclassical design of the Altes Museum (see p.56) and his paintings are meticulously drawn Gothic fantasies, often with sea settings. *Gothic Church on a Rock by the Sea* is the most moodily dramatic and didactic in purpose: the medieval knights in the foreground ride next to a prayer tablet – Schinkel believed that a rekindling of medieval piety would bring about the moral regeneration of the German nation. But more dramatic are the works of **Caspar David Friedrich**, all of which express a powerful elemental and religious approach to landscape. Particularly characteristic of the brooding drama of his Romantic sensibility is *Abbey Among Oak Trees* of 1809, perhaps the best known of his works.

Pergamonmuseum

Bodestr. 1–3 • Fri–Wed 10am–6pm, Thurs 10am–8pm • €14, €18 with all other Museum Island museums on a Bereichskarte (see p.23) • ⓦ smb.museum • S-Hackescher Markt

The **Pergamonmuseum** is accessible from Am Kupfergraben on the south bank of the River Spree. It's a massive structure, built in the early part of the twentieth century in the style of a Babylonian temple to house the treasure trove of the German archeologists who were busy plundering the ancient world, packaging it up and sending it back to Berlin.

The most important of the museum's three sections is the **Department of Antiquities** on the main floor. It contains the **Pergamon Altar**, a huge structure dedicated to Zeus and Athena, from around 170 BC, which was unearthed at Bergama in western Turkey by archeologist Carl Humann and brought to Berlin in 1903. The **frieze** shows a tremendous battle between the gods and giants, with powerfully depicted figures writhing in a mass of sinew and muscle. To the rear of the Altar is the **Telephos Frieze**, another amazing Pergamon find, which originally adorned the interior of the Pergamon Altar, depicts the life story of Telephos, the legendary founder of Pergamon, and is a bit more sedate. The section also contains other pieces of Hellenistic and Classical architecture, including the two-storey **market gate** from the Turkish town of Miletus. Built by the Romans in 120 AD, the gate was destroyed by an earthquake just under a thousand years later and brought to Berlin in fragmentary form for reconstruction during the nineteenth century.

The **Middle Eastern Section**, also on the main floor, has items dating back four thousand years to Babylonian times. The collection includes the enormous **Ishtar Gate** (see box, p.58), the **Processional Way** and the facade of the **Throne Room** from Babylon, all of which date from the reign of Nebuchadnezzar II in the sixth century BC. It's impossible not to be awed by the size and the remarkable state of preservation of the deep-blue enamelled bricks – but bear in mind that much of it is a mock-up, built around the original finds.

Pride of place in the museum's **Islamic Section** goes to the relief-decorated facade of a Jordanian **Prince's Palace** at Mshatta, from 743 AD, presented to Kaiser Wilhelm II by

A THIRTEEN-YEAR-LONG FACELIFT

At more than 2600 years old, it's perhaps high time that the **Ishtar Gate** – one of the eight fabled gates of the ancient city of Babylon, and one of the Pergamonmuseum's biggest draws – got a face lift. Partly because of the museum's humidity and lack of air conditioning, the 13m-high gate needed work in around a thousand places, mainly on the glaze that seals the enamel tiles, about one-tenth of which are original. The process involves cleaning each section then slowly injecting chemicals into it, which will happen in front of an average of two thousand visitors a day. Completing the entire process is expected to take until 2019.

the sultan of Turkey. Slightly more modest is a thirteenth-century **prayer niche** decorated with turquoise, black and gold tiles, from a mosque in Asia Minor. Another highlight is the **Aleppo Room**, a reception chamber with carved wooden wall decorations, reassembled in Berlin after being removed from a merchant's house in present-day Syria.

Bode-Museum

Am Kupfergraben • Tues, Wed & Fri–Sun 10am–6pm, Thurs 10am–8pm • €10, €18 with all other Museum Island museums on a Bereichskarte (see p.23) • Ⓦ smb.museum • S-Hackescher Markt

The stocky, neo-Baroque **Bode-Museum** at the northern tip of Museum Island suffered such heavy damage in World War II that it was scheduled for demolition in the late 1940s, until Berliners protested in the streets.

Expensive renovation over the years has created impressive results: opulent entrances and stairways, a swish first-floor **café**, and, most importantly, a seamless backdrop for one of Europe's most impressive **sculpture collections**. Wilhelm von Bode, the first director of the museum that now bears his name, would probably have approved: his ambition, to present a complete history of European sculpture and place in a proper context, led to his scouring Europe for items like fireplaces, frescoes and even whole ceilings for the museum. The present set-up isn't quite as exhaustive, but despite wartime losses the collection represents a good tour of European sculpture between the third and nineteenth centuries. A particular strength is the early **Italian Renaissance** with pieces by Luca della Robbia, Donatello, Desiderio da Settignano, Francesco Laurana and Mino da Fiesole among the highlights. Also from Italy is the unusual attraction of the **Tiepolo-Kabinett**, a small white and pastel room rich in stucco ornamentation and immaculate frescoes by Giovanni Battista Tiepolo, in a 1759 work originally located in a north Italian village.

The **German collection** is equally authoritative, particularly in sections detailing the Middle Ages – including work by masters like the late fifteenth-century woodcarver Tilman Riemenschneider, along with Hans Multscher, Hans Brüggemann, Nicolaus Gerhaert van Leyden and Hans Leinberger. Equally significant, particularly in the local context, are sculptures of several proud and imposing Prussian generals by Andreas Schlüter, created for Wilhelmplatz – a square in Berlin's former government quarter (see p.40); the imposing statue of Friedrich Wilhelm I sitting astride a horse in the museum lobby is also his work.

Also in the building is a collection of **Byzantine Art**, said to be second only to that of Istanbul's archeological museum. It's particularly strong on early Christian religious items, as well as featuring ornamental Roman sarcophagi and several intricate mosaics and ivory carvings. Finally, the museum is also home to an extraordinary **Numismatic collection**. Though mainly appealing to those with a specialist interest, it's worth a quick look for its gigantic size – around half-a-million coins – and the prize possessions, which include seventh-century coins that were among some of the first to have ever been minted.

The collection suffered greatly during the war, with many pieces in storage being irreparably damaged, such as the early sixteenth-century bust by Antonio della Porta, damaged by fire and now resembling a gruesomely disfigured figure or traumatized victim of war, which is displayed in the museum as a memorial to the others.

FERNSEHTURM AND WELTZEITUHR

Mitte: Alexanderplatz and around

With the gigantic TV tower looming above all Berlin, the adjacent, dreary Alexanderplatz – an unmistakable product of the old East Germany – is easy to find. And as a major U-Bahn, S-Bahn and tram station it's also easy to get to. During East Berlin's forty-year existence, while Unter den Linden was allowed to represent the glories of past Berlin, Alexanderplatz and its environs were meant to represent the glories of a modern socialist capital. However, it's hard to imagine that the concrete gigantism of the GDR era will wear as well as the efforts of Schinkel and his contemporaries. This is not to say that Alexanderplatz should be passed by. It's worth exploring not only the area's handful of historic buildings but also the East German creations that have their own place in Berlin's architectural chronology.

This is one part of town where there's little point in trying to spot prewar remains, as there's almost no trace of what stood here before 1945. Whole streets have vanished – the open area around the base of the TV tower, for example, used to be a dense network of inner-city streets – and today only a few survivors like the **Marienkirche** and **Rotes Rathaus** remain amid the modernity.

The nearby **Nikolaiviertel** is a pedestrian quarter that recreates a portion of Berlin's destroyed medieval heart. It is also home to the **Zille Museum**, which sketches out the life and work of cartoonist and satirist Heinrich Zille. The Nikolaiviertel backs onto an attractive stretch of the **River Spree** from where riverside paths join to form a loop past interesting modern buildings, including the **Dutch Embassy**, a clutch of secluded old buildings beside a stretch of Berlin's medieval first wall (built to keep people out rather than in) and the **Märkisches Museum**, where you can flesh out some of the city's history.

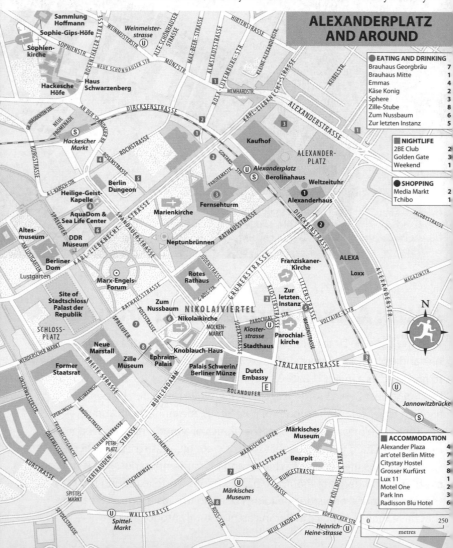

Alexanderplatz

Though long an important business and traffic centre, today's **Alexanderplatz** – a sprawling, windswept, pedestrianized plaza surrounded by high-rises – is largely the product of a 1960s GDR vision of how the centre of a modern, socialist metropolis should look. In the eighteenth century routes to all parts of Germany radiated from here, and a cattle and wool market stood on the site. It acquired its present name after the Russian tsar Alexander I visited Berlin in 1805. Today, in addition to the S-Bahn line running overhead, three underground lines cross beneath the platz, various bus routes converge on the area, and several tram lines course through it, making it one of central Berlin's busiest spots.

From the main doors at the southern end of the **train station** – which looks much the same as it did before the war despite being a 1960s rebuild – the route onto "Alex" leads through a gap between a couple of prewar survivors: the **Alexanderhaus** and the **Berolinahaus**, two buildings designed at the beginning of the 1930s by the architect and designer Peter Behrens, whose ideas influenced the founders of the Bauhaus movement. With their opaque glass towers beautifully lit at night, these are the only Alexanderplatz buildings not to have been destroyed in the war. The most intriguing communist-era landmark on the square is the **Weltzeituhr** ("World Clock") in front of the Alexanderhaus. Central Berlin's best-known rendezvous point, it tells the time in different cities throughout the world, and is a product of the same architectural school responsible for the Fernsehturm.

Loxx

Grunerstr. 20 • Daily 10am–8pm • €12 • ☎ 030 44 72 30 22, ⓦ loxx-Berlin.de • U- & S-Alexanderplatz

Tucked away on the top floor of the Alexa Centre shopping mall, **Loxx** may well be run by a fringe group of modelling enthusiasts, but it's certainly no small operation. Here a battery of forty computers and dozens of monitors equip a nerve centre that runs four hundred model trains and even a model airport: "night flights" occur every twenty minutes. The Berlin cityscape on display took 400,000 man hours to create; scores of Berlin landmarks have been faithfully reproduced on an exacting 1:87 scale, from a Fernsehturm that's well over twice human height down to mock-Byzantine enclosures of Berlin zoo and the *Plattenbau* high-rises of the GDR. Even with its creative geography it's a delight, especially for anyone who knows Berlin, and there's an undeniable pleasure in watching modellers working around the clock to create a mini version of a city famous for its tireless builders and architects.

ALEXANDERPLATZ: A TURBULENT HISTORY

Alexanderplatz has figured prominently in city **upheavals** ever since revolutionaries (including writer Theodor Fontane) set up barricades here in 1848. In 1872 it was the site of a demonstration by an army of homeless women and children, and nearly half a century later, during the revolution of 1918, sailors occupied the Alexanderplatz police headquarters (a feared local landmark just southeast of the platz – a plaque marks the spot) and freed the prisoners. Then in November 1989 it was the focal point of a million-strong demonstration and subsequent rallies when hundreds of thousands of people crammed into the square to hear opposition leaders speak.

Throughout its existence, the face of Alexanderplatz has undergone many **transformations**. A major reshaping at the end of the 1920s cleaned up what had become a rather sleazy corner of the city and turned it into one of its main shopping centres, with two expensive department stores in the vicinity: Hermann Tietz and Wertheim, Both were Jewish-owned until "Aryanized" by the Nazis. The Kaufhof department store facing the fountain was, as Centrum, one of the best-stocked shops in East Germany, though these days it's just another standard big store, now joined by several other chain stores and malls in and around the square.

Fernsehturm

Panoramastr. 1a • Daily: March–Oct 9am–midnight; Nov–Feb 10am–midnight • €12.50; you don't need a reservation for the tower, but it can be handy for the restaurant (in high season) – a VIP ticket (€19.50, available in advance online), enables you to dodge the queues and has an option for a table reservation • ⓦ tv-turm.de • U- & S-Alexanderplatz

Overshadowing every building in the vicinity, the gigantic **Fernsehturm**, or TV tower, just southwest of the Alexanderplatz S-Bahn station, looms over the eastern Berlin skyline like a displaced satellite on a huge factory chimney. The highest structure in Western Europe, this 365m-high transmitter was built during the isolationist 1960s, when the eastern part of the city was largely inaccessible to West Germans, and was intended as a highly visible symbol of the permanence of East Berlin and the German Democratic Republic. Its construction was watched with dismay and derision by West Berliners (and many in the East), who were heartily amused by the fact that sunshine reflecting off the globe on the tower forms a cross visible even in western Berlin; they dubbed it the "pope's revenge", much to the reported chagrin of the old GDR authorities. Nevertheless, after completion in 1969 the tower soon became a popular stop-off on the East Berlin tourist circuit.

Having outlasted the regime that conceived it, the Fernsehturm has now become part of the scenery, and though few would champion it on the grounds of architectural merit, it does have a certain retro appeal. Along with being an unmissable orientation point, the tower also provides a tremendous **view** (40km on a rare clear day) from the observation platform – reached by a very fast lift. Above the platform is *Sphere*, a restaurant whose key selling-point is that it revolves on its own axis twice an hour. The tower receives around a million visitors a year and the queues can be long whatever the weather; if time is short, consider investing in the VIP ticket.

Marienkirche

Karl-Liebknecht-Str. 8 • Daily: April–Oct 10am–8pm; Nov–March 10am–6pm (no visits during services) • Free • U- & S-Alexanderplatz

Once hemmed in by buildings, but now oddly alone in the shadow of the huge Fernsehturm, the **Marienkirche** is Berlin's oldest parish church. The Gothic stone-and-brick nave dates back to about 1270, but the tower is more recent, having been added in 1466, with the verdigris-coated upper section tacked on towards the end of the eighteenth-century by Brandenburg Gate designer Carl Gotthard Langhans. This uncontrived combination of architectural styles somehow makes the Marienkirche one of Berlin's most appealing churches, its simplicity a reminder of the city's village origins.

The **interior** is an excellent place to escape the increasingly frenetic street life of the area and listen to a free organ recital (Sat 4.30pm). Near the main entrance at the western end of the church is a small cross erected by the citizens of Berlin and Cölln as penance to the pope, after a mob immolated a papal representative on a nearby marketplace. There are five holes in the cross and, so the story goes, medieval convicted criminals wishing to prove their innocence could do so by inserting the fingers of one hand into the holes simultaneously – not too many escaped punishment, though, as the feat is almost an anatomical impossibility. Just inside the entrance, look out for the fifteenth-century *Totentanz*, a 22m-high frieze showing the dance of death. It's very faded, but accompanied by a representation of how it once looked, with Death shown as a shroud-clad mummy popping up between people from all levels of society.

The vaulted nave is plain and white but enlivened by some opulent decorative touches. Foremost among these is Andreas Schlüter's magnificent **pulpit**, its canopy dripping with cherubs and backed by a cloud from which gilded sunrays radiate. Complementing this are the white marble altar with a huge triptych altarpiece and the eighteenth-century organ, a riot of gilded filigree and yet more cherubs, topped by a sunburst.

Neptunbrunnen

The centrepiece of the parkland just southwest of the TV tower is the **Neptunbrunnen**, an extravagantly imaginative fountain incorporating a statue of a trident-wielding Neptune sitting on a shell. A serpent, seal and alligator spray the god of the sea with water, and he is supported by strange fish and eel-draped aquatic centaurs with webbed feet instead of hooves. Around the rim of the fountain sit four female courtiers, symbolizing what were at the time the four most important German rivers: the Rhine, the Vistula, the Oder and the Elbe. The statue was built in 1891 and was originally on Schlossplatz.

Rotes Rathaus

Rathausstr. 15 • Mon–Fri 9am–6pm • Free • ☎ 030 90 26 24 11 • U-Klosterstrasse

Across Rathausstrasse from the Neptunbrunnen is a rare survivor of Hohenzollern-era Berlin in the shape of the **Rotes Rathaus**, Berlin's "Red Town Hall". So called because of the colour of its bricks rather than its politics, the Rotes Rathaus has a solid angularity that contrasts sharply with the finicky grandeur of contemporaries like the Dom. This is perhaps because it's a symbol of the civic rather than the Imperial Berlin of the time – a city in the throes of rapid commercial expansion and industrial growth. The building has lost some of its impact now that it's been hemmed in by new structures, but it remains a grandiose, almost Venetian-looking edifice; look out for the intricate bas-relief in terracotta, illustrating episodes from the history of Berlin, that runs around the building at first-floor level. The Rathaus was badly knocked around in 1945, but made a good comeback following restoration during the 1950s. During GDR days it was headquarters of the East Berlin city administration, and since October 1991 it has housed the united city's administration. Inside a grand stairwell leads to a coat-of-arms hall with a few exhibits on the city, including some engaging aerial photos. The building also has a **cafeteria** offering low-price lunches – accessed via a door on the east side of the building.

The reconstruction of the Rathaus and thousands of other Berlin buildings is largely due to the *Trümmerfrauen* or "rubble women", who set to work in 1945 clearing up the 100 million tons of rubble created by wartime bombing and shelling. Their deeds are commemorated by the **statue** of a robust-looking woman facing the eastern entrance to the Rathaus on Rathausstrasse. Women of all ages carried out the bulk of the early rebuilding work, since most of Berlin's adult male population was dead, disabled or being held in PoW camps by the Allies. Despite this, the male contribution to the work is also marked by a statue of a man looking wistfully towards his *Trümmerfrau* counterpart from the western end of the Rathaus.

Sea Life Center

Spandauer Str. 3 • Daily 10am–7pm, last admission 6pm • €17.50, online discounts offered • ☎ 030 99 28 00, ⓦ sealifeeurope.com • S-Hackescher Markt

The large modern colossus that overlooks the Marx-Engels-Forum from the north, and incorporates the *Radisson Hotel* (see p.178), is a touristy mall that contains Berlin's

---

THE U5 EXTENSION AND THE MARX-ENGELS-FORUM

The huge building works in front of the Rotes Rathaus are part of a mighty project to extend the **U5** underground line across the heart of Berlin between Alexanderplatz and the Hauptbahnhof. Completion is planned for 2019, but in the meantime viewing platforms allow passers-by to inspect progress. Much of the work is taking place on the **Marx-Engels-Forum**, a severe plaza just west of the Rathaus. It's dedicated to the two revolutionary thinkers Karl Marx and Friedrich Engels and their landmark commemorative bronze – about five times their former real sizes – will eventually reappear here.

Sea Life Center, an overtly commercial aquarium that displays the fairly dreary aquatic life of the region's rivers and the North Atlantic. But at least the species here, highlights of which include sea horses, jellyfish, small sharks and manta rays, are elegantly displayed, particularly in the **AquaDom**, a gigantic tubular tank, located in the lobby of the *Radisson*, which you can rise through on a leisurely elevator. You can also sneak a peek at it from the hotel lobby, with its swish bar and comfy chairs.

Berlin Dungeon

Spandauer Str. 2 · Daily 10am–7pm · €19, online discounts offered; despite ticket combo deals with Madame Tussauds (see p.41), the Sea Life Centre (see p.63) and Legoland (see p.93), children under 10 are not allowed; most tours are in German, but there are regular English-language options · ☎ 01805 25 55 44, ⓦ thedungeons.com/berlin · S-Hackescher Markt

For a populist history of some of Berlin's gorier moments, visit the **Berlin Dungeon**. Hour-long tours visit theatre sets of several Berlin eras while costumed actors try to scare and amuse with tales of torture, serial killings, plagues and the like. Crucially material comes to an end with the 1920s, when, of course much of the real horror started, making the attraction seriously flaccid in a city where a former concentration camp is only a suburban train-ride away.

Heilige-Geist-Kapelle

Northwest of the Sea Life Center, en route to Hackescher Markt (see p.71), is the red-brick Gothic **Heilige-Geist-Kapelle** (Holy Ghost Chapel), one of Berlin's oldest surviving buildings. A remnant of the fourteenth century, it's now quaintly incongruous, dwarfed by a larger, newer building (part of Humboldt University) that was grafted onto it at the start of the twentieth century. The original interior has not survived, but it's a miracle that the chapel is still standing at all: it has endured the huge city fire of 1380, an enormously destructive explosion of a nearby gunpowder magazine in 1720, and, above all, wartime bombing.

DDR Museum

Karl-Liebknecht-Str. 1 · Mon–Fri & Sun 10am–8pm, Sat 10am–10pm · €6 · ☎ 030 847 12 37 31, ⓦ ddr-museum.de · S-Hackescher Markt

Tucked into the banks of the Spree, opposite the Berliner Dom, the popular **DDR Museum** is a homage to *Ostalgie* (see p.66). Using hands-on displays to reminisce on life in the GDR, it offers memories of the school system, pioneer camps and the razzmatazz with which the feats of model workers were celebrated. Less impressive were the GDR's awkward attempts to rival Western fashions, as its collection of polyester clothing and bleached jeans shows. Small wonder, perhaps, that one big GDR passion was nudism – as one very revealing display explains – which was considered as healthy as the many sports that the state unceasingly supported. The section devoted to travel is particularly good, and includes the chance to sit behind the wheel of a Trabi, where you'll quickly appreciate the "fewer parts mean less trouble" principles of the fibreglass car. The car is parked in front of video footage of East Berlin streets; for journeys further afield you can consult an Eastern Bloc road atlas, which clearly defines where the freedom of the open road ends.

The museum's highlight is the chance to mooch around a tiny reconstructed GDR apartment, ablaze with retro browns and oranges, where you can nose through cupboards and cosy up on a sofa to watch speeches by Erich Honecker: "*Vorwärts immer, rückwärts nimmer*" ("always forwards, never backwards"). Many of the remaining areas of the museum are gloomy but important, since they tackle the dark sides of the GDR era – such as censorship and repression – and help properly round off this snapshot of East German life.

FROM TOP DDR MUSEUM (P.64); NIKOLAIVIERTEL (P.66) >

Nikolaiviertel

Just southwest of the expansive open spaces that surround the Fernsehturm lie the compact network of streets of the **Nikolaiviertel**. This old district was razed overnight on June 16, 1944 but rebuilt by the GDR authorities in the early 1980s in an attempt to recreate some of Berlin's **medieval** core. One or two original buildings aside, the Nikolaiviertel consists partly of exact replicas of historic Berlin buildings and partly of stylized buildings not based on anything in particular, but with a vaguely "old Berlin" feel. Sometimes it doesn't quite come off, and in places the use of typical East German *Plattenbau* construction techniques, with prefabricated pillars and gables, isn't too convincing, but all in all the Nikolaiviertel represents a radical and welcome

3

OSTALGIE

Nostalgia for the East, or rather *Nostalgie* for the *Osten*, has produced **Ostalgie**, a hybrid word for a phenomenon that's emerged throughout the old East Germany. Though the sentiment might originate with those who can remember the collapsed country, this nostalgia for the iconography of communist East Germany has also proved immensely popular with visitors, spawning a mini-industry in Berlin.

The meaning of *Ostalgie* is a little nebulous and has slowly redefined itself since the *Wende*. What started as a melancholic craving for the securities of life in a communist state by the 16 million East Germans thrust into the turbulent and uncertain world of capitalism, became an expression of both discontent and identity. It was a protest at the quick eradication of a unique East German culture and its absorption into the West – a process that implied that all things Western were superior, and tended to mock everything from the East as laughably backward. *Ostalgie* became a way of affirming that some aspects of the GDR were worth celebrating, and that – despite the many shortcomings of the state – it had also produced rewarding moments.

These days *Ostalgie* stretches far beyond political debates and the 2003 film *Good Bye Lenin!*, with its nostalgic and comedic celebration of 1970s GDR kitsch and innocence. Visiting Berlin you'll come across a number of cult GDR icons, including the chubby, cheerful Ampelmann from East German pedestrian crossings and the cute fibreglass Trabant car. There's even been a revival of utilitarian GDR products, including foods, household products and cosmetics made by companies that went out of business when Western goods flooded the market. Some pop up in grocery stores and corner shops, but the entire range is most easily found online; try Ossiversand (Ⓦossiversand.de). Most of Berlin's *Ostalgie* shops concentrate on souvenirs, particularly the Ampelmann shop (see p.230).

Most agree that *Ostalgie* is just a good laugh, but the sentiment has its critics. Some warn of the dangers of posthumously glorifying any aspect of a totalitarian dictatorship and glossing over a dreadful chapter of Germany's history. Among them is Berlin's mayor Klaus Wowereit (see p.239) who bluntly warned of the "need to be careful that the GDR does not achieve cult status". Certainly, cheerful as the Ampelmann and Trabi may be, and as refreshing as cravings for simple pleasures and a frugal existence may seem, a balanced view of East Germany is essential. Some counterbalance may come from the film *The Lives of Others*, winner of the 2006 best foreign film Oscar, which reminded Germany and the world of the oppression, censorship, secret police and intimidation that underpinned life in communist Europe.

OSTALGIE HOTSPOTS

Drive a Trabi Unleash your inner Ossi behind the wheel of the two-stroke chariot and decide for yourself if this old East German workhorse deserves its cult status. See p.25

Ampelmann Store, Hackeshen Höfe You can buy a whole host of Ampelmann-branded items at its flagship store, from deck chairs and diaries to T-shirts and toys – and even a bicycle helmet. See p.230

DDR Museum Explore daily life in old East Germany and pick up a copy of the funny satirical film *Good Bye Lenin!*. See p.64

Verkehrsberuhigte Ost-Zone This bar is decked out in GDR memorabilia. See p.209

Ostel Nod off at the orange-and-brown furnished *Ostel* lodging. See p.181

Mondos Arts The ultimate GDR shopping temple. They are currently selling online only, at Ⓦmondosarts.de.

architectural departure from the usual East German response of levelling an area and building enormous concrete edifices.

Unfortunately, the district has barely taken seed, having the sterile feel of a living history museum that attracts only tourists and those Berliners who work in the restaurants and *Gaststätten* which, in keeping with their surroundings, tend to specialize in heavy traditional German food. Some of the most attractive **houses** – mostly pastel-facaded town houses four or five storeys high – are around the Nikolaikirche, along Propststrasse, and on the southern side of Nikolaikirchplatz, behind the church itself, where they are particularly convincing. To compare these with an original head to the Knoblauch-Haus on Poststrasse.

Nikolaikirche

Nikolaikirchplatz 5 • Tues & Thurs–Sun 10am–6pm, Wed noon–8pm • €5, free on first Wed every month • ⓦ stadtmuseum.de • U-Klosterstrasse

The centrepiece of the Nikolaiviertel is the thirteenth-century Gothic **Nikolaikirche**, a restored twin-towered church. It's one of the city's oldest churches and it was from here on November 2, 1539, that news of the Reformation was proclaimed to Berlin's citizens. The distinctive needle-like spires date from a nineteenth-century restoration, or rather their design does – the building was thoroughly wrecked during the war, as extensive patches of lighter, obviously modern masonry betray. An unusual feature of its **interior** is the bright colouring of the vault ribbings: the orange, purple, green and other vivid lines look like a Sixties Pop Art addition, but actually follow a medieval pattern discovered by a 1980s restorer. Otherwise the interior features a **museum** that traces the building's history.

Zille Museum

Propststr. 11 • April–Oct daily 11am–7pm; Nov–March Tues–Sun 11am–6pm • €6 • ☎ 030 24 63 25 00, ⓦ heinrich-zille-museum.de • U-Klosterstrasse

Propststrasse runs past the side of Nikolaikirche all the way down to the River Spree and ends in a rather clichéd statue of St George and the Dragon. Along it are a couple of places associated with Heinrich Zille – the Berlin artist who produced earthy satirical drawings of Berlin life around the turn of the twentieth century. One of his favourite watering holes – along with another Berlin artist Otto Nagel – was the sixteenth-century **Zum Nussbaum** (see p.189) pub, though in those days it stood on the opposite side of the Spree on the Spreeinsel where it was destroyed by wartime bombing. The replica is a faithful copy, right down to the walnut tree in the tiny garden. Many of Zille's drawings of early twentieth-century proletarian life were based on stories overheard in this pub, and you can explore the results further down the street at the excellent little **Zille Museum**. Though providing a fine insight into the artist's life and attitude, it makes no allowances for non-German speakers. But if you know a little of Zille's background, it's easy enough to enjoy the three rooms and short video on the artist's life, and appreciate his economical, humorous and vivid portrayals of squalid working-class life.

Gerichtslaube

Crossing Propststrasse is Poststrasse, the only other main street in the Nikolaiviertel. At its northern end is the **Gerichtslaube**, a replica of Berlin's medieval courthouse. The original was dismantled in 1870, to create space to build the Rotes Rathaus, and was moved to the grounds of Schloss Babelsberg in Potsdam where it can still be seen (see p.173).

Knoblauch-Haus

Poststr. 23 • Tues & Thurs–Sun 10am–6pm, Wed noon–8pm • Free • ⓦ stadtmuseum.de • U-Klosterstrasse

The southern end of Poststrasse features the **Knoblauch-Haus**, a Neoclassical town house built in 1759 and a rare survivor of the war. It was home to the patrician Knoblauch family, who played an important role in the commercial and cultural life of eighteenth- and nineteenth-century Berlin, and now contains an exhibition (with nothing in English) about their activities. While the careers of Eduard Knoblauch, Berlin's first freelance architect, and Armand Knoblauch, founder of a major city brewery, are mildly interesting, the real appeal is the house's **interior**, with its grand-bourgeois furnishings, which gives a good impression of upper middle-class life in Hohenzollern-era Berlin. The ground floor and vaulted basement are home to the *Historische Weinstuben*, a reconstruction of a nineteenth-century wine-restaurant once favoured by the playwrights Gerhart Hauptmann, August Strindberg and Henrik Ibsen.

Ephraim-Palais

Poststr. 16 · Tues & Thurs–Sun 10am–6pm, Wed noon–8pm · €6 · ☎ 030 24 00 21 62, ⓦ stadtmuseum.de · U-Klosterstrasse

With its elegantly curving Rococo facade, Tuscan columns, wrought-iron balconies, oval staircase and ornate ceiling crafted by Schlüter, the **Ephraim-Palais** is an exquisite place to visit. A rebuilt eighteenth-century merchant's mansion, this relic of Berlin bourgeois high life now houses a museum of Berlin-related art from the seventeenth to the beginning of the nineteenth centuries, with numerous pictures, prints and maps giving a good impression of the city in its glory days. The Ephraim-Palais was built in 1762 by Veitel Heine Ephraim, court jeweller and mint master to Frederick the Great, and all-round wheeler-dealer. He owed his lavish lifestyle primarily to the fact that – on Frederick's orders – he steadily reduced the silver content of the Prussian *thaler*. This earned a great deal of money for Frederick and Ephraim himself but ruined the purchasing power of the currency.

Molkenmarkt

The busy but soulless square just east of the Nikolaiviertel, the **Molkenmarkt**, is one of Berlin's oldest public spaces. On its eastern side, Jüdenstrasse –"Jews' Street" was Berlin's original Jewish ghetto, until they were driven out of Brandenburg in 1573. When allowed back into Berlin in 1671 they mainly settled near today's Hackescher Markt (see p.71). Glowering over the road, the large domed **Stadthaus** is reminiscent of the Französischer Dom (see p.48) but dates from as recently as 1911, a relic of the days when the area served as the administrative district of Wilhelmine Berlin. Also on the Molkenmarkt is the smooth zinc-clad **Berlinwasser Holding** building, with its fiercely angular arches and windows, which belongs to the local water company. The work of highly acclaimed local architect Christoph Langhof, it cleverly plays on the **Palais Schwerin**, the traditional building next door – one of two pompous buildings that make up the **Berliner Münze** (Berlin Mint), whose most impressive feature is a replica of a frieze depicting coining techniques by Gottfried Schadow, designer of the Brandenburg Gate quadriga.

Dutch Embassy

A couple of minutes' walk along the north bank of the Spree from the Berlin Mint sits the striking **Dutch Embassy** building, designed by Rem Koolhaas. The concept intended to blend the security and formality of the civil service with something that projects Dutch openness. The resulting building has a slightly unfinished look but is clever in the way that it circulates light and air and with its use of a cube housing the ambassadorial accommodation, which stands apart from the rest. The embassy staff's habits were used to inspire the building: in the previous embassy, the entrance hall was popular for informal meetings so the designers created an enormous hallway as a centrepiece that extends up to all eight storeys and shapes the building's internal communication and ventilation.

Klosterstrasse and around

Named after a long-gone local monastery, **Klosterstrasse** leaves the banks of the Spree and the Dutch Embassy to link several minor points of interest. The **Parochialkirche**, a sixteenth-century Baroque church, lies near its junction with **Parochialstrasse**. The bare brick interior (legacy of the usual wartime gutting) is a venue for changing, but often low-key art exhibitions (free). Parochialstrasse itself had a brief moment of importance when the building at **Parochialstrasse 1** hosted the first meeting of Berlin's post-Nazi town council, headed by future SED chief Walter Ulbricht, even as fighting still raged a little to the west. Ulbricht and his comrades had been specially flown in from Soviet exile to sow the seeds of a communist civil administration, and they moved in here, having been unable to set up shop in the still-burning Rotes Rathaus.

The northern end of Klosterstrasse is worth a quick look for the gutted thirteenth-century **Franziskaner-Kirche**, destroyed by a landmine in 1945 and left a ruin by GDR authorities as a warning against war and fascism. Another ruin from Berlin's history is behind it on Littenstrasse where a fragment of **Stadtmauer**, the thirteenth-century Berlin wall, survives. Behind it is the atmospheric old **Zur letzten Instanz**, Berlin's oldest pub (see p.190).

3

Märkisches Museum

Am Köllnischen Park 5 · Tues & Thurs–Sun 10am–6pm · €5, free on first Wed every month · ⓦ stadtmuseum.de · U-Märkisches Museum

Occupying a building that resembles a red-brick neo-Gothic cathedral, the **Märkisches Museum** feels somewhat dated in its treatment of Berlin and Brandenburg's history. Small rooms are crammed with paintings, gadgets and glass vitrines, and the text is in German only. The displays, which predate reunification, are also episodic: eighteenth- and nineteenth-century culture is definitely the museum's forte. One of the first rooms deals with Berlin's late nineteenth-century role as a centre of **barrel organ** production, an industry established by Italian immigrants. Many of these music-makers are on display, as well as their increasingly large and more intricate progeny. Organ-grinding performances are given every Sunday at 3pm.

Other rooms are divided into sections of the city – Unter den Linden, Friedrichstrasse and so on. Among them is the **Gottische Kapelle**, a room resembling a small chapel and filled with wonderful pieces of medieval sacred art from (usually) unknown local artisans. More secular is the room devoted to the "Panorama", a huge arcade-like machine, built over a hundred years ago: as you peer through the eyepiece, a huge drum rotates to show you dozens of fascinating **3D photographs** of 1890s Berlin.

Less rewarding are the early history displays, from prehistoric pottery pieces to copies of royal proclamations from Friedrich Wilhelm, the Great Elector, who died in 1688. A marvellous bronze statue of Bismarck dressed as a blacksmith manfully forging German unity is a highlight, and there are seven original sections of the Berlin Wall.

More Berliniana is on view outside the museum: a statue of Heinrich Zille and, in a leafy park behind, a **bearpit** that provides the depressing home to a couple of sleepy brown bears, Berlin's city symbol.

Mitte: The Spandauer Vorstadt

The Spandauer Vorstadt, the crescent-shaped area running north of the River Spree between Friedrichstrasse and Alexanderplatz, emerged after the *Wende* as one of the most intriguing parts of the unified city. Its appeal is based partly on its history as Berlin's prewar Jewish quarter – by the start of the twentieth century the district had become the cultural and spiritual centre of a well-established, wealthy and influential Jewish community. Things changed dramatically under the Nazis, but since the *Wende* the district has undergone a dramatic revival. Squatters and artists were the first pioneers; restoration projects soon followed, putting the infrastructure to rights and renovating the backstreets to usher in a tide of bars, boutiques, cafés and restaurants. The area now boasts a booming (if fairly touristy) shopping, dining and nightlife scene, all easily navigable on foot.

The Spandauer Vorstadt originated as one of a number of suburbs just beyond Berlin's walled centre during the seventeenth century, when the population swelled firstly with persecuted French Huguenots and then with large numbers of persecuted Eastern European Jews (see box, pp.80–81). Deportation of the Jews under the Nazis took much of the soul out of the area, which was further decimated during the GDR era when most surviving businesses shut down. From the 1950s until the *Wende* the quarter became little more than a network of decrepit prewar streets punctuated by the occasional slab of GDR-era housing. Few visitors strayed here from Unter den Linden, and apart from a couple of pockets of restoration the area was allowed to quietly decay.

Its 1990s resurrection began in earnest around the S-Bahn station and convivial square of **Hackescher Markt**, and in the adjacent courtyards of the **Hackesche Höfe** which now provide the district's main focus. The surrounding streets, particularly **Sophienstrasse**, were also attractively restored, but nowhere has the injection of energy been greater than in the youthful shops peddling cool clothes and shoes just east of here, where **Rosenthaler Strasse**, **Neue Schönhauser Strasse** and **Münzstrasse** form a de facto hub for Berlin's indie fashion scene. This zone bleeds into a residential district that, when known as the **Scheunenviertel**, was Berlin's most squalid and colourful district – Nazi demolition of this unruly and heavily Jewish enclave removed all evidence of it, however. The Nazis also left an indelible imprint on the area to the west – the heart of Berlin's prewar **Jewish district**, which is focused around **Grosse Hamburger Strasse** and the busy **Oranienburger Strasse**. Here the past is as much recalled by the absence of landmarks as their presence. At least the **Neue Synagoge** has been restored – as a museum of Jewish culture. Further up Oranienburger Strasse sits the dank, graffiti-covered **Tacheles**, an anarchic landmark arts venue that now awaits demolition. Opposite, **Auguststrasse** is a vital part of Berlin's contemporary art scene.

At its western end, around **Oranienburger Tor**, the Spandauer Vorstadt has less to offer, though it was once the hub of Berlin's industrial revolution. Almost all points of interest around here appeal to fans of **theatre**, particularly of **Bertolt Brecht**, whose house, grave and some of the venues where he worked dot the area. Finally, just beyond the district's northern fringes are a couple of Berlin's most important sights: the **Berlin Wall Memorial**, the only place in the city where a section of the Berlin Wall has been preserved in its entirety – complete with border defences and a "death strip" between two parallel walls; and a **World War II bunker** within the Gesundbrunnen U-Bahn station.

S-Bahnhof Hackescher Markt

Running the entire southern length of **Hackescher Markt** is its **S-Bahnhof**, now a protected building. A nineteenth-century construction whose original red-tile facade retains the mosaic decorative elements and rounded windows typical of the period, its architectural features are best appreciated by walking through the station itself and taking a look at the northern facade. On both sides the renovated arches under the S-Bahn tracks house trendy restaurants, bars and clothes shops.

Hackesche Höfe

Daily · S-Hackescher Markt

One of the main draws of the Spandauer Vorstadt are the **Hackesche Höfe**, a series of nine courtyards (*Höfe*) built between 1905 and 1907 to house businesses, flats and places of entertainment. Restored to their former Art Deco glory, the courtyards now bustle with crowds visiting the several cafés, stores, galleries, theatres and cinemas within. The first courtyard, decorated with blue mosaic tiles, is home to the Chamäleon (see p.222), at the forefront of the revival of the city's interwar cabaret tradition.

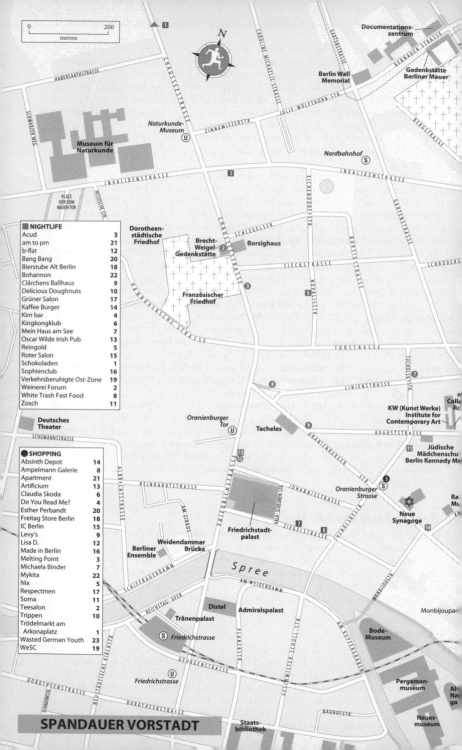

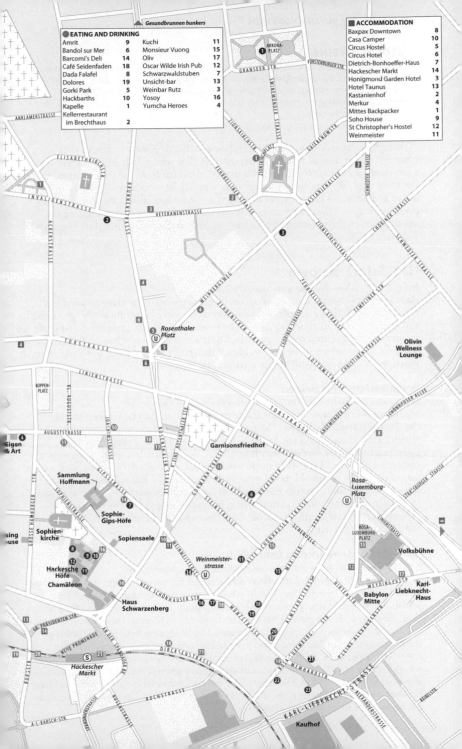

Gesundbrunnen bunkers

EATING AND DRINKING

Amrit	9	Kuchi	11
Bandol sur Mer	6	Monsieur Vuong	15
Barcomi's Deli	14	Oliv	17
Café Seidenfaden	18	Oscar Wilde Irish Pub	12
Dada Falafel	8	Schwarzwaldstuben	7
Dolores	19	Unsicht-bar	13
Gorki Park	5	Weinbar Rutz	3
Hackbarths	10	Yosoy	16
Kapelle	1	Yumcha Heroes	4
Kellerrestaurant im Brechthaus	2		

ACCOMMODATION

Baxpax Downtown	8
Casa Camper	10
Circus Hostel	5
Circus Hotel	6
Dietrich-Bonhoeffer-Haus	7
Hackescher Markt	14
Honigmond Garden Hotel	3
Hotel Taunus	13
Kastanienhof	2
Merkur	4
Mittes Backpacker	1
Soho House	9
St Christopher's Hostel	12
Weinmeister	11

STOLPERSTEINE

Look at the ground around the entrances to some Hackesche Höfe and you'll see brass-plated cobblestones known as **Stolpersteine**, or "stumbling-blocks". These are some of the nine thousand laid into footpaths around Germany as a memorial to the victims of Nazi persecution: each carries a name, birth date and their fate. See ⓦ stolpersteine.com for full information on the project.

Though thoroughly beautified today, these courtyards preserve a layout that was common in this district and much of prewar Berlin, where daily life was played out in a labyrinth of *Hinterhöfe* – courtyards that were hidden from the shops and offices on the main road. Within the *Hinterhöfe* were a warren of workshops – with housing above and behind – that together produced a microcosm of the city, with rich and poor, housing and commerce crammed together for better or worse, creating the squalid turn-of-the-twentieth-century urban culture that was satirized by Heinrich Zille (see p.67).

Haus Schwarzenberg

Rosenthaler Str. 39 • ⓦ haus-schwarzenberg.org • S-Hackescher Markt

Haus Schwarzenberg is the unapologetically grungy sidekick of the gentrified Hackesche Höfe, just a couple of doors away. It has only been minimally refurbished and at least part of its allure is provided by its atmospherically crumbling and grafittied facades around a central courtyard. It harbours a number of low-key cafés, bars, shops and galleries (street-art lovers will want to visit Neurotitan Gallery), but a trio of small **museums** relating to **Jewish life** are a particular draw.

Gedenkstätte Stille Helden

Daily 10am–8pm • Free • ☎ 030 23 45 79 19, ⓦ gedenkstaette-stille-helden.de • S-Hackescher Markt

Spreading over a couple of rooms above the hubbub of the Hackescher Markt, the **Gedenkstätte Stille Helden** (Memorial to the Silent Heroes) is a museum that remembers Germans who tried to save Jewish lives by risking their own. The high-tech interactive format uses photographs, documents and oral testimonies to uncover the faces and stories of those who worked in isolation and lived with a daily fear of discovery to uphold moral values and undermine Nazi racial decrees. The heroic successes and even the tragic failures help restore your faith in human nature in this era. If all this piques your interest, be sure to investigate the overlapping content of the more studied Gedenkstätte Deutscher Widerstand (see p.98), in the diplomatic district.

Museum Blindenwerkstatt Otto Weidt

Daily 10am–8pm • Free • ☎ 030 28 59 94 07, ⓦ museum-blindenwerkstatt.de • S-Hackescher Markt

The **Museum Blindenwerkstatt Otto Weidt** occupies the former rooms of a broom and brush factory run by one Otto Weidt, whose employees were mostly deaf, blind and Jewish. Luckily the factory was considered important to the war effort, so for a long time Weidt was able to protect his workers from deportation to concentration camps. But in the 1940s, as pressure grew, he resorted to producing false papers, bribing the Gestapo and providing food and even hiding places to keep them alive, all at considerable personal risk. One small room, whose doorway was hidden by a cupboard, was the refuge for a family of four until their secret was discovered and they were deported and murdered in Auschwitz. The exhibition has relics of the wartime factory – brushes, photos and letters from the workers – but it is all in German, so if necessary ask for the free English translation on entry.

Anne Frank Center
Tues–Sun 10am–6pm · €5 · ☎ 030 288 86 56 10, ⓦ annefrank.de

Across the courtyard from the Museum Blindenwerkstatt Otto Weidt, the **Anne Frank Center** tells the world-famous story of the bright, popular, middle-class Jewish girl who died in Bergen-Belsen, leaving behind poignant diaries of Nazi persecution. The familiarity of the tale allows the exhibition to take only a relatively superficial look at it, starting with the background to the persecution – including diagrammatic representations of the 1935 Nuremberg laws, which delineated in pointless and obsessive detail whether marriage between people is admissible based on the amount of Jewishness of a great-grandparent – before sketching out the basics of Anne's life, wonderfully photographed by her father Otto. Anne had no connection with Berlin, and the centre, partner to the Anne Frank House in Amsterdam, simply chose this site for its location in the middle of Berlin's prewar Jewish quarter. Nonetheless her story is woven into the local context in a large section of the museum that shows video interviews with Berlin teenagers, from ethnic minorities about the age Anne was when she died, as they relate their aspirations and experiences.

Scheunenviertel

Northeast of the Hackesche Hofe is the **Scheunenviertel** ("barn quarter"), now a fairly unremarkable residential area enclosed between Rosenthaler Strasse and Alexanderplatz. Despite today's appearance, its history is a fairly lively one: founded in 1672, following a decree that flammable hay could no longer be stored within the city limits, Scheunenviertel was originally a base for Berlin's poorest peasants; in later years it attracted impoverished political and religious refugees from all over Europe, with its heyday coming towards the end of the nineteenth century when it became a magnet for Jewish migrants from eastern Europe and Russia (see pp.80–81). The neighbourhood's melting-pot atmosphere made it an ideal refuge for those at odds with the Prussian and later the Imperial German establishment, making it a notorious centre of revolutionary activity. By the early twentieth century the Scheunenviertel had become an infamous slum, rife with deprivation and petty crime. In the 1930s it became a regular battleground for the street gangs of the left and right, while artists and writers – including Bertolt Brecht, Marlene Dietrich and actor Gustav Gründgens – were attracted to the area, quick to create their own bohemian enclave. The Nazis put a stop to much of the activity by pulling chunks of the Scheunenviertel down, ostensibly to make way for a U-Bahn station. At the same time they played on the district's unsavoury reputation by extending the term Scheunenviertel to include the affluent and bourgeois Jewish areas around the Oranienburger Strasse – an attempt to tar all Jews with the same brush.

Garnisonsfriedhof

Kleine Rosenthaler Str. · **Cemetery** Daily: April–Sept 7am–7pm; Oct–March 8am–4pm **Exhibition** April–Sept Sat & Sun 10am–4pm;
Oct–March Sun noon–3pm · Free

At the eastern end of Auguststrasse lies the leafy **Garnisonsfriedhof**, a military cemetery dating from the eighteenth century, full of rusting cast-iron crosses with near-obliterated inscriptions commemorating officers and men of the Prussian army. Also here is the rather grander tomb of Adolph von Lützow, a general who found fame during the Napoleonic Wars, contrasting sharply with the overgrown wooden crosses commemorating victims of the Battle of Berlin, hidden away in a far corner. Information is available from the administration offices near the entrance, which also house a small **exhibition**.

Rosa-Luxemburg-Platz and around

On the eastern side of what was once the Scheunenviertel lies **Rosa-Luxemburg-Platz**. The most prominent landmark here is the **Volksbühne** theatre, built in 1913 with money raised by public subscription. Under the directorship of the ubiquitous Max Reinhardt, it became Berlin's people's theatre and, daringly for that time, put on plays by Hauptmann, Strindberg and Ibsen. Erwin Piscator continued the revolutionary tradition from 1924 to 1927, and immediately after the war in September 1945 a production of Lessing's plea for tolerance, *Nathan the Wise*, was put on here. The venue was officially reopened in 1954; it became – and remains – one of the ex-GDR capital's best theatres (see p.220).

Nearby, at Weydingerstrasse 14 and Kleine Alexanderstrasse 28, is the **Karl-Liebknecht-Haus**, the former KPD central committee headquarters, which also housed the editorial offices of the communist newspaper *Rote Fahne* ("Red Flag"). From the late 1920s onwards this was an important centre of resistance to the increasingly powerful Nazis: 100,000 pro-communist workers demonstrated here on January 25, 1933, just days before Hitler came to power. After the Reichstag fire in February 1933 the KPD was broken up and its headquarters ransacked.

Sophienstrasse

Sophienstrasse, first settled at the end of the seventeenth century, was once the Spandauer Vorstadt's main street. Extensively restored in the 1980s, it's now the best-looking street in the Hackescher Markt district and features a mix of retailers and arts workshops. In places, however, the restoration is only skin-deep and the pastel frontages of the old apartment houses conceal rundown, crumbling courtyards.

Sammlung Hoffman

Sophienstr. 21 • Sat 11am–4pm; 90min guided tour (English tours available) • €10 • ☎ 030 28 49 91 20, 🌐 sammlung-hoffmann.de

At Sophienstrasse 21 a doorway leads to the **Sophie-Gips Höfe**, a renovated retail and office complex where large outdoor works of art announce the presence of **Sammlung Hoffman**, the private contemporary art collection of avid collectors Erika and Rolf Hoffmann. The collection, which includes painting, sculpture, photography and video, spreads over three light-filled floors. Organized subjectively – there are no names, descriptions or curatorial themes – it is changed each year, but always features internationally renowned names such as Jean-Michel Basquiat, Andy Warhol and Bruce Nauman. Tours offer a pleasantly interactive and informative way of experiencing such major works.

Handwerkervereinshaus

Sophienstr. 18

The vaguely Gothic-looking **Handwerkervereinshaus** used to be the headquarters of the old craftsmen's guild. Until the founding of the German Social Democrat Party (SPD), this had been the main focus of the Berlin workers' movement, and continued to play an important role as a frequent venue for political meetings, including, on November 14, 1918, the first public gathering of the Spartakusbund (Spartacus League), the breakaway anti-war faction of the SPD that later evolved into the KPD (Communist Party of Germany). The block now houses the **Sophiensäle**, a venue for contemporary theatre, music and dance (see p.222).

Sophienkirche

Sophienstr. 22 • May–Sept Wed 3–6pm, Sat 3–5pm

The **Sophienkirche**, built in 1712, is one of the city's finest Baroque churches, and the only central Berlin church to survive the war more or less undamaged. Its clear, simple lines come as a welcome change after the monumental Neoclassicism and fussy Gothic revivalism of so much of Berlin's architecture. The church's 70m-high tiered tower, added during the 1730s, is one of the area's most prominent landmarks. Built on ground gifted by the Jewish community to the Protestant community, who at the time were slightly financially embarrassed, the church itself was paid for by Princess Sophie Louise in order to provide a parish church for the neighbourhood. The **interior**, in washed-out shades of green and grey, is simple but pleasing; the one note of aesthetic exuberance is a pulpit with a crown-like canopy, set on a spiral pillar, which makes it look exactly like a chalice.

Grosse Hamburger Strasse

At its western end, Sophienstrasse meets **Grosse Hamburger Strasse**, a road dotted with several poignant reminders of the area's Jewish past. It's home to Berlin's oldest **Jewish cemetery**, established in 1672, and the first **Jewish old people's home** to be founded in the city. The Nazis used the building as a detention centre for Jews, and 55,000 people were held here before being deported to the camps. A memorial tablet, on which pebbles have been placed as a mark of respect (following the Jewish practice for grave-site visits), and a sculpted group of haggard-looking figures representing deportees, mark the spot where the home stood. The grassed-over open space behind is the site of the cemetery itself. In 1943 the Gestapo smashed most of the headstones and dug up the remains of those buried here, using gravestones to shore up a trench they had excavated through the site. A few cracked headstones with Hebrew inscriptions line the graveyard walls. The only freestanding monument was erected after the war to commemorate Moses Mendelssohn, the philosopher and German Enlightenment figure. Also adorned with pebbles, it's on the spot where he is thought to have been buried, with an inscription in German on one side and in Hebrew on the other. Just to the north of the cemetery at **Grosse Hamburger Strasse 27** is a former Jewish boys' school, now a Jewish secondary school for both sexes. Above its entrance a sign from prewar days reads, in German, "Jewish Community Boys' School". On the facade a plaque pays homage to Mendelssohn, who was a founder of Berlin's first Jewish school here in 1778, and who, until 1938, was commemorated by a bust in the garden.

On the other side of the street, the **Missing House** is a unique and effective monument to the wartime destruction of Berlin. A gap in the tenements marks where house number 15–16 stood until destroyed by a direct hit during an air raid. In the autumn of 1990 the French artist Christian Boltanski put plaques on the sidewalls of the surviving buildings on either side as part of an installation, recalling the names, dates and professions of the former inhabitants of the vanished house.

Oranienburger Strasse and around

Oranienburger Strasse, the centre of Berlin's affluent prewar Jewish community, still bears some reminders from this time. During its spell in East Berlin it was one of the city centre's more desolate streets, but after 1989 it became an atmospheric bar-crawling strip, and is now principally known for its restaurants and stylish watering holes, which attract locals and tourists in equal numbers. After dark, prostitutes openly solicit along much of the road; their presence alongside gawping visitors is a little reminiscent of Amsterdam's red-light district.

Monbijouplatz

Sedate **Monbijouplatz**, at the eastern end of Oranienburger Strasse, is of interest for a couple of modern buildings, at numbers 3 and 5, designed by innovative local architects Grüntuch/Ernst. Though radically different, the two buildings share a harmony in their geometric facades and attention to detail, such as in the intricacy of the small mosaic tiles on the detailing between the vertical bands at number 5, and in the play of light and shadow allowed by the aluminium louvres on the balconies of number 3.

4

Monbijoupark

Sitting next to Monbijouplatz, **Monbijoupark** was once the grounds of a Rococo royal palace, reduced to rubble by the war and, like so many Hohenzollern relics, never rebuilt. The park makes an unexpected and shady refuge and is a good place to picnic or lie out with a book. The pleasant promenade that separates it from the Spree leads to a footbridge to Museum Island (see p.55).

Ramones Museum

Krausnickstr. 23 • Mon–Thurs 9am–6pm, Fri 9am–8pm, Sat 10am–8pm, Sun noon–6pm • €3.50 (concerts vary but mostly free) • ☎ 030 75 52 88 90, ⓦ ramonesmuseum.com • S-Oranienburger Strasse

Berlin's own shrine to the American proto-punks, the **Ramones Museum** began two decades ago with little more than a few signed posters and some T-shirts. The collection has now expanded to more than three hundred items of memorabilia – an eclectic assortment, ranging from childhood photos of the group to gig set lists and flyers. The museum also hosts film screenings, the odd acoustic show and special events.

Neue Synagoge

Oranienburger Str. near the corner of Krausnickstr. • March & Oct Sun & Mon 10am–8pm, Tues–Thurs 10am–6pm, Fri 10am–2pm; April–Sept Sun & Mon 10am–8pm, Tues–Thurs 10am–6pm, Fri 10am–5pm; Nov–Feb Mon & Sun 10am–6pm, Tues–Thurs 10am–6pm, Fri 10am–2pm • €4.60 • ⓦ cjudaicum.de • S-Oranienburger Strasse

During the initial waves of Jewish immigration from the seventeenth century onwards the area around Oranienburger Strasse was a densely populated and desperately poor ghetto, but by the nineteenth century Berlin's Jews had achieved a high degree of prosperity and assimilation. This was reflected in the building of the grand **Neue Synagoge**, to a design by Eduard Knoblauch, halfway down Oranienburger Strasse just off the corner of Krausnickstrasse. The synagogue was inaugurated in the presence of Bismarck in 1866, a gesture of official recognition that, coming at a time when Jews in Russia were still enduring officially sanctioned pogroms, must have made many feel that their position in German society was finally secure. The acceptance that they had enjoyed in Wilhelmine Germany contributed to the sense of disbelief many Jews felt at the rise of Nazism during the 1920s and 1930s.

The Neue Synagoge was built in mock-Moorish style, with a bulbous gilt and turquoise dome. It was Berlin's central synagogue for more than sixty years, serving also as a venue for concerts, including one in 1930 by Albert Einstein in his lesser-known role as a violinist. A Jewish museum was opened next door on January 24, 1933, just six days before the Nazi takeover. Neither museum nor synagogue survived the Third Reich. Both were damaged on *Kristallnacht* (see p.255), though the synagogue wasn't actually destroyed thanks to the intervention of the local police chief who chased off SA arsonists and called the fire brigade to extinguish the flames. It remained in use as a place of worship until 1940 when it was handed over to the Wehrmacht, who used it as a warehouse until it was gutted by bombs on the night of November 22, 1943.

After the war the synagogue remained a ruin, and in 1958 the main hall, which was thought to be on the verge of collapse, was demolished, leaving only the building's facade and entrance rooms intact. For many years these stood here largely overlooked, a plaque on the shattered frontage exhorting the few passers-by to *Vergesst es nie* – "Never forget". The Jewish community pressed for what was left to be turned into a museum, but the authorities did not respond until 1988, when it was decided to resurrect the shell as a "centre for the promotion and preservation of Jewish culture".

A new plaque was affixed to the building amid much official pomp on November 9, 1988, the fiftieth anniversary of *Kristallnacht*, and work began on restoring the facade and reconstructing the gilded dome, which, visible from far and wide, has once again become a Berlin landmark. In 1995, the building was reopened as a museum and cultural centre, officially called **Centrum Judaicum – Neue Synagoge**. Inside are two permanent exhibitions, one on the history of the synagogue itself and another on the Jewish life and culture that was once found in the area. You'll have to pass through airport-style security to get in – a sad reflection of the continuing threat to Jewish institutions from terrorist attack.

Tacheles

The revitalization of Oranienburger Strasse pretty much began in 1990, when a group of young international artists took over **Tacheles**, a spectacularly ruined 1907 shopping centre. Its exterior festooned with works-in-progress, the building soon became the home and workplace of an ever-changing band of painters, sculptors, kindred spirits and hangers-on. It gradually moved away from its anarchic beginnings, but various venues within hosted a busy calendar of offbeat gigs and events. Sadly for the area's alternative culture, and after a lengthy struggle and numerous demonstrations, development pressure got the best of the venue in 2012 and the place was ring-fenced for demolition. While it awaits its final fate, several artists persevere in shacks in the garden behind. They welcome visitors.

Auguststrasse

Auguststrasse was the epicentre of the 1990s Berlin art scene, and though it has long since lost much of its original edge, it still features workspaces and commercial galleries. The breathtaking transformation of the street from decrepit inner-city district to thriving arts scene began in 1989 and was given legitimacy in June 1992 when city authorities stumped up enviable financial support for the "37 Rooms Exhibition", during which the whole of Auguststrasse was turned into a giant gallery. Since then the street's galleries (see p.217) continue to attract artists and their interesting and controversial work from all over the world.

4

Jüdische Mädchenschule and Berlin Kennedy Museum

Auguststr. 11-13 • Daily 10am–6pm • €7 • ☎ 030 20 65 35 70, ⓦ thekennedys.de • S-Oranienburger Strasse

In pre-Nazi days the corridors of the business-like dark-brick **Jüdische Mädchenschule** (Jewish Girls School) were pounded by some thousand Jewish schoolgirls, most of whom were later deported or murdered in concentration camps. In recent years the building has been refurbished by Berlin's art nobility both in their memory and to provide themselves with a ritzy hangout that includes three restaurants (one kosher), three floors for art and, slightly irrelevantly, the **Berlin Kennedy Museum**.

Inspired by the US president's 1963 visit to Berlin – then the front line of the Cold War – the museum is now a much broader homage to John F. Kennedy. He understood, as no other politician before him, the power of photos and then television – partly thanks to his former-photojournalist wife Jackie. As Norman Mailer put it: "America's politics ... (became) ... America's favorite movie, America's first soap opera, America's bestseller." Evidence of this carefully orchestrated media campaign (which included a ban on photos showing Kennedy wearing glasses) and resultant cult of personality abounds in the museum's three hundred **photos** and magazine covers. The dozens of other 1960s relics include JFK's old ties, cufflinks, phonebook and some preserved presidential doodles – twirling shapes casually interspersed with words like Cuba, Berlin, Eastern Europe – as well as the crocodile-skin briefcase that accompanied him on his fateful trip to Dallas. Also here is a brilliant **photomosaic** of Kennedy by American artist Rob Silvers who invented the technique: it uses hundreds of pictures from his life to build a mask.

The real highlights of the museum, however, are exhibits relating to JFK's eight-hour **Berlin visit** on June 26, 1963. The Berlin Wall had been built just two years earlier, so the city's emotions ran high, and there's wonderful footage here of ecstatic crowds – people breaking free of security cordons to shake hands with the passing

BERLIN'S JEWS

Jews have been part of Berlin's make-up since the earliest days of the twin towns of Berlin-Cölln. As elsewhere in Europe, their history has been studded by **episodic persecution**, though nothing comes close to their ruthless extermination by the Third Reich. Nevertheless, the Jewish community also has a history of determinedly and repeatedly rising to **prominence** against the odds: punching well above its weight in the city's prewar entrepreneurial and cultural scene and again today with the numbers of Jews in Berlin doubling over the past two decades.

Berlin's earliest Jewish settlers gravitated to a tight-knit area around today's Jüdenstrasse (see p.68) where, banned from most other trades, they successfully traded and lent money and slowly built a community. But in difficult times – of economic hardship or epidemics – they frequently became scapegoats. Bouts of persecution included during the plague of 1349; 1446, when they were driven from the city; and the **witch hunts** of 1510 when fifty Jews were tortured to death or burnt at the stake, with the rest again barred from the city. Though readmitted thirty years later, they found themselves barred once again in 1573 following a spate of pogroms after Joachim II was murdered and his much-disliked Jewish finance minister was accused of the crime.

Jews were permitted to return to Berlin in 1671, following the expulsion of several rich families from Vienna and given the economic woes of Brandenburg which, in the wake of the detrimental thirty-years war, sought powerful people to help with its rebuilding. Despite suffering personal restrictions and extra taxes, the Jewish population grew, so that by 1700 the city had 117 Jewish families, and in 1712 its **first synagogue** was built near today's Rosenstrasse.

The numbers of Jews in the Spandauer Vorstadt and particularly in the **Scheunenviertel** slum was greatly bolstered by a 1737 order that all Berlin's non-home-owning Jews must move there and that Jews could only enter the city through its northern gates. From that point on, and particularly in the nineteenth century, the area became a refuge for Jews fleeing pogroms in eastern Europe and Russia.

A big part of Berlin's draw was the loosening of Prussia's restrictions and the growing equality of its Jewish population, relative to the rest of Europe. By 1869 German Jews had full rights, and within years Jews rose to prominence in government, one influential group, dubbed the *"Kaiserjuden"*, becoming close advisors to the Kaiser. By the 1920s Jewish department stores, such as **Wertheim**, had become part of the landscape and Jews were also highly active in the cultural scene with musicians such as the **Comedian Harmonists** extremely popular.

By 1933, when the **Nazis** assumed power and state-backed persecution started, there were 160,564 Jews in Berlin: around four percent of the population and one third of those in the German Reich. The process of persecution began with an SA-enforced boycott of Jewish shops, businesses and medical and legal practices on April 1 of that year; many of the wealthiest Jews left the same year, as a series of laws banning them from public office, the civil service, journalism, farming, teaching, broadcasting and acting were introduced. Then in September 1935 the **Nuremberg laws** effectively deprived Jews of their German citizenship, by introducing apartheid-like classifications of "racial purity". There was a brief respite in 1936 when Berlin hosted the Olympic Games and the Nazis, wishing to show an acceptable face to the outside world, eased up on overt anti-Semitism, but by the following year large-scale expropriation of Jewish businesses began. Jews who could see the writing on the wall, and had money, escaped while they could (even though other European countries, the US and Palestine all restricted Jewish immigration), but the majority stayed put, hoping things would improve, or simply because they couldn't afford to emigrate. However, after the violent escalation of Nazi anti-Semitism of **Kristallnacht** – the night of November 9, 1938 – their

president. Kennedy's city parade included a stop at the viewing platform in front of the Brandenburg Gate – draped for the occasion by the Russians in enormous red flags and communist placards – before he retreated to Schöneberg to deliver his impassioned "Berliner" speech (see p.115). The day proved so emotional that at the end of it JFK commented to his aides "we'll never have another day like this one as long as we live".

already beleaguered position became intolerable. "Crystal Night" – named for the shattered glass from the attacks on Jewish shops and institutions – resulted in the deaths of at least 36 Berlin Jews, many beaten on the streets while passers-by looked on; the destruction of 23 of the city's 29 synagogues; and wrecking of hundreds of shops and businesses. Afterwards the Nazi government fined the German-Jewish community one billion marks – ostensibly to pay for the damage – and then forcibly "Aryanized" all remaining Jewish businesses, effectively excluding Jews from economic life. With the outbreak of war in September 1939, Jews were forced to observe a night-time curfew and forbidden to own radios. Forced transportation of Jews to the East (mainly occupied Poland) began in February 1940, and September 1941 saw the introduction of a law requiring Jews to wear the yellow Star of David, heralding the beginning of mass deportations.

In January 1942, the **Wannsee conference**, held in a western suburb of Berlin (see p.257), discussed the *Endlösung* or "Final Solution" to the "Jewish Question", drawing up plans for the removal of all Jews to the East and, implicitly, their extermination. As the Final Solution began to be put into effect, daily life for Berlin's Jews grew ever more unbearable: in April they were banned from public transport, and in September their food rations were reduced. By the beginning of 1943 the only Jews remaining legally in Berlin were highly skilled workers in the city's armaments factories, and in February deportation orders began to be enforced for this group too. Most Berlin Jews were sent to Theresienstadt and Auschwitz concentration camps, and only a handful survived the war. By the end of the war the combined effects of emigration and genocide had reduced Berlin's Jewish population by around 96 percent to about 6500; around 1400 had survived as "U-boats", hidden by gentile families at great personal risk, and the rest had somehow managed to evade the final round-ups in precariously legal conditions, usually by having irreplaceable skills vital to the war effort, or by being married to non-Jews.

Since the war Berlin's Jewish population has doubled to around **twelve thousand** today – largely by émigrés from the former Soviet Union. It's now the world's fastest-growing Jewish community and the largest in Germany, boasting eight synagogues. With the renovation of the **Neue Synagoge** as a cultural centre and the opening of several Jewish cafés, Oranienburger Strasse has regained a little of its pre-Nazi identity, yet some Jews complain that the tourist interest in this area and their community has led to a theme-park-like faux celebration of Jewish life. Jewish insignias have begun to appear where there was never a link, and restaurants and cultural events pop up simply to provide visitors with stereotypes – local toy shops even sell *menorah*, the Jewish candelabra. They also argue that although sympathy and interest in sites associated with Jewish culture and persecution is welcome, if their reason is to understand the Holocaust rather than simply indulge a ghoulish interest, then the focus should be on the perpetrators, not the victims.

Meanwhile, **anti-Semitism** in Berlin, especially towards young Jews, appears to be on the rise, with the number of incidents increasing every year – in one swastikas were scrawled on the walls of a Jewish nursery school before a smoke bomb was thrown in, though thankfully the building was empty. These days it is most often the work of disaffected children of immigrant Muslim families, but all the same, Gideon Joffe, widely regarded as head of the city's Jewish community, invites "Germans who say they want an end to the debate about the Nazi past to wear the…Star of David, so they can experience the anti-Semitism that German Jews confront on a daily basis."

Milk and Honey Tours ☏030 61 62 57 61, ⓦmilkandhoneytours.com. This operator, which specializes in tours of Jewish Europe, offers a variety of first-class guided tours of Jewish Berlin, either on foot and public transport or in a private vehicle. They can also take you to further-flung sites of Jewish interest, including concentration camp memorial sites.

me Collectors Room

Auguststr. 68 • Tues–Sun noon–6pm • €6 • ☏030 86 00 85 10, ⓦme-berlin.com • S-Oranienburger Strasse

The me **Collectors Room** was conceived and built by chemist and endocrinologist Thomas Olbricht to showcase his private art collection – which happens to be among the most comprehensive in Europe, including works by John Currin, Franz Gertsch, Marlene Dumas and Gerhard Richter – via a series of alternating exhibitions. The "me" here is not misplaced egotism but an acronym for "moving energies": the collection spans painting, sculpture, photography, installation and new media works from the early sixteenth century to the present day. The permanent Wunderkammer section rekindles the tradition, popular during the Renaissance period, of bringing together eccentric curiosities and "wonders" from around the world. The spacious **café** serves coffee and snacks (Tues–Sun 11.30am–6.30pm).

KW Institute for Contemporary Art
Auguststr. 69 • Tues–Sun noon–7pm, Thurs noon–9pm • €6 • ☎ 030 243 45 90, ⊛ kw-berlin.de • S-Oranienburger Strasse

The **KW (Kunst Werke) Institute for Contemporary Art** was one of the prime movers in the post-*Wende* transformation of Auguststrasse. Once a nineteenth-century margarine factory, KW was turned into a dedicated art space by Klaus Biesenbach in the early 1990s. The elegant facade leads into a lovely, tree-filled courtyard surrounded by six artist studios, a glass-walled café (designed by American artist Dan Graham) and a series of modern, white spaces that includes an exhibition hall by Berlin architect Hans Düttmann. The institute mainly exhibits cutting-edge international works from both up-and-coming and major names such as Doug Aitken, Dinos and Jake Chapman and Paul Pfeiffer. KW also runs Berlin's immensely popular **Art Biennale** (see p.218).

The theatre district

There's not all that much to see in Berlin's **theatre district**, though you can't fail to notice the giant **Friedrichstadt-Palast** on Friedrichstrasse, a clumsy GDR-era Jugendstil pastiche that rears up just south of U-Bahn Oranienburger Tor. This is the place to come if you're into big, splashy, scantily clad revues.

Most impressive among the more high-brow theatres dotted about is the elegant **Deutsches Theater**, at Schumannstrasse 13, founded in 1883. Max Reinhardt took over as director in 1905, thereafter dominating the theatre scene for nearly three decades. In 1922 a young and unknown Marlene Dietrich made her stage debut here, and a couple of years later Bertolt Brecht arrived from Munich to begin his energetic conquest of Berlin's theatre world.

The district's theatres are reviewed in our section on the Arts (see p.219).

Berliner Ensemble
Bertolt-Brecht-Platz 1 • Box office Mon–Fri 8am–6pm, Sat & Sun 11am–6pm • ☎ 030 28 40 81 55, ⊛ berliner-ensemble.de • U- & S-Friedrichstrasse

The austere exterior of the early 1890s **Berliner Ensemble**, tucked away on Bertolt-Brecht-Platz, hides a rewarding and opulent neo-Baroque interior. This is where, on August 31, 1928, the world premiere of **Bertolt Brecht's** *Dreigroschenoper* ("The Threepenny Opera") was staged, the first of 250 consecutive performances in a ritualistic tribute to one of the few world-famous writers East Germany could later claim as its own. After exile in America during the Nazi era, Brecht returned in 1949 with his wife, Helene Weigel, to take over direction of the theatre, marking his return by painting a still-visible red cross through the coat of arms on the royal box. During box office times you can view the foyer, but the rest of the theatre is only open to the public during shows (see p.219), which still include regular performances of Brecht's works.

Admiralspalast
A walk over the Spree on Weidendammer Brücke towards Bahnhof Friedrichstrasse brings you to the Jugendstil **Admiralspalast**, built as a variety theatre in 1910. Its partly gilded facade, fluted columns and bas-reliefs come as a surprise amid the predominantly concrete architecture of the area. As one of the few buildings in these parts to have survived bombing, it became an important political meeting hall in the

OPPOSITE HACKESCHE HÖFE (P.71) >

immediate postwar years and on April 22 and 23, 1946, it was the venue for the forced union of the social democratic SPD with the prewar Communist party, the KPD. This resulted in the birth of the SED (Sozialistische Einheitspartei Deutschlands), the GDR Communist Party that controlled the country until March 1990. The building houses Die Distel theatre (see p.222), a satirical cabaret whose performances sometimes daringly highlighted the paradoxes and frustrations of the pre-*Wende* GDR.

Bahnhof Friedrichstrasse

Opposite the Admiralspalast lies the grubby edifice of **Bahnhof Friedrichstrasse** with its mediocre shopping arcade and budget restaurants. Before the *Wende,* however, the train station was of real consequence as the main border crossing point for western visitors to East Berlin, and probably the most heavily guarded train station in Europe. There was a regular flow of mainline and S-Bahn traffic between Friedrichstrasse and West Berlin – except during the Berlin Blockade of 1948–49 (see p.124) – but until late 1989 the East German government did all it could to keep its own citizens from joining it. A tangle of checkpoints, guard posts and customs controls and, more discreetly, armed guards separated westbound platforms from the rest of the station.

Tränenpalast

Reichstagufer 17 · Tues–Fri 9am–7pm, Sat & Sun 10am–6pm · Free · ☎ 030 46 77 77 90, ⊛ hdg.de/berlin · S-Oranienburger Strasse

One structure that really stood out in the Friedrichstrasse border complex was its entrance hall, a glass-and-concrete construction between the Bahnhof and the River Spree. Grimly nicknamed the **Tränenpalast** or "Palace of Tears" by Berliners, this was the scene of many a poignant farewell as people took leave of relatives, friends and lovers here. Until 1990 an estimated eight million westbound travellers – visitors and tourists and occasionally East German citizens with exit visas – annually queued inside to get through passport and customs controls before travelling by U- or S-Bahn to West Berlin.

A glut of reminders from the era survive in an engaging **museum**, opened by Chancellor Merkel in 2011, which explores the consequences and daily restrictions of the German division right up to reunification. There are plenty of original artefacts, documents, photographs and old newsreels and many exhibits devoted to personal stories. Taking all this in, it's easy to overlook the loveless character of the building and imagine for a moment the contrastingly deep and varied emotions it's witnessed.

Chausseestrasse

Chausseestrasse was, during the nineteenth century, the location of one of Berlin's densest concentrations of heavy industry. Development began here during the 1820s with the establishment of a steam-engine factory and iron foundry and in 1837 August Borsig built his first factory – by the 1870s his successors were churning out hundreds of steam engines and railway locomotives each year.

Other industrial concerns were also drawn to the area, earning it the nickname *Feuerland* – "Fireland". However, by the end of the century most had outgrown their roots and relocated en masse to the edges of the rapidly expanding city. A reminder of the past, and of Borsig's local influence, is the **Borsighaus** at Chausseestrasse 9. Once the central administration block of the Borsig factories, this sandstone building, its facade richly decorated with bronze figures, looks like a displaced country residence.

Dorotheenstädtische Friedhof

Daily: Jan & Dec 8am–4pm; Feb & Nov 8am–5pm; March & Oct 8am–6pm; April & Sept 8am–7pm; May–Aug 8am–8pm · Free · U-Oranienburger Tor

At the **Dorotheenstädtische Friedhof**, eastern Berlin's VIP cemetery, you'll find the graves of Bertolt Brecht and Helene Weigel; architect Karl Friedrich Schinkel, his last resting place topped by an appropriately florid monument; John Heartfield, Dada luminary and interwar photomontage exponent, under a headstone decorated with a runic H; philosopher Georg Hegel, whose ideas influenced Marx; author Heinrich Mann; former president Johannes Rau; journalist Günter Gaus; and many Berlin worthies. A plan detailing who lies where is located beside the cemetery administration offices (on the right at the end of the entrance alley). The Dorotheenstädtische Friedhof also encloses the **Französischer Friedhof** (entrance on Chausseestrasse and closer to Oranienburger Tor), originally built to serve Berlin's Huguenot community.

Brecht-Weigel-Gedenkstätte

Chausseestr. 125 • **Museum** Tues 10am–3.30pm, Wed & Fri 10–11.30am, Thurs 10–11.30am & 5–6.30pm, Sat 10am–3.30pm, Sun 11am–6pm, guided tours at least every hour • €3 **Archive** Tues, Wed & Fri 9am–5pm, Thurs 9am–7pm • U-Oranienburger Tor

The **Brecht-Weigel-Gedenkstätte** preserves the final home and workplace of the playwright Bertolt Brecht and his wife and collaborator Helene Weigel. Guided tours take in the seven simply furnished rooms – an absolute must for Brecht fans, but not so fascinating if you're only casually acquainted with his works. There is also a Bertolt Brecht **archive** and the basement is home to the *Kellerrestaurant im Brechthaus* (see p.191), which dishes up Viennese specialities, supposedly according to Weigel's recipes.

A little way past the Brecht-Haus stands a brutal pillar commemorating the Spartakusbund, the breakaway anti-war faction of the SPD formed by Karl Liebknecht in 1916, which later evolved into the KPD, Germany's Communist party. The inscription, a quote from Liebknecht, says "Spartakus means the fire and spirit, the heart and soul, the will and deed of the revolution of the proletariat."

4

BERTOLT BRECHT (1898–1956)

Bertolt Brecht is widely regarded as one of the leading German dramatists of the twentieth century. Born in Augsburg, the son of a paper-mill manager, he studied medicine, mainly to avoid full military service in World War I. Working as an army medical orderly in 1918, his experiences helped shape his passionate anti-militarism. Soon he drifted away from medicine onto the fringes of the theatrical world, eventually winding up as a playwright in residence at the Munich Kammerspiele in 1921. It wasn't until the 1928 premiere of the *Dreigroschenoper* ("The Threepenny Opera"), co-written with the composer Kurt Weill, that Brecht's real breakthrough came. This marked the beginning of a new phase in Brecht's work. A couple of years earlier he had embraced Marxism, an ideological step that had a profound effect on his literary output, leading him to espouse a didactic "epic" form of theatre. The aim was to provoke the audience, perhaps even move them to revolutionary activity. To this end he developed the technique of **Verfremdung** ("alienation") to create a sense of distance between spectators and the action unfolding before them. By using effects such as obviously fake scenery, monotone lighting and jarring music to expose the sham sentimentality of love songs, he hoped to constantly remind the audience that what they were doing was watching a play – in order to make them judge, rather than be drawn into the action on stage. The result was a series of works that were pretty heavy-going. In 1933, unsurprisingly, Brecht went into self-imposed exile, eventually ending up in the States. His years away from Germany were among his most productive. The political message was still very much present in his work, but somehow the dynamic and lyrical force of his writing meant that it was often largely lost on his audience. Returning to Europe, he finally settled in East Berlin in 1949, after a brief period in Switzerland. His decision to try his luck in the Soviet-dominated Eastern sector of Germany was influenced by the offer to take over at the Theater am Schiffbauerdamm, where the *Dreigroschenoper* had been premiered more than twenty years earlier. However, before heading east, Brecht first took the precaution of gaining Austrian citizenship and lodging the copyright of his works with a West German publisher. The remainder of Brecht's life was largely devoted to running what is now known as the Berliner Ensemble and facing up to his own tensions with the fledgling GDR.

Museum für Naturkunde

Tues–Fri 9.30am–6pm, Sat & Sun 10am–6pm • €6 • ⓦ naturkundemuseum-berlin.de • U-Naturkundemuseum

Just west of where Chausseestrasse crosses Invalidenstrasse is the **Museum für Naturkunde**, one of the world's largest natural history museums; its origins go back to 1716, though the present building and the nucleus of the collection date from the 1880s.

Here you'll see a skeleton of a brachiosaurus, fossil remains of an archaeopteryx (the oldest known bird), and some entertaining rooms devoted to the evolution of vertebrates and the ape family; there's also an interesting, if slightly ghoulish, section on how the numerous stuffed animals were "prepared for exhibition". Finally, the museum boasts a vast mineralogy collection, including a number of meteorites.

The Berlin Wall Memorial

Bernauer Str. • Tues–Sun: April–Oct 9.30am–7pm; Nov–March 9.30am–6pm • Free • ⓦ berliner-mauer-gedenkstaette.de • S-Nordbahnhof

Opposite S-Bahn Nordbahnhof is the first of two buildings dedicated to the **Berlin Wall Memorial** (Gedenkstätte Berliner Mauer), which contains a bookshop and screens an introductory film. Bernauer Strasse was literally bisected by the Wall; before the Wall was built you could enter or exit the Soviet Zone just by going through the door of one of the buildings, which is why, on August 13, 1961, some citizens, who woke up to

THE BERLIN WALL

After the war, Berlin was split among Britain, France, the US and USSR, as Stalin, Roosevelt and Churchill had agreed at Yalta. Each sector was administered by the relevant country, and was supposed to exist peacefully with its neighbours under a unified city council. But, almost from the outset, antagonism between the Soviet and other sectors was high. Just three years after the war ended, the Soviet forces closed down the land access corridors to the city from the Western zones in what became known as the **Berlin Blockade**: it was successfully overcome by a massive **airlift** of food and supplies that lasted nearly a year (see p.124). This, followed by the 1953 uprising (see p.120), large-scale cross-border emigration (between 1949 and 1961, the year the Wall was built, over three million East Germans – almost a fifth of the population – fled to the Federal Republic) and innumerable "incidents", led to the building of what the GDR called an "an antifascist protection barrier".

The Wall was erected overnight on **August 13, 1961** when, at 2am, forty thousand East German soldiers, policemen and Workers' Militia went into action closing U- and S-Bahn lines and stringing barbed wire across streets leading into West Berlin to cordon off the Soviet sector. The Wall followed its boundaries implacably, cutting through houses, across squares and rivers with its own cool illogicality. Many Berliners were evicted from their homes, while others had their doors and windows blocked by bales of barbed wire. Suddenly the British, American and French sectors of the city were corralled some 200km inside the GDR, yet though they reinforced patrols, the Allies did nothing to prevent the sealing of the Wall.

Despite earlier rumours, most people in West and East Berlin were taken by surprise. Those who lived far from the border area only learned of its closure when they found all routes to West Berlin blocked. Crowds gathered and extra border guards sent to prevent trouble. There was little most people could do other than accept this latest development, though some – including a few border guards – managed to find loopholes in the new barrier and flee west. But within a few days, building workers were reinforcing the barbed wire and makeshift barricades with bricks and mortar. As an additional measure, West Berliners were no longer allowed to cross the border into East Berlin. From 1961 onwards the GDR strengthened the Wall making it an almost impenetrable barrier – in effect two walls separated by a *Sperrgebiet* (forbidden zone), dotted with watchtowers and patrolled by soldiers and dogs. It was also known as the *Todesstreifen* (**death strip**) as border troops, known as Grepos, were under instructions to shoot anyone attempting to scale the Wall, and to shoot accurately: any guard suspected of deliberately missing was court-martialled, and his family could expect severe harassment from the authorities. Over the years, over two hundred people were **killed** endeavouring to cross the Wall.

find themselves on the wrong side of the newly established "national border", leapt out of windows to get to the West. Over the years, the facades of these buildings were cemented up and incorporated into the partition itself, until they were knocked down and replaced by the Wall proper in 1979. A short section of Wall as it once was – both walls and a death-strip between – remain preserved at the corner of Bernauer Strasse and Ackerstrasse.

Down the road at Bernauer Strasse 111, the **Wall Documentation Centre** keeps the story of the Wall alive using photos, sound recordings and information terminals and has a useful viewing tower that you can climb to contemplate the barrier and the way in which it once divided the city.

The Gesundbrunnen bunkers

Gesundbrunnen U-Bahn • Tours, which start within easy walking distance of the office, are run by Berliner Unterwelten; tickets available from the office from 10am on the day • ☎ 030 49 91 05 17, ⓦ berlinerunterwelten.de • U- & S-Gesundbrunnen

Immediately north of the Spandauer Vorstadt – and two stops north on the S-Bahn from the Nordbahnhof – lies U- and S-Bahn **Gesundbrunnen**, around which several underground passages and **bunkers** are open for fascinating and unusual tours. These are organized by the non-profit **Berliner Unterwelten**; their ticket office is in the southern entrance hall of the Gesundbrunnen U-Bahn station. The company offers

Initial escape attempts were straightforward, and often successful – hollowing out furniture, ramming checkpoint barriers and simple disguise brought many people over. However, the authorities quickly rose to the challenge, and would-be escapees were forced to become more resourceful, digging tunnels and constructing gliders, one-man submarines and hot-air balloons. By the time the Wall came down, every escape method conceivable seemed to have been used – even down to passing through Checkpoint Charlie in the stomach of a pantomime cow – and those desperate to get out of the GDR preferred the long wait and complications of applying to leave officially to the risk of being gunned down by a border guard.

An oddity of the Wall was that it was built a few metres inside GDR territory; the West Berlin authorities therefore had little control over the **graffiti** that covered it. The Wall was an ever-changing mixture of colours and slogans, with occasional bursts of bitterness: "My friends are dying behind you"; humour: "Why not jump over and join the Party?"; and stupidity: "We shoulda nuked 'em in 45".

Late in 1989 the East German government, spurred by Gorbachev's *glasnost* and confronted by a tense domestic climate, realized it could keep the impossible stable no longer. To an initially disbelieving and then jubilant Europe, travel restrictions for GDR citizens were lifted on **November 9, 1989** – effectively, the Wall had ceased to matter, and pictures of Berliners, East and West, hacking away at the detested symbol filled newspapers and TV bulletins around the world. Within days, enterprising characters were renting out hammers and chisels so that souvenir hunters could take home their own chip of the Wall.

Today, especially in the city centre, it's barely possible to tell exactly where the Wall ran: odd juxtapositions of dereliction against modernity, and the occasional unexpected swathe of the erstwhile "death strip", are in most cases all that's left of one of the most hated borders the world has ever known. The simple row of **cobbles** that has been placed along much of the former course of the Wall acts as a necessary reminder. Few significant stretches remain; the sections devoted to the East Side Gallery (see p.130) and the Berlin Wall Memorial (see above) are the most notable exceptions.

One sad postscript to the story of the Wall hit the headlines in spring 1992. Two former **border guards** were tried for the murder of Chris Gueffroy, shot dead while illegally trying to cross the border at Neukölln in February 1989. Under the GDR government the guards had been treated to a meal by their superiors and given extra holiday for their patriotic actions; under the new regime, they received sentences for murder – while those ultimately responsible, the former leaders of the GDR, largely avoided punishment.

nine tours at different locations around Berlin, but their core tours, as listed below, are in the vicinity of the Gesundbrunnen. Those covered here are in **English**; tours in German, Spanish, French, Italian, Dutch and Danish are listed on the website.

Tour 1: Dark Worlds
Mon 11am & 1pm, Thurs–Sun 11am (March–Nov also Wed 11am); 90min • €10

The tour of the main Gesundbrunnen bunker, **Tour 1: Dark Worlds**, explores a large, well-preserved World War II bunker, one of hundreds of public bunkers that were used towards the end of the war by Berliners waiting out the Allied bombing raids. It was here also where many women committed suicide rather than be raped by advancing Russians. As a valuable part of the U-Bahn network the Gesundbrunnen bunker was one of the few spared from destruction during Germany's demilitarization, and today its rooms and passages contain countless artefacts from the time. Among them are various items cleverly crafted from military waste immediately after the war: helmets became pots, gas masks became oil lamps and tyres were used to sole shoes. Equally interesting are the finds from the Nazi bunker beneath the Reichskanzlei (see p.40), including paintings by SS artists and an Enigma machine. Other remnants unearthed from around town and displayed here come from the Battle of Berlin and include the contents of the pockets of two Volksturm recruits – a fifteen-year-old and a 69-year-old – killed in the fray. These items all come from modern-day excavations of Berlin, and weapons and bombs are still regularly found by building crews, sometimes with deadly consequences – as one display shows.

Tour 2: From the Flak Towers to Mountains of Debris
April–Oct Thurs–Sun 3pm; 90min • €10

Tour 2: From the Flak Towers to Mountains of Debris goes into the park opposite the Gesundbrunnen station to explore two of the seven levels of the **Humboldthain** anti-aircraft gun tower that proved too beefy for the Soviets to destroy. It is cold down there, even in summer, and you won't be welcome in flip-flops or sandals for safety reasons.

Tour 3: Subways, Bunkers & Cold War
March–Nov Tues 11am & 1pm, Wed 1pm, Thurs–Sun 1pm; Dec–Feb Thurs–Sun 1pm; 90min • €10

Tour 3: Subways, Bunkers & Cold War investigates another World War II bunker, but also goes into Cold War-era tunnels and bunkers, including refuges that were equipped for West Berliners in case of a nuclear strike, and underground labyrinths that were blocked to prevent East Germans escaping to the West.

Tour M – Breaching the Berlin Wall
April–Oct Mon–Wed 3pm • 2hr • €13

Tour M – Breaching the Berlin Wall explores tunnels dug under the Berlin Wall by would-be escapees and relates stories of success – three hundred people managed to escape the GDR in this way – and failures.

Mitte: Tiergarten

A huge swathe of peaceful green parkland, smack in the middle of Berlin, the Tiergarten stretches west from the Brandenburg Gate and Reichstag, its beautifully landscaped meadows, gardens and woodlands a great antidote to the bustle of the city. The park and its immediate surroundings form a sub-district of the city's central Mitte district, whose eastern edge, long occupied by the Berlin Wall, has flourished since the *Wende*. Huge building projects have mushroomed here, some the result of the Federal government's move to Berlin, but most simply reclaiming death-strip lands in prime locations at the centre of a unified city. The result is a formidable showcase of modern architecture around the fringes of the Tiergarten, arguably at its most breathtaking when illuminated at night. Also here is the Kulturforum, Berlin's second great collection of museums and cultural institutions.

TIERGARTEN

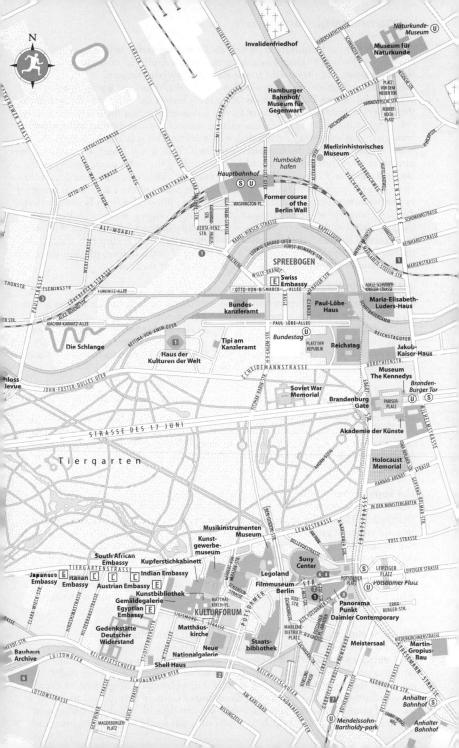

N

Naturkunde-Museum U

Invalidenfriedhof

Museum für
Naturkunde

Hamburger
Bahnhof/
Museum für
Gegenwart

Medizinhistorisches
Museum

Humboldt-
hafen

Hauptbahnhof S U

Former course
of the Berlin Wall

SPREEBOGEN

Swiss
Embassy E

Bundes-
kanzleramt

Paul-Löbe-
Haus

Maria-Elisabeth-
Lüders-Haus

Die Schlange

Tipi am
Kanzleramt

Haus der
Kulturen der Welt

Bundestag U

Platz der
Republik

Reichstag

Jakob-
Kaiser-Haus

Schloss
Bellevue

Soviet War
Memorial

Museum
The Kennedys

Branden-
Burger Tor

Brandenburg
Gate

Akademie der Künste

STRASSE DES 17 JUNI

Tiergarten

Holocaust
Memorial

Musikinstrumenten
Museum

Kunst-
gewerbe-
museum

Sony
Center

Legoland

Leipziger Strasse

South African
Embassy

Kupferstichkabinett

Indian Embassy E

Filmmuseum
Berlin

Potsdamer
Platz S

Potsdamer Platz U

Japanese
Embassy E

Italian
Embassy E

TIERGARTENSTRASSE

Austrian Embassy E

Kunstbibliothek

Egyptian
Embassy E

Gemäldegalerie

KULTURFORUM

Panorama
Punkt

Daimler Contemporary

Meistersaal

Martin-
Gropius-
Bau

Gedenkstätte
Deutscher
Widerstand

Matthäus-
kirche

Neue
Nationalgalerie

Staats-
bibliothek

Bauhaus
Archive

Shell Haus

Anhalter
Bahnhof S

Mendelssohn-
Bartholdy-park U

Anhalter
Bahnhof

Highlights of the Kulturforum include the **Gemäldegalerie**, with its internationally renowned collection of European art; the twentieth-century art of the **Neue Nationalgalerie**; and the applied arts of the **Kunstgewerbemuseum**.

Adjacent to the Kulturforum is a **diplomatic district**, where the **Bendlerblock**, site of several July Bomb Plot executions (see p.100), houses the interesting **Gedenkstätte Deutscher Widerstand**, a museum of German resistance against the Nazis. Further west, one architecturally impressive embassy flanks another as far as the **Bauhaus Archive**, a homage to that influential art and design movement. This is as good a place as any to begin an exploration of the **Tiergarten** park itself. Walk or cycle west to a couple of beer gardens or take a bus a couple of quick stops north to the park's proud centrepiece: the **Siegessäule**, a huge column that celebrates Prussian military victories and delivers fine views over the park and the city. The northeastern corner of the Tiergarten is occupied by the **Reichstag** (see p.37) and a host of other institutions that form Berlin's modern-day Regierungsviertel, or government quarter, where various cutting-edge buildings cling to a bend in the River Spree known as the **Spreebogen**. Surveying all this is the monumental glass-and-steel **Hauptbahnhof Lehrter Bahnhof**, Berlin's new main train station. It occupies a rather desolate, underdeveloped patch of town, though it's near the **Hamburger Bahnhof**, a top-notch contemporary art museum.

GETTING AROUND

By train The Hauptbahnhof and Potsdamer Platz, with its U- and S-Bahn station, are the main transport hubs for the Tiergarten district.

By bus The extremely frequent #100 and #200 buses between Bahnhof Zoo and Alexanderplatz are the best options for getting around the area. The #200 stops at the Kulturforum, while #100 stops at all the major points in the Tiergarten.

By bike The most flexible way to explore the Tiergarten, particularly the park itself, is by bike (see p.24), with CallBikes (see p.24) in invariably good supply at Potsdamer Platz.

Potsdamer Platz

Pulverized during the war, then forced into hibernation by the Berlin Wall, it is only thanks to two decades of frantic building that the busy junction of **Potsdamer Platz** has re-emerged as a temple of commercialism. The platz is worth visiting for its **modern architecture** alone, and for the excellent **Filmmuseum**, which will appeal to anyone with even a passing interest in German cinema.

The Sony Center

Potsdamer Platz · ⓦ sonycenter.de

Designed by Helmut Jahn, the **Sony Center** occupies several glass-sheathed buildings grouped around a capacious, circular courtyard. Its rotunda, topped by a conical glass roof, is easily the most impressive showpiece in the area, open to the elements but at the same time providing a remove from the surrounding urban racket. Berliners have adopted the courtyard as a place to congregate for major sporting events – particularly football matches – when big screens are rolled out and the atmosphere rivals that of many stadiums. If you want to join them, arrive early for a seat at one of the many cafés, bars and restaurants.

Deutsche Kinemathek – Museum für Film und Fernsehen

Potsdamer Str. 2 · Tues, Wed & Fri–Sun 10am–6pm, Thurs 10am–8pm · €7 · ⓦ filmmuseum-berlin.de · U- & S-Potsdamer Platz

The **Deutsche Kinemathek – Museum für Film und Fernsehen** provides an excellent introduction to the history of German cinema and television, with a free audio guide that is especially useful to those with limited German. Using a bevy of clips, reconstructions and artefacts, it plots the course of German cinema via various technical innovations, stars and major releases, starting with clips from Berlin's first public screening in 1895 (see p.275) – the first in the world – and highlighting early

5

POTSDAMER PLATZ REGENERATED

Said to have been the busiest square in prewar Europe, **Potsdamer Platz** was once a vibrant area, surrounded by stores, bars and clubs. The war left it severely battered, though it regained some of its vitality in the chaotic years immediately following as a black-market centre at the junction of the Soviet, American and British sectors. Later, West Berliners watched from their side of the dividing line as the Soviets put down the East Berlin uprising of 1953.

The Cold War was then played out here in words, with the Western authorities relaying their version of the news to East Berliners by means of an electronic newsboard – countered by an Eastern billboard exhorting West Berliners to shop in cheap East Berlin stores. This ended with the coming of the Wall, which finally put a physical seal on the ideological division of Potsdamer Platz. On the Eastern side all the buildings (which were mostly war-vintage wrecks) were razed to give the GDR's border guards a clear field of fire, while in the West only a couple of battered survivors, including the hulk of the fine old *Hotel Esplanade*, were left as a reminder of the way things used to be.

The dismantling of the Wall produced one of Europe's most valuable lots, a huge empty site in the middle of the city. It was no surprise, therefore, that – despite earlier plans for a more flexible use – in the end huge multinational corporations won out, purchasing the land and creating equally huge sprawling **commercial complexes**. Building this mini-city from scratch represented a feat of engineering. An entire power, water and sewage infrastructure was created; subway tunnels drilled and new S- and U-Bahn stations built; the surviving Weinhaus Huth, a landmark building, was picked up and trundled to another spot; and the remaining interior portions of the *Hotel Esplanade* were incorporated into a new restaurant.

Now, after years of construction work, almost everything around Potsdamer Platz is complete. Dominated by the offices and apartments of the rich, it's the most muscular display of multinational power in the city – and so not to everyone's taste – but probably exactly what Berlin needed to compete as a global metropolis.

---

pioneers and film stars. Among the latter was Henny Porten, a sturdy blond often portrayed in 1920s Germany as an ideal German woman, but who fell from grace under the Nazis when she refused to leave her Jewish husband.

The turmoil of the **Weimar years** produced some of the highpoints of German cinema, including *The Cabinet of Dr Caligari* (1920), Fritz Lang's *Metropolis* (1927) and *The Blue Angel* (1930), which launched **Marlene Dietrich** internationally. The museum is particularly strong on Dietrich, since it inherited much of her estate on her death in 1992 – and quite a haul it was too: over 3000 documents, 15,000 photos and some 3000 clothes stuffed into sixty valises. The museum's treatment of the **Nazi era** is both clever and circumspect. There's slender detail on the most famous filmmaker of the time **Leni Riefenstahl**, known for her magnificent portrayal of the 1936 Olympics in *Olympia*, but infamous for her willingness to glorify the Nazis in **propaganda** films like *Triumph des Willens*. The museum plays this and other propaganda films, including the deplorable *Jud Süss*, a tale of a dishonest Jew, on TV sets in unmarked drawers that line the walls of the room; you'll probably need to try a few drawers to find them. Propaganda was obviously a part of the Nazi era, but far more popular, particularly during the war, were **escapist** films – Hitler himself was a big fan of Mickey Mouse.

Postwar cinema receives less attention, but **television** fans will enjoy the video retrospective in which thousands of images from German television are simultaneously shown on a big screen. There's also a formidable back catalogue of TV programmes accessible in viewing booths.

Legoland Discovery Centre

Potsdamer Str. 4 • Mon–Sat 10am–7pm • €16, online discounts • ⓦ legolanddiscoverycentre.de • U- & S-Potsdamer Platz

The **Legoland Discovery Centre** obviously exists largely to promote a product, but few kids leave disappointed. It's aimed largely at 3–10 year-olds and there's a cinema, castle, dragon rides and a workshop in which to go brick-crazy – the few small freebies go

5

down very well too. A couple of things will entertain adults too – particularly a plastic mini-brick reproduction of Berlin's main landmark buildings. Earmark at least a couple of hours.

The DaimlerChrysler quarter

In the 1990s, **DaimlerChrysler** hired, among others, Renzo Piano and Richard Rogers to create an ensemble of mostly red-brick but otherwise disparate buildings that house several restaurants, a theatre, a multiplex, a 3D big-screen cinema and the obligatory shopping mall. The use of a variety of forms and facades is successful, but not that stimulating at street level.

Panorama Punkt

Potsdamer Platz • Tues–Sun 11am–8pm • €5.50 • Ⓦ panoramapunkt.de • U- & S-Potsdamer Platz

Soar above Potsdamer Platz in Europe's fastest, stomach-churning elevator to arrive at **Panorama Punkt**, the top floor of the complex's largest skyscraper. The views are among the city's best – which you'd expect given the immense height and ideal central location – and the exposed outdoor viewing deck provides an immediacy that you won't find at the Fernsehturm, the other main contender.

Daimler Contemporary

Alte Potsdamer Str. 5 • Daily 11am–6pm • Free • ☎ 030 25 94 14 20, Ⓦ collection.daimler.com • U- & S-Potsdamer Platz

The **Daimler Contemporary** art collection was set up in 1977 as a space for twentieth-century art, initially mainly focused on German artists. The museum expanded in the 1990s with the inclusion of works by other European and American artists, including Andy Warhol and Jeff Koons, and today the impressive collection includes approximately 1800 international works, showcased in rotating exhibitions across a large, attractive space. Much of the collection and most of the frequent temporary exhibitions are challenging and abstract. Ask for a leaflet or check out the website under "Sculptures" for information and a map of the sizeable works dotted around the neighbourhood.

Meistersaal

Köthener Str. 38 • Occasional tours organized by Fritz Music Tours ☎ 030 30 87 56 33, Ⓦ musictours-berlin.com • Ⓦ meistersaal-berlin.de • U- & S-Potsdamer Platz

A five-minute walk south of Potsdamer Platz is the **Meistersaal**, a former theatre that became a West Berlin recording studio for record label Hansa. For many years an almost neighbourless building set among overgrown fields, rubble and skeletal ruins – and of course with a grand view of the Berlin Wall – it became known as "Hansa by the Wall". Its cheap prices – around a twelfth of London's Abbey Road in the 1980s – and top-notch acoustics inspired scores of musicians – most famously David Bowie, U2, Iggy Pop, Nick Cave and Depeche Mode.

Leipziger Platz

Created by Berlin's expansion in the early 1700s, the civilized and beautiful **Leipziger Platz** was once almost as busy as Potsdamer Platz, thanks to the presence of shops including Alfred Messel's **Wertheim** department store. What little of the platz that hadn't been destroyed by the war was levelled in 1961 for the death-strip of the Berlin Wall, leaving behind just an octagonal footprint as a reminder. The square's new series of dreary seven-floor office blocks in monotonous light colours look like a missed opportunity to create something interesting.

Kulturforum

The **Kulturforum** offers a mixture of museums and cultural spaces that could easily fill a day of exploring. Many of the buildings were designed in the 1960s – most by Hans

Scharoun, with the exception of Mies van der Rohe's impressive Neue Nationalgalerie – but mostly the area lay dormant on the fringe of West Berlin until after the *Wende*, when building work was completed.

KULTURFORUM TICKETS

Bereichskarte A Bereichskarte (€12), available at any of the museums in the Kulturforum – the Gemäldegalerie, Kunstbibliothek, Kunstgewerbemuseum, Kupferstich-kabinett, Neue Nationalgalerie and Musikinstrumenten museum – will give you same-day entry to all of them, and includes their excellent audio tours. You will be automatically sold this ticket at all museums except the Musikinstrumenten museum. You might also consider the good-value three-day ticket that includes all Berlin's municipal museums (see p.23).

Staatsbibliothek

Mon–Fri 9am–9pm, Sat 9am–7pm • Free • ⓦ staatsbibliothek-berlin.de • U- & S-Potsdamer Platz

As you walk west from Potsdamer Platz, the first building on your left is the **Staatsbibliothek**, which has more than three and a half million books, occasional exhibitions, a small concert hall, a reasonable café and a wide selection of British newspapers. The final building to be designed by Hans Scharoun, the *Staabi* is the most popular of his works among his fans; it was used as an important backdrop in Wim Wenders' poetic film elegy to the city, *Wings of Desire*.

Berliner Philharmonie

Tours (in German and English) daily 1.30pm • €5 • ⓦ berliner-philharmoniker.de • U- & S-Potsdamer Platz

At the northeast corner of the Kulturforum, the honey-coloured **Berliner Philharmonie** is home to the Berlin Philharmonic orchestra, frequently considered to be the world's best. Conducting here is a huge privilege, and to be the resident conductor – as supremo Austrian conductor **Herbert von Karajan** (1908–89) was between 1955 and his death in 1989 – the ultimate accolade, since it's the members of the orchestra themselves that vote for this. Looking at the gaudy gold-clad building, designed in the 1960s by Hans Scharoun, and bearing in mind von Karajan's famously short temper with artists and rigid discipline that alienated many who worked under him – yet proved fabulously successful in the field of popularizing classical music – it's easy to see why Berliners nicknamed it "Karajan's circus". However, Scharoun's complicated floor plan around the orchestra offers top-notch acoustics and views, regardless of your seat. Other than on tours, you could attend a **performance** (see p.219). Free classical concerts are held most Tuesdays at 1pm in the foyer – food is available then, but there's no seating.

Musikinstrumenten museum

Tues, Wed & Fri 9am–5pm, Thurs 9am–8pm, Sat & Sun 10am–5pm • €4 or €12 with Bereichskarte (see p.23) • ⓦ sim.spk-berlin.de • U- & S-Potsdamer Platz

Overall the **Musikinstrumenten museum**, in the same building as the Philharmonie, comes as something of a disappointment, but there are a few high points in the collection of (mostly European) keyboards, wind and string instruments from the fifteenth century to the present day, including the flute Frederick the Great played to entertain his guests. Recordings give a taste of the weird and wonderful sounds of the instruments, the most memorable of which are the seventeenth-century cembalo, a nineteenth-century glass harmonica, consisting of liquid-filled glasses, and a three-storey-high 1929 Wurlitzer organ.

Kunstgewerbemuseum

Tues–Fri 10am–6pm, Sat & Sun 11am–6pm • €10 or €12 with Bereichskarte (see p.23) • ⓦ smb.museum • U- & S-Potsdamer Platz

Across the road from the Philharmonie is the **Kunstgewerbemuseum** (Museum of Applied Arts) with its encyclopedic, but seldom dull, collection of European arts and crafts. It closed in 2012 for refurbishment and is due to open in the spring of 2014, though until then some key treasures are viewable at the Bodemuseum (see p.58).

5

Normally though, the highlights include Renaissance, Baroque and Rococo pieces (wonderful silver and ceramics), along with Jugendstil and Art Deco objects, particularly furniture. Strong too are collections from the Middle Ages to Early Renaissance, including some sumptuous gold pieces. Look out for Lüneburg's municipal silver and the treasures from the Stiftskirche in Westphalian town Enger, which include an eighth-century purse-shaped **reliquary** that belonged to Duke Widikund, leader of the Saxon resistance to Charlemagne. More modern pieces include a small but great assembly of Bauhaus furniture, glittering contemporary jewellery and a display on the evolution of product design.

Gemäldegalerie

Tues, Wed & Fri–Sun 10am–6pm, Thurs 10am–8pm • €10 or €12 with Bereichskarte (see p.96) • Ⓦ www.smb.museum • U- & S-Potsdamer Platz

The jewel of the Kulturforum, the **Gemäldegalerie** (Picture Gallery) holds a stupendous collection of early European paintings. Almost nine hundred are on display, arranged in chronological order, and subdivided by region.

German work from the Middle Ages and Renaissance includes the large *Wurzach Altar* of 1437, made in the workshop of the great Ulm sculptor Hans Multscher; its figures' exaggerated gestures and facial distortions make it an ancient precursor of Expressionism. Otherwise some of the best works here are by Albrecht Altdorfer, one of the first fully realized German landscape painters, and Holbein the Younger, represented by several superbly observed portraits. Notable among the many examples of Cranach are his tongue-in-cheek *The Fountain of Youth*, and his free reinterpretation of Bosch's famous triptych *The Garden of Earthly Delights*.

Religious subjects receive a lighter treatment in the **Netherlandish section**, featuring fifteenth- and sixteenth-century work. Jan van Eyck's beautifully lit *Madonna in the Church* is crammed with architectural detail and has the Virgin lifted in the perspective for gentle emphasis. Petrus Christus is thought to have been his pupil, and certainly knew his work, as *The Virgin and Child with St Barbara and a Carthusian Monk* reveals; in the background tiny Flemish houses and street scenes carefully locate the event in Bruges. The parts of the collection from the sixteenth century include the works of Bruegel the Elder, whose *Netherlandish Proverbs* is an amusing, if hard-to-grasp, illustration of more than a hundred sixteenth-century proverbs including "armed to the teeth", "banging a head against a brick wall" and "casting pearls before swine".

The later **Dutch and Flemish collections**, with their large Van Dyck portraits, light-bathed Vermeer paintings and fleshy Rubens canvases, are another high point. The highlights are several paintings by **Rembrandt**: though *The Man in the Golden Helmet* has been proved to be the work of his studio rather than the artist himself, this does little to detract from the portrait's elegance and power.

Finally, the **Italian section**, spanning the years from the Renaissance to the eighteenth century, is particularly strong on works from the Florentine Renaissance, including, most importantly, two paintings by Botticelli: *Madonna with Saints* and *Mary with the Child and Singing Angels*. Other noteworthy painters here include Caravaggio (*Cupid Victorious*, heavy with symbolism and homoeroticism), Poussin (the important *Self-Portrait*), Claude and Canaletto.

Kupferstichkabinett

Tues–Fri 10am–6pm, Sat & Sun 11am–6pm • €6 or €12 with Bereichskarte (see p.96) • Ⓦ smb.museum • U- & S-Potsdamer Platz

Sharing its main entrance with the Gemäldegalerie, the **Kupferstichkabinett** (Engraving Cabinet) holds an extensive collection of European medieval and Renaissance prints, drawings and engravings. Founded by William Humboldt in 1831, the collection includes Botticelli's exquisite drawings for Dante's *Divine Comedy*. The museum hosts temporary exhibitions on all aspects of print-making, drawing and related design.

FROM TOP KULTURFORUM (P.94); TIERGARTEN (P.101); BAUHAUS ARCHIVE (P.100) >

5

Kunstbibliothek

Mon–Fri 10am–6pm, Sat & Sun 11am–6pm • €6, €12 with Bereichskarte (see p.98) • ⓦ smb.museum • U- & S-Potsdamer Platz

With 350,000 volumes and more than 1300 international periodicals, the **Kunstbibliothek** (Art Library), next to the Gemäldegalerie, is a gigantic resource for those with an interest in art, photography and graphic design. The library also has its own galleries for temporary exhibitions, which are almost always worth at least a quick look.

Matthäuskirche

Tues–Sun noon–6pm • Free • U- & S-Potsdamer Platz

The clear odd man out in the Kulturforum is the brick neo-Romanesque **Matthäuskirche** (Matthias Church), built between 1844 and 1846 and the only survivor of the war in the area. It now houses temporary exhibitions and you can climb the tower for aerial views of the other, far more modern and angular, Kulturforum buildings.

Neue Nationalgalerie

Tues, Wed & Fri 10am–6pm, Thurs 10am–8pm, Sat & Sun 11am–6pm • €10, €12 with Bereichskarte (see p.98) • ⓦ smb.museum • U- & S-Potsdamer Platz

By far the Kulturforum's finest building – architecturally speaking – is the **Neue Nationalgalerie**, behind the Matthäuskirche. A black-rimmed glass box, with a ceiling that seems almost suspended above the ground, it was designed by Mies van der Rohe in 1965, and has a clarity of line and detail with all the intelligent simplicity of the Parthenon. The upper section is used for temporary exhibits, often of contemporary art, while the underground galleries contain paintings from the beginning of the twentieth century onwards. Included among the permanent collection are the paintings of the "Brücke" group, such as Ernst Kirchner and Karl Schmidt-Rottluff. **Kirchner** spent time in Berlin before World War I, and his *Potsdamer Platz* dates from 1914, though given the drastic changes to it since then it might as well be in another country instead of just down the road. The galleries move on to the portraits and Berlin cityscapes of **Grosz** and **Dix**, notably Grosz's *Gray Day* and Dix's *Maler Family*. Cubism is represented by work from **Braque**, **Gris** and **Picasso**, though the latter is seen in greater number and to better effect in the Berggruen Collection in Charlottenburg (see p.156). There are also pieces by Klee, Max Beckmann and Lyonel Feininger, among others.

The diplomatic district

Immediately west of the Kulturforum is an area once filled by ostentatious residences: fine villas with long, narrow gardens overlooking the Tiergarten, before the Nazis forcibly acquired them to generate a **diplomatic district**, with many of the best plots going to close allies like Japan, Italy and Spain. The war saw most of the district destroyed, and while the West German government was in Bonn, few countries made much of their plots. But with the government back in Berlin many re-established their presence here, in preference to their East Berlin embassies, producing another of Berlin's stimulating showcases of modern architecture. It's best admired by walking along Tiergartenstrasse – which conveniently lines the way to the **Bauhaus Archive**.

Gedenkstätte Deutscher Widerstand

Stauffenbergstr. 13–14 • Mon–Wed & Fri 9am–6pm, Thurs 9am–8pm, Sat & Sun 10am–6pm • Free • ⓦ gdw-berlin.de • U-Mendelssohn-Bartholdy-Park

Along the eastern edge of the diplomatic district is Stauffenbergstrasse, which takes its name from Count Claus Schenk von Stauffenberg, one of the instigators of the July Bomb Plot (see box, p.100). Here stands the **Bendlerblock**, once the home to the Wehrmacht headquarters – where Stauffenberg was chief of staff – and now the German Defence Ministry.

5

The floors where Stauffenberg worked are occupied by the absorbing exhibition **Gedenkstätte Deutscher Widerstand** (Memorial to German Resistance), a huge collection of photos and documents covering the many and wide-ranging groups who actively opposed the Third Reich – an eclectic mix that included communists, Jews, Quakers and aristocrats. Much of the exhibition is in German, though the free English audio tour (ID required as deposit) gives a good taste by covering the highlights in around forty minutes.

Shell-Haus

At the southern end of Stauffenbergstrasse, beside the Landwehrkanal, the **Shell-Haus** – also called the BEWAG (Berlin Electric Company) building – is one of Berlin's few great modernist buildings to largely survive World War II intact. Designed by Emil Fahrenkamp in 1931, the office building's tiered levels and undulating facade were an attempt to reproduce elements of the adjacent canal and became a leading piece of modernist architecture.

The embassies

The **diplomatic district** kicks off at the northern end of Stauffenbergstrasse, site of the dignified **Egyptian Embassy**, with its polished stonework and detailed engravings, and the flamboyant **Austrian Embassy**, the work of Viennese architect Hans Hollein. West along Tiergartenstrasse, the bulky building hewn from rough-cut red sandstone is the **Indian Embassy**, a clever design that attempts to symbolize India's complexities in architectural terms. The entrance is through a gap in a cylinder that starts a contrast of void and solid that continues throughout the building, though the public can only get a closer look during rare exhibitions (check ⊕indianembassy.de for details).

Further west down Tiergartenstrasse are the two unmistakable Nazi-era edifices of Germany's closest prewar allies. The **Japanese** completed their embassy in 1942 as many other buildings in Berlin started to collapse in bombing raids. Though it has been restored and remodelled since reunification, the architects carefully respected the original design, preserving stone cladding and only removing some ornamentation – replacing it with sleek lines that tend to add to the monumentalism. The **Italian Embassy** has a similar look, as does the beautifully restored **Spanish Embassy**, though that's a little out of the way – a five-minute walk west to the corner of Lichtensteinallee and Thomas-Dehler-Strasse. Providing a sharp contrast are the bold bright lines of the area's most exciting modernist buildings around the corner on Klingelhöferstrasse.

Nordic Embassy

Rauchstr. 1 • **Exhibition hall** Mon–Fri 10am–7pm, Sat & Sun 11am–4pm **Canteen** Mon–Fri 10–11.30am & 1–4pm • U-Wittenbergplatz or bus #100

On Klingelhöferstrasse, in the stunning **Nordic Embassy**, offices for Denmark, Sweden, Finland, Iceland and Norway each occupy a separate building but share an outer skin of pre-oxidized copper panels that playfully reflect changes in light or weather – it looks particularly stunning when floodlit at night. Though each country employed different architects, all feature stone and timber designs with a light, simple elegance. The compound includes an **exhibition hall** and a **canteen** where visitors can enjoy herring, meatballs and other Nordic specialities.

Mexican Embassy

Klingelhöferstr. 3 • **Exhibitions** Mon–Fri 9am–1pm • U-Wittenbergplatz or bus #100

The avant-garde **Mexican Embassy**, next door to the Nordic Embassy, is another tribute to the simplicity and beauty of modernism, and like its neighbour is floodlit after dark to tremendous effect. Its main features are slanting supports that create a vertical blind effect and a massive concrete-and-marble entranceway. The public exhibition area in the atrium is a homage to a Maya observatory, the first cylindrical construction in the Americas.

5

ANTI-NAZI RESISTANCE AND THE JULY BOMB PLOT

Anti-Nazi resistance in Germany was less overt than in occupied Europe, but existed throughout the war, particularly in Berlin, where a group of **KPD-run communist cells** operated a clandestine information network and organized acts of resistance and sabotage. But the odds against them were overwhelming, and most groups perished. More successful for a while was the **Rote Kapelle** (Red Orchestra), headed by Harold Schulze-Boysen, an aristocrat who worked in the Air Ministry, with agents in most of the military offices, who supplied information to the Soviet Union. The **Kreisau Circle**, a resistance group led by Count Helmut von Moltke, and the groups around Carl Goerdeler (former mayor of Leipzig) and General Beck (ex-chief of staff) talked about overthrowing the Nazis and opening negotiations with the western Allies. However, the most effective resistance came from within the military. There had been attempts on Hitler's life since 1942, but it wasn't until late 1943 and early 1944 that enough high-ranking officers had become convinced defeat was inevitable, and a wide network of conspirators established.

The **July Bomb Plot** that took place in the summer of 1944 at Hitler's Polish HQ, the "Wolf's Lair" in Rastenburg, was the assassination attempt that came closest to success. The plot was led by the one-armed **Count Claus Schenk von Stauffenberg**, an aristocratic officer and member of the General Staff, with the support of several high-ranking members of the German army. Sickened by atrocities on the eastern front, and rapidly realizing that the Wehrmacht was fighting a war that could not be won, Stauffenberg and his fellow conspirators decided to kill the Führer, seize control of army headquarters on Bendlerstrasse and sue for peace with the Allies. Germany was on the precipice of total destruction; only such a desperate act, reasoned the plotters, could save the Fatherland.

On July 20, Stauffenberg was summoned to the Wolf's Lair to brief Hitler on troop movements on the eastern front. In his briefcase was a small bomb, packed with high explosive: once triggered, it would explode in under ten minutes. As Stauffenberg approached the specially built conference hut, he triggered the device. He then positioned the briefcase under the table, leaning it against one of the table's stout legs less than 2m away from the Führer. Five minutes before the bomb exploded, the Count quietly slipped unnoticed from the room. One of the officers, Colonel Brandt, then moved closer to the table to get a better look at the campaign maps and, finding the briefcase in the way of his feet under the table, picked it up and moved it to the other side of the table leg. This put the very solid support of the table leg between the briefcase and Hitler.

At 12.42pm the bomb went off. Stauffenberg, watching the hut from a few hundred metres away, was shocked by the force of the explosion; he didn't doubt that the Führer, along with everyone else in the room, was dead, and hurried off to a waiting plane to make his way to Berlin to join the other conspirators. Meanwhile, back in the wreckage of the conference hut, Hitler and the survivors staggered out into the daylight. Four people were killed, including Colonel Brandt, who had unwittingly saved the Führer's life. Hitler himself, despite being badly shaken, suffered no more than a perforated eardrum and minor injuries. After being attended to, he prepared himself for a meeting with Mussolini later that afternoon.

Bauhaus Archive

Klingelhöferstr. 14 • Wed–Mon 10am–5pm • Wed–Fri €6, Sat–Mon €7 • ⓦ bauhaus.de • U-Wittenbergplatz or bus #100

The Bauhaus school of design, crafts and architecture was founded in 1919 in Weimar by Walter Gropius. It moved to Dessau in 1925 and then to Berlin, to be closed by the Nazis in 1933 (see box, p.102). The influence of Bauhaus has been tremendous; you can get a small glimpse of this from the modest collection of the **Bauhaus Archive**, in a building designed by Gropius and completed in 1979. Marcel Breuer's seminal chair is still (with minor variations) in production today, and former Bauhaus director Mies van der Rohe's designs and models for buildings show how the modernist style has changed the face of today's cities. There's work, too, by Kandinsky, Moholy-Nagy, Schlemmer and Klee, all of whom worked at the Bauhaus.

It quickly became apparent what had happened, and the hunt for Stauffenberg was on. Hitler issued orders to the SS in Berlin to summarily execute anyone who was slightly suspect, and dispatched Himmler to the city to quell the rebellion. Back in the military Supreme Command headquarters in Bendlerstrasse, the conspiracy was in chaos. Word reached Stauffenberg and the two main army conspirators, Generals Beck and Witzleben, that the Führer was still alive. They had already lost essential hours by failing to issue the carefully planned order to mobilize their sympathizers in the city and elsewhere, and had even failed to carry out the obvious precaution of severing all communications out of the city. Goebbels succeeded in telephoning Hitler, who spoke directly to the arrest team, ordering them to obey his propaganda minister. Then Goebbels set to work contacting SS and Gestapo units, and reminding army garrisons of their oath of loyalty to the Führer. After a few hours of tragicomic scenes as the conspirators tried to persuade high-ranking officials to join them, the Bendlerstrasse HQ was surrounded by SS troops, and it was announced that the Führer would broadcast to the nation later that evening. The attempted coup was over. At 9pm, Hitler broadcast on national radio, saying he would "settle accounts the way we National Socialists are accustomed to settle them".

The conspirators were gathered together, given paper to write farewell messages to their wives, taken to the courtyard of the HQ (a memorial stands on the spot) and, under the orders of one General Fromm, shot by firing squad. Stauffenberg's last words were "Long live our sacred Germany!" Fromm had known about the plot almost from the beginning, but had refused to join it. By executing the leaders he hoped to save his own skin – and, it must be added, save them from the torturers of the SS.

Hitler's revenge on the conspirators was severe even by the ruthless standards of the Third Reich. All the colleagues, friends and immediate relatives of Stauffenberg and the other conspirators were rounded up, tortured and taken before the "People's Court" – the building where the court convened, the Kammergericht building, still stands (see p.114) – where they were humiliated and given more or less automatic death sentences, most of which were brutally carried out at **Plötzensee Prison** (see p.157). Many of those executed knew nothing of the plot and were found guilty merely by association. As the blood lust grew, the Nazi party used the plot as a pretext for settling old scores, and eradicated anyone who had the slightest hint of anything less than total dedication to the Führer. General Fromm himself was among those tried, found guilty of cowardice and shot by firing squad. Those whose names were blurted out under torture were quickly arrested, the most notable being Field Marshal Rommel, who, because of his popularity, was given the choice of a trial in the so-called People's Court – or suicide and a state funeral. He chose suicide, but other high-ranking conspirators were forced before the court for a public show trial. All were sentenced to death by the Nazi judge Ronald Freisler and hanged on meat-hooks at Plötzensee Prison, their death agonies being filmed for Hitler's private delectation.

The July Bomb Plot resulted in the deaths of at least five thousand people, including some of Germany's most brilliant military thinkers and almost all of those who would have been best qualified to run the postwar German government. (Freisler himself was killed by an American bomb.) Within six months the country lay in ruins as the Allies advanced; had events at Rastenburg been only a little different, the entire course of the war – and European history – would have been altered incalculably.

Tiergarten

S-Bahn Tiergarten – though the park is best accessed by bus #100, which cuts through it on its way between Bahnhof Zoo and Alexanderplatz

Flanking the north sides of both the Kulturforum and the diplomatic district is the **Tiergarten** park, a restful expanse of woodland and lakes that was designed by Peter Lenné as a hunting ground under Elector Friedrich III. Largely destroyed during the 1945 Battle of Berlin, after the war it was used as farmland, chiefly to grow potatoes for starving citizens; since then the replanting has been so successful that these days it's hard to tell it's not original.

The best way to appreciate the park is on foot or by bike. At the very least, try wandering along the Landwehrkanal, an inland waterway off the River Spree that separates the park from the zoo. It's an easy hour's walk between **Corneliusbrücke** – just

5

BAUHAUS

Bauhaus, a German word whose literal meaning is "building-house", has become a generic term for the aesthetically functional design style that grew out of the art and design philosophy developed at the Dessau school, in Saxony-Anhalt. The origins of the movement lie in the Novembergruppe, a grouping of artists founded in 1918 by the Expressionist painter Max Pechstein with the aim of utilizing art for revolutionary purposes. Members included Bertolt Brecht and Kurt Weill, Emil Nolde, Eric Mendelssohn and the architect **Walter Gropius**. In 1919 Gropius was invited by the new republican government of Germany to oversee the amalgamation of the School of Arts and Crafts and the Academy of Fine Arts in Weimar into the **Staatliche Bauhaus Weimar**. It was hoped that this new institution would break down the barriers between art and craft, creating a new form of applied art. It attracted more than two hundred students who studied typography, furniture design, ceramics and wood-, glass- and metalworking under exponents like Paul Klee, Wassily Kandinsky and Laszlo Moholy-Nagy.

By the end of the 1920s, the staff and students of the Bauhaus school had become increasingly embroiled in the political battles of the time, and throughout the early 1930s Nazi members of Dessau town council called for an end to subsidies for the Bauhaus. Their efforts finally succeeded in the summer of 1932, forcing the school to close down. The Bauhaus relocated to the more liberal atmosphere of Berlin, setting up in a disused telephone factory in Birkbuschstrasse in the Steglitz district. However, after the Nazis came to power, police harassment reached such a pitch that on July 20, 1933, director **Ludwig Mies van der Rohe** took the decision to shut up shop for good. He and many of his staff and students subsequently went into exile in the United States.

up Corneliusstrasse from the Bauhaus Archive (see p.100) – and Bahnhof Zoo, via the popular *Schleusenkrug* beer garden (see p.192). At Corneliusbrücke a small, odd sculpture commemorates the radical leader **Rosa Luxemburg**. In 1918, along with fellow revolutionary Karl Liebknecht, she reacted against the newly formed Weimar Republic and especially the terms of the Treaty of Versailles, declaring a new Socialist Republic in Berlin along the lines of Soviet Russia (she had played an important part in the abortive 1905 revolution). The pair were kidnapped by members of the elite First Cavalry Guards: Liebknecht was gunned down while "attempting to escape", and Luxemburg was knocked unconscious and shot, her body dumped in the Landwehrkanal.

Just north of the Landwehrkanal, and deeper inside the park, a pretty little group of ponds makes up the grand-sounding **Neuer See**. In summer there's another popular beer garden here, the *Café am Neuen See*, and it's possible to rent **boats** by the hour.

Siegessäule

April–Oct Mon–Fri 9.30am–6.30pm, Sat & Sun 9.30am–7pm; Nov–March daily 10am–5.30pm • €2.20 • U-Hansaplatz or bus #100

In the midst of the park and approached by four great boulevards stands the **Siegessäule**, a column celebrating Prussia's military victories (chiefly that over France in 1871). It was shifted from in front of the Reichstag to this spot on Hitler's orders in 1938, part of a grand design for Berlin as capital of the Third Reich; with the same forethought Hitler had the monument raised another level to commemorate the victories to come in what became World War II. Though the boulevard approaches exaggerate its size, it's still an eye-catching monument: 67m high and topped with a gilded winged victory that symbolically faces France. The summit offers a good view of the surrounding area, but climbing the 585 steps to the top is no mean feat. Have a look, too, at the mosaics at the column's base, which show the unification of the German peoples and incidents from the Franco-Prussian War. The four bronze reliefs beside them on the four sides depict the main wars and the victorious marching of the troops into Berlin; these were removed after 1945 and taken to Paris, only to be returned when the lust for war spoils had subsided.

Dotted around the Siegessäule are **statues** of other German notables, the most imposing being that of Bismarck, the "Iron Chancellor", under whom the country was united in the late nineteenth century. He's surrounded by figures symbolizing his achievements.

Strasse des 17 Juni

East and west of the Siegessäule, the broad, straight **Strasse des 17 Juni** cuts through the Tiergarten to form the continuation of Unter den Linden beyond the Brandenburg Gate (see p.35). Originally named Charlottenburger Chaussee, it was also once known as the East–West Axis and was a favourite strip for Nazi processions. Indeed, Hitler had the stretch from the Brandenburg Gate to Theodor-Heuss-Platz – formerly Adolf-Hitler-Platz (see p.157) – widened in order to accommodate these mass displays of military might and Nazi power; on his birthday in 1938, forty thousand men and six hundred tanks took four hours to parade past the Führer. Later, in the final days of the war, Charlottenburger Chaussee became a makeshift runway for aeroplanes ferrying Nazi notables to and from the besieged capital. Its current name commemorates the day in 1953 when workers in the East rose in revolt against the occupying Soviet powers (see p.120), though it later became better known as the main venue for the hedonistic Love Parade. Nowadays, though it's an ordinarily busy thoroughfare by day, by night prostitutes line its western end and the Siegessäule becomes a prime gay cruising spot. Come any big sporting event, however, like a football World Cup – which prompts the construction of a "fan-mile" – or an annual festivity such as the Berlin Gay Pride Parade (see p.236), and this stretch of road really comes alive.

Schloss Bellevue

From the Siegessäule it's a long hike to the Brandenburg Gate and Reichstag, so it's worth hopping on the #100 bus. En route, look out for **Schloss Bellevue**, an eighteenth-century building that was once a guesthouse for the Third Reich and is today the Berlin home of the Federal President. You might also catch a glimpse of the **Bundespräsidialamt** – a polished granite oval of presidential administrative offices that plays with the reflections of surrounding trees.

Haus der Kulturen der Welt

John-Foster-Dulles-Allee 10 • Exhibitions Mon & Wed–Sun 11am–7pm • ☎ 030 39 78 70, ⓦ hkw.de • U-Bundestag

The eye-catching oyster-shaped building squatting amid the greenery of John-Foster-Dulles-Allee is the **Haus der Kulturen der Welt** (House of Cultures of the World), an exhibition centre whose ambition couldn't be matched by the technology of the era: its roof collapsed in 1980. It has since been rebuilt to provide a venue for a colourful variety of non-European theatre, music, performances and exhibitions (see p.215).

Soviet War Memorial

North side of Str. des 17 Juni • U- & S-Brandenburger Tor

Built symbolically close to the Brandenburg Gate and the Reichstag, the **Soviet War Memorial** (Sowjetisches Ehrenmal) commemorates the Red Army troops who died in the Battle of Berlin. Crafted from the marble of Hitler's destroyed Berlin headquarters, the Reich Chancellery, it's flanked by two tanks that were supposedly the first to reach the city.

Spreebogen

The sharpest bend in central Berlin's River Spree, known as the **Spreebogen**, runs through one of Berlin's newest and quietest city quarters just northwest of the Reichstag (see p.37). Here the German government has built a **Regierungsviertel**,

5

or government quarter; it's also the location of Berlin's new space-age **Hauptbahnhof** train station. But a lot is still missing on a human scale, with visitors left to potter across huge empty plazas in front of giant buildings. The only exception to this is alongside the Spree where a new hangout of sorts is emerging as deck chairs colonize its banks and bars and cafés do a brisk trade, making it a pleasant place to while away an hour or two in the summer as boats cruise by.

Before the war this part of town was known as the **Alsenviertel**, an area of luxurious apartments that overlooked Königsplatz and a much shorter Siegessäule, which stood midway between the Reichstag and the Kroll Opera House, until it was moved to its present position (see p.102) to make way for a planned "Great Hall of the People". This giant structure, loosely based on Rome's Pantheon, was to be the centrepiece of Hitler and Speer's World Capital Germania, with an unfeasibly large cupola that would have been impossible to build with the technology of the time. In reality, the war gutted and largely levelled the area, its proximity to the East Berlin border deterring any redevelopment. West Berliners would come here to barbecue or learn to drive in empty lots, while boats from the East – mainly Polish freighters delivering coal to West Berlin's power stations – sailed through the only river checkpoint; all were meticulously scanned underwater for possible escapees.

Regierungsviertel

New and strikingly well-designed modern buildings form Berlin's **Regierungsviertel** (government quarter), a district built largely in the 1990s to give the German Federal government a home. Here structures straddle the Spree, symbolically linking East and West; are connected to one another, underlining the correlation of government; and are designed to be accessible and transparent, as a metaphor for the need for openness of government. These design concepts are best appreciated, in the first instance, by getting an overview from the top of the Reichstag (see p.37).

Jakob-Kaiser-Haus

The Regierungsviertel's biggest but least attention-grabbing building is administrative **Jakob-Kaiser-Haus**, immediately east of the Reichstag, whose 1750 offices make it one of Europe's largest office blocks. However, despite its size, it avoids becoming too monstrous or monotonous by following Berlin's traditional courtyard principle – almost creating a neighbourhood – and by integrating well into its surroundings.

Paul-Löbe-Haus and Maria-Elisabeth-Lüders-Haus

The offices and conference rooms of the **Paul-Löbe-Haus** and **Maria-Elisabeth-Lüders-Haus** lie just north of the Reichstag and west and east of the Spree respectively. Symbolically joined to one another via a footbridge across the river and over the former East–West border, both were designed by Stefan Braunfels and completed in 2001. Of note are the large windows that form part of the buildings' energy-efficient heating system by collecting heat – along with the roof – while interior ceilings double as cooling mechanisms.

Bundeskanzleramt

With its comb-like layout, the Paul-Löbe-Haus plays on design themes in the imposing **Bundeskanzleramt** (Federal Chancellery), opposite. A pet project of Helmut Kohl, it was cleverly designed by Axel Schultes and Charlotte Frank to contain subtle references to Le Corbusier and Luis Kahn in the studied detailing and structure. The centrepiece is a nine-storey white cube – earning the building the nickname "the washing machine" – which contains the chancellor's accommodation. Originally the building was to be connected with Paul-Löbe-Haus, to reinforce the symbolic relationship between chancellor, administration and parliament, but the project ran short of money; today the only connections are those running underground between the Reichstag and Paul-Löbe-Haus. The Bundeskanzleramt is best appreciated from the northern banks of the Spree.

Swiss Embassy

The **Swiss Embassy**, just northeast of the Bundeskanzleramt, was one of the few Neoclassical buildings to survive the war intact. Its 2001 extension, spurred on by the German government's move back to Berlin, caused some outrage, though experts judge the two buildings to be a clever play of opposites – not even the floor levels are aligned – and praise the careful exterior concreting, done in one pour so that no shuttering or expansion joints are visible.

Die Schlange

At the western end of the government quarter, and best seen from the Spree, **Die Schlange** (The Snake) is named for its unusual zigzag layout. This brick-clad apartment block has proved rather unpopular among the parliamentarians it was designed for, as some apartments stare into one another and because of the odd-shaped rooms – not to mention high rents and dull surroundings.

Hauptbahnhof

After almost a decade of planning and construction, the landmark glass-and-steel five-level **Hauptbahnhof** opened in time for the 2006 football World Cup. The look and scale of this superlative piece of architecture both impress. The Hamburg-based architects Meinhard von Gerkan and Volkin Marg produced a striking but functional station – Europe's largest ever – that can handle 300,000 travellers and 1100 trains per day. Yet it remains an oddity thanks to the barren immediate surroundings, devoid of Berlin's usual endless graffiti and the normal mix of late-night bars, gambling dens and sex shops that surround most of Europe's major train stations. Here cleanliness, sterility and peacefulness rule, escalators move noiselessly and even the bins shine.

Like London, Berlin historically had a ring of terminus stations, but as early as the 1930s plans were being drawn up to transform that impractical ring into a cross. After reunification, the opportunity was seized, and this central station at the crossing point of the two main west–east and north–south lines was planned. This was the one-time location of the old Lehrter Bahnhof, which operated from 1871 to 1952 before it was left to rot alongside Berlin's Cold War dividing line. It is now hailed as a symbolic central point of Europe, with trains running through between Rome and Copenhagen, Moscow and Paris.

The **east–west** track already existed, following an 1882 viaduct that wends its way through the city from Charlottenburg via the Zoo, Friedrichstrasse and Alexanderplatz stations to the Ostbahnhof, giving rail travellers a wonderful Mitte sightseeing tour. The new **north–south** line runs four levels further down and 15m below the Spree. The station's glass hall follows the east–west line, while the gap between two huge administrative tracts that cross it indicate the direction of the underground north–south track.

Inside, the building works well. Always quick with a nickname, Berliners soon christened it the "glass cathedral", and the basic principles of Gothic-style construction really are in evidence: supports and weights; the space's upward thrust; braces resembling Gothic clustered piers; and a series of "vaults". Though to a casual observer it may seem more like an airy shopping mall criss-crossed by trains, the main hall, with its many-layered staircase systems, elevator tubes, skylights and aperture windows, is also said to be a formal analogy to the feverish spatial fantasies of the Italian Baroque.

5

Hamburger Bahnhof/Museum für Gegenwart

Invalidenstr. 50–51 · Tues, Wed & Fri–Sun 10am–6pm, Thurs 10am–8pm · €14 · ⓦ hamburgerbahnhof.de · U- & S-Hauptbahnhof

North across Invalidenstrasse from the Hauptbahnhof lies Berlin's premier contemporary art museum, the **Museum für Gegenwart** (Museum for Contemporary Art), located in the **Hamburger Bahnhof**. Like the Anhalter Bahnhof, the Hamburger station was damaged in the war, though it had ceased functioning as a station as early as 1906. Fortunately, it didn't suffer its twin's fate in postwar redevelopment, and today the old train station and the adjoining former industrial warehouses provide superb spaces for an impressive postwar art selection: from Rauschenberg, Twombly, Warhol, Beuys and Lichtenstein right on up to Keith Haring and Donald Judd. There's an emphasis on video and film, with a vast array of 1970s video art, and an expansive Joseph Beuys archive, to which the entire west wing is dedicated.

There's a good **bookstore** and **café** on the premises, and look out too for the calendar of concerts, lectures and artist appearances.

Invalidenfriedhof

On the opposite bank of the Humboldthafen canal from the Hamburger Bahnhof, there's the opportunity for a pleasant offbeat walk along a towpath to the **Invalidenfriedhof**, a one-time important Prussian military cemetery that spent the second half of the twentieth century within the death-strip of the Berlin Wall. The earliest graves date from the mid-eighteenth century, but the most impressive belong to prominent Prussian figures, like Count Tauentzien and Generals Winterfeldt and Scharnhorst. These all remained largely undisturbed until the building of the Berlin Wall, when parish boundaries dictated that the death strip would surround the graves. Some of the graveyard was levelled and given over to access tracks, which remain, but a good number of memorials – all those here today – were preserved and provided a surreal and macabre touch to the death strip. This section of the Berlin Wall was also famed for another depressing reason; it was here that Günter Litfin, the first victim of the Wall, was shot and killed on 24 August, 1961, as he attempted to swim across the canal. An information board commemorates the event.

Medizinhistorisches Museum

Charitestr. 1 · Tues, Thurs, Fri & Sun 10am–5pm, Wed & Sat 10am–7pm · €7 · ⓦ bmm-charite.de · U- & S-Hauptbahnhof

On the southern side of Invalidenstrasse, medical textbook horrors come alive at the old-fashioned **Medizinhistorisches Museum** (Medical Museum), where two floors of a working hospital are lined with dusty shelves harbouring the pickled collection of one Rudolf Virchow (1821–1902), a local doctor and professor. Far from being dull, this surreal and disquieting collection is captivating for its freakish qualities. You won't learn much, thanks to the almost universal lack of signs and explanations (particularly for those without German), but some displays – like the smoker's tarred lungs or the alcoholic's fatty liver – need little explanation. But the grisly highlights – which will likely remain with you for some time – are the deformed foetuses and babies. As vivid as any horror filmmaker's imagination, these rows of disturbing deformities include conjoined twins, babies absurdly swollen by hydrocephalus and elephantiasis and even a cyclops. Clearly not one for expectant mothers, and, sensibly, children younger than 12 are barred – under-16s need to be accompanied by an adult.

MUSEUM FÜR FOTOGRAFIE

City West and Schöneberg

Lying immediately southwest of Berlin's Tiergarten, City West was once West Berlin's downtown but has now reverted to its prewar role as a high-end shopping area. It's focused on the famed Kurfürstendamm (or Ku'damm) and the adjoining Tauentzienstrasse where various showcase Cold War-era building projects still give the place a distinctive feel. Away from the main roads lie some of Berlin's smartest inner-city residences, which are attracting Russian investors in droves and which gather around attractive leafy squares such as Savignyplatz, the area's dining and café-culture hub. City West largely covers the most central portion of the immense, moneyed, white and rather sedate Charlottenburg-Wilmersdorf district, but on its eastern fringes it also spreads into Schöneberg, where Nollendorfplatz forms the gateway to Berlin's long-standing and world-famous gay village.

The most popular City West attraction is without doubt the well-run **Berlin Zoo and Aquarium**, but the most eye-catching is the huge **Kaiser-Wilhelm-Gedächtniskirche**, an iconic semi-ruined church tower that is one of the neighbourhood's very few remaining prewar buildings.

An easy walk from both are a smattering of good **museums** worth going out of your way for: particularly those devoted to fashion photographer Helmut Newton; anti-war artist Käthe Kollwitz, and a lively multimedia museum on Berlin's history. The **Schöneberg** neighbourhood, in contrast, has few real sights; though its city hall witnessed John F. Kennedy's famous "Ich bin ein Berliner" speech.

ARRIVAL AND GETTING AROUND

By train Bahnhof Zoo is the main transport hub in this part of Berlin, from where buses radiate to all the sights in the west.

Getting around City West is fairly easily explored on foot,

as is much of Schöneberg, where most points of interest are an easy walk from Nollendorfplatz. However, Rathaus Schöneberg is best reached by U-Bahn or bus #M46 from Bahnhof Zoo.

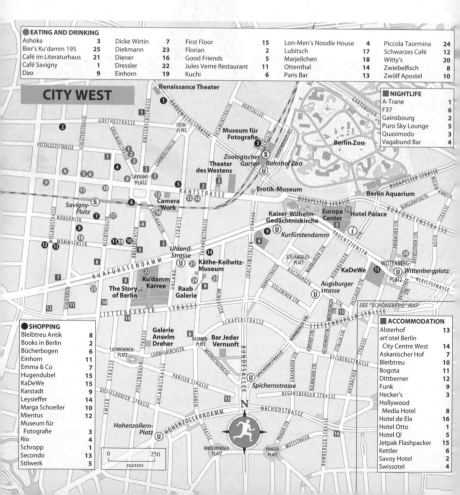

EATING AND DRINKING

Ashoka	3	Dicke Wirtin	7	First Floor	15	Lon-Men's Noodle House	4	Piccola Taormina	24
Bier's Ku'damm 195	25	Diekmann	23	Florian	2	Lubitsch	17	Schwarzes Café	12
Café im Literaturhaus	21	Diener	16	Good Friends	5	Marjellchen	18	Witty's	20
Café Savigny		Dressler	22	Jules Verne Restaurant	11	Ottenthal	14	Zwiebelfisch	8
Dao	9	Einhorn	19	Kuchi	6	Paris Bar	13	Zwölf Apostel	10

CITY WEST

Renaissance Theater

Museum für Fotografie

Berlin Zoo

Zoologischer Theater des Westens · Garten · Bahnhof Zoo

NIGHTLIFE

A-Trane	1
F37	6
Gainsbourg	2
Puro Sky Lounge	5
Quasimodo	3
Vagabund Bar	4

KANTSTRASSE

Erotik-Museum

Berlin Aquarium

Savigny-Platz

Camera Work

Kaiser-Wilhelm-Gedächtniskirche · Europa Center · Hotel Palace

Uhland-Strasse

Käthe-Kollwitz-Museum

Kurfürstendamm

KaDeWe

Wittenbergplatz

KURFÜRSTENDAMM

Ku'damm Karree

The Story of Berlin

Raab Galerie

Augsburger strasse

LIETZENBURGER STRASSE

SEE "SCHÖNEBERG" MAP

SHOPPING

Bleibtreu Antik	8
Books in Berlin	2
Bücherbogen	6
Einhorn	11
Emma & Co	7
Hugendubel	15
KaDeWe	15
Karstadt	9
Leysieffer	14
Marga Schoeller	10
Mientus	12
Museum für Fotografie	3
Rio	4
Schropp	1
Secondo	13
Stilwerk	5

Galerie Anselm Dreher

Bar Jeder Vernunft

Spichernstrasse

ACCOMMODATION

Alsterhof	13
art'otel Berlin City Centre West	14
Askanischer Hof	7
Bleibtreu	10
Bogota	11
Dittberner	12
Funk	9
Hecker's	3
Hollywood Media Hotel	8
Hotel de Ela	16
Hotel Otto	1
Hotel Q!	5
Jetpak Flashpacker	15
Kettler	2
Savoy Hotel	6
Swissotel	4

Hohenzollern-Platz

0 · 250 · metres

6

City West

Long before the term **City West** was coined for the old centre of West Berlin, its main role was as a shopping district, particularly along **Kurfürstendamm** (universally called **Ku'damm**). Even in the grim first few years after the war, a few retailers managed to struggle on here, but it was with the coming of the Berlin Wall that the area got a real boost. With Berlin's true centre snatched away by the GDR, this area quickly became an awkward surrogate. Large amounts of modern building work aimed to transform City West into the heart of a great late twentieth-century metropolis, but the work was largely in vain. Once the Wall came down the city hastily shifted back to its previous centre, abandoning West Berlin's old centre to years in the doldrums. Lately, however, its iconic avenues have been reborn, home to couture boutiques and high-street shops.

6

Bahnhof Zoo

Squeezed between a couple of scruffy shopping precincts and surrounded by third-rate modern architecture, **Bahnhof Zoo** is the district's shabby main transport hub. Pulling in here still somehow conjures up images of prewar steam trains, but that's as far as the nostalgia goes: the station is comparatively small, with no large lobby or grand portico, and its many entrances mostly harbour a retinue of urban casualties. At least a recent makeover and the presence of a few glossy and late-opening stores have helped smarten the station up a little; it's certainly a far cry from the days, just a couple of decades ago, when it was the haunt of heroin dealers and child prostitutes.

Museum für Fotografie

Jebenesstr. 2 • Tues–Sun 10am–6pm • €10, or €12 with a Bereichskarte (see p.23) • ☎ 030 266 42 42 42, ⓦ smb.museum • U- & S-Bahnhof Zoo

Behind Bahnhof Zoo, and best reached through its back door, is another of Berlin's excellent municipal museums, the **Museum für Fotografie**. The home of the **Helmut Newton Foundation**, it exhibits the work of this world-famous photographer and also sometimes has temporary exhibitions of lesser-known photographers on its upper floors.

The collection, Newton's gift to his home city shortly before his untimely death in 2004, is divided into two. The ground floor is a museum to the man himself, including a reconstruction of his quirky Monaco office and his oversized made-to-measure beach buggy – complete with monogram on the steering wheel, no doubt perfect for cruising around Monte Carlo. Most interesting among the rest of the memorabilia is his camera collection, which spans several decades. The upper floors exhibit Newton's work in regularly changing exhibits, displaying his unique and heavily stylized portrait, glamour and nude photography, his celebrity portraiture and penchant for Amazonian women. Some of the most intriguing pieces are from his personal collection of unpublished photos. Both Newton and his wife (who worked under the pseudonym Alice Springs) seem always to have had cameras to hand to chart every aspect of their life together and obsess over each other's naked forms. The images from Newton's deathbed are particularly stark. The ground-floor photography **shop** is exceptional, with a coverage that goes well beyond Newton, and with many books at reduced prices.

CITY WEST PHOTOGRAPHY GALLERIES

If you've enjoyed City West's **Museum für Fotografie** (see above) make sure to stop by the following excellent galleries, both of which are in the same neighbourhood.

Camera Work Kantstr. 149 ☎ 030 310 07 73, ⓦ camerawork.de; U-Uhlandstrasse. Just a short walk away from the main photography museum, with a variety of exhibitions (see p.217).

C/O Berlin ☎ 030 28 44 41 60, ⓦ co-berlin.com.

This superb photographic gallery hosts world-class avant-garde temporary exhibitions (usually around €8). At the time of going to press it was on the move to the Amerika Haus, Hardenbergstr. 22–24 (U-Augsburger Strasse) where it is due to reopen in 2014.

Berlin Zoo

Hardenbergplatz 8 • **Zoo** Daily: late March to mid-Sept 9am–7pm; mid-Sept to late Oct 9am–6pm; late Oct to late March 9am–5pm • €13; €20 with aquarium **Aquarium** Daily 9am–6pm • €13; €20 with zoo • ⓦ zoo-berlin.de • U- & S-Bahnhof Zoo

Step out east through the main entrance of Zoo Station and you're in a maelstrom of bright lights, traffic and high-rise buildings, but walk over the area occupied by the bus station to the other side of the plaza and you'll find yourself at the gates of the **Berlin Zoo**, or Zoologischer Garten, which contains a zoo and aquarium. Laid out in 1844 on the basis of Friedrich Wilhelm IV's private zoo from Pfaueninsel (see p.163), this survived the destruction of World War II, and subsequent pressure from a local starving populace, to become one of Europe's most important zoos, with more than 1500 species represented. It's pleasantly landscaped, with reasonably large compounds for the animals, peaceful nooks for quietly observing animal behaviour, and lots of benches that make it ideal for picnicking. Highlights include a large glass-sided hippo-pool and the **Nachttierhaus**, an underground nocturnal environment whose principal attraction is the bat cave. Sadly, the zoo's most famous resident is only viewable in the form of a bronze memorial sculpture: this was **Knut**, a rather adorable polar bear cub. Born in 2007 but rejected by his mother – a one-time GDR circus bear – he was reared by a zookeeper and became an instant celebrity, even appearing on the cover of the German edition of *Vanity Fair*, and significantly increased the zoo's revenue. He died in 2011 by drowning as the result of encephalitis.

The **aquarium** lives up to its international reputation, with more species than any other in the world. The large, humid crocodile hall is the most memorable section. Despite the attractive price of the **combined day ticket**, trying to get around both the zoo and aquarium in a day can be quite a rush.

Erotik-Museum

Joachimsthaler Str. 4 • Mon–Wed 9am–10pm, Thurs–Sat 9am–midnight, Sun 11am–10pm • €9; €16 per couple; over-18s only • ⓦ erotikmuseum.de • U- & S-Bahnhof Zoo

The **Erotik-Museum**, a short block south of Bahnhof Zoo, is run by Beate Uhse, a household name in Germany: once a Luftwaffe test pilot, she began selling sex education pamphlets after the war and now heads a multi-million-euro corporation dedicated to all things sexual. Located on two floors above her sex shop, the museum is really an assemblage rather than an organized exhibition, but with an extensive collection of prints, paintings and objects – including Japanese silk paintings, Balinese fertility shrines, Indian reliefs in wood and Chinese bordello tokens, to name but a few. The assortment of 1920s and 1930s artwork from Europe, including charcoal sketches of cabaret artist Anita Berber, and pieces by George Grosz and local favourite Heinrich Zille, is good, suggesting – albeit faintly – something of the atmosphere of Weimar Berlin. All told though, it doesn't really justify the steep entrance fee.

Breitscheidplatz

A short two-block walk east of Bahnhof Zoo, the angular concrete **Breitscheidplatz** is a magnet for vendors, caricaturists and street musicians, and often hosts fairs and festivals, including a large Christmas market. On its eastern edge is the rather generic **Europa Center** shopping mall, which was built in the 1960s as a capitalist symbol for West Berlin, topped by a huge, rotating Mercedes-Benz symbol. An intriguing sculpture entitled *Flow of Time*, an alternative clock consisting of an elaborate series of liquid-filled glass pipes, does, however, deserve some attention down in the lobby.

Kaiser-Wilhelm-Gedächtniskirche

Daily 9am–7pm; guided tours Mon, Fri & Sat 10.15am, 11am, noon, 1.15pm, 2pm & 3pm, Tues–Thurs 1.15pm, 2pm & 3pm • Free • ⓦ gedaechtniskirche-berlin.de • U-Kurfürstendamm

The focal point of Breitscheidplatz is **Kaiser-Wilhelm-Gedächtniskirche**, one of Berlin's great landmarks. Built at the end of the nineteenth century, it was destroyed by British

OPPOSITE KAISER-WILHELM-GEDÄCHTNISKIRCHE >

bombing in November 1943 and left as a reminder. It's a strangely effective memorial, the crumbling tower providing a hint of the old city. You can go inside what remains of the nave: a small exhibit shows wartime destruction and a "before and after" model of the city centre. Adjacent, a modern **chapel** contains a sad charcoal sketch by Kurt Reubers, *Stalingrad Madonna*, dedicated to those that died – on both sides – during the Battle of Stalingrad. The blue-glass campanile on the opposite side of the ruined church to the chapel has gained the nicknames the "Lipstick" or the "Soul-Silo" because of its tubular shape; in its base is a shop selling fair-trade goods.

Tauentzienstrasse

East of the Kaiser-Wilhelm-Gedächtniskirche, the Ku'damm becomes the rather bland chain-store shopping street **Tauentzienstrasse**, which is also arranged around a wide boulevard. At its eastern end is the largest department store in Europe, **KaDeWe**. An abbreviation of Kaufhaus Des Westens ("Department Store of the West"), it opened in 1907 and quickly became a temple of luxury in a rapidly modernizing city. Decades later the Nazis seized it from its Jewish owners, and in 1943 an American fighter plane crashed into it, igniting a fire that gutted the building. Almost 180,000 Berliners attended its reopening in 1950, and during the Cold War it became a symbol of West Berlin's capitalist prosperity. Some days it averages fifty thousand visitors, many of whom head to the superb sixth-floor food hall with its mouthwatering snacks.

Outside KaDeWe, **Wittenbergplatz U-Bahn station** has been likeably restored to its prewar condition both inside (1920s kitsch) and out (Neoclassical pavilion). Near the entrance, a tall sign reminds passers-by of the wartime concentration camps: it states that the German people must never be allowed to forget the atrocities that were carried out there, and lists the names of some of the camps. It's an odd memorial, neither terribly poignant nor at a significant site, and one that goes largely unnoticed by shoppers.

Käthe-Kollwitz-Museum

Fasanenstr. 24 • Daily 11am–6pm • €6 • ☎ 030 882 52 10, ⊛ kaethe-kollwitz.de • U-Uhlandstrasse

The **Käthe-Kollwitz-Museum**, just south of the Ku'damm, near Uhlandstrasse U-Bahn station, is devoted to the work of Kollwitz, who created some of the most moving works of the first half of the twentieth century. Born in 1867, the artist lived almost all her life in Prenzlauer Berg (see p.132), in the eastern part of the city, where her work developed a radical left-wing perspective. Following the death of her son in World War I, her woodcuts, lithographs and prints became explicitly pacifist, often dwelling on the theme of mother and child – her most famous print, *No More War*, a stark, furious work depicting a protesting mother, is a perfect example. Her sculptures, too, often deal with this subject: two of her bronzes, *Tower of Women* and the pietà *Mother with Dead Son*, can be seen here. When her grandson was killed in World War II her work became even sadder and more poignant. As she was a staunch pacifist and committed socialist, the Nazis watched her carefully and forced her resignation from a prestigious post at the Faculty of Arts, while at the same time using some of her work for their own propaganda purposes. She died in 1945, shortly before the end of the war.

The Story of Berlin

Kurfürstendamm 207–208 • Daily 10am–8pm, last admission 6pm • €12 • ☎ 030 88 72 01 00, ⊛ story-of-berlin.de • U-Uhlandstrasse

Just west of the Uhlandstrasse U-Bahn on Ku'damm lies **The Story of Berlin**, an excellent multimedia exhibition and an ideal first step in unravelling Berlin's history. Tucked away in the back of a mall, the museum uses its odd layout to its advantage, with each subsection extensively labelled in English. On the way round you'll be confronted with life-size dioramas, film clips, noises, flashing lights, smoke and smells, which illustrate the trawl through the highs and lows of the city's turbulent past. The end result will entertain all ages and will take at least two hours to complete, not including the additional bonus: a taste of the Cold War given on the frequent guided tours of the 1970s Allied-built nuclear bunker below the mall. It's still functional, with space for around 3500 people to shelter in the first few weeks after a nuclear attack. If you've run out of time or energy having visited the museum, you can use your ticket to return another day to view the bunker.

Schöneberg

Once a separate entity, **Schöneberg** was swallowed up by Greater Berlin as the city expanded in the late eighteenth and nineteenth centuries. Blown to pieces during the war, it's now a mostly middle-class residential area. There aren't many things to see, but there are reminders of a fascinating and moving past. The gateway to the district is **Nollendorfplatz**, a long-standing centre in the city's gay and lesbian community. Schöneberg's main drag, Potsdamer Strasse, runs a block or so east of here and was

SCHÖNEBERG

● SHOPPING

Chatwins	9
Flohmarkt Schöneberg	11
Fiona Bennett	2
Flying Colors	10
Garage	1
Herz + Stöhr	8
Körpernah	7
L&P Classics	5
Mr Dead & Mrs Free	6
Prinz Eisenherz	4
ReSales	3

■ ACCOMMODATION

Altberlin am Potsdamer Platz	2
Art Hotel Connection	3
Sylter Hof Berlin	1
Tom's Hotel	4

■ NIGHTLIFE

Connection	3
E&M Leydicke	11
Green Door	9
Hafen	4
Havanna	15
Heile Welt	6
Kumpelnest 3000	1
Mister Hu	10
Neues Ufer	13
Pinguin Club	14
Prinzknecht	5
Scheune	8
Tom's Bar	7
Victoria Bar	2
Zoulou Bar	12

● EATING AND DRINKING

Aroma	12	Edd's Thailändisches	1	Maharadscha	4
Baharat Falafel	6	Felsenkeller	20	Petite Europe	14
Café Berio	5	Garda Pizza	16	Renger-Patzsch	15
Café BilderBuch	18	Inka Eis	19	Sorgenfrei	10
Café Einstein	3	Ixthys	9	Taverna Ousies	11
Café M	7	Joseph Roth Diele	2	Winterfeldt Schokoladen	8
Ebbes	17	Kleisther	13		

once lined by the **Sportpalast** and **Kammergericht**, the scenes of several important chapters in city history. On the southern fringes of the district lies **Rathaus Schöneberg**, where on June 26, 1963 John F. Kennedy made his "Berliner" speech.

Nollendorfplatz

Long a key place for Berlin's large **gay and lesbian community**, the busy road and rail intersection of **Nollendorfplatz** throbs by night as western Berlin's main gay hub, but by day holds few specific attractions. Even so, it's worth doing a lap of the block on the south side of the square, east of the proto-Deco **Metropol Theater**, and down Massenstrasse and on to Nollendorfstrasse. Here, at no. 17, stands the building in which the writer **Christopher Isherwood** lived during his years in the prewar city, a time elegantly recounted in his famous collection of stories *Goodbye to Berlin*:

From my window, the deep solemn massive street. Cellar shops where lamps burn all day, under the shadow of top-heavy balconied facades, dirty plaster frontages embossed with scroll work and heraldic devices. The whole district is like this: street leading into street of houses like shabby monumental safes crammed with the tarnished valuables and secondhand furniture of a bankrupt middle class.

Schöneberg has since been reborn as a fancy, even chic, neighbourhood; latter-day Isherwood wannabes hang out in eastern Kreuzberg.

Kleistpark and around

On Pallasstrasse, east of Winterfeldtplatz, you'll spot a huge and undistinguished apartment building straddling the road and backing onto the northern edge of the **Kleistpark**. On the south side of the street a huge concrete cube forms the base of the structure; this began life as one of Berlin's **air-raid shelters** in case of Allied raids. After the war the tower proved impervious to demolition attempts, and the lower levels were used by NATO troops to store food and provisions in case of a Soviet invasion. Ironically, in the post-Cold War years, supplies reaching the end of their shelf life were sold off – usually on the cheap to Russia. On the northern side of the street the apartment building rests on land that until 1974 accommodated the **Sportpalast**, a sports centre that became the main venue for Nazi rallies in the 1930s. Hitler delivered some of his most famous speeches here – witness those old newsreels showing him working himself up into an oratorical fever. It was also where Goebbels asked the German people if they wanted "total war" – at which they jubilantly applauded.

Königskolonnaden

At its eastern end, Pallasstrasse finishes at Potsdamer Strasse, Schöneberg's main drag. A couple of minutes' walk south down it brings you to the **Königskolonnaden** – a colonnade from 1780 that originally stood on Alexanderplatz – which on a misty morning makes this stretch of road look a little Parisian.

Kammergericht building

On the western side of the Kleistpark looms the sturdy **Kammergericht building**, once the Supreme Court of Justice. Here Nazi show trials took place, as did the "People's Court" under the infamous Judge Freisler following the July Bomb Plot (see p.100), both preludes to the inevitable executions, which often took place in Plötzensee Prison (see p.157). Freisler met his unlamented end here in the final weeks of the war: on his way from the courtroom a bomb from an American aircraft fell on the building, dislodging a beam that crushed his skull. The building is now used by NATO.

Sankt-Matthäus-Kirchhof

Across Potsdamer Strasse from the Kleistpark, at the end of Grossgörschenstrasse, lies the **Sankt-Matthäus-Kirchhof**, a graveyard that contains the bodies of the Brothers

GAY BERLIN IN THE WEIMAR AND NAZI YEARS

Even by contemporary standards, Weimar Berlin's gay scene in the 1920s and early 1930s was prodigious: there were around forty gay bars on and near **Nollendorfplatz** alone, and gay life in the city was open, fashionable and well organized, with its own newspapers, community associations and art. The city's theatres were filled with plays exploring gay themes, homosexuality in the Prussian army was little short of institutionalized, and gay bars, nightclubs and brothels proudly advertised their attractions – there were even gay working men's clubs. All this happened at a time when the rest of Europe was smothered under a welter of homophobia and repression.

Under the Third Reich, however, homosexuality was quickly and brutally outlawed: gays and lesbians were rounded up and taken to concentration camps, branded for their "perversion" by being forced to wear pink or black triangles. (The black triangle represented "antisocial" offenders: in an attempt to ignore the existence of lesbianism, lesbians were arrested on pretexts such as swearing at the Führer's name.) As homosexuality was, at the time, still illegal in Allied countries, no Nazis were tried for crimes against gays or lesbians at Nürnberg. A red granite plaque in the shape of a triangle at Nollendorfplatz U-Bahn station commemorates the gay men and women who were murdered for their sexuality.

Cabaret Berlin ⓦ cabaret-berlin.com, ☏ 0151 25 22 03 42. Well-informed 75min English-language walking tours around Berlin's gay village with emphasis on places relating to Christopher Isherwood. Sat 11am; €12.

Grimm, united in death as they were in copyright. The bodies of Stauffenberg and his co-conspirators were also buried here following the July Bomb Plot, only to be exhumed a few days later and burned by Nazi thugs.

Rathaus Schöneberg

Martin-Luther-Str. • **Tower** April–Sept daily 10am–4pm • Free • U-Rathaus Schöneberg

Schöneberg's most famous attraction, **Rathaus Schöneberg**, actually offers very little to see. Built just before World War I, the Rathaus became the seat of the West Berlin parliament and senate after the last war, and it was outside here in 1963 that **John F. Kennedy** made his celebrated speech on the Cold War, just a few months after the Cuban missile crisis:

There are many people in the world who really don't understand, or say they don't, what is the great issue between the free world and the Communist world. Let them come to Berlin. There are some who say that Communism is the wave of the future. Let them come to Berlin. And there are some who say in Europe and elsewhere we can work with the Communists. Let them come to Berlin. And there are even a few who say it is true that Communism is an evil system, but it permits us to make economic progress. Lässt sie nach Berlin kommen. Let them come to Berlin … All free men, wherever they may live, are citizens of Berlin, and, therefore, as a free man, I take pride in the words "Ich bin ein Berliner".

Rousing stuff. But what the president hadn't realized as he read from his phonetically written text was that what he had said could also mean "I am a doughnut", since *Berliner* is a name for jam doughnuts – though not in Berlin, where it is usually known as a *Pfannkuchen*. The urban myth that peals of laughter greeted this embarrassing error only developed years later. People did laugh at the time, after applauding, but because the president thanked his interpreter, who had simply repeated his quote, for translating his German. The notion that he been laughed at for erroneously calling himself a jam doughnut was largely the work of pedants long after the event. Five months later, the day after Kennedy was assassinated, the square in front of the Rathaus was given his name – a move apparently instigated by the city's students, among whom the president was highly popular.

You can climb the **Rathaus tower** and see the replica **liberty bell** donated to the city by the US in 1950.

CHECKPOINT CHARLIE

Kreuzberg-Friedrichshain and around

Southwest of Mitte lies the mainly residential borough of Kreuzberg-Friedrichshain. The district divides into three: middle-class western Kreuzberg; unkempt eastern Kreuzberg with its large Turkish-German community and its many drop-outs and would-be bohemians; and Friedrichshain, an old East Berlin neighbourhood that lies somewhere between the two, with hip warehouse clubs rubbing shoulders with tidy residential streets. Just south of Kreuzberg-Friedrichshain lie several adjacent districts – particularly Tempelhof, Treptow and Neukölln – which hold the odd attraction. Neukölln in particular is slowly establishing itself to be as hip as eastern Kreuzberg. By day the borough has its share of sights – all in easy reach of one another on foot or via the rapid U1 underground line – but it's at night that it really comes into its own.

The well-visited **Jüdisches Museum** (Jewish Museum) and the **Berlinische Galerie** are just a couple of the many respectable museums in northwest Kreuzberg and near the world's most famous Cold War border crossing, **Checkpoint Charlie**. Just south of Kreuzberg, the adjacent districts of **Tempelhof** and **Treptow** are interesting for two huge and impressive monuments to crumbled regimes: the Nazi **Tempelhof Airport** and **Soviet Memorial** respectively.

ARRIVAL AND GETTING AROUND

Western Kreuzberg The main sights are all within walking distance of the U6 U-Bahn line, which runs south from Friedrichstrasse in Mitte. If you're feeling energetic, you could easily walk between them all in a day, in which case you might start by taking bus #248 from Alexanderplatz to the Jewish Museum and set off from there.

Eastern Kreuzberg The U-Bahn stations Kottbusser Tor or Schlesisches Tor are the best way in, after which it's mostly a matter of walking around – though the Treptower Park's Soviet Memorial is a bus ride from the latter station. **Friedrichshain** A rapid U-Bahn line travels beneath Karl-Marx-Allee from Alexanderplatz, from where the S-Bahn also leaves for the Ostbahnhof and Warschauer Str.

7

Western Kreuzberg

When in the 1830s, Berlin's industries started recruiting peasants from the outlying countryside to work in their factories and machine shops, it was to the small village of **Kreuzberg** that many came. They ended up living in low-rent buildings thrown up by speculators, making Kreuzberg a solidly working-class area and, in time, a suburb of Greater Berlin. Siemens, the electrical engineering giant, began life in a Kreuzberg courtyard. In the 1930s local trade unionists and workers fought street battles with the Nazis, and during the war it was one of the very few areas to avoid total destruction, and among the quickest to revive in the 1950s.

The nondescript modern city blocks just south of Mitte are atypical, displaying almost no evidence of Kreuzberg's countercultural roots or its preserved nineteenth-century past. Nonetheless, this part of the district is worth investigating for its museums and its most famous sight, **Checkpoint Charlie**.

Jüdisches Museum Berlin

Lindenstr, 9–14 • Mon 10am–10pm, Tues–Sun 10am–8pm • €5 • ☎ 030 25 99 33 00, ⊕ jmberlin.de • U-Hallesches Tor or bus #248 from Alexanderplatz

A phenomenal silver fortress in the midst of residential streets once levelled by wartime bombing, the **Jüdisches Museum Berlin** (Jewish Museum Berlin) is one of Berlin's most exciting pieces of architecture. Uncomfortable angles and severe lines create a disturbed and uneasy space that mirrors the difficult story portrayed inside: that of the history and culture of German Jewry.

The extraordinary **building** is by Daniel Libeskind. The ground plan is in the form of a compressed lightning bolt (intended as a deconstructed Star of David), while the structure itself is sheathed in polished metallic facing, with windows – or, rather, thin angular slits – that trace geometric patterns on the exterior. There's no front door and entry is through an underground tunnel connected to the **Kollegienhaus** – the Baroque building next door that serves as an annexe to the museum and is used for temporary exhibitions.

The **interior** is just as unusual, manifesting Libeskind's ideas about symbolic architecture, while retaining a sculptural symmetry: a "void" – an empty and inaccessible diagonal shaft – cuts through the structure, while three long intersecting corridors, each representing an element of Jewish experience, divide the space at **basement** level. At the foot of the basement stairs the "axis of exile" leads outside to a garden of pillars; the "axis of the Holocaust" crosses it, connecting with the Holocaust Tower, dimly lit and, again, completely empty; and the "axis of continuity" follows, leading to a trudge up several flights of stairs to the permanent exhibition space. Part way up the stairs, the first floor contains the **Memory Void**, an eerie space filled with the sounds of clanking as visitors walk across a space scattered with piles of thousands of grimacing iron masks; a powerful reminder of the Holocaust.

The **permanent exhibition** begins on the top floor and focuses, in a broadly chronological way, on pre-1900 German-Jewish history before moving to the second floor to deal with the painful twentieth century, and ending with the present day.

■ NIGHTLIFE

Bar Nou	8
Golgatha	9
Gretchen	2
Junction Bar	5
Melitta Sundström	7
SchwuZ	6
Serene Bar	10
Solar	1
Yorckschlösschen	4
Zyankali Bar	3

● EATING AND DRINKING

Altes Zollhaus	2
Austria	14
Bar Centrale	5
Barcomi's	13
Café Atlantic	8
Curry 36	4
E.T.A Hoffmann	6
Golgotha	15
Knofi	9, 12
Molinari & Ko	7
Mustafas	3
Pagode	11
Sale e Tabacci	
Tomasa	10

● SHOPPING

Anagramm	4
Another country	7
Ararat	8
Barcomi's	10
Colours	6
Grober Unfug	5
Luccico	9
Mad Flavor	3
Radio Art	2
Space Hall	5
Weinkeller	1

■ ACCOMMODATION

Aletto Jugendhotel	3
Angleterre Hotel	1
Hotel Am Anhalter Bahnhof	2
Hotel Transit	5
Riehmers Hofgarten	4

WESTERN KREUZBERG

Berlinische Galerie

Alte Jakobstr. 124–128 • Wed–Mon 10am–6pm • €8, €4 on 1st Mon of the month; free audio guides in German only • ☎ 030 78 90 26 00, ⓦ berlinischegalerie.de • U-Hallesches Tor

Behind the Jüdisches Museum lie the vast airy halls of a former warehouse that have been renovated to house the **Berlinische Galerie**. Some of Berlin's darkest and most tortured pieces of art are displayed here as part of a permanent collection, mostly dating from the twentieth century, when movements such as Secessionism, Dadaism and the New Objectivity called Berlin home. All challenged the accepted art world and the establishment, and reflected Europe's troubled times; consequently much of the collection is unsettling. Pieces to look for include the beautifully crafted *Berlin Street Scene* (1889) by Lesser Ury, which evokes a moody Prussian majesty in the driving night rain. Disharmony is even more central to George Grosz's *Da um* (1920) which depicts the clash between soft tradition and harsh modernity using his own union with his (much younger) wife as the metaphor. Awkward contrasts are also the subject of Otto Dix's *Kartenspieler* (Card Players, 1920). Traumatized by World War I, Dix used dry-point technique to produce ghastly caricatures of mutilated war veterans playing cards. His portrait of *Der Dichter Iwar von Lücken* (1920), showing a bedraggled poet looking unsure and lost, is equally celebrated and often seen as a social comment on the state of post-World War I Germany. A very different side to 1920s Berlin is depicted in around twenty portraits by local photographers, in which androgynous women puff on cigarettes, evoking the milieu from which Marlene Dietrich rose to fame. Werner Heldt's *Parade of the Zeros* (1935) perhaps best sums up the 1930s. Here an immense crowd of zeros are squeezed between the buildings of a big city, threatening to become a destructive and unstoppable flood.

The Berlinische collection also gives fleeting insights into postwar Berlin, though its art becomes increasingly symbolic and impenetrable. The seven gigantic avant-garde structures of Emilio Vedova's *Absurd Berlin Diary '64* recall something of West Berlin's tensions, but by the time you've moved on to the vivid oil-paint-smeared canvases by artists like Hartwig Ebersbach, the works' messages become unclear.

Checkpoint Charlie

Friedrichstr. 43–45 • U-Kochstrasse

One of the most famous names associated with the Wall and Cold War-era Berlin, the Allied military post known as **Checkpoint Charlie** marked the border between East and West Berlin and was the main gateway between the two Berlins for most non-Germans. With its dramatic "YOU ARE NOW LEAVING THE AMERICAN SECTOR" signs and unsmiling border guards, it became the archetypal movie-style Iron Curtain crossing. In the Cold War years it was the scene of repeated border incidents, including a standoff between American and Soviet forces in October 1961, which culminated in tanks from both sides growling at each other for a few days.

The site of the border crossing itself is barely recognizable now. Removed in July 1990, the original border post is in the Allied Museum (see p.162), and a **replica** now marks the original site. Around it modern offices and retail complexes have sprung up, and the derelict plots of land that surrounded the site – peopled for years by hawkers of GDR-era merchandise and souvenir bits of Wall – have been encircled by barriers, awaiting construction projects. One barrier on Zimmerstrasse, diagonally across from the Mauermuseum (see p.119), features an interesting exhibition on the Berlin Wall.

Mauermuseum

Friedrichstr. 43–45 • Daily 9am–10pm • €12.50 • ⓦ mauermuseum.de • U-Kochstrasse

For tangible evidence of the trauma of the Wall, head for the **Mauermuseum** (Wall Museum). Here you can see photos of escape tunnels and some of the home-made aircraft and converted cars by which people attempted, succeeded, and sometimes tragically failed, to break through the border. Films document the stories of some of the 230-odd people murdered by the East German border guards, and there's a section on human rights behind the Iron Curtain, but it's a jumbled, huge and rambling collection, and not quite the harrowing experience that some visitors expect. Related exhibits focus on the concept of freedom and non-violent protest in general, including the Charter 77 typewriter and Mahatma Gandhi's diary.

Dalí - The Exhibition at Potsdamer Platz
Leipziger Platz 7 • Mon – Sat noon–8pm, Sun 10am–8pm • €11 • ☎ 0700 32 54 23 75 46, ⓦ daliberlin.de • U- & S-Potsdamer Platz

Though Salvador Dalí had no real links with Germany or Berlin, **Dalí – The Exhibition at Potsdamer Platz** is among the world's best exhibitions of the surrealist maestro's work. On view are more than four hundred eccentric pieces by the versatile Catalan, including paintings, sketches, books, films, sculptures, coins and even 3D installations.

Museum für Kommunikation
Leipziger Str. 16 • Tues 9am–8pm, Wed–Fri 9am–5pm, Sat & Sun 10am–6pm • €4 • ⓦ museumsstiftung.de • U-Mohrenstrasse

On the high-rise-lined arterial road of Leipziger Strasse, a block west of its junction with Friedrichstrasse, lies the former Imperial postal ministry, now home to the **Museum für Kommunikation**. The museum traces its roots back to the world's first postal museum, which opened in Berlin in 1872 and moved into this Baroque palace to share space with the postal ministry in 1898. When the building was damaged in the war the collection was dispersed, and only after reunification and several years of renovation did it reopen in its historic home in 2000. There's a lot more here than just stamps; highlights include early examples of wax seals, postcards and stamps (such as the famous Blue Mauritius), telephones, radios, film, telegraphs and computers. Much

---

THE UPRISING OF JUNE 1953

On June 16 and 17, 1953, Leipziger Strasse was the focal point of a **nationwide uprising** against the GDR's communist government. General dissatisfaction with economic and political conditions in eastern Berlin came to a head when building workers (the traditional proletarian heroes of GDR mythology) went on strike, protesting against longer hours for the same pay. The first to protest were workers from the prestigious Stalinallee project, who downed tools to march on the city centre, joined by other workers and passers-by. At Strausberger Platz they swept aside Volkspolizei units and headed for Unter den Linden. From here, the now roughly eight thousand-strong **demonstration** marched to the Haus der Ministerien – then the seat of the GDR government. Here they demanded to speak to GDR President Otto Grotewohl and SED General Secretary Walter Ulbricht. Eventually three lesser ministers were sent out to speak to the demonstrators. Clearly alarmed at the scale of the demonstration, they promised to try and get the work hours decreased. But by now the crowd wanted more, and began calling for political freedom. After declaring a **general strike** for the next day, the protesters returned to Stalinallee, tearing down SED placards on the way. Grotewohl's announcement rescinding the new working conditions later that day failed to halt the strike, news of which had been broadcast across the GDR by Western radio stations. About 300,000 workers in 250 towns joined in, and East Berlin came to a standstill as a crowd of 100,000 people marched towards the House of Ministries once again. Clashes with the police followed as demonstrators attacked SED party offices and state food stores. The GDR authorities proved unequal to the situation, leading the city's Soviet military commandant to declared a state of emergency. When **Soviet tanks** appeared on Leipziger Strasse, they found their route blocked by a vast crowd that refused to budge. After loudspeaker warnings that martial law had been declared, the first shots rang out, leaving youths to confront the T-34s with bricks and bottles. **Street fighting** raged throughout East Berlin for the rest of the day, and it wasn't until nightfall that the Soviets reasserted control. At least 267 demonstrators, 116 policemen and 18 Soviet soldiers were killed, and some 92 civilians (including a West Berliner just passing through) were summarily shot after the **suppression of the uprising**. Some 14 death sentences and innumerable prison terms followed, and 18 Soviet soldiers were executed for "moral capitulation to the demonstrators".

is displayed with kids in mind, though not the frequently excellent temporary exhibitions of cutting-edge contemporary art.

Former Luftfahrtministerium

The city block west of the Museum für Kommunikation is marked out by Hermann Göring's fortress-like **Luftfahrtministerium** (air ministry), a rare relic of the Nazi past that has survived very much intact and once formed the southern end of the former Third Reich government quarter along Wilhelmstrasse (see p.40). Göring promised Berliners that not a single bomb would fall on the city during the war; if this were to happen, the Reichsmarschal said, he would change his name to Meyer – a common Jewish surname. Ironically, the air ministry was one of the few buildings to emerge more or less unscathed from the bombing and Red Army shelling. After the establishment of the GDR it became the SED regime's **Haus der Ministerien** (House of Ministries), and was the target of a mass demonstration on June 16, 1953 (see box, p.120), which was to be a prelude for a general but short-lived uprising against the communist government the next day. There's a historical irony of sorts in the fact that the building became, for a number of years after reunification, the headquarters of the Treuhandanstalt, the agency responsible for the privatization of the former GDR's economy. It has been tidied up again and now houses the Federal Finance Ministry.

Topography of Terror

Niederkirchnerstr. 7 • Daily 10am–8pm (outside areas until dusk) • Free • ☎ 030 25 45 09 50, ⓦ topographie.de • S- & U-Potsdamer Platz

Lurking behind central Berlin's most substantial but dilapidated stretch of Wall is a city block that between 1933 and 1945 headquartered the Reich security services, including the Gestapo and SS. Some ruined foundations remain, but the flawlessly sleek and silvery piece of memorial-chic architecture in the middle houses the **Topography of Terror**, Germany's most significant museum on the perpetrators of Nazi terror. Inside, this dreadful history is retold on numerous information panels (in both English and German) which include many reproduced black-and-white photos of Nazis and their forlorn victims at a range of miserable events – book burnings, public humiliations, the destruction of Jewish property and synagogues, the rounding-up of Jews and others to be murdered in concentration camps. It's all sadly familiar, but what many don't realize, and the exhibition goes out of its way to show, is that many of the perpetrators were never brought to justice. One exception was senior SS-man Adolf Eichmann, whose life story is extensively retold here, from his role in the Holocaust to his subsequent capture in Argentina in 1960 to his trial and hanging in Israel.

Meanwhile, in the Reich Security ruins outside, more info panels provide a potted history of the Third Reich in Berlin and reveal gruesome insights: the ground beneath the exhibition once held the cellars where prisoners were interrogated and tortured.

Martin-Gropius-Bau

Niederkirchnerstr. 7 • Wed–Mon 10am–7pm • Prices vary; around €10 • ☎ 030 25 48 60, ⓦ gropiusbau.de • S- & U-Potsdamer Platz

The magnificently restored building beside the Topography of Terror is the **Martin-Gropius-Bau**, designed in 1877 by Martin Gropius, a pupil of Schinkel and the uncle of Bauhaus guru Walter (see p.102). Until its destruction in the war the Gropius-Bau was home of a museum of applied art, but rebuilt and refurbished, it now houses changing exhibitions of art, photography and architecture.

Anhalter Bahnhof

The **Anhalter Bahnhof**, on Stresemannstrasse, is a sad reminder of a misguided civic act that some would term vandalism. Completed in 1870, this train station was once one of Europe's greatest, forming Berlin's gateway to the south. During the Holocaust it was one of the three stations used to deport Jews to Theresienstadt (or Terezín), and from there to the death camps. Nearly ten thousand Jews were deported from here, usually in groups of fifty to a hundred; the last train left on March 27, 1945. The station received only mild damage during World War II, which left it roofless but otherwise mostly intact. Despite attempts to preserve it, it was blown up in 1952 – someone had put in a good offer for the bricks. Now just a fragment of the facade stands, hinting at past glories. The patch of land that the station once covered is today a park, and includes the **Tempodrom**, a tent-shaped arts venue.

Gruselkabinett

Schöneberger Str. 23a • Mon 10am–3pm, Tues, Thurs, Fri & Sun 10am–7pm, Sat noon–8pm • €9.50 • W gruselkabinett-berlin.de • S-Anhalter Bahnhof

One of a handful of Nazi buildings left in the city, the blunt and featureless former bunker just southwest of the old Anhalter Bahnhof was built during the war by the Reichsbahn for travellers using Anhalter Bahnhof. Now it contains the **Gruselkabinett**, an amateurish "chamber of horrors", which is a strange mix of historical and playful. The most interesting section is given over to the bunker itself, with a few artefacts found here and in Hitler's bunker (see p.39) and recordings of Allied bombings.

Deutsches Technikmuseum Berlin

Trebbiner Str. 9 • Tues–Fri 9am–5.30pm, Sat & Sun 10am–6pm • €6 • W sdtb.de • U-Möckernbrücke

Opened in 1982 in the former goods depot of the Anhalter Bahnhof, the **Deutsches Technikmuseum Berlin** presents a comprehensive – some might say overwhelming – overview of technology created in Germany. The vast collection includes trains and planes, as well as computers, radios, cameras and more. There's a strong emphasis on rail, with trains from 1835 to the present day, but there are also maritime and aviation halls and exhibits on technology from the industrial revolution to the computer and space age, and on the development of the pharmaceutical and chemical industry and its impact on everyday life. A new exhibition on the history of mobility is housed in the annexe on Ladestrasse. Though much of the museum is based on viewing life-sized reproductions and actual machines, the **Science Center Spectrum annexe** at Möckernstrasse 26 is dedicated to interactive exhibits.

Bergmannstrasse and around

At the end of the nineteenth century, many buildings around Bergmannstrasse housed working-class families and survived the war to be painstakingly restored in what was West Berlin. The area is now thoroughly gentrified, though with a laid-back bohemian feel, and it's certainly a pleasant place to live. Bergmannstrasse is lined with cafés, bistros and *Trödelläden* (junk and antique shops), and boasts the **Marheineke Markthalle**, a good indoor food market.

Chamissoplatz, just south of Bergmannstrasse, is worth a look for its well-preserved, balconied nineteenth-century houses and, a block south, its water tower. The square also boasts one of Berlin's few remaining Wilhelmine *pissoirs* – ornate public toilets, characteristically dark green in colour, erected in an early attempt at sanitation. This one has been recently renovated, and is open to the public (men only).

Viktoriapark

At its western end Bergmannstrasse crosses the broad thoroughfare of Mehringdamm to become Kreuzbergstrasse. On this street lies **Viktoriapark** (the "Kreuzberg", as it's popularly known), which, draped across the slopes of a hill, is one of the city's most likeable parks, a relaxed ramble of trees and green space run through by a pretty brook. Here you'll find the *Golgotha Café* and disco (see p.196), packed with summer evenings; Germany's northernmost vineyard; and, atop the hill, the **Cross** (more a Neoclassical spire) from which Kreuzberg gets its name, designed by Schinkel to commemorate the Napoleonic Wars. The view is good, too.

FROM TOP THE SOVIET MEMORIAL (P.128); TOPOGRAPHY OF TERROR (P.121) >

Tempelhof Airport

A five-minute walk south along Mehringdamm from its intersection with Bergmannstrasse, housing fades away to the flatlands of **Tempelhof Airport** (U-Bahn Platz der Luftbrücke). The airport, opened in 1923, was once Germany's largest; the present complex was built in 1936–41 and is one of the best surviving examples of Nazi architecture. A huge bronze eagle that surmounted the building was removed in the 1960s, ostensibly to make way for a radar installation (the eagle's head can still be seen at the entrance to the airport), but you can't help thinking that its removal probably had more to do with its being an ugly reminder of the Nazi past. After the war the airport was used for visiting dignitaries and the military, and a light load of small carrier flights, until it finally closed in 2008. The old terminal buildings now serve as events venues, while the runways themselves have been turned into what is technically continental Europe's largest park (daily 6am–9.30pm) – a great place to go cycling, walking or roller-skating – or simply to have a barbecue or picnic.

It was to Tempelhof that the Allies flew supplies to beat the **Berlin Blockade** of 1948–49 (see box, p.124) and the **Luftbrückendenkmal**, a memorial in the centre of the **Platz der Luftbrücke** that forms the entrance to the airport, commemorates the airmen and crew who died in crashes. The memorial represents the three air corridors used, and forms half of a bridge: the other half, "joined by air", is in Frankfurt. Inside the airport a small exhibition shows photographs of its building and the Blockade – mostly publicity shots of gleaming USAF pilots and scruffy kids, with little on the role of Tempelhof in the war years.

THE BERLIN BLOCKADE (1948–49)

The **Berlin Blockade** was the result of an escalation in tensions between East and West in the late 1940s. These came to a head when the Western zone introduced the Deutschmark as currency in June 1948; the Soviets demanded that their own Ostmark be accepted as Berlin's currency, a move that was rejected by the city's parliament. Moscow's answer to this was an attempt to bring West Berlin to its knees by severing all road and rail links to the Western zones and cutting off the power provided by plants on the Eastern side. There was now only one month's food and ten days' coal supply left in the city.

The British and Americans realized that they had to support West Berlin, but were unwilling to use military force to push their way in overland. After some consideration it was decided to try and supply the city by air: the Soviets, it was gambled, would not dare risk an international incident – possibly even war – by shooting down Western aircraft. However, there were serious doubts as to whether it was possible to sustain two million people by an airlift. The only previous attempt on a comparable scale – maintaining the German Sixth Army at Stalingrad – had been an utter failure. Berlin's needs were calculated at 4000 tons of supplies per day, yet the available aircraft could carry fewer than 500 tons.

Nevertheless the airlift began on June 26, 1948 and at its height nine months later, it had become an around-the-clock precision operation with planes landing or taking off every thirty seconds, bringing 8000 tons of supplies to the city each day. Winter was exceptionally tough. Power cuts and severe food rationing reduced living standards to the level of the immediate postwar period. The Russians made supplies available in the eastern half of the city, but relatively few West Berliners – in a spirited show of defiance – chose to take advantage of them.

The Soviets called off the Blockade in May 1949, but they had been defeated in more ways than one. Though it cost the lives of 78 airmen and crew and millions of dollars, the airlift thwarted Stalin's attempt to expel the Allies from West Berlin. Moreover for the occupying British and Americans the propaganda value was enormous: aircrews who a few years previously had been dropping bombs on the city now provided its lifeline. Photographs of the "candy bomber" – a USAF captain who dropped chocolate bars and sweets from his plane on small parachutes for the city's children – went around the world. No longer were the occupiers seen as enemies, but rather as allies against the Soviet threat.

Eastern Kreuzberg

During the war **eastern Kreuzberg** was one of the few areas to avoid total destruction, and among the quickest to revive in the 1950s. When the Wall was built in 1961, things changed: with the neighbourhood severed from its natural hinterland in the East, families moved out, houses were boarded up and it started dying. But at the same time, by providing Berlin's cheapest rents it attracted waves of **immigrant workers** from southern Europe – particularly Turkey – who brought their families and customs. Here too, came the radicals, students and dropouts of the 1968 generation – coming to Berlin because of its national service loophole, and to Kreuzberg for its vast number of abandoned buildings in which to **squat**. It was here that the youth of the Federal Republic came to get involved in alternative politics, making it the place to hang out and hit raucous and avant-garde nightspots. Until the Wall came down, to say you lived in Kreuzberg was something of a left-wing and anti-establishment statement. Since then the atmosphere has become more apolitical – even if the annual May Day demonstration still traditionally turns into a riot between police and anarchists, extreme-leftists and anti-capitalists. Meanwhile, Turks and other immigrants still thrive and gentrification gradually takes hold.

Eastern Kreuzberg's three "underground" stops (whose tracks actually run on elevated tracks in these parts) provide focal points. U-Bahn **Kottbusser Tor** leads to the most overtly Turkish area, with a smattering of alternative businesses and several clubs. U-Bahn **Görlitzer Bahnhof** is much more the hub for "alternative" Kreuzberg. It lies between **Wiener Strasse** and its northwestern continuation Oranienstrasse, which together form eastern Kreuzberg's bohemian main drag, lined with restaurants, bike shops, café-bars, galleries and alternative boutiques. The next stop east is U-Bahn **Schlesisches Tor**, which leads to an area known as the **Wrangelkiez**, Kreuzberg's newest eating and nightlife district. This neighbourhood remains extremely gritty and doesn't generally invite relaxed exploration – muggings regularly occur in **Görlitzer Park** at its centre, the haunt of itinerant punks and drug pushers. U-Bahn Schlesisches Tor is also a handy place to get a bus to the **Soviet Memorial** in **Treptower Park**.

Kottbusser Tor

Catching U-Bahn line #1 (unkindly nicknamed the "Istanbul Express" along this stretch) to **Kottbusser Tor** is a good introduction to eastern Kreuzberg. The intersection around the U-Bahn has its own special feel – think Istanbul market in an eastern-bloc housing development – and the area around the station is a scruffy, earthy shambles of Turkish street vendors and cafés, the air filled with the aromas of southeast European cooking. Things are at their liveliest on Tuesday and Friday afternoons at the colourful oriental **food market**, a ten-minute walk south along Kottbusser Strasse – over the

---

BERLIN'S BLIGHT OR BOUNTY?

Ever since the Wall provided the world's most famous canvas for **graffiti**, this form of self-expression has thrived in Berlin, with artists from all over Europe and North America joining the hundreds of local sprayers. It's everywhere – as the S-Bahn ride through central Berlin reveals – but the greatest concentrations are in central, lower-rent neighbourhoods where older tenements have survived. Kreuzberg is particularly well smothered, with thousands of tags and the occasional more complex piece on every accessible piece of wall – and a few near-inaccessible spots too.

A form of art and a sign of a vibrant youth culture, perhaps, but certainly all this daubing costs Berlin around €8m per year to fix, triggering numerous campaigns against it, with some even involving nocturnal helicopter missions with infra-red cameras. Polls suggest at least two-thirds of Berliners hate graffiti, but there are signs too that it's becoming part of the city's identity.

Alternative Berlin See p.25. Tours of the more worthwhile pieces in the Spandauer Vorstadt and Kreuzberg; they even offer workshops where you can learn the ropes and get directions to free legal walls.

Overkill Köpenicker Str. 195 ☏030 69 50 61 26, ⓦoverkillshop.com; U-Bahn Schlesisches Tor. The professionalism and impressive array of spray cans for sale makes it hard to believe the activity is mostly illegal.

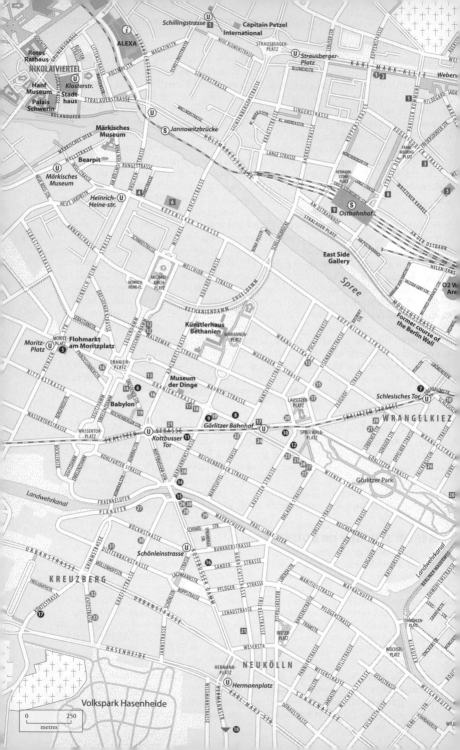

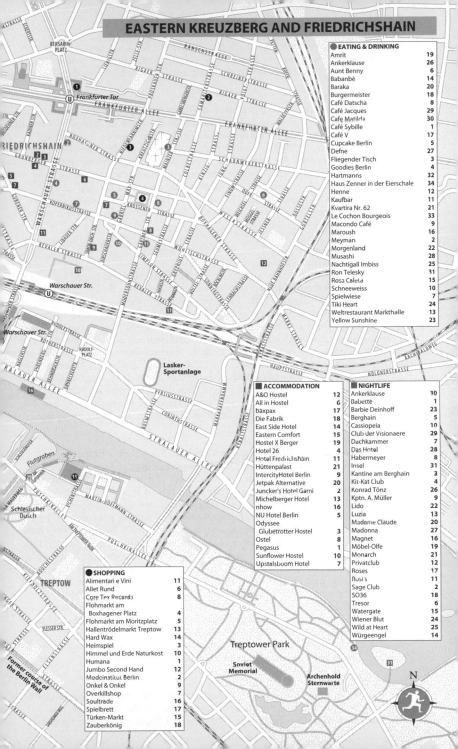

EASTERN KREUZBERG AND FRIEDRICHSHAIN

Landwehrkanal and left down Maybachufer. From here, the walk east along the leafy canal at the southern edge of the district passes along Berlin's most attractive stretches of water through a residential district: more reminiscent of Amsterdam than Berlin.

Museum der Dinge

Oranienstr. 25 • Mon & Fri–Sun noon–7pm • €4 • ☎ 030 92 10 63 11, ⓦ museumderdinge.de • U-Kottbusser Tor

Despite its nebulous mission, the **Museum der Dinge** (Museum of Things) successfully presents an interesting array of mostly everyday items. Housewares, furniture and knick-knacks and much more, from the nineteenth century to the present day, range from Manoli ashtrays and Art Deco fondue sets to World War II memorabilia. It's a design-fiend's dream, exhibited in a modern, well-organized space on the top floor of an apartment block. A star attraction is the modular "Frankfurt Kitchen" designed by Viennese architect Margarete Schütte-Lihotzky in 1926 – the forerunner of today's fitted kitchen. The exhibition text is in German, but a brochure in English is available.

7 Treptower Park

S-Bahn Treptower Park, or bus #265 from Schlesisches Tor

Now chiefly of interest for its large and sobering **Soviet Memorial** to troops killed in the Battle of Berlin, **Treptower Park** was originally built as a park for Berlin's nineteenth-century tenement-dwellers. By 1908 it had more than thirty dance halls and restaurants; later, during the interwar years, it became a well-known assembly point for revolutionary workers about to embark on demonstrations or go off to do battle with the Brownshirts.

Until the *Wende* most park visitors were either East Berliners out for a day at **Spreepark**, a GDR-era amusement park, or Soviet citizens arriving by the busload to pay their respects at the memorial. But since the 1990s increasing numbers of former West Berliners have discovered the place, and it has become a popular Sunday destination for the space-starved inhabitants of Neukölln and Kreuzberg. The pleasant harbour area close to the Treptower Park S-Bahn station is one attraction, but the main hub of activity is now on and around the Insel der Jugend, further south along the Spree.

The Soviet Memorial

At the heart of Treptower Park, the **Soviet Memorial** (Sowjetisches Ehrenmal) commemorates the Soviet Union's 305,000 estimated casualties during the Battle of Berlin in April and May 1945 and is the burial place of five thousand of them. It's best approached from the arched entrance on the south side of Puschkinallee. A little way to the south of here is a sculpture of a grieving woman representing the Motherland, to the left of which a broad concourse slopes up towards a viewing point flanked by two vast triangles of red granite, fashioned from stone bought from Sweden by the Nazis to furnish Berlin with projected victory monuments. From the viewing point, a long sunken park of mass graves of the Red Army troops is lined by sculpted frescoes of stylized scenes from the Great Patriotic War and quotes from Stalin with German translations. These lead the way to the centrepiece: a vast symbolic statue and typical piece of Soviet gigantism, built using marble from Hitler's Chancellery. More than 11m high, and set on top of a hill modelled on a *kurgan* or traditional warriors' grave of the Don region, it shows an idealized Russian soldier clutching a saved child and resting his sword on a shattered swastika. Inside the plinth is a memorial crypt with a mosaic in true Socialist Realist style, showing Soviet citizens (soldiers, mother, worker, peasant and what looks like an old-age pensioner) honouring the dead.

The rest of the park

The rest of the park conceals a couple of low-key attractions, including the **Karpfenteich**, a large carp pool just south of the memorial, and, a little to the east of here, the **Archenhold Sternwarte** (Alt-Treptow 1; Wed–Sun 2–4.30pm; tours Thurs 8pm, Sat &

Sun 3pm; museum €2.50, tours €4; ☎030 536 06 37 19, ⓦsdtb.de), an observatory with the longest refracting telescope in the world. Check the website for stargazing sessions. The park continues north of Puschkinallee, where you'll also find *Haus Zenner* (see p.200), a riverside *Gaststätte* whose origins go back to the eighteenth century.

East of here is the **Insel der Jugend**, a small island in the Spree reached via the **Abteibrücke**, an ornamental footbridge built by French prisoners of war in 1916 to link the island to the mainland. The end of Treptow's summer festival is marked by a firework display from this bridge, an event known as **Treptow in Flammen** or "Treptow in Flames". The island was originally the location of an abbey, but now the main attraction is the venue *Die Insel* (see p.214).

Returning across the bridge, you can walk northwest back to the S-Bahn station via a grass-lined boardwalk – rowing boat and paddleboat rental are available nearby (from €8/hr). At the northern tip of the boardwalk, you'll find a very tasty *Imbiss* stand serving fresh smoked fish. Southeast from the bridge lies the closed **Spreepark**, a popular GDR amusement park that awaits reinvestment. Until then the surrounding **Plänterwald** woods, which cover a couple of square kilometres, are the main draw. Just to the southwest of Neue Krug is the *Plänterwald*, a largish *Gaststätte* that makes a good stop-off. You can also take a cruise around the surrounding waterways (see p.25).

Neukölln

Much like Eastern Kreuzberg, **Neukölln** is a district dominated by Turkish-Germans and other immigrants; walking along its arterial roads **Karl-Marx-Strasse** and **Sonnenallee**, between budget department stores and Middle Eastern greengrocers, it's not hard to imagine yourself in the Istanbul suburbs. But as rents rise in Kreuzberg, the district has become the new frontier for hip young bargain-seekers, particularly along the leafy roads beside the Landwehrkanal and by Volkspark Hasenheide four blocks south. Here shabby-chic bars and associated businesses are taking hold, but besides these, and the occasional good budget ethnic restaurant, there's not much to draw visitors. The only sight as such, if you're on the look-out

---

BERLIN'S GROWING PAINS

"Yuppie scum" shouts graffiti on Weserstrasse, the Neukölln back-street near U-Bahn Hermannplatz that in 2011 was labelled "the epicentre of cool" by London's *The Guardian* newspaper. Both descriptions illustrate larger trends: as Berlin becomes a world city, **gentrification** – and the attendant legions of young, footloose foreigners – is sweeping aside many long-time incumbents while creeping from district to district.

By and large the decade-old process has been relatively smooth, but in 2011 some six thousand people took to Neukölln's streets to march against soaring rents. In the same year **Lunapark**, a large anti-capitalist festival, was organized in the Spreepark (see above) to protest against the city's increasing internationalization. While presenting a coherent argument about how the onslaught of soulless corporate venues and projects across the city is robbing it of the very ramshackle cultural landscape that makes it great, the festival also called for a tourist tax and gently ridiculed tourists themselves: one popular attraction was to have a picture taken while pretending to be a tourist at Checkpoint Charlie.

But gentrification has its own fairly inescapable logic and momentum. It's unlikely that any of the Neukölln bars displaying "no tourists or hipsters" signs in their windows can stop change, but just as inevitable was the fact that the young people who took over the Prenzlauer Berg of the 1990s grew wealthier, had kids, changed their priorities and became part of the establishment they had once eschewed.

Attacks and unpleasantness against new waves of young would-be creative types are sure to continue, which is why **Hipster Antifa Neukölln** (ⓦhipster-antifa.com) has won so much international attention. They aim to fight xenophobia in the city under the slogan: "Tourists, Hipsters, everybody is welcome – party like it's 1945!"

for somewhere to swim or sweat, is the glorious 1914 swimming bath and sauna complex **Stadtbad Neukölln** (see p.234).

Friedrichshain

East of the Spree from Kreuzberg, the former East Berlin borough of **Friedrichshain** is overwhelmingly residential. Comprehensively destroyed during the war, it lost more than two thirds of its buildings – as much as any Berlin district – and today is virtually all of GDR vintage, offering very little real sightseeing. However, the neighbourhood is a real nightlife hotspot, with dozens of bars clustered on **Simon-Dach-Strasse** and various clubs inhabiting old industrial buildings on its fringes.

The district gathers around two major arterial roads: Warschauer Strasse, which forms the link to Kreuzberg and East Side Gallery, Berlin's longest surviving stretch of Wall; and the grand **Karl-Marx-Allee**, connecting to Alexanderplatz and Mitte. Forming Friedrichshain's northwestern boundary is **Volkspark Friedrichshain**, one of the eastern city's oldest and nicest parks; it's best accessed from Prenzlauer Berg (see p.133).

East Side Gallery

Trailing the banks of the River Spree on the southern edge of Friedrichshain, a 1.3km surviving stretch of Berlin Wall is known as the **East Side Gallery** for its collection of political and satirical murals. Originally painted just after the Wall fell they resonate with the attitude and aesthetics of the time: some are imaginative, some trite and some impenetrable, but one of the most telling shows Brezhnev and Honecker locked in a passionate kiss, with the inscription, "God, help me survive this deadly love". Given their outdoor and exposed nature, all the paintings are steadily decaying; original artists have been invited back to repaint their works a couple of times, most recently to mark the twentieth anniversary of the fall of the Wall in 2009. In 2012 the removal and auctioning-off of portions of the Wall – to enable the building of a luxury block of flats – sparked outrage and protests, and for now the survival of the remaining sections seems assured. Behind the gallery, look out for the landmark **Oberbaumbrücke**, a neo-Gothic double-decker bridge that dates back to 1896 and leads over to Kreuzberg.

Warschauer Strasse and around

At the southeastern end of the East Side Gallery, **Warschauer Strasse** climbs up to cross railway tracks and become Friedrichshain's main cross street. It's fairly dull, so tram #M10 is a welcome way to speed your journey – better still to peel off at the first opportunity down Revaler Strasse where graffiti paves the way to **Cassiopeia**, a medley of skate park, climbing wall, cinema, beer garden and club that started as a squat. Opposite lies the **Simon-Dach-Strasse**, at first glance an ordinary tree-lined residential street, but also the hub of the local nightlife scene with good cafés, restaurants and bars, many with outdoor seating. At its northern end Simon-Dach-Strasse joins Boxhagener Strasse: a block to the right lies the leafy **Boxhagener Platz**, which bustles with a fleamarket on Sundays.

Karl-Marx-Allee

A vast boulevard lined with 1.5km of model 1950s and 1960s communist housing developments, **Karl-Marx-Allee** (or Stalinallee, as it was known in the 1950s) is a mixed bag. On the one hand its inhuman scale makes it hard to explore on foot and, while traffic thunders up and down the road it is devoid of buses and trams, so businesses struggle, which gives the place a bit of an eerie and empty feel. Nevertheless the monumentalist *Zuckerbäckerstil* (wedding-cake style) buildings are architecturally impressive, and their apartments among the Eastern Bloc's finest. The best way to explore is to walk (or bike) the 1km from U-Bahn Frankfurter Tor to Strausberger Platz, taking a break at **Café Sybille** at Karl-Marx-Allee 72 (see p.200), which has a good little exhibition on the history of the Stalinallee.

Prenzlauer Berg and around

Northeast of Mitte, the former East Berlin borough of Prenzlauer Berg was originally a densely populated working-class district. It was fought over street-by-street during the war, which meant that many of its hallmark turn-of-the-twentieth-century tenement blocks survived, along with its leafy cobbled streets. In the GDR days, this was a uniquely vibrant and exciting corner of East Berlin, home to artists and young people seeking an alternative lifestyle, choosing to live on the edge of established East German society (quite literally – the district's western boundary was marked by the Wall). After the *Wende*, the venerable atmosphere, central location and low rents quickly made this a lively and fashionable district. This ambience has faded a little as the first wave of migrants has aged: today health-food stores proliferate, as do young children, equipped with fair-trade garments and wooden toys.

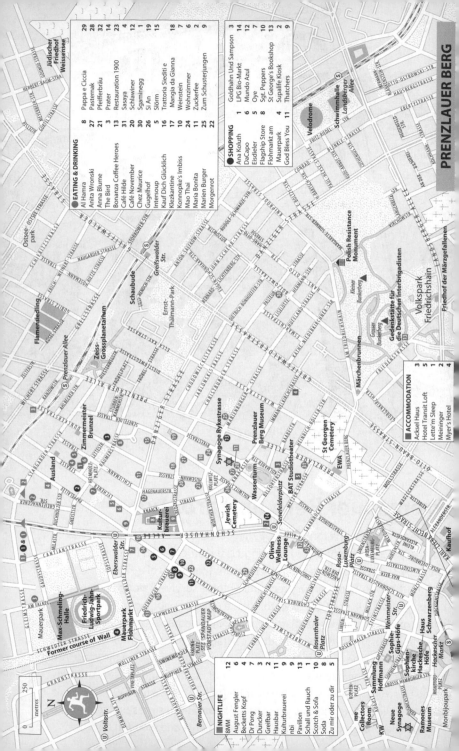

PRENZLAUER BERG

● EATING & DRINKING

Al Hamra	8	Pappa e Ciccia	29
Anita Wronski	27	Pasternak	28
Anna Blume	21	Pfeifferbräu	32
The Bird	3	Prater	14
Bonanza Coffee Heroes	13	Restauration 1900	23
Café Hilde	31	Sasaya	4
Café November	20	Schlawiner	12
Chez Maurice	30	Sgaminegg	1
Gugelhof	26	Si An	19
Intersoup	5	Slörm	15
Kauf Dich Glücklich	16	Trattoria Sieditè e	18
Klezkantine	17	Mangia da Gianna	7
Konnopke's Imbiss	10	Weinstein	6
Mao Thai	24	Wohnzimmer	2
Maria Bonita	11	Zuckerfee	9
Marien Burger	25	Zum Schusterjungen	
Morgenrot	22		

● SHOPPING

Ana Koluth	1	Goldhahn Und Sampson	3
DaCapo	6	LPG Bio-Markt	14
Eisdieler	7	Mundo Azul	12
Flagship Store	8	Oye	10
Flohmarkt am		Sgt. Peppers	13
Mauerpark	4	St George's Bookshop	13
God Bless You	11	Supalife Kiosk	9
		Thatchers	

■ ACCOMMODATION

Acksel Haus	3
Hotel Transit Loft	5
Lette'm Sleep	1
Meininger	2
Myer's Hotel	4

■ NIGHTLIFE

8MM	12
August Fengler	6
Becketts Kopf	4
Dr Pong	7
Duncker	3
Greifbar	11
Hausbar	9
Kulturbrauerei	1
nbi	13
Pavillon	10
Schall und Rauch	8
Scotch & Sofa	5
Soda	
Zu mir oder zu dir	

Prenzlauer Berg is strung out along several arterial roads that are well served by public transport from Alexanderplatz or Hackescher Markt. From Alexanderplatz, **Greifswalder Strasse** heads northeast, passing close to **Volkspark Friedrichshain**, one of the city's best parks and final resting place for victims of the 1848 revolution. From here you pass the bland, GDR-era **Ernst-Thälmann-Park**, behind which lurks the **Zeiss Planetarium** and the modest late-1920s model housing development, **Flamensiedlung**, before reaching the tidy middle-class district of **Weissensee**, where you'll find the city's largest **Jewish cemetery**. Another arterial road to the west, **Schönhauser Allee**, runs close to the former East–West border and is the main route to all the trendiest parts of Prenzlauer Berg. This is the place to explore on foot, taking in sights such as the **Kulturbrauerei** and **Kollwitzplatz**, which was once another important area for Jews, as a large nearby **cemetery** and still-functioning **synagogue** attest.

North of Prenzlauer Berg, the tidy bourgeois district of **Pankow**, once home to much of the GDR's elite, offers few significant sights. But as Berlin's northeasternmost borough before the city gives way to countryside, it has a sedate, almost village-like atmosphere and some pleasant parks, and makes for an hour or two's pleasant strolling.

GETTING AROUND

Public transport The quickest way to explore Prenzlauer Berg and around is by public transport from Alexanderplatz. Tram #M4 travels up Greifswalder Strasse to Weissensee; U-Bahn #2 heads to Senefelder Platz, which is an ideal place to start a walking tour. The same line continues up to U-Bahn Pankow, which lies a short walk from its main drag, Breite Strasse. Tram #M1 offers a good option for getting back to the centre, stopping at U-Bahn Eberswalder Strasse, the district's central hub, en route to Hackescher Markt via some of eastern Berlin's lesser-known back-streets.

8

Greifswalder Strasse and around

Greifswalder Strasse more or less forms the dividing line between Prenzlauer Berg and Friedrichshain. It still looks very neat with its freshly painted facades, and in pre-*Wende* days traffic came to a standstill along the side-streets a couple of times a day as a convoy of black Citroëns and Volvos sped by, whisking high-ranking government members (notably Erich Honecker himself) from the Palast der Republik (see p.54) to their homes in the lakeside town of Wandlitz north of Berlin. But behind the immaculate facades, the *Hinterhöfe* of Greifswalder Strasse were just as run-down as those in the back-streets.

Volkspark Friedrichshain

Just within the limits of the Friedrichshain district, **Volkspark Friedrichshain** is one of the city's oldest and largest parks. At the western entrance to the park is the **Märchenbrunnen** (Fairytale Fountain), a neo-Baroque arcade and fountain with statues of characters from Brothers Grimm stories. Intended as a gift to tenement-dwelling workers, it was put up in 1913 at the instigation of Social Democratic members of the city council, in direct contravention of the Kaiser's wishes. A few hundred metres southeast of the Märchenbrunnen stands the **Gedenkstätte für die Deutschen Interbrigadisten**, a monument to the German members of the International Brigades who fought against the fascists in Spain in the Spanish Civil War. Of the five thousand Germans (including many leading communists) who went to Spain, only two thousand returned.

There's another monument to the east of here (just off Landsberger Allee), this time to victims of an upheaval closer to home. The **Friedhof der Märzgefallenen** is where many of the 183 Berliners killed by the soldiers of King Friedrich Wilhelm IV during the revolution of March 1848 were buried, their interment attended by eighty thousand of their fellow citizens. Only a few of the original gravestones survive, but the dead of 1848 have been joined by 33 of those killed in the

November Revolution of 1918, commemorated by a statue of a *Rote Matrose* or "Red Sailor" at the cemetery entrance, reflecting the role played in the revolution by Imperial navy sailors.

The Bunkerbergs

The **Grosser Bunkerberg** and **Kleiner Bunkerberg** are two artificial hills created when a million cubic metres of rubble from bombed-out Berlin were dumped over the ruins of a flak gun and control tower respectively. In between the two is a small, tree-shaded lake, Sport und Erholungszentrum (sports centre), and giant outdoor chess sets. Set on a grassy slope a little to the east is a **Polish Resistance Monument** commemorating the joint fight of the Polish army and German resistance against the Nazis. Given the feelings most Germans and Poles had for each other, the sentiments expressed seem rather unconvincing.

St Georgen Cemetery

Opposite the westernmost corner of Volkspark Friedrichshain and on the other side of Greifswalder Strasse lies the **St Georgen cemetery**, a venerable and overgrown affair dating back to the early nineteenth century, with some elaborate tombstones and vaults. Many of the memorials bear shrapnel and bullet scars, an indication of just how intense the fighting during the Battle for Berlin must have been; even the city's graveyards were fought for inch by inch.

Ernst-Thälmann-Park and around

At the northeastern end of Greifswalder Strasse is the **Ernst-Thälmann-Park**, a prime example of former-GDR civic window-dressing. Here a model housing development is set in a small park fronted by a gigantic marble sculpture of the head and clenched fist of Ernst Thälmann, the pre-1933 communist leader who was imprisoned and later murdered by the Nazis. Floodlit and guarded around the clock by police in pre-*Wende* days, his likeness is now daubed with graffiti, and the concrete terrace on which it stands is favoured by local skateboarders. About four thousand people, mostly from the ex-GDR elite, live here in high-rise buildings with restaurants, shops, nurseries and a swimming pool all immediately at hand.

Zeiss-Grossplanetarium

Prenzlauer Allee 80 • Tues–Thurs 9am–noon & 2–4pm, Fri 9am–noon, 2–4pm & 4–9.30pm, Sat & Sun 2–9pm; show times vary – call or check online • €5 • ☎ 030 421 84 50, ⊛ sdtb.de • S-Bahn Prenzlauer Allee

A massive silver golf-ball set back from bustling Prenzlauer Allee, the **Zeiss-Grossplanetarium** was, when it was built in 1987, one of Europe's largest and most modern stellar theatres, with a giant silver dome measuring 23m across. Today its auditorium, with artificial projection of the starry skies into the roof, is host to entertaining and impressive astronomical, film and music programmes. The "Wonders of the Cosmos" astronomical show can be booked in advance in English or Russian.

Flamensiedlung

Northeast of Prenzlauer Allee's distinctive, yellow-brick 1890s S-Bahn station – one of the best-looking in the city – is the so-called **Flamensiedlung** (Flemish Colony), a model housing development built between Sültstrasse and Sodtkestrasse in 1929–30 according to plans by the architect Bruno Taut. With his associate Franz Hillinger, Taut wanted to create mass housing that broke away from the tenement-house concept. Basing their design on work already done in the Netherlands, they diffused the angularity of their apartment blocks with corner windows and balconies, and left open areas between them to create cheerful, bright back yards.

Zimmermeister Brunzel

Dunckerstr. 77 • Mon, Tues & Thurs–Sat 11am–4.30pm • €2 • ☎ 030 445 23 21, ⓦ ausstellung-dunckerstrasse.de • S-Prenzlauer Allee

Though it sits today on a leafy, very middle-class street, the apartment block of **Zimmermeister Brunzel** was once one of hundreds of *Mietskasernen*, or tenement flats, that sprouted in districts like Prenzlauer Berg to house workers in the 1890s. Virtually all followed standardized plans that were loosely based on the traditional Berlin courtyard layout of places like the *Hackesche Höfe* (see p.71). The smartest flats faced the street, while the dowdiest were tucked away on the top floors above the rear courtyard. All were pretty basic, with lavatories on the common landings. Much of this world was lost in the war and following generations of home improvements, but one apartment has been well preserved and reconstructed to help provide, along with Museum Pankow (see p.140), a rare social history of Berlin.

Inhabited until the 1990s, this particular flat had seen few renovations, making it an ideal candidate for restoration and careful furnishing to recreate the past. Short tours reveal a kitchen with an ice-powered fridge; a muted brown decor that minimized the impact of singeing from gas-powered lanterns; and a cupboard above the front door designed as a bedroom for the maid. Wall displays in German (some English translations are available) explain how, despite the basic conditions, such apartments denoted a certain social standing, with only master craftsmen and the like able to afford them. Less skilled workers slept in poor houses or became *Trockenwohner*, temporary tenants who rented digs in new damp new apartment blocks for the period they were considered too wet to be properly habitable.

Jüdischer Friedhof Weissensee

Herbert-Baum-Str. 45 • April–Oct Sun–Thurs 7.30am–5pm, Fri 7.30am–2.30pm; Nov–March Sun–Thurs 7.30am–4pm, Fri 7.30am–2.30pm; male visitors should keep their heads covered, skullcaps loaned free at the cemetery office, to the right of the entrance • U-Bahn Greifswalder Strasse or tram #M4 to Albertinenstr.

The **Jüdischer Friedhof Weissensee** lies at the end of Herbert-Baum-Strasse, ten minutes south of Berliner Allee. Opened in 1880, when the Schönhauser Allee cemetery had finally been filled, it became Europe's largest Jewish cemetery – its 115,600 graves spreading over the equivalent of 86 football pitches.

Immediately in front of the entrance, a poignant memorial "to our murdered brothers and sisters 1933–45" from Berlin's Jewish community takes the form of a circle of tablets bearing the names of all the large concentration camps.

Beyond here are the cemetery administration buildings (where information is available), with the cemetery itself stretching back from the entrance for about 1km: row upon row of headstones, with the occasional extravagant family monument including some Art Nouveau graves and mausoleums designed by Ludwig Mies van der Rohe and Walter Gropius (the grave of Albert Mendel). More moving are the four hundred urns containing the ashes of concentration camp victims (Lot G7), and the headstones on the hollow graves of those whose remains were never found or identified. A handful of well-tended postwar graves near the administration buildings are, paradoxically, symbols of survival – witness to the fact that a few thousand Berlin Jews did escape the Holocaust and that the city still has a small Jewish community (see pp.80–81).

Schönhauser Allee and around

From Senefelder Platz U-Bahn the uphill walk along **Schönhauser Allee** soon arrives at **Senefelderplatz**, previously known as Pfefferberg (Pepper Hill), but later renamed after the inventor of the lithographic process. A statue of Alois Senefelder stands on the square, with his name appearing on the base in mirror script, as though on a lithographic block. The name **Pfefferberg**, incidentally, is still in use, and applies to a former factory complex just below Senefelderplatz that features an arts centre and *Biergarten* (see p.202).

Jüdischer Friedhof

Schönhauser Allee 23–25 • Mon–Thurs 8am–4pm, Fri 8am–1pm; male visitors should keep their heads covered, skullcaps loaned free at the entrance • U-Bahn Senefelderplatz

The **Jüdischer Friedhof**, Prenzlauer Berg's Jewish cemetery, opened when space ran out at the Grosse Hamburger Strasse cemetery (see p.77). More than twenty thousand people are buried here, including painter Max Liebermann, publisher Leopold Ullstein, composer Giacomo Meyerbeer and German-Jewish banker Joseph Mendelssohn (son of philosopher Moses Mendelssohn). But for most, this last resting place is an anonymous one: in 1943 many of the gravestones were smashed and a couple of years later the trees under which they had stood were used by the SS to hang deserters found hiding in the cemetery during the final days of the war. Today many of the stones have been restored and repositioned, and a memorial stone near the cemetery entrance entreats visitors: "You stand here in silence, but when you turn away do not remain silent."

Wasserturm

From Senefelder Platz, Kollwitzstrasse runs north through quiet and almost bucolic residential streets. Adding to the relaxed atmosphere is a small urban park, a block to the east, around the huge red-brick **Wasserturm** (water tower). Constructed in 1877 by the English Waterworks Company on the site of a pre-industrial windmill, the 30m-high cylindrical brick water tower, known as "Dicker Hermann", is infamous as a site of Nazi atrocities: once the party came to power the SA turned the basement into a torture chamber and the bodies of 28 of their victims were later found in the underground pipe network. A memorial stone on Knaackstrasse commemorates them: "On this spot in 1933 decent German resistance fighters became the victims of fascist murderers. Honour the dead by striving for a peaceful world." During GDR times the tower was used to store canned fish but was later abandoned to became a "playground" for local kids. Today the refurbished tower is home to much-coveted wedge-shaped apartments (formerly belonging to the tower's operators), while the underground reservoir space is home to sporadic art and music events (see ⓦsinguhr.de).

Prenzlauer Berg Museum

Prenzlauer Allee 227–228 • Mon–Fri 9am–6pm • Free • ☎ 030 42 40 10 97 • U-Bahn Senefelderplatz

Spread across the first floor of a former school, the small but lively **Prenzlauer Berg Museum** documents the history of the district and its mainly poor working-class inhabitants from the nineteenth century to today. The permanent exhibition consists mainly of photos and text (German only) displayed along school-like corridors, though a couple of large rooms and a separate building across the courtyard are occasionally given over to more modern, multimedia exhibitions on local themes.

Synagoge Rykestrasse

Rykestr. 53 • Open for services only: Nov–March Fri 6pm; April–Oct Fri 7pm, Sat 9.30am • ⓦ synagoge-rykestrasse.de

Built by Johann Hoeniger at the start of the twentieth century, the gorgeous Neoclassical **Synagoge Rykestrasse** (inaugurated in 1904) is one of Germany's oldest and biggest – and one of Berlin's loveliest – synagogues. The building survived *Kristallnacht* in 1938 as it was located between "Aryan" apartment buildings, although precious Torah scrolls were damaged and rabbis and congregation members were deported to Sachsenhausen. The synagogue was also used as stables during the war, but was finally restored to its former glory by architects Ruth Golan and Kay Zareh in 2007, who used black-and-white photographs and a €4-million budget to lavishly recreate the remarkable original.

OPPOSITE PRENZLAUER BERG >

Kollwitzplatz and around

One block behind the Rykestrasse synagogue lies **Kollwitzplatz**, a Prenzlauer Berg focal point and home to the well-regarded *Restauration 1900*, a restaurant established long before the Wall came down (see p.203). The square is named after artist **Käthe Kollwitz**, of whom there's an unflattering statue in the little park on the square. From 1891 to 1943 she lived on nearby Kollwitzstrasse (then Weissenburgerstrasse), creating political and pacifist art that you can see in the Käthe Kollwitz Museum (see p.112).

The streets around Kollwitzplatz were among the first to be gentrified when the Wall fell in 1989 and today many of its yuppie pioneers have settled and had children, explaining the overwhelming presence of little ones in the district. It's a lovely place to come for a stroll – three playgrounds and a leafy park lie within the square and endless restaurants, cafés and smart boutiques are scattered around its perimeter. Saturdays are especially popular thanks to the extensive farmers' market that takes over three of its four streets, offering everything from organic meat and fish, fruit and veg, sweets and coffee and clothes. A smaller (and less crowded) organic market also takes place on Thursdays. In summer especially the fun carries on till late at night.

Husemannstrasse and around

The street running north from Kollwitzplatz is **Husemannstrasse**, a nineteenth-century tenement street that was restored to its former glory in late-GDR days and turned into a kind of living museum in an attempt to recall the grandeur of old Berlin. Since the *Wende*, restoration projects have transformed neighbouring streets too, covering raddled facades with fresh stucco and installing new wrought-iron balconies. A quiet stroll north on Husemannstrasse finds its abrupt end at the busy **Danziger Strasse**, where trams and traffic and shop fronts fight for space and attention.

Kulturbrauerei and around

U-Bahn Eberswalder Strasse is Prenzlauer Berg's busiest hub; under the station and the elevated railway tracks along Schönhauser Allee lies the famous **sausage kiosk** *Konnopke's* (see p.201). North of the station, Schönhauser Allee assumes its true identity as Prenzlauer Berg's main drag, an old-fashioned shopping street that, thanks to its cobbles and narrow shop facades, still retains a vaguely prewar feel. This atmosphere is also evoked by the **Kulturbrauerei** (Schönhauser Allee 36; entrances on Sredzkistr. and Danziger Str.; ⓦkulturbrauerei-berlin.de), an events centre that all but fills the city block southeast of the U-Bahn station. Built as a complex for major local brewer Schultheiss in the 1890s, it was given the pseudo-Byzantine style that was fashionable at the time. The entrance, a narrow gateway on Danziger Strasse, quickly widens to reveal a spacious inner courtyard that often serves as a live-music venue, and is flanked by old workshops which house a theatre, exhibition spaces, a couple of clubs and bars and a cinema. All of

---

SUNDAY IN THE MAUERPARK: FLEAMARKETS AND KARAOKE

One of Berlin's best loved flea markets, **Mauerpark Flohmarkt** is a city institution, popular every Sunday with hungover students, bargain-hunters, families and bemused-looking, shade-wearing clubbers who come to scan the food stalls, clothes shops and nostalgic junk that seems to extend forever. The selection is eclectic, to say the least: bikes (freshly stolen and resprayed), 1950s cutlery, faded jigsaws, new and vintage clothes, GDR memorabilia, banana telephones and record players, bibles and lots of vinyl and CDs. As with most flea markets, there's a good amount of junk among some genuine antiques. Adjacent to the market you'll find the actual **Mauerpark**, a strip of landscaped green that was once the site of a stretch of Berlin Wall and the associated death strip, loomed over by the Friedrich-Ludwig-Jahn-Sportpark and the Max-Schmeling-Halle. When the weather's warm check out the weekly **karaoke** session in the "bearpit", which attracts massive crowds on Sundays between 1.30pm and 5pm.

them have a somewhat alternative slant and there's almost always something – cultural, political or just entertaining – going on (see p.214). The southern gateway leaves the complex on Sredzkistrasse, near the bustle of Schönhauser Allee.

Crossing the main road here leads to **Oderberger Strasse** and **Kastanienalle**, both of which have some of the best **cafés**, **bars** and **restaurants** in eastern Berlin. You'll see some buildings whose facades have not been touched since the *Wende*, scarred with bullet and shell marks inflicted during the Battle of Berlin.

Pankow

From Prenzlauer Berg, Schönhauser Allee leads north to the district of **Pankow,** which during the GDR days was always much more than just another East Berlin suburb. For years its villas and well-maintained flats were home mainly to members of the upper reaches of East Berlin society: state-approved artists and writers, scientists, East Berlin resident diplomats and the *Parteibonzen* (party bigwigs) of the old regime. Up until the 1960s the area was perceived in the West as being the real centre of power in the old GDR: Schloss Niederschönhausen, an eighteenth-century palace on the edge of the *Bezirk* (district), was the official residence of the GDR's first president, Wilhelm Pieck, and later of SED General Secretary Walter Ulbricht, the man who took the decision to build the Wall. The name of the suburb was also appropriated by

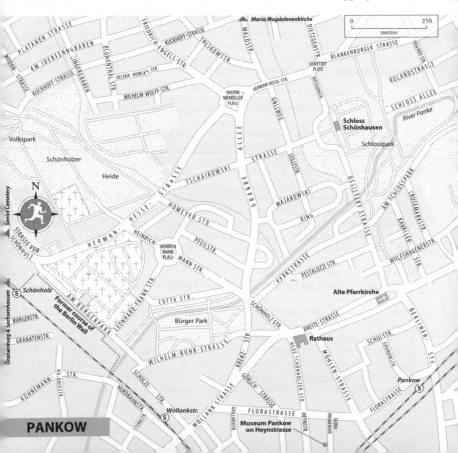

one of the ex-GDR's best-known rock bands, in a satirical dig at the social hierarchy of the workers' and peasants' state. Today, it's a pleasant, very middle-class borough, focused on the large shopping street **Breite Strasse**, and is most attractive for the belt of parks – the **Schlosspark**, **Bürgerpark** and **Volkspark Schönholzer Heide** – that lies a block or so to the north.

Breite Strasse

At the junction of Berliner Strasse and Breite Strasse, on a mid-road island that used to be the village green, is the **Alte Pfarrkirche**, Pankow's parish church and oldest building. It dates back to the fifteenth century but was extensively restored in 1832, a project in which Schinkel had a hand, resulting in an unusual-looking neo-Gothic jumble. At the western end of **Breite Strasse**, at the end of the main strip of chain stores and boutiques, is the early-twentieth-century neo-Baroque **Rathaus**, a red-brick affair of fanciful gables, towers and cupolas, with a good *Ratskeller* – a traditional German restaurant – in its basement.

Museum Pankow on Heynstrasse

Heynstr. 8 • Tues, Thurs & Sun 10am–6pm • Free • ☎ 030 481 40 47 • U- & S-Pankow

While Berlin's workers could hope to afford lodgings such as those at Zimmermeister Brunzel (see p.135), the city's wealthy could aspire to apartments like this one, beautifully preserved as a branch of **Museum Pankow on Heynstrasse**. Formerly the apartment of factory owner Fritz Heyn – who was important enough to have the street named after him – it is quite the bourgeois palace. Showy chandeliers preside over heavy furniture, while scores of decorative Prussian touches – eagles, prints of Bismarck – are all part of the rich over-decoration. None of this extends to the servants' quarters around the back, of course.

Schloss Schönhausen

Tschaikowskistr. 1 • **Palace** April–Oct Tues–Sun 10am–6pm; Nov–March Sat & Sun 10am–5pm • €6 **Garden** Daily 8am–sunset • Free • ⓦ spsg.de • S- & U-Pankow

North of Breite Strasse is the **Schlosspark**, in whose leafy grounds lurks **Schloss Schönhausen**, former home of Elisabeth Christine, the estranged wife of Frederick the Great. The Schloss was built at the beginning of the eighteenth century and given an extensive but run-of-the-mill face-lift in 1764. During GDR days it could only be admired from a distance, as it served first as official residence of GDR president Wilhelm Pieck, from 1949 to 1960, and then as the old regime's most prestigious state guesthouse. Since then it has been revamped and reopened to visitors who can admire some of the original royal residence interiors; the offices of the GDR's president; and the suites of its most honoured guests. The palace is also surrounded by a slightly dreary 1950s-era garden that you're free to wander around.

Volkspark Schönholzer Heide

The heath-like **Volkspark Schönholzer Heide** is Pankow's most impressively wild park. In its southwest corner lies a humble **cemetery**, a burial ground for civilians who died in the final days of the Battle of Berlin. Most are women or children and for many the dates of birth and death, and in some cases even names, are unknown, a stark reminder of the many untold stories that are lost in the dehumanizing chaos of war. In contrast is the grandeur of the huge **Soviet cemetery**, at the northwestern edge of the park. Here dozens of communal graves contain the remains of 13,200 soldiers killed during the same battle. Military hierarchy is observed in death as in life, with officers occupying the central lower tiers and privates around the fringes of the grounds.

NORMANNENSTRASSE

The eastern suburbs

Berlin's eastern suburbs have changed significantly since reunification. Projects designed to iron out the differences between the two sides of the city have resulted in a strange mixture of past and present: old GDR-style socialist architecture sits alongside the clean-cut lines and flashy design of new buildings, and they don't quite gel. Visiting these primarily residential areas moulded by almost fifty years of communist rule, unpleasant as it sometimes is, is an important part of getting a complete picture of Berlin – and on their southern fringes some genuine rural breathers offer a break from the city. All of the places described here are easily reached on public transport by S- or U-Bahn, though a slower tram or bus journey will allow you to get more of a feel for this part of the city.

9

The most important sights in this part of town relate to the GDR secret police, or Stasi, particularly the **Stasi Prison Hohenschönhausen** and **Stasi headquarters** in the borough of **Lichtenberg**. Both are sombre places; the rewarding **Deutsch-Russisches Museum**, in the same borough, concerns itself with twentieth-century German-Russian relations so is hardly uplifting either. Thankfully in the midst of them lies the more cheerful **Tierpark Friedrichsfelde**, eastern Berlin's sprawling zoo with its pleasant wooded grounds. East of Lichtenberg is **Marzahn-Hellersdorf**, a late-1970s satellite town and perhaps Berlin's least obvious sightseeing destination. Silo-like apartment blocks and soulless shopping precincts stretch out towards the edge of the city in what has to be

EASTERN SUBURBS

ACCOMMODATION
Campingplatz Am
Krossinsee   1

EATING
China Teehaus   1

one of the most desolate of the city's boroughs. However, this *is* the city for tens of thousands of Berliners, and worth a look for this reason alone. Probably the most pleasant day out in the eastern suburbs is **Köpenick**, in the far southeast, with its attractive small-town feel and surprisingly unspoiled **lakes**, particularly the Grosser Müggelsee with its thick belt of surrounding woods.

Lichtenberg

East of Friedrichshain lies the sprawling working-class district of **Lichtenberg**, part prefabricated postwar mass dwellings and part traditional tenement blocks, with heavy concentrations of industry in the north and south. Until the mid-nineteenth century Lichtenberg was little more than a country town and popular Sunday outing destination for Berliners. With industrialization, however, the familiar Berlin tenements sprang up and the area's rustic past was soon forgotten. Unfortunately, Lichtenberg has been hard hit by the collapse of the old order, and unemployment runs high.

Gedenkstätte Hohenschönhausen

Genslerstr. 66 • Daily 9am–4pm; tours hourly in German, 2.30pm in English • €5 • ☎ 030 98 60 82 30, ⓦ stiftung-hsh.de • Tram #M5 from Hackescher Markt or, if you're already in Lichtenberg, bus #256 from U-Bahn Lichtenberg – get off either tram or bus at Freienwalder Strasse; the entrance to the former jail is at the end of the road

A potent antidote to *Ostalgie* – nostalgia for the GDR (see p.66) – is a visit to the grim former Stasi prison at **Gedenkstätte Hohenschönhausen** (Hohenschönhausen Memorial), which offers an insight into the fear and oppression upon which the regime was founded. Hohenschönhausen began life in 1945 as a **Soviet Special Camp**, with 4200 inmates penned in together in horrendous living conditions. By 1946 around three thousand had died. Officially most of these were interned because of suspected Nazi links, but in most cases there was no evidence. Underground torture chambers became vital for acquiring "confessions" that usually led to decades of forced labour – though ultimately almost all prisoners were declared innocent by the Russian authorities in the 1990s. In 1951 the Stasi (see box, p.144) inherited the facility and turned it into a **remand prison** that was quickly blotted from city maps. The smallest sign of resistance or opposition to the state, including comments written in personal letters – which were all routinely steamed open – would earn you a spell here. Typically, you'd be caught unawares on your way to work, bundled into a van, and then brought to this site. Tours, led by former prisoners, deliver an absorbing insight into the psychological rather than physical abuse that followed in the solitary world of padded cells, tiny exercise yards, endless corridors and interrogation rooms.

Stasi Museum Berlin

Ruschestr. 103 • Mon–Fri 10am–6pm, Sat & Sun noon–6pm • €5 • ⓦ stasimuseum.de • U-Magdalenenstrasse

One building in the huge former **Stasi headquarters** complex is now the **Stasi Museum Berlin**, which uncovers the massive surveillance apparatus of the GDR's secret police. Walking along the bare, red-carpeted corridors and looking at the busts of Lenin and Felix Dzerzhinsky – founder of the Soviet Cheka, models for both the KGB and Stasi – it all seems part of a distant past, not an era that ended only in 1990. But then the obsessively neat office and apartment of **Erich Mielke**, the Stasi head from 1957 to October 1989, makes it all the more immediate. Everything is just as he left it: white and black telephones stand on the varnished wooden desk as though awaiting calls, and Mielke's white dress uniform hangs in a wardrobe. Other rooms have displays of Stasi surveillance apparatus described in German (the accompanying English-language booklet costs €3), but which mostly speak for themselves. The many bugging devices and cameras – some concealed in watering cans and plant pots – reveal the lengths the GDR went to in order to keep tabs on its citizens. You'll also find a couple of rooms stuffed with medals, badges, flags and other GDR kitsch. Sections on political terror

9

THE STASI

East Germany's infamous Staatssicherheitsdienst (State Security Service), or **Stasi**, kept tabs on everything in the GDR. It ensured the security of the country's borders, carried out surveillance on foreign diplomats, business people and journalists, and monitored domestic and foreign media. It was, however, in the surveillance of East Germany's own population that the organization truly excelled. Very little happened in the GDR without the Stasi knowing about it: files were kept on millions of innocent citizens and insidious operations were orchestrated against dissidents, real and imagined. By the time of the *Wende* the Stasi had a budget of £1 billion, 91,000 full-time employees and 180,000 informers within the East German population; figures brought into context by the more puny, albeit more ruthless, 7000-strong Nazi Gestapo.

At the beginning of 1991 former citizens of the GDR were given the right to see their Stasi files. Tens of thousands took the opportunity to find out what the organization had recorded about them, and, more importantly, who had provided the information; many a friendship and not a few marriages came to an end as a result. The process of unravelling truths from the archives also provided material for numerous stories, including Timothy Garton Ash's **book** *The File: A Personal History* (see p.273) and the **film** *Das Leben der Anderen* (Lives of Others; see p.278). Not all documents survived, though; many were briskly shredded as the GDR regime collapsed, resulting in an unenviable task for one government organization who spent literally years piecing them together to bring people to justice, thankfully with some success.

during the Stalin years and forced resettlement from border zones throw light on otherwise little-known aspects of GDR history.

Dorfkirche

Just north of the rather sinister-looking Rathaus Lichtenberg, at the junction of Normannenstrasse and Möllendorffstrasse, is an improbably rustic **Dorfkirche**, a church dating back to Lichtenberg's village origins. The stone walls date from the original thirteenth-century structure, but the rest is more modern, with the spire tacked on as recently as 1965.

Gedenkstätte der Sozialisten

Gudrunstr. • 1km or so northeast of U- & S-Lichtenberg

The **Gedenkstätte der Sozialisten** or "Memorial to the Socialists", is perhaps only for die-hard fans of GDR relics. Its centrepiece is a 4m chunk of red porphyry bearing the inscription *Die Toten mahnen uns* – "The dead remind us" – commemorating the GDR's socialist hall of fame from Karl Liebknecht and Rosa Luxemburg onwards. A tablet bears a list of names that reads like the street directory of virtually any town in pre-*Wende* East Germany, recording the esoteric cult figures of the workers' and peasants' state in alphabetical order; until 1989 the East Berlin public were cajoled and coerced into attending hundred-thousand-strong mass demonstrations here. The whole thing actually replaced a much more interesting Mies van der Rohe-designed memorial that stood here from 1926 until the Nazis destroyed it in 1935. Altogether more uncompromising, featuring a huge star and hammer and sickle, the original memorial caused problems for Mies van der Rohe when he came before Joseph McCarthy's Un-American Activities Committee in 1951. The Gedenkstätte is also the burial place of Walter Ulbricht, the man who decided to build the Berlin Wall, and Wilhelm Pieck, the first president of the GDR.

Tierpark Friedrichsfelde

Entrances on the eastern side of Am Tierpark • Daily 9am–sunset or 6pm • €12 • ⓦ tierpark-berlin.de • U-Tierpark

Lichtenberg's sprawling zoo, **Tierpark Friedrichsfelde**, ranks as one of the largest in Europe and a thorough exploration of its wooded grounds could easily absorb the better part of a day. Some visitors may balk at the traditional nature of the place; some of the animals are kept in very small cages, though others have much more space to roam around. Virtually every species imaginable, from alpaca to wisent, can be found here, including rare Przewalski horses, which have been bred here over the years, bringing the breed back from the edge of extinction.

Schloss Friedrichsfelde

Tours on the hour: Tues, Thurs, Sat & Sun 11am–5pm • €2 plus zoo entrance • ⓦ stadtmuseum.de

Hidden away in the grounds of the zoo, just beyond an enclosure of lumbering pelicans, is **Schloss Friedrichsfelde**, a Baroque palace housing an exhibition of eighteenth- and nineteenth-century interior decor. Theodor Fontane was exaggerating when he described it as the Schloss Charlottenburg of the East – the best thing about it are the pretty, ornamental grounds. To see inside you need to take a tour (German-language only).

Karlshorst

From the Tierpark, a stroll south down Am Tierpark, bearing left along Treskowerallee for about 1km, will bring you to the sub-district of **Karlshorst**. For many years you were more likely to hear Russian than German spoken here, as the area was effectively a Russian quarter, thanks to the presence of large numbers of Soviet soldiers and their dependants. The Russians accepted the unconditional surrender of the German armed forces in a Wehrmacht engineers' school here on May 8, 1945, and went on to establish their Berlin headquarters nearby. For many years, Karlshorst was fenced off and under armed guard, out of bounds to ordinary East Germans. Later, they were allowed back in part, but the area retained an exclusive cachet, its villas housing the GDR elite – scientists and writers – or used as foreign embassy residences.

Deutsch-Russisches Museum

Zwieseler Str. 4 • Tues–Sun 10am–6pm • Free • ☎ 030 50 15 08 10, ⓦ museum-karlshorst.de • S-Karlshorst

The Russians finally left Karlshorst in the summer of 1994, but a reminder of their presence endures as the **Deutsch-Russisches Museum**, in the building where the German surrender was signed. When the GDR still existed, this museum was officially known as the "Museum of the Unconditional Surrender of Fascist Germany in the Great Patriotic War 1941–45". Since then it has been renamed and rearranged to convey a self-consciously balanced view of the tumultuous German-Russian relations in the twentieth century. Its hundreds of photos and video footage make the exhibition worthwhile; if you can't read German be sure to borrow an English-language folder with translations.

Marzahn-Hellersdorf

To see the most enduring legacy of East Berlin – **Marzahn-Hellersdorf** – it's best to go by day and not look too much like a tourist, as the area has a reputation for violence. It's in places like this, all across the former GDR, that people are bearing the economic brunt of reunification's downside – unemployment – and where you'll see the worst effects caused by the collapse of a state that, for all its faults, ensured a certain level of social security for its citizens. Ironically, Marzahn was one of the GDR's model new towns of the late 1970s – part of Honecker's efforts to solve his country's endemic housing shortage by providing modern apartments in purpose-built blocks with shopping facilities and social amenities to hand. The result here was several kilometres of high-rise developments housing 250,000 people, where, like similar developments in the West, things never quite worked according to plan, with the usual crime and drugs surfacing.

Most people will see enough of the area by travelling to S-Bahn Springpfuhl and then taking tram #M8 past endless high-rises to **Alt-Marzahn**, the original, slightly quaint and now hugely incongruous district centre. Complete with a green, pub, cobbled streets, war memorial and parish church, something of a village past survives. Admittedly it's not a very pleasant past: from 1866 the fields of the area were used as *Rieselfelder*, designated for the disposal of Berlin's sewage. Marzahn acquired a Dorfkirche in neo-Gothic style a few years later, built by Schinkel's pupil Friedrich August Stüler.

9

From here you can wander to other arterial roads beside Alt-Marzahn: Landsberger Allee, to take in the immensity of all the high-rises and bus #195 to the **Gärten der Welt**, a large park with a collection of ornamental gardens. This bus goes on, though very indirectly, to the **Gründerzeitmuseum Mahlsdorf**, a museum that brings together a fine collection of late nineteenth-century furnishings from the beginning of the German Empire.

Gärten der Welt

Eisenacher Str. 99 • **Park and Chinese Garden** Daily: March & Oct 9am–6pm; April–Sept 9am–8pm; Nov–Feb 9am–4pm • Free
Japanese Garden April–Sept Mon–Fri noon–8pm, Sat & Sun 9am–8pm, Oct Mon–Fri noon–6pm, Sat & Sun 9am–6pm • €3 •
ⓦ erholungspark-marzahn.de • U-Cottbusserplatz, then bus #195

Opened in 1987 as part of the city's 750th birthday celebrations, **Gärten der Welt** (Gardens of the World) forms an attractive oasis amid Marzahn's high-rises. The park is dotted with decorative features, pleasant nooks and playgrounds, but its star turns are the trio of exotic gardens. The sprawling and ornate **Chinese Garden** is the biggest in Europe, with a restaurant, snack bar and a teahouse (see p.204), while the **Japanese Garden** is much more regimented, with water and rock features competing for space with shrubs and bonsai trees. The park also boasts several other themed gardens, including a **Balinese Garden** in a warm damp greenhouse where you'll find a traditional rural family home amid the ferns and orchids.

Gründerzeitmuseum Mahlsdorf

Hultschiner Damm 333, Mahlsdorf • Wed & Sun 10am–6pm; guided tours only – call ahead to arrange one in English • €4.50 •
☎ 030 567 83 29, ⓦ gruenderzeitmuseum.de • Tram #62 to Alt-Mahlsdorf from S-Mahlsdorf

The suburb of **Mahlsdorf**, about 5km southeast of Alt-Marzahn, is no cultural centre, but it does boast one of the city's most notable museums, the excellent **Gründerzeitmuseum Mahlsdorf**, a collection of furniture and household gear from 1880–1900, the period known as the *Gründerzeit* or "foundation time", when the newly united Germany was at its imperial peak. The founder of the museum, Lothar Berfelde (one of Berlin's better-known transvestites, better known as a writer with the pseudonym **Charlotte von Mahlsdorf**), put the collection together during GDR days when such an undertaking was by no means an easy task, creating a representative *Gründerzeit* apartment by taking the complete contents of rooms and relocating them in this eighteenth-century manor house. Depending on your tastes the result is either exquisite or over the top, but either way the museum is fascinating and certainly worth the long haul out to the suburbs – don't miss the basement, filled with furnishings from the *Mulack-Ritze*, a famous early twentieth-century Berlin *Kneipe* (pub) that originally stood on Mulackstrasse in the Scheunenviertel.

Berfelde was awarded the Bundesverdienstkreuz, Germany's equivalent of the OBE, in 1992 for his services to the preservation of the city's cultural and social heritage. He died in 2002; the following year he became the subject of the Pulitzer Prize-winning Broadway theatre piece, *I Am My Own Wife* by Doug Wright.

Köpenick

A slow-moving little place on the banks of the River Spree near the southeast edge of Berlin, **Köpenick**, easily reached by S-Bahn from Alexanderplatz, is an ideal escape from the city centre and a convenient base for exploring Berlin's southeastern lakes, in particular the **Müggelsee**, with its appealing shoreline towns of Friedrichshagen and Rahnsdorf. Also easily accessible are the **Müggelberge**, Berlin's 150m-high "mountains".

Köpenick was a town in its own right during medieval times, and though it has since been swallowed up by Greater Berlin, it still retains a distinct identity. The presence of a number of major factories meant that it always had a reputation as a "red" town. In March 1920, during the Kapp putsch attempt, workers from Köpenick took on and

9

temporarily drove back army units who were marching on Berlin to support the coup. The army later returned, but its success was shortlived as the putsch foundered – thanks mainly to a highly effective general strike. This militancy continued into the Nazi era: on January 30, 1933, the day Hitler came to power, a red flag flew from the chimney of the brewery in the suburb of Friedrichshagen. This defiance was punished during the *Köpenicker Blutwoche* ("Köpenick Week of Blood") in June that year, during which the SA swooped on Social Democrats and communists. Five hundred people were imprisoned and 91 murdered.

Altstadt

Tram #60 or #68 from S-Bahn Köpenick

To walk to Köpenick's old town from the S-Bahn station, follow Borgamannstrasse to Mandrellaplatz, location of Köpenick's **Amtsgericht** (district court), where victims of the *Köpenicker Blutwoche* were executed. From Mandrellaplatz, Puchanstrasse leads to Am Generalshof and **Platz des 23 April**, which commemorates the arrival in Köpenick of the Soviet army – liberators or conquerors, depending on your point of view. On the platz a sculpted clenched fist atop a stone tablet honours those killed by the Nazis in 1933.

From Mandrellaplatz, the Dammbrücke (boats can be rented at the foot of the bridge for €7/hr) leads across the Spree into Köpenick's **Altstadt** (old town). Situated on an island between the Spree and Dahme rivers, the Altstadt's streets run more or

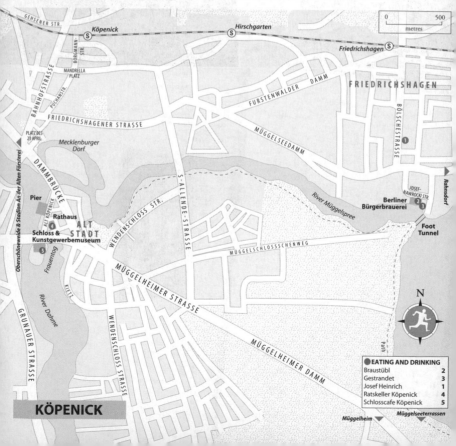

EATING AND DRINKING	
Braustübl	2
Gestrandet	3
Josef Heinrich	1
Ratskeller Köpenick	4
Schlosscafe Köpenick	5

KÖPENICK

less true to the medieval town plan and remain slightly down-at-heel – it's not hard to picture this area as it must have been a century or so ago. A number of typical nineteenth-century *Bürgerhäuser* with restored facades on **Grünstrasse** and **Böttcherstrasse** are worth a look, but the most prominent building is the early twentieth-century neo-Gothic **Rathaus** on Alt Köpenick, a typically over-the-top gabled affair with an imposing clock tower. A statue of one **Wilhelm Voigt** at the entrance to the buildings commemorates the town's most famous incident, when on October 16, 1906, unemployed shoemaker Voigt disguised himself as an army officer, commandeered a troop of soldiers, marched them to Köpenick's Rathaus and requisitioned the contents of its safe. Having ordered his detachment to take Köpenick's mayor and bookkeeper to the guardhouse in the city centre, he disappeared. Voigt was soon caught, but the story became an example of the Prussian propensity to blindly follow anyone wearing uniform. Later, playwright Carl Zuckmeyer turned the incident into a play, *Der Hauptmann von Köpenick* ("The Captain of Köpenick") and the robbery is now re-enacted every summer in the second half of June during the Köpenick summer festival.

Kunstgewerbemuseum

Schlossinsel • Tues–Sun 10am–6pm • €6; €12 with the Kulturforum's Kunstgewerbemuseum (see p.95) • ☏ 030 226 29 02, ⓦ smb.museum

At the southern end of the Altstadt a footbridge leads to the Schlossinsel, the island home of **Schloss Köpenick**, the seventeenth-century fortified Baroque manor that houses the **Kunstgewerbemuseum**, another of Berlin's fine state museums. Showcasing a collection of Renaissance, Baroque and Rococo furnishings from the sixteenth to eighteenth century, it's perhaps less impressive than the Kulturforum's Kunstgewerbemuseum (see p.95), but the Schloss has the advantage of being able to display many pieces in situ. A first-class audio tour, included in the admission price, greatly enhances a visit.

The exhibition begins with the Italian Renaissance, which sparked Europe-wide stylistic change and was quickly bolstered by the French, whose grand pieces of furniture inhabit the next room. These form a preamble to the German Renaissance, the museum's strong point, and on the first floor themes of love, marriage and fertility are intriguingly explored by arrangements of sturdy Teutonic furniture. After a brief foray into Dutch Baroque, the self-guided tour leads to a group of gigantic beer mugs, strongly underlining the Germanic nature of the collection, followed by a few Polish Renaissance pieces, which offer a distraction en route to the museum's most famous exhibit: the silver buffet from the Berliner Schloss – one of its few treasures to survive intact.

The second floor is replete with Chinese vases and commodes that seventeenth-century Dutch and British traders brought back from the Orient, which helped inspire the Rococo movement. Much of the sizeable collection belonged to Frederick II, who was clearly a big fan of the style. The *pièce de résistance* – an excessively flamboyant porcelain lampshade – was one of a series that Frederick liked to give as presents in an era when gifts like these would win friends and influence people.

Frauentog and aound

Just beside the Schloss Köpenick and its attendant Schlossplatz are views out over the **Frauentog**, a small bay where Köpenick's fishermen used to cast their nets; this becomes the Langer See further south. The sheltered bay is now home to the Solarbootpavillon, which rents out **solar-powered boats** (Mon–Fri noon–8pm, Sat & Sun 10am–8pm; from €11/hr). On the east side of the bay, just to the southeast of the Altstadt, is the **Kietz**, a cobbled street of fishing cottages dating back to the early thirteenth century. Recent renovation has brightened up the shutters and whitewashed facades of most of these cottages, making it a pleasant street for a stroll.

9

Grosser Müggelsee and around

Take a boat with Stern und Kreisschiffahrt from the quay opposite the Rathaus in Köpenick, tram #60 from Köpenick's Schlossplatz, or the S-Bahn to Friedrichshagen

Sitting just a few kilometres east of Köpenick, the **Grosser Müggelsee** is one of Berlin's main lakes, with a couple of suburbs – **Friedrichshagen** and **Rahnsdorf** – with lovely, small-town atmospheres. The shores of the lake and the surrounding woods provide welcome relief from pounding Berlin's relentless urban streets, but beware – the Müggelsee area can get crowded at any time of year – in summer, people swarm here for sun and sailing, and in winter to go ice-skating.

Friedrichshagen

Friedrichshagen is a small town founded in 1753 as a settlement for Bohemian cotton spinners who, as a condition of their being allowed to live here, were legally required to plant mulberry trees to rear silkworms. Both trams and trains stop beside Friedrichshagen's main drag, **Bölschestrasse**, where a number of single-storey houses survive from the original eighteenth-century settlement, dwarfed by later nineteenth-century blocks, and a few vestigial mulberry trees still cling to life at the roadside. About halfway down this otherwise attractive street the **Christophoruskirche**, a gloomy neo-Gothic church in red brick, puts a Lutheran damper on things.

To get away from it, make for the lake, along Josef-Nawrocki-Strasse, passing the extensive **Berliner Bürgerbrauerei**, the brewery from whose chimney the red flag flew provocatively the day Hitler was sworn in as chancellor. Following the road around leads to a small park at the point where the Spree flows into the Grosser Müggelsee. You can follow a foot tunnel under the river, and, at the other side take a path that follows the lakeshore through the woods. Perfect for strolling, it leads all the way to the Müggelberge, 2km away (see below).

Rahnsdorf

Reached by S-Bahn or tram #61 from Friedrichshagen, the little town of **Rahnsdorf** is one of eastern Berlin's more delightful hidden corners, a sprawl of tree-shaded lakeside houses with an old fishing village at its core. Head for **Dorfstrasse**, a cobbled street at the southern end of the village (bus #161 from the S-Bahn to "Grünheider Weg", then follow the signs for Altes Fischerdorf), lined by fishermen's cottages and centred around a small parish church. The best way to explore Rahnsdorf is to simply wander the lakeside and soak up the atmosphere. Just off Fürstenwalder Damm, on the western edge of town, there's an FKK (*Freikörperkultur*) **nudist beach**.

The Müggelberge

Accessed via a 2km lakeshore path from Friedrichshagen (see above) or bus #X69 from Köpenick S-Bahn, the **Müggelberge** are a series of rolling forested hills overlooking the Grosser Müggelsee. From bus stop Rübezahl, a path leads south through the woods up to the summit.

Around about the halfway mark is the **Teufelssee** (Devil's Lake), a small pool with a glass-smooth surface, from which various nature trails start. More information on these, and on the flora and fauna of the area, can be obtained at the nearby **Lehrkabinett** information centre (May–Sept Wed–Fri 10am–4pm, Sat & Sun 10am–5pm; Oct–April Wed, Thurs, Sat & Sun 10am–4pm).

Pushing on and up through the woods leads to the **Müggelturm** (closed for renovations), a functional-looking observation tower offering great views of the lake and woods, plus a café, bar and restaurant (also closed for renovations). Both the Teufelssee and Müggelturm are accessible by foot along reasonably well-surfaced tracks from the main road.

WANNSEE BEACH

The western suburbs

Berlin's smart, sleepy and wealthy western suburbs encompass a disparate group of attractions of cultural and historical interest, as well as the woodlands and lakes beyond them where hikes through dense forests and swims from sandy beaches feel a world away – not just a half-dozen S-Bahn stops – from the city centre. The closest of the main attractions to the centre is Schloss Charlottenburg – Berlin's pocket Versailles – where opulent chambers, attractive gardens and excellent art museums can easily fill a day. Elsewhere, given the easy transport links, it's possible to have a good day out visiting a Dahlem museum, going for a short hike in the Grunewald, and rounding things off with a visit to Spandau's Renaissance Zitadelle. Alternatively, you could take a private boat trip on the Havel (see p.25).

To the north of the palace and museums of **Schloss Charlottenburg**, beyond an unattractive industrial no man's land, lies the depressing **Plötzensee Prison Memorial**, Berlin's main Nazi torture site. Infinitely more pleasant is the wealthy, and properly suburban, residential **Westend** district west of the Schloss. Its significant reminders of prewar Berlin are much more upbeat, and include the Funkturm and Olympic Stadium. South of here, in the Steglitz-Zehlendorf borough, are the **Dahlem museums**, which include world-class collections of tribal and Asian art as well as European applied art. To the west lie other interesting museums, particularly the **Allied Museum**, where the

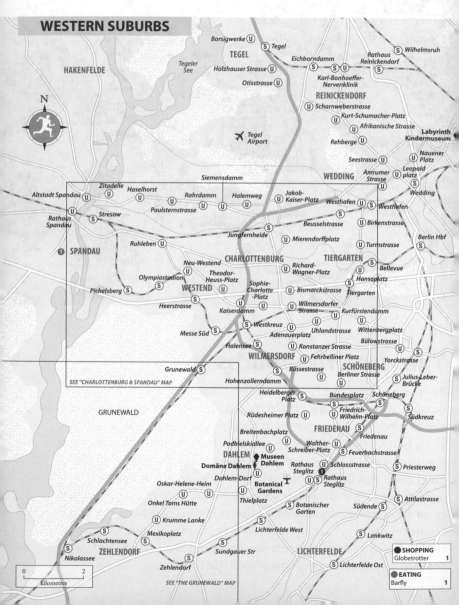

original Checkpoint Charlie booth is kept, and the verdant woodlands of the **Grunewald**, which eventually reach the banks of the huge **Havel** lake. Here, the **Wannsee** bay is famed for its large sand beach as well as for being the location of the **Wannsee villa**, where a Nazi conference sealed the fate of millions of Jews. At the northern end of the Havel, where it joins the Spree, lies **Spandau**, where the small-town feel is enhanced by the presence of its **Zitadelle**, one of the world's best-preserved Renaissance forts.

ARRIVAL AND GETTING AROUND

Thanks to the efficient U- and S-Bahn systems, it's possible to reach Berlin's western edges in 45min, but once there the main form of public transport is often the bus – the double-deckers are great for sightseeing.

10

The Westend The Westend is well served by trains, though buses rival them for speed and reveal a lot more of the city on the way. From Bahnhof Zoo #M49 heads to the Funkturm, then on to Theodor-Heuss-Platz before heading along Heerstrasse to S-Bahn Heerstrasse for the Georg-Kolbe-Museum, and on to the Flatowallee stop for the Olympic stadium. From there you have a choice of U- and S-Bahn stations to whizz you back into the centre.

The Wannsee Most destinations around the Wannsee are best reached by public transport from S-Bahn Wannsee, from where various buses radiate. The sole exception is the Strandbad Wannsee which is a 10min walk from S-Bahn Nikolassee, one stop earlier on the line from central Berlin. Cross the main road outside S-Bahn Wannsee and you're a couple of minutes' walk through a park away from regular ferries (which are part of the BVG public transport system and included in the price of a BVG day-ticket) to Alt-Kladow on the opposite side of the lake.

Spandau The hourly ferry across the Havel, linked with bus #X34 or #134 from Alt-Kladow, also makes a picturesque way of getting to Spandau.

Schloss Charlottenburg

Spandauer Damm 10–22 • The various parts of the Schloss can be visited and paid for separately, but combined day tickets are the best value (€16), if you wish to see all of it • ☎ 030 32 09 11, ⓦ spsg.de • U-Richard-Wagner-Platz or bus #M45 from Bahnhof Zoo

Commissioned as a country house by the future Queen Sophie Charlotte in 1695 (she also gave her name to the district), **Schloss Charlottenburg** was expanded and added to throughout the eighteenth and early nineteenth centuries to provide a summer residence for the Prussian kings; master builder Karl Friedrich Schinkel (see p.57) provided the final touches. Approaching the sandy elaborateness of the Schloss through the main courtyard, you're confronted with Andreas Schlüter's **statue** of Friedrich Wilhelm, the Great Elector, cast as a single piece in 1700. It's in superb condition, despite (or perhaps because of) spending the war years sunk at the bottom of the Tegeler See for safekeeping.

Altes Schloss

Tues–Sun: April–Oct 10am–6pm; Nov–March 10am–5pm; guided tours only (in German), last tour 1hr before close, free English audio-guides available • €12, €16 combined ticket for all of Schloss Charlottenburg attractions

Immediately behind the statue of Friedrich Wilhelm is the entrance to the **Altes Schloss** (Old Palace), which includes the apartment of Friedrich Wilhelm IV and the Baroque rooms of Friedrich I and Sophie Charlotte. To see these you're obliged to go on the conducted **tour**, which traipses through increasingly sumptuous chambers and bedrooms, filled with gilt and carvings. Look out for the **porcelain room**, packed to the ceiling with china, and the **chapel**, which includes a portrait of Sophie Charlotte as the Virgin ascending to heaven.

Neuer Flügel

Wed–Mon: April–Oct 10am–6pm; Nov–March 10am–5pm • €8 including audio-guide, €16 combined ticket for all of Schloss Charlottenburg attractions

It's just as well to remember that much of the Schloss is in fact a fake: a reconstruction following wartime damage. This is most apparent in the Knobelsdorff-designed **Neuer Flügel** (New Wing) to the right of the Schloss entrance as you face it; the upper rooms, such as the elegantly designed Golden Gallery, are too breathlessly perfect, the result of

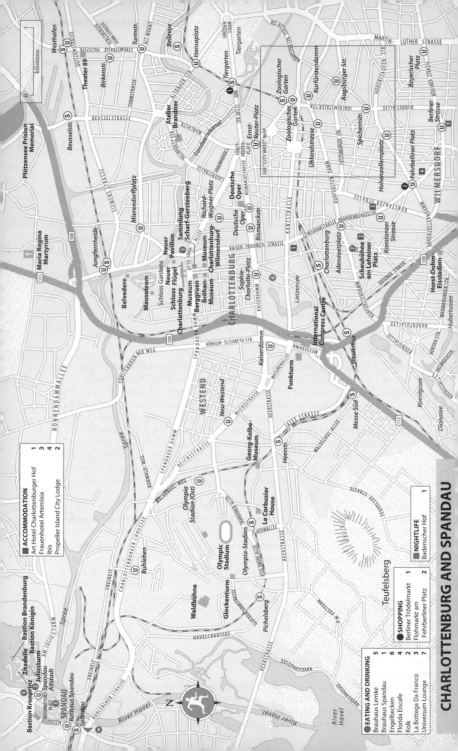

CHARLOTTENBURG AND SPANDAU

■ ACCOMMODATION
Art Hotel Charlottenburger Hof	1
Frauenhotel Artemisia	3
Ibis	4
Propeller Island City Lodge	2

● EATING AND DRINKING
Brauhaus Lemke	5
Brauhaus Spandau	1
Engelbecken	6
Florida Eiscafe	4
Kolk	3
La Bottega Da Franco	2
Universum Lounge	7

● SHOPPING
Berliner Trödelmarkt	1
Flohmarkt am Fehrbelliner Platz	2

■ NIGHTLIFE
Badenscher Hof	1

Teufelsberg

0 — 1 kilometre

intensive restoration – an effect that will no doubt be intensified by two years of further work that are due to be completed in April 2014. Better is the adjacent White Hall, whose eighteenth-century ceiling, made grungy by regular clouds of candle soot during festivities, was replaced at the end of the nineteenth century by a marble and gold confection with full electric illumination. Next door, the Concert Room contains a superb collection of works by **Watteau**, including one of his greatest paintings, *The Embarcation for Cythera*, a delicate Rococo frippery tinged with sympathy and sadness. Also here is his *The Shop Sign*, painted for an art dealer in 1720.

10

The Schloss Gardens
Daily 9am–dusk • Free; individual attractions charge a fee

Laid out in the French style in 1697, the **Schloss Gardens** were transformed into an English-style landscaped park in the early nineteenth century; after severe damage in the war, they were mostly restored to their Baroque form. Though it's possible to buy a map in the Schloss, it's easy enough to wander through the garden to the lake and the grounds behind, which do indeed have the feel of an English park.

The Neuer Pavillon
Tues–Sun: April–Oct 10am–6pm; Nov–March 10am–5pm • €4, €16 combined ticket for all of Schloss Charlottenburg attractions

The first place to head before hitting the gardens proper is the **Neuer Pavillon** (also called the Schinkel Pavillon), just to the east of the Schloss, which was designed by Schinkel (see p.57) for Friedrich Wilhelm III, and where the king preferred to live away from the excesses of the main building. Inside, furniture, decorative arts and paintings from the Romantic and Biedermeier periods are on display, including works by Carl Blechen, Schinkel and Eduard Gaertner.

The Belvedere
April–Oct Tues–Sun 10am 6pm • €3, €16 combined ticket for all of Schloss Charlottenburg attractions

Within the gardens, on the north side of the lake, is the **Belvedere**, built as a teahouse in 1788 and today housing a collection of Berlin porcelain – tea and coffee sets, dinnerware services and decorative pieces. Much of the craftsmanship is extremely delicate, and pieces commemorating the fall of Napoleon or depicting scenes from the palace and gardens have a real sense of history about them.

Mausoleum
April–Oct Tues–Sun 10am–6pm • €2, €16 combined ticket for all of Schloss Charlottenburg attractions

On the western side of the gardens, a long, tree-lined avenue leads to the hushed and shadowy **Mausoleum**, where Friedrich Wilhelm III is buried: his sarcophagus, carved with his image, makes him seem a good deal younger than his seventy years. Friedrich Wilhelm had commissioned the mausoleum to be built thirty years earlier for his wife, Queen Luise, whose own delicate sarcophagus apparently depicts her not dead but sleeping. Later burials here include Kaiser Wilhelm I, looking every inch a Prussian king.

Museums opposite the Schloss

Though you could happily spend a whole day wandering around the Schloss and its gardens, just across the way another group of excellent **museums** beckons. These in themselves could easily take an afternoon of your time.

Sammlung Scharf-Gerstenberg
Schlossstr. 70 • Tues–Sun 10am–6pm • €10 including Museum Berggruen, audio-guide included; a €12 Bereichskarte also includes the Museum für Fotografie (see p.109) • smb.museum • U-Richard-Wagner-Platz or bus #M45 from Bahnhof Zoo

The two buildings at the head of Schlossstrasse together served the palace's Garde du Corps-Regiments in the late nineteenth century. The building to the east, the former stables, has been revamped successfully and at great expense to house the **Sammlung Scharf-Gerstenberg** (Scharf-Gerstenberg Collection), the personal collection of Otto Gerstenberg, who made his fortune in the insurance industry of the early twentieth century and "liked looking at pictures", in the words of his grandson Dieter Scharf. Scharf expanded the collection (which was prodigious despite extensive losses in the war and its ransacking by Russians looking for war booty) and put it at Berlin's disposal. The collection suggests Gerstenberg had a penchant for the graphic arts and sculpture, particularly from the French Romantic and Surrealist schools; certainly the pictures Gerstenberg liked to look at tended to be unusual.

On show are the massive structures by Giovanni Battista Piranesi, some odd island-like forms by Victor Hugo and a woman copulating with a beast in Henri Rousseau's *Beauty and Beast* – who apparently uses the depiction to play with notions of the active and the passive. Other oddities include Max Klinger's local roller-skating works, which were based on his dreams, and works from Wolfgang Paalen, who painted with candle soot, and Jean Dubuffet who used coal, cement and butterfly wings. You'll also see impressive pieces by Max Ernst, René Magritte, Salvador Dalí and Paul Klee, who contributed a bit of orderly Bauhaus structure – many more of his works can be enjoyed over the road at the Museum Berggruen (see p.156). Perhaps strangest of all, maybe because they seem to fit in, is the presence of two ancient Egyptian gems: the Kalabsha Gate from around 20 BC and the Pillar of the Sahuré temple from around 2000 BC. Both are guests here until they're united with their peers in the new wing of the Pergamon museum (see p.57).

Museum Charlottenburg-Wilmersdorf

Schlossstr. 69 • Tues–Fri 10am–5pm, Sun 11am–5pm • Free • ⓦ villa-oppenheim-berlin.de • U-Richard-Wagner-Platz or bus #M45 from Bahnhof Zoo

Next door to the Scharf-Gerstenberg collection, and completely overshadowed by its neighbour, is the **Museum Charlottenburg-Wilmersdorf**. Though nothing special, this district museum can be worth ducking into for a quick look at a few evocative photos of Weimar and wartime Charlottenburg, and the occasional interesting temporary exhibition on the neighbourhood.

Museum Berggruen

Schlossstr. 1 • Tues–Sun 10am–6pm • €10 including Sammlung Scharf-Gerstenberg, audio-guide included; a €12 Bereichskarte also includes the Museum für Fotografie (see p.109) • ⓦ smb.museum • U-Richard-Wagner-Platz or bus #M45 from Bahnhof Zoo

The wonderful **Museum Berggruen** houses the collection of Heinz Berggruen, a young Jew forced to flee Berlin in 1936, who wound up as an art dealer in Paris – where he got to know Picasso and his circle – and assembled a collection of personal favourites. In 1996 Berlin gave him this building to show off his revered compilation in a comfortable and uncrowded setting. Most of the dozen or so Picassos have rarely been seen – highlights include the richly textured Cubist *The Yellow Sweater* and large-scale *Reclining Nude* – and there are also a handful of Cézannes and Giacomettis and a pair of van Goghs. The top floor is very strong on Paul Klee, with works spanning the interwar period.

Bröhan-Museum

Schlossstr. 1a • Tues–Sun 10am–6pm • €6 • ⓦ broehan-museum.de • U-Richard-Wagner-Platz or bus #M45 from Bahnhof Zoo

Just south of the Berggruen Collection, the compact and enjoyable **Bröhan-Museum** houses a fine collection of Art Deco and Jugendstil ceramics and furniture. Their assembly was the passion of Karl Bröhan (1921–2000), who donated all the pieces he had amassed to the city to commemorate his sixtieth birthday. Each of the period rooms is dedicated to a particular designer and hung with contemporaneous paintings – the best of which are the pastels of Willy Jaeckel and the resolutely modern works of Jean Lambert-Rucki.

Plötzensee Prison Memorial and around

Hüttigpfad • Daily: March–Oct 9am–5pm; Nov–Feb 9am–4pm • Free • ⓦ gedenkstaette-ploetzensee.de • Bus #123 from Hauptbahnhof to "Gedenkstätte Plötzensee"; then walk back along the route and turn right on Hüttigpfad

One of Berlin's handful of Third Reich buildings, the **Plötzensee Prison Memorial** (Gedenkstätte Plötzensee), survives in the northwest of the city centre, on the border of Charlottenburg and Wedding. Many of the former prison buildings where the Nazis brought dissidents and political opponents have been refurbished to provide a juvenile detention centre, so the memorial consists of only those buildings where executions took place. Between 1933 and 1945 more than 2500 people were hanged or guillotined here – hangings were carried out with piano wire, so that victims would slowly choke rather than die from broken necks – and their relatives were sent a bill for the execution.

Today, the execution chamber has been restored to its wartime condition: on occasion, victims were hanged eight at a time, and the hanging beam, complete with hooks, still stands. Though decked with wreaths and flowers, the atmosphere in the chamber is chilling, and in a further reminder of Nazi atrocities an urn in the courtyard contains soil from each of the concentration camps. Perhaps more than at any other wartime site in Berlin, Plötzensee conveys most palpably the horror of senseless, brutal murder.

Maria Regina Martyrum

Heckerdamm 230 • Four stops from the Plötzensee Prison Memorial on the #123 bus

Completed in 1963, the **Maria Regina Martyrum** is a purposefully sombre memorial church dedicated to those who died under the Nazis. Its brutally plain exterior, surrounded by a wide courtyard whose walls are flanked by abstract *Stations of the Cross* modelled in bronze, fronts a plain concrete shoebox, adorned only with an abstract altarpiece that fills the entire eastern wall. It's a strikingly unusual design, and successfully avoids looking dated.

The Westend

In the late nineteenth century, mansions belonging to Berlin's wealthy bourgeoisie sprung up in northwestern Charlottenburg-Wilmersdorf, in an area that became known, inspired by London's West End, as the **Westend**.

Georg-Kolbe-Museum

Sensburger Allee 25 • Tues–Sun 10am–6pm • €5 • ⓦ georg-kolbe-museum.de • S-Heerstrasse or bus #M49 from Bahnhof Zoo

The **Georg-Kolbe-Museum**, occupying the artist's former villa, displays many of his drawings and bronzes. Though Kolbe never quite achieved the eminence of his contemporary Ernst Barlach, his vigorous, modern, simplified classical style had broad appeal: it was particularly prized by the Nazis, who provided many major commissions, as well as by Mies van der Rohe, who used a Kolbe sculpture for his Barcelona Pavilion.

Le Corbusier house

Flatowallee 16 • Free • S-Olympiastadion or bus #M49 from Bahnhof Zoo to stop "Flatowallee"

The blocky **Le Corbusier** house, built by the French architect for the 1957 International Building exhibition, contains more than five hundred apartments and was heralded a modernist ideal living environment. A German-language exhibition (always open) on the ground floor tells its story and you can ride the lifts up to the shiny corridors on the top floor for views from the fire escapes.

Funkturm

Messedamm 22 • Mon 10am–8pm, Tues–Sun 10am–11pm • €4.50 • S-Messe Nord/ICC or bus #M49 from Bahnhof Zoo to stop "Haus des Rundfunks"

The **Funkturm** was built in 1928 as a radio and, eventually, a TV transmitter. One of Dr Goebbels' lesser-known achievements was to create the world's first regular TV service in 1941. Transmitted from the Funkturm, the weekly programme could only be received in Berlin; the service continued until just a few months before the end of the war. Today the Funkturm only serves police and taxi frequencies, but the mast remains popular with Berliners for the toe-curling views from its 126m-high **observation platform**. With the aluminium-clad monolith of the **International Congress Centre** (ICC) immediately below, it's possible to look out across deserted, overgrown S-Bahn tracks to the gleaming city in the distance – a mesmerizing sight at night.

10

The Olympic Stadium

Daily: late March–May & mid-Sept to Oct 9am–7pm; June to mid-Sept 9am–8pm; Nov–late March 10am–4pm • €7, including the Glockenturm; check online for details of English-language tours (1hr; €10): there's usually one at 11am, and as many as four daily in summer • ☎ 030 25 00 23 22, ⓦ olympiastadion-berlin.de • U- & S-Olympiastadion or bus #M49 from Bahnhof Zoo, stop "Flatowallee"

Built for the 1936 Games, the **Olympic Stadium** is one of Berlin's few remaining fascist-era buildings, and remains very much in use, and even well looked after thanks to a major renovation for the 2006 football World Cup. Despite its history, the building is impressive, the huge Neoclassical space a deliberate rejection of the modernist architecture that began to be in vogue in the 1930s. Inside, its sheer size comes as a surprise, since the seating falls away below ground level to reveal a much deeper auditorium than you'd imagine. On the western side, where the Olympic flame was kept and where medal winners are listed on the walls, it's easy to see how this monumental architecture, and the massive sculptures dotting the grounds outside, some of which still stand, could inspire the crowds. During the Olympics, Berliners were kept up to date with commentary on the games, interspersed with stirring music, from hundreds of loudspeakers that ran all the way from the Museum Island via Unter den Linden and the Brandenburg Gate, through the Tiergarten and out to the stadium. Standing here, looking back out to the city, you realize what an achievement this was.

As the home ground of Hertha BSC, Berlin's best football team, the stadium is regularly closed for sporting events, so it's best to check online before trudging out. Tours take you behind the scenes, to the VIP areas, locker rooms and so on; the knowledgeable guides provide interesting anecdotes along the way and after the tour you are free to wander around.

Glockenturm

Am Glockenturm • Daily: late March–May & mid-Sept to Oct 9am–7pm; June to mid-Sept 9am–8pm; Nov–late March 10am–4pm • €7 including the Olympic Stadium • U- & S-Olympiastadion or bus #M49 from Bahnhof Zoo, stop "Flatowallee"

Just a ten-minute walk from the Olympic Stadium, the **Glockenturm** (bell tower) towers above the spot where Hitler would enter the stadium each morning, state business permitting. Rebuilt after wartime damage, the building includes an exhibition about the history of the Olympic grounds here, while its tower offers stupendous views not only over the stadium but also north to the natural amphitheatre that forms the **Waldbühne**, an open-air concert site, and south to the Teufelsberg and the beginnings of the Grunewald.

Teufelsberg

A massive mound topped with a faintly terrifying fairytale castle, the **Teufelsberg** (Devil's Mountain) used to be a US signals and radar base, built to listen in to eastern bloc radio signals. No longer needed, it's scheduled to be dismantled – though no one seems in a hurry. The mountain itself is artificial: at the end of the war, the mass of debris that was once Berlin was carted to several sites around the city, most of the work being carried out by women known as *Trümmerfrauen* – "rubble women". Beneath the poplars, maples and ski runs lies the old Berlin, about 25 million cubic metres of it, perhaps awaiting the attention of some future archeologist. In the meantime, it's popular as a place for kite flying, and, in winter, skiing and tobogganing.

FROM TOP ALLIIERTEN-MUSEUM (P.162); SCHLOSS CHARLOTTENBURG (P.153) >

Dahlem and around

The mostly residential suburb of **Dahlem**, southwest of central Berlin, has the feel of a neat village-like enclave a world away from the city centre. The main draws are the exotic artefacts in the excellent **Museen Dahlem** group, but you could also visit the **Domäne Dahlem**, a working pre-industrial farm-cum-museum; the nearby **Dorfkirche St Annen**, a pretty brick church that dates back to 1220 (officially Mon, Wed & Sat 2–5pm), which boasts a Baroque pulpit and gallery and a carved wooden altar; and the city's impressive **Botanical Gardens**. You should, too, investigate the good **beer gardens** of the area (see p.205) – popular with students from the nearby Free University.

10

Museen Dahlem

The **Museen Dahlem** incorporates the **Museum of Ethnology** and the **Asian Art Museum**, and a block in the opposite direction from the underground station, the **Museum of European Cultures**.

Museum of Ethnology

Lansstr. 8 • Tues–Fri 10am–6pm, Sat & Sun 11am–6pm • €8 • ☎ 030 830 14 38 or ☎ 030 266 42 42 42, ⓦ smb.museum • U-Dahlem-Dorf

The **Museum of Ethnology** (Ethnologisches Museum) imaginatively displays just a small portion of one of the world's most extensive ethnological collections. Covering Asia, Africa, the Americas and the Pacific and South Sea islands, the museum details the varying cultures of dozens of civilizations and ethnic groups, each with their own traditions, religious beliefs and artistic forms. Look out for the dramatically lit group of sailing boats from the South Seas; the huge and macabre engraved stone stele from Guatemala; and the thoughtful exhibition on North American Indians, which not only contains artefacts such as clothing and weapons, but also examples of the non-Indian literature and ephemera – dime novels, advertising signs, rodeo posters and the like – that created many of our perceptions of indigenous American life. Equally imposing is a wall of painted ceremonial masks from South Asia and an exhibit of huts from Polynesia, Micronesia, New Guinea and New Zealand. Many of the smaller pieces, such as bronzes from Benin and carved figures from Central America, are also captivating.

Asian Art Museum

Lansstr. 8 • Tues–Fri 10am–6pm, Sat & Sun 11am–6pm • €8 • ☎ 030 83 01 43 82 or ☎ 030 266 42 42 42, ⓦ smb.museum • U-Dahlem-Dorf

The exceptional **Asian Art Museum** (Museum für Asiatische Kunst) is split into two sections – one dealing with the Indian subcontinent and one devoted to the Far East. The former includes an assortment of intricate bronze, wood or jade religious sculptures, many of which come from the Buddhist temples and monasteries along the northern Silk Route. Religious art naturally comprises the great bulk of the collection but there's also an intriguing series of miniature paintings covering secular subjects, such as court scenes and nature studies, and displaying a certain informality and playfulness. The Far East section includes an impressive Chinese calligraphy collection but many of the best exhibits are Japanese, including woodcuts, a stunning seventeenth-century gold-and-lacquer throne inlaid with mother-of-pearl, and a tearoom.

The Museum of European Cultures

Im Winkel 6 • Tues–Fri 10am–6pm, Sat & Sun 11am–6pm • €8 • ☎ 030 266 42 68 02 or ☎ 030 266 42 42 42, ⓦ smb.museum • U-Dahlem-Dorf

A short signposted walk down Archivstrasse directly opposite U-Bahn Dahlem-Dorf brings you to the **Museum of European Cultures** (Museum Europäischer Kulturen), which uses its extraordinary 275,000-item collection of handicrafts, paintings, prints and the like to put together changing exhibitions on subjects such as religious practices, modernization and commerce in various European regions. It's strong on German culture, with lots from France and Russia too.

Domäne Dahlem

Königin-Luise-Str. 49 • Wed–Mon 10am–6pm • €3 • ☎ 030 666 30 00, ⓦ domaene-dahlem.de • U-Dahlem-Dorf

Just west of and over the road from U-Bahn Dahlem-Dorf, the working farm and handicrafts centre **Domäne Dahlem** attempts to show the skills and crafts of the pre-industrial age. The old estate house has a few odds and ends, most intriguing of which are the thirteenth-century swastikas, but the collection of agricultural instruments in an outbuilding is better, with some good early twentieth-century inducements to farmers from grain manufacturers. Elsewhere are demonstrations of woodcarving, wool- and cotton-spinning and various other farm crafts, and at weekends some of the old agricultural machinery is fired up and the animals are paraded.

10

The Botanical Gardens

Königin-Luise-Str. 6–8 • **Gardens** Daily 9am–dusk, greenhouse closes 30min before garden • €6 • **Botanical Museum** Daily 10am–6pm • Included in Botanical Gardens entry, or €2.50 • ⓦ bgbm.org • S-Botanischer Garten or #X83 bus

At the **Botanical Gardens** you'll find palatial, sticky hothouses sprouting every plant imaginable (some 18,000 species, including several gruesome fly-eating plants, lots of vicious-looking cacti, and a huge variety of tulips), enticingly laid-out gardens and an uninspiring **Botanical Museum**.

The Grunewald

The **Grunewald** makes up around 32 square kilometres of mixed woodland and though more than two-thirds were cut down in the postwar years for badly needed fuel, subsequent replanting has replaced pine and birch with oak and made it more attractive and popular with Berliners for its clean air and walks.

The eastern edge of the Grunewald, where the wealthy suburb of Zehlendorf begins, is dotted with a series of modest but unusual **museums** that can be combined

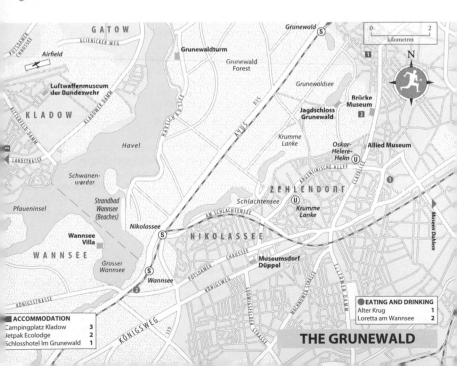

with time spent hiking in the forest to make a well-rounded day out. These include the **Brücke Museum**, which showcases German Expressionism, the **Jagdschloss Grunewald** with its small collection of old masters, the **Allied Museum**, which has important relics of Cold War Berlin, and the **Museumsdorf Düppel**, which recreates medieval village life.

Brücke Museum

Bussardsteig 9 • Wed–Mon 11am–5pm • €5 • ⓦ bruecke-museum.de • U-Fehrbeliner Platz or S-Hohenzollerndamm then bus #115 (direction Neuruppiner Strasse) to "Pücklerstrasse" stop

The **Brücke Museum** displays German Expressionist works by the group known as *Die Brücke* ("The Bridge"), active in Dresden and Berlin from 1905 to 1913, and who were banned by the Nazis. The big names are Kirchner, Heckel and Schmidt-Rottluff, who painted Expressionist cityscapes – using rich colours and playful perspectives – and who had a great influence on later artists. Many of their works were destroyed during the war, making this collection all the more interesting. Exhibitions change regularly, but tend to include early and later works from the movement.

Jagdschloss Grunewald

Hüttenweg 10 • April–Oct Tues–Sun 10am–6pm; Nov–March Sat & Sun 10am–4pm • €6 • ☎ 030 813 35 97 • U-Dahlem-Dorf, then bus X83 to "Clayallee"

From the Brücke Museum it's a ten-minute walk west along Pücklerstrasse into the depths of the Grunewald and **Jagdschloss Grunewald**, a royal hunting lodge built in the sixteenth century and enlarged by Friedrichs I and II. Today it's a museum housing old furniture and Dutch and German paintings, including works by Cranach the Elder and Rubens. There's also a small hunting museum in the outbuildings. However, walking around the adjacent lake, the **Grunewaldsee**, may prove more stimulating than the collections.

Allierten-Museum

Clayallee 135 • Tues–Sun 10am–6pm • Free • ⓦ alliertenmuseum.de • U-Oskar-Helene-Heim, then bus #115 to "Allierten-museum" stop

At the **Allierten-Museum** (**Allied Museum**) highlights include a segment of the Wall, a guardtower, and, most impressively, the original Checkpoint Charlie guardpost. The rest of the museum delivers a well-presented, somewhat turgid exhibition on Cold War Berlin, enlivened only occasionally by a spy story.

Museumsdorf Düppel

Clauertstr. 11 • Easter–Oct Thurs 3–7pm, Sun & holidays 10am–5pm • €2 • ☎ 030 802 66 71, ⓦ dueppel.de • S-Zehlendorf then bus #115 to "Ludwigsfelderstrasse" stop

With its dozen thatched buildings built on the site of a twelfth-century settlement, the reconstructed medieval country village **Museumsdorf Düppel** (Düppel Museum Village), in the far southwest of the city, gives an impression of what things might have looked like hereabouts 800 years ago. Traditional local breeds of sheep are reared and old strains of rye grown, and you can see demonstrations of handicrafts and farming techniques from the Middle Ages. Afterwards you can explore the lovely surrounding Düppel Forest.

GRUNEWALD HIKES

The Jagdschloss is a good starting point for **hikes** into the Grunewald: a 45-minute ramble along the eastern side of the Grunewaldsee brings you to S-Bahn Grunewald; or you can walk south to U-Bahn Krumme Lanke in about an hour, crossing Hutten Weg and then Onkel-Tom-Strasse to walk around the shores of Krumme Lanke lake.

Wannsee

Of the many lakes that dot the Grunewald, the best known is the **Wannsee**. The main attraction here is the **Strandbad Wannsee**, a 1km-long strip of pale sand that's the largest inland beach in Europe, and which gets packed as soon as the sun comes out. From here it's easy to wander into the forests and to smaller, less-populated beaches along the lakeside road **Havelchaussee**. The main tourist destination around the Wannsee is, however, the **Wannsee villa**. Nearby, the infinitely more pleasant **Pfaueninsel**, once a royal island playground, is now a bucolic park roamed by peacocks.

10

Strandbad Wannsee and the Havelchaussee

In essence Berlin's seaside, the **Strandbad Wannsee** has changed little in character since Heinrich Zille sketched the working classes at play here in the late nineteenth century. It's a busy commercial beach scene; if you're looking for a quieter sandy spot by the water, head north along the shore, following the **Havelchaussee**. Usefully, bus #218 from S-Bahn Wannsee and Nikolassee goes this way, running along 6km of quiet, sandy coves. This area is also good for a spot of **hiking** – both along the lakeshore and inland into the forest.

Grunewaldturm

4km north of the Strandbad • Daily 10am–10pm • €1

One possible start or terminus of a hike is the **Grunewaldturm**, a 55m-high observation tower right next to the Havel. Built at the end of the nineteenth century as a memorial to Kaiser Wilhelm I, it has a smart restaurant and fine views out across the lakes.

Wannsee villa

Am Grossen Wannsee 56–58 • Daily 10am–6pm • Free • ⓦ ghwk.de • #114 bus from S-Wannsee to "Haus der Wannsee-Konferenz" stop

While not the most enjoyable of sights, one place that should on no account be missed on a trip to the Wannsee is the **Wannsee villa** (Haus der Wannsee Konferenze) overlooking the lake, where, on January 20, 1942, the fate of European Jewry was determined (see p.257). The deeply moving exhibition here shows the entire process of the Holocaust, from segregation and persecution to the deportation and eventual murder of the Jews from Germany, its allies and all the lands the Third Reich conquered. Many of the photographs and accounts are horrific, and the events they describe seem part of a world far removed from this quiet locale – which, in many ways, underlines the tragedy. Particularly disturbing is the photograph of four generations of women – babe-in-arms, young mother, grandmother and ancient great-grandmother – moments before their execution on a sand dune in Latvia.

The room where the conference took place remains as it was, with documents from the meeting on the table and photographs of participants around the walls; biographies show that many lived to a comfortable old age. Even seventy years after the event, to stand in the room where a decision was formalized to coldly and systematically annihilate a race sends shivers down the spine.

Pfaueninsel

Museum April–Oct daily 10am–5.30pm • €3 • ⓦ spsg.de • S-Bahn Wannsee, then bus #218, then a passenger ferry (daily: March & Oct 9am–6pm; April & Sept 9am–7pm; May–Aug 9am–8pm; Nov–Feb 10am–4pm; €3)

Designed as a royal fantasy getaway on one of the largest of the Havel islands, the **Pfaueninsel** (Peacock Island) is now a conservation zone with a flock of peacocks stalking around its landscaped park. No cars are allowed on the island (nor are dogs, ghetto-blasters or smoking). Attractions include a mini-Schloss, built by Friedrich Wilhelm II for his mistress and containing a small **museum**. Most enjoyable, though, are the gardens, landscaped by Peter Lenné, the original designer of the Tiergarten.

Luftwaffenmuseum

Am Flugplatz Gatow 33 • April–Oct Tues–Sun 10am–6pm; Nov–March Tues–Sun 9am–4pm • Free • ☎ 030 36 87 26 01,
🖰 mhm-gatow.de • S-Spandau, then bus #135 to "Luftwaffenmuseum" stop, 1.5km from entrance.

The giant **Luftwaffenmuseum** (German Air Force Museum) records more than a hundred
years of air force history across several hangars on Berlin's Gatow airfield. This was one
landing place for the "raisin bombers" breaking the Berlin Blockade (see p.124), and also
where the RAF was stationed in the days of West Berlin; the exhibition itself leaves no
aileron or propeller unturned in its examination of the German military's aeronautical
past. There are dozens of planes to view, from Red Baron-era WWI aircraft to Cold
War-era fighter jets from both sides of the Iron Curtain. Though most information is in
German, enthusiasts could easily spend the best part of a day here; the café is very basic,
however, and it's a long way to come, on infrequent buses – bring supplies.

Spandau

Spandau, situated on the confluence of the Spree and Havel rivers, about 10km
northwest of its centre, is Berlin's oldest suburb. Granted a town charter in 1232, it
escaped the worst of the wartime bombing, preserving a couple of old village-like
streets – at their best during the Christmas market – and an ancient moated fort, the
Zitadelle. Though the word Spandau immediately brings to mind its jail's most famous
– indeed, in later years, only – prisoner, **Rudolf Hess**, there's little connection between
Hess and Spandau itself. The jail, 4km away from the centre, was demolished after his
death to make way for a supermarket for the British armed forces.

Spandau Altstadt

In comparison to its Zitadelle, Spandau's **Altstadt**, or old town, is of minor interest.
It begins just to the northeast of the Rathaus and is at its best around the medieval
Nikolaikirche; the **Reformationsplatz** (with a good *Konditorei*), where playful sculptures
adorn the modern marketplace; and in the restored street called **Kolk**. Also here is the
Brauhaus Spandau, a nineteenth-century brewery that produces beer to a medieval
recipe; tours are available.

Zitadelle

Daily 10am–5pm • €4.50 • 🖰 zitadelle-spandau.de • U-Zitadelle, or a 10min walk through the Altstadt from S-Spandau where the #134
from Alt-Kladow stops

The postcard-pretty **Zitadelle** (Citadel), just northeast over the Havel from the Altstadt,
was established in the twelfth century to defend the town. Its moat and russet walls
were built during the Renaissance by an Italian architect and it's an explorable, if not
totally engrossing, place with a small local history museum, a pricey restaurant and the
thirteenth-century **Juliusturm**, from which there's a good view over the ramshackle
Zitadelle interior and the countryside.

RUDOLF HESS (1894–1987)

Rudolf Hess marched in the Munich Beer Hall *putsch* of 1923 and was subsequently
imprisoned with Hitler in Landsberg jail, where he took the dictation of *Mein Kampf*. For a
time he was the **deputy leader** of the Nazi party, second only to the Führer himself. An
experienced World War I airman, he flew himself to Scotland in 1941, ostensibly in an attempt
to sue for peace with King George VI and ally Great Britain with Germany against the Soviet
Union. It remains unclear whether he did this with Hitler's blessing, but there is evidence to
suggest that the Führer knew of Hess's plans. Either way, he was immediately arrested and
Churchill refused to meet him; he was held until sentenced to life imprisonment at the
Nürnberg trials. He finally committed suicide in 1987 in his Spandau jail – the only inmate in
a jail designed for six hundred – hanging himself on a short piece of lamp flex, aged 93.

SCHLOSS SANSSOUCI

Out of the city

When Berlin's city fringes don't seem like breather enough from its bustle, a day-trip into its sleepy Brandenburg hinterland might be just the thing. This federal state is replete with gentle scenery, a patchwork of beech forests, heaths and fields of dazzling rapeseed and sunflowers, all sewn together by a multitude of rivers, lakes and waterways. Thanks to Berlin's superb transport network, the key towns of Potsdam and Oranienburg are easy and economical day-trips. And since the S-Bahn network allows you to transport a bike, you should seriously consider bringing one along, or renting one. Potsdam's parks are particularly ideal for a day's gentle exploration on two wheels coupled with a picnic. But should you wish to explore the state more widely by car, you're sure to find cruising the flat tree-lined avenues that typify Brandenburg's minor roads a pleasure.

Almost all the state's headline attractions are southwest of Berlin in **Potsdam**, a town whose size is effectively doubled by surrounding landscaped gardens dotted with royal piles and follies, which include Frederick the Great's famous Schloss **Sanssouci**. Meanwhile, just north beyond Berlin's fringes, the town of Oranienburg is far less attractive, but equally absorbing as the site of former concentration camp **Sachsenhausen**. For something completely different, the **Tropical Islands complex**, to the south of Berlin, offers a fun day out where you can enjoy the waters and beaches of warmer climes.

INFORMATION AND GETTING AROUND

Tourist information Worth investigating before you travel is the website of the regional tourism authority Tourismus Marketing Brandenburg (ⓦbrandenburg -tourism.com).

Transport and passes The Brandenburg-Berlin Ticket allows up to five people to travel together anywhere within Brandenburg for one day (9am–3am) on all regional trains (RE, IRE, RB) as well as on the entire Berlin BVG network. A second-class ticket costs €29 online, or €31 from train stations, €32 on trains; for timetables and tickets see ⓦvbb.de.

BERLIN AND BRANDENBURG

Potsdam

For most visitors **POTSDAM** means **Sanssouci**, Frederick the Great's splendid landscaped park of architectural treasures that once completed Berlin as the grand Prussian capital. However, Potsdam's origins date back to the tenth-century Slavonic settlement Poztupimi, and predate Berlin by a couple of hundred years. The castle built here in 1160 marked the first step in the town's gradual transformation from sleepy fishing backwater to **royal residence** and **garrison town**, a role it enjoyed under the Hohenzollerns until the abdication of Kaiser Wilhelm II in 1918. World War II left Potsdam badly damaged: on April 14, 1945, a bombing raid killed four thousand people, destroyed many fine Baroque buildings and reduced its centre to ruins. Less than four months later – on August 2 – the victorious Allies converged on Potsdam's **Schloss Cecilienhof** to hammer out the details of a division of Germany and Europe. Potsdam itself ended up in the Soviet zone, where modern "socialist" building programmes steadily erased many architectural memories of the town's uncomfortably prosperous imperial past. Yet it's this past that has given us its most popular sights, apart from those at Park Sanssouci; there are more across the Havel in **Babelsberg**, which is best known as the site of the most important film studio in German film history.

North from the train station beyond Lange Brücke is the **Alter Markt**, the fringe of Potsdam's town centre. From here the northbound and arterial **Friedrich-Ebert-Strasse** leads to its pedestrianized main shopping street **Brandenburger Strasse**. Part of a Baroque quarter, it's best appreciated off the main drag, but in truth the town's attractions are scant in comparison with what awaits in Park Sanssouci.

Alter Markt

The arresting outlines of the unmistakably GDR-era *Hotel Mercure* and the stately domed **Nikolaikirche** frame the triangular **Alter Markt**. Its surging traffic and extensive building work make it an unprepossessing city gateway, but for most of its life it harboured bustling squares and streets. It was here that the town's earliest fortifications were built and where the medieval town flourished, a past that the highly visible excavations continually unravel, as remnants of various crafts and the occasional buried treasure are found. But the Alter Markt is best known as the former site of the **Stadtschloss**, a Baroque residence built by the Great Elector between 1662 and 1669. World War II (specifically April 14 and 15, 1945) reduced it to a bare, roofless shell, and the GDR demolished what remained in 1960 – around eighty percent of the building – to remove the last vestiges of Potsdam's grandest imperial buildings.

Today, Brandenburg's parliament building (**Landtag**) copies the footprint of the old Schloss and incorporates many of its elements into its design: not least the reconstruction of the gate to the palace forecourt, the domed **Fortunaportal**, which completes the recreation of three domed structures that traditionally dominated the Alter Markt.

The most significant of these is the elegant, Schinkel-designed Neoclassical **Nikolaikirche** (Mon–Sat 9am–7pm, Sun 11.30am–7pm), while the third dome belongs to Potsdam's former **Rathaus** (Tues–Sun 10am–6pm, free), built in the mid-eighteenth century in Palladian Classical style. Under the GDR the building became an arts centre, a role it retains to this day. The **obelisk** in front, designed by Knobelsdorff, originally bore four reliefs depicting the Great Elector and his successors. When re-erected during the 1970s these were replaced with reliefs of the architects who shaped much of Potsdam: Schinkel, Knobelsdorff, Gontard and Persius.

Filmmuseum

Breite Str. 1a • Daily 10am–6pm • €5 • ☎ 0331 27/1 81 12, ⓦ filmmuseum-potsdam.de

Across the main road, Friedrich-Ebert-Strasse, from the Nikolaikirche, lies the squat but elegant **Marstall**, the oldest town-centre survivor. Built as an orangerie towards the end of the eighteenth century and converted into stables by that scourge of frivolity, Friedrich Wilhelm I, the building owes its current appearance to Knobelsdorff, who

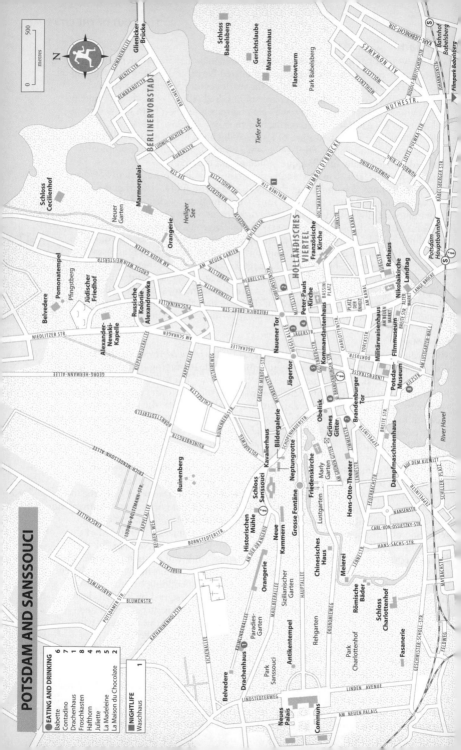

POTSDAM AND SANSSOUCI

EATING AND DRINKING
Babette 6
Contadino 7
Drachenhaus 1
Froschkasten 8
Hafthorn 4
Juliette 3
La Madeleine 5
La Maison du Chocolate 2

NIGHTLIFE
Waschhaus 1

N

0 500 metres

extended and prettified it during the eighteenth century. Today it houses Potsdam's **Filmmuseum**, which draws on material from Babelsberg's UFA studios nearby (see p.173) to present both a technical and artistic history of German film from 1895 to 1980, with some particularly fascinating material concerning the immediate postwar period. It's always been an engaging museum, with a vaguely hands-on feel, and will reopen in 2014 following a complete refurb. The museum **cinema** is the best in Potsdam and there's also a good **café**.

Just behind the Marstall, **Am Neuen Markt** leads to a few handsome and now very rare vestiges of old Potsdam, including some improbably grand eighteenth-century coaching stables with an entrance in the form of a triumphal arch.

Altstadt

North beyond Alter Markt, **Friedrich-Ebert-Strasse** passes into an area once occupied by Potsdam's **Altstadt** before it was fairly comprehensively destroyed in the war. Luckily, a couple of residential districts survived substantially intact and slowly emerge along the north end of Friedrich-Ebert-Strasse. **Brandenburger Strasse**, today's main shopping street, is the key cross street.

11

Bassinplatz

Following Brandenburger Strasse a block east of Friedrich-Ebert-Strasse brings you to **Bassinplatz**, a grand plaza and park that's disfigured by a huge modern bus station, but dominated by the nineteenth-century **Peter-Pauls-Kirche**, a replica of the campanile of San Zeno Maggiore in Verona. At the southeastern corner of the square lies the **Französische Kirche**, completed according to plans by Knobelsdorff in 1753 in imitation of the Pantheon in Rome, a recurring theme in German architecture of the period.

Holländisches Viertel

Just north of Bassinplatz lies the appealing **Holländisches Viertel** or "Dutch quarter", where 134 gabled, red-brick houses were put up by Dutch builders for immigrants from the Netherlands who were invited to work in Potsdam by Friedrich Wilhelm I. The quarter has seen periods of dereliction since, but recent restoration and gentrification has produced a small colony of trendy shops and cafés.

Brandenburger Strasse and Lindenstrasse
Gedenkstätte Lindenstr.

West of the Dutch quarter, Brandenburger Strasse leads to Park Sanssouci and forms the backbone of a **Baroque quarter** – built between 1732 and 1742 on the orders of Friedrich Wilhelm I for tradespeople as Potsdam rapidly expanded. One major cross-street is Lindenstrasse, where, at no. 54–55, the Dutch-style **Kommandantenhaus** has uncomfortable associations: until the *Wende* it served as a Stasi detention centre known as the "Lindenhotel". It now houses **Gedenkstätte Lindenstrasse**: you can view the chilling cells and an exhibition details the building's use, which included a spell as a Nazi prison and "hereditary-health court", where decisions about compulsory sterilization were made (Tues–Sun 10am–6pm; €1.50; €3 with tour; ⌨gedenkstaette-lindenstrasse.de).

Further north up Lindenstrasse is the **Jägertor** or "Hunter's Gate", one of Potsdam's three surviving town gates, surmounted by a sculpture of a stag succumbing to a pack of baying hounds. Meanwhile, the triumphal **Brandenburger Tor** marks the western end of Brandenburger Strasse built by Gontard in 1733 with a playfulness lacking in its Berlin namesake. The **Grünes Gitter** park entrance lies just beyond the northwestern corner of the adjacent **Luisenplatz**.

Park Sanssouci
Stretching west out of Potsdam's town centre, **Park Sanssouci** was built for Frederick the Great as a retreat after he decided in 1744 that he needed a residence where he

could live "without cares" – "sans souci" in the French spoken in court. The task was entrusted to architect Georg von Knobelsdorff, who had already proved himself on other projects in Potsdam and Berlin. **Schloss Sanssouci**, on a hill overlooking the town, took three years to complete, while the extensive parklands were laid out over the following five years. As a finishing touch Frederick ordered the construction of the **Neues Palais** at the western end of the park, to mark the end of the Seven Years' War. Numerous additions over the following hundred and fifty years or so included the **Orangerie**. The park is most beautiful in spring, when the trees are in leaf and the flowers in bloom, and least crowded on weekdays.

INFORMATION AND TICKETS

Park entrance Entrance to the park itself is free, although a €2 donation is suggested.

Combination tickets if you plan to visit several buildings, consider a combination ticket – a Premium-Tageskarte (€19), available only at Schloss Sanssouci, allows entry to all Park buildings. The regular Tageskarte (€15) is sold at all palaces, and the visitors' centre, and gives access to all buildings in Park Sanssouci except Schloss Sanssouci itself.

Despite calling themselves *Tageskarten* (day tickets), both the above are valid for two consecutive days.

Information The main visitors' centre for the park (daily: March–Oct 8.30am–6pm; Nov–March 8.30am–5pm; ☎ 0331 969 42 00, ⊛ spsg.de) is by the historic windmill (see p.171). The Grünes Gitter, which provides a southeastern entrance to the park, also has an information kiosk.

Friedenskirche

Late April & early Oct Mon–Sat 11am–5pm, Sun noon–5pm; May–Sept Mon–Sat 10am–6pm, Sun noon–6pm; mid-Oct to late April Sat 11am–4pm, Sun 11.30am–4pm • Free

Immediately north of the Grünes Gitter entrance lies the 1850 Italianate **Friedenskirche**, designed by Persius for Friedrich Wilhelm IV. With its 39m-high campanile and lakeside setting, it conjures up the southern European atmosphere that Friedrich Wilhelm strove for by using the St Clemente Basilica in Rome as a model, and with the design centred on the magnificent Byzantine apse mosaic from Murano. Adjoining the church, the domed Hohenzollern mausoleum contains the tombs of Friedrich Wilhelm IV and his wife Elizabeth, and Friedrich III and his wife Victoria. The garden to the west is the **Marly-Garten**, once the kitchen garden of Friedrich I, who named it, with intentional irony, after Louis XIV's luxurious Marly park.

Schloss Sanssouci

Schloss Sanssouci Tues–Sun: April–Oct 9am–6pm; Nov–March 10am–5pm; guided tours every 20min, tickets go on sale at 9am – arrive early as demand is high • April–Oct €8; Nov–March €12 **Damenflügel** May–Oct Sat & Sun 10am–6pm • €2

To approach **Schloss Sanssouci** as Frederick the Great might have done, make for the eighteenth-century **obelisk** on Schopenhauerstrasse. Beyond, Hauptallee runs through the ornate Knobelsdorff-designed **Obelisk-Portal** – two clusters of pillars flanked by the goddesses Flora and Pomona – to the **Grosse Fontäne**, the largest of the park's many fountains, around which stand a host of Classical statues, notably Venus and Mercury. The approach to the Schloss itself leads up through terraced ranks of vines that are among the northernmost in Germany.

Frederick had definite ideas about what he wanted and worked closely with Knobelsdorff on the palace design, which was to be a place where the king, who had no great love for his capital, Berlin, or his wife Elizabeth Christine, could escape both. It's a surprisingly modest one-storey Baroque affair, topped by an oxidized green dome and ornamental statues, looking out over the vine terraces towards the high-rises of central Potsdam.

The **interior** of Schloss Sanssouci can only be visited by **guided tour**. Once inside, you'll find a frenzy of Rococo in the twelve rooms where Frederick lived and entertained his guests – a process that usually entailed quarrelling with them. The most eye-catching rooms are the opulent **Marmorsaal** (Marble Hall) and the **Konzertzimmer** (Concert Room), where the flute-playing king forced eminent musicians to play his own works on concert evenings. Frederick's favourite haunt was his library where, surrounded by two thousand volumes – mainly French translations of classics and a sprinkling of contemporary French writings – he could oversee work on his tomb. One of Frederick's most celebrated house guests was Voltaire, who lived here from 1750 to 1753, acting as a kind of private tutor to the king, finally leaving when he'd had enough of Frederick's behaviour, damning the king's intellect with faint praise and accusing him of treating "the whole world as slaves". In revenge Frederick had Voltaire's former room decorated with carvings of apes and parrots.

The **Damenflügel**, the west wing of the Schloss, was added in 1840, its thirteen rooms housing ladies and gentlemen of the court. Nearby on the terrace is a wrought-iron summerhouse protecting a weatherbeaten copy of a Classical statue, while just to the south an eighteenth-century sculpture of Cleopatra looks over the graves of Frederick's horses.

Around Schloss Sanssouci

East of Schloss Sanssouci, overlooking the ornamental **Holländischer Garten**, or Dutch Garden, is the restrained Baroque **Bildergalerie** (mid-May to Oct Tues–Sun 10am–6pm; €6), which, it's claimed, was the first building in Europe built specifically as a museum. Unfortunately, wartime destruction and looting scattered the contents, but the new collection includes Caravaggio's wonderful *Incredulity of St Thomas* and several works by Rubens and Van Dyck. On the opposite side of the Schloss, from a point near the Cleopatra statue, steps lead down to the **Neue Kammern** (March Sat & Sun 10am–5pm; April–Oct Tues–Sun 10am–5pm; €4 with tour, €3 without), the architectural twin of the Bildergalerie, originally an orangerie and later a guesthouse. Immediately west is the prim **Sizilianischer Garten** or Sicilian Garden, crammed with coniferous trees and subtropical plants, complementing the **Nordischer Garten**, another ornamental garden just to the north, whose most interesting feature is the strange-looking **Felsentor** or Rock Gate, a gateway fashioned out of uncut stones and topped by a lumpen-looking eagle with outstretched wings.

Frederick was prepared to go to some lengths to achieve the desired carefree rural ambience for Sanssouci and retained an old wooden windmill as an ornament just north of the Neue Kammern. Four years after his death, this was replaced by a rustic-looking stone construction, the **Historische Mühle**, now a restaurant.

The Orangerie and around

April Sat & Sun 10am–6pm; May–Oct Tues–Sun 10am–6pm • €4

From the western corner of the Sizilianischer Garten, **Maulbeerallee**, a road open to traffic, cuts through the park past the **Orangerie**. This Italianate Renaissance-style structure with its belvedere towers is one of the most visually impressive buildings in the Sanssouci park. A series of terraces with curved retaining walls sporting waterspouts in the shape of lions' heads leads up to the sandy-coloured building, whose slightly down-at-heel appearance adds character. It was built at the behest of Friedrich IV and, like the Friedenskirche (see p.170), inspired by architecture seen on his Italian travels. The facade is lined with allegorical statues set in niches, such as "Industry" who holds a cog wheel. The western wing of the building is still used as a refuge for tropical plants in winter, and during the summer it's possible to ascend the western tower for views of the Neues Palais and vistas of Potsdam's high-rises. The Orangerie also houses a gallery, the **Raphaelsaal**, with copies of paintings looted by Napoleon.

The Belvedere and around

From the western wing of the Orangerie, the arrow-straight Krimlindenallee, lined with lime trees, leads towards a Rococo **Belvedere**, the last building to be built under Frederick the Great. It was the only building in the whole of Sanssouci park to suffer serious war damage, but has now been restored to its former glory. A couple of hundred metres short of the Belvedere, a path off to the left leads to the **Drachenhaus**, a one-time vintner's house built in the style of a Chinese pagoda for the small vineyard nearby.

There's a café inside (see p.174). Southwest of the Drachenhaus, a pathway leads to the **Antikentempel**, built in 1768 to house part of Frederick the Great's art collection. This domed rotunda is now the last resting place of a number of Hohenzollerns, including the Empress Auguste Victoria, and Hermine, whom Wilhelm II married in exile, and who became known as the "last Empress".

Neues Palais
Wed–Mon: April–Oct 10am–6pm; Nov–March Wed–Mon 10am–5pm • €8

Rising through the trees at the western end of Park Sanssoucci, the **Neues Palais** is another massive Rococo extravaganza from Frederick the Great's time, built between 1763 and 1769 to reaffirm Prussian might after the Seven Years' War. At the centre of the palace is a huge green-weathered dome, topped by a crown, while the edges of the roof around the entire building are adorned by lines of Classical figures, mass-produced by a team of sculptors. The main entrance is in the western facade, and once inside, you'll find the interior predictably opulent, particularly as you enter the vast and startling **Grottensaal** on the ground floor, which is decorated entirely with shells and semi-precious stones to form images of lizards and dragons. The equally huge **Marmorsaal** is the other highlight, with its beautiful floor of patterned marble slabs. The southern wing contains Frederick's apartments and theatre where he enjoyed Italian opera and French plays. The last imperial resident of the Neues Palais was Kaiser Wilhelm II, who packed sixty train carriages with the palace contents before fleeing with his family in November 1918, following the revolution and abdication. Facing the Neues Palais entrance are the **Communs**, a couple of Rococo fantasies joined by a curved colonnade. They look grandiose, but their purpose was mundane: they housed the palace's serving and maintenance staff.

Rehgarten and Park Charlottenhof

From the Neues Palais, Ökonomieweg leads east between the **Rehgarten** or Deer Garden, the former court hunting ground (and still home to a few deer) and **Park Charlottenhof**, created by Friedrich Wilhelm III as a Christmas present for his son, and today one of Sanssouci's quieter corners.

A path leads over a bridge past a small farm building to the **Römische Bäder** (May–Oct Tues–Sun 10am–5pm; €4), built by Schinkel and Persius in convincing imitation of a Roman villa. Across the lawns to the south is **Schloss Charlottenhof** (May–Oct Tues–Sun 10am–6pm; €4), another Roman-style building, again designed by Schinkel and Persius for Friedrich IV. Though designated a palace, it is, in reality, little more than a glorified villa, but its interior, unlike most Sanssouci buildings, is original. The effect is impressive: the hallway is bathed in blue light filtered through coloured glass decorated with stars, a prelude to the **Kupferstichzimmer**, or print room, whose walls are now covered in copies of Italian Renaissance paintings. Immediately east of Schloss Charlottenhof is the **Dichterhain** (Poets' Grove), an open space dotted with busts of Goethe, Schiller and Herder, among others. West of here through the woods and across a racetrack-shaped clearing called the **Hippodrom** is the **Fasanerie**, another Italian-style edifice built between 1842 and 1844.

On the Ökonomieweg – en route back to the Grünes Gitter entrance – you'll pass the slightly kitsch **Chinesisches Haus** (May–Oct Tues–Sun 10am–6pm; €2), a kind of Rococo pagoda housing a small museum of Chinese and Meissen porcelain and surrounded by eerily lifelike statues of Oriental figures.

Neuer Garten

Immediately northeast of Potsdam's centre lies the **Neuer Garten,** a large park where the **Marmorpalais** (Marble Palace) was built for Friedrich Wilhelm II. He died a premature death here in 1797, allegedly as a consequence of his dissolute lifestyle. The palace has now been restored to an approximation of its original royal condition and the sumptuous rooms can be seen (March–Oct Tues–Sun 10am–6pm; Nov–March Sat & Sun 10am–4pm; April Sat & Sun 10am–6pm; €5).

Schloss Cecilienhof

Tues–Sun: April–Oct 10am–6pm; Nov–March 10am–5pm • €6 • ⓦ spsg.de • Tram #92 or #96 to "Reiterweg/Alleestrasse" stop then change to bus #603 to Schloss Cecilienhof

In the grounds of the Neuer Garten, looking like a mock-Elizabethan mansion, is **Schloss Cecilienhof**; the last palace to be commissioned by the Hohenzollerns, it was begun in 1913 and completed in 1917, the war evidently doing nothing to change the architectural style. Cecilienhof would only rate a passing mention were it not for the fact that the **Potsdam conference** – confirming earlier decisions made at Yalta about the postwar European order – was held here from July 17 to August 2, 1945. The conference was heavily symbolic, providing a chance for Truman, Stalin and Churchill (replaced mid-conference by Clement Attlee) to show the world that they had truly won the war by meeting in the heart of the ruined Reich. As a result, the main attraction inside is the **Konferenzsaal**, or conference chamber, where the Allies worked out details of the division of Europe. Everything has been left pretty much as it was in 1945, with the huge round table, specially made in Moscow for the conference, still in place. It's also possible to visit the delegates' workrooms, furnished in varying degrees of chintziness. Cecilienhof has been used as an expensive hotel and restaurant since 1960.

11

Babelsberg

On the eastern bank of the Havel is **Babelsberg**, once a town but now officially part of Potsdam. Lining the banks of the Tiefer See is **Park Babelsberg**, Potsdam's third great park complex, designed by Lenné, but not as popular. Tracks lead through the hilly, roughly wooded park to **Schloss Babelsberg** (closed for renovation; ⓦ spsg.de), a neo-Gothic architectural extravaganza, built by Schinkel at the behest of Prince Wilhelm, brother of Friedrich Wilhelm IV, and inspired by England's Windsor Castle. But Babelsberg's real claim to fame is as the one-time heart of the German film industry. Founded in 1917, it was here that the **UFA film studios** rivalled Hollywood during the 1920s.

Filmpark Babelsberg

Grossbeerenstr., Potsdam-Babelsberg • Late March–Oct daily 10am–6pm • €21 • ☎ 0331 721 27 55, ⓦ filmpark.de • Buses #690 and #601 from S-Babelsberg

Today, the huge old UFA film studios complex – films produced here during its heyday included *Das Kabinett des Dr Caligari*, *Metropolis* and *Der Blaue Engel* – has reinvented itself as a theme park, **Filmpark Babelsberg**. Mainly of interest to those with a good knowledge of the German film industry, it offers the chance to wander through costume and props departments and watch technicians going through the motions of shooting film scenes. It's also possible to visit the hangar-like studio where Fritz Lang may have filmed *Metropolis* (no one is quite sure) and admire a reproduction of his futuristic set. Aside from film-related attractions are fairground rides and animal shows.

ARRIVAL AND DEPARTURE — POTSDAM

By train All services, including the S-Bahn from Berlin (around 30min) arrive in Potsdam's Hauptbahnhof.

Tickets Potsdam's local bus and tram services are included in the BVG ticket (see p.22) that include zone C, so buying an ABC day-ticket is the most economical option for daytrips from Berlin.

GETTING AROUND

By bus and tram The city's main bus station lies beside the Hauptbahnhof, from where Verkehrsbetrieb Potsdam (ViP; ⓦ vip-potsdam.de) bus #X15 runs straight to Schloss Sanssouci. Take #X5 or bus #605 to "Neues Palais" to walk from the furthest reaches of the park via its attractions back to the Altstadt. Tram #92 heads from the Hauptbahnhof to the Altstadt, though it's more interesting to simply walk

10min via Lange Brücke and Alter Markt.

Bike rental Potsdam per Pedales at the train station (May–Sept daily 9.30am–7pm; ☎ 0331 748 00 57, ⓦ potsdam-per-pedales.de) rents bikes (€10.50/day), as well as Potsdam audio guides (€6/day). However, you can only cycle on a single loop within the park and are not allowed to park your bike within it.

INFORMATION

Tourist office In the train station (April–Oct Mon–Sat 9.30am–8pm, Sun 10am–4pm; Nov–March Mon–Fri 9.30am–6pm, Sun 10am–4pm) and at Brandenburger Str. 3, by Potsdam's own Brandenburger Tor (April–Oct Mon–Fri 9.30am–6pm, Sat & Sun 9.30am–4pm; Nov–March Mon–Fri 10am–6pm, Sat & Sun 9.30am–2pm; ☎0331 27 55 88 99, ⓦpotsdam-tourism.com).

EATING AND DRINKING

CAFÉS AND BARS

Babette Brandenburger Str. 71 ☎0331 29 16 48. Pleasant café with outdoor seating, in the shadow of the Brandenburger Tor, that's a good place to rest weary feet and have an indulgent *Torte* after trekking around Sanssouci Park. The large menu, available in English, features simple snacks (€7) and main meals (€10) though the quality of both is fairly ordinary. Mon–Sat 9am–late, Sun 10am–late.

Drachenhaus Maulbeerallee 4a ☎0331 505 38 08. Genteel little café in the grounds of Schloss Sanssouci, housed in a pagoda-style building once used by royal vintners. You can eat well here, with a choice of sturdy Brandenburg specialities or just a piece of *Torte*. March–Oct daily 11am–7pm; Nov–Feb Tues–Sun 11am–6pm.

★ **Hafthorn** Friedrich-Ebert-Str. 90 ☎0331 280 08 20. Hip and happening pub with snacks (€2–7) including superb burgers, rösti and potato pancakes. A fashionable but very mixed crowd packs the place out until late, even when there's no live music, and there's also a busy beer garden. Daily 6pm–midnight.

RESTAURANTS

Contadino Luisenplatz 8 ☎0331 951 09 23. The casual surroundings overlooking a plaza and Brandenburger Tor make this mid-priced Italian restaurant a perfect place to eat before or after tackling Sanssouci. Along with pasta and pizza there's a wealth of good alternatives: chops, steaks and pan-fried Iberian and South American food. Some items and daily specials cost as little as €3.50. Daily noon–late.

Froschkasten Kiezstr. 4 ☎0331 29 13 15, ⓦfroschkasten.de. One of the oldest and most authentic inns in Potsdam serves good, traditional German food, with several great fish dishes including a delicious grilled salmon fillet (€19). Mon–Sat noon–midnight, Sun noon–10pm.

★ **Juliette** Jägerstr. 39 ☎0331 270 17 91. Cosy gourmet place that's probably Potsdam's best restaurant thanks to its French flair (and wines) and an unpredictable range of dishes that might include the exotic likes of loach with couscous and avocado puree or steak with truffles and foie gras. Expect to pay around €70/person including drinks. Daily noon–3.30pm & 6–10pm.

La Maison du Chocolat Benkertstr. 20 ☎0331 237 07 30. Café-restaurant with outdoor seating on the pavements of the pretty Dutch quarter. Good spot for breakfast or regional and seasonal specialities (from around €9); but it's the rich, indulgent, and frankly unmissable, hot chocolates that really put the place on the map. Great cakes too. Cash only. Daily 10am–10pm.

La Madeleine Lindenstr. 9 ☎0331 270 54 00. Smart *crêperie* with a good selection of delicous French crêpes from €8 – the buckwheat versions are particularly good – such as the Nordic, with salmon and radish, or the ratatouille version. Daily noon–10pm.

NIGHTLIFE AND ENTERTAINMENT

Waschhaus Schiffbauergasse 1 ☎0331 271 56 26, ⓦwaschhaus.de. Large cultural venue where there's always something going on. It lies just off Berliner Str. on the way into town from the Glienicker Brücke, and incorporates galleries, an open-air cinema, beer-garden, live music stages and Fabrik (☎0331 280 03 14, ⓦfabrikpotsdam.de), a theatre for contemporary dance and music.

Gedenkstätte Sachsenhausen

Str. der Nationen 22, Oranienburg • Daily: mid-March to mid-Oct 8.30am–6pm; mid-Oct to mid-March 8.30am–4.30pm • Free, audio tour €3, leaflet €0.50 • ⓦstiftung-bg.de/gums/en/index.htm • Trains (hourly; 25min) from Berlin–Hauptbahnhof and S-Bahn from Friedrichstr. (frequent; 42min) travel to Oranienburg train station; if you don't fancy the signposted 20min walk from just north of the square beside the station, take buses #M804 and #M821 to the Gedenkstätte (BVG day-tickets valid for whole journey)

The former concentration camp of Sachsenhausen on the fringes of the small town of Oranienburg, 35km north of Berlin, has been preserved as the unremittingly miserable **Gedenkstätte Sachsenhausen** (Sachsenhausen Memorial) to remind of the crimes of two of the last century's most powerful and terrible regimes. This early Nazi camp was a prototype upon which others were based. It was never designed for large-scale mass extermination; nonetheless around half of the 220,000 prisoners who passed through its gates never left, and at the end of the war the camp was used to systematically kill thousands of Soviet POWs and Jewish prisoners on death marches. After the war the Soviets used the infrastructure for similar purposes. At the entrance to the camp, its largest structure, the impossibly detailed **New Museum**, charts the camp's origins from defunct brewery to a Nazi political prison; the local Nazis filled it with many of their classmates, colleagues and neighbours.

The camp proper begins under the main watchtower and beyond a gate adorned with the ominous sign *Arbeit macht frei* ("Work frees") and within the perimeter walls and former high-voltage fence – site of frequent inmate suicides. Within the camp many parts have been chillingly well preserved or reconstructed: a number of prison blocks, which now house a museum telling the stories of selected inmates; the camp prison, from which internees seldom returned; the former kitchen and laundry where harrowing films show the camp on liberation. Just outside the perimeter lie pits where executions took place and bodies were incinerated.

At the northern tip of the camp an exhibition in a guard tower investigates what the local populace knew and thought of the camp, via video interviews, while the jumbled hall next door examines the postwar Soviet Special Camp (1945–50), when the Russians imprisoned sixty thousand people with suspected Nazi links – though most were innocent – of which at least 12,000 died.

11

TROPICAL ISLANDS

An old hangar for zeppelins 60km south of Berlin now houses **Tropical Islands** (☎035477 60 50 50, ⓦ tropical-islands.de), an indoor landscaped water park, the size of four football fields, containing pools, lagoons, water slides, waterfalls, whirlpools and saunas as well as a clutch of bars, restaurants and shops. The quality of the landscaping is first class, and the tropical shrubbery and birds that flit around its undergrowth get to luxuriate in the constant 27ºC temperature. A Disneyesque quality is added by interior buildings and monuments – like the Bali, Borneo, Thai and Samoan pavilions – and regular evening dance shows, but what really sets the place apart is its laid-back convenience. A wristband received when you enter electronically tallies all purchases – you settle up on leaving – but best of all, the place is open all day, every day and allows you to stay overnight. Tents (€24.50/person) can be rented, but most people just crash on the beach with a mat and blanket, which costs an additional €15 per night on top of the one-off complex entry charge of €29.50. Other one-off additional charges valid for your entire stay include use of waterslides (€4.50) and the immense, nudist sauna area (€8). Tropical Islands lies off the A13 motorway from Berlin (exit Staakow), and near Brand (Niederlausitz) train station where free shuttle buses to the complex meet every train.

Accommodation

Berlin has a good selection of guesthouses, hotels, hostels and campsites, along with a glut of private rooms and apartments for both long and short-term rental. In typically Berlin fashion there is considerable overlap between all these categories, so even if you don't want to sleep in a dorm, for example, it's worth scanning our hostel listings for private single or double rooms. Prices tend to be good value, despite the city's ever-increasing popularity: competition is extremely keen everywhere, which has kept things affordable. Even the smart hotels offer online deals that have been known to rival hostel rates. If you're camping, you have a couple of good options to choose from, though these are quite far from the centre.

With Berlin a city of distinct districts, deciding **where to stay** may be your most important choice. While the public transport network is excellent, staying in the area of town that suits you best will make your visit easier. **Mitte** is the most obvious area to stay, particularly if you're after a major hotel. Within this area, the **Spandauer Vorstadt** around Oranienburger Strasse is best for smaller-scale or budget accommodation, with a good selection of hostels and boutique hotels which, as well as being within walking distance of many city-centre attractions, have good eating and nightlife options nearby. If you are going to be in Berlin a little longer than a weekend or prefer a quieter, less touristy but equally happening residential neighbourhood, **Prenzlauer Berg** is a good choice, as is **Schöneberg** – the latter particularly for gay travellers (see p.237). If you're hell-bent on clubbing, try to lay your head in **Friedrichshain** or **Kreuzberg**, where you'll find the most cutting-edge nightlife. The other major concentration of accommodation in the city is in **City West** – the old centre of West Berlin – where you'll find plenty of options in every category, with a particularly good range of affordable guesthouses. It's a little away from Berlin's brightest lights, so nightlife is very thin, but the restaurant scene is generally very good here and transport links first-class.

ESSENTIALS

Reservations If you can, try to book at least a couple of weeks in advance – or even further ahead during important festivals (see p.26) – to be assured of getting exactly what you want. The online reservation service of Visit Berlin (☎ 030 25 00 25, ⒲ berlin-tourist-information .de) is great for hotel and pension bookings, and has hostel beds and private rooms too. There are also several websites where you can search and pay in advance for a dorm bed or private room in a hostel. These often take their commission from the hostels rather than the customer, so there is nothing extra to pay – you may even find that online deals beat what you'd be offered at a hostel reception. Check out

ⓦ gomio.com, ⓦ hostelbookers.com, ⓦ hostelworld.com and ⓦ hostelz.com.

Prices The prices at the end of our hotel and pension reviews indicate the cost of the least expensive double room, mid-week and in high season (May–Sept). Note that while rates at the less expensive hotels don't vary much across the week, many of the more upmarket hotels slash their rates at the weekend. For hostels, we quote prices for the cheapest dorm beds, singles and doubles in the same period.

Minimum stays Wherever you stay minimum-stay requirements are unusual but not unheard of, particularly at busy times such as New Year.

HOTELS AND PENSIONS

A **pension** is usually smaller and cheaper than a **hotel**, although the categories do overlap and there are also "Hotel-Pensions", which may be either or both, so don't take too much notice of the labels. But do look out for the good deals at the swankier hotels, especially at weekends. Note that **single rooms** are usually only a third cheaper than doubles and breakfast is rarely included in the price of a room, particularly at the more expensive places – we've stated exceptions in the reviews below.

UNTER DEN LINDEN AND AROUND

★ **Adlon** Unter den Linden 77 ☎ 030 22 61 11 11, ⓦ hotel-adlon.de; S-Unter den Linden; map p.36. The jewel of Berlin's prewar luxury hotels has been recreated in all its excessive splendour. Prices are fit for a Kaiser – you'll part with at least €15000 per night for the royal suite. **€216**

Arcotel John F Werderscher Markt 11 ☎ 030 405 04 60, ⓦ arcotelhotels.com; U-Hausvogteiplatz; map p.36. Close to Gendarmenmarkt, this 190-room hotel is a slightly cheaper option than the neighbouring big guns but has all the facilities you'll need – gym, sauna, meeting rooms, restaurant, bar. **€142**

Hilton Mohrenstr. 30 ☎ 030 20 23 00, ⓦ hilton.com; U-Stadtmitte; map p.36. Luxurious, expensive and not very different to any other Hilton hotel, apart from its fine view of the Gendarmenmarkt. Facilities include sauna, swimming pool and squash court. **€107**

Hotel de Rome Behrenstr. 37 ☎ 030 460 60 90, ⓦ roccofortecollection.com; U-Französische Strasse; map p.36. Occupying a nineteenth-century former Dresdner Bank building, this high-class hotel mixes history with a swanky interior, luxurious rooms, an expansive spa and a fantastic restaurant and cocktail bar. **€243**

Westin Grand Friedrichstr. 158–164 ☎ 030 202 70, ⓦ westin.com/berlin; U-Friedrichstrasse; map p.36. Fully living up to its name, this GDR-era hotel originally

TOP 5 BOUTIQUE HOTELS

Hotel Q! See p.180
Luise Kunsthotel See p.179
Michelberger Hotel See p.181
Nhow See p.181
Propeller Island City Lodge See p.182

12

served party bigwigs but has since been overhauled to provide oodles of traditional upmarket luxury with a refined Belle Époque interior and beautifully appointed rooms and suites. €120

ALEXANDERPLATZ AND AROUND

Alexander Plaza Rosenstr. 1 ☎ 030 24 00 10, ⓦ alexander-plaza.com; S-Hackescher Markt; map p.60. Once housing a fur atelier, this building survived the war and the GDR, and has been beautifully renovated to become a sleek, bright, dynamic hotel. Some rooms have kitchenettes and all are decorated with modern art. Breakfast included. €99

★ **art'otel Berlin Mitte** Wallstr. 70–73 ☎ 030 24 06 20, ⓦ artotel.de; U-Märkisches Museum; map p.60. Smart, lively, quirky hotel – lots of contemporary and modern art, including an impressive range of Georg Baselitz paintings – in a quiet corner of Berlin, close to the U-Bahn. When reserving, you can pick the colour of your room: green, blue, red or aubergine. €63

Grosser Kurfürst Neue Rossstr. 11–12 ☎ 030 24 60 00, ⓦ deraghotels.de; U-Märkisches Museum; map p.60. Sleek hotel in a renovated early twentieth-century building, with straightforward, spotless rooms and suites. Facilities include laundry, wi-fi and sauna and steambath. Discounts for longer stays. €71

Lux 11 Rosa-Luxemburg-Str. 11 ☎ 030 936 28 00, ⓦ lux-eleven.com; U-Weinmeisterstrasse; map p.60. This designer apartment-hotel, oozing style, has big, comfy rooms (with kitchenettes and spacious, open bathrooms), a decent restaurant-bar (*Luchs*) and an Aveda salon. €109

★ **Motel One** Alexanderplatz ☎ 030 20 05 40 80, ⓦ motel-one.com; U- & S-Alexanderplatz; map p.60. German hotel group whose stylish lobbies – flatscreen TVs and modular 70s furniture – suggest far higher prices than its cheerfully straightforward en-suite rooms command. The location, a couple of minutes' walk from Alexanderplatz, makes it a downtown bargain; the chain has seven other locations in Berlin. Free wi-fi. €84

Park Inn Alexanderplatz ☎ 030 238 90, ⓦ parkinn-berlin.com; U- & S-Alexanderplatz; map p.60. Big, ugly block bang in the middle of things, with brilliant views over the city and hard to beat for convenience. Of the nine hundred en-suite rooms, the newly renovated business-class ones are a clear notch above the rest. Gym, sauna and top-floor casino too. €80

Radisson Blu Hotel Karl-Liebknecht-Str. 3 ☎ 030 23 82 80, ⓦ radissonblu.com/hotel-berlin; S-Hackescher Markt; map p.60. Impressive central modern hotel that offers rooms either with views over the Spree and the Dom, or facing inwards, onto a vast aquarium of 2500 tropical fish in the lobby-cum-atrium, which is part of the Sea-Life Center (see p.63). Spa and good restaurant. €134

SPANDAUER VORSTADT

Casa Camper Weinmeisterstr. 1 ☎ 030 20 00 34 10, ⓦ casacamper.com; U-Weinmeisterstrasse; map pp.72–73. Smart boutique hotel whose solid-wood interiors try to mirror a bit of Berlin's quirkiness. Breakfast included in rates, as are around-the-clock snacks and drinks at the hotel restaurant with its impressive rooftop views. Wi-fi, sauna and bike rental available. €191

★ **Circus Hotel** Rosenthalerstr. 1 ☎ 030 20 00 39 39, ⓦ circus-berlin.de; U-Rosenthaler Platz; map pp.72–73. More upmarket and eco-friendly than the *Circus Hostel*, its sister establishment over the road, with sixty rooms, including junior suites and apartments, decorated in striking colours with wooden floors and antique furniture. Restaurant *Fabisch* serves organic and locally sourced German cuisine. Buffet breakfast €4–8. Beer garden and wi-fi. €105

Dietrich-Bonhoeffer-Haus Ziegelstr. 30 ☎ 030 28 46 70, ⓦ hotel-dietrich-bonhoeffer.de; U- & S-Friedrichstrasse; map pp.72–73. This small, church-affiliated hotel and conference centre is where the first round of talks between the GDR regime and the opposition – which led to free elections and reunification – were held in December 1989. The airy en-suite rooms are simple, quiet and equipped with desks and TVs. A good buffet breakfast is included in the rate. €139

★ **Hackescher Markt** Grosse Präsidentenstr. 8 ☎ 030 28 00 30, ⓦ hotel-hackescher-markt.com; S-Hackescher Markt; map pp.72–73. Quirky little hotel on a quiet side-street, in the middle of the Hackescher Markt bar scene. It has an eclectic mix of furnishings and some pleasant touches, including underfloor heating in the en-suite bathrooms and some non-smoking rooms. Rooms overlooking the courtyard are quieter. €99

Honigmond Garden Hotel Invalidenstr. 122 ☎ 030 28 44 55 77, ⓦ honigmond-berlin.de; U-Naturkunde museum; map pp.72–73. Downtown bargain in a charming 1845 building. The rooms are sparsely furnished, but their original wooden floors help generate an authentic elegance. Guests have access to the relaxing back garden. Breakfast included. €169

★ **Hotel Taunus** Monbijouplatz 1 ☎ 030 283 52 54, ⓦ hoteltaunus.com; S-Hackescher Markt; map pp.72–73. No-frills budget hotel with clean and simple, if cramped, rooms at extraordinarily low prices for the location – arguably as good as it gets in central Berlin. En-suite rooms cost an extra €10. €59

Kastanienhof Kastanienallee 65–66 ☎ 030 44 30 50, ⓦ kastanienhof.biz; U-Senefelderplatz; map pp.72–73. This slightly old-fashioned hotel in an elegant nineteenth-century tenement house has 35 rooms with decorative touches that nod to Berlin's fascinating history, including photos, illustrations and maps. Great location for Prenzlauer Berg and Mitte nightlife. €80

Merkur Torstr. 156 ☎ 030 282 95 23, ⓦ hotel-merkur-berlin.de; U-Rosenthaler Platz; map pp.72–73. Budget

12

place with vague Old Berlin styling and fairly comfortable rooms, most of which have showers and some toilets too. There are a small number of good-value singles; rates include breakfast. **€54**

Soho House Torstr. 1 ☎030 405 04 40, ⓦsohohouseberlin.com; U-Rosa-Luxemburg-Platz; map pp.72–73. Private members' club in a restored Bauhaus building with forty rooms that range from tiny to extra-large. Decor is quirky and fun, hinting at the faded glamour of the late 1920s. There's also a lovely spa, gym, rooftop pool, restaurant, bars, screening room and private dining area. Cheap offers from €100 are sometimes available. **€210**

Weinmeister Weinmeisterstr. 2 ☎030 755 66 70, ⓦthe-weinmeister.com; U-Weinmeisterstrasse; map pp.72–73. Hotel with 88 spacious and stylish rooms sporting large beds and modern gadgetry – in-room Apple TVs, iPads for rent. The restaurant-bar serves decent German cuisine and breakfast from €5, and there's a spa/beauty salon. **€88**

TIERGARTEN

★ **Das Stue** Drakestrasse 1 ☎030 311 72 20, ⓦdas-stue.com; U-Wittenbergplatz; map pp.90–91. Lodge in luxury at the severely stylish prewar Danish embassy, where views of the zoo's antelopes and ostriches from the elegant 1920s-themed bar add to the charm. Rooms have smart modern furnishings and detailing and share a small pool, spa and first-class restaurant. **€170**

Grand Esplanade Lützowufer 15 ☎030 25 47 80, ⓦesplanade.de; U-Nollendorfplatz; map pp.90–91. Sleek top-class hotel close to the Tiergarten park with good facilities (including sauna, pool, fitness centre and spa), a flashy New York-style cocktail bar, three restaurants and even a private yacht. **€99**

Hansablick Flotowstr. 6 ☎030 390 48 00, ⓦhotel-hansablick.de; S-Tiergarten; map pp.90–91. Riverside hotel a short hop from the Tiergarten whose rooms sport cheerful multicoloured furnishings, art by the likes of Otmar Alt and Heinrich Zille, and all the usual mod cons. The rate includes a good buffet breakfast, wi-fi and parking. **€89**

Intercontinental Budapester Str. 2 ☎030 260 20, ⓦinterconti.com; U- & S-Zoologischer Garten; map pp.90–91. Modern luxury for high-powered business people in a relatively dull corner of town, but with many amenities, among them a fully equipped fitness centre, sauna and pool. **€147**

Luise Kunsthotel Luisenstr. 19 ☎030 28 44 80, ⓦluise-berlin.com; U- & S-Friedrichstrasse; map pp.90–91. Each room here is an eccentric, and impressive, work of art: one comes with bananas all over the walls and hot-pink velvet bedding, while another is *Alice in Wonderland*-themed with oversized furniture. The elegant rooms at the front tend to suffer from train noise (earplugs provided) but the quieter rooms at the back are a bit blander. Not all are en suite. **€53**

Ritz Carlton Potsdamer Platz 3 ☎030 33 77 77, ⓦritzcarlton.com; U- & S-Potsdamer Platz; map pp.90–91. Distinctive skyscraper hotel with 303 rooms (some with views of the Sony Centre atrium) sporting cherry wood closets and watercolours. Amenities include a glamorous spa, a great brasserie, lounges and five-star service. **€185**

★ **Scandic** Potsdamer Platz, Gabriele-Tergit-Promenade 19 ☎030 700 77 90, ⓦscandichotels.com; U-Mendelssohn-Bartholdy-Park; map pp.90–91. Smart yet informal homage to Scandinavian design, part of the international hotel chain, in a no man's land south of Potsdamer Platz that's surprisingly close to much greenery and very handy for the U-Bahn. Floors and rooms are successfully themed by season, and the chain's eco-friendly policies are much in evidence: no disposable sachets; local ingredients – even down to the breakfast honey, from rooftop hives – in the restaurant; bikes available to rent. On-site gym and bar. **€82**

CITY WEST

Alsterhof Augsburgerstr. 5 ☎030 21 24 20, ⓦalsterhof.com; U-Augsburger Strasse; map p.108. Central enough, though away from the bustle of the Ku'damm, this is a pleasant modern hotel with a top-notch gym, sauna and sauna. **€87**

art'otel Berlin City Centre West Lietzenburger Str. 85 ☎030 887 77 70, ⓦartotel.de; U-Uhlandstrasse; map p.108. Sleek hotel, one for Andy Warhol fans, with more than two hundred of his originals scattered about the place. His style extends to the staff uniforms and the furniture: white leather beds and purple chairs. **€76**

Askanischer Hof Kurfürstendamm 53 ☎030 881 80 33, ⓦaskanischer-hof.de; S-Savignyplatz; map p.108. *Askanischer Hof* exudes an authentically vintage atmosphere with period rooms (sixteen in total), eccentric decor – gramophones, Prussian-era furnishings – and drawings and photos on the walls. Breakfast included. **€103**

Bleibtreu Bleibtreustr. 31 ☎030 88 47 40, ⓦbleibtreu.com; U-Uhlandstrasse; map p.108. With an interior designed by Herbert Jacob Weinand and eco-minded furnishings handcrafted in Germany and Italy, this unique and discreet hotel has bright white rooms, a café, florist and a different scent on every floor. **€93**

Bogota Schlüterstr. 45 ☎030 881 50 01, ⓦbogota.de; S-Savignyplatz; map p.108. Pleasant, down-to-earth place offering a touch of affordable luxury in an historic nineteenth-century building – which once served as the Nazi Chamber of Culture. The photos on the third floor are by the photographer known only as YVA, who tutored Helmut Newton in the 1930s. The cheapest rooms share facilities; add €30 per night for an en-suite room. Rates include breakfast. **€69**

Dittberner Wielandstr. 26 ☎030 884 69 50, ⓦhotel-dittberner.de; S-Savignyplatz; map p.108. Friendly

12

old-fashioned pension, run by Frau Lange since 1958, boasting spacious rooms, stuccoed ceilings, tasteful antiques and plush upholstery. Breakfast included. €115

★ **Funk** Fasanenstr. 69 ☎030 882 71 93, ⊛hotel-pensionfunk.de; U-Uhlandstrasse; map p.108. Interesting recreation of a prewar flat, with furnishings from the 1920s and 1930s, when Danish silent-movie star Asta Nielsen lived here. Given this, its location, and the breakfast buffet (included in rates), it's a bargain. The cheapest rooms share bathrooms. Free wi-fi. €89

Hecker's Grolmannstr. 35 ☎030 889 00, ⊛heckers-hotel.de; U-Uhlandstrasse; map p.108. Swanky boutique hotel near the Savignyplatz restaurants. Rooms include three luxurious themed suites (Bauhaus, Tuscany and Colonial), starting at €340 per night. Free wi-fi. €129

Hollywood Media Hotel Kurfürstendamm 202 ☎030 88 91 00, ⊛filmhotel.de; U-Uhlandstrasse; map p.108. Owned by German film producer Artur Brauner, this modern hotel is a shrine to films of all sorts. It's all classily understated: rooms – themed by movie star – are tastefully decorated with just one headshot and bio in each. There's a sauna and steam room in every room and a huge buffet breakfast included in the rates. Wi-fi costs extra. €99

Hotel de Ela Landshuter Str. 1 ☎030 23 63 39 60, ⊛hotel-de-ela.de; U-Viktoria-Luise-Platz; map p.108. A mix of twenty-first-century design in a nineteenth-century Victorian building, family-friendly *de Ela* has large, comfortable rooms with a classic feel at decent rates, with wi-fi and breakfast included. €55

Hotel Otto Knesebeckstr. 10 ☎030 54 71 00 80, ⊛hotelotto.com; U-Ernst-Reuter-Platz; map p.108. *Otto* eschews the traditional for a cheery, modern experience that's all blues, magentas and greens. The 46 rooms are chic and individually designed and the organic food at the restaurant is good too. €115

Hotel Q! Knesebeckstr. 67 ☎030 810 06 60, ⊛loock-hotels.com; S-Savignyplatz; map p.108. Very swanky, even for über-cool Berlin: all Bauhaus-inspired elegance and quirks (bathtubs in bedframes!), plus chocolate massages, great buffet breakfasts (though these cost extra) and affable staff. €185

★ **Kettler** Bleibtreustr. 19 ☎030 883 49 49, ⊛brunnenfee.de; S-Savignyplatz; map p.108. Tiny, charming 1920s-style pension on a lively, café-lined street. A multitude of knick-knacks, Berliniana and

patterned wallpaper give the place character. Rooms are themed by artist or performer (choose between the likes of Callas or Toulouse-Lautrec) and have showers but share toilets. €65

Savoy Hotel Fasanenstr. 9–10 ☎030 31 10 30, ⊛hotel-savoy.com; U- & S-Zoologischer Garten; map p.108. Luxury hotel whose traditional, old-world atmosphere has been happily married with some Cuban decorative flair – there's even a cigar shop in the lobby. €98

Swissotel Augsburger Str. 44 ☎030 22 01 00, ⊛swissotel.com; U-Kurfürstendamm; map p.108. Smart 316-room international chain hotel in an extraordinary building amid the bright lights of the Ku'damm. Vertical louvres bristle around the exterior; the interior is equally impressive thanks to a bright and welcoming glass-roofed lobby and a restaurant with superb views of Berlin's main shopping strip. With eco-friendly credentials, bar/lounge, sauna and fitness facilities. €106

SCHÖNEBERG

Altberlin am Potsdamer Platz Potsdamer Str. 67 ☎030 261 29 99, ⊛altberlin-hotel.de; U-Kurfürstenstrasse; map p.113. Large pension in a turn-of-the-twentieth-century, Wilhelminian-era hotel with old-world decor in its "grandma"-style rooms and long-forgotten Berlin specialities served at its restaurant. Large buffet breakfast included. €90

Sylter Hof Berlin Kurfürstenstr. 116 ☎030 212 00, ⊛sylterhof-berlin.de; U-Wittenbergplatz; map p.113. Well-appointed eighteen-storey hotel just behind Wittenbergplatz and the Ku'damm. The suites are spacious and well priced, and come with kitchens. Free wi-fi. €78

WESTERN KREUZBERG

Angleterre Hotel Friedrichstr. 31 ☎030 20 21 37 00, ⊛hotel-angleterre.de; U-Kochstrasse; map p.118. Close to Checkpoint Charlie and the Jewish Museum, the "English Hotel" has a restaurant and bar/lounge, 24hr room service and lots of charming old detailing, including restored murals, stuccoed ceilings, wood finishes and wall mirrors. €169

Hotel Am Anhalter Bahnhof Stresemannstr. 36 ☎030 258 00 70, ⊛hotel-anhalter-bahnhof.de; S-Anhalter Bahnhof; map p.118. Not a pretty hotel, but a pleasant one, with friendly staff. The cheaper rooms share bathrooms, but all are a good deal considering the location, just south of Potsdamer Platz and the Kulturforum. €47

Riehmers Hofgarten Yorckstr. 83 ☎030 78 09 88 00, ⊛riehmershofgarten.com; U-Mehringdamm; map p.118. There's a low-key, residential atmosphere at this hotel in a historic building. The 23 rooms and apartments have a nineteenth-century feel and there's a delightful living room for relaxation. €128

TOP 5 STEP BACK IN TIME

Altberlin am Potsdamer Platz See p.180
Askanischer Hof See p.179
Funk See p.180
Kettler See p.180
Riehmers Hofgarten See p.180

EASTERN KREUZBERG AND FRIEDRICHSHAIN

East Side Hotel Mühlenstr. 6 ☎ 030 29 38 33, ⓦ eastsidehotel.de; U- & S-Warschauer Strasse; map pp.126–127. Small, laid-back modern hotel just over the Spree from Kreuzberg in southern Friedrichshain and overlooking the East Side Gallery. Exceptional service and a 24hr check-in, room service and café. Original artwork in the hotel includes quirky murals by Birgit Kinder, who famously painted the Trabant on the East Side Gallery. **€83**

Hotel 26 Grünberger Str. 26 ☎ 030 297 77 80, ⓦ hotel26 .de; U- & S-Warschauer Strasse; map pp.126–127. Simple, bright and modern hotel close to Friedrichshain's many bars. All rooms are en suite and rates include breakfast. **€99**

Hotel Friedrichshain Warschauer Str. 57 ☎ 030 97 00 20 30, ⓦ hotel-friedrichshain-berlin.de; U- & S-Warschauer Strasse; map pp.126–127. Straightforward modern hotel with uncluttered rooms – some share bathrooms – and a kitchen on every floor. A good deal for longer stays: prices drop after your third night and almost halve after your fifteenth. Reception is unmanned in the evening so you need to arrange in advance if you are arriving after 6pm. **€57**

★ **IntercityHotel Berlin** Am Ostbahnhof 5 ☎ 030 29 36 80, ⓦ berlin.intercityhotel.de; S-Ostbahnhof; map pp.126–127. Sleek, budget-conscious business hotel at the Ostbahnhof, very convenient for the S-Bahn and the Friedrichshain scene. Rooms are of the usual international business standard, and rates include buffet breakfast and a public transport pass (zones A, B & C) for the duration of your stay. Rates vary depending on events and demand. **€62**

Juncker's Hotel Garni Grünberger Str. 21 ☎ 030 293 35 50, ⓦ junckershotel.de; U-Frankfurter Tor; map pp.126–127. Small, family-run hotel with medium-sized but high-quality rooms, friendly staff and a quiet atmosphere only occasionally interrupted by the hostel next door. **€48**

★ **Michelberger Hotel** Warschauer Str. 39 ☎ 030 29 77 85 90, ⓦ michelbergerhotel.com; U- & S-Warschauer Strasse; map pp.126–127. Modern, trendy and urbane, this relaxed haunt with its cool warehouse-style interior provides anything but workaday accommodation. Apart from enjoying its improvised feel – cuckoo clocks on raw concrete walls, exposed wiring – you're also likely to find the all-night bar and lobby friendly, relaxing and unpretentious hangouts. Excellent buffet breakfast (€9) **€80**

nhow Stralauer Allee 3 ☎ 030 290 29 90, ⓦ nhow -hotels.com; U-Warschauer Strasse; map pp.126–127. This four-star concept hotel merges a music theme with designer hotel rooms. There's a health club, sauna and gym, and some rooms have great views over the river. **€86**

NU Hotel Berlin Gubener Str. 46 ☎ 030 68 81 12 20, ⓦ nuhotel.de; U-Frankfurter Tor; map pp.126–127. Close to the East Side gallery and O2 World, this three-star hotel has 28 rooms, all of them functional with lots of natural light and decent amenities. Breakfast included. **€71**

★ **Ostel** Wriezener Karree 5 ☎ 030 25 76 86 60, ⓦ ostel.eu; S-Ostbahnhof; map pp.126–127. Step back into the GDR of the 1970s amid a haze of browns and oranges at this themed budget hotel a short walk from the Ostbahnhof. The rendition is creepily accurate, but thankfully the whole thing's done with a sense of humour and just the thing for those needing an *Ostalgie* fix (see p.66). Some rooms share bathrooms; there's also a six-person apartment (€120/night). **€54**

Upstalsboom Hotel Gubener Str. 42 ☎ 030 29 37 50, ⓦ upstalsboom-berlin.de; U- & S-Warschauer Strasse; map pp.126–127. Upmarket hotel whose strong point is its spa. The rooms are bland, if spacious: all four categories have wi-fi and the largest have kitchenettes. Breakfast included. **€87**

NEUKÖLLN

Hüttenpalast Hobrechtstrasse 65–66 ☎ 030 37 30 58 06, ⓦ huettenpalast.de; U-Hermannplatz; map pp.126–127. Satisfyingly eccentric place where you get to camp in vintage caravans or mountain huts inside a converted factory. All have been stylishly overhauled so you won't be roughing it, though bathrooms are shared. Pleasant garden, too, and a great café serving breakfast and other home-made treats later on. Also a few en-suite doubles. **€87**

PRENZLAUER BERG

★ **Acksel Haus** Belforter Str. 21 ☎ 030 44 33 76 33, ⓦ ackselhaus.de; U-Senefelderplatz; map p.132. Small offbeat hotel on an attractive residential street in the heart of the lively Prenzlauer Berg scene. Besides rooms, it offers fully equipped and individually themed apartments with broadband access and spacious kitchens. **€130**

Hotel Transit Loft Immanuelkirchstr. 14 ☎ 030 48 49 37 73, ⓦ transit-loft.de; U-Senefelderplatz; map p.132. Part budget hotel, part hostel, this modern hotel occupies a nineteenth-century, yellow-brick factory close to Kollwitzplatz. The 47 rooms (singles and dorms included) are airy and well lit with basic furnishings and en-suite showers. Buffet breakfast is included. The same owners run *Hotel Transit* in Kreuzberg (see p.184). Dorms **€21**; singles **€52**; doubles **€62**

Myer's Hotel Metzer Str. 26 ☎ 030 44 01 40, ⓦ hotel .de; U-Senefelderplatz; map p.132. Small upmarket hotel in a renovated nineteenth-century Neoclassical building. The 51 rooms, arranged around a glass-roofed courtyard, come in a range of shapes and sizes (some quite small) but are all elegant and tastefully furnished. There's a lounge, art gallery and garden. **€103**

WESTERN SUBURBS

Frauenhotel Artemisia Brandenburgische Str. 18 ☎ 030 873 89 05, ⓦ frauenhotel-berlin.de; U-Konstanzer Strasse; map p.154. Popular

12

women-only hotel in Wilmersdorf, with modern rooms (most en suite), a range of artworks and a sociable roof garden and. Fills quickly in high season, so book well in advance. Free wi-fi. **€59**

Ibis Brandenburgische Str. 11 ☎030 86 20 20, ⓦibishotel.com; U-Fehrbelliner Platz; map p.154. This Wilmersdorf hotel is one of ten Berlin branches of the international chain. Rooms are small but inexpensive. **€55**

★ **Propeller Island City Lodge** Albrecht-Achilles-Str. 58 ☎030 891 90 16, ⓦpropeller-island.de; U-Adenauerplatz; map p.154. Entertainingly wacky Wilmersdorf hotel where the furnishings in every room have been handcrafted by the owner according to individual themes: check the website to choose from among the likes of the Space Cube, the Mirror Room, Electric Wallpaper or Upside Down. **€79**

Schlosshotel Im Grunewald Brahmsstr. 10 ☎030 89 58 40, ⓦschlosshotelberlin.com; S-Hohenzollerndamm; map p.161. Escape the grittiness of Berlin in grand country house style in a peaceful and upmarket residential area where driveways are filled with Porsches. Much of the hotel's classical decor was given a modern design twist by Karl Lagerfeld and is matched by its seamless service. Meanwhile the large swathe of pleasant Grunewald woodland on the doorstep is perfect for a walk or run before enjoying the lovely spa, sauna, steam room and pool facilities. **€239**

HOSTELS

Hostel accommodation in Berlin is very good. The recent breed of new, **independent hostels**, with their stock of private rooms, have swept aside many pensions and set new standards for existing HI hostels. All hostels welcome travellers of any age, though most mainly cater to 20-somethings and larger ones are periodically overwhelmed by school groups. Reception desks are almost always bountiful sources of information and frequently double as late-night bars; common rooms and the universal absence of curfews also add to the party atmosphere. Traditional facilities, such as a laundry and kitchens, have become unusual, but the nearest launderette or snack bar is never far away – and you'll almost certainly have free wi-fi and internet. **Rates** depend on the number of people sharing: a twenty-bed dorm may cost around €10 per person, while five sharing a room might each pay double that; we quote the cheapest dorm rates available for each hostel, plus the cheapest rates for singles and doubles where available. Bedding is provided in most places – though sometimes there's a one-off fee of around €3 for this – or you may be able use a sleeping bag. Most hostels offer a simple buffet breakfast for around €5; at some places it is included in the rate.

ALEXANDERPLATZ

★ **Citystay Hostel** Rosenstr. 16 ☎030 23 62 40 31, ⓦcitystay.de; S-Hackescher Markt; map p.60. Berlin's best-located hostel for sightseeing – within walking distance of the S-Bahn, Hackescher Markt and Museum Island – is a large well-run place spreading over several immaculate floors. It has a good selection of private rooms, some en suite, and pleasant communal areas including a leafy courtyard. Facilities include an all-night bar, summer-only restaurant (great *Flammkuchen*), and free wi-fi. It's also a hub for walking and cycling tours and bar crawls. Breakfast buffet extra. Dorms **€19**; twins **€55**

SPANDAUER VORSTADT

Baxpax Downtown Ziegelstr. 28 ☎030 27 87 48 80, ⓦbaxpax.de; S-Oranienburger Strasse; map pp.72–73. Great hostel with busy communal areas in a handy yet relatively quiet location, with all the usual facilities – internet, bar, breakfast buffet, games room, bike rental – and a relaxed vibe. Avoid the 24-bed dorm (€17) if you are a light sleeper in favour of those with eight beds (€21) or fewer. Dorms **€17**; singles **€29**; doubles **€98**

★ **Circus Hostel** Weinbergsweg 1a ☎030 20 00 39 39, ⓦcircus-berlin.de; U-Rosenthaler Platz; map 72–73. Top-notch hostel in fantastic location, with particularly helpful staff and good facilities. Rooms are plain but bright, with large windows and high ceilings, and they don't have bunk beds. The hostel also has its own, decent bar, *Goldmans*, downstairs. Bicycles for rent and free walking tours, too. Dorms **€23**; singles **€50**; doubles **€100**

Mittes Backpacker Chausseestr. 102 ☎030 28 39 09 65, ⓦbaxpax.de; U-Naturkundemuseum; map pp.72–73. Imaginatively decorated converted factory within walking distance of the Scheunenviertel bar scene. Facilities include bike rental and a communal kitchen. Dorms **€18**; doubles **€70**

St Christopher's Hostel Rosa-Luxemburg-Str. 39–41 ☎030 81 45 39 60, ⓦst-christophers.co.uk; U-Rosa-Luxemburg-Platz; map pp.72–73. Well-run branch of a British hostel chain, with 24hr opening and the perfect layout for partying all night in its big bar, with chill-out areas and billiards. There's also pub grub, free wi-fi and occasional live events, but the staff and guests are a motley international crew, so there's little to remind that you're in Germany. Rates include a basic breakfast. Dorms (some single-sex) **€24**; singles **€50**; doubles & twins **€78**

CITY WEST

★ **Jetpak Flashpacker** Pariserstr. 58 ☎030 784 43 60, ⓦjetpak.de; U-Spichernstrasse; map p.108. Western Berlin's best hostel is scrupulously clean and in a quiet residential neighbourhood a short walk from the Ku'damm shops and close to the U-Bahn. Amenities include free

FROM TOP CIRCUS HOTEL (P.178); HOTEL ADLON (P.177) >

internet and wi-fi; access to printers, iPod chargers and speakers; a sociable café-bar, with rockbottom prices, and a common room with all sorts of film and gaming entertainment. Breakfast included. Dorms €20; doubles €80

WESTERN KREUZBERG
Aletto Jugendhotel Grunewaldstr. 33 ☎ 030 21 00 36 80, ⓦ aletto.de; U-Eisenacher Strasse; map p.118. One of three colourful and lively *Aletto* hostels in the city (the others are in Schöneberg and City West); with singles, doubles and dorms for up to eight people. Table football, video games and a large DVD library keep guests entertained when they're not roaming Berlin. Breakfast included. Dorms €18; singles €44; doubles €58

Hotel Transit Hagelberger Str. 53 ☎ 030 789 04 70, ⓦ hotel-transit.de; U-Mehringdamm; map p.118. Bright, breezy hostel in a former factory building with fifty basic spacious rooms and an upbeat atmosphere. Breakfast is included and served until noon, but sadly there's no online booking. Dorms €21; singles €59; doubles €69

EASTERN KREUZBERG-FRIEDRICHSHAIN
A&O Hostel Friedrichshain Boxhagener Str. 73 ☎ 030 809 47 54 00, ⓦ aohostels.com; S-Ostkreuz; map pp.126–127. A good choice if you're travelling with kids, since, alongside dorms, singles and doubles there are family rooms, a children's games room and a large garden – childcare is even offered at weekends. Dorms €15; singles €43; doubles €49; family rooms €96

All in Hostel Grünberger Str. 54 ☎ 030 288 76 83, ⓦ all -in-hostel.com; U- & S-Warschauer Strasse; map pp.126–127. Clean, modern and well-managed hostel just metres from the nocturnal goings-on of Simon-Dach-Str. All the usual facilities are offered, with breakfast included in rates. Though frequently beset by German school groups, it's a good choice for its hotel-standard private en-suite rooms and rockbottom off-season prices, when dorm beds go for €7.77. Dorms €13; singles €99; twins €110

baxpax Skalitzer Str. 104 ☎ 030 69 51 83 22, ⓦ baxpax .de; U-Görlitzer Bahnhof; map pp.126–127. Cheerful beatnik hostel in a happening area of Kreuzberg. The USP here is the bed in a pink VW Beetle, parked in one of the rooms; otherwise it's unremarkable, and the communal facilities are a bit overstretched. Dorms €17; single €37; doubles €50

Die Fabrik Schlesische Str. 18 ☎ 030 611 71 16, ⓦ diefabrik.com; U-Schlesisches Tor; map pp.126–127. Hip, quiet hostel in an old factory. Unusually, the dorm beds aren't bunks. Dorms €18; singles €38; doubles €58

★ **Eastern Comfort** Mühlenstr. 73–77 ☎ 030 66 76 38 06, ⓦ eastern-comfort.com; U- & S-Warschauer Strasse; map pp.126–127. Sleep swaying on the River Spree in a range of accommodation – from spacious doubles through cabin bunks to tents on deck. All cabins except dorms are en

suite and the boat has internet and free wi-fi. Highly unconventional and lots of fun, with a social area and lively bar. Tents €12; bunks €16; doubles €78

Hostel X Berger Schlesische Str. 22 ☎ 030 69 53 18 63, ⓦ hostelxberger.com; U-Schlesisches Tor; map pp.126–127. Dowdy, but clean and friendly hostel a hop, skip and a stagger from several of Berlin's best clubs. Common areas include a basic kitchen but little else. Free wi-fi. Dorms €16; singles €37; doubles €48

★ **Jetpak Alternative** Görlitzerstr. 38 ☎ 030 62 90 86 41, ⓦ jetpak.de; U-Schlesisches Tor; map pp.126–127. Slick branch of Berlin's best hostel chain that offers a pretty stark contrast to Kreuzberg's gritty but happening Wrangelkeitz neighbourhood. All rooms have high-end fittings such as underfloor heating in en-suite bathrooms. Other perks include a cheap bar, free on-street parking, free wi-fi, and a free buffet breakfast. Dorms €22

Odyssee Globetrotter Hostel Grünberger Str. 23 ☎ 030 29 00 00 81, ⓦ globetrotterhostel.de; U-Frankfurter Tor; map pp.126–127. Imaginatively decorated and sociable hostel hard by the Friedrichshain scene and with a happening bar of its own. Facilities include kitchen and free wi-fi. Dorms €16; single €69; doubles €78

Pegasus Str. der Pariser Kommune 35 ☎ 030 297 73 60, ⓦ pegasushostel.de; U-Weberwiese; map pp.126–127. Well-run establishment set around a garden-cum-courtyard that comes into its own in the summer as a place to enjoy your free welcome drink. The location is a bit out of the way, though the U-Bahn is just a 5min walk away. Linen costs extra. Dorms €13; singles €45; doubles €50

Sunflower Hostel Helsingforserstr. 17 ☎ 030 44 04 42 50, ⓦ sunflower-hostel.de; U-& S-Warschauer Strasse; map pp.126–127. Sociable hostel tucked away in a residential part of Friedrichshain. The reception doubles as a bar, and the hostel itself is quite handy for transport and the local bar scene. The dorms are good value, but the singles and doubles are dingy and uninviting. Dorms €17; singles €38; doubles €45

PRENZLAUER BERG
Lette'm Sleep Lettestr. 7 ☎ 030 44 73 36 23, ⓦ backpackers.de; U-Eberswalder Strasse; map p.132. Quirky hostel with clean and comfy, if basic, rooms, just steps away from the action in Prenzlauer Berg. Big plus points include the cosy living room with free wi-fi, coffee and tea; DVD evenings; summer beer garden and communal kitchen. Discounts for stays of three nights or more. Dorms €13; twins €49; doubles €69

Meininger Schönhauser Allee 19 ☎ 030 66 63 61 00, ⓦ meininger-hotels.de; U-Hallesches Tor; map p.132. Part hotel, part hostel, this smart, well-run and well-located 70-bed place is part of an international chain (there are three others in Berlin alone). A little more sterile and less happening than many other hostels, but with a lounge, games room and café-bar nonetheless. Free wi-fi. Dorms €18; singles €53; doubles €66

THE GRUNEWALD

★ **Jetpak Ecolodge** Pücklerstr. 54 ☎ 030 832 250 11, ⓦ jetpak.de; U-Fehrbelliner Platz then bus #115 to Pücklerstrasse; map p.161. One-of-a-kind hostel with a laid-back international vibe, in the woods on the southwestern edge of Berlin. The large communal spaces have plenty on offer, including free nightly big-screen movies and lots of indoor and outdoor games. Bring supplies, though, as there are no shops in the vicinity. Free internet and wi-fi; bike rental offered. Note some #115 buses don't go as far as Pücklerstrasse, but night buses from the Zoo stop a 10min walk from the hostel. Dorms €16; twins €42; doubles €45

CAMPSITES

Berlin's **campsites** are not close to the centre, and, if you're looking to cut costs, bear in mind hostels will probably work out cheaper once you've added the cost of travel into town. That said, the campsites are both well run and inexpensive.

Campingplatz Am Krossinsee Wernsdorfer Str. 38 ☎ 030 675 86 87, ⓦ campingplatz-berlin.de; S-Grünar, then tram #68 to Schmöckwitz, then bus #733; map p.142. Pleasantly set in the woods near the southeastern suburb of Schmöckwitz, with easy access to local lakes. Bungalows available (€75). Tent plus one person €12.50

Campingplatz Kladow Krampnitzer Weg 111–117, Gatow ☎ 030 365 27 97, ⓦ dccberlin.de; U-Rathaus Spandau, then bus #134 or #X34 to Alt-Kladow stop; map p.161. Friendly campsite on the western side of the Havel lake, with good facilities including a crèche, bar, restaurant, shop and showers. Tent plus one person €12.50

LIVING LIKE A LOCAL: ROOMS AND APARTMENTS

Private rooms are usually of a good standard in Berlin: clean and simple, often self-contained, and offering quite a lot of privacy – you may barely see your hosts. Breakfast is sometimes included, in which case you'll probably just be helping yourself to bread and what's in the fridge. The typical charge for a private room is €25–35 per person per night, while monthly rents for a self-contained apartment start at €400, or about €300 if you're prepared to share kitchen and bathroom. Accommodation agencies tend to specialize in either short-term – up to about a month – or long-term lets, for longer periods. In the case of the latter, there are often agency fees to pay on top, to a maximum of 25 percent of the monthly rent.

12

MOSTLY SHORT-TERM

9flats ⓦ 9flats.com. Berlin internet start-up that aims to help you find "affordable private accommodations, rented out by friendly locals all over the world".

Airbnb ⓦ airbnb.de. A good variety of Berlin properties and timescales.

Be My Guest wbe-my-guest.com. Short-stay apartments, B&Bs and guest rooms for all budgets.

Bed & Breakfast in Berlin ☎ 030 44 05 05 82, ⓦ bed-and-breakfast-berlin.de. Single and double rooms and apartments.

Bed & Breakfast Privatzimmervermittlung ⓦ bed-and-breakfast.de. Part of a national chain, offering rooms ranging from the simple to the luxurious.

Brilliant Apartments ⓦ brilliant-apartments.de. Specializes in apartments in the Prenzlauer Berg district.

Citybed ☎ 030 23 62 36 10, ⓦ citybed.de. Online accommodation booking, with prices starting at around €20 per person.

Ferienwohnung Berlin ⓦ ferienwohnungen-berlin.de. A wide range of rooms and apartments all over the city with a vast online booking engine.

Oh Berlin ⓦ oh-berlin.com. Berlin apartments to suit all tastes and budgets.

Roomsurfer ⓦ roomsurfer.com. The most casual and low-budget accommodation site: much like ⓦ couchsurfing.com, but with money changing hands.

Stadtbett ☎ 030 69 56 50 00, ⓦ stadtbett.de. Another good way of finding rooms and apartments online, via a request service.

Wimdu ⓦ wimdu.com. Another big international database for apartments, holiday homes and B&Bs.

MOSTLY LONG-TERM

Agentur Wohnwitz ☎ 030 861 82 22, ⓦ wohnwitz.com. Rooms in shared flats and apartments.

Berlin Inn ☎ 030 339 88 77 82, ⓦ berlin-inn.de. A good selection of rooms and apartments, short- and long-term lets.

Fine & Mine ☎ 030 235 51 20, ⓦ fineandmine.de. International agency with some short-term lets too.

Zeitraum Wohnkonzepte ☎ 030 441 66 22, ⓦ zeit-raum.de. Helpful agency with rooms and apartments for short- and long-term let.

ZUR LETZTEN INSTANZ

Eating and drinking

Berlin has all the restaurants, cafés and bars you'd expect from a major European capital, with virtually every imaginable cuisine: indeed, the national gastronomy generally takes a back seat to Greek, Turkish, Balkan, Indian and Italian specialities. Berliners tend to eat out regularly, so prices are reasonable – a main dish typically costs around €6 to €10 – though you can easily triple this figure by dining at top-end places serving "Neue Deutsche Küche". In line with Berlin's rolling nightlife timetable, you can pretty much eat and drink around the clock. Most restaurants happily serve until around 11pm, and even later it's not hard to find somewhere in most neighbourhoods.

Another common feature of Berlin's dining scene is how many places **morph** from one type of venue into another through the day. A good place to sip a morning coffee and read a paper may well become a restaurant later on, before bringing out the DJ decks until the wee small hours, then closing only to start the cycle again two or three hours later. Throughout the city the distinction between restaurants, cafés, bars and even clubs can be difficult to make: outside busy periods, many restaurants are perfectly happy to serve you just a coffee, and some of the tastiest food you'll eat on your trip may be in a café.

Berlin still has its share of traditional places, including male-oriented bare-bones **Kneipen** – or pubs – as well as classic **cafés** specializing in coffee and rich mid-afternoon cakes. Meanwhile, the **Imbiss** (see p.195) or snack stand is even more ubiquitous in Berlin than elsewhere in Germany. Conversely, **beer gardens** are comparatively thin on the ground, although, emerging from hibernation around the end of March, they still play a significant role as convivial outdoor gathering points. Some of the best are in the suburbs, particularly on lakeshores in Köpenick and Zehlendorf. Local **microbreweries** (*Hausbrauereien*) often have a similar feel; the house beers are generally top-quality, and the decor is suitably shiny brewery-chic.

Despite the difficulties inherent in pinning establishments down as any one type of place, our **listings** are divided into **cheap eats** – mostly *Imbiss* places (see p.195) – **cafés** and **bars** that are good places to hang out irrespective of your appetite, **beer gardens** and **microbreweries** that offer the kind of concerted beer drinking Germany is famous for, and **restaurants** recommended for a full meal. Bars that tend to be best as nightspots are reviewed in the nightlife section (see p.206); they may also do food, but generally not of the sort you would go out of your way for.

ESSENTIALS

Costs Eating at Berlin's cafés and restaurants is inexpensive by international standards: main courses start at around €6 in each, and drinks aren't much pricier than in bars. When it comes to tipping, you need only add a euro or so to the bill, since a fifteen percent service charge is already added – always give the tip directly to your server, rather than leaving on the table.

Reservations For most restaurants reviewed below you can just walk in, though on weekend nights or at the most expensive places, booking is recommended.

UNTER DEN LINDEN AND AROUND

CAFÉS AND BARS

Café Einstein Unter den Linden 42 ☎030 204 36 32; U-Brandenburger Tor; map p.36. The younger sibling to the famous *Einstein* (see p.195) lacks its elder's panache, but it's popular with Berlin's cultural elite and serves excellent Austro-Hungarian specialities. Also handy for coffee and cake. Daily 7am–10pm.

EATING YOUR WAY AROUND BERLIN

You can find more or less every type of restaurant, café, bar and *Imbiss* in every Berlin district, but a few generalizations stand. Places around **Unter den Linden** and all the way to **Alexanderplatz** largely provide sightseers with coffee and big slabs of rich cake and traditional German meals, with the latter particularly well represented in the **Nikolaiviertel**, Berlin's old quarter. The **Spandauer Vorstadt**, particularly the stretch along Oranienburger Strasse, is far more eclectic and hip, but still caters primarily to visitors so standards tend to be lower and prices higher than further out of the centre. But it's still a good district for browsing if you're unsure what you're after.

Outside Mitte, traditional coffee houses still congregate in **City West** where Savignyplatz has become the hub of a busy dining district. In **Schöneberg** and **Kreuzberg** the scene revolves around three distinct and fairly bohemian areas, which attract an older, less image-conscious crowd: Winterfeldplatz is a popular gay centre, Bergmanstrasse a relatively bohemian strip, and Oranienstrasse and the Wrangelkiez are two grittier counter-cultural areas – you could spend weeks exploring these districts before exhausting the possibilities. The gastro scene in **Friedrichshain**, Berlin's clubland and student nightlife quarter, has started to come of age and is good for inexpensive meals. Berlin's moneyed bohemian district, **Prenzlauer Berg**, is also a good place to explore, with its great mix of cafés and smarter restaurants.

13

RESTAURANTS

Bocca di Bacco Friedrichstr. 167 ☎030 20 67 28 28, ⓦboccadibacco.de; U-Französische Strasse; map p.36. *Bocca di Bacco* blends a down-to-earth atmosphere with high-quality cuisine that takes its inspiration from Tuscany and other parts of Italy. The menu includes pasta, game and fish and plenty of wonderful desserts. The three-course lunch is a pretty good deal at €19.50. Mon–Sat noon–midnight, Sun 6pm–midnight.

★ **Café Nö!** Glinkastr. 23 ☎030 201 08 71, ⓦcafe-noe.de; U-Französische Strasse; map p.36. This wine bar-restaurant serves quality South German and Mediterranean food at very reasonable prices. The menu includes *Flammkuchen* and the like, a huge mixed plate for two featuring almost everything on the menu is €23, and the wine list is vast enough for most tastes. Service is pleasant and not too formal. Mon–Fri noon–1am, Sat 7pm–1am, kitchen till midnight.

Chipps Jägerstr. 35 ☎030 280 88 06, ⓦchipps.eu; Hausvogteiplatz; map p.36. This venture from the owner of *Cookies Cream* features panoramic windows, a light-filled, sleek interior and terrace. The open kitchen serves seasonal and regional ingredients. You can mix and match your dishes (meat and fish are served as side orders – evening dishes from €12), while hearty breakfasts include the "hangover". A second *Chipps* is at Friedrichstr. 120. Mon–Fri 8am–late, Sat & Sun 9am–late.

Cookies Cream Behrenstr. 55 ☎030 27 49 29 40, ⓦcookiescream.de; U-Französische Strasse; map p.36. Deliberately difficult to find (see website for creative directions – walk down the service road and past the dustbins of the *Westin Grand* off Behrenstr.) this stylish vegetarian restaurant, one of the best in the city, is worth seeking out. At €32 for a three-course menu and €18 for a main, it's pricey but far from prohibitive, and the seasonal, inventive food is well worth it. Tues–Sat 7pm–midnight.

Fischers Fritz The Regent, Charlottenstr. 49 ☎030 20 33 63 63, ⓦfischersfritzberlin.com; U-Französische Strasse; map p.36. *Fischers Fritz* is the domain of Christian Lohse, whose way with fish and seafood has earned him numerous accolades (including two Michelin stars). This is imaginative stuff, bursting with originality in terms of presentation, flavours and ideas. There's a price, naturally, namely €110 for four courses; for a cheaper option, check the lunch deals. Daily noon–2pm & 6.30–10.30pm.

Ishin Mittelstr. 24 ☎030 20 67 48 29, ⓦishin.de; U- & S-Brandenburger Tor; map p.36. There are four *Ishin* restaurants in Berlin. The interior of this central one is slightly functional but the decent, fresh sushi, good prices and quick service make it very popular, especially for lunch. There's a happy hour every day until 4pm (all day Wed & Sat), with €2–3 off sushi, and full menus from €5. Plenty of veggie dishes and free green tea. Mon–Sat 11am–10pm (kitchen till 9.30pm).

★ **Käfer Dachgarten** Platz der Republik 1 ☎030 22 62 99 33; U- & S-Brandenburger Tor; map p.36. Famous for its location on the roof of the Reichstag and its 180-degree view of eastern Berlin, this restaurant specializes in gourmet renditions of regional German dishes (mains €8–30). A reservation here also means you get to nip in a side entrance and avoid the consistently long lines at the front. Daily 9am–midnight; last orders 10pm.

Lutter & Wegner Charlottenstr. 56 ☎030 202 95 40, ⓦl-w-berlin.de; U-Französische Strasse; map p.36. This refined, airy Austro-German restaurant is the finest of the *Lutter & Wagner* mini empire. It was here the wine merchant started (in 1811) – there's a high-end wine store alongside. Prices are high (set menus around €37, mains from €15) but that's what happens when the *New York Times* crowns your *Wiener Schnitzel* the best outside Vienna (though in truth the *Sauerbraten* is the real highlight). There's a cheaper bistro with a shorter menu and the same list of around 750 wines. Daily 11am–3am, kitchen till 1am.

GERMAN CUISINE

To enjoy traditional **German cuisine**, it does help if you share the national penchant for heavy meat dishes accompanied by healthy fresh vegetables and salad. The **pig** is the staple of the German menu – it's prepared in umpteen different ways, and just about every part gets eaten. Sausages are the country's most popular snack, while *Kassler Rippen* (smoked and pickled pork chops) and *Eisbein* (pigs' trotters) are Berlin favourites – although the fatty *Eisbein* tends to be more of a winter speciality. *Königsberger Klopse* (meat dumplings in a caper- and lemon-flavoured sauce) also appear on many menus.

   Potatoes are used imaginatively, too: try *Kartoffelpuffer* (flour and potatoes mixed into a pancake) or *Pellkartoffeln mit Quark und Leinöl*, a combination of baked potatoes, low-fat cheese and linseed oil that's best digested with lashings of beer or schnapps.

   Surprisingly for a country known for its cakes, **desserts** in Berlin's German restaurants are an anticlimax. *Rote Grütze* (mixed soft berries eaten hot or cold with vanilla sauce) is one of the few distinctive dishes; if you have a sweet tooth, you may be best off heading for a café that serves one of the delicious cakes or *Torten* of which Germans are so fond.

13

BERLIN OHNE SPECK – A GUIDE FOR VEGETARIANS

In the 1930s, Berlin had more than thirty **vegetarian restaurants**, and while the city can't field anything like that amount today, it's still the best place for a vegetarian in a country that seems overwhelmingly to sustain itself on dead pig. There's a list of exclusively vegetarian places below: otherwise, you should generally steer clear of pubs and German restaurants, whether traditional or modern; lard and beef stock are used prodigiously, and there's an unwritten convention that no meal is really complete until sprinkled with small pieces of *Speck* (bacon). Thankfully, the city's cosmopolitan spread of cuisines means that choosing an Italian, Indian or Thai option will usually yield something without meat on the menu, and most upmarket cafés have a flesh-free option.

USEFUL PHRASES

I am a vegetarian (feminine ending in parenthesis) Ich bin Vegetarier(in)
I don't eat meat or fish Ich esse keinen Fleisch oder Fisch
I don't want to eat bacon or meat stock Ich möchte keinen Speck oder Fleischbrühe essen
Has it got meat in it? Gibt's Fleisch drin?
Do you have anything without meat in it? Gibt's was ohne Fleisch?

VEGETARIAN RESTAURANTS

Café V See p.199
Cookies Cream See p.188

Einhorn See p.193
Yellow Sunshine See p.199

Margaux Unter den Linden 78, entrance on Wilhelmstr. ☎030 22 65 26 11, ⓦmargaux-berlin.de; U- & S-Brandenburger Tor; map p.36. Onyx walls, marble floors and burgundy upholstery set the stage for this upscale restaurant, whose daily menu is dictated by the quality of available supplies. Mains €26–45, with better-value set meals including three-course lunches (€35) and dinners (€95). The gracious maitre d' will happily recommend wines from their selection of 700. Mon–Sat 7pm until late (kitchen until 10.30pm).
VAU Jägerstr. 54–55 ☎030 202 97 30, ⓦvau-berlin.de;

U-Hausvogteiplatz; map p.36. Acclaimed (and expensive) restaurant run by chef Kolja Kleeberg – a famous TV chef who produces fantastic, modern takes on classic international cuisine, specializing in using ingredients from the Berlin area. The menu changes often, but expect to see intriguing combinations such as scallops, red beets, dove and polenta, or halibut, spiced *tabouleh*, carrot and apple – with mains at around €35. The six-course menu costs €120, three-course lunches are €85, and the wine list is superb. Reservations essential. Mon–Sat noon–2.30pm & 7–10.30pm.

ALEXANDERPLATZ AND AROUND

CHEAP EATS

Käse König Panoramastr. 1 ☎030 25 29 50 98, ⓦkaesekoenig.de; U- & S-Alexanderplatz; map p.60. Join locals at this basic cafeteria serving simple, decent German and Central European food at low prices from a small daily menu – schnitzel or goulash with boiled potatoes, say, for around €6. Two branches share the same block; the larger is further from the bustle of the street and has more outdoor seating. Mon–Sat 8am–7pm, Sun 10am–7pm.

BARS AND MICROBREWERIES

Brauhaus Georgbräu Spreeufer 4 ☎030 242 42 44, ⓦbrauhaus-georgbraeu.de; U-Klosterstrasse; map p.60. This microbrewery attracts a merry, touristy crowd, and is also popular among locals for its excellent beer and traditional German food. Daily 10am–midnight.
Brauhaus Mitte Karl-Liebknecht-Str. 13 ☎030 24 78 38 31 11, ⓦbrauhaus-mitte.de; U- & S-Alexanderplatz;

map p.60. All the trappings of a Bavarian beer hall, including excellent beers – try the delicious *Weissen*, a cloudy Bavarian speciality – recreated in this city-centre microbrewery in the heart of Berlin. Good for basic pub food, with well-priced lunch specials for €6. Mon–Sat 10am–midnight, Sun 11am–midnight.
Zum Nussbaum Am Nussbaum 3 ☎030 242 30 95; U-Klosterstrasse; map p.60. In the heart of the Nikolaiviertel, this is a convincing copy of a prewar bar – destroyed in an air raid – that stood on the Fischerinsel and was favoured by the artists Heinrich Zille and Otto Nagel. This replica verges on the expensive, but it's a good place to soak up a bit of (ersatz) old Berlin ambience. Mon–Sat 9am–6pm.

RESTAURANTS

Emmas Heiligegeistkirchplatz 1 ☎030 24 63 17 32; S-Hackescher Markt; map p.60. Smart bistro specializing in simple fresh German food of the meat and potatoes

13

variety, but with the addition of more fresh veggies and modern twists to make things less stodgy. It's a particularly good choice for inexpensive lunches (€6.50), such as carrot and ginger soup followed by a rich goulash. Daily 11.30am–midnight.

Sphere Panoramastr. 1A ☎ 030 242 59 22, ⌨ tv-turm .de; U- & S-Alexanderplatz; map p.60. The smart, revolving restaurant at the top of the TV tower (p.62) serves a reasonable enough menu of traditional Berlin and international dishes aimed squarely at tourists. You might have to pay €12 to access the restaurant and another €15 for a plate of ravioli, but where else can you get to see all of Berlin in half an hour? Daily: March–Oct 9am–midnight; Nov–Feb 10am–midnight.

Zille-Stube Spreeufer 3 ☎ 030 242 52 47; U-Klosterstrasse; map p.60. Traditional German restaurant and homage to Berlin life – and to artist Heinrich Zille, who used to drink nearby at *Zum Nussbaum*

(see p.189) and whose illustrations line the wood-clad walls. Particularly good on the menu of old Berlin favourites are the *Rinderroulade* (beef-stuffed cabbage leaves) and *Sauerbraten* (marinated pot roast), both around €13. Daily noon–10pm.

★ **Zur letzten Instanz** Waisenstr. 14–16 ☎ 030 242 55 28; U-Klosterstrasse; map p.60. Berlin's oldest *Kneipe*, with a wonderfully old-fashioned interior, including a classic tiled oven, and a great beer garden. The reasonably priced traditional dishes all have law-themed names, like *Zeugen-Aussage* ("eyewitness account") – a reminder of the days when people used to drop in on the way to the nearby courthouse. It's considered so authentically German that foreign heads of state are often brought here to dine. If the meaty dishes (€9–14) look too heavy, try the simpler *Boulette*, Berlin's home-made mince-and-herb burger, done here to perfection. Mon–Sat noon–11pm, Sun noon–9pm.

SPANDAUER VORSTADT

CHEAP EATS

Dada Falafel Linienstr. 132 ☎ 030 27 59 69 27, ⌨ dadafalafel.de; U-Oranienburger Tor; map pp.72–73. Tiny Middle Eastern *Imbiss* with sleek decor, some seating and excellent falafel and *shawarma* sandwiches – the best of a clutch of cheap and cheerful options at this end of Oranienburger Str. Sun–Thurs 10am–2am, Sat 10am–3pm.

Dolores Rosa-Luxemburg-Str. 7 ☎ 030 28 09 95 97, ⌨ dolores-online.de; U-Rosa-Luxemburg-Platz; map pp.72–73. As good a burrito as you'll find in Berlin, dished up in a small, funky and generally overcrowded cafeteria at staggeringly low prices. You'll leave very full, €4–6 poorer and maybe a bit bewildered by the à la carte menu system. Mon–Sat 11.30am–10pm, Sun 1–10pm.

CAFÉS AND BARS

Barcomi's Deli Sophienstr. 21 ☎ 030 28 59 83 63, ⌨ barcomis.de; U-Weinmeisterstrasse; map pp.72–73. Situated in a pleasant courtyard, accessible from both Sophienstr. and Gipsstr., *Barcomi's* is a nice place to rest while gallery-hopping; it serves interesting soups and American-style baked goodies, as well as great breakfasts. Mon–Fri 8am–6pm, Sat 10am–6pm, Sun noon–6pm.

Gorki Park Weinbergsweg 25 ☎ 030 448 72 86, ⌨ gorki-park.de; U-Rosenthaler Platz; map pp.72–73. Tongue-in-cheek Soviet-themed café with 1970s Eastern Bloc-style furnishings and tasty and affordable Russian dishes like *blini* and *pelmeni* (mains average €9). A large *Milchcafé* comes with a delicious molasses cookie, and the weekend brunch buffet (€10) is a treat. Free wi-fi. Mon–Sat 9.30am–2am, Sun 10am–2pm.

Hackbarths Auguststr. 49a ☎ 030 282 77 04; U-Weinmeisterstrasse; map pp.72–73. Dominated by a

huge triangular bar, *Hackbarths* attracts a very mixed crowd. The good choice of food includes tasty breakfasts and excellent tapas (from €2). Daily 10am until late.

Kapelle Zionskirchplatz 22–24 ☎ 030 44 34 13 00, ⌨ cafe-kapelle.de; U-Rosenthaler Platz; map pp.72–73. High ceilings and apricot walls in the shadow of the hulking Zionskirche. A little off the beaten track but worth the detour – particularly if you're heading to the Arkonaplatz flea market. Breakfasts, snacks, cakes and great frozen fruit juices available. Daily 9am–3am.

Oliv Münzstr. 8 ☎ 030 89 20 65 40, ⌨ oliv-cafe.de; U-Rosa-Luxemburg-Platz; map pp.72–73. With a modern interior, great coffee and decent, unpretentious food (sandwiches, quiches, soups, cakes), this is a pleasant spot for breakfast or lunch, and very convenient for a respite from boutique shopping. Cash only. Mon–Fri 8.30am–7pm, Sat 9.30am–7pm, Sun 10am–6pm.

Oscar Wilde Irish Pub Friedrichstr. 112a ☎ 030 282 81 66, ⌨ oscar-wilde-irish-pub.de; U-Oranienburger Tor; map pp.72–73. Generic Irish bar and something of a social club for Berlin's English-speaking community. The all-day breakfasts are good if you're craving a fry-up, and the Irish stews aren't bad either. Mon–Fri noon–1am, Sat 1pm–3am, Sun 1pm–2am.

Yosoy Rosenthaler Str. 37 ☎ 030 28 39 12 13, ⌨ yosoy .de, S-Hackescher Markt; map pp.72–73. Inexpensive tapas bar, with beautiful tile work and Spanish staff, perfectly placed for before-drinking or after-clubbing dinners (€9–15). Daily 11am until late.

RESTAURANTS

Amrit Oranienburger Str. 45 ☎ 030 28 88 48 40, ⌨ amrit.de; U-Oranienburger Tor; map pp.72–73. A cut above most of Berlin's very average Indian restaurants, delivering quality ingredients and fresh spices at reasonable prices (mains €8–13) in clean-cut contemporary surroundings. Lots of veggie choices. Sun–Thurs noon–1am, Fri & Sat noon until late.

Bandol sur Mer Torstr. 167 ☎030 67 30 20 51; U-Rosenthaler Platz; map pp.72–73. A former kebab kiosk refurbished into a tiny but casually upmarket and hugely popular French restaurant. The menu, chalked up on the all-black walls, consists of fine French cuisine like snails, entrecôte and foie gras. There's not too much innovation for the price (mains around €18) but the food is consistently good. Daily 6pm–11pm.

Kellerrestaurant im Brechthaus Chausseestr. 125 ☎030 282 38 43, ⓦbrechtkeller.de; U-Oranienburger Tor; map pp.72–73. Atmospheric restaurant in the basement of Brecht's old house, decorated with Brecht memorabilia, including models of his stage sets. The Viennese specialities (mains €9–15) are from recipes dreamt up by Brecht's wife Helene Weigel, a busy actress with only East German ingredients at her disposal, so don't expect anything too elaborate or expensive. Reservations recommended. Daily 6pm until late.

Kuchi Gipsstr. 3 ☎030 28 38 66 22, ⓦkuchi.de; U-Rosenthaler Platz; map pp.72–73. *Kuchi* might not serve the best sushi in Berlin, but it's definitely the buzziest place to eat it, with a classy interior, hipster clientele and upbeat atmosphere. The menu ranges beyond sushi (nigiri from €4) to noodles and tempura. At peak times expect to share a table. Mon–Sat noon–midnight, Sun 6pm–midnight.

★ **Monsieur Vuong** Alte Schönhauser Str. 46 ☎030 30 87 26 43, ⓦmonsieurvuong.de; U-Weinmeisterstrasse; map pp.72–73. Snazzy Vietnamese place with delicious soups and noodle dishes (€8–11) from a tiny menu – look out also for the daily specials on the blackboard, which are available without meat. Bench seating means you'll sometimes have to squeeze together with other diners – expect queues at peak times. Don't miss the delicious jasmine and artichoke teas, or the zesty fruit smoothies. Daily noon–midnight.

Schwarzwaldstuben Tucholskystr. 48 ☎030 28 09 80 84, ⓜschwarzwaldstuben-berlin.com; S-Oranienburger Strasse; map pp.72–73. This Mitte mainstay doubles as a

TOP 5 SWEET TREATS
Anna Blume See p.202
Café BilderBuch See p.195
Café Buchwald See p.192
Café Einstein (Schöneberg) See p.195
Zuckerfee See p.202

casual restaurant serving hearty Swabian food – think *Sauerkraut, Maultaschen* (filled pasta) and *Flammkuchen* (a type of thin-crust pizza, from €8) – and a friendly bar in the evenings with decent German beers on draught. Daily 9am–midnight.

Unsicht-bar Gormannstr. 14 ☎030 24 34 25 00, ⓦunsicht-bar-berlin.de; U-Weinmeisterstrasse; map pp.72–73. Hugely successful novelty restaurant (run by an organization of the blind and visually impaired), where you eat in total darkness. First, pick from one of several three- or four-course fixed menus (€40–57), including a vegetarian option, then follow your blind or partially sighted waiter into the pitch black for your meal. The idea is that without your eyesight, your other senses will be heightened, but you're likely to make other discoveries, too, including how hard it is to judge the amount of food that's on your plate or fork, or even down your front. Fri & Sat 6pm–1am, Sun–Thurs 5pm–1am.

Weinbar Rutz Chausseestr. 8 ☎030 24 62 87 60, ⓦrutz-weinbar.de; U-Naturkundemuseum; map pp.72–73. Michelin-starred cuisine on the second floor and more than a thousand international wines offered in the ground-floor bar make this a de rigueur stop for foodies. It's expensive – multi-course menus €90–122 – but the bar sells slightly cheaper (but still great) home-style dishes. Tues–Sat: wine bar 4–11pm; restaurant 6.30–10.30pm.

Yumcha Heroes Weinbergsweg 8 ☎030 76 21 30 35, ⓦyumchaheroes.de; U-Rosenthaler Platz; map pp.72–73. With the same owners as nearby Portuguese café *Galao*, this is *the* place in Mitte for dumplings – steamed, baked or in a tasty broth. The food is handmade and MSG-free, cooked in an open kitchen and served in a small, but stylish interior. Two-course daily menu €7.50. Daily noon–midnight.

TIERGARTEN AND AROUND

CHEAP EATS

Salomon Bagels Potsdamer Platz Arkaden, 1st floor ⓦsalomon-bagels.de; U- & S-Potsdamer Platz; map pp.90–91. Good selection of bagels, sandwiches and desserts (including a tasty New York-style cheesecake), but as with all the cheap eating places in this mall – they're concentrated in the basement – the noise and bustle don't exactly create a relaxing atmosphere. There are sofas, however, and prices are reasonable. Daily 9am–9pm.

Sushi Express Potsdamer Platz 2 ☎030 25 75 18 63, ⓦsushi-expressberlin.de; U- & S-Potsdamer Platz; map pp.90–91. Tricky to find – it's off the Sony Center courtyard on a passage to the S-Bahn – but worthwhile for a decent range of conveyor-belt sushi, especially when there are half-price offers (Mon–Fri noon–6pm). Hot dishes and lunchboxes also available, though it's usually packed at lunchtimes. Main courses €5. Mon–Sat 11.30am–10pm, Sun 2–10pm.

13

CAFÉS, BARS AND BEER GARDENS

★ **Café am Neuen See** Lichtensteinallee 2 ☎ 030 254 49 30, ⓦ cafeamneuensee.de; S- & U-Zoologischer Garten; map pp.90–91. A little piece of Bavaria in the middle of the Tiergarten; this beer garden is next to a picturesque lake where you can rent a rowing boat. The usual snacks – and superb pizzas (€9–15) – are served alongside frothing jugs. Daily 9am–late.

Café Buchwald Bartningallee 29 ☎ 030 391 59 31, ⓦ konditorei-buchwald.de; S-Bellevue; map pp.90–91. This old-fashioned *Konditorei* has been serving its famed *Baumkuchen,* a kind of layered cake, since 1852 (€2.90) and used to supply the royal court. A perfect break from a stroll around the Tiergarten. Mon–Sat 9am–6pm, Sun 10am–6pm.

Schleusenkrug Müller-Breslau-Str. ☎ 030 313 99 09, ⓦ schleusenkrug.de; S- & U-Zoologischer Garten; map pp.90–91. Wedged between a canal lock, the zoo and Tiergarten, this beer garden is a great spot to spend a last hour before hopping on a train at Zoo Bahnhof. Chairs are easy to move around for optimal sunning, and anything from the small daily menu (mains €9–15) is a safe bet. Inside, it is modern diner chic. Daily: March–Oct 10am until late; Nov–Feb 10am–6pm.

RESTAURANTS

Angkor Wat Paulstr. 22 ☎ 030 393 39 22, ⓦ angkorwat .kambodschareise.de; S-Bellevue; map pp.90–91. Excellent place, serving subtle variations on traditional Cambodian food at moderate prices (mains €10–15). The two-person set meals (from €30) are a great way to sample a cross-section of delicious dishes, and the Cambodian

fondue is great. Mon–Fri 6pm–midnight, Sat & Sun noon–midnight.

Facil Mandala Hotel, Potsdamer Str. 3 ☎ 030 590 05 ext. 1234, ⓦ facil.de; U-Potsdamer Platz; map pp.90–91. Michael Kempf's restaurant in the *Mandala Hotel* not only offers amazing food but also splendid views from the fifth floor despite its lush bamboo garden. Popular with business types, politicos and serious foodies, Kempf's Michelin-starred, fish-heavy menu has become justly famous. Dinner costs €16–55 per course; try a lunch reservation for something slightly cheaper overall (€18–39 per course). Mon–Fri noon–3pm & 7–11pm.

Hugos Hotel InterContinental, Budapester Str. 2 ☎ 030 26 02 12 63, ⓦ hugos-restaurant.de; U–Wittenbergplatz; map pp.90–91. In a gorgeously appointed room at the top of the *Hotel InterContinental,* superstar chef Thomas Kammeier creates Michelin-starred "New German-Mediterranean" food that you can sample – for a price – while enjoying the restaurant's panoramic views (mains €44–52). Mon–Sat 6–10.30pm; closed mid-July to mid-Aug.

Paris-Moskau Alt-Moabit 141 ☎ 030 394 20 81, ⓦ paris-moskau.de; S-Hauptbahnhof; map pp.90–91. Housed in a nineteenth-century rail signalman's house on the Paris to Moscow line, this French gourmet restaurant offers a curious mix of old Berlin and contemporary elegance and serves hearty dishes like deer and rabbit, fish and vegetarian lasagne with beetroot and chestnuts (€39–65), all backed up by a great wine list. Popular with politicians and civil servants from the nearby government district, and elegant without being too snooty. Mon–Fri noon–3pm & 6–11pm, Sat & Sun 6pm–midnight.

CITY WEST

CHEAP EATS

Bier's Ku'damm 195 Kurfürstendamm 195; map p.108. Neon-lit place famed for its *Currywurst* and its popularity with German politicians and celebrities

(you can even get champagne), although its prices remain everyday. Also serves meat skewers and meatballs. Mon–Thurs 11am–5am, Fri & Sat 11am–6am, Sun noon–5am.

BREAKFAST AND SUNDAY BRUNCH

Breakfast (*Frühstück*) will often be provided by your hotel, but many cafés serve it throughout the day. Prices start around €3 for a basic bread, eggs and jam affair, rising to €15 for more exotic, champagne-swigging delights.

Typically, you'll be offered a small platter of **cold meats** (usually sausage-based) and **cheeses**, along with a selection of marmalades, jams and honey, and, occasionally, muesli or another cereal. You're also generally given a variety of **breads**, one of the most distinctive features of German cuisine. Both brown and white rolls are popular, often baked with caraway, coriander, poppy or sesame seeds. The rich-tasting black rye bread, known as *Pumpernickel*, is a particular favourite. Freshly brewed **coffee** is the normal accompaniment, though plain or herbal **tea** and **hot chocolate** are also common. A glass of orange **juice** is sometimes included as well.

Sunday brunch is a very popular affair, offering first-class people-watching and often excellent food – and proves particularly good value when offered as part of a **buffet**. Expect to pay €6–10 for unlimited food; drinks are paid for separately.

Einhorn Mommsenstr. 2 ☎030 881 42 41, ⓦeinhornonline.de; U-Uhlandstrasse; map p.108. Vegetarian wholefood at its best, with a daily changing international menu – dishes might include lentils with goat's cheese – and a fabulous lunch bar where food is priced by weight (€1.50/100g). Often standing-room only, but the atmosphere remains friendly and relaxed. Mon–Fri 10am–5pm.

Lon-Men's Noodle House Kantstr. 33 ☎030 31 51 96 78, ⓦlon-men.de; S-Savignyplatz; map p.108. A relaxed, tiny Taiwanese noodle shop run by friendly grandmas who make excellent dumplings and noodle soups (small and large portions available). Try the "Chinese Maultaschen" – fried ravioli-style pasta packets filled with pork and vegetables (€5–6) – and ask for the home-made noodles (not on the menu). Daily noon–midnight.

Piccola Taormina Uhlandstr. 29 ☎030 881 47 10, ⓦpiccola-taormina.net; U-Uhlandstrasse; map p.108. Enduringly popular wafer-thin pizza specialist with a strange set-up: order and pay at the bar, find a seat in the back room, listen out for a tannoy announcement; then head back to the bar to collect. It's all a bit chaotic and very Italian, but well worth it for the food – slices from €1.50. Daily 11am–2am.

Witty's Wittenbergplatz 5 ☎030 211 94 96, ⓦwittys -berlin.de; U–Wittenbergplatz; map p.108. One of the city's first and finest organic sausage stands, *Witty's* has customers lined up along the square for their *Currywurst* and crispy fries. Eat here, then cross the street for an exquisite chocolate or two from KaDeWe (see p.230). Mon–Sat 11am–8pm, Sun noon–7pm.

CAFÉS AND BARS

Café im Literaturhaus Fasanenstr. 23 ☎030 882 54 14, ⓦliteraturhaus-berlin.de; U-Uhlandstrasse; map p.108. Every bit as classic and elegant as the name suggests. The spacious interior or beautiful summer garden are great spots for coffee and cake, lunch or dinner: the organic menu changes weekly (€5.30 soup, €24.50 steak) and has vegetarian options. Daily 9.30am–1am.

Café Savigny Grolmanstr. 53 ☎030 44 70 83 86; S-Savignyplatz; map p.108. A small, classic spot that's been serving great breakfasts and coffee for more than a decade. Lunches start at €5.50 (soups) with a hearty Burgundy stew for €13.50. Service is good and it's also nice for an evening drink. Daily 9am–1am.

Dicke Wirtin Carmerstr. 9 ☎030 312 49 52, ⓦdicke -wirtin.de; S-Savignyplatz; map p.108. Traditional Berlin *Kneipe*, here since the 1920s, but spruced up a little since to appeal to Berlin visitors who can pick from nine draught beers and basic snacks like *Schmalzbrot* (lard on bread; €2.50). Daily noon until late.

Schwarzes Café Kantstr. 148 ☎030 313 80 38, ⓦschwarzescafe-berlin.de; S-Savignyplatz; map

TOP 10 BRUNCH SPOTS

Aroma Schöneberg. See p.196
Café Datscha Friedrichshain. See p.200
Café November Prenzlauer Berg. See p.202
Kleisther Schöneberg. See p.195
Macondo Café Friedrichshain. See p.201
Morgenland Eastern Kreuzberg. See p.200
Pasternak Prenzlauer Berg. See p.203
Restauration 1900 Prenzlauer Berg.
See p.203
Schneeweiss Eastern Kreuzberg. See p.201
Zwölf Apostel City West. See p.194

p.108. The slightly ragged charm of the "Black Café" makes it feel like it would be better placed in the east. Downstairs is small and intimate, but upstairs the large, airy room has a relaxed, convivial vibe. Food is served 24hr, including breakfasts (from €4.50) – but it comes into its own as a night-owl place. Daily 24hr.

Zwiebelfisch Savignyplatz 7 ☎030 312 73 63, ⓦzwiebelfisch-berlin.de; S-Savignyplatz; map p.108. Corner bar and 1970s throwback for would-be arty and intellectual types. Jazz, earnest debate and good cheap grub (€5–11), including goulash and Swabian *Maultaschen* (ravioli), served until 1am. Daily noon–6am.

RESTAURANTS

Ashoka Grolmanstr. 51 ☎030 31 01 58 06; S-Savignyplatz; map p.108. Ashok Sharma opened this restaurant in 1975 as he was missing the food from his home in Punjab. It offers well-priced, decent food (curries around €8.50) in a small *Imbiss*-style place. Vegetarian options and friendly staff. Daily 11am–midnight.

Dao Kantstr. 133 ☎030 37 59 14 14, ⓦdao-restaurant .de; S-Savignyplatz; map p.108. Opened by a Berliner and his Thai wife Dao in the 1970s, this Thai spot serves tasty dishes that brim with flavour. Alongside *pad Thai* (€8.90) and fish and duck dishes (up to €18) there are specials like "Bloodnoodlesoup". Daily noon–midnight.

Diekmann Meinekestr. 7 ☎030 883 33 21, ⓦdickmann-restaurants.de; U-Kurfürstendamm; map p.108. Longstanding Berlin bistro, with French colonial touches in the decor and on the menu; the €10 three-course business lunches are a bargain, otherwise you'll pay €17–23 for oft-changing mains that are always fresh and reliable – the oysters are particularly good. Mon–Sat noon until late, Sun 6pm until late.

Diener Grolmanstr. 47 ☎030 881 53 29, ⓦdiener -tattersall.de; S-Savignyplatz; map p.108. This Berlin ale house is a local institution – not only because it was opened in 1954 by former German heavyweight boxer Franz Diener, but also because it serves dishes like *Königsberger Klopse* (meatballs in white sauce with capers;

13

€9.20) and has an atmosphere as old-school as the menu. Daily 6pm–3am.

Dressler Kurfürstendamm 207–208 ☎030 883 35 30, ⓦrestaurant-dressler.de; U-Uhlandstrasse; map p.108. German take on a French brasserie with an old-fashioned feel and an Art Nouveau interior – formal but friendly. The seasonal food is very good, and the small front bar is perfect for a quick coffee or lunch (three courses €13.50). Daily 8am–1am (kitchen till midnight).

★ **First Floor** Hotel Palace, Budapester Str. 45 ☎030 25 02 10 20, ⓦfirstfloor.hotel-palace.biz; U-Kurfürstendamm; map p.108. Matthias Diether is the mastermind behind one of Berlin's most celebrated restaurants. His inventive French/European menu is seasonal and changes regularly, and though it's not cheap (mains average €40) you get your money's worth. Four-, six- or eight-course menus from €110, with a two- or four-course lunch menu (€28/€56). Mon–Fri noon–3pm & 6.30–11pm, Sat & Sun 6.30–11pm.

Florian Grolmanstr. 52 ☎030 313 91 84, ⓦrestaurant-florian.de; S-Savignyplatz; map p.108. Leading light among Berlin's modern German restaurants, serving fresh, light and innovative versions of traditional combinations from a weekly menu that includes the likes of boiled veal with radish, beetroot, potato and leeks, or rump steak with green beans and rosemary potatoes. Prices are fair (mains €16.50–24.50), the interior coolly bland and the service excellent. It's as much a place for Berlin's beautiful people to be seen as it is a place to eat. Daily 6pm–3am (kitchen until 2am).

Good Friends Kantstr. 30 ☎030 313 26 59, ⓦgoodfriends-berlin.de; S-Savignyplatz; map p.108. One of Berlin's few really authentic Cantonese restaurants, with plain decor and a full range of classics (mains €7–19). It's always busy; evening bookings recommended. Daily noon–2am.

Jules Verne Restaurant Schlüterstr. 61 ☎030 31 80 94 10, ⓦjules-verne-berlin.de; S-Savignyplatz; map p.108. The interior feels classically French but the menu is aptly global, ranging from *Flammkuchen* (a thin-crusted, pizza-like Alsatian speciality) and *schnitzel* to couscous and satay. Lunchtime deals (€6–8) change weekly. Daily 9am–1am, kitchen till 11.45pm.

Kuchi Kantstr. 30 ☎030 31 50 78 15, ⓦkuchi.de; S-Savignyplatz; map p.108. With a sister restaurant in Mitte (see p.191), this place sells the same range of innovative sushi, sashimi and yakitori, as well as some Thai, Chinese and Korean recipes. It gets busy at peak times,

when it's best to reserve. Happy hour (5–6pm) includes noodle soups for €6 and sushi for €7. Daily noon–midnight.

★ **Lubitsch** Bleibtreustr. 47 ☎030 882 37 56, ⓦrestaurant-lubitsch.de; S-Savignyplatz; map p.108. Named after German film director Ernst Lubitsch, this slick bistro has a wonderfully old-school Berlin feel. The food is generous and hearty – dumplings, *schnitzel*, cucumber salad – and though the ambience is vaguely formal (linen tablecloths) and popular with business people, it's also a friendly place. A daily lunch dish is available for €5; three-course lunches €10; dinner mains €12–18. Mon–Sat 10am–late, Sun 6pm–late (kitchen daily to 11pm).

Marjellchen Mommsenstr. 9 ☎030 883 26 76, ⓦmarjellchen-berlin.de; S-Savignyplatz; map p.108. It's obvious from the window displays – books, photos and other paraphernalia – that this is a timewarped kind of place. Indeed, *Marjellchen* specializes in cuisine from East Prussia, Pomerania and Silesia, all served up in a cosy, traditional atmosphere. Portions are generous and service is friendly. Mains €12.50–20.20. Daily 5pm–midnight.

Ottenthal Kantstr. 153 ☎030 313 31 62, ⓦottenthal.com; S-Savignyplatz; map p.108. White-clothed tables and relatively sparse white walls lend this place an unfussy, classic feel that ties in well with the Austrian cuisine – simple, yet some of the best in the area. Organic ingredients feature on the menu, which includes fish, risotto and a famed *Wiener Schnitzel*; dishes €4–7. Good Austrian wine list too. Daily 6pm–1am.

Paris Bar Kantstr. 152 ☎030 313 80 52, ⓦparisbar.net; U-Uhlandstrasse; map p.108. Once the city's most famous meeting place for artists, writers and intellectuals, and now, due to its high prices, the preserve of the moneyed middle classes and visiting celebrities including Madonna, Robert de Niro and Mikhail Gorbachev. The decidedly average food is French and Viennese in style but the service immaculate. Mains around €18–26; weekday lunches a bargain at €8–12 each. Daily noon–2am.

Zwölf Apostel Bleibtreustr. 49 ☎030 312 14 33, ⓦ12-apostel.de; S-Savignyplatz; map p.108. Deluxe and very popular pizzeria with a smart, Baroque-style interior and kitsch religious frescoes. Mains (€7–20) include five types of calzone and huge thin-crust pizzas with unusual toppings like smoked salmon and cream cheese. The €6.50 weekday lunch (11.30am–4pm) is excellent, and the terrific Sunday brunch buffet (€18) comes with a glass of sparkling wine and a hot drink. Booking recommended in the evenings. Daily 8am–1am.

SCHÖNEBERG

CHEAP EATS

★ **Baharat Falafel** Winterfeldtstr. 37 ☎030 216 83 01; U-Nollendorfplatz; map p.113. A bare-bones falafel joint, you might think; but these are the best

falafels this side of Baghdad. With some seating. Daily noon–2am.

Ebbes Crellestr. 2 ☎030 70 09 48 13, ⓦebbes-in-berlin.de; S-Julius-Leber-Brücke; map p.113. This quirky

13

THE IMBISS

The German term **Imbiss** was originally coined for little food stalls at medieval markets, and Berliners are certainly past masters in serving inexpensive food for eating on the hoof. The city's immigrant population has built on the tradition, adapting recipes to produce quick portable meals. Today virtually every Berlin street has an *Imbiss*, with major concentrations in commercial areas and at train stations. Some have limited seating, but many only offer a couple of high tables on which to lean. It's pretty much guaranteed that a local *Imbiss* will be more interesting than the international fast-food places that dot the city (though the national fish and seafood specialist chain *Nordsee* is worth a try). All the *Imbisses* reviewed in this chapter are listed under "cheap eats".

The simple sausage has traditionally been the most popular *Imbiss* item and in Berlin it's been transformed into the local speciality **Currywurst** – a chubby smoked pork sausage smothered in curried ketchup – often served with French fries (*pommes frites*). Another local *Imbiss* speciality is the **Boulette**, a hamburger patty made from ground beef, eggs, butter, herbs and onions, which was introduced by the French Huguenots in the late 1600s. These days, however, the most common of all are **Greek**, **Turkish** and **Middle Eastern** *Imbiss* stands selling *döner*, *gyros* or *shawarma* respectively – all essentially kebabed meat or chicken bundled into a pitta, tortilla or ciabatta-style bread sandwich with salad and a sauce – usually hot (*scharf*), herb (*Kräuter*) or garlic (*Knoblauch*). All are likely to be delicious and fill you up for around €3. The standard of *Imbiss* food throughout Berlin is very good since most rely on local business, so in general it's not worth going out of your way to track down a particular place. That said, if you want to make sure you are having as good a *Currywurst* as the city can offer, try **Bier's Kudamm 195** (see p.108), **Konnopke's Imbiss** (see p.201) or **Curry 36** (see p.196).

Swabian deli is crowded with rings of venison salami and trays of fresh *spätzle* (pasta) from southern Germany. Buy a picnic and wander north to Kleistpark, or grab a stool outside and try one of the daily specials, including *Maultaschen* (ravioli) in broth (€2.50). Mon–Fri 10am–7.30pm, Sat 9am–4pm.

Garda Pizza Crellestr. 48 ☎030 78 09 79 70; U-Julius-Leber-Brücke; map p.113. Locals flock here for thin-crust Roman-style (elongated) pizza, particularly the version with fresh aubergine, mushroom, sheep's salami and artichokes. A tray (€15) will feed a hungry group of four. Join the crowd on the pavement, or, with kids, mosey down a few metres to the neighbouring playground. Daily 11.30am–9pm; Dec–Feb closed Sun.

CAFÉS AND BARS

Café BilderBuch Akazienstr. 28 ☎030 78 70 60 57, ⓦ cafe-bilderbuch.de; S-Julius-Leber-Brücke; map p.113. Lovely rambling café in the Viennese tradition. It doesn't look particularly special from outside, but the comfortable back parlour may well hold you captive for hours. Great breakfasts, lovely cakes, elegant coffees and courtyard seating, too. Mon–Sat 9am–midnight, Sun 10am–midnight.

Café Einstein Kurfürstenstr. 58 ☎030 261 50 96; U-Nollendorfplatz; map p.113. Housed in a seemingly ancient German villa, with parquet floors and leather banquettes, this is about as close as you'll get to the ambience of a prewar Berlin *Kaffeehaus*, with international newspapers, breakfast served until 2pm and occasional live music. On sunny afternoons make a beeline for the spacious garden and sip bellinis as shadows lengthen. Expensive, though (daily specials €13.50), and a little snooty. Daily 8am–1am.

Café M Goltzstr. 33 ☎030 216 70 92, ⓦ cafe-m.de; U-Nollendorfplatz; map p.113. Littered with tatty plastic chairs and precious little else, *M* is a favoured rendezvous for self-styled creative types and the conventionally unconventional. Usually packed, particularly for its famous breakfasts; cocktails €5.50 during happy hour (8–10pm). Daily 8am–2am.

Felsenkeller Akazienstr. 2 ☎030 781 34 47; S-Julius-Leber-Brücke; map p.113. Perfect for when you're nostalgic for old Berlin. Founded in 1923, this unpretentious old bar is famous for its eight beers on tap drawn the old-fashioned way, so be prepared to wait. Hearty, simple food includes lentil soup and swede stew (€5). No music, but plenty of atmosphere and a hip young crowd. Mon–Fri 4pm–1am, Sat noon–2am.

Inka Eis Belziger Str. 44 ☎030 78 09 70 50, ⓦ inka-eis.eu; U-Eisenacher Strasse; map p.113. A little taste of Latin America in a quiet corner of Schöneberg, *Inka Eis* serves scrumptious scoops of tamarind ice cream, Peruvian grilled chicken (€5) and *empanadas* (€3.50). Closed Jan & Feb. Daily 11am–8pm.

Kleisther Hauptstr. 5 ☎030 784 67 38, ⓦ kleisther.de; U-Kleistpark; map p.113. Neighbourhood institution, perennially crowded with style-conscious alternative types, and offering a good Sunday buffet brunch (10am–4pm; €8.50). Thurs–Sat 9am–5pm, Sun–Wed 9am–1pm.

TOP 5 TRADITIONAL LOCAL FOOD

Altes Zollhaus See p.198
Marjellchen See p.194
Ratskeller Köpenick See p.204
Zum Schusterjungen See p.204
Zur letzten Instanz See p.190

Sorgenfrei Goltzstr. 18 ☏030 30 10 40 71; U-Nollendorfplatz; map p.113. This gay-friendly café will take you straight back to the 1950s, with Hawaiian-style toast on the menu and Bing Crosby on the speakers. The Bakelite radios and kidney-shaped tables aren't just for decoration – most items are for sale. Tues–Fri noon–7pm, Sat 10am–6pm, Sun 1–6pm.

Winterfeldt Schokoladen Goltzstr. 23 ☏030 23 62 32 56, ⊛winterfeldt-schokoladen.de; U-Nollendorfplatz; map p.113. Once an apothecary, this café-chocolate shop now serves a lovely selection of pastries to cure all ills. Scones with clotted cream and jam and warm chocolate fondant cake (both €3) are popular. Mon–Fri 9am–8pm, Sat & Sun 9am–6pm.

RESTAURANTS

Aroma Hochkirchstr. 8 ☏030 782 58 21, ⊛cafe-aroma.de; U- & S-Yorckstrasse; map p.113. Rustic Italian gem tucked away on a sleepy residential street and the unofficial headquarters for Berlin's slow food movement. The antipasti spread at Sunday brunch (until 4pm; €12) is legendary, while dried cod with polenta (€7.50) and squid with baby chard (€15.50) satisfy the dinner crowd. The terrace is a peaceful haven in summer. Mon–Fri from 6pm, Sat from 3pm, Sun brunch 11am–2pm, à la carte from 2pm.

Edd's Thailändisches Lutzowstr. 81 ☏030 215 52 94, ⊛edds-thairestaurant.de; U-Kurfürstenstrasse; map p.113. Huge portions of superbly cooked fresh Thai food make this sumptuous place popular all week. Bearing in mind the quality and authenticity – many family recipes stem from Edd's gran (including the signature banana blossom salad), who cooked in Bangkok's Royal Palace – the prices are reasonable, with mains around €16–25. Booking essential and credit cards not accepted. Tues–Fri

11.30am–3pm & 6pm–midnight, Sat 5pm–midnight, Sun 2pm–midnight.

Ixthys Pallasstr. 21 ☏030 81 47 47 69; U-Nollendorfplatz; map p.113. A tiny café run by two Korean widows who've festooned the walls with Biblical slogans, this place is all about great home-style cooking. Guests squeeze in to enjoy home-made noodles with vegetables (€5) or seafood (€7.50) and the fiery, sizzling *bibimbap* (€7.50). Mon–Sat noon–10pm.

Joseph Roth Diele Potsdamer Str. 75 ☏030 26 36 98 84, ⊛joseph-roth-diele.de; U-Kurfürstenstrasse; map p.113. Quirky restaurant that pays homage to the life and work of inter-war Jewish writer Joseph Roth and adds a splash of charm and colour to a fairly nondescript corner of central Berlin. Very popular, with very reasonably priced daily specials (€3.95–8), though the food is fairly basic. Mon–Fri 10am–midnight, Sat 6pm–midnight.

Maharadscha Fuggerstr. 21 ☏030 213 88 26; U-Nollendorfplatz; map p.113. Though the ambience is that of a German farmhouse, the food is pure Indian, with dishes (€7–11) from every part of the subcontinent. It gets packed out for the Sun buffet (noon–5pm; €9.90). Daily noon–midnight.

Petite Europe Langenscheidtstr. 1 ☏030 781 29 64; U-Kleistpark; map p.113. Unpretentious Italian place that dishes up filling home-made pastas and stone-oven pizzas (average €7) in an informal, lively atmosphere. Booking advised. Daily 5pm–1am.

Renger-Patzsch Wartburgstr. 54 ☏030 784 20 59, ⊛renger-patzsch.com; U-Eisenacher Strasse; map p.113. Rustic restaurant, with dark wood interiors and white tablecloths covering long communal tables, serving excellent cuisine from the Alsace region – a mix of French and German. In spring, don't miss the dandelion salad with lardons (€8); in winter, try the braised ox cheeks with bacon-wrapped plums, turnips and mashed potatoes (€18). Look out too, for wild boar. Mains €14–18. Booking advised. Daily 6pm–1am.

Taverna Ousies Grunewaldstr. 16 ☏030 216 79 57, ⊛taverna-ousies.de; U-Eisenacher Strasse; map p.113. This kitschy, raucous Greek taverna is a perennial favourite. There are no real duds, so go wild with the mezze menu (€4–7) and be entertained by the jolly staff. Reservations essential at weekends. Daily from 5pm.

WESTERN KREUZBERG

CHEAP EATS

Curry 36 Mehringdamm 36 ☏030 251 73 68, ⊛curry36.de; U-Mehringdamm; map p.118. Everyone in Berlin has a favourite place to eat *Currywurst* – sausage doused in curry sauce – but *Curry 36* (along with *Konnopke's* (see p.201) is cited more often than most; it's a buzzy place to grab a snack (around €2). Mon–Fri 9am–4pm, Sat

10am–4pm, Sun 11am–3pm.

Knofi Bergmannstr. 11 & 98 ☏030 69 56 43 59, ⊛knofi.de; U-Gneisenaustrasse; map p.118. There are two *Knofis* opposite each other. At no. 11 you'll find a small *Imbiss* serving tasty Turkish food – stuffed vine leaves, hummus and more (mixed platter €6). Over the road is a Turkish deli. Daily 7am–midnight.

OPPOSITE CAFÉ AM NEUEN SEE (P.192) >

13

TOP 5 RAINY-DAY HANGOUTS
Al Hamra See p.201
Café BilderBuch See p.195
Macondo Café See p.201
Spielwiese See p.201
Wohnzimmer See p.202

Mustafas Mehringdamm 32 ⊛mustafas.de; U-Mehringdamm; map p.118. People will wait in line for an hour at any time of day at this cult *Imbiss* kiosk; all the fuss is about delicious kebabs (around €3) made with lots of fried vegetables (some cooked within the meat itself), feta cheese and plenty of garlic and coriander. Daily 8am–midnight.

Pagode Bergmannstr. 88 ☎030 619 26 40; U-Gneisenaustrasse; map p.118. Crowded, noisy and steamy place where the Thai meals enjoy a high reputation among Berlin's *Imbiss* aficionados. Daily noon–midnight.

CAFÉS, BARS AND BEER GARDENS
Barcomi's Bergmannstr. 21 ☎030 694 81 38, ⊛barcomis.de; U-Gneisenaustrasse; map p.118. American-style coffee house with thirteen exotic blends accompanied by bagels, brownies and other oversized American baked goods – great cheesecake and carrot cake. Scattered copies of the New Yorker too. Mon–Sat 8am–9pm, Sun 9am–9pm.

Café Atlantic Bergmannstr. 100 ☎030 691 92 92; U-Gneisenaustrasse; map p.118. Large, classic café, with colourful paintings in the back and bar stools in the front, serving an abundant weekend breakfast (eleven ways to scramble your eggs, from €6) till 5pm, and with daily lunch specials and dinner options too. Mon–Thurs & Sun 9am–1am, Fri & Sat 9am–2am.

Golgotha Dudenstr. 48–64 ☎030 785 24 53; U- & S-Yorckstrasse; map p.118. Enormous and hugely popular summer-only beer garden and disco (from 10pm) perched in the Viktoriapark near the top of Kreuzberg's hill. Mixed-grill platter €6.50; 0.5 litre beer €3; Breakfast served until 3pm. April–Sept daily 10am until late.

Molinari & Ko Riemannstr. 13 ☎030 691 39 03, ⊛molinari-ko.de; U-Gneisenaustrasse; map p.118. Welcoming Italian café/bar/restaurant hidden away on a residential street. With a wooden interior and friendly staff it offers a menu of breakfasts, snacks, pasta and pizza, with a decent wine and beer selection that makes it good for evenings too. Mon–Fri 8am–1pm, Sat & Sun 9am–1pm.

EASTERN KREUZBERG

CHEAP EATS
Babanbè Oranienplatz 2 ⊛babanbe.tumblr.com; U-Görlitzer Bahnhof; map pp.126–127. This chic,

Sale e Tabacci Rudi-Dutschke-Str. 23 ☎030 252 11 55, ⊛sale-e-tabacchi.de; U-Kochstrasse; map p.118. Authentic and beautiful Italian café near Checkpoint Charlie where journalists and architects linger over espresso. The contemporary food uses top-notch ingredients, but is perhaps a little overpriced, with mains around €9–25. It's known particularly for its excellent seafood (tuna €11.50, sea bass €19) and impressive Italian wine list. Garden seating out back. Mon–Fri 9am–2am, Sat & Sun 10am–2am.

RESTAURANTS
Altes Zollhaus Carl-Herz-Ufer 30 ☎030 692 33 00, ⊛altes-zollhaus-berlin.de; U-Prinzenstrasse; map p.118. Very classy place in an old half-timbered building overlooking a canal, serving modern German food such as duck from Brandenburg with *Kartoffelpuffer*, and zander, a pike-like fish, from the Havel. Three-course set menus €38. Tues–Sat 6pm–1am.

Austria Bergmannstr. 30 ☎030 694 44 40, ⊛austria-berlin.de; U-Gneisenaustrasse; map p.118. Generous portions of excellent Austrian food – particularly the huge *Wiener Schnitzel* (mains €13.50–17.50)– served on solid wood tables in dark, rustic surrounds where the mounted antlers evoke the feel of a hunting lodge. Mains €9–18. Daily 6pm–1am.

Bar Centrale Yorckstr. 82 ☎030 786 29 89, ⊛bar-centrale.ne; U-Mehringdamm; map p.118. Chic Italian locale, popular with affluent young people and exiled Italians. Lots of fresh antipasti, pasta, fish and meat dishes (mains €14–23) and an international wine list. Daily noon–1am, kitchen opens 2pm.

E.T.A Hoffmann Yorckstr. 83 ☎030 78 09 88 09, ⊛restaurant-e-t-a-hoffmann.de; U-Mehringdamm; map p.118. Upmarket bistro overseen by Thomas Kurt, who serves rich European dishes like entrecote with braised cabbage and red wine shallots (€28) and scallops with foie gras (€21), or a set menu for €42. The interior is classic and comfortable, and there's a lovely courtyard. Mon & Wed–Sun 5–11pm.

Tomasa Kreuzbergstr. 62 ☎030 81 00 98 85, ⊛tomasa.de; U-Mehringdamm; map p.118. This old-school villa, on the edge of Viktoriapark, is a particularly pleasant place for a relaxed breakfast or lunch. The classic interior, good, seasonal menu (from tapas to pasta and Asian dishes) and friendly service attract a mixed clientele, families included. Business lunches are available daily (noon–3pm) from €5, otherwise most dishes cost around double that. Sun–Thurs 9am–1am, Fri & Sat 9am–2am.

glass-walled fast-food joint may be German-run, but the speciality dish of *banh mi* – fluffy white bread buns filled with fresh vegetables and flavoursome meats – are pure

Saigon. The menu also features *pho bo* (noodle soup) and more (dishes €5–10). Mon–Sat noon–8pm.

★ **Burgermeister** Oberbaumstr. 8 ⓦ burger-meister .de; U-Schlesisches Tor; map pp.126–127. Cult burger joint in a converted old Prussian public toilets, by the elevated underground station at Schlesisches Tor, serving fresh and delicious burgers (€2–3.50) that could hold their own in far classier surroundings. There are a couple of places to sit, but mostly it's standing room only and often packed. Fri & Sat 11am–4am, Sun–Thurs 11am–3am.

Maroush Adalbertstr. 93 ⓣ 030 69 53 61 71, ⓦ maroush-berlin.de; U-Kottbusser Tor; map pp.126–127. Cosy Lebanese café with authentically Middle Eastern decor and above-average sandwiches, kebabs, falafels and fresh salads. Daily 11am–2am.

Nachtigall Imbiss Ohlauerstr. 10 ⓣ 030 611 71 15; U-Görlitzer Bahnhof; map pp.126–127. Middle Eastern specialities, including the delicious *shawarma* kebab – lamb and hummus in pitta bread. Good salads for vegetarians as well. Daily 11am–midnight.

Yellow Sunshine Wiener Str. 19 ⓣ 0178 21 46 00 66, ⓦ yellow-sunshine.de; U-Görlitzer Bahnhof; map pp.126–127. Vegetarian and organic self-service burger bar, with set meals including fries and a drink for €6. The toasties are good breakfast options. Fri & Sat noon–1am, Sun–Thurs noon–midnight.

CAFÉS AND BARS

Ankerklause Kottbusser Damm 104 ⓣ 030 693 56 49; U-Kottbusser Tor; map pp.126–127. This nautically themed pub overlooking a bucolic canal has been transformed into a hip bar playing a mixture of techno and easy listening. Great breakfast choices (served until 4pm) with first-class French toast and a Mexican breakfast that will tide you over until dinner. Usually packed by 11pm. Tues–Sun 10am–4am, Mon 4pm–4am (kitchen open until 11pm).

Cafe Matilda Graefestr. 12 ⓣ 030 81 79 72 88; U-Schönleinstrasse; map pp.126–127. Choose a table in the front or grab a comfy sofa in the back room. There are several good breakfast options as well as yummy sandwiches (€3–9), coffee and cakes. The owners play soul and funk vinyl during the day, DJs play at weekends, and there are regular bingo and crime TV nights. Daily 9am–2am.

Café V Lausitzer Platz 12 ⓣ 030 612 45 05; U-Görlitzer Bahnhof; map pp.126–127. Cosy, dimly lit, bohemian place beside a leafy Kreuzberg park and as good a hangout as it is a place to eat. Though it serves fish, everything else is vegetarian, with plenty of tofu and seitan (wheat gluten) on offer in anything from pizzas to salads; the fennel nut salad is particularly good. Mains €8–12. Menus change weekly. Daily 10am–2am.

Kvartira Nr. 62 Lübbener Str. 18 ⓣ 0179 134 33 43; U-Schlesisches Tor; map pp.126–127. Atmospheric Russian café with 1920s-era dark red and gold décor, serving Russian classics such as *borscht* (stew; €3), delicious *pelimi* (dumplings; €4.50) and tea flavoured with jam – as well as some great chocolate cake. Daily 4pm–late (kitchen daily 5–11pm).

Ron Telesky Dieffenbachstr. 62 ⓣ 030 61 62 11 11; U-Schönleinstrasse; map pp.126–127. Canadian pizza served from a canoe – how could you refuse? Especially when toppings include walnut, mango, feta and maple syrup. The interior also features national emblems like a moose head. Vegan options available. Mon–Fri noon–10pm, Sat & Sun 3–10pm.

Tiki Heart Wiener Str. 20 ⓣ 030 61 07 47 03, ⓦ tikiheart.de; U-Görlitzer Bahnhof; map pp.126–127. Hawaiian-rockabilly themed joint with an unapologetically kitsch interior and innovative menu. The breakfasts, served until 5pm, feature items like the "Oi-Fast" – a heady mix of scrambled eggs and chorizo (€7). There are veggie burgers and – one for the serious rockers – a Lemmy burger grilled in whisky. Strong cocktails, too. Mon–Fri 11am–late, Sat & Sun 10am–late.

RESTAURANTS

Amrit Oranienstr. 202 ⓣ 030 612 55 50, ⓦ amrit.de; U-Görlitzer Bahnhof; map pp.126–127. The seating is always a bit of a squeeze at this busy Indian restaurant, where the huge portions are inexpensive (mains €8–15) and delicious. Not the sort of place to linger after a meal; reservations are recommended in the week and essential at weekends. Daily noon–midnight.

Baraka Lausitzer Platz 6 ⓣ 030 612 63 30, ⓦ baraka -berlin.de; U-Görlitzer Bahnhof; map pp.126–127. One for North African food fans with tasteful authentic decor and food – tagines, chicken skewers, *shawarma* – that's some of the best in town, and at decent prices (mains €5–12). The mixed plate for two is immense. Mon–Thurs 11am–midnight, Fri & Sat 11am–1am.

Café Jacques Maybachufer 8 ⓣ 030 694 10 48; U-Schönleinstrasse; map pp.126–127. Traditional French cuisine is the mainstay here on the leafy banks of the Landwehr canal, but other foods like pasta and couscous also make an appearance, as do seasonal ingredients including asparagus and globe artichokes. Mains around €10. Daily 6pm–midnight.

Defne Planufer 92 ⓣ 030 81 79 71 11, ⓦ defne -restaurant.de; U-Kottbusser Tor/Schönleinstrasse;

TOP 5 FOOD WITH A VIEW
Café am Neuen See See p.192
Hugos See p.192
Käfer Dachgarten See p.188
Schlosscafe Köpenick See p.204
Sphere See p.190

13

map pp.126–127. A great menu of Turkish/Mediterranean food using fresh ingredients. Classics include "Imam Fainted" (aubergines with pine nuts, peppers and tomato-herb sauce; €8.60) and lamb skewers (€11.90). The interior is simple and spacious; the terrace, overlooking the Landwehrkanal, is lovely in summer. Daily: April–Sept 4pm–1am; Oct–March 5pm–1am (kitchen till midnight all year).

Hartmanns Fichtestr. 31 ☎030 61 20 10 03, ⓦhartmanns-restaurant.de; U-Südstern; map pp.126–127. Chef Stefan Hartmann creates innovative French-Mediterranean cuisine that's devilishly rich – think goose liver, pork chops and quail – in a romantic and tasteful setting. Three- to seven-course menus (€47–76) or à la carte (mains €29–32). Mon–Sat 6pm–midnight.

Henne Leuschnerdamm 25 ☎030 614 77 30, ⓦhenne-berlin.de; U-Moritzplatz; map pp.126–127. Pub-style restaurant serving the best fried chicken (€7.50) in Berlin, served with cabbage and potato salad sides. The interior hasn't been changed, the owners claim, since 1905. Reservations essential. Tues–Sat 7pm until late, Sun 5pm until late.

Le Cochon Bourgeois Fichtestr. 24 ☎030 693 01 01, ⓦlecochon.de; U-Südstern; map pp.126–127. One of the more romantic Kreuzberg places, in an elegant old house and serving high-end French food – oysters, frogs'

legs, juicy steaks – but little for vegetarians. Choose fixed-price (from €40) or à la carte. Reservations necessary. Daily 6pm–late.

★ **Morgenland** Skalitzer Str. 35 ☎030 611 32 91, ⓦmorgenland-berlin.de; U-Görlitzer Bahnhof; map pp.126–127. Relaxed café with a welcoming vibe, which serves a mix of European snacks. The amazing brunch buffet (Sat & Sun 10am–4pm; €11.50) seems to attract most of the neighbourhood. Mon–Fri 9am until late, Sat & Sun 10am until late.

Rosa Caleta Muskauer Str. 9 ☎030 69 53 78 59, ⓦrosacaleta.com; U-Görlitzer Bahnhof; map pp.126–127. Jamaican/European fusion restaurant that's created quite a buzz in a city hopelessly devoid of Caribbean cuisine. There's plenty of Jerk-style food on the menu, but also dishes like oven-roast pork fillet, mango-ginger lentil salad and tofu and vegetable stew (mains from €8). It also functions as an art space and hosts DJs. Tues–Sat 6pm–1am, Sun 2pm–1am.

Weltrestaurant Markthalle Pücklerstr. 34 ☎030 617 55 02, ⓦweltrestaurant-markthalle.de; U-Görlitzer Bahnhof; map pp.126–127. Spacious restaurant that attracts a young crowd with its long communal tables and hearty portions of German food. Look out for the €8.50 daily special and leave space for the phenomenal cakes. Daily 10am–midnight.

NEUKÖLLN

CHEAP EATS

Musashi Kottbusser Damm 102 ☎030 693 20 42; U-Schönleinstrasse; map pp.126–127. Tiny spot serving decent sushi in a refreshingly designer-free space,

decorated with posters of sumo wrestlers and with just a few bar tables. The Japanese chefs prepare fresh, tasty and well-priced (€6.50 for a set menu) *makis* and inside-out rolls. Mon–Fri & Sun noon–10.30pm, Sat 2–10pm.

TREPTOW

BEER GARDENS

Haus Zenner in der Eierschale Alt-Treptow, Treptow 14–17 ☎030 533 72 11, ⓦeierschale-zenner.de;

S-Treptower Park; map pp.126–127. A large and popular beer garden by the Spree River. Don't be thrown off by the *Burger King* on the ground floor. Daily 10am–midnight.

FRIEDRICHSHAIN

CAFÉS

Aunt Benny Oderstr. 7 ☎030 66 40 53 00, ⓦauntbenny.com; U-Samariterstrasse; map pp.126–127. Welcoming modern café run by a German-Canadian team. The range of teas and coffees (€2–3) is good, there are bagels, daily soups and other breakfast and lunch options available (most around €5), plus free wi-fi and home-made baked treats. Mon–Fri 9am–7pm, Sat & Sun 10am–7pm.

Café Datscha Gabriel-Max-Str. 1 ☎030 70 08 67 35, ⓦcafe-datscha.de; U-Samariterstrasse; map pp.126–127. Built in the style of a smart traditional Russian home – wooden furniture, tall ceilings – with a rich spread of Russian and Ukrainian dishes like *borscht*, *blini* and *solyanka* (a spicy, sour soup). There's a daily changing lunch

menu (€6) and Sunday brunch (10am–3pm; €9.80). Daily 10am–late.

Café Sybille Karl-Marx-Allee 72 ☎030 29 35 22 03, ⓦcafe-sibylle-berlin.de; U-Strausberger Platz; map pp.126–127. Airy café with a fin-de-siècle feel – it's been here more than a century – and a diverting exhibition about the socialist origins of the Karl-Marx-Allee in the back. Worth a visit for the cakes (€2–3) and ice creams alone. Mon–Fri 10am–8pm, Sat & Sun 11am–8pm.

Cupcake Berlin Krossener Str. 12 ☎030 25 76 86 87, ⓦcupcakeberlin.de; U-Samariterstrasse; map pp.126–127. Café dedicated to cupcakes, all home-made by the American owner. Vegan cupcakes, brownies, fantastic New York cheesecake and pecan pie also available (all around €2.50). Mon & Tues 1–7pm, Wed–Sun noon–7pm.

Goodies Berlin Warschauer Str. 69 ☎ 0151 53 76 38 01, ⓦ goodies-berlin.de; U-Frankfurter Tor; map pp.126–127. Tiny café that serves wholesome home-made baked goods, sandwiches and bagels (€2–4.50). The organic soup changes daily and there's a small but varied selection of salads and vegan options. Free wi-fi, and children's area. Cash only. Mon–Fri 7am–8pm, Sat & Sun 9am–8pm.

Kaufbar Gärtnerstr. 4 ☎ 030 29 77 88 25, ⓦ kaufbar -berlin.de; U-Samariterstrasse; map pp.126–127. Breezy neighbourhood favourite whose charm extends well beyond its gimmick – that everything in the café, from the chairs to the artwork, is for sale. A great spot to play games, read a book or drink tea or wine. Light snacks (salads, soups) are available (from €1.80), and a garden opens in summer. Tues–Thurs 3pm–midnight, Fri–Mon 10am–midnight.

Macondo Café Gärtnerstr. 14 ☎ 0151 10 73 88 29, ⓦ macondo-berlin.de; U-Samariterstrasse; map pp.126–127. Kitted out with fraying vintage furniture, this local chill-out spot offers a good selection of books and board games and a great atmosphere for lounging. Serves brunch (€7) at weekends; otherwise snacks run from €3–6. Mon–Fri 3pm–late, Sat & Sun 10am–late.

Spielwiese Kopernikusstr. 24 ☎ 030 28 03 40 88, ⓦ spielwiese-berlin.de; U- & S-Warschauer Strasse; map pp.126–127. Advertising itself as a "game library", this café stocks more than 1200 games, from chess to Risk. For a small fee (€0.50–3), you can play games in the café or rent them (€1–3/day) to take home. A great place to lose yourself for a couple of hours. Food and drink here is nothing special – such as waffles from packet mixes – but it's inexpensive (snacks €2–5). Mon & Thurs–Sat 2pm–midnight, Sun 2–9pm.

RESTAURANTS

Fliegender Tisch Mainzer Str. 10 ☎ 030 29 77 64 89, ⓦ fliegender-tisch.de; U-Samariterstrasse; map pp.126–127. "The flying table" is a small, cosy place with just a few wooden tables. It's justly popular thanks to tasty Italian staples like thin-crust pizza and risotto for decent prices (€6–7). Mon–Fri & Sun noon–midnight, Sat 5pm–midnight.

Meyman Krossener Str. 11A ☎ 016 38 06 16 36; U-Samariterstrasse; map pp.126–127. Unassuming restaurant that's great for late-night cravings or for a break between bar hops. They specialize in tasty Moroccan and Middle Eastern dishes along with pizza. Ingredients are fresh, prices are reasonable (€3–7 for a main), and there's usually a table free. Mon–Thurs & Sun noon–2am, Fri & Sat noon–3am.

Schneeweiss Simplonstr. 16 ☎ 030 29 04 97 04, ⓦ schneeweiss-berlin.de; U-Warschauer Strasse; map pp.126–127. One of Friedrichshain's few upmarket restaurants, "Snow White" is an understated and minimalist place offering what it calls an "Alpine" menu: Italian, Austrian and south German dishes such as *schnitzel* and pasta. There's also a decent Sunday brunch, fireplace lounge and a low-key bar vibe in the evening. Mon–Fri 6pm–1am, Sat & Sun 10am–1am.

PRENZLAUER BERG

CHEAP EATS

★ **Kiezkantine** Oderberger Str. 50 ☎ 030 448 44 84, ⓦ kiezkantine-berlin.de; U-Eberswalder Strasse; map p.132. Choose from just two or three excellent daily specials for under €5 in this hugely popular bistro with plenty of outdoor seating. There's always something vegetarian, and students get a discount – order and pay at the till, the food will then be brought to your seat. Mon–Fri 9am–4pm.

Konnopke's Imbiss Schönhauser Allee 44a, beneath U-Eberswalder Strasse ☎ 030 442 77 65, ⓦ konnopke -imbiss.de; map p.132. *Pommes* and *Wurst* served from a pre-fab cabin beneath the S-Bahn lines since 1930; surviving fascism, communism and World War II. Incredibly it's been run by the same family all that time, and remains one of the best places in the area for a quick bite. Mon–Fri 5.30am–7pm, Sat 11.30am–7pm.

CAFÉS AND BARS

Al Hamra Raumerstr. 16 ☎ 030 42 85 00 95; U-Eberswalder Strasse; map p.132. Comfortable Middle Eastern café with shabby decor but decent Mediterranean food (€3–10), beer, water pipes, backgammon and chess, plus internet terminals and free wi-fi. Daily 10am–3am.

WILL BERLINERS BUTT OUT?

With one-third of Berliners smoking, and typically puffing on their first cigarette aged 13, Germany's smoking ban, introduced after much deliberation in 2008, was always going to prove hard to enforce. Technically this introduced a general **ban on smoking** in bars and restaurants, except in separate smoking rooms, though local pubs smaller than 75 square metres are exempt. So too are clubs, though there is technically a ban on lighting-up on the dancefloor. Many other places have elected to continue to allow smoking, by declaring themselves a *Raucherclub* (smokers' club) with a sign in the window. An illegal compromise, but one police seem happy to tolerate.

13

Anita Wronski Knaackstr. 26–28 ☎ 030 442 84 83; U-Senefelderplatz; map p.132. Opposite the Wasserturm, with a welcoming, established feel. It serves very good breakfasts (€6–9) and brunches, and while busy at weekends, is usually quiet enough through the week to enjoy a newspaper or a good book in peace. Daily 9am–2am.

Anna Blume Kollwitzstr. 83 ☎ 030 44 04 87 49, ⓦ cafe -anna-blume.de; U-Eberswalder Strasse; map p.132. Part flower shop, part café, part bakery, this Art Deco classic – named after a Kurt Schwitters poem, whose lines are elegantly inscribed on the walls inside – is one of the area's best-known cafés. Slide into one of the red leather banquettes and sample one of their superb cakes (€4) or a daily special (€7.50). Daily 8am–2am.

Bonanza Coffee Heroes Oderberger Str. 35 ☎ 017 81 44 11 23, ⓦ bonanzacoffee.de; U-Eberswalder Strasse; map p.132. Coffee connoisseurs flock to tiny *Bonanza* to sample the creations of their famed baristas: perfect lattes and flat whites knocked up on a fancy Synesso Cyncra machine (one of only three in Europe). The cool staff are friendly. Mon–Fri 8.30am–7pm, Sat & Sun 10am–7pm.

Café Hilde Metzer Str. 22 ☎ 030 040 50 41 72, ⓦ hilde -berlin.com; U-Senefelderplatz; map p.132. This sizeable café on the corner of busy Prenzlauer Allee is a lovely spot to unwind, with books and magazines to read during the day, home-made cakes and lunches (€4–9), plus film screenings and book readings in the evenings. They also serve up a hearty Irish breakfast at weekends. Mon–Fri 9am–11pm, Sat & Sun 9.30am–11pm.

Café November Husemannstr. 15 ☎ 030 442 84 25, ⓦ cafe-november.de; U-Senefelderplatz; map p.132. Uncluttered, exposed-wood place, just north of Kollwitzplatz, with imaginative German daily specials (€8–14), a reasonable Sun brunch (9am–4pm; €11) and outdoor seating in a pleasantly quiet residential street. Free wi-fi. Mon–Fri 10am–2am, Sun 9am–2am.

Intersoup Schliemannstr. 31 ☎ 0151 29 11 18 98, ⓦ intersoup.de; S-Prenzlauer Allee; map p.132. Mellow den with a huge selection of excellent soups (€3.50–5) and a relaxing vibe. The place's trademark soup – Thai lemon grass, bean sprouts, noodle, coconut milk with chicken, tofu, fish or shrimp – is well worth a try. It's also one of the few bars in the area regularly promoting local and international DJs (upstairs) and bands (downstairs). Mon–Fri 6pm–3am, Sat & Sun 6pm–5am.

Kauf Dich Glücklich Oderberger Str. 44 ☎ 030 44 35 21 82, ⓦ kaufdichgluecklich.de; U-Eberswalder Strasse; map p.132. Come here for waffles with ice cream (around €4) – and a spot of cutely kitsch capitalism. "Buy yourself happy" is an irrepressibly cheerful place where you can not only get great coffee and sweet treats, but also buy any of the secondhand furniture – tables, chairs, lamps, sunglasses – you see around you. Mon–Fri noon–1am, Sat & Sun 10am–1am.

★ **Morgenrot** Kastanienallee 85 ☎ 030 44 31 78 44, ⓦ cafe-morgenrot.de; U-Eberswalder Strasse; map p.132. Bohemian Berlin hits its stride in this collective café where G8 riots are planned and vegan breakfasts consumed. Everything is organic and the vegetarian buffet breakfast (until 3pm) is excellent (€4–8: pay according to how wealthy you consider yourself). Tues–Thurs noon–1am, Fri & Sat 11am–3am, Sun 11am–midnight.

Sgaminegg Seelower Str. 2 ☎ 030 44 73 15 25, ⓦ sgaminegg.de; U-Schönhauser Allee; map p.132. There is a dearth of decent cafés north of Stargarderstr., but *Sgaminegg* is an absolute treasure thanks to its delicious coffees, home-made lunches – couscous, lentil and south German dishes (two Munich Weisswürste – sausages served with a Pretzel – cost €5.20) and a little shop that sells local produce. Mon–Fri 8.30am–7pm, Sat 10am–6pm.

Slörm Danziger Str. 53 ☎ 030 70 08 36 87, ⓦ sloerm .net; U-Prenzlauer Allee; map p.132. With parrots at the back, hip hop on rotation and a collection of comfy old furniture, *Slörm* is unique even by Prenzlauer Berg's café standards. The coffees are excellent, as are the inventive fruit juices, which come with b-boy titles like Nas and MC Hammer. Mon–Sat 8am–6pm.

Wohnzimmer Lettestr. 6 ☎ 030 445 54 58, ⓦ wohnzimmer-bar.de; U-Eberswalder Strasse; map p.132. The rumpled and ramshackle living room atmosphere helps make this a relaxed and sociable hangout at any time – and the comfy sofas make it difficult to leave. At weekends a cocktail bar pops up between its two rooms. Breakfast served until 4pm; a simple coffee and croissant or roll costs only €2.90. Daily 9am–4am.

Zuckerfee Greifenhagener Str. 15 ☎ 030 52 68 61 44, ⓦ zuckerfee-berlin.de; U-Schönhauser Allee; map p.132. Gastronomic concept based on Tchaikovsky's *The Nutcracker* and named after the Sugar Plum fairy. The immaculate interior – all Victorian dolls and tasteful ornamentation – reflects the menu, which features delicious waffles, cakes and uniquely presented breakfasts and lunches (€6–13; book ahead at weekends). Tues–Sun 10am–6pm.

MICROBREWERIES AND BEER GARDENS

Pfefferbräu Schönhauser Allee 176 ☎ 030 44 35 48 53, ⓦ pfefferbraeu.de; U-Senefelderplatz; map p.132. Popular outdoor beer garden, in the courtyard of an 1841 brewery that was resurrected in 2013 to create its own range of draught beers. With a good restaurant along with the usual beer garden snacks and daily specials (around €9 for mains). Tues–Sun 5–11pm.

Prater Kastanienallee 7–9 ☎030 44 48 56 88, ✆pratergarten.de; U-Eberswalder Strasse; map p.132. In summer you can swig beer, feast on *Bratwurst* and other native food, and listen to 1970s German rock in the traditional beer garden (dates back to 1837); in winter the beer hall offers a similarly authentic experience. Mon–Sat 6–11pm, Sun noon–11pm.

RESTAURANTS

The Bird Am Falkplatz 5 ☎030 51 05 32 83, ✆thebirdinberlin.com; U-Schönhauser Allee; map p.132. Hugely popular New York-style steakhouse with punk-rock attitude, an international staff and gigantic tasty burgers, spicy chicken wings, steaks, hand-cut fries and so on. Mains €10–20, other dishes around half that. Finish with a sumptuous cheesecake, if you can manage it. Cash only. Mon–Sat 6pm–late, Sun noon–late.

Chez Maurice Botzowstr. 39 ☎030 425 05 06, ✆chez-maurice.com; S-Griefswalder Strasse; map p.132. Finer dining spot that's a little out of the way but worth it for the authentic food and theatrics of the energetic French chef Maurice. Service can be slow, so count on spending the better part of an evening here, enjoying the huge wine list with more than 200 varieties from France alone. The *plat du jour* specials (noon–3.30pm) are good value: two courses €10, three courses €15. Reservations recommended. Tues–Sat noon–4pm & from 6pm, Sun & Mon from 6pm.

Gugelhof Knaackstr. 37 ☎030 442 92 29, ✆gugelhof.de; U-Senefelderplatz; map p.132. Lively Alsatian restaurant put on the map by Bill Clinton's surprise visit in 2000, and successful ever since. It serves inventive and beautifully presented German, French and Alsatian food (mains €8–18) – worth trying is the unusual Flammkuchen, a thin-crust Alsatian pizza. Mon–Fri 4pm–1am, Sat & Sun 10am–1am.

Mao Thai Wörther Str. 30 ☎030 441 92 61, ✆maothai.de; U-Senefelderplatz; map p.132. Perhaps a bit overpriced, but the Thai food, garnished with delightful little sculpted vegetables, is excellent – tasty classics like *tom ka gai*, spring rolls, glass noodle salads. Staff, in traditional garb, are unfailingly polite. Mains €10–20. Daily noon–11.30pm.

Maria Bonita Danziger Str. 33 ☎0176 70 17 94 61, ✆maria-bonita.com; U-Eberswalder Strasse; map p.132. Tucked away amid the *Imbisses* and kebab shops hereabouts, *Maria Bonita* stands out for above average Mexican street food. You couldn't swing an enchilada inside, but the burritos, tacos and quesadillas – and the guacamole for that matter – are all winners. Daily noon–11pm.

Marien Burger Marienburger Str. 47 ☎030 30 34 05 15, ✆marienburger-berlin.de; U-Senefelderplatz;

TOP 10 GOURMET DINING   **13**

E.T.A Hoffmann See p.198
Facil See p.192
First Floor See p.194
Fischers Fritz See p.188
Hugos See p.192
Le Cochon Bourgeois See p.200
Lutter & Wegner See p.188
Margaux See p.189
VAU See p.189
Weinbar Rutz See p.191

map p.132. This diminutive but buzzy burger hangout lures locals back again and again with huge, delicious beef, chicken, fish or vegetable burgers (the €5.50 Marienburger is almost too big to eat in one sitting). Organic options available. Daily 11am–10pm.

Pappa e Ciccia Schwedter Str. 18 ☎030 61 62 08 01, ✆pappaeciccia.de; U-Senefelderplatz; map p.132. Bored with the usual Berlin brunch formula? Check out Sundays at this smart-casual Italian restaurant, where chefs dole out freshly baked lasagne and salmon, tomato and mozzarella and other scrumptious dishes, and diners gather at the long communal tables outside. It's all organic and there are decent vegetarian and vegan options. Ice cream, cakes and more are on offer at the adjacent organic deli. Mon–Thurs 9.30am–midnight, Fri 9.30am–1am, Sat 11am–1am, Sun 11am–11pm.

Pasternak Knaackstr. 22–24 ☎030 441 33 99, ✆restaurant-pasternak.de; U-Senefelderplatz; map p.132. Long-standing Jewish-Russian restaurant, named after the author of *Doctor Zhivago*, and best known for its incredible Sunday brunch (10am–4pm; €13): a regal spread of blini, caviar, fish and much more; it's so popular you'll need to wake up early to find a seat (no reservations). Evenings feature live piano music and fixed price menus. Daily 9am–1am.

★ **Restauration 1900** Husemannstr. 1 ☎030 442 24 94, ✆restauration-1900.de; U-Eberswalder Strasse; map p.132. A Kollwitzplatz culinary highlight, serving traditional German dishes that spring a few surprises, as well as some pasta and vegetarian options (€10–19). It's also another excellent choice for a Sunday buffet brunch (10am–4pm; €11). Check out the photographs of the neighbourhood before and after reunification. Daily 10am until late.

Sasaya Lychener Str. 50 ☎030 44 71 77 21, ✆sasaya-berlin-de.tumblr.com; U-Schönhauser Allee; map p.132. Delicious, traditional and innovative Japanese food using fresh, high-quality ingredients. Swift service ensures this a serious contender for best sushi spot in the city. Mon, Tues & Thurs–Sun noon–3pm & 6–10.30pm.

13

Schlawiner Hagenauer Str. 9 ☎030 44 03 70 59; U-Eberswalder Strasse; map p.132. Austrian spot whose simple, unfussy interior – just a few simple wooden tables and some black-and-white photos on the walls – disguises the fact that the Austrian chef serves up the best *Wiener Schnitzel* in the neighbourhood. Daily specials are chalked on the blackboard behind the bar. Mains from €8. Daily from 6pm.

Si An Rykestr. 36 ☎030 40 50 57 75, ⓦsian-berlin.de; U-Eberswalder Strasse; map p.132. One of the most popular Vietnamese spots in the area. The interior is cosy, subtly upscale yet traditional (oak tables, handmade lamps) and the menu, while small, changes twice weekly and is generally fresh (all dishes are guaranteed glutamate-free). In summer sit outside by the immaculately landscaped street garden. Daily noon–midnight.

Trattoria Siediti e Mangia da Gianna Sredzki Str. 43 ☎030 83 10 94 60; U-Eberswalder Strasse; map p.132. Nearby *Trattoria Paparazzi* gets all the attention, but this smaller Italian place serves superior food – simple, home-style and fresh – and has a more intimate atmosphere. Its handful of tables are spread over two tiers inside, but you can also sit out on the pavement in summer. Pasta dishes from €7.50. Cash only. Mon–Fri 4pm–midnight, Sat noon–midnight.

Weinstein Lychener Str. 33 ☎030 441 18 42, ⓦweinstein.eu; U-Eberswalder Strasse; map p.132. This intimate wine bar and restaurant, all sturdy wooden tables and wine barrel decoration, is a bit of a local secret. It serves up food as traditional as the interior, but has a strong emphasis on local produce and German wines, as well as imported high-quality products like French cheeses and Iberian ham. Mains start at €9, and from Monday to Wednesday you can get eight small courses for €40. Mon–Sat 5pm–2am, Sun 6pm–2am; kitchen 6–11.30pm.

Zum Schusterjungen Danziger Str. 9 ☎030 442 76 54, ⓦzumschusterjungen.com; U-Eberswalder Strasse; map p.132. Large portions of no-nonsense German food served in the back room of a locals' *Kneipe*. The plastic-and-formica decor has echoes of the GDR and, at around €8 per dish, the prices are almost as cheap as back then, too. Daily noon–midnight.

EASTERN SUBURBS

CAFÉS, BARS AND BEER GARDENS

Braustübl Müggelseedamm 164, Köpenick ☎030 37 44 67 69, ⓦbraeustuebl-mueggelsee.de; S-Friedrichshagen; map p.148. Waterside pub of the Berliner Bürgerbräu brewery, serving German and well-priced international dishes (mains around €8) and the fine local beer, Rot Händel. Daily 11am–midnight.

China Teehaus Eisenacher Str. 99, Marzahn ☎0179 394 55 64, ⓦchina-teehaus.de; U-Cottbusser Platz then bus #195 to "Gärten der Welt" stop; map p.142. Chinese Garden teahouse in the Gärten der Welt (p.146); where you can take part in a traditional tea ceremony (reservations necessary and six person minimum; €8). April–Oct daily 10.30am–6pm; Nov–March Sat & Sun 10.30am–6pm in fine weather.

Gestrandet Am Müggelsee 216, Köpenick/Friedrichshagen ☎0176 97 52 81 49, ⓦgestrandet-am-mueggelsee.de; S-Friedrichshagen; map p.148. It had to happen sooner or later – a central Berlin beach bar landing on the shores of the Müggelsee. Deck chairs, beer and cocktails in a pleasant spot at the end of the Spreetunnel, ideally placed for before or after a wander along the lakeshore. Mon–Fri noon–late, Sat & Sun 10am–late.

Josef Heinrich Bölschestr. 11, Köpenick ☎030 95 99 27 27, ⓦjosefheinrich.de; S-Friedrichshagen; map p.148. Simple modern café-bar, at the southern end of Friedrichshagen's main drag, with basic modern pub grub – soups, nachos and a cheese platter (all around €6), and a good Sun buffet brunch (€11.50). Mon–Fri 6pm until late.

Schlosscafe Köpenick Schlossinsel, Köpenick ☎030 65 01 85 85, ⓦschlosscafe-koepenick.de; S-Spindlersfeld; map p.148. Elegant café beside Schloss Köpenick, with lake views and excellent fresh daily dishes (mains €8–17), good cakes and a wonderful Sunday brunch (10am–2pm; €15). May–Sept Thurs–Sun 10am–6pm; Oct–April Sun 10am–7pm.

RESTAURANTS

Ratskeller Köpenick Alt Köpenick 21, Köpenick ☎030 655 51 78; S-Köpenick; map p.148. Authentic *Ratskeller* full of locals and serving decent, good-value German food from €6 per dish. Regular live jazz on Fri and Sat. Mon–Sat 11am–11pm, Sun 11am–10pm.

WESTERN SUBURBS

CAFÉS AND BARS

Barfly Brüderstr. 47, Spandau ☎030 331 55 55, ⓦcafe-barfly.de; U- & S-Rathaus Spandau; map p.154. Laid-back, living room-style café with a good, ever-changing selection of food. All meats are organic and the weekend brunch buffet (10am–2pm; €11.50) a winner. Mon–Fri 8am–3am, Sat & Sun 9am–3am.

Florida Eiscafe Klosterstr. 15, Spandau ☎030 331 56 66, ⓦflorida-eiscafe.de; U- & S-Rathaus Spandau; map p.154. Ice-cream parlour with a Berlin-wide reputation; you'll need to wait in line to see what the fuss is all about, but that gives you time to choose from the 41 flavours. Daily noon–11pm.

Universum Lounge Kurfürstendamm 153

13

BERLINER WEISSE

Berlin's most famous and distinctive beer is **Berliner Weisse**. The brew is only just fermented and still quite watery and sour, so it's traditionally drunk with a shot of fruity syrup, or *Schuss*. Ask for it *mit grün* and you get a dash of woodruff, creating a green beverage with a herby taste; *mit rot* secures a raspberry-flavoured drink that works wonders on a breakfast-time hangover.

☎030 89 06 49 95, ⓦuniversumlounge.com; U-Adenauerplatz; map p.154. Located in the stunning Bauhaus-era Universum Cinema, this café-bar is an oddity even by Berlin standards. A curved main bar decorated in golds and browns and lunar-themed wallpaper lend it a futuristic feel. The menu includes pumpkin soup and burgers (mains €15–32) and the cocktails are well mixed. Daily 6pm–3am.

MICROBREWERIES AND BEER GARDENS

Alter Krug Königin-Luise-Str. 52, Zehlendorf ☎030 84 31 95 40, ⓦalter-krug.com; U-Dahlem-Dorf; map p.161. Rustic pub opposite Domäne Dahlem and close to the U-station. The large beer garden makes it an ideal counterbalance to the nearby museums, or you could prepare yourself for your culture fix with a breakfast or Sun brunch buffet (10am–2pm; €11). Later on there's lots of traditional meat-and-potatoes type food to choose from: mains around €12. Daily 10am–11pm.

Brauhaus Lemke Luisenplatz 1, Charlottenburg-Wilmersdorf ☎030 30 87 89 79, ⓦbrauhaus-lemke .com; U-Richard-Wagner-Platz; map p.154. Large microbrewery offering a menu of reasonably priced (most mains around €13) traditional staples – sausage salad, pepper steak, pork chops – until 11pm. Daily 11am–late.

Brauhaus Spandau Neuendorfer Str. 1, Spandau ☎030 353 90 70, ⓦbrauhaus-spandau.de; U-Altstadt Spandau; map p.154. Brewery with beer garden, various beer halls and lots of shiny brewing equipment; reliable for

schnitzels and the like. April–Oct Sun–Thurs 10am–midnight, Fri & Sat 10am–1am; Nov–March Mon 4pm–midnight, Tues–Thurs 11am–midnight, Fri & Sat 11am–1am, Sun 10am–midnight.

Loretta am Wannsee Kronprinzessinweg, Zehlendorf 260 ☎030 803 51 56, ⓦloretta-berlin.de; S-Wannsee; map p.161. Inviting tree-lined beer garden with Wannsee views enjoyed by a mixed crowd digging into snacks and beer. Daily 11pm until late.

RESTAURANTS

Engelbecken Witzlebenstr. 31 ☎030 615 28 10, ⓦengelbecken.de; U-Sophie-Charlotte-Platz; map p.154. A quality restaurant that serves Bavarian and Alpine cuisine – *schnitzel*, goulash – with an emphasis on organic products and home-made sauces (mains €8.50–22). The park-facing terrace is nice in the summer. Mon–Fri 5pm–1am, Sat 4pm–1am, Sun noon–1am.

Kolk Hoher Steinweg 7, Spandau ☎030 333 88 79, ⓦkolk.im-netz.de; U-Altstadt Spandau; map p.154. Popular family-run restaurant in an old fire station, serving regional dishes, including good vegetarian versions (mains €8–16). Its outdoor seating is beside the old city walls. Daily 11am–11pm.

La Bottega Da Franco Breite Str. 56–58, Spandau ☎030 36 75 01 71; U-Altstadt Spandau; map p.154. Unpretentious Italian trattoria with exceptional food and prices for every budget: mains €7–18. Great home-made pasta. Daily 9am–midnight.

Nightlife

Since the days of the Weimar Republic, and even through the lean postwar years, Berlin's nightlife has had the reputation for being some of the best – and steamiest – in Europe, an image fuelled by the savage caricatures of George Grosz and films like Cabaret. Today the main focus is on the clubs that have grown out of the city's techno scene – in a remarkably short space of time these places, many in abandoned East German industrial buildings, have spawned one of the most exciting scenes in Europe. The city also has a wide range of more traditional clubs, ranging from slick hangouts to raucous punky dives. Lively, varied and inexpensive, the live music scene is bolstered by the city's unpretentious grittiness – in addition to the music venues, all but the most committed techno clubs will often have live performances too.

There are several distinct **nightlife districts**, making it easy to spend an evening trawling the bars of a particular area before ending up in a late-night club nearby. That said, with the U- and S-Bahn running nonstop on Friday and Saturday nights – and restarting from about 4am on other nights – jumping between areas of town could hardly be easier. Most of the "in" places are to the east, where glitz is out and raving in. **Friedrichshain** and **eastern Kreuzberg** are good areas for the grungiest and most cutting-edge clubs. More established places are in **Prenzlauer Berg** and the **Spandauer Vorstadt**, and also in **Schöneberg** and **western Kreuzberg**, where they tend to attract a slightly older crowd. However, like in most major cities, Berlin's nightspots change rapidly: although we've included reviews of both well-established and newer places, the scene changes rapidly, so be prepared for some places to have changed by the time you arrive.

The distinction between cafés, bars, clubs and arts venues in Berlin is notoriously fluid, with **considerable overlap** between each, meaning that many cafés, bars and beer gardens listed in "Eating and drinking" (see p.186) may well double as venues of some sort into the small hours. The places we've reviewed here are particularly good for a night out. Gay bars and clubs are covered in "Gay and lesbian Berlin" (see p.236).

14

ESSENTIALS

Listings To find out what's on where check listings magazines *Tip* (ⓦ tip-berlin.de) and *Zitty* (ⓦ zitty.de), available at any newsstand, and the free magazine *030* (ⓦ berlin030.de), mainly distributed in bars and cafés.

Opening times Opening times are very relaxed and there are no last orders. Typically bars will close between 1am and 5am, often depending on how busy they are and the mood of the staff, and then may reopen around 9am. Club hours are also open-ended – it's rare for any to get going

before midnight and some stay open beyond 6am.

Admission policies Berlin's clubs are smaller, cheaper and less exclusive than their counterparts in London or New York. And don't worry too much about a dress code – the city's prevalent shabby-chic aesthetic means you can get into most places without making much of an effort.

Costs Clubs are often free – though cover charges tend to run from €5 to €11 on weekends and can change dramatically depending on the event.

BARS, CLUBS AND MUSIC VENUES

UNTER DEN LINDEN AND AROUND

Newton Bar Charlottenstr. 57 ☎030 20 61 29 99; U-Stadtmitte; map p.36. Helmut Newton's lifesize shots of nude Amazons stare out at the leather and marble interior of this chic bar, popular with a mature, well-heeled crowd. Watch Berlin's sharp dressers puff on cigars and sip well-made cocktails. Daily 10am until late.

Shochu Bar Behrenstr. 72 ☎030 301 11 73 28, ⓦ shochubar.de; U-Brandenburger Tor; map p.36. This swanky bar offers flamboyant yet elegant cocktails made from the Japanese spirit it's named after. Japanese food is served until 11pm and there are sometimes live jazz performances. Expect a dressy, upmarket crowd. Mon–Sat 6pm–2am.

Tausend Schiffbauerdamm 11 ☎030 41 71 53 96, ⓦ tausendberlin.com; U- & S-Friedrichstrasse; map p.36. Signposted by an enormous eye emitting a golden glow over the tunnel-shaped space, this upmarket club attracts a decidedly dapper crowd – so be sure to look the part. Inside you'll find a mix of upbeat disco and 1980s nights. Entry €10. Tues–Sat 7.30pm–late.

Windhorst Dorotheenstr. 65 ☎030 20 45 00 70; U- & S-Friedrichstrasse; map p.36. This little cocktail haven is tucked away, and though it's not a residential area, feels like a neighbourhood spot. It's a smart, fairly simple place, but the cocktails are above average and go well with the jazz (on vinyl) that they love to play. Mon–Fri 6pm–late, Sat 9pm–late.

PUB CRAWLS

If the idea of venturing into Berlin's legendary nightlife seems daunting, or you fancy the company of young visitors, consider a **pub crawl tour**. For around €12 (cover charges included) you'll be taken to half-a-dozen or so watering holes and a club. You'll be given free shots on the street along the way, so it's not the most dignified way to spend an evening, but it can be good fun if the crowd's right. Pub crawls trawl Berlin every night and companies include: New Berlin Tours (ⓦ newberlintours.com), Insider Tours (ⓦ insiderberlintours.com) and Alternative Berlin (ⓦ alternativeberlin.com). The last offers something a bit different, hitting more unusual nightspots than the competition and with smaller group sizes.

TOP 5 PLACES TO START A NIGHT OUT

Cassiopeia See p.213
Oscar Wilde Irish Pub See p.209
Verkehrsberuhigte Ost-Zone See p.209
Zoulou Bar See p.210
Zu mir oder zu dir See p.215

14

ALEXANDERPLATZ AND AROUND

2BE Club Klosterstr. 44 ☎030 89 06 84 10, ⓦ2be-club .de; U-Klosterstrasse; map p.60. Arguably Berlin's premier hip-hop club, spread over two big dance floors, with a playlist that encompasses reggae, ragga and r'n'b. Attracts many big-name DJs and artists. Entry €10. Sat 11pm until late.

★ **Golden Gate** Dirckenstr. 77–78 ☎030 282 92 95, ⓦgoldengate-berlin.de; S-Jannowitzbrücke; map p.60. Lurking beneath the S-Bahn tracks, this club consists of two wilfully shabby rooms kitted out in secondhand furniture and is dedicated to two- or three-day-long free-for-alls. The crowds here tend to be a dressed down, unpretentious lot who arrive well after midnight to try their luck with the difficult bouncers. Music is mostly house and techno with some surprises. Wed from 10pm, Thurs–Sat from 11pm.

Weekend Alexanderplatz 5 ☎030 24 63 16 76, ⓦweek-end-berlin.de; U- & S-Alexanderplatz; map p.60. Occupying the former GDR state travel agency, this club is typical of Berlin's creative transformations. The twelfth-floor views over central Berlin are spectacular and the roof terrace wonderful. All this makes up for the coolly offhand manner of many of its patrons as they groove to house and techno. Very popular Sun gay night. Entry €10–12. Thurs–Sat 11pm until late.

SPANDAUER VORSTADT

Acud Veteranenstr. 21 ☎030 44 35 94 99, ⓦacud.de; U-Rosenthaler Platz; map pp.72–73. Rock and blues are the mainstay of this ramshackle venue, with hip-hop and drum 'n' bass thrown in. There's also a gallery and movie theatre tucked inside. Entry €3–5. Daily 11pm until late.

am to pm Am Zwirngraben 2 ☎030 24 08 53 01, ⓦamtopm.de; S-Hackescher Markt; map pp.72–73. Though it's nothing special, this non-stop café-cum-bar-cum-club under the S-Bahn tracks is a good people-watching spot during the day, and a handy spot to start, or finish, a night out. Daily 24hr.

Bang Bang Neue Promenade 10 ☎030 60 40 53 10, ⓦbangbangclub.net; S-Hackescher Markt; map pp.72–73. Small venue, a stone's throw from Hackescher Markt, that packs a punch when it comes to live music: expect everything from avant-garde to British and US indie acts as well as soul, rock and electro DJs. Attracts a youngish, muso crowd. Tues–Sat 9pm–late.

Bierstube Alt Berlin Münzstr. 23 ☎030 281 96 87; U-Weinmeisterstrasse; map pp.72–73. A traditional corner pub, *Alt Berlin* has successfully resisted time (and gentrification) in an area that hasn't. Traditional jazz or Tom Waits features on the stereo, and since it's a small place that values atmosphere, don't show up in a large group as you'll probably be turfed out. Daily from 8pm.

Bohannon Dircksenstr. 40 ☎030 69 50 52 87, ⓦbohannon.de; S-Hackescher Markt; map pp.72–73. Named after funk legend Hamilton Bohannon, this club is one of the few places in the city with regular hip-hop, funk and dancehall sets, though the sound system could be better. Entry €5–10. Mon, Fri & Sat 10pm–late.

★ **Clärchens Ballhaus** Auguststr. 24 ☎030 282 92 95, ⓦballhaus.de; S-Hackescher Markt; map pp.72–73. Opened in 1913, providing a hedonistic venue throughout the 1920s and just about surviving fascism and communism, this dancehall is back in style, hosting a range of dance nights, from swing to tango and waltz, with instruction provided (times on website). Sun afternoons see the upstairs mirror room – unused during GDR days for being too glitzy – acting as a concert venue. Great pizza, too. Daily 10am until late.

Delicious Doughnuts Rosenthaler Str. 9 ☎030 28 09 92 74, ⓦdelicious-doughnuts.de; U-Rosenthaler Platz; map pp.72–73. The one place in Mitte open to anybody, at any time of night: part club, part dive bar, it comes into its own in the small hours, when it fills with post-club casualties, the odd transvestite and anyone looking to drink themselves to bed. Daily 9pm–late.

Grüner Salon Rosa-Luxemburg-Platz 2 ☎030 24 59 89 36, ⓦgruener-salon.de; U-Rosa-Luxemburg-Platz; map pp.72–73. Club beside the *Roter Salon* (see p.209) that preserves something of the 1920s in its chandeliers and velvet. Renowned for salsa courses and Fri tango evenings, but with a varied programme of live music, comedy and cabaret besides. Entry €4–15. Thurs 9pm–4am, Fri & Sat 11pm–4am.

Kaffee Burger Torstr. 60 ☎030 28 04 64 95, ⓦkaffeeburger.de; U-Rosa-Luxemburg-Platz; map pp.72–73. Russian-owned smoky 1970s retro-bar legendary for its Russian-themed disco nights, but good at any time, not least for the mad mix of genres – Balkan, surf rock, samba, rockabilly – that fills the small dance floor. Readings and poetry often start evenings off, but it really fills up later on. Entry €1–5. Mon–Thurs from 8pm, Fri & Sat from 9 or 10pm, Sun from 7pm.

Kim bar Brunnenstr. 10 ⓦkim-bar.com; U–Rosenthaler Platz; map pp.72–73. Art space, bar and locals' hangout, *Kim* is a firm favourite among Mitte's trend-conscious residents. There's no sign on the door, just a glass facade (the entrance is through the adjacent courtyard) onto a perpetually dark, white-walled space. Check the website for information on art, film and DJ nights. Tues–Sat 8pm–late.

Kingkongklub Brunnenstr. 173 ☎030 91 20 68 60, ⓦking-kong-klub.de; U-Rosenthaler Platz; map pp.72–73. Rock club with massive tattered dark leather sofas, kitsch B-movie paraphernalia and DJs spinning just about any genre of rock and electro. Popular with students and local eccentrics but generally drawing a 30-something crowd. Entry €2. Daily 9pm–late.

Mein Haus Am See Brunnenstr. 197–198 ☎030 23 88 35 61, ⓦmein-haus-am-see.blogspot.com; U-Rosenthaler Platz; map pp.72–73. Spacious café/bar stumbling distance from Rosenthaler Platz. Filled with comfy flea-market furnishings, it's a great spot for reading or chatting during the day, and for a more upbeat drink late at night when DJs play anything from disco to Latin. Daily 24hr.

Oscar Wilde Irish Pub Friedrichstr. 112a ☎030 282 81 66, ⓦoscar-wilde-irish-pub.de; U-Oranienburger Tor; map pp.72–73. Perennially popular and sociable Irish bar with all the usual ingredients: Guinness, Kilkenny and Strongbow on draught (German beers too), various whiskies, Irish breakfasts and SkySports on the big screen. All this makes it a hub for Berlin's English-speaking expats, with quiz nights (Mon), karaoke (every other Fri), and live music on most weekend nights. Mon–Thurs noon–2am, Fri & Sat noon–3am, Sun noon–midnight.

Reingold Novalisstr. 11 ☎030 28 38 76 76; U-Oranienburger Tor; map pp.72–73. Sophisticated Art Deco cocktail lounge with a 20- and 30-something clientele lounging on the leather and velvet seating. Plays jazz, trip-hop, house and the like. Tues–Sat 7pm–4am.

Roter Salon Rosa-Luxemburg-Platz 2 ☎030 24 06 58 06, ⓦvolksbuehne-berlin.de; U-Rosa-Luxemburg-Platz; map pp.72–73. Tatty club within the Volksbühne theatre, with lurid red decor and chintzy furniture giving it the feel of a 1950s brothel. Readings, concerts and club nights are held here. Wed is soul and funk night, other nights offer a mix of electronica, ska and Britpop. Entry €6–7. Mon & Wed–Sat 11pm–4am.

Schokoladen Ackerstr. 169 ☎030 282 65 27, ⓦschokoladen-mitte.de; U-Rosenthaler Platz; map pp.72–73. The spartan, bare-brick interior of this former chocolate factory is a hangover from its time as a squatted

building in the early post-Wende days. Now a venue for theatrical and art events, live indie-pop and up-and-coming singer/songwriters. Mon–Thurs 8pm–4am, Fri & Sat 9pm–4am, Sun 7pm–4am.

Sophienclub Sophienstr. 6 ⓦsophienclub-berlin.de; S-Hackescher Markt; map pp.72–73. Small, functional and rather nondescript club with a couple of cramped, well-populated dance floors and a mixed crowd. At its best on Tues Britpop nights; at other times patrons survive on a medley of soul, funk, house and indie. Entry €3–6. Tues & Thurs–Sat 10pm until late.

Verkehrsberuhigte Ost-Zone Monbijouplatz, S-Bahnbogen 153 ☎030 24 62 87 81, ⓦveboz.de; S-Hackescher Markt; map pp.72–73. Great little bar if you are looking for a dose of *Ostalgie* (see p.66) with your beer – there's an abundance of GDR memorabilia. It's hidden away in the arches of the S-Bahn overlooking the Spree, which might be what keeps it from being touristy. Daily 8pm–3am.

Weinerei Forum Bar: Fehrbelliner Str. 57; Shop: Veteranenstr. 14; ☎030 440 69 83, ⓦweinerei.com; U-Rosenthaler Platz; map pp.72–73. This members' club-style wine shop and bar operates on an honesty-box system after 8pm: pay what you feel is fair for your drinks when you leave. This makes it popular with a mix of leftie sympathizers, students and freeloaders. The wine is decidedly average but the atmosphere friendly. The owners run similar ventures nearby – *Perlin* (Griebenowstr. 5) and *Fra Rosa* (Zionskirchstr. 40). All bars: 8pm–midnight; shop: Mon–Fri 1–8pm, Sat 11am–8pm.

White Trash Fast Food Schönhauser Allee 6–7 ☎030 50 34 86 68, ⓦwhitetrashfastfood.com; U-Rosa-Luxemburg-Platz; map pp.72–73. With a Wild West saloon meets Chinese restaurant theme, this perennially popular den of kitsch acts as restaurant, bar and club/live venue. The food – mostly burgers and nachos – is decent enough and matches the informal nature of the crowd, who come to check out the regular DJs and bands who play mostly country, punk and 50s and 60s-era tunes. Entry €1–8. Mon–Fri noon–late, Sat & Sun 6pm–late.

Zosch Tucholskystr. 30 ☎030 280 76 64, ⓦzosch-berlin.de; U-Oranienburger Tor; map pp.72–73.

14

OUTDOOR VENUES

International **big-name acts** visiting town regularly play at one of several stadiums and larger venues around town and generally the act rather than the venue will be the big draw. The exceptions to this are those performing in the Olympic Stadium (see p.158) and at the two other suburban venues below.

Parkbühne Wuhlheide ☎030 53 07 95 30, ⓦwuhlheide.de; S-Wuhlheide; map p.142. Small outdoor venue, tucked away in the forest near Köpenick, and a favourite for summertime festivals.

Waldbühne Glockenturmstr./Passenheimer Str.

☎030 305 72 50, ⓦwaldbuehne-berlin.de; S-Pichelsberg; map p.154. Near the Olympic stadium, this open-air natural amphitheatre regularly attracts big-name acts in the summer and is great fun on a warm evening.

Alternative place that started as a squat when the Wall came down, and has retained much of that feel. A good place for gigs and club nights in the cellar, where a fun-loving local Creole jazz band often plays amid the smoky ambience and constant chatter. Daily 4pm–5am.

TIERGARTEN

40seconds Potsdamer Str. 58 ☎030 890 64 20, ⓦ40seconds.de; U- & S-Potsdamer Platz; map pp.90–91. Named after the amount of time it takes the elevator to get to its top-floor location, this part futurist, part 1980s throwback bar has great views over Potsdamer Platz. There are three lounge areas, lit by Verner Panton lamps, and balconies for summer. The mood is glamorous, the music is standard r'n'b, house and electronica, and the dress code is smart-casual or sporty-elegant. Entry €10. Fri & Sat 11pm–late.

CITY WEST

F37 Fasanenstr. 37 ☎030 881 49 08; U-Spichernstr; map p.108. Pricey cocktail bar and art gallery that hails from the 1950s. Some interior features are by Hans Scharoun, architect of the Berlin Philharmonie (see p.219). A meeting point for lounge lizards, actors and artists. Mon–Sat 8pm until late.

Gainsbourg Jeanne-Mammen-Bogen 576/577 ☎030 313 74 64; S-Savignyplatz; map p.108. The name may pay homage to the master of risqué *chanson*, but the cocktails (€8–10) and food are more mainstream. Nevertheless, they're some of the best drinks in the neighbourhood. Daily 4pm until late.

Puro Sky Lounge Tauentzienstr. 11 ☎030 26 36 78 75, ⓦpuro-berlin.de; U-Zoologischer Garten; map p.108. Probably Berlin's snazziest club with as its main selling point a twentieth-storey location in the Europa Centre, with great views of the City West nightscape. But it's an elitist place and one of the few clubs in Berlin with any kind of dress code: if it's not designer, you won't get in – and if it's not a 1980s classic it probably won't be played. Tues–Sat 8pm until late.

SCHÖNEBERG

E&M Leydicke Mansteinstr. 4 ☎030 216 29 73; U- & S-Yorckstrasse; map p.113. Claiming to be the oldest *Kneipe* in western Berlin – though some of the decor looks suspiciously modern – this place is famed for its fruit wines and theme nights: from rockabilly to belly-dancing. Daily 6pm–late.

Green Door Winterfeldtstr. 50 ☎030 215 25 15; U-Nollendorfplatz; map p.113. Somewhat snobby, dimly lit cocktail bar, attracting a well-dressed crowd of young professionals and party-goers. Press the buzzer to get in;

once you're past the pretension the place can be fun, and they mix a really good cocktail. Sun–Thurs 6pm–3am, Fri & Sat 6pm–4am.

Havanna Hauptstr. 30 ☎030 784 85 65, ⓦhavanna-berlin.de; S-Julius-Leber-Brücke; map p.113. Upbeat Latin club, with seven bars and four dancefloors: one for salsa and merengue, and the others to groove to funk and r'n'b. Dance classes available; entry €3–7. Wed 9pm–4am, Fri & Sat 10pm–4am.

★ **Kumpelnest 3000** Lützowstr. 23 ☎030 261 69 18, ⓦkumpelnest3000.com; U-Kurfürstenstrasse; map p.113. Carpeted walls and a mock-Baroque effect attract a rough-and-ready crew of 30- and 40-somethings to this erstwhile brothel, which gets going around 2am, when there's standing room only. The best place in the area, it's good fun and infamous as a hook-up bar for people of all sexual orientations. Daily 7pm–late.

Mister Hu Goltzstr. 39 ☎030 217 21 11; U-Eisenacher Strasse; map p.113. Warm red cocktail bar with a relaxed atmosphere and great range of drinks (€6–11) mixed by some of the city's best bartenders. Fri & Sat 6pm–4am, Sun–Thurs 6pm–3am.

Pinguin Club Wartburgstr. 54 ☎030 781 30 05; U-Eisenacher Strasse; map p.113. Tiny and friendly bar – with 1950s and 1960s Americana decor – which doesn't really get going until after midnight. Daily 7pm–3am.

Victoria Bar Potsdamer Str. 102 ☎030 25 75 99 77, ⓦvictoriabar.de; U-Kurfürstenstrasse; map p.113. Much-loved cocktail bar that's great for a low-key and decently mixed drink in the week or a livelier weekend night. With a long bar, subdued lighting and discreet but upbeat music. Mon–Thurs & Sun 6.30pm–3am, Fri & Sat 6.30pm–4am.

Zoulou Bar Hauptstr. 4 ☎030 70 09 47 37, ⓦzouloubar.de; U-Kleistpark; map p.113. Wonderfully low-key bar packed after 11pm with sociable Schönebergers, quaffing draught *Kölsch*, Cologne's famous beer, and a few good cocktails. Sun–Thurs 8pm–5am, Fri & Sat 8pm–6am.

WESTERN KREUZBERG

Bar-Nou Bergmannstr. 104 ☎030 74 07 30 50, ⓦbar-nou.com; U-Mehringdamm; map p.118. Discreet cocktail bar in a Bergmannstrasse basement. Expect red lighting, stylish decor and very good drinks served by friendly staff. A good spot for a tête-à-tête. Daily 8pm–4am.

Golgatha Dudenstr. 48–64 ☎030 785 24 53; U- & S-Yorckstrasse; map p.118. Kreuzberg's popular hillside café hosts a daily alfresco disco from 10pm April–Sept, which is good fun on warm evenings. April–Oct daily 9am until late.

14

Gretchen Obentrautstr. 19–21 ☎030 25 92 27 02, ⓦgretchen-club.de; U-Mehringdamm; map p.118. A bit off the beaten track, but few clubs can boast that they occupy the 1854 stables of Queen Victoria's Prussian 1st guards. This mid-sized club has a pedigree too, as it rose from the ashes of the legendary *Icon* club, a late-1990s club-scene pioneer. Drum'n'bass is big here, but all species of innovative electronic music thrive. Entry €5–12. Hours vary, usually Thurs–Sat 11.30pm–late.

Junction Bar Gneisenaustr. 18 ☎030 694 66 02, ⓦjunction-bar.de; U-Gneisenaustrasse; map p.118. Nightly live music covering the full spectrum of sounds, played to a very mixed crowd in a basement club. Always busy, and DJs keep the night going after the bands finish. Entry €3–6. Sun–Thurs 9pm–4am, Fri & Sat 10pm–4am.

★ **Solar** Stresemannstr. 76 ☎0163 765 27 00, ⓦsolarberlin.com; S-Anhalter Bahnhof; map p.118. Swanky lounge bar whose seventeenth-floor location provides exceptional views over the city. There's also a pricey restaurant, but the place to be is among the beautiful people grooving to ambient techno in the bar above. The entrance is slightly hidden at the back of a small parking lot opposite Anhalter Bahnhof and the door policy can be stringent and unpredictable: there's no need to dress up, but don't dress down either. Mon–Thurs noon–2am, Fri noon–4am, Sat 6pm–4am, Sun 6pm–2am.

Zyankali Bar Grossbeerenstr. 64 ☎030 251 63 33, ⓦzyankali.de; U-Mehringdamm; map p.118. Pharmacy-themed bar that's brimming with its own weird science – odd even by Berlin standards. Glass-topped coffins with fake skeletons serve as tables; drinks (more than 200 cocktails) contain some unusual ingredients, sometimes home-made and served in laboratory ware. Movie-themed nights take place in the back room. Daily 8pm–late.

EASTERN KREUZBERG

Club der Visionaere Am Flutgraben 1 ☎030 69 51 89 42, ⓦclubdervisionaere.com; U-Schlesisches Tor; map pp.126–127. Legendary summer-only techno bar enjoying a unique setting on the intersection of the Spree and Flutgraben canal. The bar and DJ booth is in an old ceramic-tiled boathouse, and punters stand (and dance) on the floating docks outside. It's minimal techno all the way and a fantastically upbeat place. Entry €1–5. Food daily 6pm–1am. May–Sept Mon–Fri 2pm–late, Sat & Sun noon–late.

TOP 5 TECHNO CLUBS

Berghain See p.213
Gretchen See p.212
Tresor See p.213
Weekend See p.208
Watergate See p.213

Das Hotel Mariannenstr. 26a ☎030 84 11 84 33; U-Kottbusser Tor; map pp.126–127. Split-level spot where crowds gather to drink, chat and watch the odd TV documentary. Divided into three areas, it features a main bar, occasional DJs playing Latin and 1960s music and a rustic bar with a more relaxed vibe with wooden tables and candlelight. Daily 2pm until whenever.

Kit-Kat Club Köpenicker Str. 76 (entrance on Brückenstr.) ☎030 787 18 96, ⓦkitkatclub.de; U-Heinrich-Heine-Strasse; map pp.126–127. Famously debauched club, sharing premises with the *Sage Club* (see below), for people looking for casual and public liaisons – voyeurs are not welcome. The door policy is strict: wear something revealing or fetishistic – check the website for guidelines, and for details of theme evenings. Fri & Sat 11pm until late, Sun 8am until late.

Konrad Tönz Falckensteinstr. 30 ☎030 612 32 52, ⓦkonradtoenzbar.de; U-Schlesisches Tor; map pp.126–127. Cheesy bar with 1970s trappings; sip cocktails (€4–8) while grooving to retro sounds and easy listening. Tues–Sun 8.15pm until late.

Lido Cuvrystr. 7 ☎030 69 56 68 40, ⓦlido-berlin.de; U-Schlesisches Tor; map pp.126–127. Old-school club in a former theatre that's been championing new indie music – with the occasional techno or house event – for more than a decade. Attracts a younger crowd. Entry €5–€9. Fri & Sat 10pm–late.

Luzia Oranienstr. 34 ☎030 61 10 74 69; U-Kottbusser Tor; map pp.126–127. Oranienstrasse's key hipster hangout, *Luzia* is styled in the manner of an industrial loft, with exposed brickwork, velvet armchairs, wall paintings by street artists, rough wallpaper and a bizarre upstairs space that you have to climb a ladder to get to. Decent drinks and cocktails mean it's buzzing most nights. Daily 10am–3am.

Madame Claude Lübbener Str. 19 ☎030 84 11 08 61, ⓦmadameclaude.de; U-Görlitzer Bahnhof; map pp.126–127. This student hangout has shows five days a week, ranging from indie-rock and experimental to folk. Be prepared to feel slightly unsettled by the decor, much of which hangs upside down from the ceiling. Pay what you want to enter. Daily 7pm–late.

Madonna Wiener Str. 22 ☎030 611 69 43; U-Görlitzer Bahnhof; map pp.126–127. Longstanding, grimy and perennially "in" bar; check out the ceiling fresco of the seven deadly sins, pick from the extensive whisky selection and vibrate to the loud music. Daily 3pm until late.

Magnet Falckensteinstr. 48 ⓦmagnet-club.de; U-Schlesisches Tor; map pp.126–127. Formerly a Prenzlauer Berg rock'n'roll mainstay, *Magnet* moved to more suitably grungy Kreuzberg in 2010. It hosts regular DJ parties and live shows, ranging from pop to rock and from metal to electro. Mon–Sat 10pm–late.

Möbel-Olfe Reichenberger Str. 177 ☎030 23 27 46 90; U-Kottbusser Tor; map pp.126–127. Sandwiched

between a string of Turkish snack bars in a rundown building behind Kottbusser Tor, this unusual, smoky, local bar attracts gays, hipsters, ageing drunks and more. There are regular DJ nights but it's more about experiencing the diversity of the Kreuzberg crowds. Tues–Sun 6pm–late.
Monarch Skalitzerstr. 134 ⓦ kottimonarch.de; U-Kotbusser Tor; map pp.126–127. Unpretentious and slightly ragged place that attracts a hip crowd who groove to a wide range of tunes – swing, rockabilly, folk, punk, indie (no techno) – and enjoy views over Kotbusser Tor from huge windows. Entrance is via an unmarked door and stairwell opposite kebab shop *Misir Casisi*. Entry €3. Tues–Sat 9pm–late.
Privatclub Pücklerstr. 34 ☎ 030 611 30 02, ⓦ privatclub-berlin.de; U-Görlitzer Bahnhof; map pp.126–127. Cellar club below *Weltrestaurant Markthalle*, which is notable for weekend theme parties – attracting a wide range of ages – ranging from 1970s disco trash and new wave to blaxploitation funk. Local bands often play here as well. €6–7. Fri & Sat 11pm until late.
Sage Club Köpenicker Str. 76 ☎ 030 278 98 30, ⓦ sage-club.de; U-Heinrich-Heine-Strasse; map pp.126–127. One of Berlin's premier clubs, with multiple dance floors and a good range of sounds – particularly rock, but also hip-hop, r'n'b, mainstream and techno. Always a good vibe and popular with a younger set. Thurs–Sun 11pm–5am.
SO36 Oranienstr. 190 ☎ 030 61 40 13 06, ⓦ so36.de; U-Görlitzer Bahnhof; map pp.126–127. Legendary club, named after the district's old postcode, which has its roots in punk, post-punk and alternative music – a string of musical heroes have played here, including Iggy, Bowie and Einstürzende Neubauten. Nowadays it hosts alternative and electronic shows, including monthly parties like "Gayhane", a Turkish "homoriental" party, and "Ich bin ein Berliner", where you can catch an exquisite array of Berlin-based artists playing everything from garage to synth-pop. Entry €3–10. Usually from 11pm.
Tresor Köpenicker Str. 70 ☎ 030 695 37 70, ⓦ tresorberlin.de; U-Heinrich-Heine-Strasse; map pp.126–127. A key player in Berlin's electronic music scene with thumping techno booming in every nook of this convoluted bunker-style club and attracting clubbers from all over Europe. The volume, intensity and light show all have to be experienced to be believed. Entry Wed €5–8, Fri & Sat €10–15. Wed–Sat midnight until late.
Watergate Falckensteinstr. 49 ☎ 030 61 28 03 96, ⓦ water-gate.de; U-Schlesisches Tor; map pp.126–127. A top Berlin nightspot, with a glorious riverside location by the Oberbaumbrücke. The futuristic club with its impressive light installations sprawls over two levels with a large main floor and another with a lounge; music is varied but mostly electronic. Some big-name DJs. Entry €8–15. Wed, Fri & Sat 11pm–late, occasional Tues & Thurs events.

TOP 5 LIVE MUSIC CLUBS
Acud See p.208
Magnet Club See p.212
Schokoladen See p.209
SO36 See p.213
Wild at Heart See p.213

Wiener Blut Wiener Str. 14 ☎ 030 618 90 23; U-Görlitzer Bahnhof; map pp.126–127. Former studenty bar that has aged along with its clientele, though there's still table football and a buoyant, spirited atmosphere. Bundesliga football or dancing depending on the night. Daily 6pm until late.
Wild at Heart Wiener Str. 20 ☎ 030 611 70 10, ⓦ wildatheartberlin.de; U-Görlitzer Bahnhof; map pp.126–127. Cornerstone live music venue for rock 'n' roll, indie and punk, with something always going on well into the small hours. Daily 8pm until late.
Würgeengel Dresdener Str. 122 ☎ 030 615 55 60; U-Kottbusser Tor; map pp.126–127. One of the best bars in Kreuzberg, "the exterminating angel" has red walls, great tapas, decadent decor and an extensive cocktail and wine list. The feel is timeless, though with a trendy clientele. Daily 7pm–late.

FRIEDRICHSHAIN
Babette Karl-Marx-Allee 36 ☎ 0176 38 38 89 43, ⓦ barbabette.com; U-Schillingstrasse; map pp.126–127. Cool and sparsely furnished bar in the glass box building of a former cosmetics shop. At night, its only identifying feature is the warm glow of the interior lights. The upstairs former treatment rooms occasionally have live music. Daily 6pm–late.
★ **Berghain** Am Wriezener Bahnhof ⓦ berghain.de; S-Ostbahnhof; map pp.126–127. This vast, artfully scuzzy old power plant with a fantastic sound system is considered by many people to be the best club in the world. Minimal techno and house cannonball around the gigantic dancefloors that are packed largely with shirtless guys. More laid-back bars and murky backrooms cater to other desires of an evenly mixed gay and straight crowd. The club ensures and abuses its legendary status with a picky, indefinable door policy: avoid looking like a tourist or arriving in any kind of group. And remember headline acts often start at noon – so there's no rush to get here early; about 5am is ideal, when the wait to get in generally drops below an hour. Entry €14. Fri & Sat midnight until late (usually late afternoon the next day).
Cassiopeia Reveler Str. 99 ☎ 030 47 38 59 49, ⓦ cassiopeia-berlin.de; U- & S-Warschauer Strasse; map pp.126–127. Yet another former squat where the shambolic vibe has been preserved to produce a venue that's as odd, grungy and as hip and nebulous as any: there's a

14

**TOP 5 PLACES TO END
A NIGHT OUT**
Berghain See p.213
Delicious Doughnuts See p.208
Golden Gate See p.208
Kumpelnest 3000 See p.210
Möbel-Olfe See p.212

skate-park, climbing wall, outdoor cinema, beer garden and four dancefloors. Entry €3–7, more when bands play. Tues–Fri 6pm until late, Sat–Mon 3pm until late.

Dachkammer Simon-Dach-Str. 39 ☎030 296 16 73; U- & S-Warschauer Strasse; map pp.126–127. The largest and possibly most sociable place on the strip – the combination of rustic bar downstairs and retro bar upstairs has made this a local classic. Free wi-fi. Mon–Fri noon–1am, Sat & Sun 10pm–1am.

Habermeyer Gärtnerstr. 6 ☎030 29 77 18 87, ⊛habermeyer-bar.de; U-Samariterstrasse; map pp.126–127. This smoky, dark, low-key, dive-style hangout is a Friedrichshain classic. Slightly off the main path, it offers table football and pinball machines, a miscellany of seating and DJs playing anything from Northern soul to electronica. Best late on weekends. Daily 7pm until late.

Kantine am Berghain Rüdersdorfer Str. 70 ☎030 29 36 02 10; S-Ostbahnhof; map pp.126–127. Its friendly atmosphere and tiny, jolly summer beer garden mean that this venue is now far more than simply a haven for people rejected by the neighbouring *Berghain* club – to which its music compares. Entry €5–10. Sat noon until late, Sun 9am until late.

Kptn. A. Müller Simon-Dach-Str. 32; U- & S-Warschauer Strasse; map pp.126–127. Ramshackle, sociable and very popular budget bar on the Simon-Dach-Str. strip, with free table football – though you'd better be good to challenge the locals. Daily 6pm until late.

Rosi's Revalerstr. 29 ⊛rosis-berlin.de; S-Warschauer Strasse; map pp.126–127. Oddball upbeat club that sports Berlin's classic unfinished and improvised feel in a mix of semi-derelict buildings. There's a definite sense of crashing a house party here, with even a small kitchen and living room to hang out in between bouts on the dancefloors – where indie or techno pounds. Outside table tennis is also a big attraction. Thurs–Sat 11pm–late.

NEUKÖLLN AND TREPTOW
Ankerklause Kottbusser Damm 104, Neukölln ☎030 41 71 75 12, ⊛ankerklause.de; U-Kottbusser Tor; map pp.126–127. This little café, perched by the Landwehr canal, turns into a hip and crowded funk and soul club by night. Thurs is Sixties night. Mon 4pm–4am, Tues–Sun 10am–4am.

Insel Alt-Treptow 6, Treptow ☎030 20 91 49 90; S-Plänterwald; map pp.126–127. Reliable venue for

thrash/punk gigs and club nights, on a Spree island that's part of Treptower Park. Occasional outdoor raves on the large terrace in summer. Times vary, usually Sat & Sun from 3pm.

PRENZLAUER BERG
8MM Schönhauser Allee 177 ☎030 40 50 06 24, ⊛8mmbar.com; U-Senefelderplatz; map p.132. This small, blacked-out room with a little bar, a DJ spinning anything from rock to northern soul and 8mm films projected onto one wall is a superb place for low-key, late-night hedonism. Daily 9pm–close.

August Fengler Lychener Str. 11 ☎030 44 35 66 40; U-Eberswalder Strasse; map p.132. Classic neighbourhood bar – with table football and even a *Kegelbahn* (German nine-pin bowling; call ahead to book; €14/hr) – that's been taken over by a trendy set who dance in the small back room to soul, disco and funk. Daily 7pm–5am.

Becketts Kopf Pappelallee 64 ☎016 22 37 94 18, ⊛becketts-kopf.de; U- & S-Schönhauser Allee; map p.132. It would be easy to walk straight past this clandestine cocktail bar – but you'd be missing out. Look out for the glowering head of Mr Beckett staring at you from the darkness, and enter to find a sophisticated and intimate space with one of the best cocktail lists in town. Tues–Sun 8pm–4am.

Dr Pong Eberswalder Str. 21 ⊛drpong.net; U-Eberswalder Strasse; map p.132. The action here revolves – literally – around the ping-pong table in the middle of the main room. Rent a bat (or bring your own) and join the crowd as they move slowly around the table, bats in one hand, beer bottles in the other, playing a communal game. DJs grace the sound system from time to time, though be warned the bar is on the tourist beer crawl route and can get packed. Mon–Sat 8pm–late, Sun 2pm–late.

Duncker Dunckerstr. 64 ☎030 445 95 09, ⊛dunckerclub.de; S-Prenzlauer Allee; map p.132. Indie, industrial and unashamedly Goth refuge from the mainstream and techno. Aptly enough it's located in a striking neo-Gothic church. Entry €3–5. Mon 9pm–late, Tues, Thurs & Sun 10pm–late, Fri & Sat 11pm–late.

Hausbar Rykestr. 54 ☎030 44 04 76 06; U-Senefelderplatz; map p.132. It might be small, but this unpretentious, dimly lit bar, across from the Wasserturm and a couple of doors down from the synagogue, is a great deal of fun on the right nights – and a late-night drinking spot. Daily 7pm–5am.

Kulturbrauerei Knaackstr. 97 ☎030 48 49 44, ⊛kulturbrauerei-berlin.de; U-Eberswalder Strasse; map p.132. Nineteenth-century brewery that's been turned into a multi-venue arts and cultural centre attracting local and emerging bands. Its two clubs, *Alte Kantine* and *Soda*, both attract a 30-plus crowd; the former is pretty mainstream and rock-oriented, the latter best known for salsa nights, but also house and r'n'b. Entry €3–8. Daily 10pm–late.

nbi Schönhauser Allee 36 ☎030 67 30 44 57, ⓦneueberlinerinitiative.de; U-Eberswalder Str; map p.132. In a residential neighbourhood, this lounge-cum-club has to keep the volume down; it's used this to its advantage, creating a comfortable environment to appreciate cutting-edge electronic music. DJs come here to hear each other experiment. Entry €3. Daily 8pm until late.

Pavillon Friedenstr. in Volkspark ☎0172 750 47 24, ⓦpavillon-berlin.de; U-Strausberger Platz; map p.132. Beer garden by day and club by night, surrounded by the laid-back greenery of Volkspark Friedrichshain, this venue is best in the summer when its hundred-person dancefloor packs out to the sounds of funk, Nu Jazz and soul. March–Oct Mon–Fri 11am until late, Sat & Sun 10am until late.

Scotch & Sofa Kollwitzstr. 18 ☎030 44 04 23 71; S-Senefelderplatz; map p.132. This highly agreeable, quietly hip neighbourhood bar is a fine spot for sinking into

an old sofa, sipping on a decently made cocktail and having a tête-à-tête. They always play interesting music – everything from Elvis to rap – and smokers and ping-pong fans can indulge their passions downstairs. Daily 2pm–any time.

Soda Knaackstr. 97 ☎030 44 31 51 44, ⓦsoda-berlin .de; U-Eberswalder Strasse; map p.132. Club in the Kulturbrauerei cultural centre, located in a former brewery. The usual diet of soul, house and funk is interrupted on Thurs & Sun by well-attended salsa nights, and occasional live acts, too. Marred by some of Berlin's highest bar prices. Thurs 8pm until late, Fri & Sat 11pm until late, Sun 7pm until late.

Zu mir oder zu dir Lychener Str. 15 ☎0176 24 42 29 40; U-Eberswalder Strasse; map p.132. Groovy, very Seventies lounge-bar with a sociable vibe and lots of sofas to crash out on. A good place to start a night out, even if the cheeky name– translating to "your place or mine?" – suggests you might end it here. Daily 8pm until late.

14

JAZZ, BLUES AND WORLD MUSIC

SPANDAUER VORSTADT

b-flat Rosenthaler Str. 13 ☎030 283 31 23, ⓦb-flat -berlin.de; U-Weinmeisterstrasse; map pp.72–73. This cosy jazz bar, with windows facing onto the street and small bar at the back, offers a mix of local musicians and the occasional international act. Popular at weekends, and there's also a busy free jam session on Wed. Entry €12. Mon–Sat 9pm until late.

TIERGARTEN

Haus der Kulturen der Welt John-Foster-Dulles-Allee 10 ☎030 39 78 70, ⓦhkw.de; S-Hauptbahnhof; map pp.90–91. The city's number-one venue for world music is always worth checking out.

CITY WEST

A-Trane Bleibtreustr./Pestalozzistr. ☎030 313 25 50, ⓦa-trane.de; U-Savignyplatz; map p.108. Small and smoky jazz den; a good place for both up-and-coming and well-known jazz artists. Best during Sat-night jams, when musicians arrive from other venues and join in at will throughout the evening. Entry €6–21. Daily 9pm until late.

Quasimodo Kantstr. 12a ☎030 312 80 86, ⓦquasimodo.de; U- & S-Zoologischer Garten; map

p.108. Casual cellar bar that's one of Berlin's best jazz spots, with black-and-white photos, low ceilings, intimate tables and nightly programmes. A high-quality mix of international, usually American, stars and up-and-coming names. Also funk, blues and Latin. Often free on weekdays, otherwise €7–28. Daily 9pm–2am.

WESTERN KREUZBERG

Yorckschlösschen Yorckstr. 15 ☎030 215 80 70, ⓦyorckschloesschen.de; U-Mehringdamm; map p.118. Century-old local institution that's preserved a 1970s feel and is still famous as an artists' drinking den and a place to enjoy free live jazz, swing, blues and country. Basic food served. Summer daily 10am–3am; rest of year Mon–Sat 5pm–3am, Sun 10am–3am.

WILMERSDORF

Badenscher Hof Badensche Str. 29 ☎030 861 00 80, ⓦbadenscher-hof.de; U-Blissestrasse; map p.154. Lively café-restaurant and long-standing jazz venue that draws in the Schöneberg crowd for its frequent concerts. Expect any type of jazz – from mainstream to modern – or blues. Mon–Fri 4pm until late, Sat 6pm until late.

JAZZ IN BERLIN

Though long-standing and high-quality, Berlin's **jazz and blues** scene lacks the reputation it deserves. Much of it was spawned in the Cold War days in those parts of Berlin occupied by American forces, where a discerning and experienced audience could add authenticity to proceedings. But the scene has long outlived this era, generally maintaining its own momentum in traditional haunts that survive well outside the rest of Berlin's nightlife landscape. Jazz fans should make sure to check out **Jazzfest Berlin** (ⓦjazzfest-berlin.de) in late Oct/early Nov. Running since the 1960s, with a varied programme attracting big names at venues throughout the city, it's traditional and progressive in equal parts, focusing on big bands and large ensembles.

HAMBURGER BAHNHOF

The arts

When Berlin was a divided city, the West German government poured arts subsidies into their half to the value of more than fifty percent of the federal budget for culture for the entire United States. Then unification left Berlin with a "doubling" of facilities, three magnificent opera houses and one of the liveliest arts scenes in Europe. However, in the mood of glum post-unification realism, things changed: almost all subsidies disappeared and many companies folded. Even so, Berlin's scene remained buoyant: the city maintained its appetite for culture and creative types gravitate here in ever-greater numbers. Today, high-quality dance and theatre groups perform everything from classic to avant-garde experimental works; mainstream and art-house cinemas thrive; the gallery scene is particularly vibrant; and the city still has one of the world's finest symphony orchestras.

ESSENTIALS

Information Listings magazines *Zitty* and *Tip* (see p.33) are good for what's on information, as is the city's tourist information website (⬤visitberlin.de). For art shows, check the English/German bi-monthly magazine *artery berlin* (€3; ⬤artery-berlin.de), found in most galleries, where you can also usually pick up the free *Galerien Berlin* listings brochure (⬤berliner-galerien.de). Look out too for a similar leaflet produced by Index (⬤indexberlin.de) whose website centres on a useful browsable city map of all the galleries with all the latest exhibition details.

Booking You can book for most events through the ⬤visitberlin.de site and at BTM offices (see p.33).

Otherwise ticket offices (*Theaterkassen*) are usually the easiest way of buying tickets for all major arts events, though they often charge a hefty commission; try *Ko Ka 36* Oranienstr. 29, Kreuzberg (☎030 61 10 13 13, ⬤koka36.de; U-Kottbusser Tor).

Discounted tickets The first place to try, however, for just about anything, is Hekticket (☎030 230 99 30, ⬤hekticket.de); which sells half-price tickets from 2pm. Offices include Hekticket am Zoo (Hardenberg Str. 29a; Charlottenburg, U- & S-Zoologischer Garten) and Hekticket am Alex (Karl-Liebknecht-Str. 13, Mitte; U- & S-Alexanderplatz).

CONTEMPORARY ART

Complementing the superb, state-owned **Hamburger Bahnhof**, Berlin's local art scene is astoundingly good, with an estimated five thousand artists regularly opening their studios or exhibiting at hundreds of galleries around town. For a long time, the city's art scene was divided between east and west: the west contained the more expensive and established **Charlottenburg** galleries, while the east was the focus of energy and attention. Immediately after the *Wende*, the area around **Auguststrasse** in the Spandauer Vorstadt (see p.79) became a breeding ground of experimental art, but now is as settled and commercialized as Charlottenburg once was, which in turn has become more avant-garde and daring. Today, you can find art shows in any neighbourhood, though the city's less commercial and more rough-and-ready scene operates outside the mainstream galleries and moves from one improvised space to the next. You'll stumble upon places in less polished neighbourhoods, such as Kreuzberg and Neukölln, or check the website ⬤kunstberlin.eu.

15

GALLERIES

Atelier Brandner Helmholtzstr. 2–9, Entrance E, Charlottenburg ☎030 30 10 05 75, ⬤atelier-brandner.de; U-Turmstrasse. Southern German Matthias Brandner is among the most successful of the many painters who have been drawn to live and work in Berlin, drawn by the city's energetic, liberal atmosphere and cheap studio space. Though famed for his murals on building exteriors, it's his powerful abstract watercolours and oils that are on show at his studio. Daily noon–8pm.

★ **Camera Work** Kantstr. 149, Charlottenburg ☎030 310 07 73, ⬤camerawork.de; U-Uhlandstrasse. Hidden in a courtyard and blessed with huge north-facing windows and wonderfully even light, this relaxed photography gallery spreads over two floors. Exhibitions often focus on big names like Man Ray, Irving Penn, Horst P. Horst, Peter Lindbergh and Helmut Newton but the occasional up-and-coming name also gets a look-in. Visitors welcome, even if you can't afford the work. Tues–Sat 11am–6pm.

Capitain Petzel Karl-Marx-Allee 45, Friedrichshain ☎030 24 08 81 30, ⬤capitainpetzel.de; U-Strausberger Platz. Joint venture between two art dealers from Cologne and New York. With an eye-catching location in a Soviet modernist glass cube, this was an Eastern Bloc showcase in GDR days. It's now far more international, and the cornerstone of a new area in the Berlin art scene. Tues–Sat 11am–6pm.

Carlier Gebauer Markgrafenstr. 67, Mitte ☎030 280 81 10, ⬤carliergebauer.com; U-Kochstrasse. Superb art gallery where you never quite know if you'll find home-grown or international art; either way, it's sure to be cutting-edge. Tues–Sat 11am–6pm.

Contemporary Fine Arts Am Kupfergraben 20, Mitte ☎030 288 78 70, ⬤cfa-berlin.com; U- & S-Friedrichsstrasse. Contemporary art and sculpture specialist founded in Charlottenburg but now conveniently close to Museum Island. The large gallery is a great place to feel the pulse of the Berlin art scene and see the work of locals like Marc Brandenburg as well as International big names like Daniel Richter and Georg Baselitz. Tues–Fri 11am–6pm, Sat 11am–4pm.

DAAD Galerie Zimmerstr. 90/91, Mitte ☎030 261 36 40, ⬤daadgalerie.de; U-Kochstrasse. Exhibitions and occasional readings by big-name artists working in the city on fellowships. Mon–Sat 11am–6pm.

EIGEN+ART Auguststr. 26, Mitte ☎030 280 66 05, ⬤eigen-art.com; S-Hackescher Markt. Run by Gerd Harry Lybke, who opened the first private gallery in the GDR back in the 1980s, this is one of the most important Auguststrasse galleries. Though originally a showcase for East German talent, the programme now covers painting, installations and photography by predominantly young international artists. Tues–Sat 11am–6pm.

Galerie Anselm Dreher Pfalzburger Str. 80, Wilmersdorf ☎030 883 52 49, ⬤galerie-anselm-dreher.com; U-Hohenzollernplatz. Long-standing city gallery, showing international avant-garde artists and particularly keen on sound installations. Tues–Fri 2–6pm, Sat 11am–2pm.

BERLIN'S ART AND FASHION EVENTS

Berlin's big annual art and fashion events, often on the cutting edge, draw in hundreds of international curators and designers.

The first major date on Berlin's contemporary art calendar is **Gallery Weekend Berlin** (ⓦgallery-weekend-berlin.de) in early May, when some forty galleries co-ordinate their efforts to startle and impress. The biggest dates, however, fall close together in late September: **Berlin Art Week** (ⓦberlinartweek.de), involves all of Berlin's large contemporary art museums; **Art Berlin Contemporary** (ⓦartberlincontemporary.com), where collectors from around the world gather at Stadion Berlin in northwest Kreuzberg (U-Gleisdreieck); and the artist-led and more offbeat **Berliner Liste** (ⓦberliner-liste.org), which focuses on showcasing new local talent in a different venue each year.

July is the key month for **fashion shows**; the headliner tends to be **Mercedes Benz Fashion Week Berlin** (ⓦberlin.mbfashionweek.com), a glitzy spectacular dominated by big-name international designers and their sycophantic retinue, but also with slots for new names. Held in tandem, the **Premium** (ⓦpremiumexhibitions.com) trade fair also showcases many fashionable brands. More offbeat and arguably more in step with Berlin is the **Bread & Butter** (ⓦbreadandbutter.com) fashion festival, which takes over the defunct Tempelhof airport to showcase streetwear of the sort that you'll probably see in Berlin's subway the following month. Meanwhile the smallest, least predictable, but often most interesting event is also held in early July: **Projektgalerie** (ⓦprojektgalerie.net) sees many city art galleries open their doors to fashion designers of all stripes.

Another spate of fashion excitement takes place in Berlin in **mid-January**, with Bread & Butter, Berlin Fashion Week and Projektgalerie all reappearing in smaller form and with different seasonal collections.

Galerie Barbara Thumm Markgrafenstr. 68, Mitte ☏030 128 39 03 47, ⓦbthumm.de; U-Kochstrasse. British and Berlin-based artists working in all media; one of several galleries on or around this city block. Tues–Sat 11am–6pm.

Galerie Thomas Schulte Charlottenstr. 24, Charlottenburg ☏030 20 60 89 90, ⓦgaleriethomas schulte.de; S-Charlottenburg. Well-presented conceptual art, photography and sculpture; frequently featuring established artists from America. Tues–Sat noon–6pm.

Hamburger Bahnhof/Museum für Gegenwart Invalidenstr. 50–51, Tiergarten ⓦhamburger bahnhof.de; U- & S-Hauptbahnhof. The state-owned Hamburger Bahnhof (see p.106), the flagship venue for contemporary art in Berlin, has an exciting, heavyweight post-1950s collection that includes the likes of Andy Warhol, Marcel Duchamp and Joseph Beuys. Entry €14. Tues, Wed & Fri–Sun 10am–6pm, Thurs 10am–8pm.

★ **Kunst-Werke Berlin** Auguststr. 69, Mitte ☏030 243 45 90, ⓦkw-berlin.de; U-Oranienburger Tor. High-profile gallery (see p.82) in a former factory building, where exhibits often include astute reflections on contemporary Berlin. Principal organizer of the Berlin Biennale (ⓦberlinbiennale .de). Entry €6. Wed–Mon noon–7pm, Thurs noon–9pm.

★ **Kunstraum Bethanien** Mariannenplatz 2, Kreuzberg ☏030 902 98 14 55, ⓦkunstraumkreuzberg .de; U-Görlitzerbahnhof. An attempt to match offbeat neighbourhood art in a wing of a giant old hospital in a Kreuzberg park. There's space for graffiti art, local fashion and artists from developing countries who'd struggle to get space elsewhere. Daily noon–7pm.

Loock Wohnmaschine Potsdamer Str. 63, Mitte ☏030 394 09 68 50, ⓦloock.info; U-Kurfürstenstrasse. Young gallery owner Friedrich Loock opened his first gallery in his flat in the Spandauer Vorstadt and now specializes in promoting the works of young, predominantly local, artists. Tues–Sat 11am–6pm.

Raab Galerie Fasanenstr. 72, Charlottenburg ☏030 261 92 18, ⓦraab-galerie.de; S-Savignyplatz. Avant-garde and contemporary art at this popular meeting place for the art in-crowd. Mon–Fri 10am–7pm, Sat 10am–4pm.

Zwinger Galerie Mansteinstr. 5, Mitte ☏030 28 59 89 07, ⓦzwinger-galerie.de; U-Weinmeisterstrasse. One of the city's most important galleries, presenting a mixture of avant-garde and conventional art. Tues–Fri 2–7pm, Sat noon–6pm.

CLASSICAL MUSIC

For years classical music in Berlin meant one man and one orchestra: Herbert von Karajan and the Berlin Philharmonic. Since his death in 1989, the **Philharmonie** has had its former supremacy questioned by the rise of the excellent **Deutsches Symphonie Orchester**. Yet the Philharmonic still remains arguably the world's best orchestra, directed since 2002 by Simon Rattle. In addition, many smaller orchestras play at sites in and around the city, and museums and historic buildings often host chamber concerts and recitals. A major annual music festival is the **Festtage** in late March, which is organized by the Staatsoper, but staged both there and at the Berlin Philharmonic. Also popular is the **Musikfest Berlin** (Ⓦberlinerfestspiele.de), an acclaimed international music festival during the first half of September, when guest orchestras arrive from around the world to take part in a programme that features innovative modern works.

ORCHESTRAS AND VENUES

Berliner Symphoniker Ⓦberliner-symphoniker.de. Founded in 1952 and based in the Konzerthaus (see below), this used to be East Berlin's main symphony orchestra, and it maintains its fine reputation today, conducted by Lior Shambadal, though it does not compare to the Philharmonic. Tickets €9–39.

Deutsche Oper Bismarckstr. 35, Charlottenburg ☎030 34 38 43 43, Ⓦdeutscheoperberlin.de; U-Deutsche Oper. Formerly West Berlin's premier opera house, built in 1961 after the Wall cut access to the Staatsoper. Once the city's most prestigious venue in terms of visiting performers, it now shares that honour with its eastern cousin. Tickets €17–162.

Deutsches Symphonie Orchester Ⓦdso-berlin.de. Currently under conductor Tugan Sokhiev since 2012 and with no permanent base, though often at the Philharmonic. Tickets €20–59.

Komische Oper Behrenstr. 55–57, Mitte ☎030 47 99 74 00, Ⓦkomische-oper-berlin.de; S-Unter den Linden. Less traditional than the Staatsoper, but a reliable venue for well-staged operatic and dance productions. The building doesn't look like much from the outside, but the interior is a wonderful 1890s frenzy of red plush, gilt and statuary and a great place to enjoy cutting-edge interpretations of modern works alongside more traditional shows. Tickets €10–149.

Konzerthaus Berlin (Schauspielhaus) Gendarmenmarkt, Mitte ☎030 20 30 90, Ⓦkonzerthaus.de; U-Stadtmitte. Regarded to be among the best classical concert venues in the world, this super venue often serves visiting musicians, orchestras and ensembles but is also the home of the Konzerthausorchester Berlin. Two concert spaces occupy the Schinkel-designed building: the Grosser Konzertsaal for orchestras and its Kammermusiksaal for smaller groups and chamber orchestras. Look out for performances on the Konzerthaus's famed organ. Daily 75min tours of the building cost €3; times vary. Tickets €10–99.

★ **Philharmonie** Herbert-von-Karajan-Str. 1, Mitte ☎030 25 48 80, Ⓦberlin-philharmonic.de; U- & S-Potsdamer Platz. Home to the world-famous Berlin Philharmonic, Hans Scharoun's controversially ugly building is acoustically near-perfect. Conductor Simon Rattle has created his own distinctive sound with the orchestra, moving them away from their traditional Germanic comfort zone of Brahms and Beethoven and into more contemporary music like that of the Finnish composer Magnus Lindberg. The Philharmonie also contains the smaller, more intimate Kammermusiksaal. Your best chance of getting a ticket is when guest orchestras are playing. Tickets €34–138.

Rundfunk Symphonieorchester Berlin Ⓦrsb -online.de. The second-oldest orchestra in Berlin after the Philharmonic, and a little more daring than its older sister. The orchestra appears at both the Philharmonie and the Konzerthaus, and director Marek Janowski often lends his baton to talented guest conductors. Tickets €14–59.

Staatsoper Unter den Linden 5–7, Mitte ☎030 20 35 45 55, Ⓦstaatsoper-berlin.de; U-Friedrichstrasse. The city's oldest and grandest music venue, built for Frederick the Great in 1742 to a design by Knobelsdorff. During the GDR years, political isolation meant that performers didn't match the glamour of the venue, but the appointment of Daniel Barenboim in 1992 as musical director gradually helped bring the Staatsoper to the forefront of the international opera scene. Tickets €14–160.

THEATRE

Mainstream **civic and private theatres** in Berlin tend to be dull, unadventurous and expensive – though last-minute tickets can cut costs – but the **fringe** scene is exciting. The thousands of eager young Germans that flock to the city every year, rent a space, and stage their productions, make Berlin a major venue for **experimental work**, and if your German is up to it, a number of such groups are worth the ticket price. The scene is active, though it's worth remembering that many theatre companies take a break in August; check under "Off-Theater" in Tip or Zitty (see p.33) for up-to-the-minute listings. Groups that have the word Freie in their name are not dependent on city or state subsidies, and thus are not subject to the same creative constraints.

CIVIC AND PRIVATE THEATRES

★ **Admiralspalast** Friedrichstr. 101, Mitte ☎030 47 99 74 99, Ⓦadmiralspalast.de; U- & S-Friedrichstrasse. The Admiralspalast provides much the same round-the-clock entertainment as it did in its 1920s heyday – though without the brothel it incorporated then. These days it's the eclectic events programme, including comedy, live music, burlesque and operas, plus a casino, that draws in the punters. Tickets €22–63.

Berliner Ensemble Bertolt-Brecht-Platz 1, Mitte ☎030 28 40 81 55, Ⓦberliner-ensemble.de; U- & S-Friedrichstrasse. Brecht's old theatre still features a lot of his work, though thankfully the productions are a little livelier than in GDR days and much of the rest of the programme is given over to a range of reliable pieces by Henrik Ibsen, Friedrich Schiller and the like. There are also occasional experimental productions on the Probebühne (rehearsal stage). Tickets €5–30.

Deutsches Theater Schumannstr. 13a, Mitte ☎ 030 28 44 12 25, ☒ deutsches-theater.de; U-Oranienburger Tor. Good, solid productions taking in everything from Schiller to Mamet make this one of Berlin's best theatres and frequently sold out. Also includes a second theatre, the Kammerspiele. Tickets €4–48.

Maxim-Gorki-Theater Am Festungsgraben 2, Mitte ☎ 030 20 22 11 15, ☒ gorki.de; U- & S-Friedrichstrasse. This 1827 theatre, one of Berlin's largest, puts on consistently good literary and filmic adaptations. The work of Russian socialist-realist author Maxim Gorky is regularly featured, as you might expect, along with contemporary pieces from the likes of Fassbinder. The Studiobühne stage shows more experimental works. Tickets €12–30.

Renaissance Theater Knesebeckstr. 100, Charlottenburg ☎ 030 312 42 02, ☒ renaissance-theater .de; U-Ernst-Reuter-Platz. Contemporary international theatre, mainly productions with strong social or emotional themes. Also readings and musical revues. Tickets €14–48.

Schaubühne am Lehniner Platz Kurfürstendamm 153, Wilmersdorf ☎ 030 89 00 23, ☒ schaubuehne.de; U-Adenauerplatz. State-of-the-art theatre that hosts performances of the classics and some experimental pieces, with plenty of young energy and an accent on dance. Advance booking advisable. Tickets €7–43.

Theater des Westens Kantstr. 12, Charlottenburg ☎ 030 31 90 30, ☒ theater-des-westens.de; U- & S-Zoologischer Garten. Musicals and light opera, and the occasional Broadway-style show, sometimes in English. Housed in a beautiful fin-de-siècle building. Tickets €40–120.

Theater im Palais Am Festungsgraben, Mitte ☎ 030 201 06 93, ☎ theater-im-palais.de; U- & S-Friedrichstrasse. Traditional pieces performed with a contemporary spin

– conversational delivery, music, storytelling – while preserving theatrical simplicity. Expect pieces by the likes of Fontane, Heine or E.T.A. Hoffmann. Ticket €5–25.

★ **Volksbühne** Linienstr. 227, Mitte ☎ 030 24 06 57 77, ☒ volksbuehne-berlin.de; U-Rosa-Luxemburg-Platz. One of Berlin's most adventurous and interesting theatres, often with highly provocative performances: nudity and throwing things at audiences crop up fairly regularly; a second stage also shows modern adaptations of classics. Tickets €10–27.

EXPERIMENTAL AND FREE THEATRE

BAT Studiotheater Belforter Str. 15, Prenzlauer Berg ☎ 030 755 41 77 77, ☒ bat-berlin.de; U-Senefelder Platz. Originally a "workers' and students' theatre", founded in 1975, this can usually be relied on to come up with challenging experimental offerings. Tickets €8.

English Theatre Berlin Fidicinstr. 40, Kreuzberg ☎ 030 691 12 11, ☒ etberlin.de; U-Platz der Luftbrücke. Tiny courtyard theatre specializing in English-language fringe productions: theatre, comedy and even films and concerts. Tickets €5–14.

Hebbel Am Ufer Hallesches Ufer 32, Kreuzberg ☎ 030 25 90 04 27, ☒ hebbel-am-ufer.de; U-Hallesches Tor. Spread across three neighbouring locations, this is the place for short runs of varied theatre, performance and dance productions, sometimes in English. Often interesting, modern and experimental. The theatre also features four major annual contemporary dance festivals. Tickets €8–25.

★ **Schaubude** Greifswalder Str. 81–84, Prenzlauer Berg ☎ 030 423 43 14, ☒ schaubude-berlin.de; S- & U-Greifswalder Strasse. Former GDR puppet theatre now presenting shows for adults and children – from Hansel and Gretel to Faust to performances on atomic physics. The kids' programme starts aged 4 and their tickets are €4. Tickets €9.50–12.50.

Theater 89 Torstr. 216, Mitte ☎ 030 282 46 56, ☒ theater89.de; U-Oranienburger Tor. A small venue putting on modern works and literary adaptations in a simple and unaffected style. Tickets €15.

CABARET

In the 1920s and 1930s, Berlin had a rich and intense **cabaret scene**: hundreds of small clubs presented acts that were often deeply satirical and political. When the Nazis came to power these quickly disappeared, to be replaced by anodyne entertainments in line with Party views. Sadly, the cabaret scene never recovered: most of what's on show today is drag or semi-clad titillation for tourists. However, a few places are worth trying, notably the Chamäleon, which plays host to eclectic acts. Be warned, though, that most cabaret venues make their money by charging very high prices at the bar.

CABARET VENUES

★ **Ausland** Lychener Str. 60 ☎ 030 447 70 08, ☒ ausland-berlin.de; U-Prenzlauer Allee. Non-profit experimental club in an undecorated bunker in front of an apartment block. It's committed to promoting performances and events that struggle to find a home

anywhere else, so the range is huge, from free jazz and sound art gigs to movies and installations. Door fees go directly to the artists. Tickets around €7.

Bar Jeder Vernunft Scharperstr. 24, Wilmersdorf ☎ 030 883 15 82, ☒ bar-jeder-vernunft.de; U-Spichernstrasse. Hip young venue for all manner of

FROM TOP CHAMÄLEON (P.222); PHILHARMONIE (P.219) >

modern cabaret and comedy with the occasional chanson act too; a good bet, though a good knowledge of German is often needed. Tickets €15–30.

Chamäleon Rosenthaler Str. 40–41 (in the Hackeschen Höfe), Mitte ☎030 400 05 90, ⓦchamaeleonberlin.de; S-Hackescher Markt. Lively, innovative cabaret and vaudeville shows with jugglers, acrobats and the like. Seating is around tables and there's a bar, so there's no harm in turning up early. Tickets €36–49.

Distel Friedrichstr. 101, Mitte ☎030 203 00 00, ⓦadmiralspalast.de; U- & S-Friedrichstrasse. Long-standing satirical cabaret theatre in the Admiralspalast (see p.219) whose performances once even daringly highlighted the paradoxes and frustrations of the pre-Wende GDR. You'll need German. Tickets €14–28.

Friedrichstadtpalast Friedrichstr. 107, Mitte ☎030 23 26 23 26, ⓦfriedrichstadtpalast.de; U-Oranienburger Tor. Big, flashy variety shows with leggy chorus girls and fantastical costumes. Tickets €17–105.

Kleine Nachtrevue Kurfürstenstr. 116, Schöneberg ☎030 218 89 50, ⓦkleine-nachtrevue.de; U-Wittenbergplatz. Berlin burlesque, intimate and dimly lit, going for that 1920s feel; much titillation but pretty hit-or-miss in terms of quality. Tickets €30.

La Vie en Rose Flughafen Tempelhof, Kreuzberg ☎030 69 51 30 00, ⓦlavieenrose-berlin.de; U-Platz der Luftbrücke. A drag variety revue with lots of glitter and lots of skin, magic and comedy in one of the old Tempelhof airport buildings. There's also a piano bar. Tickets €25–32.

Roter Salon and Grüner Salon in the Volksbühne Rosa-Luxemburg-Platz, Mitte. Lots of interesting and varied goings on, with occasional performances in English.

Scheinbar Variete Monumentenstr. 9, Schöneberg ☎030 784 55 39, ⓦscheinbar.de. U- & S-Yorckstrasse. Experimental and fun; open stage on many nights. Tickets €8–11.

Tipi am Kanzleramt Grosse Querallee, Tiergarten ☎030 39 06 65 50, ⓦtipi-am-kanzleramt.de; U–Bundestag. Mixed cabaret performances in a huge permanent tent. Shows start with gourmet food and then progress to lightweight, but often entertaining galas. Shows Mon–Fri 8pm, Sun 7pm. Tickets €15–45.

Wintergarten Potsdamer Str. 96, Tiergarten ☎030 588 43 40, ⓦwintergarten-variete.de; U-Kurfürstenstrasse. Glitzy attempt to recreate the Berlin of the 1920s, with live acts from all over the world – cabaret, musicians, dance, mime, magicians. Meals served while you watch. Tickets €26–60.

DANCE

Apart from those regular venues listed below, expect dance performances to pop up at various theatres, particularly the more experimental ones. You can also see modern ballet and experimental works at the **Komische Oper** (see p.219).

DANCE COMPANIES AND VENUES

★ **Sophiensaele** Sophienstr. 18, Mitte ☎030 283 52 66; U-Weinmeisterstrasse. Experimental and avant-garde dance stronghold in a refurbished 1905 craftsmen's association centre – its programme also incorporates unconventional fringe theatre, music and performance art. Many plays are in English. Tickets around €15.

Staatsballett ⓦstaatsballett-berlin.de. Berlin's premier ballet company performs at the Staatsoper and Deutsche Oper (see p.219). Tickets €14–86.

Tanzfabrik Berlin Möckernstr. 68, Kreuzberg ☎030 786 58 61, ⓦtanzfabrik-berlin.de; U- & S-Yorckstrasse. Experimental and contemporary works, usually fresh and exciting. This is also Berlin's biggest contemporary dance school. Tickets free–€13.

FILM

When the all-night drinking starts to get too much, it's always possible to wind down in front of the silver screen. The independent film scene is thriving in Berlin, and art house cinemas abound. *Tip* and *Zitty* have detailed film listings; if a film is listed as **OF** or **OV** (*Originalfassung*) it's in its original language; **OmU** (*Originalfassung mit Untertiteln*) indicates that it has German subtitles. Otherwise, the film will have been dubbed into German. Occasionally films are listed as **OmE** – original with English subtitles. The small selection of cinemas below are either particularly strong on screening English-language versions of films or just particularly atmospheric. **Ticket prices** range from €7 to €11, but there are always reductions for children and sometimes for students, too. Also, one day a week, designated *Kinotag* ("KT" in the listings magazines), normally a Mon, Tues or Wed, the price generally halves. Much smaller than the huge **Berlinale** film festival (see p.223), but equally global, is the **Jewish Film Festival** (ⓦjffb.de) held in Berlin and Potsdam in April.

CINEMAS

Babylon Dresdener Str. 126, Kreuzberg ☎030 61 60 96 93, ⓦyorck.de; U-Kottbusser Tor. New films in English, with and without subtitles. There are another dozen cinemas in the same cinema group in central Berlin; check the website. *Kinotag* Mon.

★ **Babylon Mitte** Rosa-Luxemburg-Str. 30, Mitte ☎030 242 59 69, ⓦbabylonberlin.de; U-Rosa-

THE BERLINALE

Every February, the **Berlinale** film festival (ⓦ berlinale.de) dominates the city's cultural life. Second only to Cannes among European film festivals, it offers a staggering number of movies from around the world and is much more accessible to the public than the French festival. The programme includes many premieres, usually shown in their original versions with German (sometimes English) subtitles. Action is concentrated around the Potsdamer Platz multiplexes (see below), though many screenings are repeated across the city. A limited number of season tickets (around €150) go on sale a week before the opening. Otherwise, advance tickets can be bought at the ticket booths in the Potsdamer Platz Arkaden shopping mall, the second floor of the Europa Center (see p.110) or at the *International* cinema (see below). Tickets for the day of the show must be purchased at the cinema box office. During the festival, programming information is available in the regular listings magazines or the festival's own daily magazine, *Berlinale*, available at all participating theatres.

Luxemburg-Platz. Central Berlin's best rep cinema in a landmark theatre. A mix of indie, trash and cult movies, as well as concerts; films regularly have English subtitles.

Central Rosenthalerstr. 39, Mitte ⓣ 030 28 59 99 73, ⓦ kino-central.de; S-Hackescher Markt. The main programme is almost all German, but quirky midnight events are often held and are often in English. Beside Hackeschen Höfe. *Kinotag* Tues & Wed.

Cinestar Sony Center Potsdamer Str. 4, Tiergarten ⓣ 030 26 06 62 60, ⓦ cinestar.de; U- & S-Potsdamer Platz. Eight-screen cinema in the bowels of the Sony Center, with almost every screening — mostly Hollywood blockbusters — in the original (usually English) language.

Hackesche Höfe Rosenthalerstr. 40–41 (in Hackeschen Höfe), Mitte ⓣ 030 283 46 03, ⓦ hoefekino.de, S-Hackescher Markt. Five-screen multiplex, on the top floor of the busy Hackeschen Höfe, showing upscale independent foreign films and documentaries, some in English. Often sold out at weekends, but they take phone reservations. *Kinotag* Mon & Tues.

International Karl-Marx-Allee 33, Mitte ⓣ 030 24 75 60 11, ⓦ yorck.de; U-Schillingstrasse. Big, comfortable GDR cinema showing new releases — of interest in part because of its status as a landmark. *Kinotag* Mon, smaller discounts Tues & Wed.

Odeon Hauptstr. 116, Schöneberg ⓣ 030 78 70 40 19, ⓦ yorck.de; U-Innsbrucker Platz. If you're after the more intelligent English-language releases, the *Odeon* will often have them first. *Kinotag* Mon, smaller discounts Tues & Wed.

★ **Zeughaus-Kino** Unter den Linden 2, Mitte ⓣ 030 20 30 44 21, ⓦ dhm.de/kino; S-Hackescher Markt. Cinema in the Zeughaus, which often unearths fascinating films from the pre- and postwar years.

15

BERLINER KUNSTMARKT

Shopping

In addition to the usual multi-storey department stores that you can find all around Europe, Berlin has many small, interesting shops that are perfect for browsing. A remarkable number of quirky specialist stores are thriving; we've reviewed some of the more interesting and distinctive places. As a rule the level of customer service is excellent – and if a shop can't supply you with what you need the assistants will not hesitate to suggest alternatives. Unsurprisingly, too, Berlin is an excellent place for secondhand shopping. If you like foraging you'll love the city's many flea markets – a number of which are veritable treasure troves of Eastern Bloc relics – and its interesting vintage clothes shops.

Glitz and dazzle are the prerogatives of **City West**, with its 3km of large chain stores on or around the **Kurfürstendamm; Friedrichstrasse** in the east, though more modest in size, is just as opulent. The largest and best central malls are the Potsdamer Platz Arkaden and the Alexa Centre just southeast of **Alexanderplatz**. Meanwhile, many of the city's funkiest speciality shops and expensive boutiques are concentrated in **Charlottenburg**, **Mitte** and **Prenzlauer Berg**. Ethnic foods and "alternative" businesses are mostly to be found in **Kreuzberg**, along Oranienstrasse and Bergmannstrasse.

ESSENTIALS

Listings Though we've selected the best of Berlin's shops below, the list is far from exhaustive. The yellow pages (*Gelbe Seiten*; ⓦ gelbeseiten.de) can be useful in finding further specialist shops, but an even better idea is to ask around at similar places.

Opening hours Large shops in central Berlin are generally open from Monday to Saturday from 10am to 8pm, while smaller shops or those outside the centre will tend to close two hours earlier. Supermarkets and other shops in main stations, particularly the Hauptbahnhof, are open longer hours, daily from around 8am to 10pm. We've included individual opening hours in the reviews below.

Credit cards In most larger places credit cards are widely accepted, but don't rely on being able to use them everywhere.

BOOKS AND MAGAZINES

Berlin boasts a great variety of new and secondhand bookstores, and it's an ideal city for leisurely browsing. Quite a few places sell **English-language books**, most of them on or around Knesebeckstr., Berlin's main street for book shopping.

ENGLISH-LANGUAGE AND GENERAL

Another Country Riemannstr. 7, Kreuzberg ☎ 030 69 40 11 60, ⓦ anothercountry.de; U-Gneisenaustrasse; map p.118. English-language secondhand books sold in this intimate living-room-like space, where you can borrow any book for €1.50. Tues–Fri 11am–8pm, Sat & Sun noon–4pm.

Books in Berlin Goethestr. 69, Charlottenburg ☎ 030 313 12 33, ⓦ booksinberlin.de; U-Ernst-Reuter-Platz; map p.108. Small bookstore with a good selection of English-language history and popular fiction, some secondhand. Mon–Fri noon–8pm, Sat 10am–4pm.

⭐ **Dussmann** Friedrichstr. 90, Mitte ☎ 030 20 25 11 11, ⓦ kulturkaufhaus.de; U- & S-Friedrichstrasse; map p.36. Giant emporium with five levels of books, CDs and ... more books. A small shop at the back also features books about music. Mon–Sat 10am–midnight.

Hugendubel Potsdamer Platz Arkaden, Mitte (U- & S-Potsdamer Platz; map pp.90–91; Tauentzienstr. 21–24, City West (U-Wittenbergplatz; map p.108); ☎ 0181 48 44 84, ⓦ hugendubel.de. Huge general bookstore with a section devoted to English-language paperback fiction. Potsdamer Platz Mon–Sat 9.30am–9pm; Tauentzienstr. Mon–Sat 9.30am–8pm.

Marga Schoeller Knesebeckstr. 33, City West ☎ 030 881 11 12, ⓦ margaschoeller.de; S-Savignyplatz; map p.108. Opened in 1929 by Frau Schoeller, this bookstore is one of the longest-running in Europe, and was once a focal point for West Berlin's postwar literary scene. Schoeller's son now runs the store, which continues to sell a fantastic range of German- and English-language books on the arts as well as fiction, history and biographies; with lots on Berlin. Mon–Wed 9.30am–7pm, Thurs & Fri 9.30am–8pm, Sat 9.30am–6pm.

St George's Bookshop Wörther Str. 27, Prenzlauer Berg ☎ 030 81 79 83 33; U-Eberswalder Strasse; map p.132. Delightful British-run bookstore selling a fine selection of new and used English-language books. There's a sofa to chill on and free wi-fi; they also buy used books. Mon–Fri 11am–8pm, Sat 11am–7pm.

LOCAL INTEREST

Berlin Story Unter den Linden 26, Mitte ☎ 030 20 45 38 42, ⓦ berlinstory.de; U- & S-Friedrichstrasse; map p.36. The city's most extensive bookshop on Berlin itself, with everything from travel guides to specialist histories, and offered in a range of languages. Daily 10am–8pm.

THE ARTS

Artificium Rosenthaler Str. 40–41, in the Hackeschen Höfe, Mitte ☎ 030 30 87 22 80, ⓦ artificium.com; S-Hackescher Markt; map pp.72–73. Nineteenth- and twentieth-century art, architecture, photography and the like. Mon–Thurs 10am–8pm, Fri & Sat 10am–9pm.

Bücherbogen Stadtbahnbogen 593, Charlottenburg ☎ 030 31 86 95 11, ⓦ buecherbogen.com, S-Savignyplatz; map p.108. Airy and spacious spot under the S-arches where you can spend hours browsing books on art, architecture, film and photography. Plenty of English-language books – all non-fiction. Mon–Fri 10am–8pm, Sat 10am–6pm.

⭐ **Museum für Fotografie** Jebensstr. 2, City West ☎ 030 20 90 55 66; U- & S-Zoologischer Garten; map p.108. Small bookshop in the museum foyer, where you can browse a glut of books on photography, art and design – many at reduced prices – without having to enter the museum itself. Wed & Fri–Sun 10am–6pm, Thurs 10am–10pm.

16

Onkel & Onkel Oranienstr. 195, Kreuzberg ☎030 61 07 39 57; U-Kottbusser Tor; map pp.126–127. This magazine shop specializes in graphic design, photography and street art and also publishes its own titles. Mon–Sat 10am–6pm.

★ **Overkillshop** Köpenicker Str. 195a, Kreuzberg ☎030 69 50 61 26; U-Schlesisches Tor; map pp.126–127. An essential spot for street art and graffiti fans with lots of graffiti-related books and magazines along with all the paraphernalia you need to make your mark. Mon–Sat 11am–8pm.

MAGAZINES AND COMICS

★ **Do You Read Me?** Auguststr. 28, Mitte ☎030 69 54 96 95; S-Rosenthaler Platz; map pp.72–73. A magazine lover's paradise, this multilingual store offers a vast assortment of reading material from around the world, covering fashion and photography, art and architecture. Check the website for regular readings and events. Mon–Sat 10am–7.30pm.

Grober Unfug Zossener Str. 33, Kreuzberg ☎030 69 10 14 90, ⓦgroberunfug.de; U-Gneisenaustrasse; map p.118. Large display of international comics, plus T-shirts and cards on sale. Often hosts exhibitions of cartoonists' work in the small gallery upstairs. Mon–Fri 11am–7pm, Sat 11am–6pm.

TRAVEL

Chatwins Goltzstr. 40, Schöneberg ☎030 21 75 69 04, ⓦchatwins.de; U-Nollendorfplatz; map p.113. Friendly bookshop run for and by travellers, with a vast array of guidebooks and travel writing. Mon–Fri 10am–7pm, Sat 10am–4pm.

Schropp Hardenbergstr. 9a, City West ☎030 23 55 73 20, ⓦlandkartenschropp.de, U- & S-Zoologischer Garten; map p.108. Specialist store with a large, well-chosen selection of travel books and maps, including detailed cycling maps of Berlin and Germany. Mon–Fri 10am–8pm, Sat 10am–6pm.

MUSIC

Berlin has plenty of small **record shops**, generally dedicated to just one style of music, and many of which are thriving alongside the city's dynamic clubbing scene.

16

Core Tex Records Oranienstr. 3, Kreuzberg ☎030 61 28 00 50; U-Görlitzer Bahnhof; map pp.126–127. The best place in the city to stock up on punk or hardcore music, as well as related T-shirts, accessories and books. Mon–Fri 11am–7pm, Sat 11am–4pm.

DaCapo Kastanienallee 96, Prenzlauer Berg ☎030 448 17 71, ⓦda-capo-vinyl.de; U-Eberswalderstrasse; map p.132. New and used vinyl shop with a wide selection of jazz, 1960s–80s rock and releases on East German label Amiga. Tues–Fri noon–7pm, Sat noon–6pm.

Dussmann Friedrichstr. 90, Mitte ☎030 20 25 11 11, ⓦkulturkaufhaus.de; U- & S-Friedrichstrasse; map p.36. Good selection of rock, jazz, dance, world and international vocalists. The basement is devoted entirely to classical. You can spend a whole afternoon listening to CDs without being interrupted by a salesperson. Mon–Sat 10am–midnight.

Hard Wax Paul-Lincke-Ufer 44a, Kreuzberg ☎030 61 13 01 11, ⓦhardwax.com; U-Görlitzer Bahnhof; map pp.126–127. Premier electronic music specialist. Techno, trance: you name it, they should have it, and if they haven't, they'll get it for you. Mon–Sat noon–8pm.

L&P Classics Welserstr. 28, Schöneberg ☎030 88 04 30 43, ⓦlpclassics.de; U-Wittenbergplatz; map p.113. Store devoted entirely to classical music with extremely knowledgeable and helpful staff. Mon–Sat 10am–8pm.

Melting Point Kastanienallee 55, Mitte ☎030 44 04 71 31; U-Rosenthaler Platz; map pp.72–73. This place is

well established, having been a techno and house stalwart since the 1990s; there's also funk, Afro, Latin and more. Masses of vinyl and some CDs. Mon–Sat noon–8pm.

Mr Dead & Mrs Free Bülowstr. 5, Schöneberg ☎030 215 14 49, ⓦdeadandfree.com; U-Nollendorfplatz; map p.113. Lovely, dusty little music shop crammed full of everything from the latest imports to rare vintage albums: primarily pop, folk, indie and country vinyl on independent labels. Mon–Fri noon–7pm, Sat 11am–4pm.

Oye Oderberger Str. 4, Prenzlauer Berg ☎030 66 64 78 21; U-Eberswalder Strasse; map p.132. Originally devoted to Latin, soul and funk vinyl, but now covering an impressive range of styles, from Afrobeat and blip-hop to Berlin house and techno. Mon–Fri 1–8pm, Sat noon–8pm.

Soultrade Sanderstr. 29, Neukölln ☎030 694 52 57, ⓦsoultrade.de; U-Schönleinstrasse; map pp.126–127. Specialists in soul, hip-hop, funk, house and jazz. Mon & Wed 11am–7pm, Tues, Thurs & Fri 11am–8pm, Sat noon–6pm.

★ **Space Hall** Zossener Str. 33 & 35, Kreuzberg ☎030 53 08 87 18; U-Gneisenaustrasse; map p.118. This two-store, multi-roomed record shop is one of the best stocked in the city, with a large CD collection at no. 33 (rock, pop, electronic, rap) and DJ-friendly vinyl at no. 35. No. 33: Mon–Sat 11am–8pm; No. 35: Mon–Wed & Sat 11am–8pm, Thurs & Fri 11am–10pm.

CLOTHING AND ACCESSORIES

Although they like to think of themselves as such, Berliners aren't exactly trendsetters, and despite the many innovative designers in the city their work is mostly small-scale and tends to lack international impact. Still, it's possible to pick up **bargains** at the many **secondhand** clothes stores: you'll find unusual (and stylish) pieces here – including many odd items from the East – at low prices. The main **shopping areas** at Wilmersdorferstrasse U-Bahn, and Walter-Schreiber-Platz U-Bahn, Steglitz, have plenty of inexpensive own-brand styles. Ku'damm and Friedrichstrasse boast designer clothes shops targeting the rich and conservative, as well as several leather outlets with cheap but good-quality jackets, and some excellent shoe shops. For the most cutting-edge boutiques head to the Hackescher Markt area, where urban styles dominate: think funky trainers, not glamorous heels. Many specialize in a sort of 1970s-revival-meets-GDR-*Ostalgie* look.

FASHION

Allet Rund Dresdener Str. 16, Kreuzberg ☎ 0163 440 72 89; U-Kottbusser Tor; map p.126–127. Women's fashion for larger sizes (42–60): everything is fairtrade; the fabrics are European and the clothes are made in Kreuzberg. Tues–Fri noon–7pm, Sat noon–5pm.

Apartment Memhardstr. 8, Mitte ☎ 030 28 04 22 51, ⓦ apartmentberlin.de. S- & U-Alexanderplatz; map pp.72–73. You'll have to be careful not to walk right past what looks like an all-white art space: the goods lie downstairs (follow the spiral staircase), where you'll find jeans, jackets, shoes and accessories with a distinctly Berlin twist. For retro styles, check out *Cash* around the corner. Mon–Fri 11am–7pm, Sat noon–7pm.

Claudia Skoda Mulackstr. 8, Mitte ☎ 030 40 04 18 84, ⓦ claudiaskoda.com; U-Weinmeisterstrasse; map pp.72–73. Berlin's knit-master and most famous designer, whose shop is filled with her renowned and instantly recognizable knitwear. Chic and expensive and geared mostly towards women. Mon–Sat 11.30am–7.30pm.

Eisdieler Kastanienallee 12, Prenzlauer Berg ☎ 030 28 38 12 91, ⓦ eisdieler.de; U-Eberswalder Strasse; map p.132. Innovative international urban streetwear along with its own custom clothing (hoodies, sneakers, T-shirts) and an impressive range of vintage shades from the likes of Cartier, Porsche and Ray Ban. Mon–Fri noon–8pm, Sat 11am–7pm.

Esther Perbandt Almstadtstr. 3, Mitte ☎ 030 88 53 67 91; U-Weinmeisterstrasse; map pp.72–73. The Berlin fashion scene veteran specializes in pricey avant-garde and androgynous clothing; complemented by bags, belts, jewellery and more. Mon–Fri 10am–7pm, Sat noon–6pm.

★ **Flagship Store** Oderberger Str. 53, Prenzlauer Berg ☎ 030 43 73 53 27, ⓦ flagshipstore-berlin.de; U-Eberswalderstrasse; map p.132. Great one-stop shop to explore the urbane collections of some thirty local designers with a vast range of clothing and accessories (for women and men), plus shoes, magazines and more. Mon–Sat noon–8pm.

God Bless You Kastanienallee 31, Prenzlauer Berg ☎ 030 29 66 68 80; U-Eberswalder Strasse; map p.132. Quirky dressers will adore this store, which stocks unusual street designs for men and women as well as iron-on-patches (guitars, grenades) so you can customize your own clothing. Mon–Sat 11am–8pm.

Herz + Stöhr Winterfeldtstr. 52, Schöneberg ☎ 030 216 44 25; U-Nollendorfplatz; map p.113. Intelligent, elegant designs from this German fashion duo – the dresses and suits are grown-up but not dowdy, and everything can be altered to fit. Mon–Fri 11am–7pm, Sat 11am–4pm.

Lisa D. Rosenthaler Str. 40–41 (in the Hackeschen Höfe), Mitte ☎ 030 282 90 61, ⓦ lisad.com; S-Hackescher Markt; map pp.72–73. One of Berlin's very few local designers to have made a name for herself, Lisa D. favours fitted dresses in muted colours. Mon–Sat 11am–7pm, Sun 11am–5pm.

Mientus Wilmersdorfer Str. 73, City West ☎ 030 323 90 77, ⓦ mientus.com; U-Wilmersdorfer Strasse; map p.108. Casual and formal up-to-the-minute menswear, ranging in price from reasonable to outrageously expensive. Mon–Sat 10am–7pm.

Nix Oranienburger Str. 32, Mitte ☎ 030 281 11 80 44, ⓦ nix.de; S-Oranienburger Strasse; map pp.72–73. Unusual, robust and practical designs for women from a couple of young east Berliners. Mon–Sat 11am–8pm.

Respectmen Neue Schönhauser Str. 14, Mitte ☎ 030 283 50 10, ⓦ respectmen.de; S-Hackescher Markt; map pp.72–73. Good tailoring and nice design mark out the suits and casual wear of this men's store. Mon–Fri noon–8pm, Sat noon–7pm.

Soma Alte Schönhauser Str. 27, Mitte ☎ 030 281 93 80, ⓦ soma-berlin.de; S-Hackescher Markt; map pp.72–73. Young Berlin designers and clubwear in the front of the shop, secondhand gear in the rear. Mon–Fri noon–8pm, Sat noon–6pm.

Wasted German Youth Memhardstr. 1, Mitte ☎ 0177 248 48 58; U-Weinmeisterstrasse; map pp.72–73. New Zealand-born designer and artist Paul Snowden has made a name for himself in Berlin with his savvy, techno-influenced slogans on T-shirts, hoodies and more. Ravers rejoice. Tues–Fri 2–7pm, Sat noon–7pm.

WeSC Münzstr. 14–16 (entrance Max-Beer-Str.), Mitte ☎ 030 60 05 92 19; U-Weinmeisterstrasse; map pp.72–73. Swedish collective that caters for the skate- and snowboard community with a broad line of clothing, shades and other cool accessories. Mon–Sat 11am–8pm.

16

SHOES

Luccico Bergmannstr. 8, Kreuzberg ☎ 030 216 65 17, ⓦ luccico.de; U-Mehringdamm; map p.118. Wild and wacky Italian shoes, plus plainer varieties. Four other Berlin locations, including Oranienburger Str. 23. All stores: Mon–Fri noon–8pm, Sat 11am–8pm.

Mad Flavor Solmsstr. 33, Kreuzberg ☎ 030 312 49 63, ⓦ madflavor.de; U-Gneisenaustrasse; map p.118. Trendy sneakers for the hip-hop and club crowd. Mon–Sat noon–8pm.

Thatchers Kastanienallee 21, Prenzlauer Berg ☎ 030 24 62 77 51; U-Eberswalder Strasse; map p.132. Upmarket fashion store for women who like their dresses, skirts and shirts classy and sexy but not over the top. Perfect place for sensual evening dresses and sophisticated club wear. Mon–Fri 11am–7pm, Sat noon–6pm.

★ **Trippen** Hackeschen Höfe, Rosenthaler Str. 40, Mitte ☎ 030 28 39 13 37, ⓦ trippen.com; S-Hackescher Markt; map pp.72–73. Hot Berlin design company specializing in wooden-soled shoes with a rounded toe, but selling men's and women's shoes for every occasion in a range of materials. This is the flagship store, with several other branches in the city. Footwear can be made to order. Mon–Fri 11am–7pm, Sat 10am–5pm.

ACCESSORIES AND UNDERWEAR

Fiona Bennett Potsdamer Str. 81–83, Schöneberg ☎ 030 28 09 63 30, ⓦ fionabennett.com; U-Kurfürs -tenstrasse; map p.113. Avant-garde designer hats for men and women. Mon–Wed 10am–6pm, Thurs & Fri noon–8pm, Sat noon–6pm.

Freitag Store Berlin Max-Beer-Str. 3, Mitte ☎ 030 24 63 69 61; ⓦ freitag.ch; U-Weinmeisterstrasse; map pp.72–73. Swiss merchant of bags, wallets and the like all made from old truck tarps. Each is unique and their fatigued, reused look very at home in Berlin. Plus a small number of fixed-speed bikes to loan out for the day for free; arrive early to secure one. Mon–Fri 11am–8pm, Sat 11am–7pm.

IC Berlin Max-Beer-Str. 17, Mitte ☎ 030 417 17 70, ⓦ ic-berlin.de; U-Weinmeisterstrasse; map pp.72–73. Internationally famous spectacles thanks to the wonderful designs of the handmade screwless frames, and worn by a wide range of celebs from Tom Cruise to Shakira. Pricey. Mon–Sat 11am–8pm.

Körpernah Massanenstr. 8, Schöneberg ☎ 030 215 74 71, ⓦ koerpernah-berlin.de; U-Nollendorfplatz; map p.113. Fashionable underwear and lingerie for both sexes in every possible size. Mon–Fri 10am–6.30pm. Sat 10am–3pm.

Michaela Binder Gipsstr. 13, Mitte ☎ 030 28 38 48 69, ⓦ michaelabinder.de; U-Weinmeisterstrasse; map pp.72–73. Smart shop stocking Binder's stylish rings, bracelets, ear studs and necklaces in clean, basic shapes, from silver and gold. There's also a line of (cheaper) steel and stone vases. Tues–Fri noon–7pm, Sat noon–4pm.

Mykita Rosa-Luxemburg-Str. 6, Mitte ☎ 030 67 30 87 15, ⓦ mykita.com; U- & S-Alexanderplatz; map pp.72–73. Berlin-based company that has achieved international fame due to the stylish twists of its sunglasses and spectacles. Mon–Fri 11am–6pm, Sat noon–6pm.

Rio Bleibtreustr. 52, City West ☎ 030 313 31 52, ⓦ rio-modeschmuck-berlin.de; S-Savignyplatz; map p.108. Decorative costume jewellery, with lots of unusual offerings from Paris and Milan, as well as their own line, named "after 5pm" for its natural evening-wear flamboyance and glamour. Also specializes in affordable earrings. Mon–Wed & Fri 11am–6.30pm, Thurs 11am–7pm, Sat 11am–6pm.

VINTAGE

Colours Bergmannstr. 102, Kreuzberg ☎ 030 694 33 48; U-Mehringdamm; map p.118. A retro fan's paradise with secondhand clothes spanning the 1960s to 1980s, but particularly good on the 1970s, as well as new designs. Mon–Fri 11am–8pm, Sat 10am–4pm.

Garage Ahornstr. 2, Schöneberg ☎ 030 211 27 60, ⓦ kleidermarkt.de; U-Nollendorfplatz; map p.113. The largest secondhand clothes store in Europe – good for jackets, coats and jeans. You pay according to weight (the clothes', not yours), with a 30 percent discount offered Wed 11am–1pm. Mon–Fri 11am–7pm, Sat 11am–6pm.

Humana Frankfurter Tor 3, Friedrichshain ☎ 030 422 20 18; ⓦ humana-de.org; U-Frankfurter Tor; map pp.126–127. Gigantic branch of a local secondhand chain that has a dozen stores in Berlin, offers great bargains on items that are (back) in style. Mon–Sat 10am–8pm

Jumbo Second Hand Wiener Str. 63, Kreuzberg ☎ 030 218 96 60; U-Görlitzer Bahnhof; map pp.126–127. A bewildering amount of clothes, from dresses to bags, sunglasses and more. Can be a little overpriced and it's worth trying to bargain. Mon–Sat 11am–7.30pm

Made in Berlin Neue Schönhauser Str. 19, Mitte; ☎ 030 21 23 06 01; U-Weinmeisterstrasse; map pp.72–73. One of four shops in the city that sell cutting-edge, mostly vintage clothes for girls and boys. You'll find everything from hats and shoes to blouses and faintly bizarre appendages. Tuesday noon till 3pm is happy hour (20 percent off all vintage). Mon–Sat noon–8pm.

Modeinstitut Berlin Samariterstr. 8, Friedrichshain ☎ 030 42 01 90 88; U-Samariterstrasse; map pp.126–127. An Aladdin's Cave of vintage clothes, accessories, bags, colourful shoes, disco lamps, leather jackets, rare magazines and old books. Mon–Sat noon–7pm.

★ **ReSales** Potsdamer Str. 105, Schöneberg ⓦ secondhandandmore.com; U-Kurfürstenstrasse;

KADEWE (P.230) >

map p.113. This north German chain of secondhand stores has half a dozen branches in central Berlin, each with a vast array of garments that range from hip streetwear to glamorous, silky evening dresses. All tend to be fairly priced, too. Mon–Fri 9.30am–7pm, Sat 9.30am–4pm.

Secondo Mommsenstr. 61, City West ☎ 030 881 22 91, ⓦ secondoberlin.de; S-Savignyplatz; map p.108. Exclusively designer clothes at massively knocked down prices: most items are in top condition, though of course many designs are a bit dated – which is half the fun for vintage nuts.. You'll find a number of similar shops further up and down the street. Mon–Fri 11am–6.30pm, Sat 11am–3.30pm.

Sgt. Peppers Kastanienallee 91, Prenzlauer Berg ☎ 030 448 11 21, ⓦ sgt-peppers-berlin.de; U-Eberswalder Strasse; map p.132. Mixed bag of vintage 1960s and 1970s gear, along with its own-label retro-wear. Mon–Sat 11am–8pm.

SOUVENIRS AND GIFTS

★ **Ach Berlin** Markengrafstr. 39, Mitte ☎ 030 92 12 68 80, ⓦ achberlin.de; U-Stadtmitte; map p.36. Very good source of offbeat Berlin memorabilia where classy designs celebrate local life and culture– cookie-cutters of the TV tower, brooms that look like the Brandenburg Gate – along with stylish souvenir T-shirts. Mon–Sat 11am–7pm.

Ararat Bergmannstr. 9, Kreuzberg ☎ 030 694 95 32, ⓦ ararat-berlin.de; U-Gneisenaustrasse; map p.118. Postcards, cards and a wealth of gimmicky gifts. It's easy to lose yourself here; when you've finished you can head over the road to where another branch sells picture frames and artworks. Mon–Sat 10am–8pm.

Ampelmann Galerie Hackeschen Höfe V, Mitte ☎ 030 44 72 64 38, ⓦ ampelmann.de; S-Hackescher Markt; map pp.72–73. Joyous celebration of the traffic-light man (Ampelmann) that reigns supreme on the eastern side of the city. After being threatened with replacement by his svelte West Berlin counterpart he became the subject of protests and a cult figure. Pick up T-shirts, mugs, lights and the like at the original shop here. Five other branches in central Berlin. Mon–Sat 9.30am–10pm, Sun 10am–7pm.

Heimspiel Niederbarnimstr. 18, Friedrichshain ☎ 030 20 68 78 70; U-Samariterstrasse; map pp.126–127. This cute little store s always worth stopping by, offering a fresh assortment of trendy women's clothing, kitsch Berlin-themed postcards and games and locally produced artworks. Mon–Fri 11am–8pm, Sat 11am–6pm.

Supalife Kiosk Raumerstr. 40, Mitte ☎ 030 44 67 88 26; U-Eberswalder Strasse; map p.132. This funky little boutique sells the wares of Berlin urban artists, from comics and fanzines to silkscreen prints and paintings. They're well connected to some of the city's best-known artists, so expect one-offs too. Mon–Sat noon–7pm.

ELECTRONICS, RADIOS AND RECORD PLAYERS

Media Markt Grunerstr. 20, Mitte ☎ 030 263 99 70, ⓦ mediamarkt.de; U- & S-Alexanderplatz; map p.60. Electrical superstore with aggressively priced phones, cameras, memory cards, iPads, computers and the like. This is the most central of 15 Berlin branches. Mon–Sat 10am–9pm.

Radio Art Zossener Str. 2, Kreuzberg ☎ 030 693 94 35; U-Mehringdamm; map p.118. Fantastic and visually satisfying shop for radio fans, musos and lovers of nostalgia, with shelves brimming with vintage (and some modern) radio sets and record players. Thurs & Fri noon–6pm, Sat 10am–1pm.

TRAVEL EQUIPMENT

Globetrotter Schlossstr. 78–82, Steglitz-Zehlendorf ☎ 030 850 89 20, ⓦ globetrotter.de; U- & S-Rathaus Steglitz; map p.152. Massive, well-stocked outdoor shop with several gimmicks – a pool to try out kayaks, and a -25°C freezer to try out jackets and sleeping bags. A bit of a trek from the centre, but directly above the station. Mon–Fri 10am–8pm, Sat 9am–8pm.

DEPARTMENT STORES AND MALLS

There are no surprises inside Berlin's department stores and, with the exception of KaDeWe and Galeries Lafayette, they're only worth popping into for essentials. The Stilwerk mall, however, is a classy place.

Galeries Lafayette Friedrichstr. 76, Mitte ☎ 030 20 94 80, ⓦ lafayette-berlin.de; U-Französische Strasse; map p.36. Branch of the upscale Paris-based department store. Surprisingly small, but packed with beautiful and expensive things and including a food department with French imports. Mon–Sat 10am–8pm.

★ **KaDeWe** Tauentzienstr. 21, Schöneberg ☎ 030 212 10, ⓦ kadewe-berlin.de; U-Wittenbergplatz; map p.108. Content rather than flashy interior decor rules the day here. From surprisingly well-priced designer labels to the extraordinary displays at the international delicatessen, where you can nibble on exotica, there's everything the consumer's heart desires at this, the largest department store on the continent. Mon–Thurs 10am–8pm, Fri 10am–9pm, Sat 9.30am–8pm.

Karstadt Kurfürstendamm 231, City West ☎030 88 00 30, ⓦ karstadt.de; U-Kurfürstendamm; map p.108. A smaller and cheaper version of KaDeWe. Everything is nicely laid out, with a good menswear department. Other

branches dotted around Berlin. Mon–Thurs & Sat 10am–8pm, Fri 10am–9pm.

Stilwerk Kantstr. 17, City West ☎030 31 51 50, ⓦ stilwerk.de; S-Savignyplatz; map p.108. Swanky designer mall, located near Zoologischer Garten, featuring shops dedicated to home decoration, jewellery and fashion. Expect high-end stores like Bang & Olufsen, with one or two cheaper options as well. There's a café and even a babysitting service. Mon–Fri 10am–8pm, Sat 10am–6pm.

FOOD AND DRINK

COFFEE, TEA AND CHOCOLATE

Barcomi's Bergmannstr. 21, Kreuzberg ☎030 28 59 83 63, ⓦ barcomis.de; U-Gneisenaustrasse; map p.118. Good selection of top-notch, house-roasted coffee, including organic and caffeine-free varieties. Mon–Sat 8am–9pm, Sun 9am–9pm.

Leysieffer Kurfürstendamm 218, City West Wilmersdorf ☎030 885 74 80; U-Uhlandstrasse; map p.108. This Ku'damm branch of the famed German chocolateria does a brisk trade. Aside from the usual sweet goodies, there's also a small coffee bar. Mon–Fri 9am–7pm, Sat 10am–5pm.

Tchibo Alexanderplatz 2, Mitte ☎030 24 72 06 96; U-Alexanderplatz; map p.60. The city's most popular stand-up coffee place with good-quality beans and the chance to mix your own blend from a small choice at the counter. Many other branches. Mon–Sat 8am–8pm.

Teesalon Invalidenstr. 160, Mitte ☎030 28 04 06 60, ⓦ tee-import.de; U-Rosenthaler Platz; map pp.72–73.

A glut of exotic teas and all the paraphernalia they cry out for in order to be enjoyed in style. Mon–Fri 10am–7pm, Sat 10am–4pm.

DELIS AND FOOD MARKETS

Alimentari e Vini Skalitzer Str. 23, Kreuzberg ☎030 611 49 81, ⓦ alimentari.de; U-Kottbusser Tor; map pp.126–127. A slick shop in scruffy Kreuzberg offering wines, pastas and other Italian deli items. Mon–Fri 9am–8pm, Sat 9am–4pm.

Goldhahn Und Sampson Dunckerstr. 9, Prenzlauer Berg ☎030 41 19 83 66; U-Eberswalder Strasse; map p.132. Foodies' paradise selling herbs, spices and other tasty delicacies from all over the world, plus cookbooks and kitchen utensils. Regular wine tasting and cooking courses. Mon–Sat 8am–8pm.

Türken-Markt Kottbusser Damm/Maybachufer, Neukölln; U-Kottbusser Tor; map pp.126–127. Definitely worth a visit, especially on Fri. Handy for all things Turkish,

16

BERLIN FOR FOODIES

Berliners love their **food**. Not only is the variety on offer extremely good, the quality is high and prices reasonable. The key player at the top end is the food court on the sixth floor of the luxurious **KaDeWe** department store (see p.230) where a mind-boggling array of gourmet delights arrive daily from around the world. You can choose from 400 types of bread, 1200 cheeses and 1400 meats, never mind the bewildering number of cakes and confectionery. But probably its best feature is its many counters where you can sample freshly prepared goodies. **Galeries Lafayette** (see p.230) also has a good gourmet food section with delectables from around the world.

One of the city's greatest passions is locally sourced **organic** food, as evidenced by the success here of Europe's largest organic supermarket, the **LPG Bio-Markt** (see p.232), along with the health-food shops (*Naturkostläden*) with their vegetarian goodies, that thrive in almost every neighbourhood. In some ways the success of these places is surprising given Berlin's terrific **food markets**, which have been selling well-priced, good-quality fruit, veg and local produce in every district for generations. Particularly good are western Kreuzberg's **Marheineke Markthalle** (see p.122), the Saturday market on Schöneberg's **Winterfeldplatz** and the **Türken-Markt** in eastern Kreuzberg (see p.231).

Also not to be missed are the small neighbourhood **bakeries** scattered throughout the city: wholemeal bread, multigrain rolls and simple cakes fresh from the oven are real foodie delights. Of the city's **supermarkets** Pennymarkt, Netto, Lidl, Aldi and Plus are by far the cheapest, although they offer limited choice. **Ullrich**, on Hardenbergstr., underneath the railway bridge by Zoo Station, has an excellent selection of foods, wines and spirits, keeps long hours and is cheap despite its central location. **Speciality food shops** are spread throughout the city, with the majority of dedicated ethnic places in Kreuzberg.

especially cheese, bread, olives and dried fruits, all at rockbottom prices. Tues & Fri noon–6pm.

HEALTH FOOD

Einhorn Mommsenstr. 2, City West ☎ 030 88 14 241, ⓦ einhornonline.de; U-Uhlandstrasse; map p.108. Excellent wholegrain breads and cakes, baked in-house, at this popular veggie caff (see p.193). Mon–Fri 10am–6pm.

Himmel und Erde Naturkost Skalitzer Str. 46, Kreuzberg ☎030 611 60 41, ⓦhimmelerde.de; U-Görlitzer Bahnhof; map pp.126–127. Excellent organic supermarket that's been around for over two decades. Mon–Fri 9am–7pm, Sat 9am–4pm.

LPG Bio-Markt Kollwitzstr. 17, Prenzlauer Berg ☎030 322 97 14 00, ⓦlpg-naturkost.de; U-Senefelderplatz; map p.132. Europe's largest organic supermarket with a staggering 18,000 products, many from the countryside around Berlin. There are another five branches in central Berlin. Mon–Sat 9am–9pm.

WINES AND SPIRITS

Absinth Depot Weinmeisterstr. 4, Mitte ☎ 030 281 67 89; U-Weinmeisterstrasse; map pp.72–73. All kinds of "Green Fairy" liquor but also a wide variety of props for the true absinthe experience. You can even have a little taste. Mon–Fri 2pm–midnight, Sat 1pm–midnight.

Weinkeller Blücherstr. 22, Kreuzberg ☎030 693 46 61, ⓦweinkeller-berlin.de; U-Gneisenaustrasse; map p.118. A good selection of Spanish, French, Italian and German wines, plus sherries and whiskies from the cask. Mon–Fri 10am–8pm, Sat 10am–4pm.

MARKETS, JUNK SHOPS AND ANTIQUES

If you're looking for antiques, hunting around Berlin's flea markets can be fruitful but hard work. A good bet for junk shops and antiques is **Suarezstrasse** in Charlottenburg: get off at U-Sophie-Charlotte-Platz and work your way along the street. Gotzstrasse in Schöneberg and Bergmannstrasse in Kreuzberg are also good bets.

FLEA MARKETS

Berliner Kunstmarkt By the Bode and Pergamon museums, Mitte; S-Hackescher Markt; map p.53. A good mix of real antiques, schlocky souvenirs, used books and bootleg CDs. Sat & Sun 11am–5pm.

Berliner Trödelmarkt Str. des 17 Juni, Charlottenburg; S-Tiergarten; map p.154. Pleasant enough for a Sun morning stroll, but it's the most expensive of the flea markets, and geared toward tourists. Good for embroidery and lace, though. Sat & Sun 10am–5pm.

Flohmarkt am Boxhagener Platz Boxhagener Platz, Friedrichshain; U- & S-Warschauer Strasse; map pp.126–127. Small flea market catering to the needs of the student quarter. Good Eastern Bloc memorabilia. Sun 9am–4pm.

★ **Flohmarkt am Fehrbelliner Platz** Fehrbelliner Platz 1, Charlottenburg-Wilmersdorf; U-Fehrbelliner Platz; map p.154. Small but very good fleamarket for reasonably priced antiques and collectables with a local flavour. There's a pleasant café too, but the large number of Thai families selling fantastic street food in the adjacent park are a bigger attraction. Sat & Sun 10am–4pm.

Flohmarkt am Mauerpark Bernauer Str. 63–64, Prenzlauer Berg; U-Bernauer Strasse; map p.132. Huge fleamarket on the edge of Prenzlauer Berg with a bit of everything that's cheap, including a legion of freshly stolen and spray-painted bikes. Few real antiques, but a good place to make a day of it, with good ethnic food stalls and a fun open-air karaoke at 3pm. Sun 8am–6pm.

Flohmarkt am Moritzplatz Moritzplatz, Kreuzberg; U-Moritzplatz; map pp.126–127. An integral part of Kreuzberg's social fabric, with all that entails. Lots of Turkish goods and some pretty rough-and-ready clutter to sift through for gems. Sun 8am–4pm.

Flohmarkt Schöneberg John-F.-Kennedy-Platz 1, Schöneberg; U-Rathaus Schöneberg; map p.113. Some professionals selling books and collectables, but also amateur vendors who have cleared out the garage or attic and are selling the motley results. Sat & Sun 8am–4pm.

Hallentrödelmarkt Treptow Eichenstr. 4, Treptow; S-Treptower Park; map pp.126–127. Ideal rainy-day option: there's something of everything in this huge indoor flea market. The stalls are all permanent fixtures and thoroughly chaotic. Head north along Hoffmannstr., parallel to the Spree River. Sat & Sun 10am–5pm.

Trödelmarkt am Arkonaplatz Arkonaplatz, Mitte, ⓦtroedelmarkt-arkonaplatz.de; U-Bernauer Strasse; map pp.72–73. Popular flea market in the city's yuppie district, thick with 1960s and 70s junk and cult objects in equal measure. Sun 10am–4pm.

ANTIQUES

Berliner Antik und Flohmarkt Bahnhof Friedrichstr., under the railway arches, 190–203, Mitte ☎ 030 208 26 55, ⓦantikmarkt-berlin.de; U- & S-Friedrichstrasse; map p.36. Tending more toward the antique end of things, with several shops selling everything from books to jewellery. Not particularly cheap. Daily 11am–6pm.

Bleibtreu Antik Schlüterstr. 54 ☎030 883 52 12; S-Savignyplatz; map p.108. Well-established shop with a great selection of antiques from 1900 to the 1960s, plus stylish 1960s and 1970s jewellery. Mon–Fri noon–7pm, Sat 11am–3pm.

16

OLYMPIC STADIUM

Sports and outdoor activities

While Berliners go in for healthy eating in a big way, they're not famous for being fitness fanatics – they need all their energy for the frenetic nightlife. Nonetheless there is a surprising variety of participatory sports available in the city. Municipal facilities for many sports are excellent, partly because this was one area the GDR was always keen to invest in. Berlin is also cycle-friendly (see p.24). Meanwhile, despite a shortage of top-flight teams, the spectator sports scene is vibrant, with some fanatical support for virtually every team. Major and some minor sporting events are listed in the *Tip* and *Zitty* what's-on magazines (see p.33), but the best index of facilities and events is on the web at the German-only ⓦcitysports.de.

17

PARTICIPATORY SPORTS

JOGGING

With so many parks it's easy to find a good place to jog in Berlin. Best are the Tiergarten, Volkspark Friedrichshain, Treptower Park and the gardens of Schloss Charlottenburg. The lakes around the city are also popular with joggers: try the Schlachtensee, Krumme Lanke or Grunewaldsee. If you're into long-distance running there's always the Berlin Marathon (see p.27) on the last weekend in September.

GYMS, POOLS, SAUNAS AND SPAS

Berlin's private gyms are usually members-only and you'll usually need to be a guest of a member to qualify for a day pass, which is likely to be around €15. However, if you are in Berlin for a few weeks it should be fairly easy to get a short-term membership at your nearest gym. One chain with several branches in Berlin is Fit Sportstudio (⟳ fit -sportstudios.de). Most city districts have both indoor and outdoor swimming pools, the majority of which are municipal (⟳ berlinerbaederbetriebe.de), charge around €4 for a swim and have complicated opening hours – from as early as 7am to as late as 10pm on some days, with some closing in the summer and some offering men- and women-only times and family times. Look out too for *Warmbadetag*, when the water is warmer than usual – and admission is usually more. Many pools also have saunas which cost around €15 for three hours, and require you to leave any Anglo-Saxon prudishness at home, for they are inevitably naked and mixed-sex. Women uncomfortable with this arrangement should look out for women-only sessions offered regularly at most facilities, while men should be aware that men-only sessions, where offered, are frequently cruisey – anywhere advertising itself as a men's sauna is an out-and-out gay venue. If you're looking for a waterpark, you could head outside the city to Tropical Islands (see p.175), a luxurious indoor complex with a constant temperature of 27ºC.

Bad am Spreewaldplatz Wiener Str. 59h, Kreuzberg ☎ 030 695 35 20, ⟳ berlinerbaederbetriebe.de; U-Görlitzerbahnhof. Popular 25m indoor pool complete with wave machine that makes it popular with families. Also a good sauna. Approx Mon–Fri 2.30–10pm, Sat & Sun 11am–6.30pm.

Hamam Mariannenstr. 6, Kreuzberg ☎ 030 615 14 64, ⟳ hamamberlin.de; U-Kottbusser Tor. Women-only (but not lesbian) Turkish-style bathhouse in women's centre Schokofabrik (see p.237). Various beauty treatments available. Mon 3–11pm, Tues–Sun noon–11pm.

★ **Liquidrom** Möckernstr. 10, Kreuzberg ☎ 030 258 00 78 20, ⟳ liquidrom-berlin.de; S-Anhalter Bahnhof. Cutting-edge health spa, whose claim to fame is its atmospheric saltwater pool into which ambient music is piped. The amazing underwater sound experience is complemented by mildly psychedelic projections on the ceiling and floors. There's also a couple of hot tubs – one outdoor – a sauna, steam room and a civilized bar. Sun–Thurs 10am–midnight, Fri & Sat 10am–1am.

Sommerbad Olympia-Stadion Olympischer Platz (Osttor), Charlottenburg ☎ 030 663 11 52, ⟳ berlinerbaederbetriebe.de; U-Olympia Stadion. Outdoor pool that's part of the impressive 1930s-era Olympic Stadium complex. With a 50m pool and several diving boards. Mid-May to mid-Sept daily 7am–7pm.

Stadtbad Charlottenburg (Alte Halle) Krumme Str. 10, Charlottenburg ☎ 030 34 38 38 60, ⟳ berlinerbaederbe triebe.de; U-Bismarckstrasse. A delightful, old-fashioned tiled pool, seldom crowded, with three saunas and a steam room. Hours vary wildly by day and season.

Stadtbad Neukölln Ganghoferstr. 3, Neukölln ☎ 030 68 24 98 12, ⟳ berlinerbaederbetriebe.de; U-Rathaus Neukölln. Swim and relax in a setting that resembles a Hungarian spa. Two pools (one heated, one cool) decorated with fountains and mosaic tiles, encased in a maze of archways and colonnades. Sauna and steam room available. Approx. daily 6.30am–10.30pm; but hours vary wildly.

Strandbad Wannsee Wannseebadweg 25, Zehlendorf ☎ 030 70 71 38 33, ⟳ strandbadwannsee.de; S-Nikolassee. Berlin's famed beach, with lots of activities in summer – volleyball, table tennis, basketball, boat rental – when it is usually packed. There are *Strandkörbe* (stylish beach cabanas that seat two; €8) for rent. Entry €4.50. April–Sept daily 10am–6pm, with varying but extended hours June–Aug.

Thermen am Europa-Center Nürnberger Str. 7, Charlottenburg ☎ 030 257 57 60, ⟳ thermen-berlin .de; U-Wittenbergplatz. Big sauna complex with no less

---

BADESCHIFF

A dip in the River Spree might not sound like such a good idea until you visit **Badeschiff** (daily 8am–midnight; €5 pool, €14 sauna; ☎ 030 533 20 30, ⟳ arena-berlin.de; U-Schlesiches Tor), an old industrial barge converted into a clear blue, 20m-long swimming pool that bobs in the river. A wooden jetty that's perfect for sunbathing connects the pool to a beach – complete with a happening beach bar that hosts various events – that's been constructed on the bank. Look out for early-morning yoga sessions. The entrance is hidden behind a maze of old tram sheds beside the Arena complex. In winter the pool gets a roof and its two saunas are popular.

than nine saunas, as well as indoor and outdoor saltwater pools, fitness rooms and beauty treatments. Towels available for rent. Mon–Sat 10am–midnight, Sun 10am–9pm.

IN-LINE SKATING

Skate Night ⓦberlin.skatebynight.de. In-line skating is extremely popular in Berlin, as evidenced by Skate Night, when thousands take to cordoned-off streets in the city centre. Setting off at 7pm on selected summer Sundays (June–Sept), the event costs €2 and runs until dusk, with skaters returning in a loop back to the starting point. It's a magnificent opportunity to see some of Berlin's streets from an unusual viewpoint. If you need to rent skates, arrive early – they have a limited number of free rentals – or visit Ski Shop Charlottenburg, Schustehrusstr. 1 (ⓣ030 341 48 70, ⓦski-shop-charlottenburg.de; U-Richard-Wagner-Platz), who rent out skates for €10/day.

SKATEBOARDING

The most obvious place for skateboarders to head is the Skatehalle Berlin, but other skate-parks, ramps and pipes are scattered around the city's parks, with some of the best at the old Radrennbahn in Weissensee and Grazer Platz in Schöneberg. A full overview is given at ⓦskate-spots.de.

Skatehalle Berlin Revaler Str. 99, Friedrichshain ⓦskatehalle-berlin.de. The city's main skate-park, within the Cassiopeia complex (see p.213). Do check online in advance as some times are reserved for BMXers. €5 entry Mon 2–8pm, Tues, Wed & Fri 2pm–midnight, Thurs 2–10pm, Sat noon–midnight, Sun noon–8pm.

ICE-SKATING

Small open-air rinks sprout near Christmas markets in the centre of town, but the proper rinks are all a little way out. These usually have several 3hr sessions per day which cost around €4 and the same again to rent skates.

Horst-Dohm-Eisstadion Fritz-Wildung-Str. 9, Wilmersdorf ⓣ030 89 73 27 34, ⓦeissport-service.de; U-Heidelberger Platz. The city's largest rink is an outdoor facility, with a track surrounding the central rink.

SPECTATOR SPORTS

Though no Berlin sports team is world-class, all play in competitive leagues and have a loyal and entertaining fan base. The most high-profile is Hertha BSC, the city's major **football team**, though most other Berlin teams tend to do better in their respective leagues. The biggest sporting spectacles, however, are the city's annual events, including the **Six-Day Non-Stop Cycle Race** (see p.26) in late January and the late September **Berlin Marathon** (see p.27).

TEAMS AND VENUES

Alba Berlin ⓣ030 300 90 50, tickets ⓣ01805 57 00 11, ⓦalbaberlin.de; S-Ostbahnhof. Berlin's premier basketball team, and one of the top dozen in Europe, competes in the German League and the Euroleague, and plays in the O2 World Arena in Friedrichshain. Tickets €8–65. Oct–June.

EHC Eisbären ⓣ030 97 18 40 40, ⓦeisbaeren.de; S-Ostbahnhof. Fanatically supported eastern Berlin ice hockey team, which has been competing at the very top of the premier German division for years. The razzmatazz surrounding the teams and players brings it close to the likes of an NHL, and the game quality is not too far off either. The Eisbären, or polar bears, play in the O2 World Arena. Tickets €15–40. Season Sept–March.

Hertha BSC ⓣ01805 18 92 00, ⓦherthabsc.de; U-Olympia Stadion. Berlin's Bundesliga also-rans, who have never quite achieved real glory, despite lots of promise and the occasional successful European outing. But the Olympic Stadium is glorious whatever the team or result. Tickets are generally easy to come by, either online or via the Hertha fan shop in the Europa Center (see p.110). Tickets €15–89. Aug–May.

Trabrennbahn Karlshorst Treskow allee 129, Lichtenberg ⓣ030 740 12 12, ⓦberlintrab.de; S-Karlshorst. Enjoy a day at the races Berlin-style, watching harness racing. The racetrack is to the left of Treskow allee, just south of the S-bridge. Tickets €3. Year-round.

Union Berlin ⓣ030 656 68 80, tickets ⓣ030 65 66 88 93, ⓦfc-union-berlin.de; S-Köpenick. Eastern Berlin's football team, with a fiercely loyal working-class following, plays in the second division. Despite some shock success in German cup matches and even in Europe, the day-to-day picture is less exciting. Matches are played in the Stadion An der Alten Försterei and An der Wuhlheide in Köpenick. Tickets €9–31. Aug–May.

CHRISTOPHER STREET DAY PARADE

Gay and lesbian Berlin

Berlin's gay and lesbian scenes are world-class – certainly on a par with those of San Francisco or New York – and the city is a huge magnet for gay men and women from all over Germany and Europe. This has been the case since the 1920s, when Christopher Isherwood and W.H. Auden both came here, drawn to a city where, in sharp contrast to oppressive London, the gay community did not live in fear of harassment and legal persecution. The easy-going, easy-living attitude stretches into the straight community, too, and it's not uncommon to see transvestites at their glitziest dancing atop tables at even the most conservative bashes. The best time to arrive and plunge yourself into the hurly-burly is Gay Pride Week, centred on the Christopher Street Day parade (ⓦcsd-berlin.de) in late June.

GUIDES AND LISTINGS

Magazines and guides The German/English-language *Berlin von Hinten* ("Berlin from behind"; €12) is the city's most useful gay guide. *Siegessäule* (ⓦsiegessaeule.de), a monthly gay magazine, has listings of events and an encyclopedic directory of gay and lesbian contacts and groups; it's available free from information centres and most gay bars. They also produce an online city guide in both German and English: ⓦout-in-berlin.de.

INFORMATION CENTRES

AHA–Berlin Monumentenstr. 13, Schöneberg ☎030 692 36 00, ⓦaha-berlin.de; U-Yorckstrasse. Non-profit cooperative that organizes workshops and events for gay and lesbian groups.

Begine Potsdamer Str. 139, Schöneberg ☎030 215 14 14, ⓦbegine.de; U-Bülowstrasse. Women's centre with a mixed programme ranging from earnest lectures and films, through excellent performances by women musicians and dancers to televised women's soccer and disco evenings. Mon–Fri 5pm–late, Sat 7pm–late, Sun 3pm–late.

EWA Prenzlauer Allee 6, Prenzlauer Berg ☎030 442 55 42, ⓦewa-frauenzentrum.de; U-Rosa-Luxemburg-Platz. The first post-Wall women's centre in east Berlin, EWA offers courses and counselling, as well as various

cultural events and computer and media facilities. It also has an airy women-only café-gallery with a children's play area. Good for events information and flyers. Mon–Thurs 10am–11pm, Fri–Sun varies according to programme.

Frauenzentrum Schokofabrik Mariannenstr. 6, eastern Kreuzberg ☎030 615 29 99, ⓦschokofabrik .de; U-Kottbusser Tor. One of Europe's largest women's centres, with a café/gallery, sports facilities, including a women-only Turkish bath (see p.234) and diverse events. Mon–Thurs 10am–2pm, Fri noon–4pm.

Mann-O-Meter Bülowstr. 106, Schöneberg ☎030 216 80 08, ⓦmann-o-meter.de; U-Nollendorfplatz. One of the city's main gay information centres and meeting points. Tues–Fri 5–10pm, Sat & Sun 4–8pm.

GALLERIES AND MUSEUMS

Das Verborgene Museum Schlüterstr. 70, Charlottenburg ☎030 313 36 56, ⓦdasverborgene museum.de; S-Savignyplatz. A gallery founded by women artists for the research, documentation and exhibition of women's art. Entry €2. Thurs & Fri 3–7pm, Sat & Sun noon–4pm.

Schwules Museum Lützowstr. 73, Schöneberg ☎030 69 59 90 50, ⓦschwulesmuseum.de; U-Kurfürstenstrasse. Interesting gay museum with changing exhibitions on local

and international gay history, and library material to browse through. Entry €6. Mon, Wed–Fri & Sun 2–6pm, Sat 2–7pm.

Spinnboden Anklamer Str. 38, Mitte ☎030 448 58 48, ⓦspinnboden.de; U-Bernauer Strasse. A comprehensive archive of every aspect of lesbian experience, with a beautifully housed collection of books, videos, posters and magazines. Wed & Fri 2–7pm.

ACCOMMODATION

Most **accommodation** in Berlin is gay-friendly, and there are some places, listed below, that are run for and by the gay community. There are no hotels or pensions in Berlin specifically for **lesbians**, though there are women-only hotels including the *Artemisia* (see p.181).

Art Hotel Charlottenburger Hof Stuttgarter Platz 14, Charlottenburg ☎030 32 90 70, ⓦcharlottenburger-hof.de; S-Charlottenburg; map p.154. Bright contemporary hotel, replete with modern art, Bauhaus design and multicoloured furniture. Perks include free internet access in every room and a 24hr café. Rates can often be slashed by booking specials online. Breakfast extra. €82

Art Hotel Connection Fuggerstr. 33, Schöneberg ☎030 210 21 88 00, ⓦarthotel-connection.de; U-Wittenbergplatz; map p.113. Located above the

well-known gay club *Connection*. Most rooms are large and en suite, bright, pleasant and ordinary – the "playrooms", however, come with chains, slings and rubber sheets. Breakfast included. €82

Tom's Hotel Motzstr. 19, Schöneberg ☎030 219 66 04, ⓦtoms-hotel.de; U-Nollendorfplatz; map p.113. One of the largest gay hotels in town, with a great location in Berlin's gay village and its own vibrant café. Bright simple rooms, with free wi-fi and a bowl of fruit provided along with a pass for discounts at a number of local businesses. €120

CAFÉS

You'll find the majority of gay and lesbian **hangouts** in Schöneberg, Kreuzberg and Prenzlauer Berg. In addition to the cafés there are several very active and convivial mixed-use venues, popular within the lesbian scene. Gay women might also want to check out any possible happenings at the Begine women's centre (see above).

18

18

Café Berio Maassenstr. 7, Schöneberg ☎030 216 19 46; U-Nollendorfplatz; map p.113. This gay café is an ideal spot for *Kaffee und Kuchen* in the Viennese tradition; later on the drinks specials (7–9pm) are the main draw. Occasional exhibitions, too. Mon–Thurs 7am–midnight, Fri 7am–1am, Sat 8am–1am, Sun 8am–midnight.

Café Seidenfaden Dircksenstr. 47, Mitte ☎030 283 27 83, ⊚frausuchtzukunft.de; U-Weinmeisterstrasse; map pp.72–73. Calm women-only café with inexpensive lunch specials (€3–5) and a no alcohol policy. Mon–Fri 10am–6pm.

Melitta Sundström Mehringdamm 61, Kreuzberg ☎030 692 44 14; U-Mehringdamm; map p.118. Small, low-key and comfortable mixed café – often a warm-up for the legendary *SchwuZ* club (see below) in the basement. Food served until 11pm. Daily 10am–4am.

BARS AND CLUBS

The longest-standing and most concentrated area of **gay bars** is in Schöneberg between Wittenbergplatz and Nollendorfplatz, though in the last decade or so the area south of Kleiststrasse, along Schönhauser Allee in Prenzlauer Berg, has become an eastern gay centre. Many mainly straight clubs have gay nights – see *Tip*, *Zitty* or the dedicated gay magazine *Siegessäule* for details. *Berghain* (see p.213), *Kit Kat Club* (see p.212) and *Kumpelnest 3000* (see p.210) are all mixed venues with a strong gay presence that have become legendary. Other nights not to miss are the **GMF** events (⊚gmf-berlin.de), which pop up at different venues around town, and have over the years become a stalwart of the Berlin scene – think stripped-to-the-waist revellers dancing to pounding house music. As in many other large cities, **lesbians** in Berlin have a much lower profile than gay men. Perhaps because of this, there's no real distinction between bars and cafés for lesbians and straight women, and many of Berlin's women-only bars have a strong lesbian following.

CITY WEST

Vagabund Bar Knesebeckstr. 77 ☎030 881 15 06, ⊚vagabund-berlin.com; U-Uhlandstrasse; map p.108. This popular mixed gay bar opened in 1968 but has recently had a facelift. It gets crowded after 3am and has an anything goes, trashy aesthetic – very flirty, very fun, and not only for men. Mon–Thurs 6pm–8am, Fri & Sat midnight–late, Sun midnight–8am.

SCHÖNEBERG
MOSTLY MEN

Connection Fuggerstr. 33 ☎030 23 62 74 44, ⊚connectionclub.de; U-Wittenbergplatz; map p.113. Gay entertainment complex including an American-style sports bar – *Prinzknecht* (see below). Very popular house and techno club at weekends. Daily 3pm–late.

★ **Heile Welt** Motzstr. 5 ☎030 21 91 75 07, ⊚heile -welt-berlin.de; U-Nollendorfplatz; map p.113. A convivial second living room for many local gay men and the women who love them. During the week, it's all about lounging on the sofas, drinking famously strong cocktails; at weekends the action picks up and it gets crowded, with music running the gamut from soul and dance to house and home-grown "Schlager", a folksy German pop genre. Daily 6pm–late.

Neues Ufer Hauptstr. 157 ☎030 78 95 97 00, ⊚neuesufer.de; U-Kleistpark; map p.113. Lovely neighbourhood gay bar. Bowie used to drink here in the 1970s, when it was *Anderes Ufer*. Daily 11am–2am.

Prinzknecht Fuggerstr. 33 ☎030 23 62 74 44, ⊚prinzknecht.de; U-Wittenbergplatz; map p.113. A refined version of an American sports bar, all bare brick and gleaming chrome, attracting a broad range of middle-aged gay men and some women. The men-only cellar darkroom is underused. Daily 3pm–3am.

Scheune Motzstr. 25 ☎030 213 85 80, ⊚scheune -berlin.de; U-Nollendorfplatz; map p.113. Very popular leather club with regular theme parties for devotees of rubber, uniforms or stark nakedness. Darkroom, baths and other accoutrements. Mon–Thurs 9pm–7am, non-stop Fri 9pm–Mon 7am.

★ **Tom's Bar** Motzstr. 19 ☎030 213 45 70, ⊚tomsbar .de; U-Nollendorfplatz; map p.113. Dark, sweaty and debauched men-only cruising establishment with a large darkroom. Among Berlin's most popular gay bars, and a great place to finish off a night out. Drinks are two for the price of one on Mon. Daily 10pm–late.

MIXED

Hafen Motzstr. 19 ☎030 211 41 18, ⊚hafen-berlin.de; U-Nollendorfplatz; map p.113. Long-established cruisey mixed bar for 30- and 40-somethings. Always packed and a great place to start a night out. Daily 8pm until late.

WESTERN KREUZBERG
MIXED

★ **SchwuZ** Mehringdamm 61 ☎030 69 50 78 89, ⊚schwuz.de; U-Mehringdamm; map p.118. Dance club much loved by all stripes of the gay community, and always crowded and convivial. One floor has the usual 1980s and disco mixes, the other more experimental tunes. Fri & Sat 11pm–late.

WOMEN

Serene Bar Schwiebusser Str. 2 ☎030 69 04 15 80, ⊚serenebar.de; U-Platz-der-Luftbrücke; map p.118. Great lesbian hangout, particularly on Sat when the big dance floor gets packed. The bar is also used by many special interest groups as a meeting point:

WOWI

Oozing can-do attitude, Berlin's flashy and openly gay mayor **Klaus Wowereit** or "Wowi", as Berliners call him, is used to courting controversy. In June 2001 he became Germany's first high-level politician to announce his homosexuality, coining the now famous German phrase "Ich bin schwul, und das ist auch gut so" ("I'm gay, and that's all right, too"). But he caused quite a stir when he zealously welcomed Folsom-Europe, a sado-masochism festival, to Berlin in 2005. Attracting ten thousand leather- and chain-clad revellers to the city, it caused outrage among conservatives in the city's parliament, but Wowi shot back that Berlin in particular must, above all, be tolerant. Berliners appear to agree, and Wowi was re-elected as mayor in 2006, despite widespread dissatisfaction with his mainstream political party the SPD, and then again in 2011, despite all the bad press relating to delays in the construction of Berlin-Brandenburg Airport.

18

table tennis, amateur photography and so on. The entrance is a little tucked away down an alley. Tues 6pm until late, Wed & Thurs 8pm until late, Sat 10pm until late.

EASTERN KREUZBERG
MIXED
Barbie Deinhoff Schlesische Str. 16 ⓦbarbiedeinhoff .de; U-Schlesisches Tor; map pp.126–127. Colourful and fun-loving dive bar that attracts a heady mix of transvestites, gay men and curious onlookers. The decor runs from deliberately kitsch to colourfully futuristic and there are regular DJs and events. Popular two-for-one happy hour Mon–Fri 6–9pm, Sat & Sun from 4pm. Mon– Fri 6pm–6am, Sat & Sun 4pm–6am.
★ **Roses** Oranienstr. 187 ☎030 615 65 70; U-Kottbusser Tor; map pp.126–127. Legendary kitsch gay club with a strong lesbian presence. The fun vibe makes it one of the venues of choice for a solo night out for either

sex. Sun is the main day – and the "gayest" – but women are welcome anytime. Daily 10pm–5am.

PRENZLAUER BERG
MOSTLY MEN
Greifbar Wichertstr. 10 ☎030 444 08 28, ⓦgreifbar .com; U-Schönhauser Allee; map p.132. This wicked cruising den is the cornerstone of gay debauchery in Prenzlauer Berg. Attracts the full range of the gay community, gets them in the mood with videos and provides an area around the back to release mutual tension. Daily 10pm–6am.

MIXED
Schall und Rauch Gleimstr. 23 ☎030 443 39 70, ⓦschall-und-rauch.de; U-Schönhauser Allee; map p.132. Tasteful, designer elegance in this hip young mixed bar. A place to see and be seen – and eat, thanks to an imaginative and ever-changing menu. Daily 9am–2am.

CINEMAS

Kino International Karl-Marx-Allee 33, Friedrichshain ☎030 24 75 60 11, ⓦyorck.de; U-Schillingstrasse. The "Mongay" event every Mon involves a screening of a cult gay or lesbian film – the bar opens at 9pm, the film is at 10pm and the party really starts afterwards.

Xenon Kolonnenstr. 5, Schöneberg ☎030 78 00 15 30, ⓦwww.xenon-kino.de; U-Kleistpark. Gay cinema that often screens English-language independent films. Tickets €7.

BOOKSHOPS

Ana Koluth Schönhauser Allee 124, Prenzlauer Berg ☎030 87 33 69 80, ⓦanakoluth.de; U-Schönhauser Allee; map p.132. Well-stocked lesbian bookstore, which also puts on regular exhibitions and readings. Mon–Fri 10am–8pm, Sat 10am–6pm.
Prinz Eisenherz Lietzenburger. 9a, Schöneberg

☎030 313 99 36, ⓦprinz eisenherz.com; U-Wittenbergplatz; map p.113. Friendly and informative gay bookstore with helpful assistants. Excellent for relaxed browsing, free magazines and posters and leaflets about current gay happenings. Mon–Sat 10am–8pm.

SPORT

Vorspiel Martin-Luther-Str. 56, Schöneberg ☎030 44 05 77 40, ⓦvorspiel-berlin.de; S-Papestrasse. Berlin's gay and lesbian sports club, offering a variety of activities

for every level of fitness and ability. Mon 1–3pm, Tues 5–7pm, Thurs 10am–1pm.

ZEBRAS AT THE ZOOLOGISCHER GARTEN

Kids' Berlin

Attitudes to young children in Berlin can strike outsiders as oddly ambivalent. While the city has a large number of single-parent families and excellent social services provisions, Berliners aren't too tolerant of kids in "adult" places, such as restaurants or bars, and though the city boasts a higher proportion of lakes, parks and woodland than any other European capital, there are few official attractions in those places directly geared towards entertaining children. If you're bringing kids, be prepared to do Berlin versions of the obvious things – zoos, museums, shops – rather than anything unique to the city. In addition to browsing the selections that we have covered here, you should also check the "Kinder" sections of listings magazines *Tip* and *Zitty* (see p.33) for details of what's on.

SIGHTSEEING

Tours Depending on your children's level of interest, some sightseeing might be enjoyable. A ride on the #100 or #200 bus doesn't cost much, and will take in all the main sights between Alexanderplatz and Bahnhof Zoo, connecting several key places and offering superb views of Berlin from on high (see box, p.242). Most other bus tours will end up being a bit too much for younger kids, but boat tours (see p.25) are a possibility.

Cycling With its many cyclepaths, Berlin is also a bike-friendly city for kids – those who can be relied on to stop at junctions, at least. However, few bike rental places offer children's bikes– among the few that do is Yaam Bike, Stralauer Platz 35 (☎0178 804 97 54, ⓦrent-a-bike -berlin.net; April–Oct; S-Ostbahnhof) at the start of the East Side Gallery (see p.130).

THE GREAT OUTDOORS

With more than a third of Berlin being forest or parkland, often with playgrounds dotted around, there's no shortage of spaces for children to let off steam. The most central and obvious choice is the **Tiergarten**, northeast of Bahnhof Zoo, though this is rather tame compared to the rambling expanses of the **Grunewald** (S-Grunewald). In both parks, paddle and rowing boats can be rented. The Grunewald borders the **Wannsee** beach, and it's fun to take the ferry over to the **Pfaueninsel**, or Peacock Island (see p.163), where there's a castle and strutting peacocks. Alternatively, **Freizeitpark Tegel** (U-Alt-Tegel; walk to the lake, then turn right) has playgrounds, trampolines, table tennis and paddle boats, while the **Teufelsberg** (Devil's Mountain; a 20min walk south down Teufelsseechaussee from S-Heerstr.), a large hill to the west of the city, is the place to go kite-flying at weekends. On the southeastern edge of the city, the woods around the **Grosser Müggelsee** (S-Bahn to Friedrichshagen) offer lakeside walking trails, and, just to the south, there's also a good nature trail around the **Teufelssee** (S-Bahn to Köpenick, then bus #X69 to Rübezahl).

19

MUSEUMS

Almost all the city's museums give discounts for children; those listed here are particularly recommended for kids, mainly thanks to fun interactive exhibits.

Deutsches Technikmuseum Berlin See p.122. The German Technology Museum has lots of highly diverting gadgets to experiment with, plus a great collection of old steam trains and carriages.

Düppel Museum Village See p.162. Reconstruction of a medieval country village, with demonstrations of traditional handicrafts and farming methods. Better for older children.

Juniormuseum im Ethnologischen Museum See p.160. The children's section of the Ethnological Museum teaches about different cultures through playful activities and interactive temporary exhibits.

Labyrinth Kindermuseum Berlin Osloer Str. 12, Wedding ☎030 800 93 11 50, ⓦkindermuseum -labyrinth.de; U-Pankstrasse; map p.152. Converted factory building that offers temporary exhibits, usually very inventive and thoughtful, geared towards hands-on

learning and fun. Admission €4.50. Outside school holidays Fri & Sat 1–6pm, Sun 11am–6pm; in school holidays Mon–Fri 9am–6pm, Sat 1–6pm, Sun 11am–6pm.

Museum für Kommunikation Berlin See p.120. Robots career around the main lobby in this hands-on communications museum, which offers older kids lots of computers and devices to play with.

Museum für Naturkunde See p.86. This natural history museum has a gigantic Brachiosaurus skeleton, plus plenty more to keep animal-crazy kids happy for an hour or so.

The Story of Berlin See p.112. Easily the most captivating of the city's history museums, with lots of multimedia gimmicks to bring the experience alive for kids.

BABYSITTING AND CHILD CARE

Berlin has several reliable agencies for English-speaking **babysitters**, but one that stands out for professionalism and convenience is Kinderinsel, Eichendorffstr. 17 (☎030 41 71 69 28, ⓦkinderinsel.de; U-Naturkundemuseum). Here parents can leave their children (aged up to 14 years) in good hands, for anything from a couple of hours to several days. The programme of outings and activities offered by the friendly and dynamic centre ensures the kids won't get bored; rates are €15/hr, €75 for an overnight stay. Not only can they provide a pick-up and drop-off service, but they can also supply babysitters if you'd rather keep the kids at your place.

TOP VIEWS FOR KIDS

Fernsehturm The viewing area has mind-blowing dimensions and an otherworldly feel. See p.62.
Panorama Punkt The most exciting views, though it does require a head for heights. See p.94.
Reichstag dome This unusual structure with its many mirrors is always entertaining for kids. See p.37.
Siegessäule Lots of steps make this slightly hard work for little legs but great for energetic youngsters. See p.102.

ZOOS AND AQUARIUMS

As a hangover from the old East-West days, Berlin has two full-sized **zoos**. The aquariums, meanwhile, are very good wet-weather options.

Sea-Life Centre See p.63. A much smaller variety of species than at the Zoologischer Garten, but with some flashy tanks and good activities for kids, including quiz questions (in English) and the chance to touch manta rays and starfish in a tank.
Tierpark Friedrichsfelde See p.144. The old eastern zoo is only really worth the trek for zoo fanatics or if you happen to be in the area.
Zoologischer Garten See p.110. City West's zoo is the best for kids of the two city zoos, with an underground nocturnal area (where varieties of gerbil-like creatures, and bats, do their thing) and a good playground. It also boasts a very good aquarium featuring all sorts of fish plus interesting creatures from crocodiles to bees to snakes.

PLAYGROUNDS, LEISURE COMPLEXES AND CHILDREN'S FARMS

Berlin has a number of rag-tag **adventure playgrounds** featuring creative wooden structures that are perfect to charge around and explore – many of them are supervised, too. Information on these along with the location of the city's children's farms are at the German-only website ⓦakib.de.

Domäne Dahlem Königin-Luise-Str. 49, Zehlendorf ☎030 666 30 00, ⓦdomaene-dahlem.de; U-Dahlem-Dorf; map p.161. Working farm and craft museum with plenty to entertain kids besides farmyard animals, especially during weekend craft fairs when there are games and shows especially for children. Daily 8am–7pm.
FEZ Wuhlheide An der Wuhlheide 197, Köpenick ☎030 53 07 10, ⓦfez-berlin.de; S-Wuhlheide; map p.142. A large GDR-era recreation park, packed with play and activity areas for kids of all ages and unusual features such as a BMX track (rentals available) and a popular narrow-gauge railway, the 7km-long Berliner *Parkeisenbahn* (ⓦparkeisenbahn.de). Hours vary according to school terms, but core times: Tues–Fri & Sun 9am–10pm, Sat 1–6pm, Sun noon–6pm.
Kinderbauernhof auf dem Görlitzer Görlitzer Park, Wiener Str. 59, Kreuzberg ⓦkinderbauernhofberlin .de; U-Görlitzer Bahnhof; map pp.126–127. The most central of several of Berlin's educationally oriented children's farms, which can still be fun even if you don't know the language. Mon, Tues, Thurs & Fri 10am–7pm (5pm in winter), Sat & Sun 11am–6pm (5pm in winter).

CIRCUSES

Cabuwazi Zirkus Weiner Str. 59h, Kreuzberg ☎030 29 04 78 40, ⓦcabuwazi.de; U-Görlitzer Bahnhof. Resident circus, and one in which youngsters perform. Also a popular venue for visiting circuses. Another three venues in Berlin. Opening hours vary.
UFA-Fabrik Viktoriastr. 10, Tempelhof ☎030 75 50 30, ⓦufafabrik.de; U-Ullsteinstrasse; map pp.126–127. Resident circus offering an inventive alternative – jugglers, acrobats, magicians – to the usual lions-and-clowns stuff. Show times vary, usually Wed–Sat 8pm with daytime shows on Sat.

THEATRES AND CINEMAS

Most cinemas show **children's films** during the school holidays but these are likely to be German-language only. The one time you're likely to catch English-language kids' films is during the Berlinale Film Festival in February (see p.223), as part of its children's programme (*Kinderprogramm*). Berlin supports a remarkable number of **puppet theatres**, most of which put on worthwhile performances that kids don't need a knowledge of German to enjoy. For details of children's films and theatre performances, check the listings magazines (see p.33).

Die Schaubude See p.220. Longstanding top-quality puppet theatre that presents a range of sophisticated pieces for kids aged 4 and up.

Grips Theater Altonaer Str. 22, Tiergarten ☎030 39 74 74 77, ⓦgrips-theater.de; U-Hansaplatz; map pp.90–91. Very good children's and young people's theatre that's been going since the 1960s to become a world leader in the art. Shows are often improvised.

SHOPS

There's a fair but not overwhelming selection of **children's shops** in Berlin, with an emphasis on wooden toys, ecological themes and multicultural education.

Anagramm Mehringdamm 50, Kreuzberg ☎030 785 95 10, ⓦanagramm-buch.de; U-Mehringdamm; map p.118. Neighbourhood bookstore with an excellent children's section and a reading corner. Mon–Fri 9am–7pm, Sat 10am–4pm.

Emma & Co Niebuhrstr. 2, City West ☎030 88 67 67 87, ⓦemmaundco.de; S-Savignyplatz; map p.108. Lovingly decorated store with a relaxed atmosphere and attentive staff. Designer knitwear and other children's fashions, lots of unique and interesting pieces, and a good selection of shoes as well as wooden toys. Mon–Fri 11am–7pm, Sat 11am–4pm.

Flying Colors Eisenacher Str. 81, Schöneberg ☎030 78 70 36 36, ⓦflying-colors.de; U-Eisenacher Strasse; map p.113. Suberb kite shop – the place to come before heading off for the Teufelsberg hill (see p.158). Mon–Fri 10am–6.30pm, Sat 10am–2pm.

Grober Unfug See p.118. Large display of international comics.

Levy's Rosenthalerstr. 40–41, in the Hackesche Höfe, Mitte ☎030 280 82 03; S-Hackescher Markt; map pp.72–73. One half of this store is dedicated to Judaica, the other half to wooden toys, sophisticated puzzles and children's books. Mon–Sat 11am–7pm.

Mundo Azul Choriner Str. 49, Prenzlauer Berg ☎030 49 85 38 34; U-Senefelderplatz; map p.132. "Blue world" stocks beautiful books for kids in French, Spanish, German and English, and also runs events and workshops. A must for visiting parents. May–Sept Mon 10am–6pm, Tues–Fri 10am–7pm, Sat 10am–4pm; Oct–April Mon 10am–6pm, Tues–Fri 10am–7pm, Sat 11am–6pm.

Spielbrett Körtestr. 27, Kreuzberg ☎030 692 42 50; U-Südstern; map pp.126–127. Massive selection of games and puzzles with some picture books too. Mon–Fri 10am–6.30pm, Sat 10am–4pm.

Zauberkönig Hermannstr. 84, Neukölln ☎030 49 20 57 51, ⓦzauberkoenig-berlin.de; U-Leinestrasse; map pp.126–127. Illusions and tricks for magicians and their apprentices. Tues–Sat 11am–7pm.

19

THE REICHSTAG IN RUINS AFTER WORLD WAR II

Contexts

History

As the heart of the Prussian kingdom, cultural centre of the Weimar Republic, headquarters of Hitler's Third Reich and a key Cold War flashpoint, Berlin has long been a weather vane of European and even world history. But World War II left the city devastated, with bombs razing 92 percent of all its shops, houses and industry, so it's the latter half of the twentieth century that shaped much of what's visible today. This was a period when the world's two most powerful military systems stood, glaring face to face, over that most tangible object of the Iron Curtain, the Berlin Wall. As the Wall fell in November 1989, Berlin was again at the forefront of world events, ushering in a period of change as frantic, confused and significant as any in the city's history.

All this historic turmoil provides a troubling fascination, and understanding it unlocks the secrets of a cityscape that is only just beginning to settle down from the slew of post-unification building work that once again made Berlin Germany's capital. In its wake, the city has successfully cultivated a fashionable and cosmopolitan outlook, and is now firmly established as a hothouse of contemporary trends and dilemmas, where the hopes and challenges of not only eastern and western Europe, but also increasingly the world, collide as Berlin again becomes a world city to be reckoned with.

Beginnings

Archeologists believe people have lived in the vicinity of modern-day Berlin for about 60,000 years. Traces of hunter-gatherer activity dating from about 8000 BC and more substantial remains of Stone Age farming settlements from 4000 BC onwards have been discovered. The Romans regarded this as barbarian territory and left no mark. Although **Germanic tribes** first appeared during the fifth and sixth centuries AD, many left during the great migrations of later centuries, and the vacated territories were occupied by **Slavs**. Germanic ascendancy only began in the twelfth and thirteenth centuries, when Saxon feudal barons of the Mark (border territory) of Brandenburg expelled the Slavs. The **Saxons** also granted municipal charters to two humble riverside towns – where the Berlin story really begins.

The twin towns

Sited on marshlands around an island (today's Spreeinsel) at the narrowest point on the River Spree, **Berlin** and **Cölln** were on a major trade route to the east and began to prosper as municipalities. Despite many links (including a joint town hall built in 1307), they retained separate identities throughout the fourteenth century.

Black Death struck the twin towns in 1348 – the first of many major devastations – killing ten percent of the population and unleashing anti-Jewish pogroms as part of a

720	948	983
The region known today as Berlin is settled by Slavic and Germanic tribes.	Germans take control over the area of present-day Berlin.	The Slavs rebel (successfully) against German rule.

search for a scapegoat. Things looked up twenty years later with the admission of Berlin and Cölln to the powerful **Hanseatic League** of city-states in 1369, confirming their economic and political importance. Powerful trade guilds and prosperous burghers ran the towns and, by 1391, made them virtually autonomous from the Mark of Brandenburg, which grew ever more chaotic in the early fifteenth century. Order was eventually restored by **Friedrich Hohenzollern**, burgrave of Nürnberg, when in 1411 the Holy Roman Emperor invited him to take over – the start of a dynasty that would rule Berlin for half a millennium. Friedrich's subjugation of the province was initially welcomed by the burghers of Berlin and Cölln. However, when his son Johann attempted to follow suit, they forced him to withdraw to Spandau. It was only divisions in their ranks that enabled **Friedrich II**, "Irontooth" Johann's brother, to take over the two cities. Some guilds offered him the keys to the gates in return for backing them against the Berlin-Cölln magistrates. Friedrich obliged, then built the **Berliner Schloss** (see p.53) and instituted his own harsh rule, forbidding any further union between Berlin and Cölln.

After swiftly crushing a 1448 **rebellion**, Friedrich imposed new restrictions. To symbolize the **consolidation of Hohenzollern power**, a chain was placed around the neck of Berlin's heraldic symbol, the bear, which remained on the city's coat of arms until 1875. After the Hohenzollerns moved their residence and court here, Berlin-Cölln assumed the character of a *Residenzstadt* (royal residence city) and rapidly expanded, its old wattle-and-daub dwellings replaced with substantial stone buildings – culminating in a Renaissance Schloss finished in 1540. Yet life remained hard; despite being involved in the Reformation, Berlin-Cölln lagged behind the great cities of western and southern Germany, and in 1576 was ravaged by plague.

The **Thirty Years' War** (1618–48) marked another low point: Europe was riven by Protestant-Catholic conflicts and national rivalries, and leaders who could ill afford to pay their mercenary armies promised them loot instead. Both Catholic Imperial troops and Protestant Swedes occupied and ransacked the twin towns who lost half their population and one third of their buildings by the end of the war.

The Great

The monumental task of postwar reconstruction fell to the Mark's new ruler, Elector **Friedrich Wilhelm of Brandenburg** (1620–88), who was barely out of his teens. Massive fortifications were constructed, besides the residences and public buildings necessary to make Berlin-Cölln a worthy capital for an Elector. (Seven Electors – three archbishops, a margrave, duke, count and king – were entitled to elect the Holy Roman Emperor.) In recognition of his achievements, Friedrich Wilhelm came to be known as the **Great Elector**. After defeating the Swedes at the Battle of Fehrbellin in 1675, the Mark of Brandenburg was acknowledged as a force to be reckoned with, and its capital grew accordingly. Recognizing the value of a cosmopolitan population, the Elector permitted Jews and South German Catholics to move here and enjoy protection as citizens.

A later wave of immigrants affected Berlin-Cölln even more profoundly. Persecuted in France, thousands of **Protestant Huguenots** sought new homes in England and Germany. The arrival of five thousand immigrants – mostly skilled craftsmen or traders – revitalized Berlin-Cölln, whose own population was just twenty thousand. French became an almost

1100s	**1244**	**1247**
Germans take over the land again.	Berlin is first mentioned in written records.	The city of Cölln is founded right next to Berlin.

obligatory second language, indispensable for anyone looking for social and career success. Another fillip to the city's development was the completion of the **Friedrich Wilhelm Canal**, linking the Spree and the Oder, which boosted it as an east–west trade centre.

Carrying on from where his father had left off, Friedrich III succeeded in becoming king of Prussia to boot (thus also gaining the title Friedrich I), while Berlin continued to expand. The **Friedrichstadt** and **Charlottenburg** quarters and the **Zeughaus** (now the Deutsches Historisches Museum) were created during this period, and Andreas Schlüter revamped the Elector's palace. In 1709, Berlin-Cölln finally became a single city named **Berlin**. None of this came cheap, however. Both Berlin and the Mark of Brandenburg were heavily in debt by the end of Friedrich's reign, to the point where he even resorted to alchemists in the hope of refilling his treasury.

Berlin under the Soldier King

The next chapter in the city's history belongs to Friedrich I's son, **Friedrich Wilhelm I** (1688–1740). Known as the **Soldier King** and generally reckoned to be the father of the Prussian state, he dealt with the financial chaos by enforcing spartan conditions on his subjects and firing most court servants. As much as eighty percent of state revenues were then directed to building up his army, and culture took a back seat to parades (eventually he even banned the theatre). While the army marched and drilled, the populace had a draconian work ethic drubbed into them – Friedrich took to walking about Berlin and personally beating anyone he caught loafing.

Friedrich tried to introduce conscription but had to make an exception of Berlin when the city's able-bodied young men fled en masse to escape the army. Despite this, Berlin became a **garrison town** geared to maintaining the army: the Lustgarten park of the royal palace was transformed into a parade ground, and every house was expected to have space available for billeting troops. Much of modern Berlin's shape and character can be traced back to Friedrich – squares like **Pariser Platz** (the area in front of the Brandenburg Gate) began as parade grounds, and **Friedrichstrasse** was built to link the centre with the Tempelhof parade ground. When Friedrich died after watching rehearsals for his own funeral (and thrashing a groom who made a mistake), few Berliners mourned.

Frederick the Great and the rise of Prussia

His son, Friedrich II – known to historians as **Frederick the Great** (1712–86) and to his subjects as "Der alte Fritz" – enjoyed a brief honeymoon as a liberalizer, before reverting to his father's ways. Soon Prussia was drawn into a series of wars that sent Berlin taxes through the roof, while the king withdrew to Sanssouci Palace in Potsdam, where only French was spoken, leaving the Berliners to pay for his military adventurism. Friedrich's saving grace was that he liked to think of himself as a philosopher king, and Berlin's **cultural life** consequently flourished. This was thanks in part to the work of the leading German Enlightenment figures, like playwright Gotthold Ephraim Lessing and philosopher Moses Mendelssohn, both of whom enjoyed royal patronage.

It was the **rise of Prussia** – particularly the invasion and subsequent annexation of Silesia in 1740 – that alarmed Austria, Saxony, France and Russia into starting the **Seven Years' War** in 1756. Four years later they occupied Berlin and demanded a tribute

1307

Cölln and Berlin become known simply as "Berlin", the larger of the two cities.

1451

Berlin becomes the royal residence of the Brandenburg Electors and has to give up its status as a free Hanseatic city.

of four million thalers, causing city president Kirchstein to faint on the spot. This was later reduced to 1.5 million when it was discovered that the city coffers were empty. Berlin was eventually relieved by Frederick, who, with British aid, went on to win the war (if only by default) after Russia and France fell out. A general peace was concluded in 1763 and victory confirmed Prussia's power in Central Europe, but keeping the peace meant maintaining a huge standing army.

Besides direct taxation, Frederick raised money by establishing **state monopolies** in the trade of coffee, salt and tobacco. Citizens were actually required to buy set quantities of these commodities whether they wanted them or not. Thus were born some of Berlin's most celebrated dishes: sauerkraut, *Kassler Rippchen* (salted pork ribs) and pickled gherkins were all invented by people desperate to use up their accumulated salt. Popular discontent was muffled by Frederick's **secret police** and **press censorship**.

Unter den Linden came into its own during Frederick's reign, as grandiose new edifices like the **Alte Bibliothek** sprang up. Just off the great boulevard, the **Französischer Dom** was built to serve the needs of the Huguenot population, while the construction of Schloss Bellevue in the Tiergarten sparked off a new building boom, as the wealthy flocked into this newly fashionable area.

Decline and occupation

After Frederick's death Prussia went into a **decline**, culminating in the defeat of its once-invincible army by French revolutionaries at the Battle of Valmy in 1792. The decline went unchecked under Friedrich Wilhelm II (1744–97), continuing into the Napoleonic era. As Bonaparte's empire spread across Europe, the Prussian court dithered, appeasing the French and trying to delay the inevitable invasion. Life in Berlin continued more or less as normal, but by August 1806 citizens were watching Prussian soldiers set off on the march west to engage Napoleonic forces. On September 19, the king and queen left the city, followed a month later by Count von der Schulenburg, the city governor, who had assured Berliners that all was going well right up until he learned of Prussia's defeat at Jena and Auerstadt.

Five days later French troops marched through the **Brandenburg Gate** and Berlin was occupied. On October 27, 1806, Napoleon himself arrived to head a parade down Unter den Linden – greeted as a liberator by the Berliners, according to some accounts. **French occupation** forced state reform: ministries were streamlined, nobles could engage in trade and guild membership became more accessible. And during this time Berlin embraced the **Romantic movement** – a rebellious celebration of German spirit and tradition in opposition to the cold rationality of the French Enlightenment. From the movement sprouted notions of what it meant to be German and the idea that all Germans should be unified in a single state – though this wouldn't happen until 1871.

The rebirth of Prussia

After his defeats in Russia and at the 1813 Battle of Leipzig, Napoleon's empire began to collapse, allowing Prussia to pull out of their forced alliance and resume self-rule. Symbolically, the **Quadriga** (the Goddess of Victory in her chariot) was restored to the Brandenburg Gate, but despite high hopes for reform the people of Berlin gained only the promise of a constitution for Prussia, which never materialized. Otherwise the pre-Napoleonic status quo was restored, and the real victor was the **Prussian state**,

1539

1576

The city becomes officially Lutheran.

Nearly five thousand inhabitants of Berlin are wiped out by the bubonic plague.

which acquired tracts of land along the Rhine, including the Ruhr, that contained the iron and coal deposits on which its military might would be rebuilt.

The war was followed by an era of reaction and oppression, which did so much to stifle intellectual and cultural life in Berlin that the philosopher Wilhelm von Humboldt resigned from the university in protest at the new authoritarianism. Gradually this mellowed out into the **Biedermeier years**, characterized by the retreat into private and family life, tranquil art and Neoclassical architecture. Meanwhile, Prussia's industrial fortunes began to rise, laying the foundation of its Great Power status. Berlin continued to grow: factories and railways and the first of the city's *Mietskaserne*, or **tenement buildings**, were constructed – foreshadowing what was to come with full industrialization.

Revolution and reaction

Berlin enjoyed more than thirty years of peace and stability after 1815, but shared the revolutionary mood that swept Europe in **1848**. Influenced by events in France and the writings of Karl Marx (who lived here from 1837 to 1841), Berliners demanded a say in the running of their own affairs. King Friedrich Wilhelm IV (1795–1861) refused to agree. On March 18, citizens gathered outside his palace to present their demands. The soldiers who dispersed them accidentally fired two shots and the demonstration became a **revolution**. Barricades went up and a fourteen-hour battle raged, with rich and poor alike joining in. During the fighting 183 Berliners and eighteen soldiers died.

Aghast at his subjects' anger, Friedrich Wilhelm IV ordered his troops to withdraw to Spandau, leaving the city in the hands of the revolutionaries, who established a parliament and citizens' militia, but lacked direction: rather than assaulting Spandau, declaring a republic or seizing public buildings, the new assembly concerned itself with law and order. On March 21, the king appeared in public wearing the tricolour black, red and gold emblem of the revolution. Having failed to suppress it, he now proposed to join it. He spoke, promising nothing much but paying lip service to the idea of German unity, which impressed the assembled liberals. Order was fully restored, then in October, a Prussian army under General Wrangel entered Berlin and forced the **dissolution of parliament**. Berliners either gave up or followed millions of fellow Germans into exile.

Suppression followed. Friedrich gave up the tricolour and persecuted liberals, before going insane shortly afterwards. His brother Prince Wilhelm – who had led the troops against the barricades – became king. **Otto von Bismarck** was appointed chancellor (1862), despite the almost universal loathing he inspired among Berliners. Meanwhile, Berlin continued to grow apace, turning into a cosmopolitan, modern industrial city. Its free press and revolutionary past exerted a liberal influence on Prussia's emasculated parliament, the **Reichstag**, to the irritation of Bismarck and the king (who was soon to proclaim himself emperor, or Kaiser). However, Bismarck became a national hero after Prussian victory at the **Battle of Königgrätz** (1866) smashed Austrian military power, clearing the way for Prussia to unite – and dominate – Germany. Although militaristic nationalism caused liberalism to wither elsewhere, Berlin continued to elect liberal Reichstag deputies, which became the parliament of the whole nation after **German unification** in 1871.

Berlin remained a maverick city. It was here that three attempts were made to kill Emperor Wilhelm I; the final one on Unter den Linden (1878) left him with thirty

1618

The Thirty Years' War begins. It has a devastating impact on Berlin with a third of houses damaged and half of the population left dead.

1685

Friedrich Wilhelm offers asylum to the Huguenots. More than 15,000 come to Brandenburg and six thousand settle in Berlin.

pieces of shrapnel in his body. While the Kaiser recovered, Bismarck used the event to justify a **crackdown on socialists**, closing newspapers and persecuting trade unionists. The growth of unionism was a direct result of relentless urbanization. Between 1890 and 1900, Berlin's population doubled to two million and thousands of tenement buildings sprang up in working-class districts like **Prenzlauer Berg** and **Wedding**. The poor conditions here meant its residents were solidly behind the Social Democratic Party (**SPD**), whose deputies were the chief dissenters within the Reichstag. By 1890 Wilhelm II had become Kaiser and dropped Bismarck, but the country continued to be militaristic and authoritarian. While Berlin remained defiantly liberal, it steadily acquired the attributes of a modern capital. Now an established centre for commerce and diplomacy, it boasted electric trams, an underground railway, and other technical innovations of the age. In the arts Berlin also moved forward, developing its own form of Modernism, in the **Berlin Secession** movement, which rejected the art establishment and included artists Max Liebermann, Edvard Munch and Walter Leistikow.

World War I and its aftermath

The arms race and alliances that polarized Europe during the 1890s and the first decade of the twentieth century led inexorably towards **World War I**. Its 1914 outbreak was greeted with enthusiasm by most German civilians – only pacifists and communists resisted the heady intoxication of patriotism. In Berlin, Kaiser Wilhelm II spoke "to all Germans" from the balcony of his palace, and shop windows across the city were festooned with national colours. Military bands played *Heil dir im Siegerkranz* ("Hail to you in the Victor's Laurel") and *Die Wacht am Rhein* ("The Watch on the Rhine") in cafés, while Berliners threw flowers to the Imperial German army, or Reichswehr, as it marched off to war. The political parties agreed to a truce, and even the Social Democrats voted for war credits.

The General Staff's calculation that France could be knocked out before Russia fully mobilized soon proved hopelessly optimistic, and Germany found itself facing a war on two fronts – the very thing Bismarck had dreaded. As casualties mounted on the stalemated western front, 350,000 German men perished in the war. Rationing and food shortages began to hit poorer civilians and **disillusionment** set in. By the summer of 1915 housewives were demonstrating in front of the Reichstag, a portent of more serious popular unrest to come. Ordinary people were beginning to see the war as an exercise staged for the rich at the expense of the poor.

In December 1917, nineteen members of the SPD announced that they could no longer support the war and formed an independent socialist party known as the USPD. This party joined the "International Group" of **Karl Liebknecht** and **Rosa Luxemburg** – later known as the Spartacists – which had opposed SPD support for the war since 1915. This grouping later formed the nucleus of the postwar Kommunistische Partei Deutschlands, or **KPD**. Meanwhile, fuel, food and even beer shortages added to growing hardships on the home front.

Defeat and revolution

With their last great offensive spent, and America joining the Allied war effort, even Germany's supreme warlord, Erich von Ludendorff, recognized that **defeat** was inevitable

1699	1701
Inauguration of Schloss Charlottenburg, commissioned by Sophie Charlotte, wife of Friedrich I.	Berlin becomes the capital of Prussia.

by the autumn of 1918. Knowing the Allies would refuse to negotiate with the old absolutist system, he declared (on September 9) a democratic, **constitutional monarchy**, whose chancellor would be responsible to the Reichstag and not the Kaiser. A government was formed under Prince Max von Baden, and extensive reforms agreed. But it was too little, too late for the bitter sailors and soldiers on the home front, where the contrast between privilege and poverty was most obvious. At the beginning of November the Kiel Garrison led a **naval mutiny** and revolutionary **Workers' and Soldiers' Soviets** mushroomed across Germany. Elements of this revolutionary unrest were mirrored in the Dada art movement, which put down firm roots in the city in 1919, while the fresh, functional **Bauhaus** design movement (see p.61) began to tidy some of the chaos.

Caught up in this wave of unrest, Berliners took to the streets on November 8–9, where they were joined by soldiers stationed in the capital. Realizing that the game was up, **Kaiser Wilhelm II abdicated**, producing a situation of dual power: almost at the same time as Philipp Scheidemann of the SPD declared a "**German Republic**" from the Reichstag's balcony, Karl Liebknecht was proclaiming a "Free Socialist Republic" from a balcony of the royal palace just 2km away. In the face of increasing confusion, SPD leader Friedrich Ebert took over as head of the government. A deal was struck with the army, which promised to protect the republic if Ebert forestalled a full-blooded socialist revolution by the Spartacists. Ebert ruled Berlin for nearly three months but many of the revolutionary soldiers, sailors and workers who controlled the streets favoured a Soviet-style government and refused to obey his orders. Things came to a head with the **Spartacist uprising** in Berlin during the first half of January 1919. This inspired lasting dread among the bourgeoisie, who applauded when the Spartacists were eventually crushed by the militarily superior **Freikorps**: armed bands of right-wing officers and NCOs from the old Imperial army, dedicated to protecting Germany from "Bolshevism". The torture and **murder of Liebknecht and Luxemburg** by Freikorps officers (who threw their bodies in the Landwehrkanal) remained unpunished once the fighting was over. This hardly augured well for the future of the **new republic**, whose National Assembly elections were held on January 19.

The Weimar Republic

The elections gave the SPD 38 percent of the vote and confirmed them the new political leaders of the country. Ebert was made president, Scheidemann chancellor. **Weimar**, the small country town that had seen the most glorious flowering of the German Enlightenment, was chosen in preference to Berlin as the place to draft a national constitution, which was tinged by monarchic and military associations.

The **constitution** drawn up was hailed as the most liberal, democratic and progressive in the world. While it incorporated a highly complex system of checks and balances to prevent power becoming too concentrated in either particular parts of government or regions, it crucially lacked clauses outlawing parties hostile to the system. This opened the way for savage attacks on the republic by extremists at both ends of the political spectrum. With public opinion divided between a plethora of parties promoting sectional interests, all Weimar-era governments became unwieldy coalitions that often pursued contradictory policies in different ministries and had an average life of only about eight months, providing a weak framework that later readily allowed the Nazis to take control.

1740	1745–47
Friedrich II – known as Frederick the Great – comes to power and rules until 1786. He turns Berlin into a centre of Enlightenment.	Schloss Sanssouci is built as the summer palace of Frederick the Great.

1920s Berlin

Much of Germany's **1920s** history was dictated by the Allies and the harsh terms of the **Treaty of Versailles:** Alsace-Lorraine was handed back to France. In the east, Germany lost a large chunk of Prussia to Poland, giving the latter access to the Baltic, but cutting off the German province of East Prussia from the rest of the country. The overseas empire was dismantled; the Rhineland occupied. But what aggrieved Germans most was the treaty's war guilt clause that held Germany responsible "for causing all the loss and damage" suffered by the Allies in the war. This was seen as a cynical victors' justice, yet provided the validation for a gigantic bill of reparation payments: a total of 132 billion gold marks.

The early 1920s was a bad time for Berlin. As the mark began to plunge in value, the government was shocked by the **assassination of Walter Rathenau.** As foreign minister, he had just signed the Treaty of Rapallo, aimed at promoting closer economic ties with the Soviet Union, since the western powers remained intransigent. Rathenau was killed at his own Grunewald house by Freikorps officers. When France and Belgium occupied the Ruhr in response to alleged defaults in the reparations payments, a **general strike** was called across Germany in January 1923.

The combination of reparations and strikes sent the mark plummeting, causing the worst **inflation** ever known. As their savings were wiped out and literally barrowloads of paper money weren't enough to support a family, Berliners experienced the terrors of hyperinflation. In working-class districts, street fighting between right and left flared up. Foreigners flocked in to pay bargain prices for carpets and furs that even rich Germans could no longer afford, and fortunes were made and lost by speculators. In the midst of all this, on November 8, Berliners' attention was briefly diverted to Munich, where a motley crew of right-wing ex-army officers including General Ludendorff attempted to mount a putsch. It failed, but Berliners were to hear of one of the ringleaders again – **Adolf Hitler.**

The mark was finally stabilized under the supremely able foreign minister, **Gustav Stresemann,** who believed relief from reparation payments was more likely to come from cooperation than stubborn resistance. The Allies too moderated their stance, realizing Germany needed to be economically stable in order to pay. So, under the **1924 Dawes Plan,** loans poured into Germany, particularly from America, leading to an economic upsurge.

Nightlife and the arts

Economic recovery transformed the social life of Berlin. For many people the centre of the city had shifted from Friedrichstrasse and Unter den Linden to the cafés and bars of the Kurfürstendamm. Jazz hit the **nightclubs** in a big way, along with drug abuse (mainly cocaine) and all kinds of sex. There were clubs for transvestites, clubs where you could watch nude dancing, or dance naked yourself – and usually the police didn't give a damn. This was the legendary era later to be celebrated by writer **Christopher Isherwood** and others, when Berlin was briefly the most open, tolerant city in Europe, a spiritual home for anyone who rejected conventions and traditions.

The 1920s was also a boom time for the arts, as the Dada shockwave rippled through the decade. **George Grosz** satirized the times in savage caricatures, while **John Heartfield** used photomontage to produce biting political statements. Equally striking, if less didactic, was the work of artists like **Otto Dix** and **Christian Schad.** Producer **Max**

1788–91	1806	1810
The Brandenburg Gate is built.	Napoleon conquers Berlin but grants self-government to the city.	Humboldt University is founded by Prussian educational reformer and linguist Wilhelm von Humboldt.

Reinhardt continued to dominate Berlin theatre, as he'd done since taking over at the Deutsches Theater in 1905. **Erwin Piscator** moved from propaganda into mainstream theatre at the Theater am Nollendorfplatz, without losing his innovative edge, and in 1928 **Bertolt Brecht**'s *Dreigroschen Oper* ("Threepenny Opera") was staged for the first time. Appropriately, Berlin also became a centre for the very newest of the arts. Between the wars the **UFA film studios** (see p.173) at Babelsberg was the biggest in Europe, producing legendary films like **Fritz Lang**'s *Metropolis, The Cabinet of Doctor Caligari* and *The Blue Angel* (starring Berlin-born **Marlene Dietrich**).

Middle- and lowbrow tastes were catered for by endless all-singing, all-dancing **musicals**, featuring platoons of women in various states of undress. This was also the heyday of the Berlin **cabaret** scene, when some of its most acidic exponents were at work.

Political extremism and the Nazis

With inflation under control, Germany returned to relative **political stability**. The 1924 elections demonstrated increased support for centre-right and republican parties. When President Ebert died (February 28, 1925) and was succeeded by the former commander of the Imperial army, **General Field Marshal von Hindenburg**, monarchists and conservatives rejoiced. Nevertheless, it was now that the extreme right, particularly the **National Socialist German Workers' Party** (NSDAP), or Nazis, began gradually gaining ground, starting in Bavaria.

Germany's late-1920s economic upsurge would last only until the **Wall Street Crash** in October 1929. That suddenly ended all American credit and wiped out Germany's economic stability. The poverty of the immediate postwar period returned with a vengeance. Everyone suffered: hyperinflation wiped out middle-class savings, and by 1932 there were six million unemployed. Increasingly people sought radical solutions in political extremism, and started supporting two parties that bitterly opposed one another but shared a desire to end democracy: the **Communists** and the National Socialist German Workers' Party. While red flags and swastika banners hung from neighbouring tenements, gangs from the left and right fought in the streets in ever-greater numbers, with the brown-shirted Nazi **SA** (*Sturmabteilung*) Stormtroopers, fighting endless pitched battles against the communist **Rote Frontkämpferbund** (Red Fighters' Front). The threat of a return to the anarchy of the postwar years increased Nazi support among the middle classes and captains of industry (who provided heavy financial support) who feared for their lives and property under communist rule. Fear of the reds also helped the Nazis ensure little or nothing was done to curb their violence against them. Growing Nazi popularity was also attributable to Hitler's record as a war veteran, his identification of Jews as scapegoats and a charisma that promised to restore national pride. Meanwhile, the Communists found it difficult to find support beyond the German working classes.

By September 1930, the Communists and Nazis together gained nearly one of every three votes cast and in the July 1932 **parliamentary elections** the Nazis took 37 percent of the vote – their biggest total in any free election – making them the largest party in the Reichstag; the Communists took fifteen percent. Very soon, Nazi thugs began attacking Jewish shops and businesses throughout Germany and intimidating liberals into muted criticism or silence. But what eventually brought the Nazis to power in

1841	**1861**	**1871**
Berlin's Museum Island is dedicated to "art and science" by Friedrich Wilhelm IV of Prussia.	Wedding, Moabit and several other suburbs are incorporated into Berlin.	Berlin becomes the capital of a unified German Empire, under Otto von Bismarck's chancellorship.

1933 was in-fighting among conservatives, who persuaded the virtually senile Hindenburg to make Hitler chancellor. This move was based on a gamble that the Nazis would usefully crush the left but fail to form an effective government – so that within a few months Hitler could be nudged aside. Hitler became chancellor on January 4, 1933 and Berlin thronged with Nazi supporters bearing torches. For the vast majority of Berliners it was a nightmare come true: three quarters of the city had voted against the Nazis at the last elections.

Nazi takeover

The pretext for an all-out **Nazi takeover** was provided by the **Reichstag fire** (February 28, 1933), which was likely started by them, rather than the simple-minded Dutch communist Marius van der Lubbe on whom it was blamed. An **emergency decree** the following day effectively legalized a permanent state of emergency, which the Nazis quickly used to start crushing the communists and manipulate the 1933 **elections** in which the Nazis won 43.9 percent of the vote. Though short of a majority, this need was quickly rendered unnecessary by the arrest of communist deputies and SPD leaders to pass an **Enabling Act** that gave the Nazis dictatorial powers. Hitler was only just short of the two-thirds majority he needed to legally abolish the Weimar Republic. The SPD salvaged some self-respect by refusing to agree, but Catholic centrists meekly supported the Bill in return for minor concessions. It was passed by 441 votes to 84, hammering the final nails into the coffin of German parliamentary democracy. With Hindenburg's death in the summer of 1934, Hitler merged the offices of president and chancellor declaring himself **Führer** of the German Reich and producing an absolute dictatorship.

Nazi terror begins

Once in absolute power Hitler quickly consolidated his control by removing opposition and tightening the Nazi grip on all areas of society. Rival political parties were effectively banned, unions quickly disbanded, and leaders of both arrested and sent to **concentration camps**. Then the persecution of Nazi opponents was extended to embrace "active church members, freemasons, politically dissatisfied people … abortionists and homosexuals". On May 11, 1934, they shocked the world by **burning thousands of books** that conflicted with Nazi ideology on Opernplatz (now Bebelplatz) in central Berlin. The **exodus from Berlin** of known anti-Nazis and those with reasons to fear them began in earnest. Well-known names including Bertolt Brecht, Kurt Weill, Lotte Lenya and Wassily Kandinsky all left the city, joining the likes of Albert Einstein and George Grosz in exile.

Nazi ruthlessness extended to their own, and in 1934 the party was purged during a night later called the **"Night of the Long Knives"**. Under **Ernst Röhm**, the SA had grown

JEWISH BERLIN

Though commonly remembered in the context of their persecution under the Third Reich, **Jews** had had a far longer and happier history in Berlin, which, as one of the most progressive cities in Europe, had fostered a large Jewish population between the late seventeenth century and the 1930s (see box, pp.80–81).

1894	1901
The Reichstag is completed after ten years of building work.	Actress and singer Marlene Dietrich is born in Schöneberg.

to 500,000 men and their power worried big business, the regular army and rival Nazis like Himmler and Göring. United in their hostility towards the SA they persuaded Hitler that Röhm and his allies were conspiring against him with the result that on the night of June 30, the SA leaders were taken to Stadelheim Prison and shot in the courtyard by SS troopers; it came as such a surprise that some believed it was an army coup, and died shouting "Heil Hitler!" In Berlin alone, 150 SA leaders were executed. Other victims included conservative politicians such as General Schleicher and several of von Papen's assistants, while local police and Gestapo chiefs added personal enemies to death lists. Meanwhile, the Nazis put their own men into vital posts throughout local governments – in Berlin and the rest of Germany. This was the first stage of Gleichschaltung ("coordination"), whereby the machinery of state, and then society itself, would be Nazified.

The other big night of Nazi savagery in the prewar period was **Kristallnacht** (November 9, 1938) when the **boycott of Jewish** businesses, medical and legal practices in Berlin – enforced by the SA since April 1, 1934 – turned into bare-faced **attacks on Jewish shops and institutions**. Just as the Reichstag fire was used as an excuse to consolidate power, the Nazis used the assassination of Ernst vom Rath, a German official in Paris, by Herschel Grynszpan, a young German-Jewish refugee, as an excuse to unleash a general pogrom on German Jews. Grynszpan was protesting his parents' forced deportation to Poland with ten thousand other Jews. (Ironically, vom Rath was an anti-Nazi whom Grynszpan had mistaken for his intended target, the German ambassador.) In retaliation the Nazis organized "spontaneous" anti-Jewish demonstrations – directing the police to ensure that attacks on the Jewish community, mainly by SA men in civilian clothes, were not hindered. After *Kristallnacht* the Nazi government enacted anti-Semitic laws confiscating property and making life difficult and dangerous for German Jews, paving the way for the greater horrors to come.

Daily life and the Olympics

Given the suppression, fear, exodus and the tightening grip of Nazi control on all areas of life, the atmosphere in Berlin changed irrevocably. The unemployed were drafted into labour battalions, set to work on the land or building autobahns; the press and radio were orchestrated by Goebbels; children joined Nazi youth organizations; and every tenement building had Nazi-appointed wardens who doubled as Gestapo spies. It was even decreed that women should eschew make-up as an "un-German" artifice – one of the few edicts that wasn't taken seriously. Anti-Nazi criticism – even of the mildest kind – invited a visit from the Gestapo. Although Germans might avoid joining the NSDAP itself, it was difficult to escape the plethora of related organizations covering every aspect of life, from riding clubs and dog breeders to the "Reich Church" or "German League of Maidens". This was the second stage of *Gleichschaltung* – drawing the entire population into the Nazi net.

As the capital of the Reich, Berlin became a showcase city of banners, uniforms and parades. An image of order and dynamism, of a "new Germany" on the march, was what the Nazis tried to convey. This reached its zenith during the **1936 Olympics**, held at a vast purpose-built stadium in suburban Berlin, which helped raise Germany's international standing and temporarily glossed over the realities of Nazi brutality.

1918	1920
Berlin witnesses the end of World War I and the proclamation of the Republic.	Berlin is established as a separate administrative zone under the Greater Berlin Act. A dozen villages and estates are incorporated into the city to expand it.

World War II

Throughout the 1930s the Nazis made **preparations for war**, expanding the army and gearing the economy for war readiness by 1940, to dovetail with Hitler's foreign policy of obtaining *Lebensraum* ("living space") from neighbouring countries by intimidation. From 1936 onwards Hitler even spent much time with his favourite architect, **Albert Speer**, drawing up extensive plans for a remodelled and grandiose Berlin, to be called "Germania", that would reflect a postwar role as world capital of the "Thousand Year Reich". His megalomania inspired hours of brooding on how future generations might be awed by Germania's monumental ruins, in the way that contemporaries venerated the ruins of ancient Roman and Middle Eastern civilizations – hence the need to build with the finest materials on a gigantic scale.

The road to war was swift. In 1936 the German army occupied the Rhineland (demilitarized under the terms of the Treaty of Versailles) to token protests from the League of Nations. The **Anschluss** ("annexation") of Austria in 1938 was likewise carried off with impunity, and a few months later Britain and France agreed to dismember Czechoslovakia. Encouraged by their appeasement, Hitler made new demands on Polish territory in 1939, probably hoping for a similar collapse of will by the western powers, the more so since he had pulled off the spectacular coup of signing a nonaggression pact with his ultimate enemy, the Soviet Union, thus ensuring that Germany could avoid a war on two fronts. But two days after the German invasion of Poland began on September 1, Britain and France declared war in defence of their treaty obligations.

Outbreak and early success

The outbreak of **World War II** was greeted without enthusiasm by Berliners, despite German victories in Poland. There were few signs of patriotic fervour as the troops marched off to war through the streets, and Hitler cancelled further parades out of pique. Only the spectacle of the military parade to mark the fall of France (July 18, 1940), when German troops marched through the Brandenburg Gate for the first time since 1871, really attracted the crowds.

Initially, Berlin suffered little from the war. Although citizens were already complaining of meagre rations, delicacies and luxury goods from occupied Europe gravitated towards the Reich capital. What remained of the diplomatic and foreign press community and all the Nazi bigwigs continued to maintain chic lifestyles. Open dissent seemed impossible, with Gestapo informers believed to lurk everywhere, while much wartime misery was softened by Nazi welfare organizations and a blanket of propaganda.

Air raids

Göring had publicly boasted that Germans could call him "Meyer" (a Jewish surname) if a single bomb fell on Berlin. Notwithstanding, the British RAF dropped some for the first time on August 23, 1940, and a further night raid on August 28–29 killed ten people – the first German civilian casualties. These raids had a marked demoralizing effect on Berliners, who had counted on a swift end to the war, and Hitler had to reassure the populace in a speech at the Sportpalast. Holding up a Baedeker travel guide to Britain, he thundered that the Luftwaffe would raze Britain's cities to the ground one by one.

However, these early **bombing raids** on Berlin caused little real damage and it wasn't until March 1, 1943 – when defeat in the Western Desert and difficulties on the

1928	**1933**
British novelist Christopher Isherwood arrives in Berlin.	Adolf Hitler comes to power shortly after a fire devastates the Reichstag.

THE WANNSEE CONFERENCE

The conference at the **Wannsee villa** on January 20, 1942, was held at the instigation of Reinhard Heydrich, Chief of Reich Security Head Office, who had been ordered by Göring to submit plans for rounding up, deporting and destroying all Jews in Reich territory. Heydrich summoned SS and government officials, including Adolf Eichmann and Roland Freisler, who later gained infamy as the judge at the Volksgerichthof (see p.101). Eichmann kept a complete set of minutes of the meeting, and these documents, discovered after the war – despite the fact that all recipients had been requested to destroy their copies – played an important part in the Nürnberg trials of war criminals.

The problem Heydrich delineated was that Europe contained eleven million Jews: the "Final Solution" to the "Jewish Question" was that these people should be taken to camps and worked to death, if they were able-bodied, or murdered on arrival if not. Those who survived would eventually be executed, since, under Nazi principles of natural selection, they would be the toughest, and in Heydrich's words could be "the germ cell of a new Jewish development". In these early stages systematic killing machines like Auschwitz and Treblinka were not yet fully operational. More discussion was spent on how the Jews should be rounded up: deception would prevent panic and revolt, so the pretence that Jews were being moved for "resettlement" extremely important. Heydrich charged Eichmann with this task, which eventually cost him his life when he was sentenced to death for war crimes in Israel in 1960.

At no time during the conference were the words "murder" or "killing" written down; careful euphemisms shielded the enormity of what was being planned. Reading the minutes, it's difficult not to be shocked by the matter-of-fact manner in which the business was discussed, and the way in which politeness and efficiency absorb and absolve all concerned. When sterilization was suggested as one "solution" it was rejected as "unethical" by a doctor present, and there was much self-congratulation as various officials described their areas as "Judenfrei" (free of Jews).

Heydrich died following an assassination attempt in Prague a few months later; some of the others present did not survive the war either, but, in contrast to the millions who were destroyed by their organizational ability, many of the Wannsee delegation lived on to gain a pension from the postwar German state.

eastern front had already brought home the fact that Germany was not invincible – that Berlin suffered its first heavy raids. The British bombed by night, the Americans by day, establishing a pattern that would relentlessly reduce Berlin to ruins. "We can wreck Berlin from end to end if the USAAF will come in on it. It will cost us between 400 and 500 aircraft. It will cost Germany the war", the head of Bomber Command, Sir Arthur "Bomber" Harris, had written to Churchill in 1943. The first buildings to go were the Staatsoper and Alte Bibliothek on Unter den Linden. On December 22, the Kaiser-Wilhelm-Gedächtniskirche was reduced to a shell. By the year's end, daily and nightly bombardments were a feature of everyday life.

During the 363 air raids until the end of the war, 75,000 tons of high-explosive or incendiary bombs killed between 35,000 and 50,000 people and rendered 1,500,000 Berliners homeless. Yet despite the colossal destruction that filled the streets with 100 million tons of rubble, at the war's end seventy percent of the city's industrial capacity was still functioning.

Apart from chipping away at Nazi power, the destruction also intensified **underground resistance**. Despite the Gestapo stranglehold some groups managed

1936

The Olympic Games are held in Berlin.

1938

Jewish shop windows are smashed and businesses attacked throughout Germany on Kristallnacht, also called the Night of Broken Glass.

minor successes and several failed attempts on Hitler's life were made, most notably the **July Bomb Plot** (see p.100). But resistance was piecemeal and included assistance given to **Jews** to help them evade being rounded up onto trains bound for concentration camps, as part of the Nazi "**Final Solution**" to the Jewish question as decided in a villa beside Berlin's Wannsee (see p.257).

The fall of Berlin

Enjoy the war while you can! The peace is going to be terrible…

Berlin joke shortly before the fall of the city.

By autumn 1944, it was obvious to all but the most fanatical Nazis that the end was approaching fast. Even so, Hitler would hear no talk of surrender or negotiation. But by January 1945, distance between the Allied forces was narrowing inexorably and on January 27, Soviet forces crossed the Oder 160km from Berlin. Only Hitler now really believed there was any hope for Germany. The Nazis threw all they could at the eastern front and mobilized the Volkssturm, an ill-equipped home guard of old men, boys and cripples. Thirteen- and fourteen-year-old members of the **Hitler Youth** were briefly trained in the art of using the Panzerfaust bazooka, then sent into the fray against tanks and battle-hardened infantrymen. As thousands died at the front to buy a little time for the doomed Nazi regime, life in Berlin became a nightmare. The city was choked with refugees and terrified of the approaching Russians; it was bombed day and night, and the flash of Soviet artillery could be seen on the horizon.

Behind the lines, **flying court martials** picked up soldiers and executed anyone suspected of "desertion" or "cowardice in the face of the enemy". On February 1, 1945, Berlin was declared *Vertedigungsbereich* (a "zone of defence") – to be defended to the last man and the last bullet. The civilian population – women, children and forced labourers – were set to work building tank traps and barricades; stretches of the U- and S-Bahn formed part of the fortifications. Goebbels trumpeted a "**fortress Berlin**", while Hitler planned the deployment of phantom armies, which existed on battle charts, but hardly at all in reality.

As Berlin frantically prepared to defend itself, the Russians consolidated their strength. On April 16, at 5am Moscow time, the **Soviet offensive** began with a massive bombardment lasting 25 minutes. When the artillery fell silent, 143 searchlights spaced 200m apart along the entire front were switched on to dazzle the enemy as the Russians began their advance. Three army groups totalling over 1.5 million men moved forward under marshals Zhukov, Konev and Rokossovsky – and there was little the vastly outnumbered Germans could do to halt them. By April 20 – Hitler's 56th birthday (celebrated with tea and cakes in the *Führerbunker*) – the Red Army was on the edge of Berlin. The next day the city centre came within range of their guns, and several people queuing outside the Karstadt department store on Hermannplatz were killed by shells. On April 23, Soviet troops were in the Weissensee district, just a few kilometres east of the centre.

Hitler's birthday party was the last time the Nazi hierarchy assembled before going – or staying – to meet their respective fates. The dictator and his partner Eva Braun chose to remain in Berlin, and Goebbels elected to join them in the **Führerbunker** with his family. It was a dank, stuffy complex of reinforced concrete cells beneath the garden of the Reich Chancellery. Here Hitler brooded over Speer's architectural models of

1938–45

1939

Thousands of Jews (and other minorities) living in Berlin are sent to death camps.

World War II begins.

unbuilt victory memorials, subsisting on salads, herbal tisanes and regular injections of dubious substances by one Dr Morell. To hapless generals and faithful acolytes, he ranted about traitors and the unworthiness of the German *Volk*, and after learning that General Steiner's army had failed to stop Zhukov's advance declared that the war was lost and that he would stay in the bunker to the end.

The final days
By April 25, Berlin was completely **encircled by Soviet troops**, which met up with US forces advancing from the west. Over the next two days, the suburbs of Dahlem, Spandau, Neukölln and Gatow fell to the Russians, and the city's telephone system failed. On April 27, the Third Panzer Army was completely smashed; survivors fled west, leaving Berlin's northern flank virtually undefended. The obvious hopelessness of the situation didn't sway the top Nazis' fanatical **refusal to surrender**. As the Red Army closed in, Goebbels called hysterically for "rücksichtslose Bekämpfung" – fight without quarter – and SS execution squads worked around the clock, killing soldiers, Volkssturm guards or Hitler Youth who tried to stop fighting.

In the city the horrors mounted. The **civilian population** lived underground in cellars and air-raid shelters, scavenging for food wherever and whenever there was a momentary lull in the fighting. Engineers blasted canal locks, flooding the U-Bahn to prevent the Russians from advancing along it and drowning scores of sheltering civilians in the process. On April 27, the Ninth Army was destroyed attempting to break out of the Russian encirclement to the south, and unoccupied Berlin had been reduced to a strip 15km long from east to west, and 5km wide from north to south, constantly under bombardment. Next the Russians captured the Tiergarten, reducing the **last pocket of resistance** to the *Regierungsviertel*, where fighting focused on the Reichstag and Hitler's Chancellery, and on Potsdamer Platz, only a few hundred metres from the *Führerbunker*, by now under constant shellfire.

Hitler still hoped one of his phantom armies would relieve Berlin, but on April 28 his optimism evaporated when he heard that Himmler had been suing for unconditional surrender with the western Allies. In the early hours of the following day, he married Eva Braun, held a small champagne reception, and dictated his will. As the day wore on, savage fighting continued around the Nazi-held enclave. At a final conference the commandant of Berlin, General Weidling, announced that the Russians were in the nearby *Adlon Hotel*, and that there was no hope of relief.

A breakout attempt was proposed, but Hitler declared that he was staying put. On the afternoon of April 30, after testing the cyanide on his pet German shepherd dog, **Hitler and Eva Braun committed suicide**: he with a revolver, she by poison. The bodies were taken to the Chancellery courtyard and doused with two hundred litres of petrol; Hitler's followers gave the Nazi salute as the corpses burned to ashes. Meanwhile, Soviet troops battled for the Reichstag, and at 11pm two Russian sergeants raised the red flag on its rooftop.

After Hitler's death, chief of staff Krebs was sent out to parley with the Russians. After hasty consultation with Stalin, General Chuikov replied that only unconditional surrender was acceptable. When Krebs returned to the bunker, Goebbels rejected this and ordered the fighting to continue. That night he and his wife killed themselves, having first poisoned their six children. Almost all the rest of the eight hundred or so

1943–45	1945
Over ninety percent of Berlin is destroyed in air raids.	The Allies take Berlin, and divide it into Russian, American, French and British zones.

bunker occupants decided to try and break out. Weidling agreed not to surrender until the following dawn in order to give the fugitives time to **escape** through the railway tunnels towards northern Berlin; about a hundred made it – the rest were either killed or captured.

Capitulation and surrender

At 5am, Weidling offered the **capitulation of Berlin** to General Chuikov, who broadcast his surrender proclamation from loudspeaker vans around the city. At 3pm, firing in the city centre stopped, although sporadic, sometimes fierce, fighting continued on the outskirts, where German troops tried to break out to the west to surrender to the more merciful British or Americans rather than the vengeful Russians. The **official surrender of German forces** occurred at a Wehrmacht engineers' school in the Berlin suburb of Karlshorst on May 8, 1945. By then Berliners had already emerged from their shelters and started to clear the dead and the rubble from the streets.

With the final act of surrender complete, it was time to count the **cost** of the Battle of Berlin. It had taken the lives of 125,000 Berliners (including 6400 suicides and 22,000 heart attacks), and innumerable German soldiers from the 93 divisions destroyed by the Red Army. The Soviets themselves had suffered some 305,000 casualties in the battle, while the city was left in ruins, without even basic services. But for those civilians who remained in the city, this was just the start of the worst as the Soviets unleashed an **orgy of rape and looting** on the capital.

Occupation

During the immediate postwar months, civilian rations of food, fuel and medicine, if forthcoming at all, were cut to the bone to support the two-million-strong **Soviet occupation forces**. Civilians had to use all their wits to stay alive. The Soviet Union had taken steps towards establishing a civilian, communist-dominated administration even before the war was over. On April 30, a group of exiled German communists were brought to Berlin to establish a temporary headquarters in Lichtenberg. Directed by **Walter Ulbricht**, the future leader of the GDR's communist party, they set about tracking down old Berlin party members and setting up a new **municipal administration**.

The **western occupation sectors** had been demarcated by the Allies as far back as 1943, but the troops didn't move in until July 1–4, 1945, when fifty thousand British, American and French soldiers replaced the Red Army in western Berlin. Here, the food situation improved marginally once American supplies began to find their way through, but public health remained a huge problem. Dysentery and TB were endemic, and there were outbreaks of typhoid and paratyphoid, all exacerbated by an acute shortage of hospital beds. British and American soldiers had endless opportunities to profit from the burgeoning **black market**: trading cigarettes, alcohol, gas, NAAFI and PX supplies for antiques, jewellery or sexual favours. Huge black-market centres sprang up around the Brandenburg Gate and Alexanderplatz.

From July 17 to August 3 the **Potsdam conference** took place at Cecilienhof Palace. It was to be the last great meeting of the leaders of the Big Three wartime alliance. Churchill took the opportunity to visit the ruins of the Reich's Chancellery, followed by a mob of fascinated Germans and Russians. Mid-conference he returned to Britain

June 1948

The Russians cut off all overland routes between West Germany and West Berlin, so the Berlin airlift begins, with Allied planes delivering essential supplies around the clock.

1949

The Federal Republic of Germany is founded in West Berlin and the German Democratic Republic in East Berlin.

to hear the results of the first postwar election – and was replaced by the newly elected Labour prime minister, Clement Attlee, who could do little but watch as Truman and Stalin settled the fate of postwar Europe and Berlin.

Starvation and unrest

For Berliners, things stayed miserable. German agriculture and industry had virtually collapsed, threatening acute **shortages of food and fuel** just as winter approached. Mass graves were dug and coffins stockpiled for the expected wave of deaths, and thousands of children were evacuated to the British occupation zone in the west, where conditions were less severe. To everyone's surprise the winter turned out to be uncommonly mild. Christmas 1945 was celebrated after a fashion, and mothers took their children to the first postwar *Weihnachtsmarkt* (Christmas fair) in the Lustgarten.

Unfortunately the respite was only temporary, for despite the good weather, food supplies remained overstretched. In March rations were reduced drastically, and the weakened civilian population fell prey to typhus, TB and other **hunger-related diseases**; the lucky ones merely suffered enteric or skin diseases. The Allies did what they could, sending government and private relief, but even by the spring of 1947 rations remained at malnutrition levels. **Crime and prostitution** soared. In Berlin alone, two thousand people were arrested every month, many from the juvenile gangs that roamed the ruins murdering, robbing and raping. Trains were attacked at the Berlin stations, and in the countryside bandits ambushed supply convoys heading for the city. The winter of 1946–47 was one of the coldest since records began. Wolves appeared in Berlin and people froze to death aboard trains. There were rumours of cannibalism and Berlin hospitals treated 55,000 people for frostbite.

Allied tensions

Meanwhile, **political developments** that were to have a lasting impact on Berlin were occurring. In March 1946, parts of the SPD were forced into a shotgun merger with the KPD, to form the **SED** (Sozialistische Einheitspartei Deutschlands – "Socialist Unity Party of Germany"), or future **communist party** of East Germany, underlining the political division of the city as the wartime alliance between the western powers (France had also been allotted an occupation zone) and the Soviet Union fell apart, ushering in a new era of conflict that would all too often focus on Berlin. The Allied Control Council met for the last time on March 20, when Marshal Sokolovsky, the Soviet military governor, protested British and American attempts to introduce economic reform in their zones.

Tension mounted over the next few months as the Allies went ahead with economic reform, while the Russians demanded the right to board Berlin-bound Allied trains, and on June 16 walked out of the four-power *Kommandantura* that had ultimate control over Berlin. Things came to a head with the **introduction of the D-Mark** in the western zone (June 23, 1948). On that day, the Soviets demanded from Berlin's mayor that he accept their Ostmark as currency for the whole city. But the city's parliament voted overwhelmingly against it. Everyone knew that this was asking for trouble, and trouble wasn't long in coming. On the night of June 23–24, power stations in the Soviet zone cut off electricity supplies to the western half of Berlin, and road and rail links between the western part of Germany and Berlin were severed. This was the beginning of the **Berlin blockade**, the USSR's first attempt to force the western Allies

June 1953	1961
An uprising of industrial workers against the Communist regime in the East is brutally put down; at least 200 people die.	Germany signs an agreement that grants Turks temporary work visas; many start to settle in Berlin.

out of the city. SPD politician Ernst Reuter, soon to be mayor of West Berlin, addressed a crowd at the Gesundbrunnen football field, promising that Berlin would "fight with everything we have". In the end the greatest weapon proved to be American and British support when on June 26, 1948, they began the **Berlin airlift**, flying supplies into the city to keep it alive against the odds for almost a year (see p.124).

The 1950s: the birth of two Germanys

Within six months, the political division of Germany was formalized by the creation of two rival states. First, the British, French and American zones of occupation were amalgamated to form the **Federal Republic of Germany** (May 1949); the Soviets followed suit by launching the **German Democratic Republic** on October 7. As Berlin lay deep within GDR territory, its eastern sector naturally became the official GDR capital. However, much to the disappointment of many Berliners, the Federal Republic chose Bonn as their capital. West Berlin remained under the overall control of the Allied military commandants, although it was eventually to assume the status of a Land (state) of the Federal Republic.

Political tension remained a fact of life in a city that had become an arena for superpower confrontations. The Soviets and GDR communists had not abandoned the idea of driving the Allies out of Berlin, and mounted diverse operations against them, just as the Allies ran spying and sabotage operations in East Berlin. In this cradle of **Cold War espionage**, the recruitment of former Gestapo, SD or Abwehr operatives seemed quite justifiable to all the agencies concerned. On one side were Britain's SIS (based at the Olympic Stadium) and the American CIA, which fostered the Federal Republic's own intelligence service, the Gehlen Bureau, run by a former Abwehr colonel. Opposing them were the Soviet KGB and GRU (based at Karlshorst), and the GDR's own foreign espionage service and internal security police. The public side of this rumbling underground war was a number of **incidents** in 1952. An Air France plane approaching West Berlin was fired upon by a Russian MiG; and East German authorities blocked streets leading from West to East Berlin and expropriated property owned by West Berliners on the outskirts of the eastern sector.

The economic miracle and the Berlin Wall

Throughout the 1950s important events took place in **West Germany** under Chancellor Konrad Adenauer. Foremost among them was the so-called "**economic miracle**", which saw West Germany recover from the ravages of war astonishingly quickly and go on to become Europe's largest economy. Although West Berlin's **economic recovery** was by no means as dramatic as that of West Germany, the city did prosper, particularly in comparison to East Berlin. **Marshall Plan aid** and West German capital were transforming West Berlin into a capitalist showcase, whereas the GDR and East Berlin seemed to languish, partly the result of the Soviets' ruthless **asset-stripping** – removing factories, rolling stock and generators to replace losses in the war-ravaged USSR. The **death of Stalin** on March 5, 1953 raised hopes that the situation in Berlin could be eased, but these were soon dashed. In the eastern sector, the communists unwittingly fuelled smouldering resentment by announcing a ten percent **rise in work norms** on June 16, leading to a widespread uprising that was brutally suppressed (see p.120).

August 1961	**June 1963**
The tension between East and West culminates in the building of the Berlin Wall.	US President John F. Kennedy visits West Berlin, delivering his famous "Ich bin ein Berliner" speech.

So, as the economic disparity between East and West Germany (and their respective halves of Berlin) worsened throughout the 1950s, West Berlin became an increasingly attractive destination for East Germans and East Berliners, who were able to cross the **zonal border** more or less freely at this time. Many moved over and found work in the western half of the city, benefiting from the purchasing power of the D-Mark – others at the very least went over at night to enjoy entertainment and culture lacking in the more spartan East. This steady **population drain** undermined the GDR, as young and highly skilled workers headed west for higher living standards and greater political freedom. Roughly 2,500,000 people quit the GDR during the 1950s, mostly via the open border with West Berlin, which an average of nineteen thousand East Germans crossed every month.

Both the GDR and Soviet governments saw this as a threat to East Germany's existence, and on November 10, 1958, Soviet leader Nikita Khrushchev demanded that the western Allies relinquish their role in Berlin to "normalize" the GDR. Two weeks later, he suggested the Allies should withdraw and make Berlin a free city – coupled with a broad hint that if no agreement was reached within six months, a blockade would be reimposed. The Allies rejected the ultimatum, and the Kremlin allowed the deadline to pass without incident.

By 1961, Ulbricht's regime was getting desperate, and rumours that the border might be sealed began to circulate. In mid-June Ulbricht assured the world that no one had "the intention of building a wall". Simultaneously, however, border controls were tightened, while the flood of people voting with their feet continued to rise. It was obvious that something was about to happen. Shortly after midnight on August 13, 1961, East Germany sealed the border, dividing the city with the **Berlin Wall** (see pp.86–87).

Reaction in the West

Despite public outrage throughout West Germany and formal **diplomatic protests** from the Allies, everyone knew that a firmer line risked nuclear war. The West had to fall back on symbolic gestures: the Americans sent over General Lucius Clay, organizer of the Berlin airlift, and Vice-President Lyndon Johnson on August 18. The **separation of families** plunged morale in East Berlin to new depths and **economic problems** hit West Berlin, which was suddenly deprived of sixty thousand skilled workers who formerly commuted in from the GDR. They could only be replaced by creating special tax advantages to attract workers and businesses from the Federal Republic. American support for West Berlin was reaffirmed in August 1963 by President **John F. Kennedy**'s "Berliner" speech (see p.115), but for all its rhetoric and rapturous reception, the West essentially had to accept the new status quo.

The 1960s

The **gradual reduction of political tension** that occurred after the Wall had been standing a couple of years was partly due to improved relations between the superpowers, but mostly to local efforts. Under SPD mayor **Willy Brandt**, talks were opened up between the West Berlin Senate and the GDR government, resulting in the "**Pass Agreement**" of December 1963, whereby 730,000 West Berliners were able to pay brief visits to the East at the end of the year. Three more agreements were concluded over the next couple

1971	1976
Access is guaranteed across East Germany to West Berlin with the Four Powers agreement.	David Bowie moves to Schöneberg and starts work on his Berlin trilogy.

BERLIN ON BERLIN

Remarkably, Berlin doesn't really have one single great **museum** all about its own history. But maybe this isn't even desirable, since the process of exploring its scattered single-perspective museums is so rewarding and revealing.

With little or no background knowledge of the city, the obvious place to start is the flashy but relatively superficial **Story of Berlin** (see p.112). Another good starting point is the more formal, less Berlin-centric approach of the **Deutsches Historisches Museum** (see p.46).

Undoubtedly Berlin's most fascinating epoch began with the industrial revolution and the best places to get a feel for this are two nineteenth-century apartments: Zimmermeister Brunzel's **Mietshaus** (see p.135) and **Museum Pankow** (see p.140). For a more art-centric perspective, the **Zille Museum** (see p.67) shows industrial Berlin portrayed by its most famous cartoonist, and the **Berlinische Galerie** (see p.119) gathers together local art for a revealing insight into the early twentieth-century city. The **Filmmuseum** (see p.92) is most fascinating for its coverage of the same era.

The Nazi era effectively destroyed much of all this, and several collections provide insights into the regime. Foremost among them is the **Sachsenhausen Concentration Camp Memorial** (see p.174) and the **Wannsee Villa** (see p.163), where the Jewish Holocaust was planned; both lie on the edge of Berlin. In the centre you can complete the picture with the **Topography of Terror** exhibition on Nazi terror apparatus (see p.121), the **German Resistance museum** (see p.98), the **Holocaust Memorial** (see p.38), and the **Blindenwerkstatt** (see p.74), a brushmaker's workshop where a Jewish family went into hiding. The best insights into the war in Berlin itself are provided by the **bunker tours** of Berliner Unterwelten (see p.87).

Essential to Berlin's Cold War chapter is the last remaining complete section of the Berlin Wall at the **Berlin Wall Memorial** (see p.86); the **Tränenpalast** (see p.84), the city's main former border crossing; the former GDR secret police headquarters at **Normanenstrasse** (see p.143) and the eerily well-preserved Stasi prison **Hohenschönhausen** (see p.143). For an overview of all this and reminders of the GDR's better sides, visit the **DDR Museum** (see p.64), while to see it all from the West's point of view visit the **Allied Museum** (see p.162) or the **Kennedy Museum** (see p.79).

As Berlin busies itself with closing previous chapters of its history, it still awaits a single museum to properly record the post-reunification era. Until such a place exists, the story is all around; talking a **walking tour** (see p.25) should reveal much.

of years until the GDR decided to use border controls as a lever for winning **diplomatic recognition** (which the Federal Republic and its Western allies refused to give). Access to West Berlin via routes through GDR territory was subject to official hindrance; on one occasion, deputies were prevented from attending a plenary session of the Bundestag, held in West Berlin in 1965. New and more stringent **passport and visa controls** were levied on all travellers from June 1968 onwards.

As the direct threat to its existence receded, West Berlin society began to fragment along generational lines. Partly because Berlin residents could legally evade West German conscription, young people formed an unusually high proportion of the population – many gravitating towards squats and cheap digs in Kreuzberg. The immediate catalyst was the 1967–68 wave of **student unrest**, when grievances over unreformed, badly run universities soon spread to embrace wider disaffection with West Germany's materialistic culture. As in West Germany, the APO, or **extra-parliamentary opposition**, emerged as a strong and vocal force in West Berlin, criticizing what many people saw as a failed

1982

US President Ronald Reagan visits Berlin for the first time.

1987

During his second Berlin visit, Reagan makes a speech in front of the Brandenburg Gate, demanding Mr Gorbachev "tear down this Wall!"

attempt to build a true democracy on the ruins of Nazi Germany. Another powerful strand was anti-Americanism, fuelled by US policy in Southeast Asia, Latin America and the Middle East. Both these viewpoints tended to bewilder and enrage older Germans.

The police reacted to street demonstrations in Berlin with a ferocity that shocked even conservatives. On June 2, 1967, a student was shot by police during a protest against a state visit by the Shah of Iran. When someone tried to kill student leader **Rudi Dutschke** (April 11, 1968), there were huge and violent demonstrations. Although the mass-protest movement fizzled out towards the end of the 1960s, a new and deadlier opposition would emerge in the 1970s – partly born from the West German establishment's violent response to what was initially a peaceful protest movement.

Ostpolitik and détente

The international scene and Berlin's place in it changed considerably around the turn of the decade. Both superpowers now hoped to thaw the Cold War and agree to a détente, while elections in the Federal Republic brought to power Willy Brandt, a chancellor committed to rapprochement with the GDR. On February 27, 1969, US President Richard Nixon called for an easing of international tension during his visit to Berlin. Soon afterwards, **Four Power Talks** were held in the former Allied Control Council building in the American sector. Participants decided to set aside broader issues in an effort to fashion a workable agreement on the status of the divided city resulting in the **Quadripartite Agreement** (September 3, 1971), followed in December by inter-German agreements regarding transit routes to West Berlin and travel and traffic regulations for West Berliners. In 1972, the Federal Republic and the GDR signed a **Basic Treaty**, which bound both states to respect each other's frontiers and de facto sovereignty. In return for diplomatic recognition, the GDR allowed West Germans access to friends and family across the border, which had effectively been denied to them (barring limited visits in the mid-1960s). However, the freedom to move from East to West was restricted to disabled people and senior citizens.

The 1970s

During the 1970s Berlin assumed a new identity, breaking with the images and myths of the past. Thanks to the easing of Cold War tensions, West Berlin was no longer a frontline city, and East Berlin lost much of its intimidating atmosphere. Throughout the decade, **West Berlin** had similar problems to those of West Germany: economic upsets triggered by the quadrupling of oil prices in 1974, and a wave of terrorism directed against the establishment. In addition, West Berlin suffered from a deteriorating stock of housing and rising unemployment – both alleviated to some extent by financial help from West Germany. **East Berlin** remained relatively quiet. A new East German leader, **Erich Honecker**, who was regarded as a "liberal", succeeded Ulbricht in 1971. Living standards improved and there was some relaxation of the tight controls of the Ulbricht days. However, most people regarded the changes as essentially trivial, and escapes continued to be attempted, although by now the Wall was formidably deadly. In 1977, a rock concert in Alexanderplatz turned into an explosion of street unrest, which the authorities suppressed with deliberate brutality.

1989	**November 9, 1989**
The first Love Parade is organized in Berlin; just 150 people take part.	Following a series of mass demonstrations across East Berlin, and a confused government press conference, border crossings in the Wall finally open.

The 1980s

Throughout the 1970s and early 1980s, the Quadripartite Agreement and the inter-German treaties formed the backdrop to relations between West and East Berlin. The main irritant was the **compulsory exchange** of D-Marks for Ostmarks, which the GDR raised in value from DM6.50 to DM25 in 1980, deterring significant numbers of visitors. But on the whole, a degree of stability and normality had been achieved, enabling both cities to run relatively smoothly. Even after the partial resumption of the Cold War following the Soviet invasion of Afghanistan in 1979, Berlin remained relatively calm. The only notable event was the shooting of an American officer on an alleged spying mission in Potsdam in the spring of 1985.

As elsewhere in West Germany, Berlin witnessed a crystallization of issues and attitudes and the flowering of new radical movements. Concern about the arms race and the environment was widespread; feminism and gay rights commanded increasing support. Left-wing and Green groups formed an **Alternative Liste** to fight elections, and a left-liberal newspaper, *Tageszeitung*, was founded. Organized squatting was the radical solution to Berlin's **housing crisis**. In 1981, the new Christian Democrat administration (elected after a financial scandal forced the SPD to step down) tried to evict the squatters from about 170 apartment buildings, and police violence sparked rioting in Schöneberg. The administration compromised by allowing some of the squatters to become legitimate tenants, which had a big effect on life in West Berlin. For the first time since the late 1960s, the social divisions that had opened up showed signs of narrowing. Alternative Liste delegates were elected to the Berlin Senate for the first time in May 1981, and the same year witnessed a boom in **cultural life**, as the arts exploded into new vitality.

The **early 1980s** saw a resumption of frostiness in US–Soviet relations, which heightened concern about **nuclear weapons**. Anti-nuclear activists protested during the Berlin visit of President Ronald Reagan in June 1981. But the tension and sabre-rattling of the 1950s and 1960s Cold War didn't return to Berlin even though ideological hostility prevented the two halves of the city from jointly celebrating Berlin's 750th **anniversary** in 1987. In East Berlin anniversary celebrations were preceded by a massive **urban renewal project**, in both the city centre and the inner suburbs; the reconstructed Nikolaiviertel (see p.66) stems from this time. In West Berlin, the elections of spring 1989 swept the CDU administration from power, and an **SPD/Alternative Liste coalition** took over, with Walter Momper as mayor. In Kreuzberg, demonstrations against what many regarded as an Alternative Liste sell-out were put down with unwarranted force, sparking running street battles.

When, in 1985, **Mikhail Gorbachev** became the new Soviet leader and began campaigns for *glasnost* and *perestroika*, their initial impact on East Germany was slight. The SED regarded them with deep suspicion, so while Poland and Hungary embarked on the road to democracy, Erich Honecker declared that the Berlin Wall would stand for another fifty or one hundred years if necessary.

Die Wende

The year 1989 ranks as both one of the most significant years in German history and one of the most unforeseeable. Within twelve months **die Wende** ("the turning") transformed Germany completely. With little warning East Germany suddenly

October 3, 1990	**1997**
The two parts of Berlin are unified within the Federal Republic of Germany.	Peter Eisenman's controversial design for a Memorial to the Murdered Jews of Europe is chosen.

collapsed in the wake of the general easing of communism in the Eastern Bloc of the late 1980s. The Berlin Wall was breach on **November 9, 1989**, symbolizing an end to the Cold War, making a lifetime's dream come true for most Germans – above all, for those living in the East. Several events then fairly logically and briskly followed: the union of the two Germanys; the reassertion of Berlin as capital; and the start of the lengthy process of putting those responsible for the GDR's crimes on trial.

The first holes in the Iron Curtain

Despite the unyielding position of the GDR government, as the 1980s wore on things started to happen. The **Protestant Church** provided a haven for **environmental and peace organizations**, whose members unfurled protest banners calling for greater freedom at an official ceremony in East Berlin in January 1988. They were immediately arrested, imprisoned, and later expelled from the GDR. The end of the regime didn't seem nigh – so when Chris Gueffroy was shot dead trying to cross the Berlin border at Neukölln on February 6, 1989, no one fathomed that he would be the last person killed in such an attempt. However, the impetus for East German collapse came from other Eastern European countries: in 1988 Hungary began taking down the barbed wire fence along their Austrian border, creating a **hole in the Iron Curtain**, across which many East Germans fled. A similar pattern emerged in Czechoslovakia.

The October revolution

The East German government's disarrayed response to these goings-on galvanized into action thousands who had previously been content to make the best of things. Fledgling **opposition groups** like the **Neues Forum** emerged, and unrest begun in Leipzig and Dresden soon spread to Berlin. Then, at the beginning of October, at the pompous official celebration of the GDR's **fortieth anniversary**, Gorbachev stressed the need for new ideas and stunningly announced that the USSR would not interfere in the affairs of fellow socialist states. Protests and scuffles along the cavalcade route escalated into a huge demonstration as the day wore on, which the police and Stasi (the East German secret police) brutally suppressed. Thousands of arrests were made, and prisoners were subjected to the usual degrading treatment. The following week, **nationwide demonstrations** came close to bloodshed in **Leipzig**, where seventy thousand people marched through the city, forcing the sudden replacement of Erich Honecker with **Egon Krenz** as party secretary, who immediately announced that the regime was ready for dialogue.

The final week of October saw a growing exodus of GDR citizens via other Eastern Bloc countries, while pressure on the streets kept rising. Then on November 4, East Berlin saw more than one million citizens demonstrate, forcing authorities to make hasty **concessions**, including dropping the requirement for GDR citizens to get visas to visit Czechoslovakia – in effect, permitting emigration. People swarmed across the Czech border, and within two days fifteen thousand had reached Bavaria – bringing the number of East Germans who had fled the country in 1989 to 200,000.

The Wall opens

The **opening of the Berlin Wall** was announced almost casually, on the evening of Thursday November 9, when EastBerlin party boss Günter Schabowski told a televised press conference that East German citizens were free to leave the GDR with valid exit

1999	2005
Berlin becomes capital of reunified Germany.	Openly gay mayor Klaus Wowereit dubs Berlin "poor but sexy", which becomes a slogan for the city.

visas, which would henceforth be issued without delay. Hardly daring to believe the announcement, Berliners on both sides of the Wall started heading for border crossings.

Huge crowds converged on the **Brandenburg Gate**, where the Volkspolizei gave up checking documents and simply let thousands of East Germans walk into West Berlin. An impromptu **street party** broke out, with West Berliners popping champagne corks and Germans from both sides of the Wall embracing. The scenes of joy and disbelief flashed around a world taken by surprise. West German Chancellor **Helmut Kohl** interrupted a state visit in Warsaw to rush to West Berlin, where the international press was arriving in droves. Inside the GDR, disbelief turned to joy as people realized that the unimaginable had happened. On the first weekend of the opening of the Wall – November 11 and 12 – 2.7 million exit visas were issued to East Germans, who formed kilometre-long queues at checkpoints. West Germans – and TV-viewers around the world – gawped at streams of Trabant cars pouring into West Berlin, where shops enjoyed a bonanza as East Germans spent their DM100 "welcome money", given to each of them by the Federal Republic. By the following weekend, **ten million visas** had been issued since November 9 – an incredible number considering the entire population of the GDR was just sixteen million.

The road to Reunification

Despite the opening of the border East German demonstrations continued and anti-government feelings still ran high, forcing the immediate dismantling of the formidable Stasi security service and an agreement to have free elections, for which the **SED** hastily repackaged itself as a new, supposedly voter-friendly **PDS** – Partei des Demokratischen Sozialismus (Democratic Socialist Party), partly by firing the old guard. But the next initiative came from the West when **Chancellor Kohl** visited Dresden on December 19, addressing a huge, enthusiastic crowd as "dear countrymen", and declaring a **united Germany** his ultimate goal. East Germans began to agree as they discovered that West Germany's standard of living eclipsed anything in the GDR, and found out exactly how corrupt their government had been – with the result that the GDR's first free elections on March 18, 1990 returned a victory for a right-wing alliance dominated by the CDU and Kohl.

The **economic union** was hammered out almost immediately and the GDR began rapidly to fade away. Eastern produce vanished from shops to be replaced by western consumer goods, and superficially it seemed as though a second "economic miracle" had begun. Yet for many East Germans, the excitement was tempered by fears of rent increases and factory closures during the transformation to a market economy. Already the first legal claims by former owners of apartment buildings in East Berlin were being lodged.

With confirmation that a united Germany would respect its post-World War II boundaries, the wartime allies agreed to reunification. After an all-night Volkskammer session on August 23 it was announced that the GDR would become part of the Federal Republic on **October 3, 1990**.

Street-level changes

The two Berlins, meanwhile, were already drawing together as the border withered away during the course of the year. Passport and customs controls for German citizens had ceased early in 1990 and, by the time of currency union, nationals of other

2006	2006
Demolition begins on the former East German parliament, the Palast der Republik.	The new Hauptbahnhof is opened.

countries, although nominally still subject to control, could cross the border unhindered. During the course of the year most of the central sections of **the Wall** were demolished and numerous cross-border streets linked up once again.

As border controls in Berlin and elsewhere throughout the former Soviet bloc eased, Berlin became a magnet for the restless peoples of eastern Europe. The first arrivals had been the **Poles**, who set up a gigantic impromptu street market on a patch of wasteland near the Wall, much to the chagrin of Berliners, who felt the order of their city threatened by the influx of thousands of weekend street traders selling junk out of suitcases. They were followed by **Roma**, fleeing alleged persecution at home and hoping, by taking advantage of visa-free access to what was still the GDR, to secure a place for themselves in the new Germany. Post-unification visa regulations were to put a stop to the commuting activities of the Poles, but as asylum-seekers the Romanians had the right to remain, and the sight of Roma begging on the streets of Berlin became commonplace.

Reunification and the 1990s

On **October 3, 1990**, the day of **reunification**, Chancellor Kohl spoke to assembled dignitaries and massive crowds in front of the Reichstag. A conscious effort was made to rekindle the spontaneous joy and fervour that had gripped the city on the night the Wall was opened and during Berlin's first post-*Wende* new year, but for many ordinary people already experiencing the economic side-effects of the collapse of the GDR the celebrations left a bitter taste. On the sidelines anti-unification demonstrators marched through the streets, precipitating minor **clashes with the police**.

Just over a month later, on the night of November 13, the reunited Berlin experienced its first **major upheaval** when SPD mayor Walter Momper ordered the police to evict **West Berlin squatters** who had occupied a number of tenement blocks in the eastern Berlin district of Friedrichshain. The violent tactics of the police, coupled with the uncompromising stance of the radical Autonome squatters, who responded with petrol bombs and a hail of missiles from the rooftops, resulted in the fiercest **rioting** seen in the city since 1981, with dozens of police injured and more than three hundred squatters arrested. Politically, the unrest resulted in the **collapse** of the fragile Red-Green SPD/Alternative Liste coalition that had governed West Berlin for the previous twenty months.

December 2, 1990 saw Germany's first nationwide elections since 1933. Nationally the CDU, in coalition with the FDP (Free Democrats), triumphed easily. One surprise was that the PDS secured 25 percent of the vote in East Berlin on an anti-unemployment and anti-social inequality ticket. At the start of 1991, with the celebrations of the first united Christmas and New Year over, it was time for the accounting to begin in earnest. The new year brought vastly unpopular tax increases in western Germany to pay for the spiralling cost of unification. As the year wore on, and unemployment continued to rise, Kohl's honeymoon with the East ended. He became reluctant to show himself there, and when he finally did, in April, he was greeted by catcalls and egg-hurlers.

Ill-feeling between easterners and westerners also became apparent and increased throughout the decade. West Germans resented the tax increases and caricatured easterners as naive and lazy. East Germans resented patronizing western attitudes and economic inequalities that made them second-class citizens, so mocked westerners for

2006

The football World Cup is held in Germany, with the final played in Berlin's Olympic stadium.

2008

Tempelhof airport is officially closed; the surrounding area is later turned into a public park.

their arrogance and materialism. Feelings got worse as it became apparent that the ever-increasing cost of reunification had pushed the German economy into recession. As the instability of the transitional period began to ebb, witch-hunts for those responsible for the crimes of the GDR's repressive regime began in earnest, many resulting from an increasing access to old Stasi files. **Trials** throughout the 1990s brought Politbüro members, border guards, and even sports coaches who had doped players without their knowledge, before the courts. On June 20, 1991, a Bundestag decision to relocate the national government to Berlin ushered in a new era: a tremendous task, and one undertaken in the late 1990s with the usual German thoroughness.

Berlin today

Since the start of the twenty-first century Berlin has been a city on the move, with **building sites** everywhere, particularly along the old east–west border. Today the city is finally coming out of an era of transition and beginning to complete the rebuilding work that began in the aftermath of World War II and the Cold War. Magically this has almost wound back the clock to the 1920s, before Nazism struck, with Berlin once again a cosmopolitan and upbeat **city**. But also like the 1920s, the city is plagued by **economic and social problems** to which there are no easy solutions. Berlin's underperforming economy is perhaps the hardest nut to crack, despite signs that things are improving, with the hope that the knock-on effect will be to stem the small-scale resurgence of **neo-Nazism** and improve the lot of the city's marginalized **immigrants**.

Party capital

As host of the 2006 football **World Cup finals**, Berlin was able to project its friendly and youthful dynamism to the world, hosting several games, including the final, in the fine old Olympic Stadium. Visiting fans quickly realized that the city deserved its reputation for partying hard – earned in part as a consequence of the annual **Love Parade** (see p.271) – and since then barely a week has passed without a big event. Twenty-somethings from all over Europe continually jet in on low-cost airlines for the all-night club scene that continues to be as wild and cutting-edge as it ever was. The gay scene too is thriving, and Berlin's sociable, gay mayor **Klaus Wowereit** or "Wowi", as Berliners call him, has become one of Germany's best-known public figures (see p.239).

The economy

Greatly weakened by the costs of pulling the two Germanys together, and heavy investment in construction projects like the Hauptbahnhof and the much-delayed Berlin-Brandenburg Airport, the city has long been teetering on the edge of recession. Almost half of all Berliners live on benefits, despite the rich political elite at the city's heart that now controls Europe's mightiest economy.

Part of the problem has been the **death of manufacturing** which now employs fewer than 100,000 of a population of 3.4 million. Meanwhile, the legacy of state subsidies that once shored up uncompetitive firms on both sides of the city has been detrimental to entrepreneurism and new initiatives tend to be mired by a huge bureaucracy. Even so, Berlin is helped by its increasingly central location as the European Union has expanded east and by the fact that Berlin has an increasingly

2009	2010
Celebrations mark the twentieth anniversary of the fall of the Wall. Work begins on a major restoration of original paintings at the Berlin Wall's East Side Gallery.	The original date for the opening of Berlin-Brandenburg airport comes and goes.

THE LOVE PARADE

Nowhere was the spirit of unity and excess in a newly self-confident post-*Wende* Berlin celebrated as hard as at the **Love Parade**, an annual Techno-fest that grew into a 1990s institution, before becoming a victim of its own success. The event spawned copy-cat parades around the globe – including Leeds, Vienna, Tel Aviv and Cape Town – and elsewhere in Germany.

The event began modestly enough in 1989, as an extravagant birthday party for local DJ **Dr Motte**, who, as co-founder of the Ufo club near Schlesisches Tor, had already been instrumental in bringing techno and acid house music from Chicago to Berlin. He played records from a float followed down Berlin's streets by a hundred or so of his friends who chanted "Friede, Freude, Eierkuchen" (peace, joy and pancakes), bemusing onlookers. Later that year the Berlin Wall fell and somehow the event captured the mood of the time, gathering , unbelievable momentum in subsequent years. By 1995 attendance was up to 300,000, gridlocking city-centre streets for an entire weekend. In 1996 the crowd doubled and the parade rerouted to end in the Tiergarten: a natural home for pill-poppers gyrating to the thud of a €15 million sound system and indulging in generous amounts of no-holds-barred sexual activity of all types. Annual cancellation rumours were no more than that until 2004, when the organizers couldn't find the money demanded by the city for the immense operation needed to clean up the aftermath of a million loved-up ravers. The parade reappeared in 2006, but that was Berlin's last. The event carried on in other countries until the 2010 Duisburg parade, where the death of 21 people in a crowd surge prompted the organizers to cancel all further events.

hip image, helping firms to lure skilled workers here so that both can benefit from the city's relatively **cheap real estate**. A clutch of small fashion designers have moved in around the Hackescher Markt and the banks of the River Spree have become the base for Universal Music, MTV and other media firms, including scores of tiny tech startups. Meanwhile information technology parks in the southern suburbs have grown fast, as has the research and development sector, thanks largely to the presence of three universities in the city. **Tourism** has also become a major growth area, with Berlin overtaking Rome in terms of visitor numbers (22 million annually: making it third in Europe after London and Paris).

International Berlin

Berlin's economic green shoots and the doubling of visitor numbers over the last decade have helped ignite its **property market** since 2006. Some Berliners grumble about Russians buying up much of ritzy Charlottenburg; others bemoan the influx of hip young Europeans to bedraggled districts like Kreuzberg and Neukölln, with all the consequent changes in atmosphere, rent increases and general gentrification (see p.129).

All these growing pains seem part of the general process of Berlin turning itself back into a key world city, but they have also stimulated older frictions. Among them are complaints from the disadvantaged in the former east who blame foreigners for their plight and are attracted to right-wing extremism and neo-Nazi ideals. Just as disadvantaged and angry are many descendants of Turkish Muslim "guest workers" who arrived in Berlin in the 1960s and preferred to settle rather than return home. But in truth Berlin's problems with gentrification, racism and radical Islam remain minor by world standards. This is still a comparatively **safe** city whose tolerance, unrivalled creativity and increasingly anglophone nature will no doubt assure it a bright future.

2011	2013
Six thousand people march on Neukölln's streets to protest rent increases; a large anti-capitalist festival in Lunapark protests Berlin's growing internationalization.	Demonstrations at the East Side Gallery highlight the threat developers pose to Berlin's heritage.

Books

Huge numbers of books have been written about Berlin. The collection below shows a bias towards unravelling the evil mysteries of the Third Reich, the double-dealing of the Cold War and getting to grips with the Wende. But Berlin has also attracted dozens of specialist guides, the most useful of which are books on its architecture, new and old. Books marked with a ★ are particularly recommended.

HISTORY

GENERAL HISTORY AND PRE-THIRD REICH

Otto Friedrich *Before the Deluge: A Portrait of Berlin in the 1920s*. An engaging social history, full of tales and anecdotes, of the city when Dada and decadence reigned. An excellent history of Berlin's most engaging period.

Anton Gill *A Dance Between Flames*. Gill's dense but readable account of Berlin in the 1920s and 1930s has lots of colour, quotation and detail but leans so heavily on a single source – The Diary of Henry Kessler – that you feel he should be sharing the royalties. Even so, one of the best books on the period.

Mark Girouard *Cities and People*. A well-illustrated social and architectural history of European urban development that contains knowledgeable entries on Berlin, particularly the eighteenth- and nineteenth-century periods.

Alex De Jong *The Weimar Chronicle*. While not the most comprehensive of accounts of the Weimar Republic, this is by far the liveliest. A couple of chapters focus on Berlin, and the book is spiced with eyewitness memoirs and a mass of engaging detail, particularly about the arts in the city.

Giles MacDonogh *Berlin*. The book's thematic rather than chronological organization can initially be a bit baffling – and doesn't really work in uncovering themes from the city's past as it intends – but there's a wealth of fascinating anecdotes on aspects of daily life here that's ignored by traditional histories.

Andreas Nachama et al *Jews in Berlin*. Packed with source material of every kind, this well-illustrated book charts the troubled history of Berlin's Jewish community between 1244 and 2000.

Alexandra Richie *Faust's Metropolis*. A thick and thorough general history of Berlin, beginning with the very first settlers and ending in the 1990s. Richie debunks a number of myths about the city – such as its supposed anti-Nazism – but her conservatism too often intrudes on the narrative.

Ronald Taylor *Berlin and Its Culture*. Profusely illustrated survey of the cultural movements and personalities that constituted the artistic life of the city; especially good on Weimar writing and cinematography.

THIRD REICH

Allied Intelligence Map of Key Buildings. This large, detailed map published by After The Battle is an excellent resource for anyone searching for Nazi and prewar remains in the city.

★ **Anonymous** *A Woman in Berlin*. Remarkable war diary kept by a female journalist who vividly describes the pathetic lot of Berlin's vanquished in the closing days of the war, when looting and gang rape were part of daily life. The honesty of the book caused such an uproar when it was first published in 1950s Germany – when society was unprepared to face its recent trauma – that it wasn't reprinted again during the author's lifetime; she died in 2001.

Antony Beevor *Berlin the Downfall 1945*. Berlin doesn't actually start to fall until the middle of the book, but once there a synthesis of many sources provides a riveting account of how the city's defences crumbled and its civilians suffered, with few harrowing details spared. Beevor was congratulated by many female victims of brutal rapes by Soviet troops for at last telling their story as in *A Woman in Berlin* (see above).

Christabel Bielenberg *The Past is Myself*. Bielenberg, the niece of Lord Northcliffe, married German lawyer Peter Bielenberg in 1934 and was living with her family in Berlin at the outbreak of the war. Her autobiography (serialized for TV as *Christabel*) details her struggle to survive the Nazi period and Allied raids on the city, and to save her husband, imprisoned in Ravensbrück as a result of his friendship with members of the Kreisau resistance group.

George Clare *Berlin Days 1946–1947*. "The most harrowing and yet most fascinating place on earth" is how Clare begins this account of his time spent as a British army translator. This is Berlin at what the Germans called the *Nullpunkt* – the zero point – when the city, its economy, buildings and society began to rebuild almost from scratch. Packed with characters and observation, it's a captivating – if at times depressing – read.

D. Fisher and A. Read *The Fall of Berlin*. Superb and essential account of the city's *Götterdämmerung*, carefully researched with a mass of anecdotal material you won't find elsewhere.

Bella Fromm *Blood and Banquets*. Fromm, a Jewish aristocrat living in Berlin, kept a diary from 1930 until 1938. Her job as society reporter for the *Vossische Zeitung* gave her inside knowledge on the top figures of Berlin society, and the diaries are a chilling account of the rise of the Nazis and their persecution of Berlin's Jews.

Tony Le Tissier *The Battle of Berlin*. Soldierly (the author is a retired lieutenant-colonel) shot-by-shot account of Berlin's final days. Authoritative, if a little dry. The same author's *Berlin Then and Now* is a collection of photographs of sites in the city during the war years, contrasted with the same places today. This extraordinary book is the best way to find what's left of Berlin's Nazi buildings – a startling number have barely changed.

Martin Middlebrook *The Berlin Raids*. Superbly researched account of the RAF's campaign to destroy the capital of the Third Reich by mass bombing. Based on interviews with bomber crews, Luftwaffe fighter pilots and civilians who survived the raids – a moving, compassionate and exciting read.

★ **William Shirer** *The Rise and Fall of the Third Reich*. Shirer was an American journalist stationed in Berlin during the Nazi period, and his history of the German state before and during the war has long been recognized as a classic. Notwithstanding its length and occasionally outdated perceptions, this book is full of insights and is ideal for dipping into, with the help of its exhaustive index.

Hugh Trevor-Roper *The Last Days of Hitler*. A brilliant reconstruction of the closing chapter of the Third Reich, set in the Bunker of the Reich's Chancellery on Potsdamer Platz.

Marie Vassiltchikov *The Berlin Diaries*. These diaries, written by the daughter of a Russian émigré family, provide a vivid portrait of wartime Berlin and the July 1944 bomb-plot conspirators – whose members numbered among her friends.

Peter Wyden *Stella*. Stella Goldschlag was a young, very "Aryan"-looking Jew who avoided deportation and death by working for the SS as a "catcher", hunting down Jews hiding in wartime Berlin – including former friends and even relatives. The author, who knew the young Stella, traces her life story and tries to find some explanation for the motives behind what seem incalculably evil actions. A gripping, terrifying story.

POSTWAR HISTORY AND SOCIAL STUDIES

★ **Anna Funder** *Stasiland: True Stories From Behind the Berlin Wall*. Engrossing account of the experiences of those East Germans who found themselves tangled in the web of the State Security Service (Stasi) in the GDR.

★ **Timothy Garton Ash** *The File: A Personal History*. Garton Ash lived and worked as a journalist in East Berlin in 1980, making him the subject of surveillance and a Stasi file. In this book he tracks down the file and interviews informers using an informal style to weave everything together and marvellously evoke the era. His book *We the People* (US title: *The Magic Lantern*) is an equally enjoyable first-hand account of the fall of the Wall.

Norman Gelb *The Berlin Wall*. The definitive account of the building of the Wall and its social and political aftermath up until 1986. Includes a wealth of information and anecdotes that you won't find in other books.

Anne McElvoy *The Saddled Cow*. Thorough and witty analysis of the GDR by Berlin's *Times* correspondent who witnessed the fall of the Wall. The book also draws on the author's time in East Germany before and after the *Wende*: its title is a quote from Stalin, who once said that "Communism fits Germany as a saddle fits a cow".

David E. Murphy, Serfei A. Kondrashev and George Bailey *Battleground Berlin: CIA vs KGB in the Cold War*. A detailed account by participants of the tense skirmishes in Berlin between the spies of the two superpowers.

Hermann Waldenburg *The Berlin Wall Book*. A collection of photographs of the art and graffiti the Wall inspired, with a rather self-important introduction by the photographer.

ART AND ARCHITECTURE

Peter Adam *The Art of the Third Reich*. Engrossing and well-written account of the officially approved state art of Nazi Germany – a subject that for many years was ignored or deliberately made inaccessible. Includes more than three hundred illustrations.

★ **Karl Baedeker** *Berlin and its Environs*. First published in 1903, the learned old *Baedeker* is an utterly absorbing read, describing a grand imperial city now long vanished. There's advice on medicinal brine-baths, where to buy "mourning clothes", the location of the Estonian embassy, and beautiful fold-out maps that enable you to trace the former course of long-gone streets. An armchair treat.

★ **Duane Philips and Alexandra Geyer** *Berlin: A guide to recent architecture*. Ideal pocket guide to many key Berlin buildings, with good photographs and an interesting commentary, even if it's occasionally mired in opaque architectural snobbery.

Michael Z. Wise *Capital Dilemma: Germany's Search for a New Architecture of Democracy*. Engaging discussion of the historical, political and architectural considerations in the rebuilding of Berlin.

GUIDES AND TRAVEL WRITING

Stephen Barber *Fragments of the European City*. Written as a series of interlocking poetic fragments, this book explores the visual transformation of the contemporary European city, focusing on Berlin. An exhilarating evocation of the intricacies and ever-changing identity of the city.

★ **Heather Reyes, Katy Derbyshire (eds)** *City Lit Series Berlin.* Superb anthology that provides an intellectual tour of Berlin in some hundred pieces written by various historians, journalists and writers; among them Christopher Isherwood, Ian McEwan and David Bowie. Great for a quick sense of the city's historical context, its ongoing cultural and architectural evolution and its countercultural vibe.

Uwe Seidel *Berlin & Potsdam.* Illustrated guide to the city, with much detail on places that you can't see anymore. Useful if you're after knowledge of the what-stood-where kind.

Ian Walker *Zoo Station.* A personal recollection of time spent in Berlin in the mid-1980s. Perceptive, engaging and well informed, it's the most enjoyable account of pre-*Wende* life in the city.

FICTION

Len Deighton *Winter: A Berlin Family 1899–1945.* Fictional saga tracing the fortunes of a Berlin family through World War I, the rise of Nazism and the collapse of the Third Reich: a convincing account of how a typical upper-middle-class family fared. Better known is *Funeral in Berlin*, a spy-thriller set in the middle of Cold War Berlin and based around the defection of an Eastern chemist, aided by hard-bitten agent Harry Palmer (as the character came to be known in the film starring Michael Caine). *Berlin Game* pits British SIS agent Bernard Samson (whose father appears in *Winter*) against an arch manipulator of the East Berlin secret service, and leaves you hanging for the sequels *Mexico Set* and *London Match.*

Alfred Döblin *Berlin-Alexanderplatz.* A prominent socialist intellectual during the Weimar period, Döblin went into exile shortly after the banning (and burning) of his books in 1933. This is his weightiest and most durable achievement, an unrelenting stream-of-consciousness epic of the city's proletariat.

Theodor Fontane *Effi Briest.* This story of a woman's adultery in the second half of the nineteenth century offers a vivid picture of Prussian mores, with the sort of terrible and absurd climax that's virtually unique to Fontane and to German literature. One of the few classics to come out of Berlin.

Hugo Hamilton *Surrogate City* is a love story between an Irish woman and a Berliner and strongly evocative of pre-*Wende* Berlin. *The Love Test*, the tale of a journalist researching the history of a woman's involvement with the Stasi, gives a realistic account of 1990s Berlin.

Robert Harris *Fatherland.* A Cold War novel with a difference: Germany has conquered Europe and the Soviet Union, and the Cold War is being fought between the Third Reich and the USA. Against this background, Berlin detective Xavier March is drawn into an intrigue involving murder and Nazi officials. All this owes much to Philip Kerr (see below) but Harris's picture of Nazi Berlin in 1964 is chillingly believable.

Lillian Hellman *Pentimento.* The first volume of Hellman's memoirs contains "Julia", supposedly (it was later accused of being heavily fictionalized) the story of one of her friends caught up in the Berlin resistance. This was later made into a finely acted, if rather thinly emotional, film of the same name.

★ **Christopher Isherwood** *Goodbye to Berlin.* Set in the decadent atmosphere of the Weimar Republic as the Nazis steadily gain power, this collection of stories brilliantly evokes the period and brings to life some classic Berlin characters. It subsequently formed the basis of the films *I Am a Camera* and the later remake *Cabaret.* See also Isherwood's *Mr Norris Changes Trains*, the adventures of the eponymous overweight hero in pre-Hitler Berlin and Germany.

★ **Wladimir Kaminer** *Russian Disco, Tales of Everyday Lunacy on the Streets of Berlin.* Collection of stories that are snapshots of Berlin through the eyes of a Russian immigrant from Moscow. Unusual, entertaining and well written: Kaminer has since become a local celebrity, DJing *Russendisko* nights at *Kaffee Burger* (see p.208).

Philip Kerr *Berlin Noir: March Violets, The Pale Criminal* and *A German Requiem.* Three great novels on Berlin in one omnibus edition. The first is a well-received detective thriller set in the early years of Nazi Berlin. Keen on period detail – nightclubs, the Olympic Stadium, building sites for the new autobahn – and with a terrific sense of atmosphere, the book rips along to a gripping denouement. Bernie Gunther, its detective hero, also features in the second title – a wartime Berlin crime novel. But the best, *A German Requiem*, has Gunther travelling from ravaged postwar Berlin to run into ex-Nazis in Vienna.

Ian McEwan *The Innocent.* McEwan's novel brilliantly evokes 1950s Berlin as seen through the eyes of a post office worker caught up in early Cold War espionage – and his first sexual encounters. Flounders in its obligatory McEwan nasty final twist, but laden with a superbly researched atmosphere.

Ulrich Plenzdorf *The New Sufferings of Young W.* A satirical reworking of Goethe's *Die Leiden des jungen Werthers* set in 1970s East Berlin. It tells the story of Edgar Wibeau, a young rebel without a cause adrift in the antiseptic GDR, and when first published it pushed the borders of literary acceptability under the old regime with its portrayal of alienated, disaffected youth.

Holly-Jane Rahlens *Becky Bernstein Goes Berlin.* A young Jewish girl from Queens falls in love with a German, emigrates to Berlin and discovers a new love for the city. A bouncy and funny novel full of New York wit.

Film

Berlin's cinema history goes back to some of the very first experiments in the medium. It rapidly became the cornerstone of Germany's film industry, a position consolidated in the 1920s and then throughout the Nazi era, despite the mass exodus of many of the country's key stars and directors. After World War II East Germany quickly made the most of all the equipment that had fallen into their hands in the Soviet-controlled suburbs of Berlin to produce a programme of tightly controlled filmmaking. Meanwhile, generous subsidies lured many of Germany's most cutting-edge filmmakers to West Berlin. But it's since the Wende that the city's film industry has really begun to blossom again.

The beginnings: showmen and inventors

Berlin first whirred into cinema history on November 1, 1895 when former fairground showman Max Skladanowsky and his brother Emil put on a show with their home-made film projector – which they called a *Bioskop* – at the city's Wintergarten music hall. It was quickly replaced by better methods and techniques in Paris later that year, but Berlin continued to play a crucial role, with locals like Oskar Messter pioneering and setting standards for many production techniques.

Once established, Germany's early twentieth-century film industry grew steadily. The outbreak of World War I and subsequent boycott of French films stimulated growth, and Berlin consolidated its role in 1917 with the founding of the giant and partially nationalized **Universum Film AG** (UFA) studio – which was established largely to imitate the very effective Allied propaganda films.

Boom in Weimar Germany

After the war, movies became a popular form of escapism in the hard times of **Weimar Germany**, with new genres emerging to portray forbidden love, myths, and other populist themes. The film industry boomed, churning out vast quantities of celluloid – six hundred feature films a year in the 1920s – thanks partly to hyperinflation, which allowed filmmakers to borrow money that would vastly devalue before repayment. Even so, studio bankruptcies were common and film budgets relatively tight, forcing directors to work with less and so helping to prompt the rise of **German Expressionist cinema**. The genre relied on symbolism and artistic imagery, as evidenced in the era's most famous film, *Das Kabinett des Doktor Caligari* (*The Cabinet of Dr Caligari*; 1920), shot in Berlin. Here, the wild, non-naturalistic and exaggeratedly geometric sets, with images painted on floors and walls evoking objects, light and shadow, complemented the highly stylized performances to create affecting psychological yarns. The era's other great filmmaking landmark was Fritz Lang's futuristic **Metropolis** (1927), a gigantic project for which UFA was massively expanded and which included 750 extras, becoming Weimar Germany's most expensive film and a commercial flop. The film's exploration and critique of social power structures and hierarchies was common to many of the overwhelmingly left-wing films made at the time, which the Nazis would quickly quash. The arrival of sound at the end of the 1920s produced a final artistic flourish for German film before the collapse of the Weimar Republic. **Der Blaue Engel** (*The Blue Angel*; 1930), directed by Josef von Sternberg, was Germany's first talking film and, shot simultaneously in German and English, made an international star of Marlene Dietrich, a local girl discovered at a Berlin variety show.

Film in Nazi Germany

Marlene Dietrich was one of many performers to leave the country after the Nazi seizure of power in 1933. The uncertain economics and politics of Weimar Germany had already prompted many to leave the country, primarily for the USA, but after 1933 this turned into a flood. Around 1500 directors, producers, actors and other film professionals fled the Third Reich, among them Fritz Lang. All those in exile were either excluded from or rejected the *Reichskulturkammer*, the Nazi cultural organization that excluded Jews and anyone politically questionable and defined who could work in the media, effectively bringing to an end the glory days of German cinema. Nevertheless, even the Nazi period produced a few cinematic masterpieces, particularly by **Leni Riefenstahl**: *Triumph des Willens* (*The Triumph of the Will*; 1935), which documented the 1934 Nuremberg Rally, and *Olympia* (1938), an awe-inspiring tribute to Berlin's 1936 Summer Olympics, both of which obviously remain controversial for propagandizing Nazi ideals.

Evolution in a divided Germany

After the war **East Germany** was quick to capitalize on the fact that much of Germany's film infrastructure, notably the former UFA studios, lay in the Soviet occupation zone. Film production quickly got off the ground with Soviet encouragement and Berlin's cinemas were reopened in May 1945, within three weeks of German capitulation. However, strict controls limited topics to those directly contributing to the communist state project. A particular strength turned out to be **children's films**, notably fairytale adaptations such as *Drei Haselnüsse für Aschenbrödel* (*Three Nuts for Cinderella*; 1973), but also genre works, such as *Der schweigende Stern* (*The Silent Star*; 1960), an adaptation of a Stanislaw Lem sci-fi novel, and "red westerns" such as *The Sons of the Great Mother Bear* (1966) in which the heroes tended to be Native American.

Meanwhile the **West German** film industry of the 1950s could no longer measure up to those of France, Italy or Japan. German films were perceived as provincial and only rarely distributed internationally. Cinema attendance began to stagnate and drop in the 1950s, and plummeted in the 1960s. One reaction to this, and a perceived artistic stagnation, was the 1962 **Oberhausen Manifesto** in which a group of young filmmakers proclaimed "Der alte Film ist tot. Wir glauben an den neuen" ("The old cinema is dead. We believe in the new"), rejecting the commercial dictates of the German film industry and resolving to build a new industry based on artistic excellence and experimentation. Many up-and-coming filmmakers allied themselves with this group, among them Volker Schlöndorff, Werner Herzog, Wim Wenders, Hans-Jürgen Syberberg and Rainer Werner Fassbinder. The lure of new subsidies quickly brought many to Berlin, where the **New German Cinema** movement returned the country's film industry to international acclaim: *The Tin Drum* (1979), by Schlöndorff, became the first German film to win the Academy Award for Best Foreign Language Film, and *Das Boot* (1981) still holds the record for most Academy Award nominations for a German film (six).

A post-Wende renaissance

During the 1980s the vitality of the New German Cinema movement ebbed and the country's film industry struggled against a glut of private TV channels, videos and DVDs. Not until almost ten years after the *Wende* did it really begin to find its feet again. Unlike the more sober and artistic films of the 1970s, this time success has been based on an ability to marry arthouse sensibilities with a more commercial outlook, yet still addressing difficult topics from Germany's history and the country's contemporary issues. **Good Bye Lenin!** (see p.278) was a particularly important landmark in relaunching German cinema abroad, grossing $80m, most of it from overseas. Appropriately the film was first screened at the internationally recognized **Berlinale film festival**, where it won a coveted Golden Bear award as the best European film of 2003. The festival itself has also become a symbol of the city's cinematic prowess, steadily growing and attracting international talent, critics and filmgoers in increasing numbers.

But it's at ground level that Berlin's cinema is arguably most vibrant; there are more than 260 cinemas – not counting the dozens of venues where a projector is often set up for the occasional screening of avant-garde local works. Many have come from the city's burgeoning underground film scene, which is defined by serious and socially aware themes. Given their penetrating, realistic studies of relationships and characters, these films don't tend to travel far internationally, but have enjoyed critical success in France, where the term **Nouvelle Vague Allemande** is used for the work of a group of mostly Berlin-based directors, including Christian Petzold, Thomas Arslan, Valeska Grisebach and Christoph Hochhäusler.

A BERLIN FILMOGRAPHY

Over the years Berlin has provided the inspiration and setting for a great many films, which now offer a valuable glimpse of a city that vanished in the mayhem of its twentieth century. The following filmography is laid out in chronological order; films marked with a ★ are particularly recommended.

Berlin: Sinfonie einer Grosstadt (*Berlin: Symphony of a Great City*; Walter Ruttmann; 1927). Expressionist silent documentary that magnificently captures a day in the life of 1920s Berlin.

★ **Metropolis** (Fritz Lang; 1927). Futuristic classic and masterpiece of film architecture that was both inspired by and filmed in Berlin.

Mutter Krausens Fahrt ins Glück (*Mother Krause's Journey to Happiness*; Phil Jutzi; 1929). Film version of the working-class Berlin portrayed and caricatured by Heinrich Zille (see p.67). Set in Wedding, where most of the actors came from.

M (Fritz Lang; 1931). Dark Berlin thriller and one of the forerunners of *film noir*.

Olympia (Leni Riefenstahl; 1938). Olympic majesty as never captured on film before or since, based on literally hundreds of kilometres of footage taken during the 1936 Berlin Olympics.

The Big Lift (George Seaton; 1950). Dramatized version of the Berlin Air Lift, starring Montgomery Clift. Of middling quality, but filmed on location.

Funeral in Berlin (Guy Hamilton; 1966). Spy film in which Michael Caine stars as a British agent sent to Berlin. Much cloak and dagger action, but a little slow.

Cabaret (Bob Fosse; 1972). Weimar Berlin as glimpsed through the peepholes of the famed Kit Kat Klub, described by Christopher Isherwood, then reinterpreted by Bob Fosse and made iconic by Liza Minnelli.

Die Legende von Paul und Paula (*The Legend of Paul and Paula*; Heiner Carow; 1973). Love story set in East Berlin and filmed in Marzahn. Good for a dose of genuine *Ostalgie*.

★ **Berlin Alexanderplatz** (Rainer Werner Fassbinder; 1980). Epic portrayal – all 931 minutes of it– of 1920s Berlin, based on the Alfred Döblin novel of the same name. It follows a small-time criminal on his journey into Berlin's underworld.

Christiane F. – Wir Kinder vom Bahnhof Zoo (Christiane F.; Uli Edel; 1981). Gritty, dark and disturbing fictionalized film about heroin addiction in the underbelly of 1970s West Berlin. It pulls no punches.

Berlin Tunnel 21 (Richard Michaels; 1981). Reasonable made-for-TV-movie about a former American officer who leads an attempt to build a tunnel underneath the Wall in 1961; not bad at providing a feel of early-1960s Berlin.

Taxi zum Klo (Frank Ripploh; 1981). Groundbreaking film documenting gay culture in West Berlin directed by the lead, who possibly plays himself: an oversexed shaggy-haired teacher who has an interest in filmmaking.

Octopussy (John Glen; 1983). Probably Roger Moore's best outing as James Bond – who arrives in Berlin to investigate 009's death.

Der Himmel über Berlin (*Wings of Desire*; Wim Wenders; 1987). Iconic classic – which inspired the imaginations of countless filmmakers – about love in a divided city, where angels swoop in on postwar Berlin.

Linie 1 (Reinhard Hauff; 1988). Musical based on a girl from the country arriving in the big city, meeting various oddball and low-life characters and travelling extensively up and down U-Bahn Line 1: based on a play created by the GRIPS theatre (see pp.90–91).

★ **Lola Rennt** (*Run Lola Run*; Tom Tykwer; 1998). Fast-paced film set to a pounding techno soundtrack, evoking a real sense of city life and speckled with wry examples of Berlin humour.

Sonnenallee (Leander Haussmann; 1999). Well-received teen comedy set in 1970s East Berlin, and one of the earliest examples of *Ostalgie*.

⭐ **Berlin Babylon** (Hubertus Siegert; 2001). Fascinating documentary on the rebuilding projects after the fall of the Wall, based on four years of footage.

Invincible (Werner Herzog; 2001). True story of a Jewish strongman in Weimar Berlin who becomes convinced he's been chosen by God to warn his people of imminent danger.

Berlin is in Germany (Hannes Stöhr; 2001). A look back at the GDR era through the eyes of a convict released after the *Wende* and struggling to come to terms with the new Germany he faces.

Was Tun, Wenn's Brennt? (Gregor Schnitzler; 2002). A tale of anarchists squatting in 1980s Berlin, going their separate ways and then being reunited a dozen years later when charged with a crime. Neat insights into the time and Berlin's grittier aspects.

⭐ **Good Bye Lenin!** (Wolfgang Becker; 2003). Arguably the finest *Ostalgie* film, with dozens of humorous moments and a melancholy look at the *Wende* and its influence on daily lives.

Der Untergang (*Downfall*; Oliver Hirschbiegel; 2004). Much-debated film portraying the last days of Hitler (played by Bruno Ganz) in his bunker, it also believably depicts scenes from the Battle of Berlin.

Die Fetten Jahre sind vorbei (*The Edukators*; Hans Weingartner; 2004). *Good Bye Lenin*'s Daniel Brühl plays one of three activists who kidnap a businessman in one of Berlin's affluent suburbs. The film at times takes itself a bit too seriously but delivers some fun snatches of life in Noughties Berlin, and the plot has several interesting twists.

Gestpenster (*Ghosts*; Christian Petzold; 2005). Modern urban alienation in Mitte, focusing on the life of a late-teenage orphan with mental problems.

⭐ **Das Leben der Anderen** (*The Lives of Others*; Florian Henckel von Donnersmarck; 2005). Highly evocative Stasi drama set in an East Berlin that's riddled by agents, informers and bugging devices. The film became an international success, potently informing the world about Stasi crimes.

Ich bin ein Berliner (Franziska Meyer Price; 2005). Fluffy but watchable comedy by one of Germany's foremost female directors.

Valkyrie (Bryan Singer; 2008). American dramatization of the July Bomb Plot (see p.100) in which Tom Cruise stars as Klaus Schenk von Stauffenberg.

Russendisko (Oliver Ziegenbalg; 2012). Film version of Wladimir Kaminer's book (p.274); panned by critics but watchable nonetheless.

Architecture

"Berlin is a new city; the newest I have ever seen," remarked Mark Twain in 1891. A curious thing for an American to say, but the statement still rings true. Certainly, by European standards the city is relatively young – founded in the thirteenth century and only blossoming from the late sixteenth – but it's the obliterating destruction of World War II that has made it so new. Few buildings hark back to before this time (those that appear to are mostly replicas), and the city has become a haven for modern architecture and experimentation.

Prussia's imperial capital

A chronological tour of Berlin's architecture kicks off in the Nikolaiviertel, with the medieval **Nikolaikirche** (see p.67). This is followed by the ornate Baroque buildings of the seventeenth century – the best examples are the grand **Schloss Charlottenburg** (see p.153) and the **Brandenburg Gate** (see p.35). South of here, magnificent churches with splendid domes stand on the **Gendarmenmarkt** (see p.47). These and many other buildings – such as the **Neue Wache** (see p.47) and the **Altes Museum** (see p.56) – were later adorned by Karl Friedrich Schinkel (1781–1841), with his unmistakable Neoclassical touch. As all these grand edifices were assembled, the industrial revolution in Berlin's suburbs was leading to an explosion in the population: to combat the need for housing a system of tenements around a series of courtyards was developed – the **Hackeschen Höfe** (see p.71) are a good example of this design.

The founding of the German empire in 1871 ushered in *Gründerzeit* architecture, whose premise was largely to recycle earlier styles, and then to add ostentatious flourishes – the **Reichstag** (see p.254) and the **Berliner Dom** (see p.54) are models of the style.

Modernism to Third Reich

As a backlash against all this nostalgia, **Modernism** arrived in Berlin in the early twentieth century. Foremost among the Modernist architects was Peter Behrens (1868–1940), who removed ornamentation and favoured glass, concrete and steel building materials. One of the finest buildings from the period is Emil Fahrenkamp's **Shell-Haus** (see p.99). The Nazis brought any Modernist enterprises to an end, preferring powerful-looking Neoclassical buildings for their **Third Reich**. An imposing remodelling of Berlin was envisaged but defeat in the war scuppered the plans – however a few Nazi buildings remain, including the magnificent **Tempelhof airport** (see p.124) and the **Olympic Stadium** (see p.158).

The divided city

Postwar town planners and architects on both sides of the divided city were presented with a relatively blank canvas. East Berlin continued monumentalist traditions with its enormous **Karl-Marx-Allee** (see p.130) housing schemes built in Stalin's favourite *Zuckerbäckstil* (wedding cake style), while its top project was the **Fernsehturm** (see p.62). Meanwhile, planners in West Berlin did the opposite, in an effort to project a modern yet sensitive image: the use of greenery around buildings was as important as the architecture itself, as at the **Kongresshalle** (see p.103), and Scharoun's **Philharmonie** (see p.95). Prestige projects aside, both Berlins needed affordable housing and both approached this in similarly dismal ways, illustrated by the high-rises of Marzahn. More sensitive **regeneration projects** followed in areas like Prenzlauer Berg in the east and Kreuzberg in the west.

Reunification

After the *Wende*, attention shifted to the building projects in areas where the Berlin Wall once stood. The Sony Center and skyscrapers of **Potsdamer Platz** (see p.92) are the most striking, but impressive too are the developments on **Pariser Platz** (see p.36), in the **Regierungsviertel** (Government quarter; see p.104), and those that fringe the Tiergarten, such as the Nordic and Mexican **embassies** (see p.99) and the immense **Hauptbahnhof** (see p.105). Most recent are monuments and museums designed to help Berlin address its past, including Daniel Libeskind's **Jüdisches Museum** (see p.117) and the **Holocaust Memorial** (see p.38).

Though the pace of building work in Berlin is slowing, there's much more to do. **Berlin-Brandenburg airport** is the largest project, but the reconstruction of the **Schloss** likely to be the most eye-catching. Campaigns are also being waged to reconstruct various other historic buildings – cranes will be an integral part of the city's skyline for some time yet.

Language

English speakers approaching German for the first time have one real initial advantage, which is that German – as a close linguistic relative of English – shares with it a lot of basic vocabulary. It doesn't take long to work out that the Milch for your breakfast Kaffee comes from a Kuh that spends its life eating Gras in a Feld, or that Brot is nicer when spread with Butter.

Two things conspire to give German a fearsome reputation among non-native speakers, however. The first is the **grammar:** it *is* complex – many Germans never really master it properly – but for the purposes of a short stay you shouldn't need to wade too deeply into its intricacies. The second is the **compound noun** – the German habit of creating enormously long words to define something quite specific. These aren't as difficult as they first appear, since they're composed from building blocks of basic vocabulary, so that, if you break them down into their component parts, you can often puzzle out the meaning without a dictionary. (All nouns in German are written with a capital letter, by the way.) German uses the same **alphabet** as English, with the exception of the letter ß ("scharfes S"), pronounced like "ss", with which it is phonetically interchangeble and so has been replaced by ss in this guide. The vowels o, a and u can be modified by using the Umlaut to ö, ä and ü, changing the pronunciation.

Pronunciation and grammar

Unlike English, German is written more or less **phonetically**, so that once you understand how the vowels and consonants are pronounced there's rarely any ambiguity. Exceptions include foreign words that have been incorporated into German – including, in recent years, a great many from English (see p.281). The equivalent sounds detailed below are in British English.

Vowels and umlauts

a long "a" as in farther (eg sagen); short "a" as in hat (eg Hand)

e long "e" as in lay (eg wenig); short "e" as in ten (eg gelb)

i "i"as in meek (eg Tiger); short "i" as in pin (eg Tipp)

o long "o" as in open (eg oben); short "o" as in hop (eg offen)

u long "u" as in in loot (eg Kuh); short "u" as in foot (eg und)

ä is a combination of "a" and "e", sometimes pronounced like "e" in set (eg Hände) and sometimes like "ai" in laid (eg Gerät)

ö roughly like a long or short version of the vowel in sir (eg möchte)

ü no exact equivalent; roughly a long or short version of the vowel sound in few (eg über)

ENGLISH IN BERLIN

With tourism on the up, it's got to the point where in central Berlin you're as likely to hear **English** as German spoken, and some Berlin businesses now even maintain English-language-only websites. But the roots of the language in Berlin mainly go back to the start of the Cold War, when British and American military personnel settled here in numbers. English became a compulsory subject in West Berlin's schools and, since reunification, the trend has been for all German kids to learn English from an increasingly early age – even in Kindergarten. So most West Berliners, and all Berliners under the age of about 30, will have a good grounding – good enough that English words are often and increasingly used in spoken and written German, and particularly in magazine headlines. All this is good news for English speakers trying to get by – but it does make it harder to practise your German.

Vowel combinations

au as in mouse (eg Haus)
ie as in tree (eg Bier)
ei as in pie (eg mein)

eu as in boil (eg Freude)
ai as in pie (eg Kaiser)

Consonants and consonant combinations

ch is pronounced like Scottish "loch" (eg ich)
g is always a hard "g" sound, as in "go" (eg Gang), except in words ending with -ig (eg Leipzig), when it is like a very soft German "ch"
j is pronounced like an English "y" (eg ja)
s is pronounced similar to English "z" at the end of a word like "s" in glass (eg Glas), and like "sh" before a consonant (eg Sport)

sch is like English "sh"
th is pronounced like English "t"
v is roughly "f" (eg von)
w is pronounced like English "v" (eg wann), except at the end of the word, as in the Berlin place names Kladow and Gatow, which rhyme with "pillow"
z is pronounced "ts"

Gender and adjective endings

German nouns can be one of three **genders**: masculine, feminine or neuter (the = der, die or das). Sometimes the gender is obvious – it's der Mann (the man) and die Frau (the woman) – but sometimes it seems baffling: a girl is das Mädchen, because Mädchen – "little maiden" – is a diminutive, and diminutives are neutral. There are some hard and fast rules to help you know which is which: nouns ending in -er (der Böcker, der Sportler) are masculine; the female form ends in -in (die Böckerin, die Sportlerin). Words ending in -ung, -heit, -keit or -schaft are feminine (die Zeitung, die Freiheit, die Fröhlichkeit, die Mannschaft). Definite (der; "the") and indefinite (ein; "a") **articles** and **adjective endings** can change according to the precise grammatical role in the sentence of the noun, which is where things start to get complex. If in doubt, stick to "der" or "das" for single items: once there is more than one of anything, it becomes "die" anyway.

Politeness

You can address children, animals and, nowadays, young people (but only in relaxed social situations, and really only if you're the same age) with the familiar "**du**" to mean "you". For anyone else – and particularly for older people or officials – stick to the polite "**Sie**"; if they want to be on familiar terms with you, they'll invite you to be so – "Duzen wir?". Incidentally, unmarried German women often prefer to be addressed as "**Frau**", the word "**Fräulein**" to describe a young, single woman being considered nowadays old-fashioned and rather sexist.

WORDS AND PHRASES

GREETINGS AND BASIC PHRASES

Good morning	Guten Morgen
Good evening	Guten Abend
Good day	Guten Tag
Hello (informal)	Hallo
Goodbye (formal)	Auf Wiedersehen
Goodbye (informal)	Tschüss (but also Servus)
Goodbye (on the telephone)	Auf Wiederhören
How are you? (polite)	Wie geht es Ihnen?
How are you? (informal)	Wie geht es dir?
Yes	Ja
No	Nein
Please/ You're welcome	Bitte/Bitte schön
Thank you/Thank you very much	Danke/Danke schön

Do you speak English?	Sprechen Sie Englisch?
I don't speak German	Ich spreche kein Deutsch
Please speak more slowly	Könnten Sie bitte langsamer sprechen?
I understand	Ich verstehe
I don't understand	Ich verstehe nicht
I'd like ...	Ich möchte ...
I'm sorry	Es tut mir leid
Where?	Wo?
When?	Wann?
How much?	Wieviel?
Here	Hier
There	Da
Open	Geöffnet/offen/auf
Closed	Geschlossen/zu
Over there	Drüben

This one	Dieses	100	hundert
That one	Jenes	1000	tausend
Large	Gross		
Small	Klein	**DAYS, MONTHS, TIME AND SEASONS**	
More	Mehr	Today	Heute
Less	Weniger	Yesterday	Gestern
A bit	Ein bisschen	Tomorrow	Morgen
A little	Ein wenig	The day before yesterday	Vorgestern
A lot	Viel	The day after tomorrow	Übermorgen
Cheap	Billig	Day	Tag
Expensive	Teuer	Night	Nacht
Good	Gut	Week	Woche
Where is …?	Wo ist …?	Month	Monat
How much does that cost?	Wieviel kostet das?	Year	Jahr
What time is it?	Wieviel Uhr ist es?/	Weekend	Wochenende
	Wie spat ist es?	In the morning	Am Vormittag/Vormittags
The bill, please	Die Rechnung, bitte!	Tomorrow morning	Morgen früh
	(or Zahlen, bitte!)	In the afternoon	Am Nachmittag/
Separately or together?	Getrennt oder zusammen?		Nachmittags
Receipt	Quittung	In the evening	Am Abend
Where is the toilet?	Wo ist die Toilette, bitte?	Seven thirty	Halb acht (ie half before
Women's toilets	Damen/Frauen		eight)
Men's toilets	Herren/Männer	Quarter past seven	Viertel nach sieben
		Quarter to eight	Viertel vor acht
NUMBERS		Now	jetzt
1	eins	Later	später
2	zwei	Earlier	früher
3	drei	At what time?	Um wieviel Uhr?
4	vier	Monday	Montag
5	fünf	Tuesday	Dienstag
6	sechs	Wednesday	Mittwoch
7	sieben	Thursday	Donnerstag
8	acht	Friday	Freitag
9	neun	Saturday	Samstag/Sonnabend
10	zehn		(northern Germany)
11	elf	Sunday	Sonntag
12	zwölf	January	Januar
13	dreizehn	February	Februar
14	vierzehn	March	März
15	fünfzehn	April	April
16	sechszehn	May	Mai
17	siebzehn	June	Juni
18	achtzehn	July	Juli
19	neunzehn	August	August
20	zwanzig	September	September
21	einundzwanzig	October	Oktober
22	zweiundzwanzig	November	November
30	dreissig	December	Dezember
40	vierzig	Spring	Frühling
50	fünfzig	Summer	Sommer
60	sechzig	Autumn	Herbst
70	siebzig	Winter	Winter
80	achtzig	Holidays	Ferien
90	neunzig	Bank holiday	Feiertag

TRANSPORT AND SIGNS

Abflug	Departure (airport)
Abreise/Abfahrt	Departure (more generally)
Ankunft	Arrivals
Ausfahrt	Motorway exit
Ausgang	Exit
Ausgang freihalten	Keep clear/no parking in front of exit
Autobahn	Motorway
Baustelle	Roadworks (on Autobahn etc)
Einbahnstraße	one-way street
Eingang	Entrance
Fähre	Ferry
Führerschein	Driver's licence
Kein Eingang	No entrance
Nicht rauchen/ Rauchen verboten	No smoking
Notausgang	Emergency exit
Plakette	Colour-coded sticker for cars, needed if travelling in the city centre (see p.23).
Reisepass/Pass	Passport
Tankstelle	Petrol station
Umleitung	Diversion
Unfall	Accident
Verboten	Prohibited
Vorsicht!	Attention!/Take care!
Zoll	Customs

A FOOD AND DRINK GLOSSARY

BASIC TERMS

Breakfast	Frühstück
Lunch	Mittagessen
Coffee and cakes	Kaffee und Kuchen – a mid-afternoon ritual
Supper, dinner	Abendessen/Abendbrot (bread with cold toppings)
Knife	Messer
Fork	Gabel
Spoon	Löffel
Plate	Teller
Cup	Tasse
Mug	Becher
Bowl	Schüssel
Glass	Glas
Menu	Speisekarte
Wine list	Weinkarte
Set menu	Menü
Course	Gang
Starter	Vorspeise
Main course	Hauptgericht
Dessert	Nachspeise
Restaurant bill	Rechnung
Tip	Trinkgeld
Vegetarian	vegetarisch

COOKING TERMS

blau	boiled
eingelegt	pickled
frisch	fresh
gebacken	baked
gebraten	fried, roasted
gedämpft	steamed
gefüllt	stuffed
gegrillt	grilled
gekocht	boiled (also more generally means "cooked")
geräuchert	smoked
geschmort	braised, slow-cooked
gutbürgerlich	traditional German
hausgemacht	home-made
heiss	hot
lauwarm	lukewarm
kalt	cold
roh	raw
am Spiess	skewered
Topf, Eintopf	stew, casserole
überbacken	with a hot topping (especially cheese)
zart	tender (eg of meat)

BASICS

Belegtes Brot	sandwich
Bio	organic
Brot	bread, loaf
Brötchen	bread roll
Butter	butter
Ei	egg
Essig	vinegar
Fisch	fish
Fleisch	meat
Gemüse	vegetables
Honig	honey
Joghurt	yoghurt
Kaffee	coffee
Käse	cheese
Marmelade	jam
Milch	milk
Obst	fruit
Öl	oil
Pfeffer	pepper
Sahne	cream
Salatsoße	salad dressing
Salz	salt
scharf	spicy
Schrippe	bread roll (in Berlin)

Senf	mustard
Soße	sauce
Süßstoff	artificial sweetener
Tee	tea
Wasser	water
Zucker	sugar

SOUPS AND STARTERS

Blattsalat	green salad/salad leaves
Bohnensuppe	bean soup
Bunter Salat	mixed salad
Erbsensuppe	pea soup
Flädlesuppe/ Pfannkuchensuppe/ Frittatensuppe	clear soup with pancake strips
Fleischsuppe	meat soup
Gulaschsuppe	spicy thick meat soup with paprika
Gurkensalat	cucumber salad
Hühnersuppe	chicken soup
Kartoffelsalat	potato salad
Leberknödelsuppe	clear soup with liver dumplings
Linsensuppe	lentil soup
Sülze	brawn
Suppe	soup
Wurstsalat	sausage salad

MEAT AND POULTRY

Backhähnchen	roast chicken
Bockwurst	chunky boiled sausage
Bratwurst	grilled sausage
Cordon Bleu	a Schnitzel stuffed with ham and cheese
Currywurst	sausage served with tomato ketchup and curry powder
Eisbein	boiled pigs' hock
Ente	duck
Frikadelle/Bulette	German burger
Gans	goose
Geschnetzeltes	shredded meat
Gyros/Dönerkebap	kebab
Hackfleisch	minced meat
Hirsch, Reh	venison
Huhn/Hähnchen	chicken
Jägerschnitzel	cutlet in wine and mushroom sauce
Kassler Rippen	smoked and pickled pork chops
Kohlroulade	cabbage leaves stuffed with mincemeat
Kotelett	cutlet, chop
Lamm	lamb

Leber	liver
Leberkäse	baked meatloaf
Lunge	lungs
Rindfleisch	beef
Sauerbraten	braised pickled beef (or horse, in which case the menu description will specify "vom Pferd")
Schaschlik	diced meat with piquant sauce
Schinken	ham
Schweinebraten	roast pork
Schweinefleisch	pork
Schweinshaxe	roast pig's hock (knuckle)
Speck	bacon
Truthahn/Puter	turkey
Weisswurst	Veal sausage seasoned with lemon zest and parsley
Wiener Schnitzel	thin cutlet in breadcumbs: either veal (vom Kalb) or pork (vom Schwein)
Wienerwurst	boiled pork sausage
Wild	wild game
Wildschwein	wild boar
Wurst	sausage
Zigeunerschnitzel	cutlet in paprika sauce

FISH

Aal	eel
Forelle	trout
Garnelen	prawns
Hecht	pike
Hering/Matjes	herring
Hummer	lobster
Kabeljau	cod
Karpfen	carp
Krabben	shrimps
Lachs	salmon
Muscheln	mussels
Rotbarsch	rosefish
Saibling	char
Scholle	plaice
Schwertfisch	swordfish
Seezunge	sole
Thunfisch	tuna
Tintenfisch	squid
Zander	pike-perch

PASTA, DUMPLINGS AND NOODLES

Kloß/Knödel	potato dumpling
Semmelknödel	bread dumpling
Maultaschen	a form of ravioli
Reis	rice

Spätzle	German pasta

VEGETABLES

Blumenkohl	cauliflower
Bohnen	beans
Bratkartoffeln	fried potatoes
Champignons	button mushrooms
Dicke Bohnen	broad beans
Erbsen	peas
Grüne Bohnen	green beans
Gurke	cucumber or gherkin
Karotten/Möhren	carrots
Kartoffelbrei	mashed potatoes
Kartoffelpüree	creamed potatoes
Kartoffelsalat	potato salad
Knoblauch	garlic
Kopfsalat	lettuce
Lauch/Porree	leek
Maiskolben	corn on the cob
Paprika	green or red peppers
Pfifferling/Eierschwamm	chanterelle mushroom
Pellkartoffeln	jacket potatoes
Pilze	mushrooms
Pommes frites	chips/French fries
Reibekuchen/ Kartoffelpuffer	fried potato cake
Rosenkohl	Brussels sprouts
Rote Rübe	beetroot
Rotkohl	red cabbage
Rübensalat	turnip salad
Salzkartoffeln (Petersilienkartoffeln)	boiled potatoes (with parsley)
Sauerkraut	pickled cabbage
Spargel	asparagus
Weisskohl	white cabbage
Wok-Gemüse	stir-fried vegetables
Zwiebeln	onions

FRUIT

Ananas	pineapple
Apfel	apple
Aprikose	apricot
Birne	pear
Brombeeren	blackberries
Datteln	dates
Erdbeeren	strawberries
Feigen	figs
Himbeeren	raspberries
Johannisbeeren	redcurrants
Kirschen	cherries
Kompott	stewed fruit
Melone	melon
Obstsalat	fruit salad
Pampelmuse	grapefruit
Pfirsich	peach
Pflaumen	plums
Rosinen	raisins
Schwarze Johannisbeeren	blackcurrants
Trauben	grapes
Zitrone	lemon

CHEESES

Käseplatte	cheese board
Quark	low-fat soft cheese
Schafskäse	sheep's cheese
Weichkäse	cream cheese
Ziegenkäse	goat's cheese

DESSERTS AND BAKED GOODS

Apfelstrudel (mit Sahne)	apple strudel (with cream)
Pfannkuchen	jam doughnut
Dampfnudeln	yeast dumplings served hot with vanilla sauce
Eierkuchen	pancake
Eis	ice cream
Gebäck	pastries
Käsekuchen	cheesecake
Keks	biscuit
Kuchen	cake
Lebkuchen/Printen	spiced gingerbread
Nüsse	nuts
Nusskuchen	nut cake
Obstkuchen	fruitcake
Schlagsahne	whipped cream
Schokolade	chocolate
Schwarzwälder Kirschtorte	Black Forest gateau
Torte	gateau, tart

Glossary of German terms

Altstadt Old part of a city.
Auskunft Information.
Ausländer Literally "foreigner", the word has come to be a pejorative term for any non-white non-German.
Ausstellung Exhibition.
Bäckerei Bakery.
Bahnhof Station.

Bau Building.
Berg Mountain or hill.
Berliner Schnauze Sharp and coarse Berlin wit.
Bezirk City district.
Brücke Bridge.
Burg Mountain or hill.
Bushaltestelle Bus stop.

Denkmal Memorial.
Dom Cathedral.
Dorf Village.
Einbahnstrasse One-way street.
Feiertag Holiday.
Flughafen Airport.
Fluss River.
Fremdenzimmer Room for short-term let.
Gasse Alley.
Gastarbeiter "Guest worker": a foreigner who comes to Germany to do menial work.
Gasthaus, Gasthof Guesthouse, inn.
Gaststätte Traditional bar that also serves food.
Gemälde Painting.
Grünen, die The Greens: political party.
Haupteingang Main entrance.
Hof Court, courtyard, mansion.
Insel Island.
Jugendherberge Youth hostel.
Jugendstil German version of Art Nouveau.
Junker Prussian landowning class.
Kaiser Emperor.
Kammer Room, chamber.
Kapelle Chapel.
Kaufhaus Department store.
Kino Cinema.
Kirche Church.
Kneipe Bar.
Konditorei Cake shop.
Krankenhaus Hospital.
Kunst Art.
Markt Market, market square.
Motorrad Motorbike.
Not Emergency.
Platz Square.
Quittung Official receipt.
Rathaus Town hall.

Reich Empire.
Reisebüro Travel agency.
Rundgang Way round.
S-Bahn Suburban train network.
Sammlung Collection.
Schicki Abbreviation of "Schicki-Micki": yuppie.
Schloss Castle, palace.
See Lake.
Staatssicherheitsdienst (STASI) The "State Security Service" or secret police of the GDR.
Stadt Town, city.
Stammtisch Table in a pub or restaurant reserved for regular customers.
Stiftung Foundation.
Strand Beach.
Strassenbahn Tram.
Tankstelle Petrol station.
Tor Gate, gateway.
Trabi The Trabant, East Germany's two-cylinder, two-stroke people's car.
Turm Tower.
U-Bahn Network of underground trains.
Verkehrsamt/Verkehrsverein Tourist office.
Viertel Quarter, district.
Volk People, folk; given mystical associations by Hitler.
Vopo Slang for Volkspolizei, a member of the East German police force.
Wald Forest.
Weimar Republic Parliamentary democracy, established in 1918, which collapsed with Hitler's assumption of power in 1933.
Wende Literally, "turning point" – the term used to describe the events of November 1989 and after.
Zeitschrift Magazine.
Zeitung Newspaper.
Zeughaus Arsenal.
Zimmer Room.

Acronyms

BRD (Bundesrepublik Deutschland) Official name of former West Germany.
CDU (Christlich Demokratische Union) Christian Democratic (Conservative) Party.
DDR (Deutsche Demokratische Republik) Official name of former East Germany.
GDR (German Democratic Republic) English equivalent of DDR.
NSDAP (Nationalsozialistische Deutsche Arbbeiterpartei) "National Socialist German Workers' Party", the official name for the Nazis.

PDS (Partei des Demokratischen Sozializmus) The revamped SED after the collapse of the Wall.
SED (Sozialistische Einheitspartei Deutschlands) "Socialist Unity Party of Germany", the official name of the East German communist party before December 1989.
SPD (Sozialdemokratische Partei Deutschlands) Social Democratic (Labour) Party.

Small print and index

A ROUGH GUIDE TO ROUGH GUIDES

Published in 1982, the first Rough Guide – to Greece – was a student scheme that became a publishing phenomenon. Mark Ellingham, a recent graduate in English from Bristol University, had been travelling in Greece the previous summer and couldn't find the right guidebook. With a small group of friends he wrote his own guide, combining a highly contemporary, journalistic style with a thoroughly practical approach to travellers' needs.

The immediate success of the book spawned a series that rapidly covered dozens of destinations. And, in addition to impecunious backpackers, Rough Guides soon acquired a much broader readership that relished the guides' wit and inquisitiveness as much as their enthusiastic, critical approach and value-for-money ethos.

These days, Rough Guides include recommendations from budget to luxury and cover more than 120 destinations around the globe, as well as producing an ever-growing range of eBooks.

Visit **roughguides.com** to find all our latest books, read articles, get inspired and share travel tips with the Rough Guides community.

Rough Guide credits

Editor: Samantha Cook
Layout: Jessica Subramanian
Cartography: Ashutosh Bharti
Picture editors: Tim Draper, Mark Thomas
Proofreader: Stewart Wild
Managing editor: Monica Woods
Assistant editor: Prema Dutta
Production: Charlotte Cade

Cover design: Nicole Newman, Jessica Subramanian
Editorial assistant: Olivia Rawes
Senior pre-press designer: Dan May
Operations coordinator: Helen Blount
Creative operations manager: Jason Mitchell
Publisher: Joanna Kirby
Publishing director (Travel): Clare Currie

Publishing information

This tenth edition published March 2014 by
Rough Guides Ltd,
80 Strand, London WC2R 0RL
11, Community Centre, Panchsheel Park,
New Delhi 110017, India
Distributed by Penguin Random House
Penguin Books Ltd,
80 Strand, London WC2R 0RL
Penguin Group (USA)
345 Hudson Street, NY 10014, USA
Penguin Group (Australia)
250 Camberwell Road, Camberwell,
Victoria 3124, Australia
Penguin Group (NZ)
67 Apollo Drive, Mairangi Bay, Auckland 1310,
New Zealand
Penguin Group (South Africa)
Block D, Rosebank Office Park, 181 Jan Smuts Avenue,
Parktown North, Gauteng, South Africa 2193
Rough Guides is represented in Canada by Tourmaline
Editions Inc. 662 King Street West, Suite 304, Toronto,
Ontario M5V 1M7
Printed in Singapore by Toppan Security Printing Pte. Ltd.

MIX
Paper from
responsible sources
FSC™ C018179

Help us update

We've gone to a lot of effort to ensure that the tenth
edition of **The Rough Guide to Berlin** is accurate and up-
to-date. However, things change – places get "discovered",
opening hours are notoriously fickle, restaurants and
rooms raise prices or lower standards. If you feel we've got
it wrong or left something out, we'd like to know, and if
you can remember the address, the price, the hours, the
phone number, so much the better.

Please send your comments with the subject line
"Rough Guide Berlin Update" to ✉ mail@uk.roughguides
.com. We'll credit all contributions and send a copy of the
next edition (or any other Rough Guide if you prefer) for
the very best emails.

Find more travel information, connect with fellow
travellers and plan your trip on ⓦ roughguides.com

ABOUT THE AUTHOR

Christian Williams grew up in a divided Berlin and has been fascinated by the city ever since. As a freelance writer he has written or worked on various other Rough Guides, including Germany, Austria, Tenerife, Canada, the USA and Colorado.

Acknowledgements

Christian Williams wants to extend a big thank you to Neil and Gülnur at Jetpak for their bottomless hospitality and to all those others who helped with insights and advice. Particularly Francesca in Potsdam, Rachele at Mustafas and Patrick at Kumpelnest 3000. At Rough Guides thanks go to all those involved in the book including Monica Woods and particularly Samantha Cook, who displayed unceasing editorial energy even when wi-fi wasn't free.

Photo credits

All photos © Rough Guides except the following:
(Key: t-top; c-centre; b-bottom; l-left; r-right)

p.1 Corbis: Jon Hicks
p.2 Corbis: Aris (Kyriakos) Chatzistefanou
p.4 Getty Images: spreephoto.de
p.7 Corbis: Ludovic Maisant (c); Florian Monheim (b)
p.8 Getty Images: Kieran Scott
p.9 Alamy: Iain Masterton
p.10 Getty Images: Siegfried Layda
p.11 Corbis: Wolfgang Kumm (b)
p.12 Alamy: travelstock44 (t); Bildagentur-online/Klein (c). Getty Images: Sean Gallup (b)
p.13 Getty Images: Buena Vista Images (t); Adam Berry (b). Corbis: Patrick Pleul (c)
p.14 Alamy: Bon Appetit (t); F1online digitale Bildagentur GmbH (b). Corbis: FABRIZIO BENSCH (c)
p.15 Corbis: Michele Falzone (tl); Michael Sohn (tr); Massimo Borchi (bl). Alamy: Iain Masterton (br)
p.16 Alamy: JLImages
p.17 Robert Harding Picture Library: Image Broker
p.43 Corbis: Sylvain Sonnet
p.51 Alamy: Right Perspective Images
p.59 Corbis: Paul Seheult
p.65 Corbis: Wolfgang Kumm (t); Julie Woodhouse (b)
p.97 Corbis: Rene Mattes (t). Alamy: dpa picture alliance (b)
p.107 Getty Images: Carsten Koall
p.123 Alamy: Brian Harris (t); Adam Eastland (b)
p.131 Alamy: Iain Masterton
p.137 Alamy: Imagebroker

p.141 Alamy: Caro
p.151 Corbis: Britta Pedersen
p.159 Alamy: Peter Stroh (b)
p.165 Getty Images: Danita Delimont
p.175 Corbis: Patrick Pleul
p.176 Getty Images: Sean Gallup
p.183 Alamy: Eden Breitz (t); Caro (b)
p.197 Alamy: Julie G Woodhouse
p.206 Alamy: travelstock44
p.211 Alamy: Caro (t); Juergen Henkelmann Photography (b)
p.216 Corbis: Thomas Peter
p.221 Alamy: Eden Breitz (t); Juergen Henkelmann Photography (b)
p.224 Alamy: Iain Masterton
p.229 Alamy: Juergen Henkelmann Photography
p.233 Alamy: Caro
p.236 Alamy: VPC Travel Photo
p.240 Getty Images: Wilfried Krecichwost
p.244 Alamy: Interfoto

Front cover East Side Gallery © Luca Da Ros/ SIME/4Corners Images
Back cover East Side Gallery © Alamy/LOOK Die Bildagentur der Fotografen GmbH (t); Berliner Dom © Rough Guides/Diana Jarvis (bl); Sony centre roof © Alamy/Dime Dimov (br)

Index

Maps are marked in grey

W

U

V

Y

Z

T

Maps

Index

Listings key

- ■ Accommodation
- ● Eating and drinking
- ■ Drinking and nightlife
- ● Shopping

City plan

The **city plan** on the pages that follow is divided as shown:

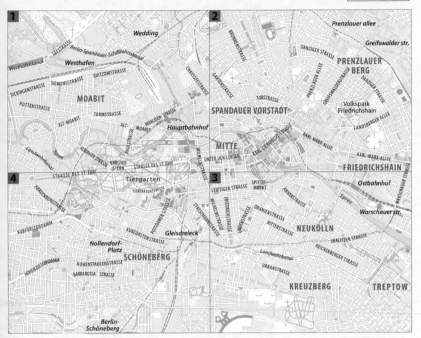

Map symbols

▦▦ Railway	Ⓤ U-Bahn station	▲ Peak	⬛ Church				
- - - Path	Ⓢ S-Bahn station	🏛 Monument	⬭ Stadium				
▦▦ River	◆ Place of interest	⚲ Museum	Christian cemetery				
···· Wall	⊙ Statue	✡ Synagogue	Jewish cemetery				
⌣ Bridge	ⓘ Tourist office	⊤ Garden	Park				
✈ Airport	E Embassy	▦ Building	Beach				

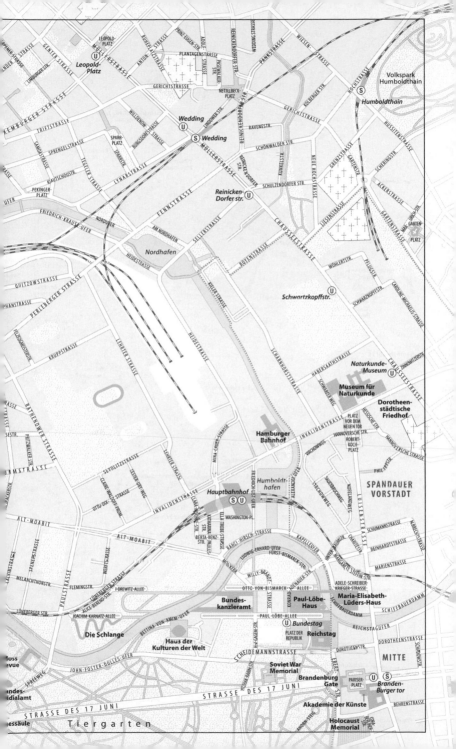

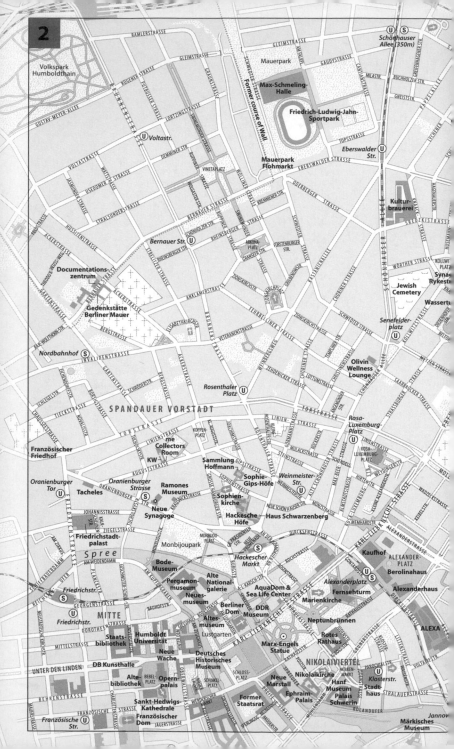

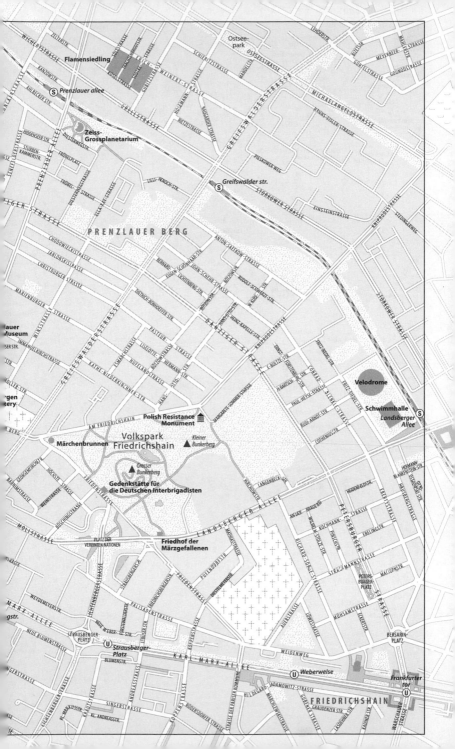

THE U- AND S-BAHN

- **U1** Warschauer Strasse ◄► Uhlandstrasse
- **U2** Pankow ◄► Ruhleben
- **U3** Nollendorfplatz ◄► Krumme Lanke
- **U4** Nollendorfplatz ◄► Innsbrucker Platz
- **U5** Hönow ◄► Alexanderplatz
- **U55** Brandenburger Tor ◄► Hauptbahnhof
- **U6** Alt-Tegel ◄► Alt-Mariendorf
- **U7** Rathaus Spandau ◄► Rudow
- **U8** Wittenau ◄► Hermannstrasse
- **U9** Osloer Strasse ◄► Rathaus Steglitz

171 Airport bus

ROUGH GUIDES

WE GET AROUND

ONLINE start your journey at roughguides.com

EBOOKS & MOBILE APPS

GUIDEBOOKS from Amsterdam to Zanzibar

PHRASEBOOKS learn the lingo

MAPS so you don't get lost

GIFTBOOKS inspiration is our middle name

LIFESTYLE from iPads to climate change

...SO YOU CAN TOO

BOOKS | EBOOKS | APPS

Start your journey at **roughguides.com**
MAKE THE MOST OF YOUR TIME ON EARTH[TM]